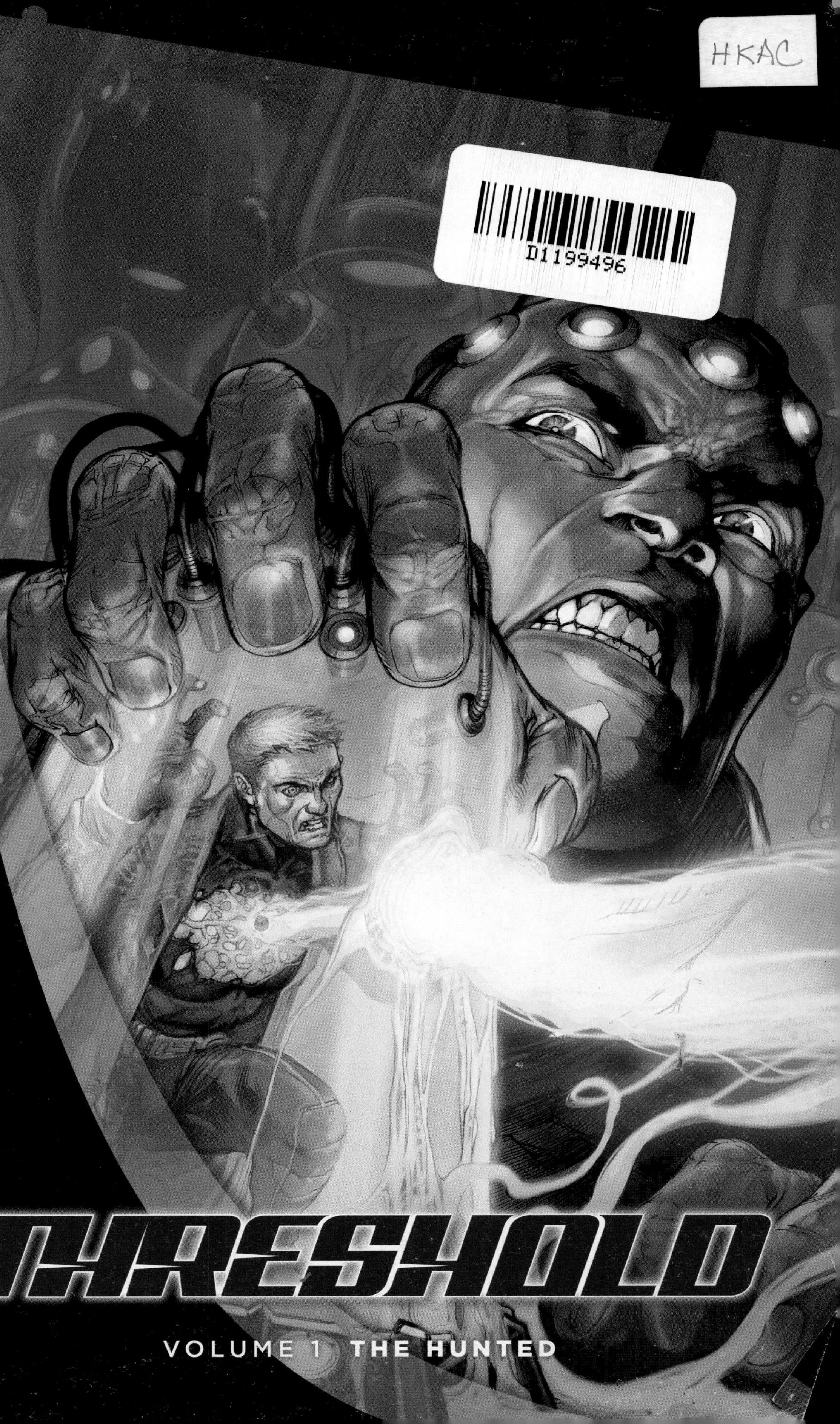

THRESHOLD

VOLUME 1 THE HUNTED

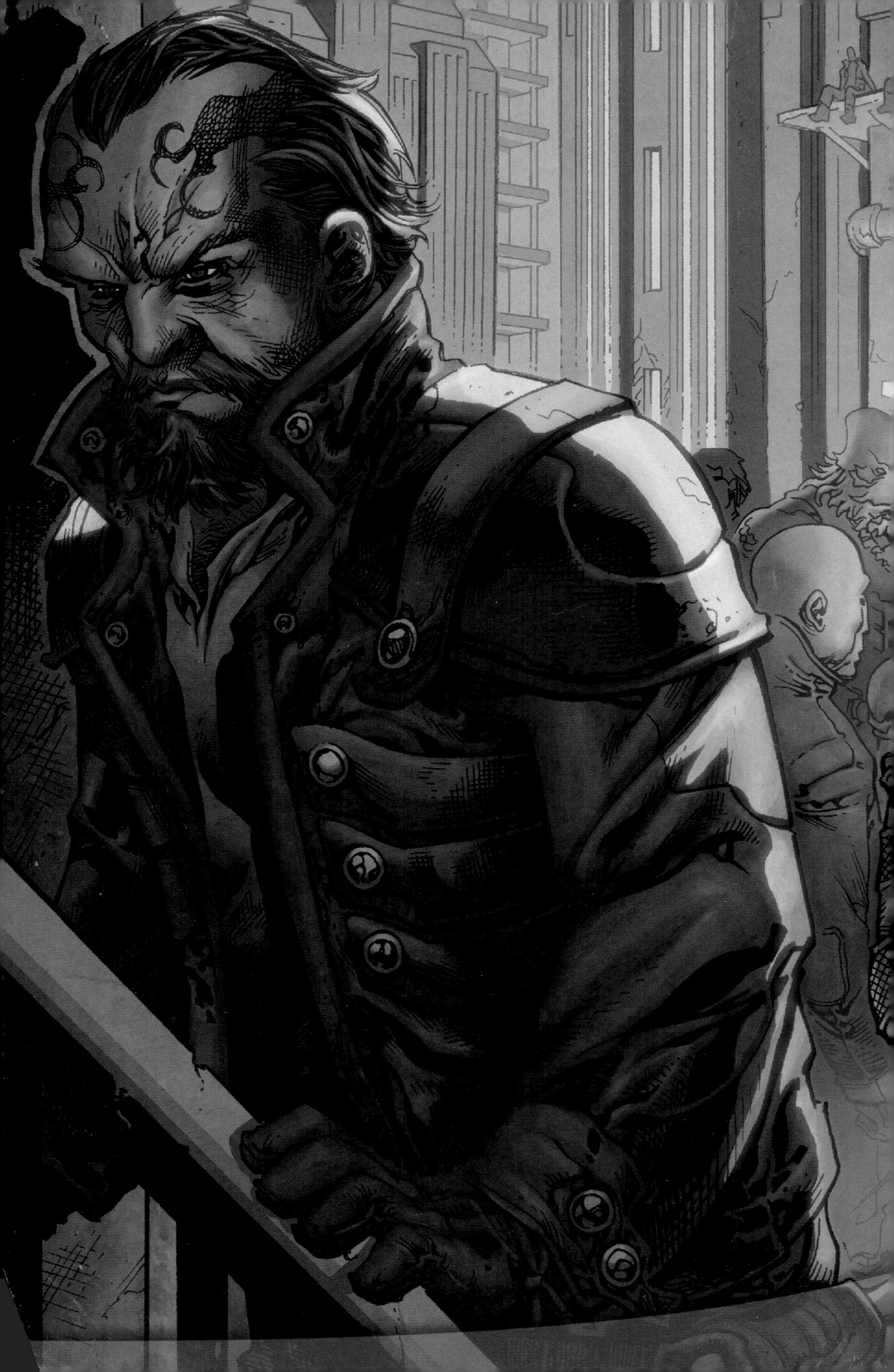

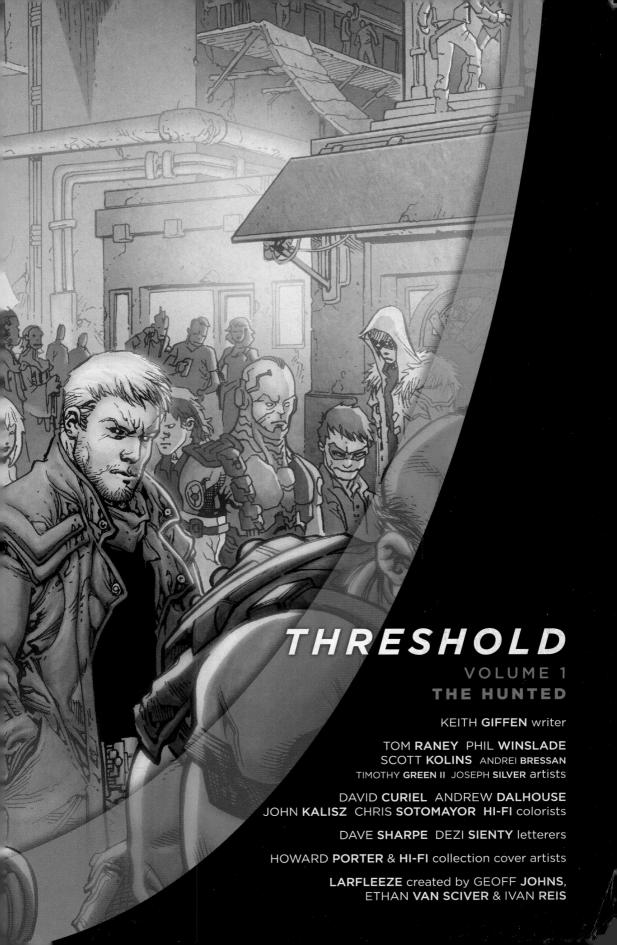

THRESHOLD

VOLUME 1
THE HUNTED

KEITH **GIFFEN** writer

TOM **RANEY** PHIL **WINSLADE**
SCOTT **KOLINS** ANDREI **BRESSAN**
TIMOTHY **GREEN II** JOSEPH **SILVER** artists

DAVID **CURIEL** ANDREW **DALHOUSE**
JOHN **KALISZ** CHRIS **SOTOMAYOR** HI-FI colorists

DAVE **SHARPE** DEZI **SIENTY** letterers

HOWARD **PORTER** & HI-FI collection cover artists

LARFLEEZE created by GEOFF **JOHNS**,
ETHAN **VAN SCIVER** & IVAN **REIS**

JOEY CAVALIERI Editor – Original Series KATE STEWART & KYLE ANDRUKIEWICZ Assistant Editors – Original Series
ROWENA YOW Editor
ROBBIN BROSTERMAN Design Director – Books

BOB HARRAS SENIOR VP – Editor-in-Chief, DC Comics

DIANE NELSON President DAN DIDIO and JIM LEE Co-Publishers
GEOFF JOHNS Chief Creative Officer
JOHN ROOD Executive VP – Sales, Marketing and Business Development
AMY GENKINS Senior VP – Business and Legal Affairs NAIRI GARDINER Senior VP – Finance
JEFF BOISON VP – Publishing Planning MARK CHIARELLO VP – Art Direction and Design
JOHN CUNNINGHAM VP – Marketing TERRI CUNNINGHAM VP – Editorial Administration
ALISON GILL Senior VP – Manufacturing and Operations HANK KANALZ Senior VP – Vertigo & Integrated Publishing
JAY KOGAN VP – Business and Legal Affairs, Publishing JACK MAHAN VP – Business Affairs, Talent
NICK NAPOLITANO VP – Manufacturing Administration SUE POHJA VP – Book Sales
COURTNEY SIMMONS Senior VP – Publicity BOB WAYNE Senior VP – Sales

THRESHOLD VOLUME 1: THE HUNTED

DC Comics, 1700 Broadway, New York, NY 10019
A Warner Bros. Entertainment Company.
Printed by RR Donnelley, Salem, VA, USA. 1/24/14. First Printing.
ISBN: 978-1-4012-4333-3

Library of Congress Cataloging-in-Publication Data

Giffen, Keith, author.
Threshold. Volume 1, The Hunted / Keith Giffen ; [illustrated by] Tom Raney, Scott Kolins.
pages cm. -- (The New 52!)
Summary: "Introducing Jediah Caul, a disgraced Green Lantern stripped of his power ring, who is hunted for sport
on a televised reality show! Forced to battle aliens from across the galaxy, Caul must band together his own group of
rebels to storm the metaphorical castle of their abductees before the game ends and they lose. Plus, Larfleeze, the
Orange Lantern goes on a quest across the galaxy when someone steals his stuff--and NO ONE steals from Larfleeze!
Collects Threshold 1-8 and Green Lantern New Guardians Annual 1"-- Provided by publisher.
ISBN 978-1-4012-4333-3 (paperback)
1. Graphic novels. I. Raney, Tom, illustrator. II. Kolins, Scott, illustrator. III. Title. IV. Title: Hunted.
PN6728.T646G54 2014
741.5'973--dc23
2013045592

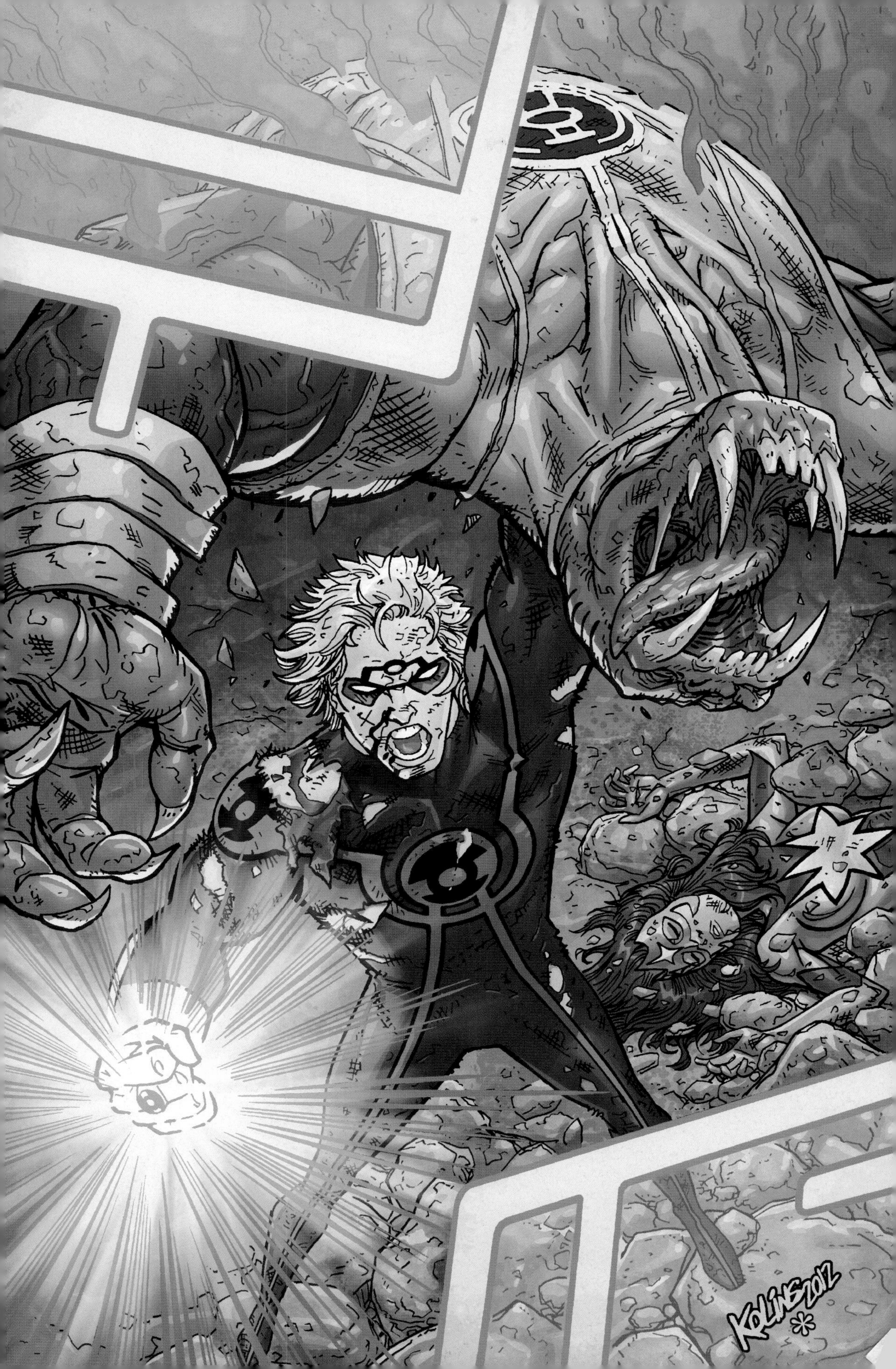
KOLINS 2012

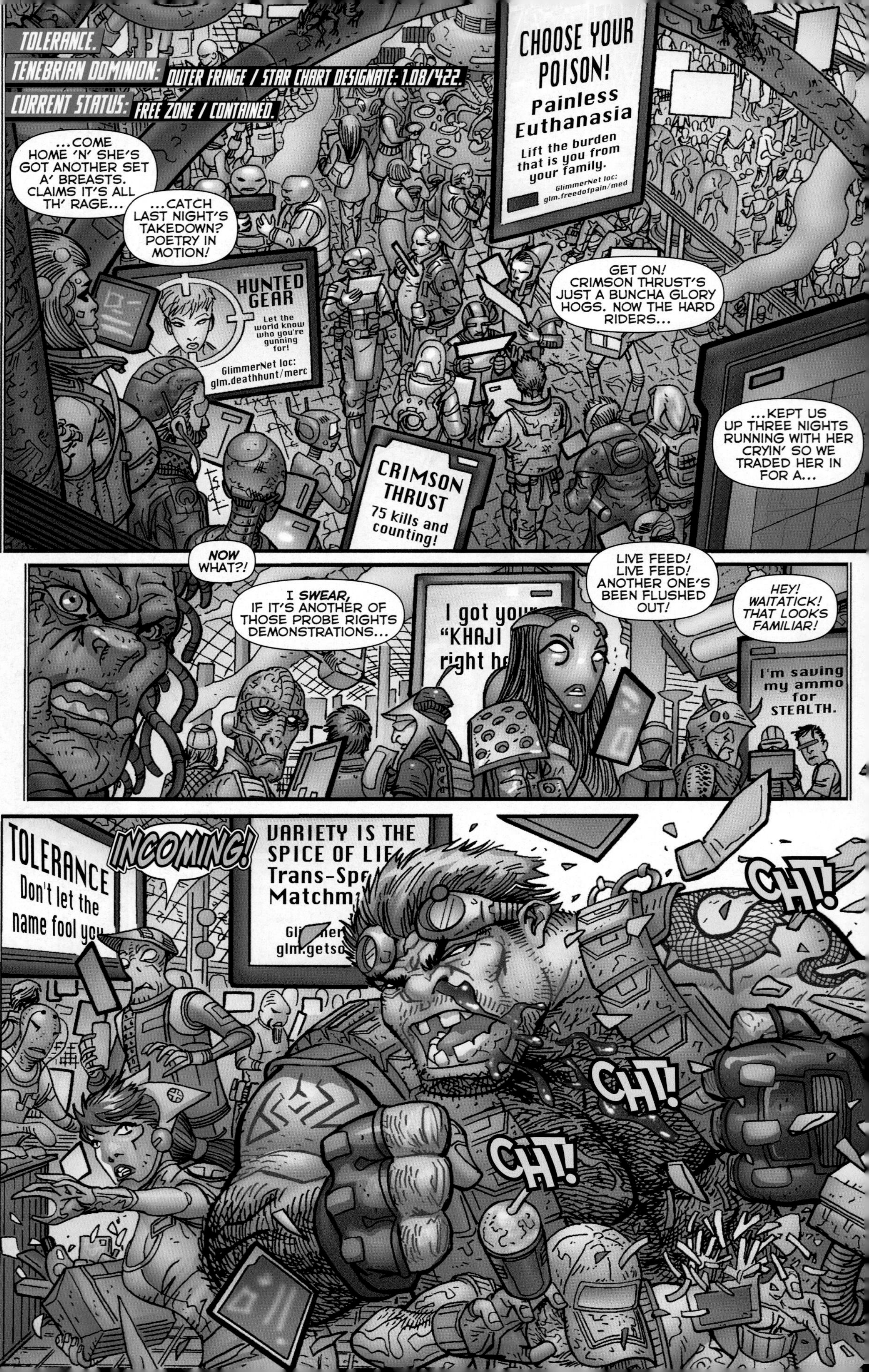
TOLERANCE.
TENEBRIAN DOMINION: OUTER FRINGE / STAR CHART DESIGNATE: 1.08/422.
CURRENT STATUS: FREE ZONE / CONTAINED.
CHOOSE YOUR POISON! Painless Euthanasia Lift the burden that is you from your family. GlimmerNet loc: glm.freedofpain/med
...COME HOME 'N' SHE'S GOT ANOTHER SET A' BREASTS. CLAIMS IT'S ALL TH' RAGE...
...CATCH LAST NIGHT'S TAKEDOWN? POETRY IN MOTION!
HUNTED GEAR Let the world know who you're gunning for! GlimmerNet loc: glm.deathhunt/merc
GET ON! CRIMSON THRUST'S JUST A BUNCHA GLORY HOGS. NOW THE HARD RIDERS...
CRIMSON THRUST 75 kills and counting!
...KEPT US UP THREE NIGHTS RUNNING WITH HER CRYIN' SO WE TRADED HER IN FOR A...
NOW WHAT?!
I SWEAR, IF IT'S ANOTHER OF THOSE PROBE RIGHTS DEMONSTRATIONS...
I got you
"KHAJI
right he
LIVE FEED! LIVE FEED! ANOTHER ONE'S BEEN FLUSHED OUT!
HEY! WAITATICK! THAT LOOKS FAMILIAR!
I'm saving my ammo for STEALTH.
TOLERANCE Don't let the name fool you
INCOMING!
VARIETY IS THE SPICE OF LIF Trans-Spe Matchm
glm.getso
CHT!
CHT!
CHT!

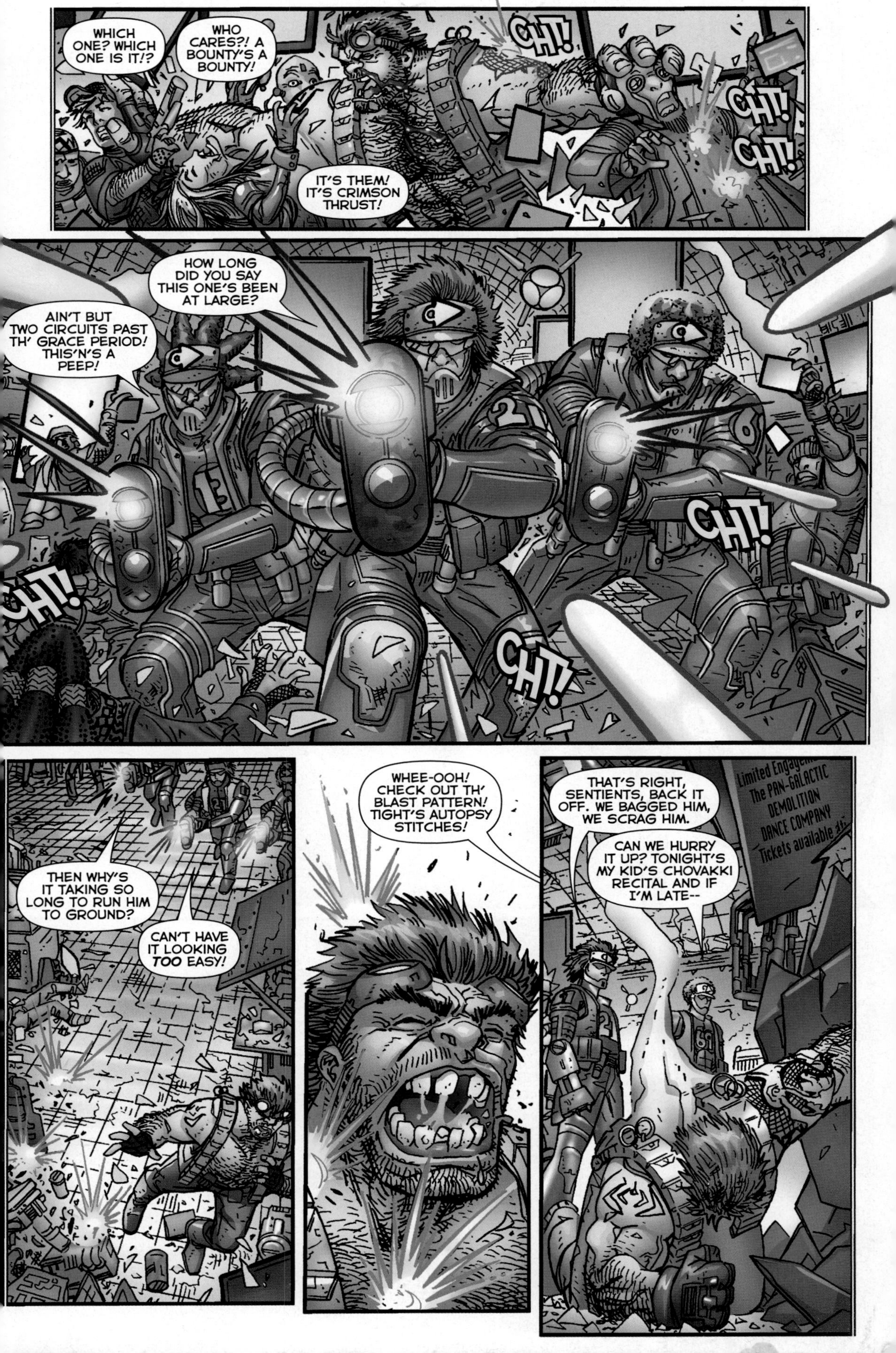
WHICH ONE? WHICH ONE IS IT!?
WHO CARES?! A BOUNTY'S A BOUNTY!
CHT!
CHT!
CHT!
IT'S THEM! IT'S CRIMSON THRUST!
HOW LONG DID YOU SAY THIS ONE'S BEEN AT LARGE?
AIN'T BUT TWO CIRCUITS PAST TH' GRACE PERIOD! THIS'N'S A PEEP!
CHT!
CHT!
CHT!
THEN WHY'S IT TAKING SO LONG TO RUN HIM TO GROUND?
CAN'T HAVE IT LOOKING *TOO* EASY!
WHEE-OOH! CHECK OUT TH' BLAST PATTERN! TIGHT'S AUTOPSY STITCHES!
THAT'S RIGHT, SENTIENTS, BACK IT OFF. WE BAGGED HIM, WE SCRAG HIM.
CAN WE HURRY IT UP? TONIGHT'S MY KID'S CHOVAKKI RECITAL AND IF I'M LATE--
The PAN-GALACTIC
DEMOLITION
DANCE COMPANY
Tickets available

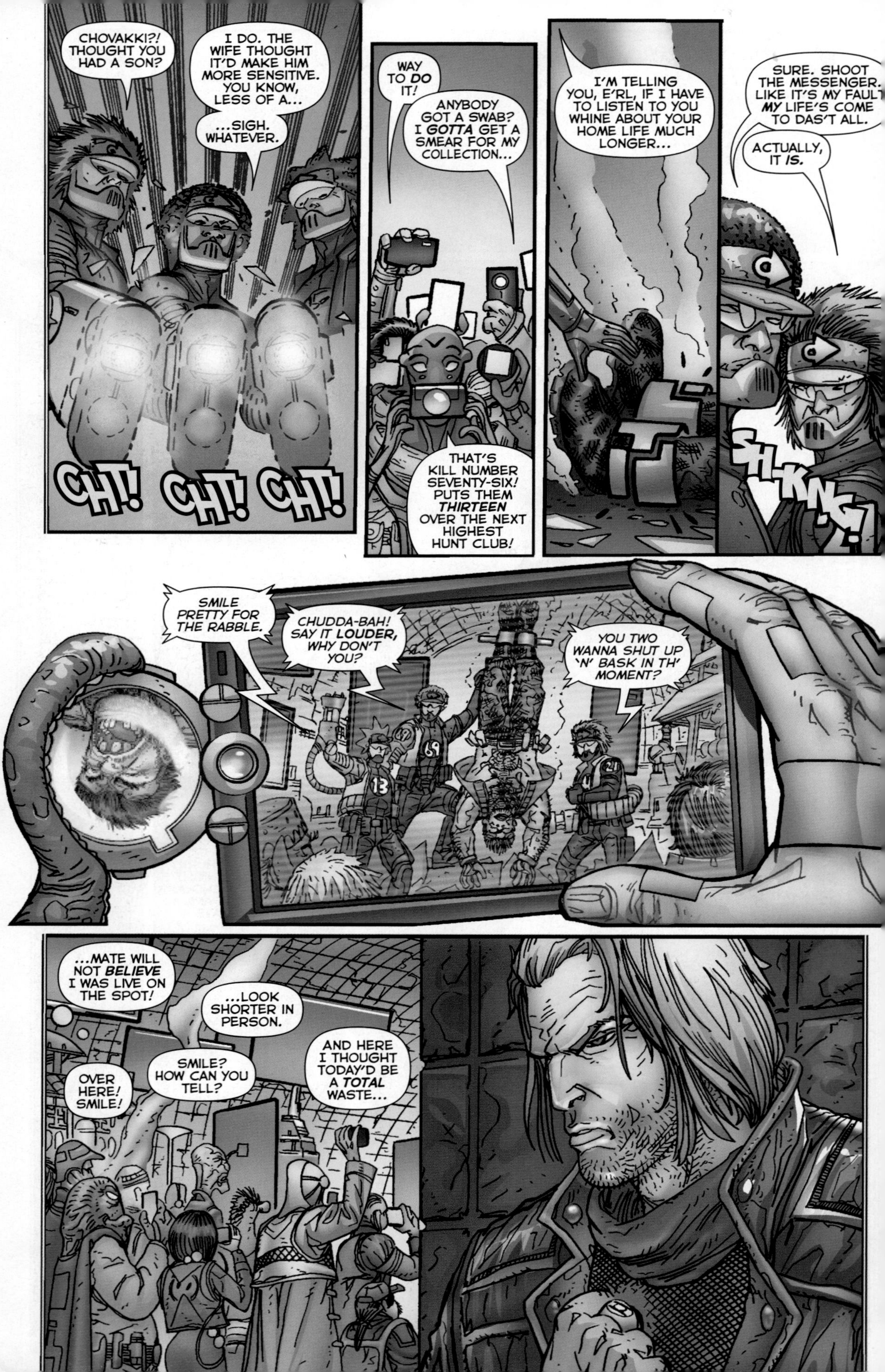
CHOVAKKI?! THOUGHT YOU HAD A SON?
I DO. THE WIFE THOUGHT IT'D MAKE HIM MORE SENSITIVE. YOU KNOW, LESS OF A...
...SIGH. WHATEVER.
CHT! CHT! CHT!
WAY TO *DO* IT!
ANYBODY GOT A SWAB? I *GOTTA* GET A SMEAR FOR MY COLLECTION...
THAT'S KILL NUMBER SEVENTY-SIX! PUTS THEM *THIRTEEN* OVER THE NEXT HIGHEST HUNT CLUB!
I'M TELLING YOU, E'RL, IF I HAVE TO LISTEN TO YOU WHINE ABOUT YOUR HOME LIFE MUCH LONGER...
SURE. SHOOT THE MESSENGER. LIKE IT'S MY FAULT *MY* LIFE'S COME TO DAS'T ALL.
ACTUALLY, IT *IS.*
SHLKNG!
SMILE PRETTY FOR THE RABBLE.
CHUDDA-BAH! SAY IT *LOUDER,* WHY DON'T YOU?
YOU TWO WANNA SHUT UP 'N' BASK IN TH' MOMENT?
...MATE WILL NOT *BELIEVE* I WAS LIVE ON THE SPOT!
...LOOK SHORTER IN PERSON.
OVER HERE! SMILE!
SMILE? HOW CAN YOU TELL?
AND HERE I THOUGHT TODAY'D BE A *TOTAL* WASTE...

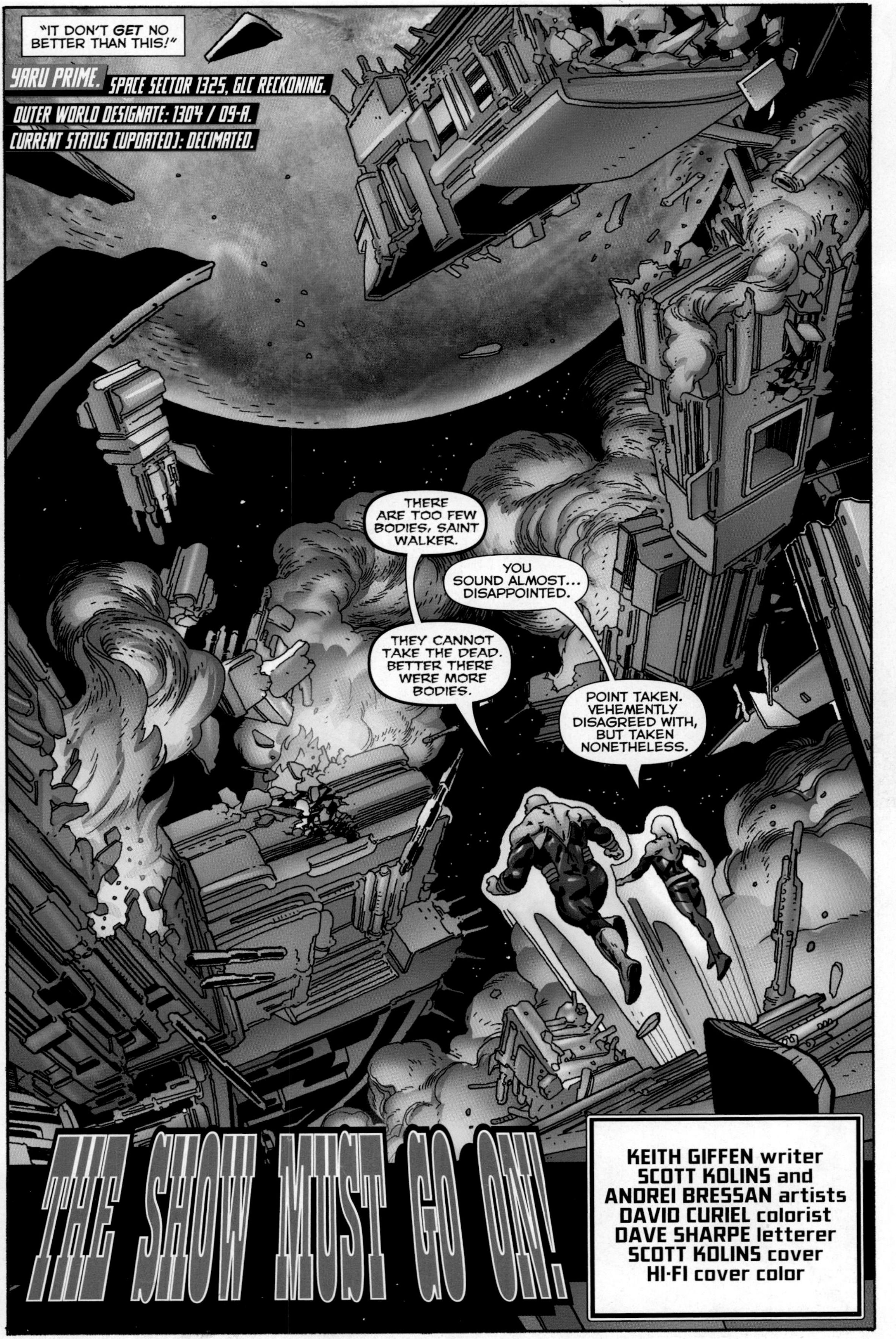
"IT DON'T GET NO BETTER THAN THIS!"
YARU PRIME. SPACE SECTOR 1325, GLC RECKONING.
OUTER WORLD DESIGNATE: 1304 / 09-A.
CURRENT STATUS [UPDATED]: DECIMATED.
THERE ARE TOO FEW BODIES, SAINT WALKER.
YOU SOUND ALMOST... DISAPPOINTED.
THEY CANNOT TAKE THE DEAD. BETTER THERE WERE MORE BODIES.
POINT TAKEN. VEHEMENTLY DISAGREED WITH, BUT TAKEN NONETHELESS.
THE SHOW MUST GO ON!
KEITH GIFFEN writer
SCOTT KOLINS and
ANDREI BRESSAN artists
DAVID CURIEL colorist
DAVE SHARPE letterer
SCOTT KOLINS cover
HI-FI cover color

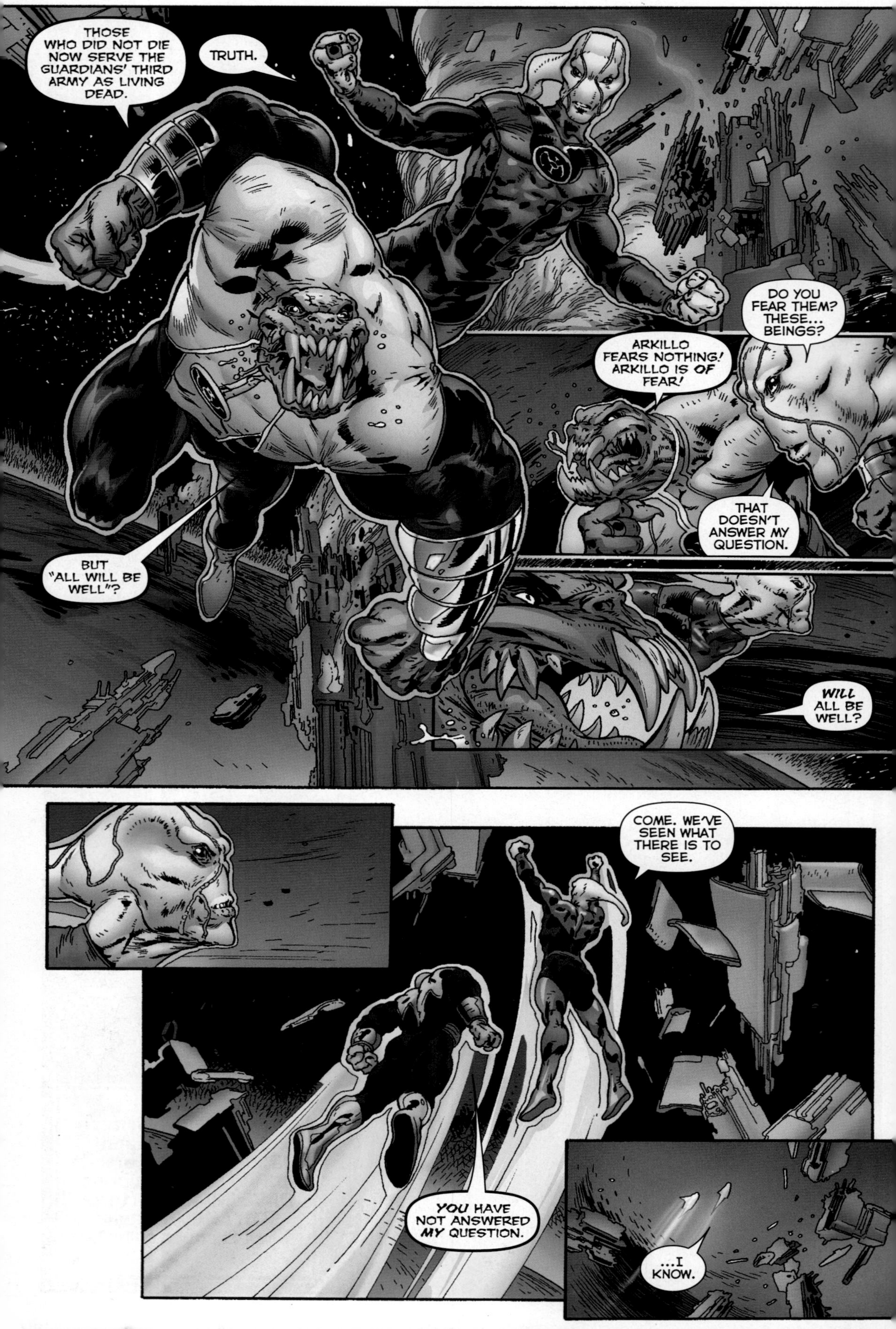

THOSE WHO DID NOT DIE NOW SERVE THE GUARDIANS' THIRD ARMY AS LIVING DEAD.
TRUTH.
BUT "ALL WILL BE WELL"?
DO YOU FEAR THEM? THESE... BEINGS?
ARKILLO FEARS NOTHING! ARKILLO IS OF FEAR!
THAT DOESN'T ANSWER MY QUESTION.
WILL ALL BE WELL?
COME. WE'VE SEEN WHAT THERE IS TO SEE.
YOU HAVE NOT ANSWERED MY QUESTION.
...I KNOW.

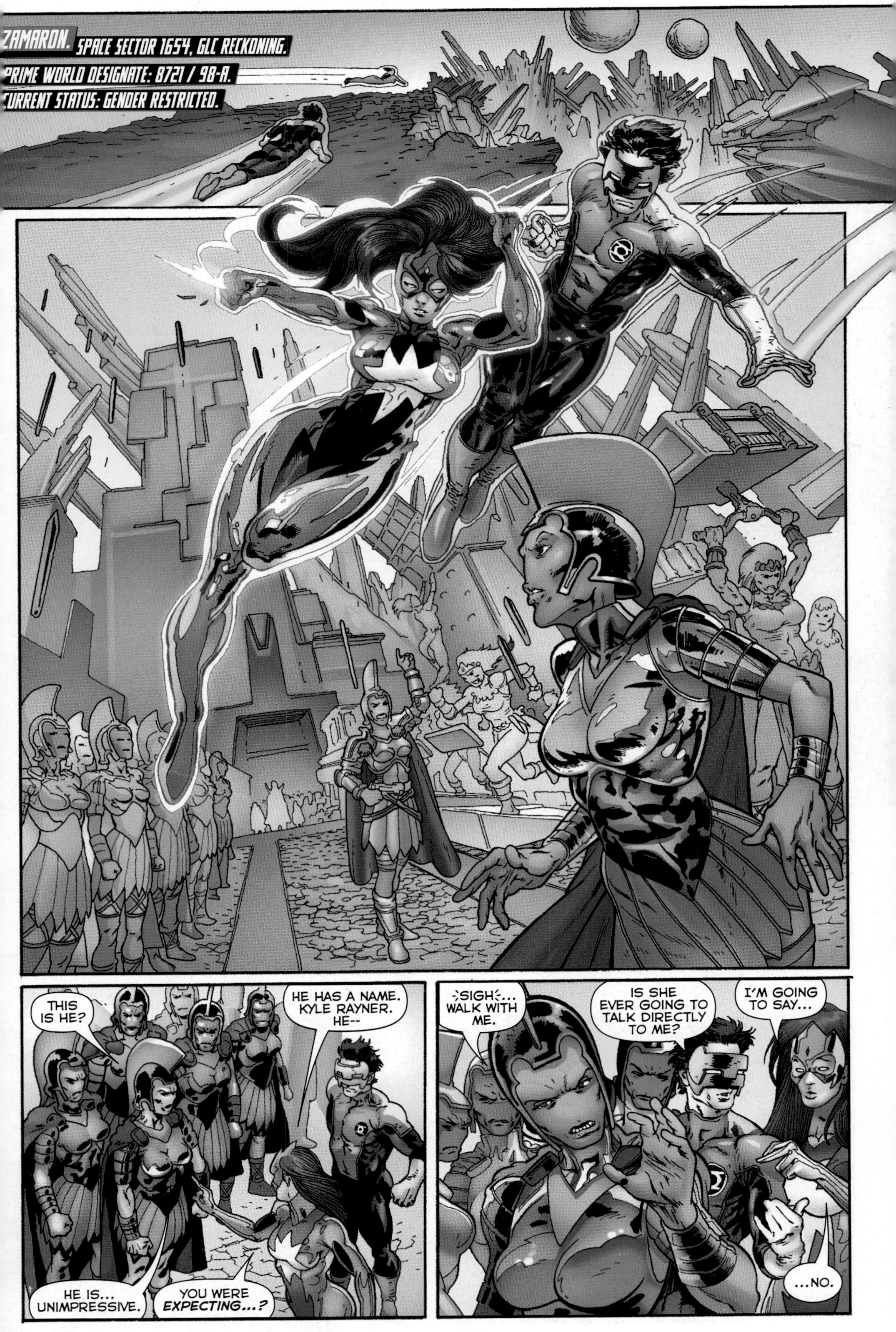

ZAMARON. SPACE SECTOR 1654, GLC RECKONING.
PRIME WORLD DESIGNATE: 8721 / 98-A.
CURRENT STATUS: GENDER RESTRICTED.
THIS IS HE?
HE HAS A NAME. KYLE RAYNER. HE--
HE IS... UNIMPRESSIVE.
YOU WERE *EXPECTING*...?
SIGH... WALK WITH ME.
IS SHE EVER GOING TO TALK DIRECTLY TO ME?
I'M GOING TO SAY...
...NO.

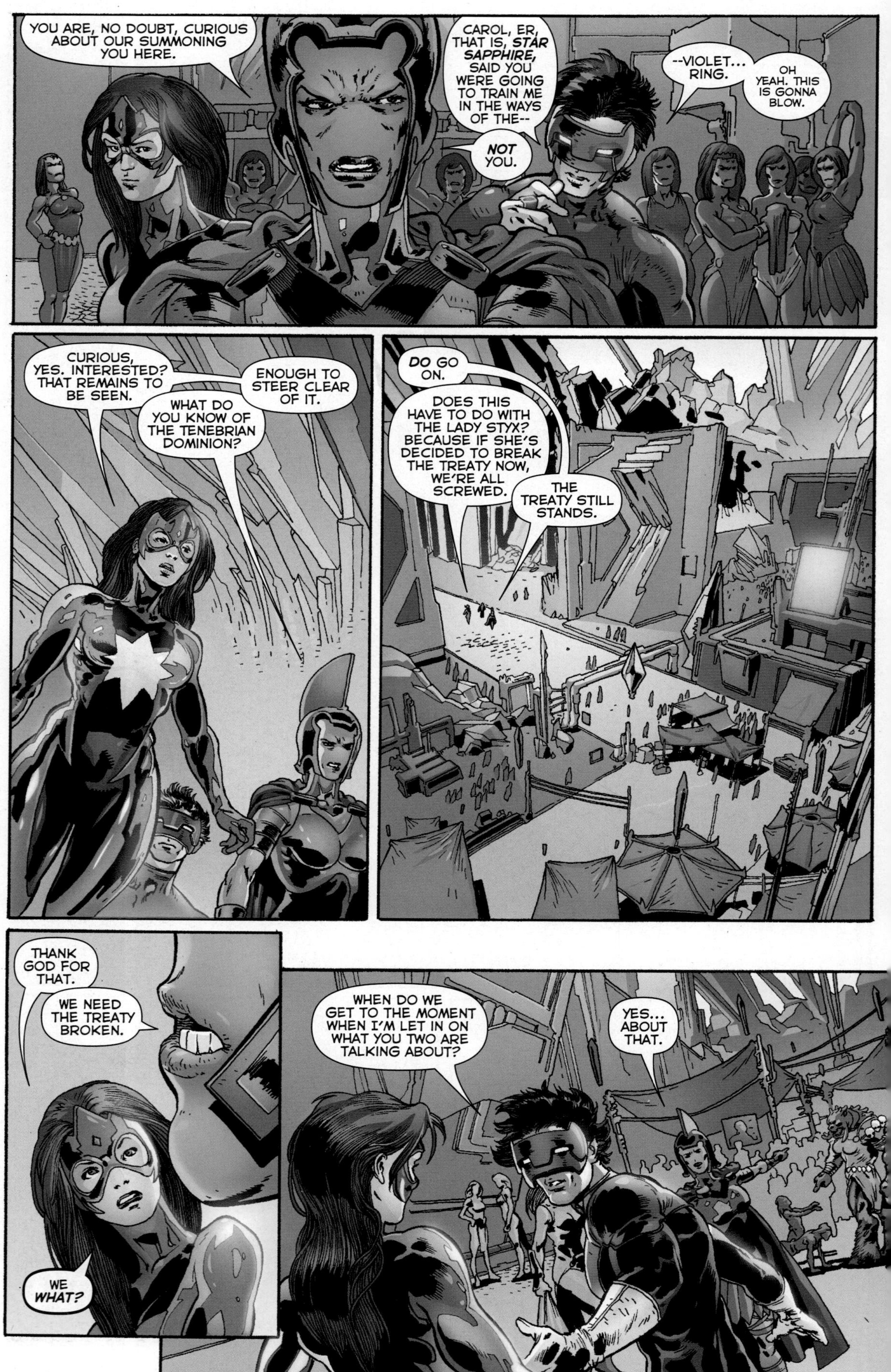
YOU ARE, NO DOUBT, CURIOUS ABOUT OUR SUMMONING YOU HERE.
CAROL, ER, THAT IS, STAR SAPPHIRE, SAID YOU WERE GOING TO TRAIN ME IN THE WAYS OF THE--
NOT YOU.
--VIOLET... RING.
OH YEAH. THIS IS GONNA BLOW.
CURIOUS, YES. INTERESTED? THAT REMAINS TO BE SEEN.
ENOUGH TO STEER CLEAR OF IT.
WHAT DO YOU KNOW OF THE TENEBRIAN DOMINION?
DO GO ON.
DOES THIS HAVE TO DO WITH THE LADY STYX? BECAUSE IF SHE'S DECIDED TO BREAK THE TREATY NOW, WE'RE ALL SCREWED.
THE TREATY STILL STANDS.
THANK GOD FOR THAT.
WE NEED THE TREATY BROKEN.
WE WHAT?
WHEN DO WE GET TO THE MOMENT WHEN I'M LET IN ON WHAT YOU TWO ARE TALKING ABOUT?
YES... ABOUT THAT.

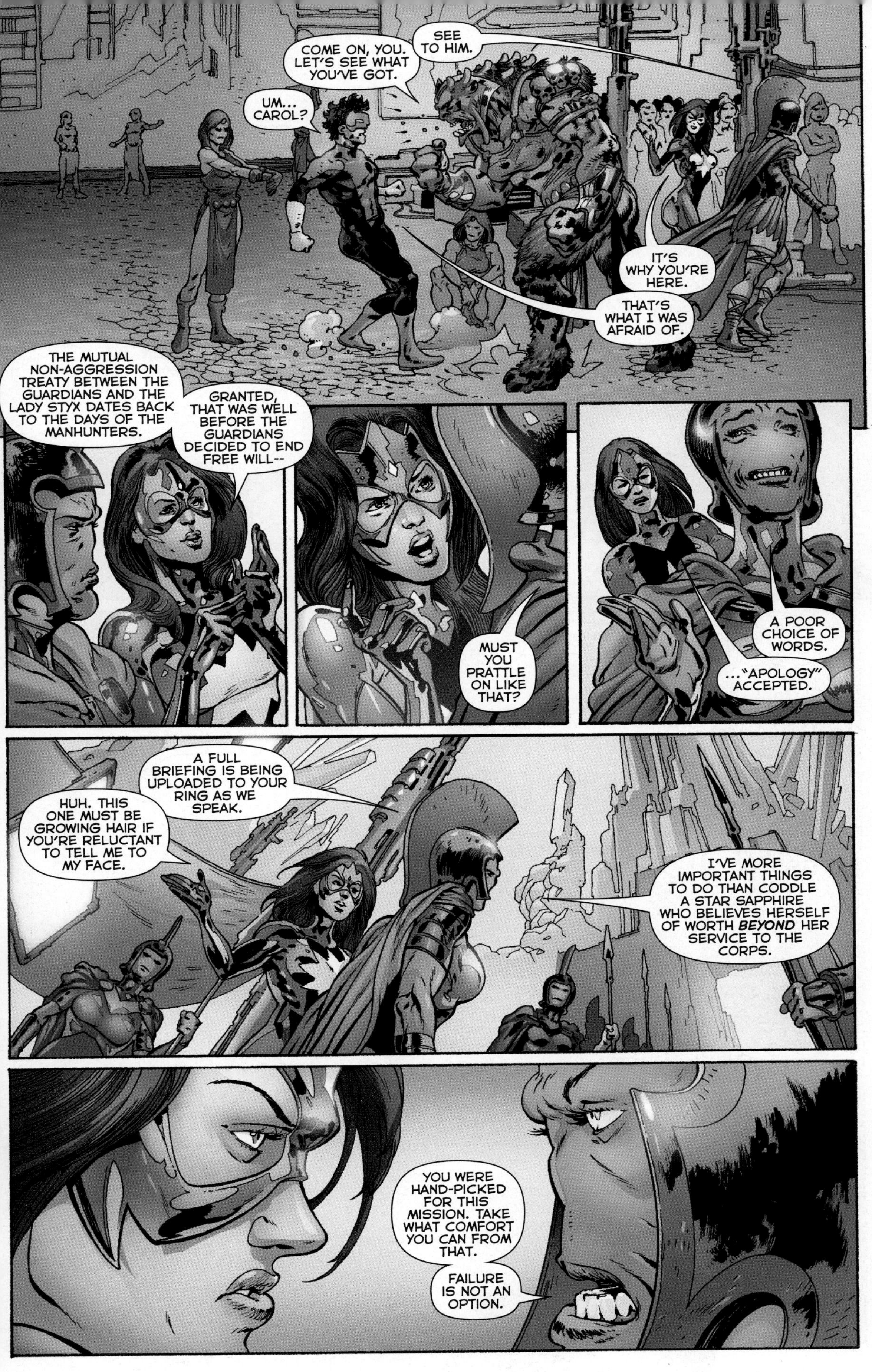
COME ON, YOU. LET'S SEE WHAT YOU'VE GOT.
SEE TO HIM.
UM... CAROL?
IT'S WHY YOU'RE HERE.
THAT'S WHAT I WAS AFRAID OF.
THE MUTUAL NON-AGGRESSION TREATY BETWEEN THE GUARDIANS AND THE LADY STYX DATES BACK TO THE DAYS OF THE MANHUNTERS.
GRANTED, THAT WAS WELL BEFORE THE GUARDIANS DECIDED TO END FREE WILL--
MUST YOU PRATTLE ON LIKE THAT?
A POOR CHOICE OF WORDS.
..."APOLOGY" ACCEPTED.
A FULL BRIEFING IS BEING UPLOADED TO YOUR RING AS WE SPEAK.
HUH. THIS ONE MUST BE GROWING HAIR IF YOU'RE RELUCTANT TO TELL ME TO MY FACE.
I'VE MORE IMPORTANT THINGS TO DO THAN CODDLE A STAR SAPPHIRE WHO BELIEVES HERSELF OF WORTH BEYOND HER SERVICE TO THE CORPS.
YOU WERE HAND-PICKED FOR THIS MISSION. TAKE WHAT COMFORT YOU CAN FROM THAT.
FAILURE IS NOT AN OPTION.

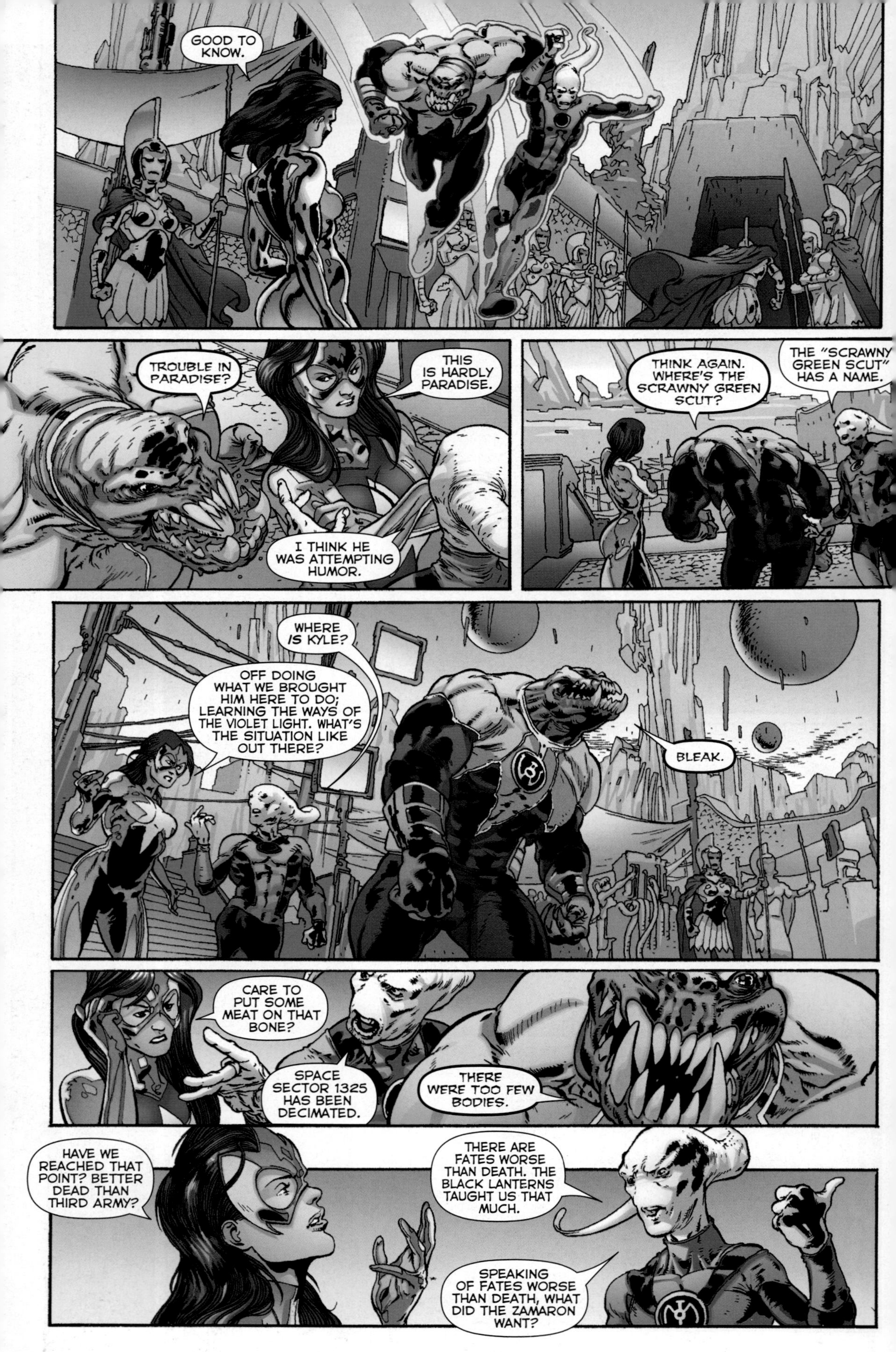
GOOD TO KNOW.
TROUBLE IN PARADISE?
THIS IS HARDLY PARADISE.
I THINK HE WAS ATTEMPTING HUMOR.
THINK AGAIN. WHERE'S THE SCRAWNY GREEN SCUT?
THE "SCRAWNY GREEN SCUT" HAS A NAME.
WHERE IS KYLE?
OFF DOING WHAT WE BROUGHT HIM HERE TO DO; LEARNING THE WAYS OF THE VIOLET LIGHT. WHAT'S THE SITUATION LIKE OUT THERE?
BLEAK.
CARE TO PUT SOME MEAT ON THAT BONE?
SPACE SECTOR 1325 HAS BEEN DECIMATED.
THERE WERE TOO FEW BODIES.
HAVE WE REACHED THAT POINT? BETTER DEAD THAN THIRD ARMY?
THERE ARE FATES WORSE THAN DEATH. THE BLACK LANTERNS TAUGHT US THAT MUCH.
SPEAKING OF FATES WORSE THAN DEATH, WHAT DID THE ZAMARON WANT?

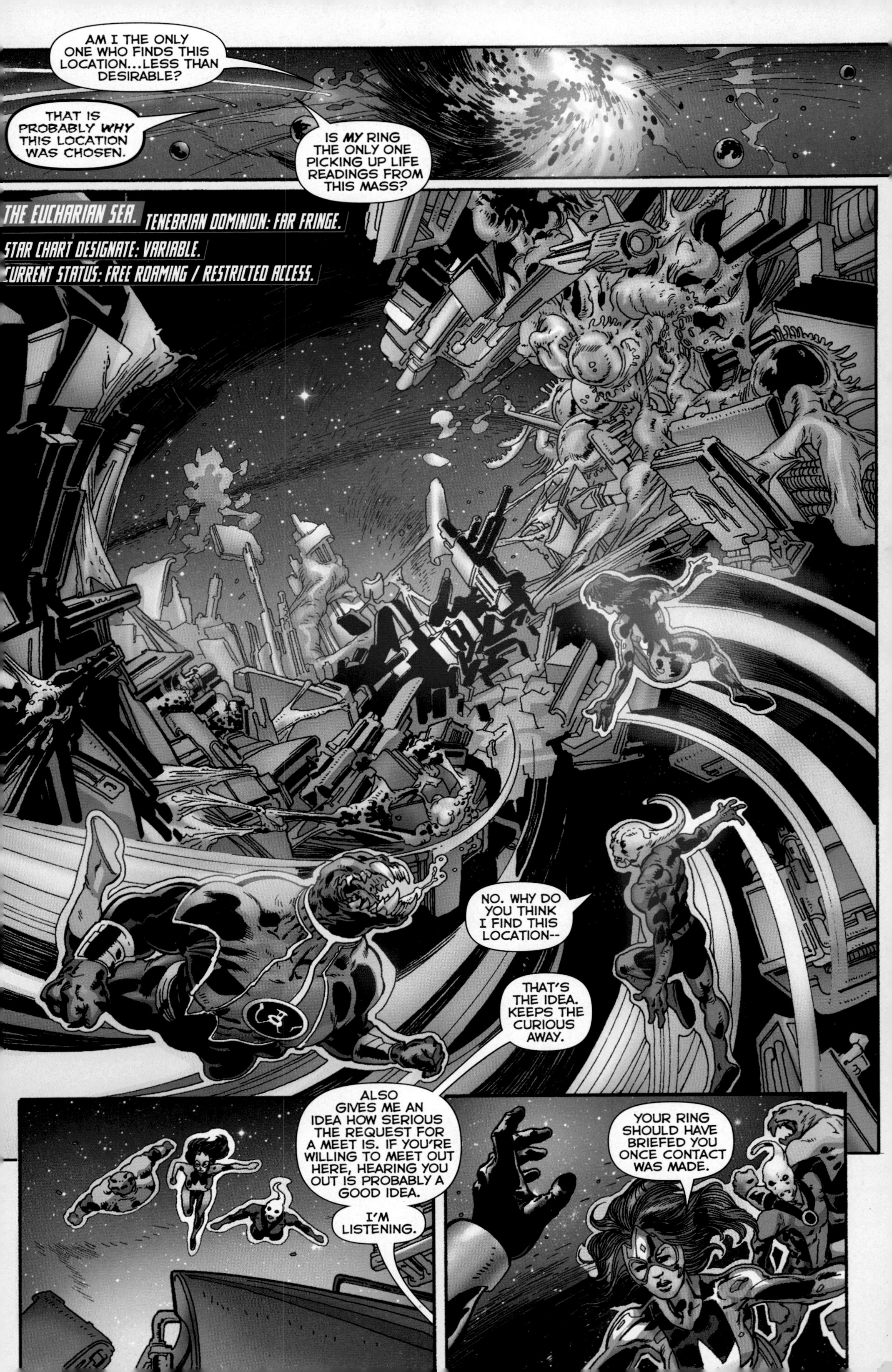
AM I THE ONLY ONE WHO FINDS THIS LOCATION...LESS THAN DESIRABLE?
THAT IS PROBABLY WHY THIS LOCATION WAS CHOSEN.
IS MY RING THE ONLY ONE PICKING UP LIFE READINGS FROM THIS MASS?
THE EUCHARIAN SEA.
TENEBRIAN DOMINION: FAR FRINGE.
STAR CHART DESIGNATE: VARIABLE.
CURRENT STATUS: FREE ROAMING / RESTRICTED ACCESS.
NO. WHY DO YOU THINK I FIND THIS LOCATION--
THAT'S THE IDEA. KEEPS THE CURIOUS AWAY.
ALSO GIVES ME AN IDEA HOW SERIOUS THE REQUEST FOR A MEET IS. IF YOU'RE WILLING TO MEET OUT HERE, HEARING YOU OUT IS PROBABLY A GOOD IDEA.
I'M LISTENING.
YOUR RING SHOULD HAVE BRIEFED YOU ONCE CONTACT WAS MADE.

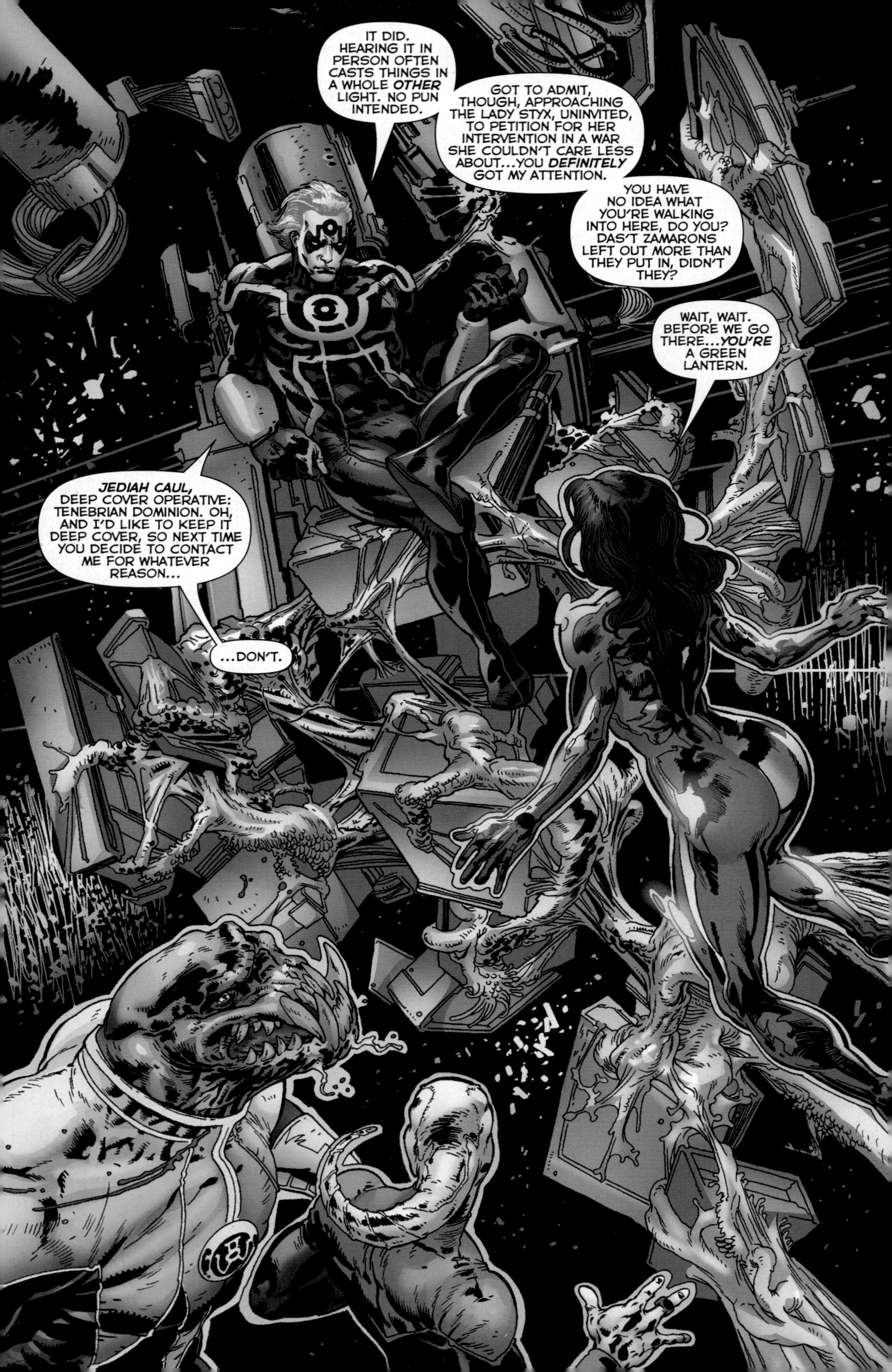
IT DID. HEARING IT IN PERSON OFTEN CASTS THINGS IN A WHOLE *OTHER* LIGHT. NO PUN INTENDED.
GOT TO ADMIT, THOUGH, APPROACHING THE LADY STYX, UNINVITED, TO PETITION FOR HER INTERVENTION IN A WAR SHE COULDN'T CARE LESS ABOUT...YOU *DEFINITELY* GOT MY ATTENTION.
YOU HAVE NO IDEA WHAT YOU'RE WALKING INTO HERE, DO YOU? DAS'T ZAMARONS LEFT OUT MORE THAN THEY PUT IN, DIDN'T THEY?
WAIT, WAIT. BEFORE WE GO THERE...*YOU'RE* A GREEN LANTERN.
JEDIAH CAUL, DEEP COVER OPERATIVE: TENEBRIAN DOMINION. OH, AND I'D LIKE TO KEEP IT DEEP COVER, SO NEXT TIME YOU DECIDE TO CONTACT ME FOR WHATEVER REASON...
...DON'T.

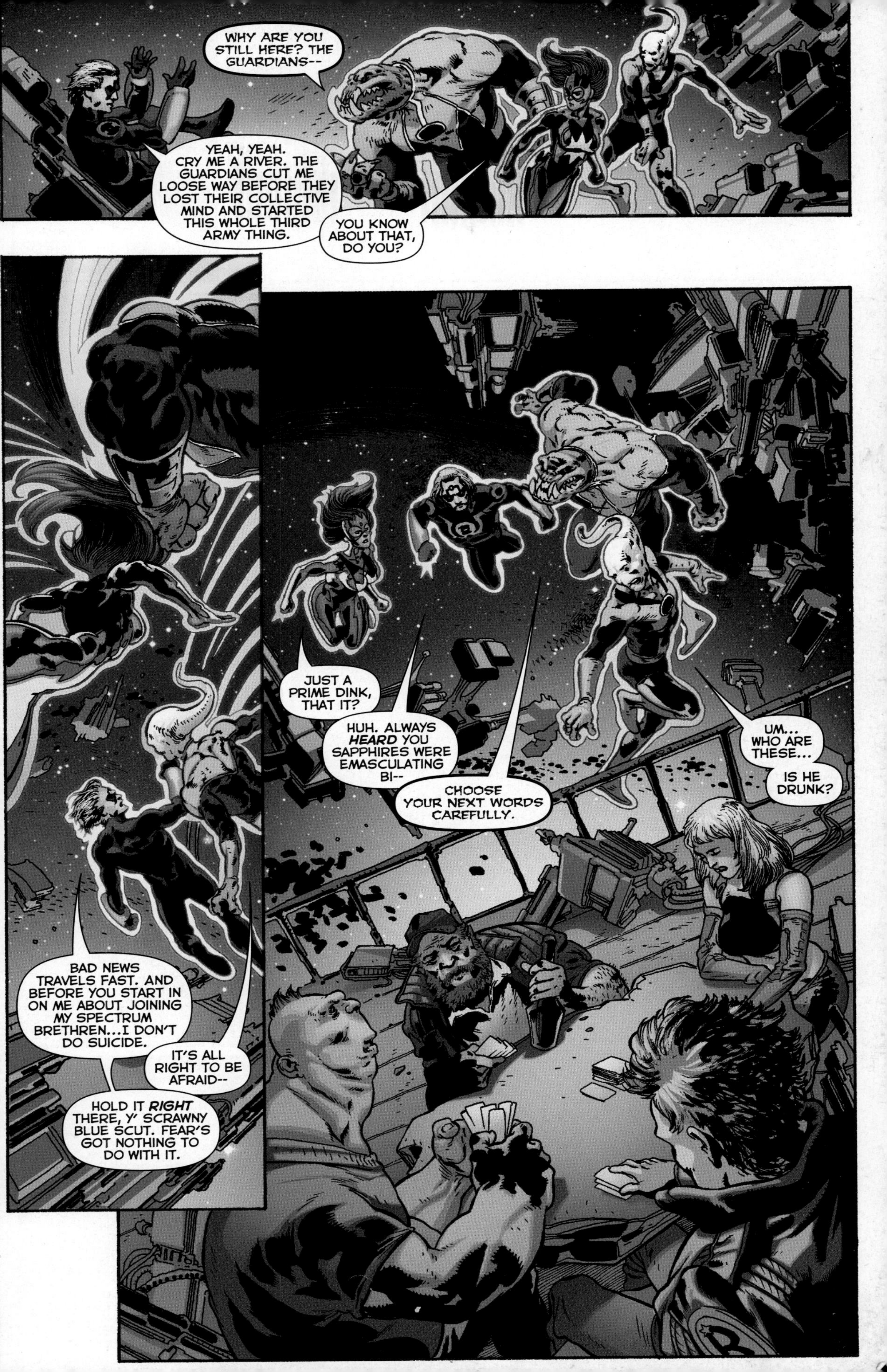
WHY ARE YOU STILL HERE? THE GUARDIANS--
YEAH, YEAH. CRY ME A RIVER. THE GUARDIANS CUT ME LOOSE WAY BEFORE THEY LOST THEIR COLLECTIVE MIND AND STARTED THIS WHOLE THIRD ARMY THING.
YOU KNOW ABOUT THAT, DO YOU?
BAD NEWS TRAVELS FAST. AND BEFORE YOU START IN ON ME ABOUT JOINING MY SPECTRUM BRETHREN...I DON'T DO SUICIDE.
IT'S ALL RIGHT TO BE AFRAID--
HOLD IT *RIGHT* THERE, Y' SCRAWNY BLUE SCUT. FEAR'S GOT NOTHING TO DO WITH IT.
JUST A PRIME DINK, THAT IT?
HUH. ALWAYS *HEARD* YOU SAPPHIRES WERE EMASCULATING BI--
CHOOSE YOUR NEXT WORDS CAREFULLY.
UM... WHO ARE THESE...
IS HE DRUNK?

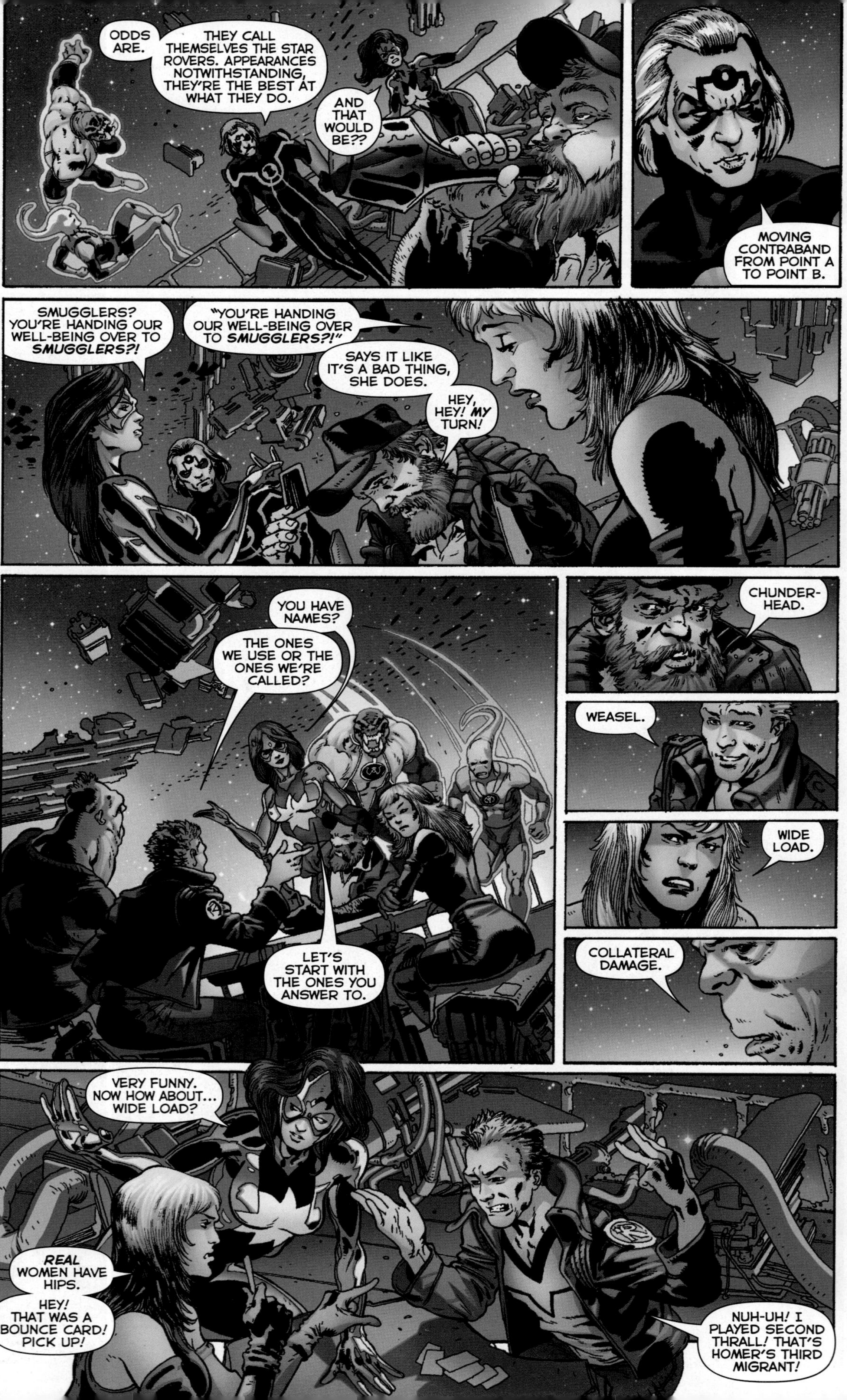

ODDS ARE.
THEY CALL THEMSELVES THE STAR ROVERS. APPEARANCES NOTWITHSTANDING, THEY'RE THE BEST AT WHAT THEY DO.
AND THAT WOULD BE??
MOVING CONTRABAND FROM POINT A TO POINT B.
SMUGGLERS? YOU'RE HANDING OUR WELL-BEING OVER TO SMUGGLERS?!
"YOU'RE HANDING OUR WELL-BEING OVER TO SMUGGLERS?!"
SAYS IT LIKE IT'S A BAD THING, SHE DOES.
HEY, HEY! MY TURN!
YOU HAVE NAMES?
THE ONES WE USE OR THE ONES WE'RE CALLED?
LET'S START WITH THE ONES YOU ANSWER TO.
CHUNDER-HEAD.
WEASEL.
WIDE LOAD.
COLLATERAL DAMAGE.
VERY FUNNY. NOW HOW ABOUT... WIDE LOAD?
REAL WOMEN HAVE HIPS.
HEY! THAT WAS A BOUNCE CARD! PICK UP!
NUH-UH! I PLAYED SECOND THRALL! THAT'S HOMER'S THIRD MIGRANT!

WELL *SOMEBODY'D* BETTER PICK UP.

SHOULDN'T WE BE SEEING TO GETTING THE STAR SAPPHIRE INTO TENEBR--?

AH, AH, AH. MERCHANDISE SHOULD BE SEEN BUT NOT HEARD.

...

KTASSH!

WHAT WAS *THAT* ALL ABOUT?!

NOW THAT I HAVE YOUR UNDIVIDED ATTENTION...

UNDIVI... I OUGHT TO GUT YOU GOOD FOR PULLING A STUNT LIKE THAT!

NOW THAT I WOULD LIKE TO SEE.

HAH?

IF ONLY FOR THE LOOK ON YOUR FACE AS SHE SLOWLY DISSOLVES YOU.

UM... THANKS FOR THE TIP?

HOW MUCH DO THEY KNOW?

THEY KNOW THEY'VE GOT TO GET YOU WELL WITHIN THE DOMINION.

AND THEN?

AND THEN YOU'RE ON YOUR OWN. GOOD LUCK WITH THAT.

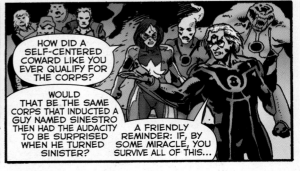

HOW DID A SELF-CENTERED COWARD LIKE YOU EVER QUALIFY FOR THE CORPS?

WOULD THAT BE THE SAME CORPS THAT INDUCTED A GUY NAMED SINESTRO THEN HAD THE AUDACITY TO BE SURPRISED WHEN HE TURNED SINISTER?

A FRIENDLY REMINDER: IF, BY SOME MIRACLE, YOU SURVIVE ALL OF THIS...

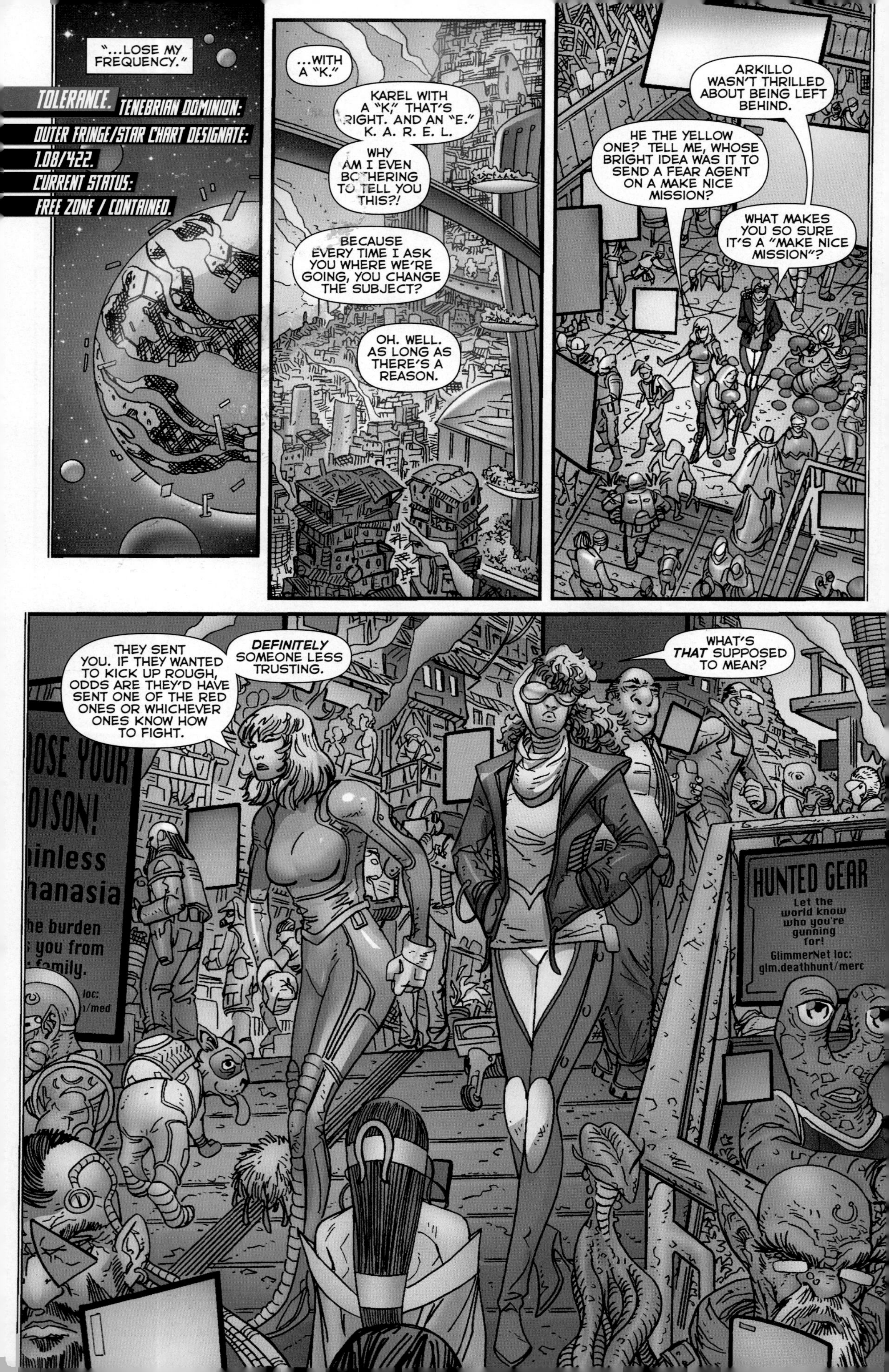
"...LOSE MY FREQUENCY."
TOLERANCE. TENEBRIAN DOMINION: OUTER FRINGE/STAR CHART DESIGNATE: 1.08/422. CURRENT STATUS: FREE ZONE / CONTAINED.
...WITH A "K."
KAREL WITH A "K," THAT'S RIGHT. AND AN "E." K. A. R. E. L.
WHY AM I EVEN BOTHERING TO TELL YOU THIS?!
BECAUSE EVERY TIME I ASK YOU WHERE WE'RE GOING, YOU CHANGE THE SUBJECT?
OH. WELL. AS LONG AS THERE'S A REASON.
ARKILLO WASN'T THRILLED ABOUT BEING LEFT BEHIND.
HE THE YELLOW ONE? TELL ME, WHOSE BRIGHT IDEA WAS IT TO SEND A FEAR AGENT ON A MAKE NICE MISSION?
WHAT MAKES YOU SO SURE IT'S A "MAKE NICE MISSION"?
THEY SENT YOU. IF THEY WANTED TO KICK UP ROUGH, ODDS ARE THEY'D HAVE SENT ONE OF THE RED ONES OR WHICHEVER ONES KNOW HOW TO FIGHT.
DEFINITELY SOMEONE LESS TRUSTING.
WHAT'S *THAT* SUPPOSED TO MEAN?
HUNTED GEAR
Let the world know who you're gunning for!
GlimmerNet loc: glm.deathhunt/merc

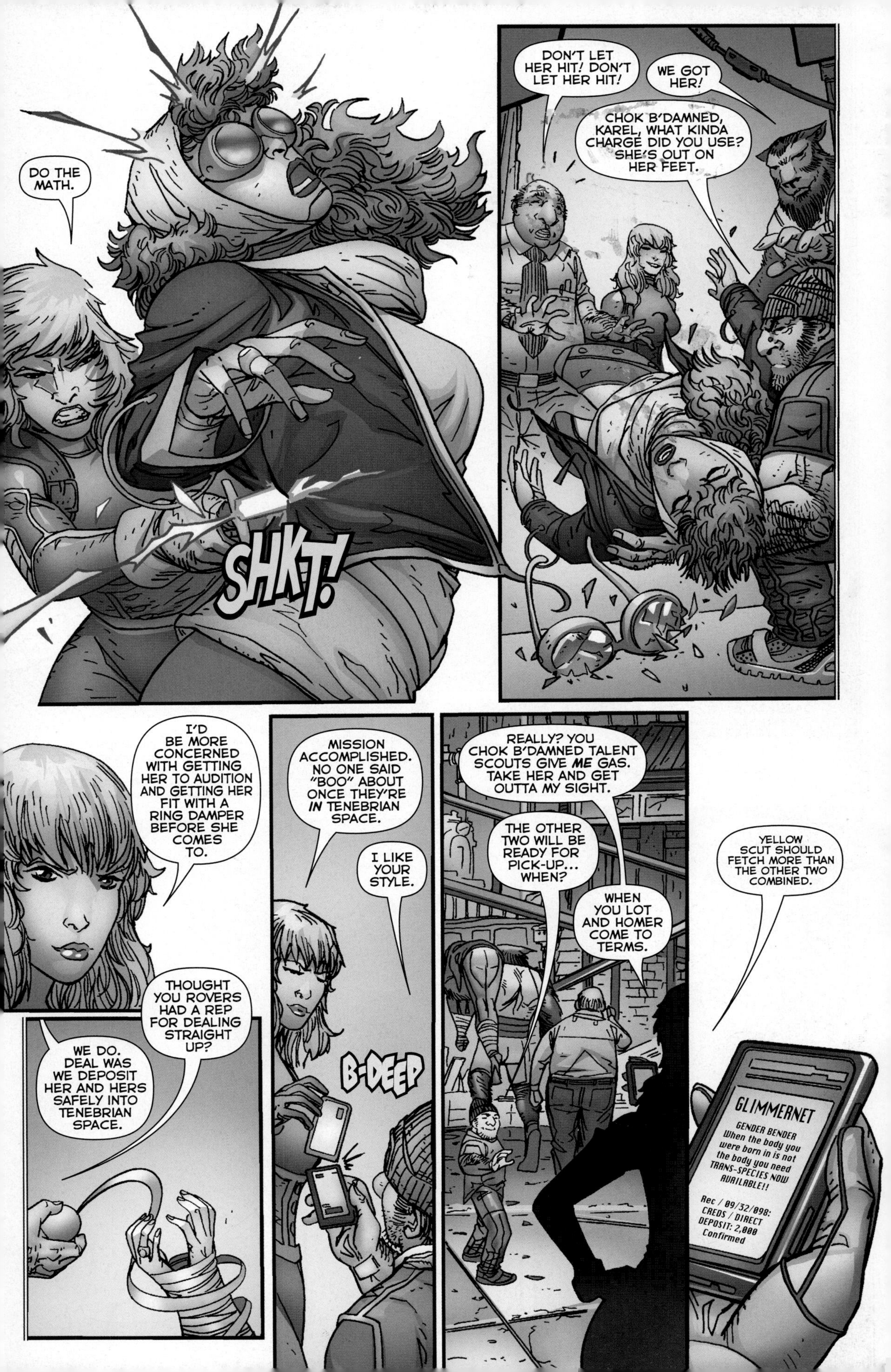
DO THE MATH.
SHKT!
DON'T LET HER HIT! DON'T LET HER HIT!
WE GOT HER!
CHOK B'DAMNED, KAREL, WHAT KINDA CHARGE DID YOU USE? SHE'S OUT ON HER FEET.
I'D BE MORE CONCERNED WITH GETTING HER TO AUDITION AND GETTING HER FIT WITH A RING DAMPER BEFORE SHE COMES TO.
THOUGHT YOU ROVERS HAD A REP FOR DEALING STRAIGHT UP?
WE DO. DEAL WAS WE DEPOSIT HER AND HERS SAFELY INTO TENEBRIAN SPACE.
MISSION ACCOMPLISHED. NO ONE SAID "BOO" ABOUT ONCE THEY'RE IN TENEBRIAN SPACE.
I LIKE YOUR STYLE.
B-DEEP
REALLY? YOU CHOK B'DAMNED TALENT SCOUTS GIVE ME GAS. TAKE HER AND GET OUTTA MY SIGHT.
THE OTHER TWO WILL BE READY FOR PICK-UP... WHEN?
WHEN YOU LOT AND HOMER COME TO TERMS.
YELLOW SCUT SHOULD FETCH MORE THAN THE OTHER TWO COMBINED.
GLIMMERNET
GENDER BENDER
When the body you were born in is not the body you need
TRANS-SPECIES NOW AVAILABLE!!
Rec / 09/32/098:
CREDS / DIRECT
DEPOSIT: 2,000
Confirmed

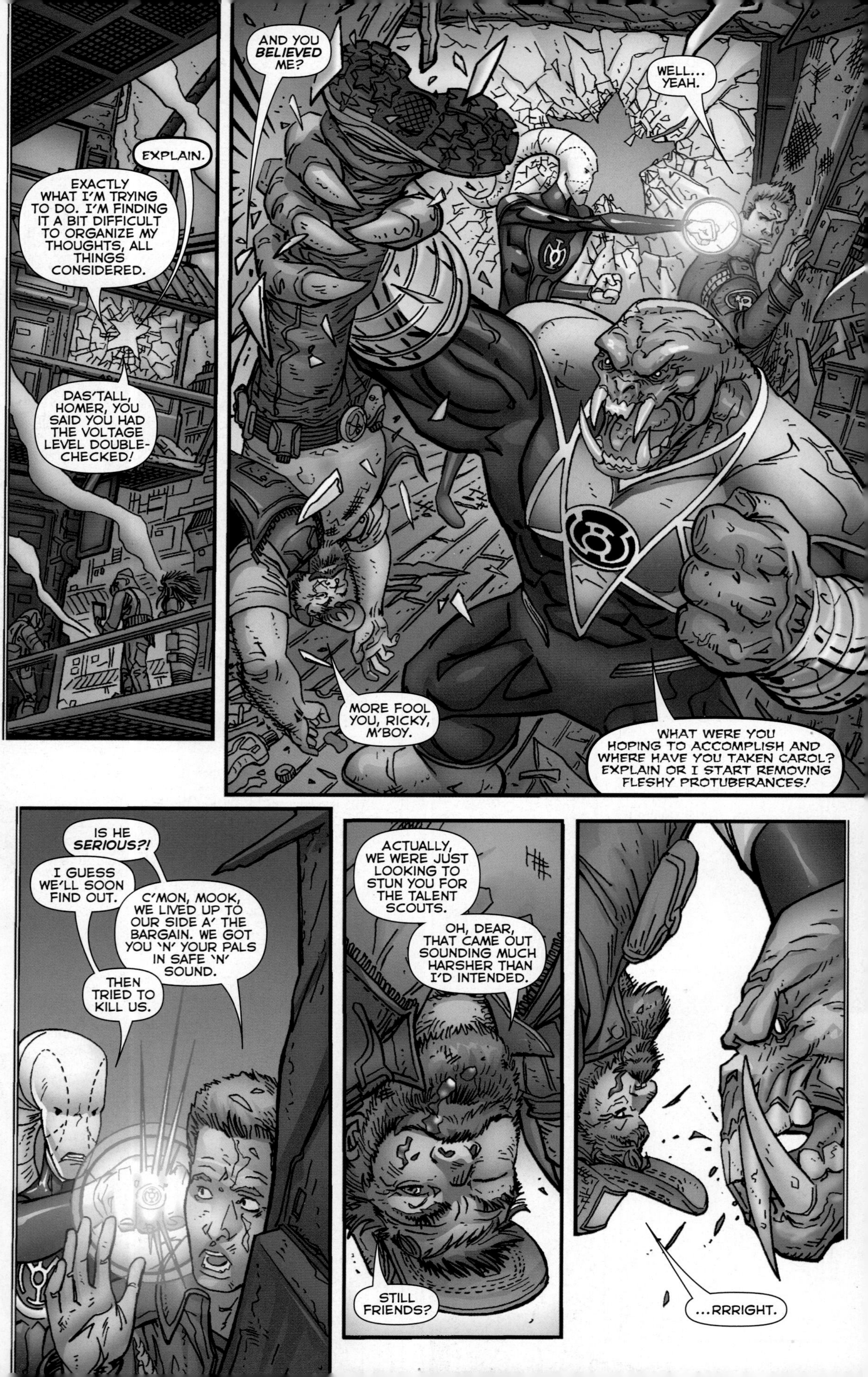
EXPLAIN.
EXACTLY WHAT I'M TRYING TO DO. I'M FINDING IT A BIT DIFFICULT TO ORGANIZE MY THOUGHTS, ALL THINGS CONSIDERED.
DAS'TALL, HOMER, YOU SAID YOU HAD THE VOLTAGE LEVEL DOUBLE-CHECKED!
AND YOU BELIEVED ME?
WELL... YEAH.
MORE FOOL YOU, RICKY, M'BOY.
WHAT WERE YOU HOPING TO ACCOMPLISH AND WHERE HAVE YOU TAKEN CAROL? EXPLAIN OR I START REMOVING FLESHY PROTUBERANCES!
IS HE SERIOUS?!
I GUESS WE'LL SOON FIND OUT.
C'MON, MOOK, WE LIVED UP TO OUR SIDE A' THE BARGAIN. WE GOT YOU 'N' YOUR PALS IN SAFE 'N' SOUND.
THEN TRIED TO KILL US.
ACTUALLY, WE WERE JUST LOOKING TO STUN YOU FOR THE TALENT SCOUTS.
OH, DEAR, THAT CAME OUT SOUNDING MUCH HARSHER THAN I'D INTENDED.
STILL FRIENDS?
...RRRIGHT.

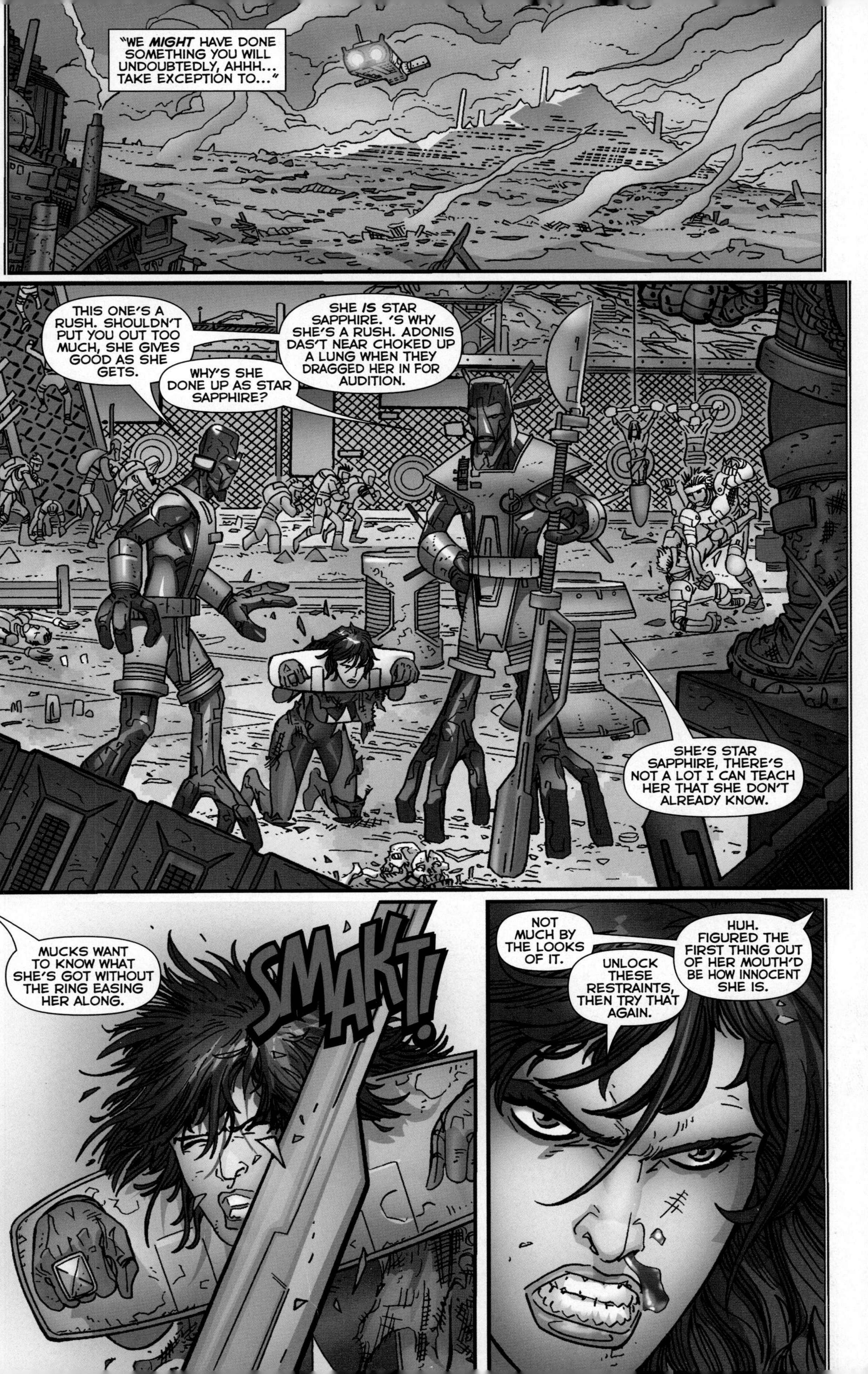
"WE *MIGHT* HAVE DONE SOMETHING YOU WILL UNDOUBTEDLY, AHHH... TAKE EXCEPTION TO..."
THIS ONE'S A RUSH. SHOULDN'T PUT YOU OUT TOO MUCH, SHE GIVES GOOD AS SHE GETS.
WHY'S SHE DONE UP AS STAR SAPPHIRE?
SHE *IS* STAR SAPPHIRE. 'S WHY SHE'S A RUSH. ADONIS DAS'T NEAR CHOKED UP A LUNG WHEN THEY DRAGGED HER IN FOR AUDITION.
SHE'S STAR SAPPHIRE, THERE'S NOT A LOT I CAN TEACH HER THAT SHE DON'T ALREADY KNOW.
MUCKS WANT TO KNOW WHAT SHE'S GOT WITHOUT THE RING EASING HER ALONG.
SMAKT!
NOT MUCH BY THE LOOKS OF IT.
UNLOCK THESE RESTRAINTS, THEN TRY THAT AGAIN.
HUH. FIGURED THE FIRST THING OUT OF HER MOUTH'D BE HOW INNOCENT SHE IS.

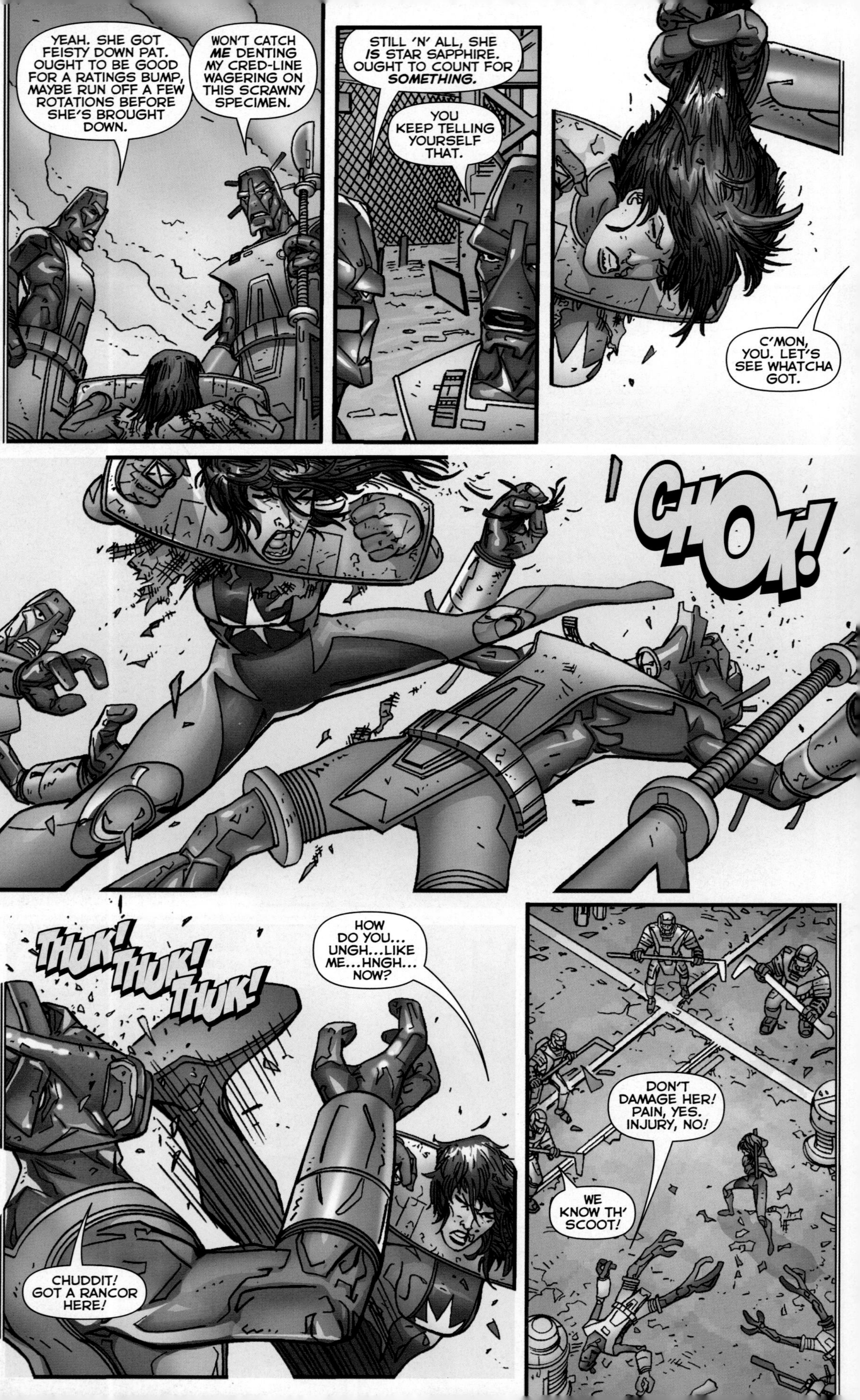
YEAH. SHE GOT FEISTY DOWN PAT. OUGHT TO BE GOOD FOR A RATINGS BUMP, MAYBE RUN OFF A FEW ROTATIONS BEFORE SHE'S BROUGHT DOWN.
WON'T CATCH *ME* DENTING MY CRED-LINE WAGERING ON THIS SCRAWNY SPECIMEN.
STILL 'N' ALL, SHE *IS* STAR SAPPHIRE. OUGHT TO COUNT FOR *SOMETHING.*
YOU KEEP TELLING YOURSELF THAT.
C'MON, YOU. LET'S SEE WHATCHA GOT.
CHOK!
THUK! THUK! THUK!
HOW DO YOU... UNGH...LIKE ME...HNGH... NOW?
CHUDDIT! GOT A RANCOR HERE!
DON'T DAMAGE HER! PAIN, YES. INJURY, NO!
WE KNOW TH' SCOOT!

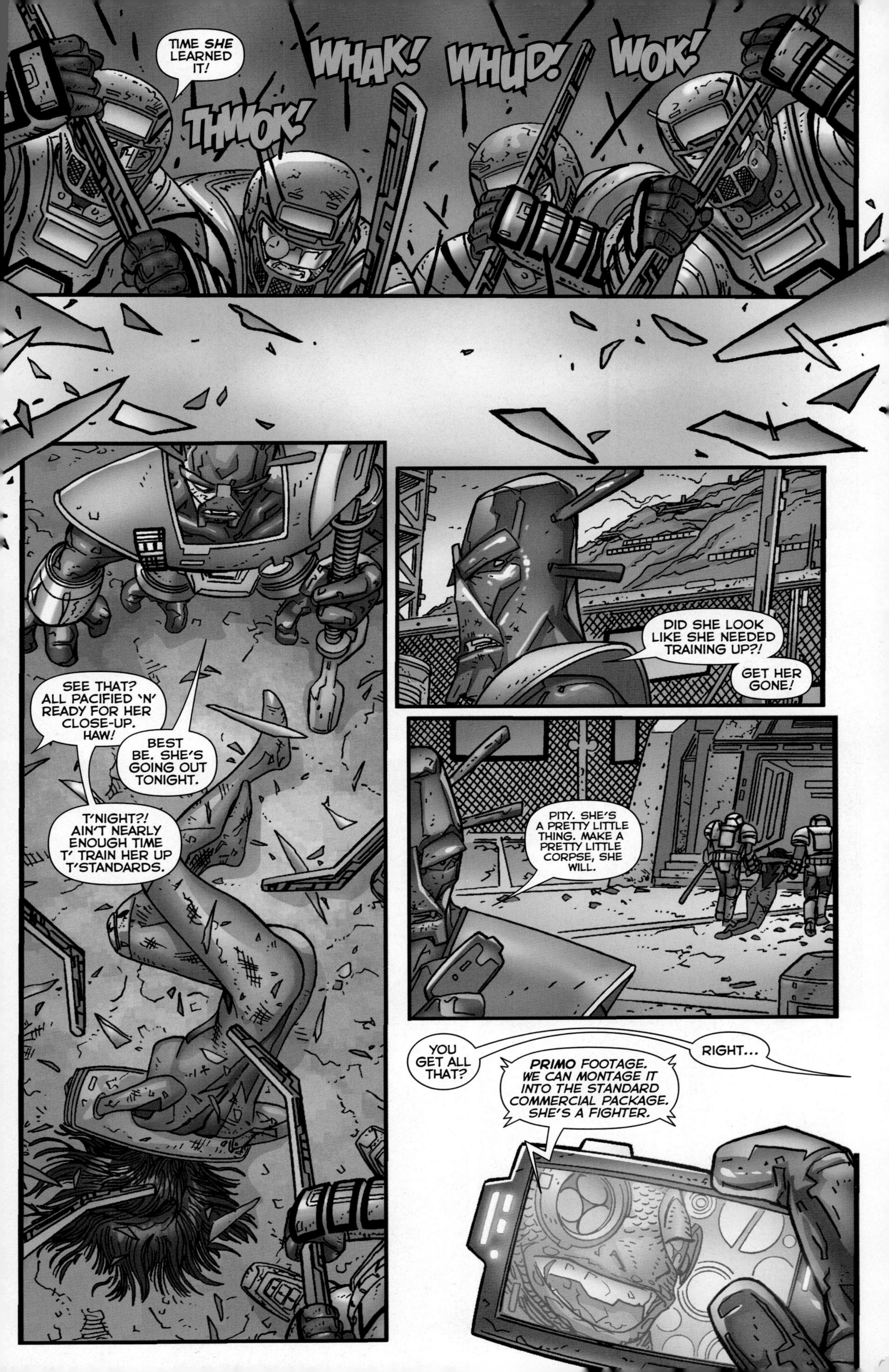
TIME *SHE* LEARNED IT!
WHAK! WHUD! WOK!
THWOK!
SEE THAT? ALL PACIFIED 'N' READY FOR HER CLOSE-UP. HAW!
BEST BE. SHE'S GOING OUT TONIGHT.
T'NIGHT?! AIN'T NEARLY ENOUGH TIME T' TRAIN HER UP T'STANDARDS.
DID SHE LOOK LIKE SHE NEEDED TRAINING UP?!
GET HER *GONE!*
PITY. SHE'S A PRETTY LITTLE THING. MAKE A PRETTY LITTLE CORPSE, SHE WILL.
YOU GET ALL THAT?
RIGHT...
PRIMO FOOTAGE. WE CAN MONTAGE IT INTO THE STANDARD COMMERCIAL PACKAGE. SHE'S A FIGHTER.

"LIKE SHE HAS A CHOICE."

CHRIS KL-99
New Season Starts
10/09/898
Glimmernet loc:
lm.him?really?/ent

EROMONES
FOR ALL
CCASIONS
ve him or
athe him,
him know.
mmerNet
loc:
.fragrance
/ret

HABITATS 4
RENT
Contained
atmospheres
to order.

GLIMMERNET

 night on
HUNTED

LOVE
URTS!

...TERRAN INTERCEPT LITERATURE WILL TELL YOU "LOVE HATH NO FURY," BUT THIS CONTESTANT HAS FURY TO SPARE!

HUH. SUCKS TO BE HER.

PRIMARY PORTAL REQUESTS ATTENTION.

NOT HOME.

RELAYING MESSAGE.

WHRR -UNCH!

DAS'TALL, HOMER! I TOLD YOU TO PLAY THIS ONE STRAIGHT!

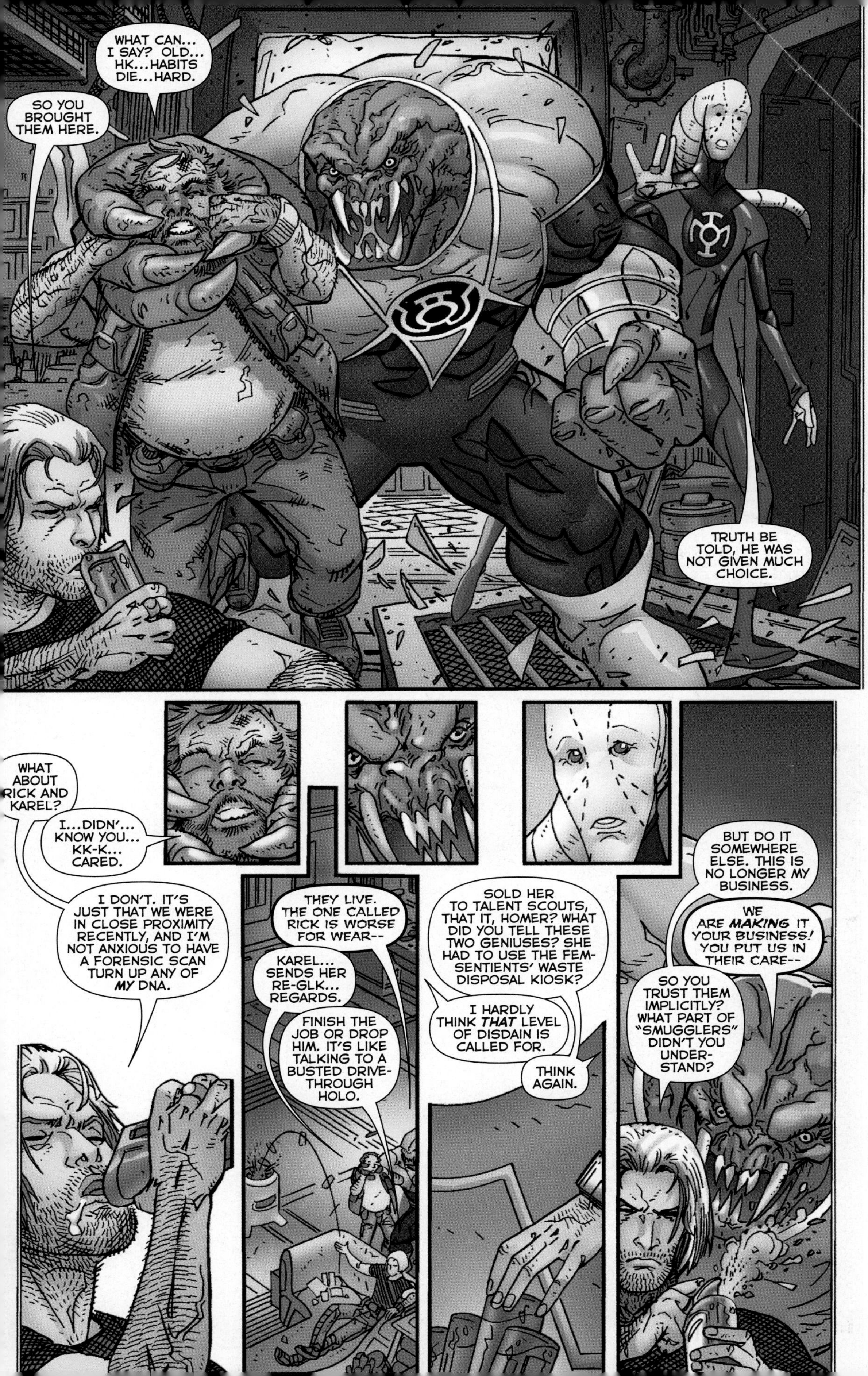
SO YOU BROUGHT THEM HERE.
WHAT CAN... I SAY? OLD... HK...HABITS DIE...HARD.
TRUTH BE TOLD, HE WAS NOT GIVEN MUCH CHOICE.
WHAT ABOUT RICK AND KAREL?
I...DIDN'... KNOW YOU... KK-K... CARED.
I DON'T. IT'S JUST THAT WE WERE IN CLOSE PROXIMITY RECENTLY, AND I'M NOT ANXIOUS TO HAVE A FORENSIC SCAN TURN UP ANY OF *MY* DNA.
THEY LIVE. THE ONE CALLED RICK IS WORSE FOR WEAR--
KAREL... SENDS HER RE-GLK... REGARDS.
FINISH THE JOB OR DROP HIM. IT'S LIKE TALKING TO A BUSTED DRIVE-THROUGH HOLO.
SOLD HER TO TALENT SCOUTS, THAT IT, HOMER? WHAT DID YOU TELL THESE TWO GENIUSES? SHE HAD TO USE THE FEM-SENTIENTS' WASTE DISPOSAL KIOSK?
I HARDLY THINK *THAT* LEVEL OF DISDAIN IS CALLED FOR.
THINK AGAIN.
BUT DO IT SOMEWHERE ELSE. THIS IS NO LONGER MY BUSINESS.
WE ARE *MAKING* IT YOUR BUSINESS! YOU PUT US IN THEIR CARE--
SO YOU TRUST THEM IMPLICITLY? WHAT PART OF "SMUGGLERS" DIDN'T YOU UNDER-STAND?

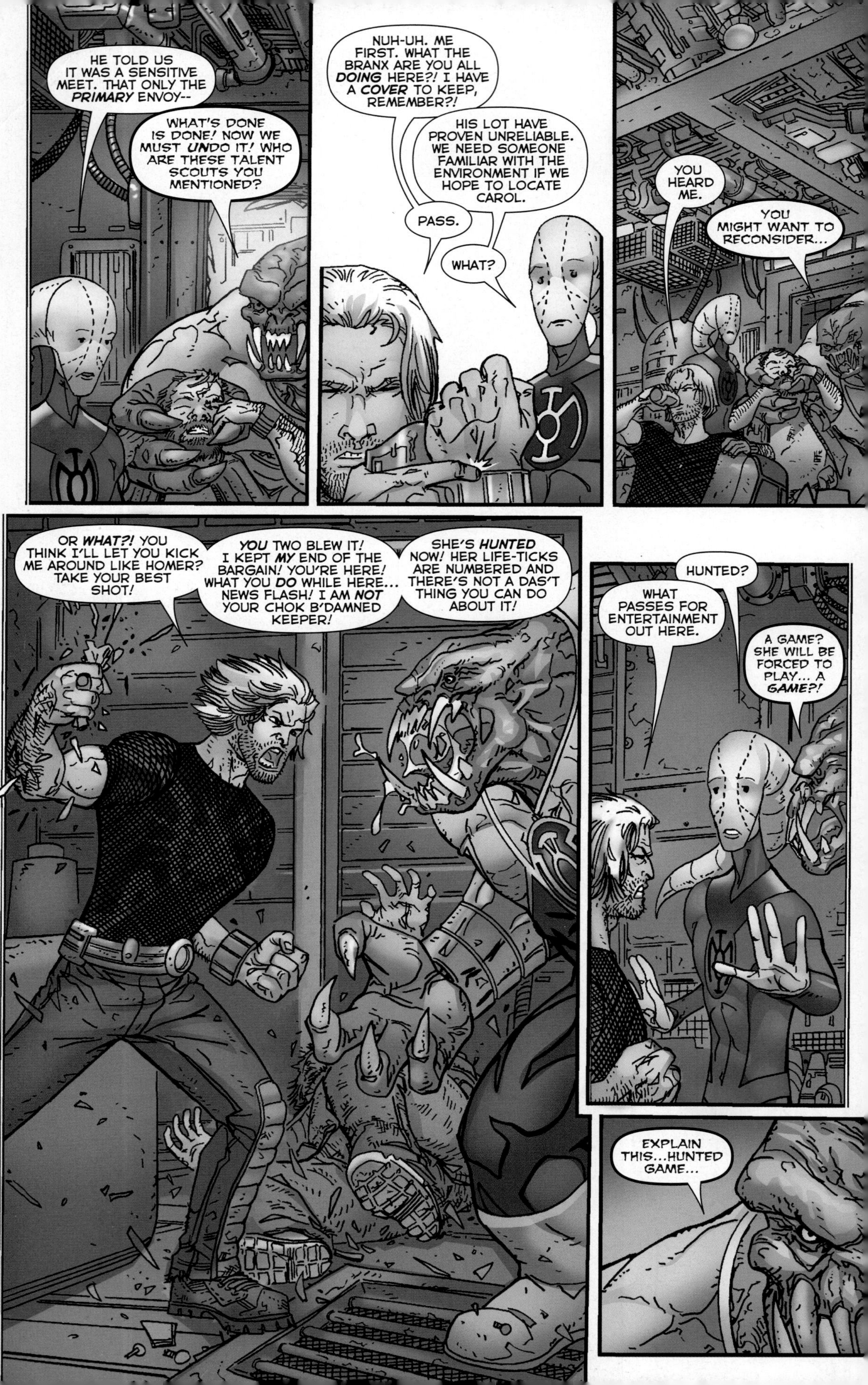

HE TOLD US IT WAS A SENSITIVE MEET. THAT ONLY THE PRIMARY ENVOY--
WHAT'S DONE IS DONE! NOW WE MUST UNDO IT! WHO ARE THESE TALENT SCOUTS YOU MENTIONED?
NUH-UH. ME FIRST. WHAT THE BRANX ARE YOU ALL DOING HERE?! I HAVE A COVER TO KEEP, REMEMBER?!
HIS LOT HAVE PROVEN UNRELIABLE. WE NEED SOMEONE FAMILIAR WITH THE ENVIRONMENT IF WE HOPE TO LOCATE CAROL.
PASS.
WHAT?
YOU HEARD ME.
YOU MIGHT WANT TO RECONSIDER...
OR WHAT?! YOU THINK I'LL LET YOU KICK ME AROUND LIKE HOMER? TAKE YOUR BEST SHOT!
YOU TWO BLEW IT! I KEPT MY END OF THE BARGAIN! YOU'RE HERE! WHAT YOU DO WHILE HERE... NEWS FLASH! I AM NOT YOUR CHOK B'DAMNED KEEPER!
SHE'S HUNTED NOW! HER LIFE-TICKS ARE NUMBERED AND THERE'S NOT A DAS'T THING YOU CAN DO ABOUT IT!
HUNTED?
WHAT PASSES FOR ENTERTAINMENT OUT HERE.
A GAME? SHE WILL BE FORCED TO PLAY... A GAME?!
EXPLAIN THIS...HUNTED GAME...

WELCOME TO THE HUNTED, THE GLIMMERNET'S MOST POPULAR STREAMING PROGRAM. YOU HAVE BEEN CONSCRIPTED TO SERVE AS A CONTESTANT. THIS IS NOT AN HONOR.

YOU HAVE BEEN CHOSEN BECAUSE YOU REPRESENT A THREAT TO THE TENEBRIAN DOMINION AND ITS AFFILIATED HOLDINGS. THE RULES ARE AS FOLLOWS.

YOU WILL BE ASSIGNED A BOUNTY, RELEASED FROM CUSTODY AND GRANTED A FULL PLANETARY ROTATION GRACE PERIOD, AFTER WHICH YOU WILL BE HUNTED BY ANYONE WHO CHOOSES TO HUNT YOU FOR WHATEVER REASON.

THE COMPETITION IS OPEN TO ALL REGISTERED CITIZENS OF THE TENEBRIAN DOMINION, REGARDLESS OF AGE. IF YOU ARE TAKEN DOWN BY A MINOR, THE BOUNTY WILL BE PLACED IN STATE TRUST UNTIL THE CHILD COMES OF AGE.

THE HUNT WILL CONTINUE UNTIL DEATH. THERE IS NO REPRIEVE. THERE ARE NO CONDITIONS UNDER WHICH THE HUNT, ONCE BEGUN, WILL BE SUSPENDED.

DELIBERATE FORFEITURE OF THE HUNT BY WAY OF SUICIDE OR A REFUSAL TO DEFEND ONESELF WILL RESULT IN THE CONTESTANT'S IMMEDIATE FAMILY AND / OR FRIENDS REPLACING THE CONTESTANT AS HUNTED.

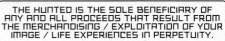

COLLATERAL DAMAGE, WHETHER GENERATED BY HUNTED OR HUNTER, IS ACKNOWLEDGED AS BEING PART AND PARCEL OF THE GAME EXPERIENCE.

COLLATERAL DAMAGE IN SERVICE TO THE GAME WILL NOT BE CONSIDERED A PUNISHABLE OFFENSE. FAMILIES WILL RECEIVE THE STANDARD WRONGFUL DEATH BENEFITS PACKAGE SHOULD A LOVED ONE DIE DURING A LIVE FEED.

THE HUNTED IS THE SOLE BENEFICIARY OF ANY AND ALL PROCEEDS THAT RESULT FROM THE MERCHANDISING / EXPLOITATION OF YOUR IMAGE / LIFE EXPERIENCES IN PERPETUITY.

BY LISTENING TO THIS RECORDING, YOU AGREE TO THE TERMS AS STATED.

WE NOW RETURN YOU TO REALITY AS YOU PERCEIVE IT.

YOU HAVE GOT TO BE KIDDING ME!

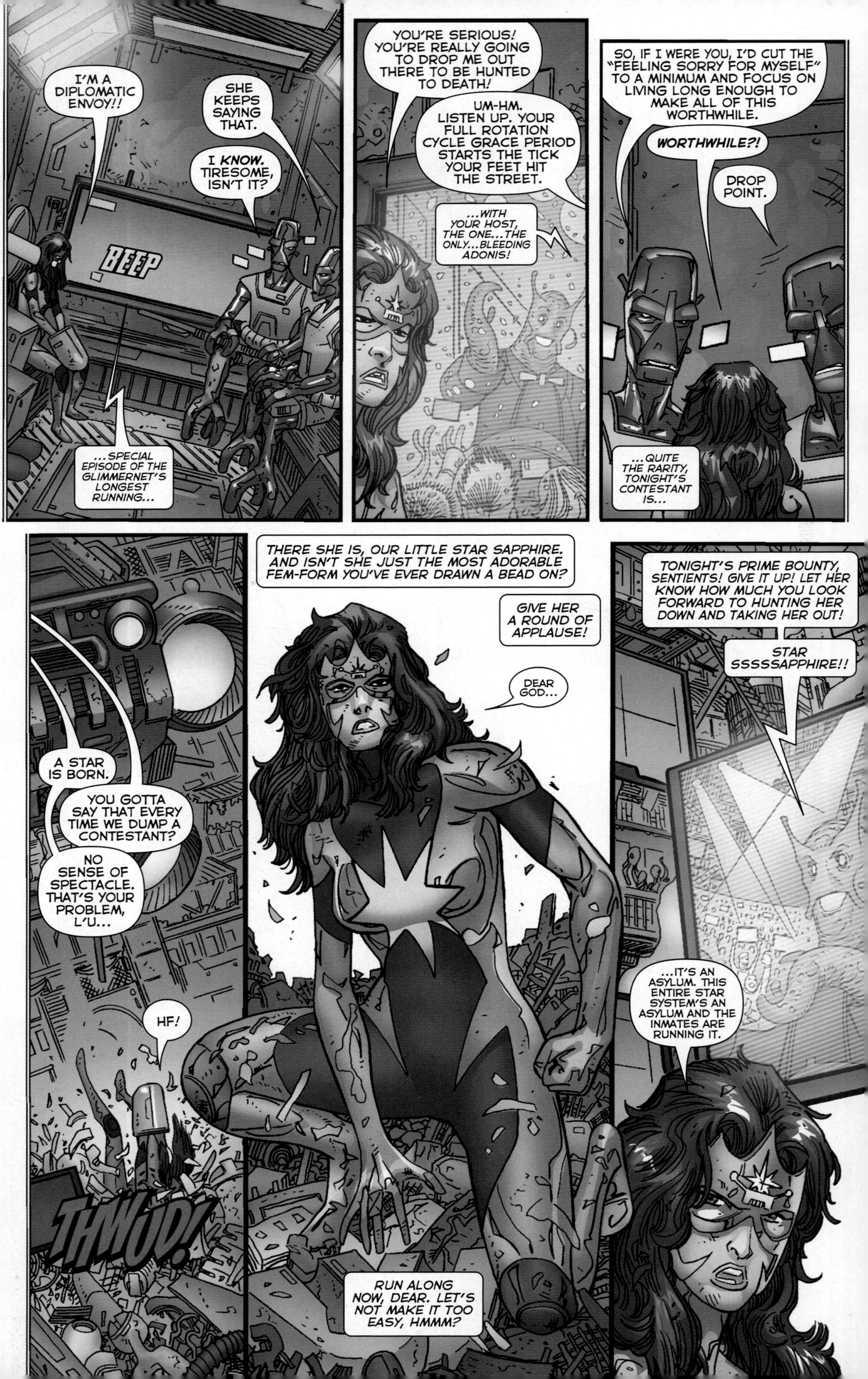
I'M A DIPLOMATIC ENVOY!!
SHE KEEPS SAYING THAT.
I KNOW. TIRESOME, ISN'T IT?
BEEP
...SPECIAL EPISODE OF THE GLIMMERNET'S LONGEST RUNNING...
YOU'RE SERIOUS! YOU'RE REALLY GOING TO DROP ME OUT THERE TO BE HUNTED TO DEATH!
UM-HM. LISTEN UP. YOUR FULL ROTATION CYCLE GRACE PERIOD STARTS THE TICK YOUR FEET HIT THE STREET.
...WITH YOUR HOST, THE ONE...THE ONLY...BLEEDING ADONIS!
SO, IF I WERE YOU, I'D CUT THE "FEELING SORRY FOR MYSELF" TO A MINIMUM AND FOCUS ON LIVING LONG ENOUGH TO MAKE ALL OF THIS WORTHWHILE.
WORTHWHILE?!
DROP POINT.
...QUITE THE RARITY, TONIGHT'S CONTESTANT IS...
A STAR IS BORN.
YOU GOTTA SAY THAT EVERY TIME WE DUMP A CONTESTANT?
NO SENSE OF SPECTACLE. THAT'S YOUR PROBLEM, L'U...
HF!
THWUD!
THERE SHE IS, OUR LITTLE STAR SAPPHIRE. AND ISN'T SHE JUST THE MOST ADORABLE FEM-FORM YOU'VE EVER DRAWN A BEAD ON?
GIVE HER A ROUND OF APPLAUSE!
DEAR GOD...
RUN ALONG NOW, DEAR. LET'S NOT MAKE IT TOO EASY, HMMM?
TONIGHT'S PRIME BOUNTY, SENTIENTS! GIVE IT UP! LET HER KNOW HOW MUCH YOU LOOK FORWARD TO HUNTING HER DOWN AND TAKING HER OUT!
STAR SSSSSAPPHIRE!!
...IT'S AN ASYLUM. THIS ENTIRE STAR SYSTEM'S AN ASYLUM AND THE INMATES ARE RUNNING IT.

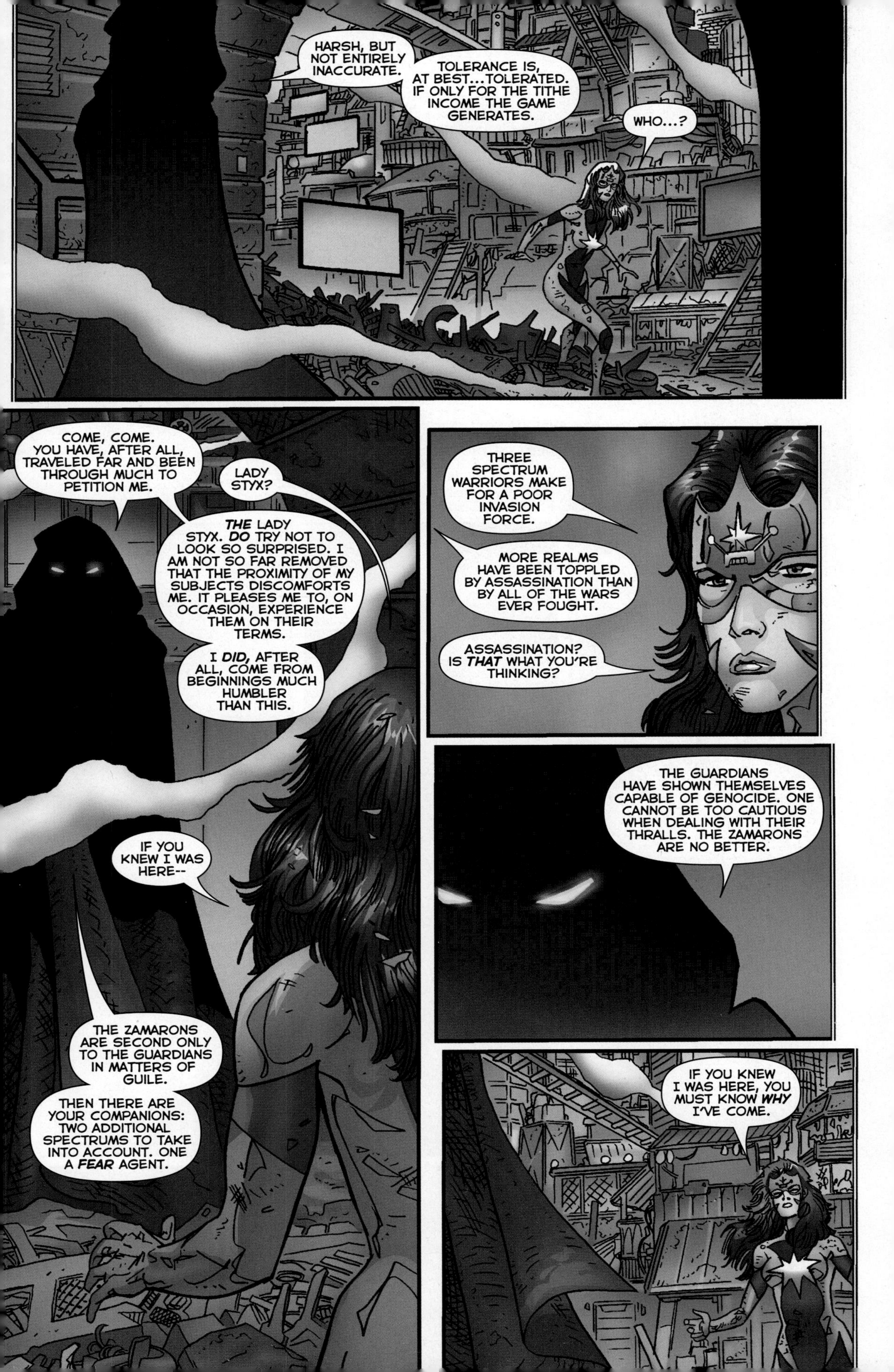

HARSH, BUT NOT ENTIRELY INACCURATE.
TOLERANCE IS, AT BEST...TOLERATED. IF ONLY FOR THE TITHE INCOME THE GAME GENERATES.
WHO...?
COME, COME. YOU HAVE, AFTER ALL, TRAVELED FAR AND BEEN THROUGH MUCH TO PETITION ME.
LADY STYX?
THE LADY STYX. DO TRY NOT TO LOOK SO SURPRISED. I AM NOT SO FAR REMOVED THAT THE PROXIMITY OF MY SUBJECTS DISCOMFORTS ME. IT PLEASES ME TO, ON OCCASION, EXPERIENCE THEM ON THEIR TERMS.
I DID, AFTER ALL, COME FROM BEGINNINGS MUCH HUMBLER THAN THIS.
IF YOU KNEW I WAS HERE--
THE ZAMARONS ARE SECOND ONLY TO THE GUARDIANS IN MATTERS OF GUILE.
THEN THERE ARE YOUR COMPANIONS: TWO ADDITIONAL SPECTRUMS TO TAKE INTO ACCOUNT. ONE A FEAR AGENT.
THREE SPECTRUM WARRIORS MAKE FOR A POOR INVASION FORCE.
MORE REALMS HAVE BEEN TOPPLED BY ASSASSINATION THAN BY ALL OF THE WARS EVER FOUGHT.
ASSASSINATION? IS THAT WHAT YOU'RE THINKING?
THE GUARDIANS HAVE SHOWN THEMSELVES CAPABLE OF GENOCIDE. ONE CANNOT BE TOO CAUTIOUS WHEN DEALING WITH THEIR THRALLS. THE ZAMARONS ARE NO BETTER.
IF YOU KNEW I WAS HERE, YOU MUST KNOW WHY I'VE COME.

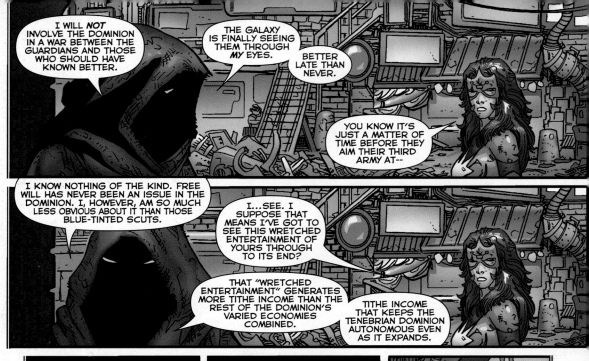

I WILL **NOT** INVOLVE THE DOMINION IN A WAR BETWEEN THE GUARDIANS AND THOSE WHO SHOULD HAVE KNOWN BETTER.

THE GALAXY IS FINALLY SEEING THEM THROUGH **MY** EYES.

BETTER LATE THAN NEVER.

YOU KNOW IT'S JUST A MATTER OF TIME BEFORE THEY AIM THEIR THIRD ARMY AT--

I KNOW NOTHING OF THE KIND. FREE WILL HAS NEVER BEEN AN ISSUE IN THE DOMINION. I, HOWEVER, AM SO MUCH LESS OBVIOUS ABOUT IT THAN THOSE BLUE-TINTED SCUTS.

I...SEE. I SUPPOSE THAT MEANS I'VE GOT TO SEE THIS WRETCHED ENTERTAINMENT OF YOURS THROUGH TO ITS END?

THAT "WRETCHED ENTERTAINMENT" GENERATES MORE TITHE INCOME THAN THE REST OF THE DOMINION'S VARIED ECONOMIES COMBINED.

TITHE INCOME THAT KEEPS THE TENEBRIAN DOMINION AUTONOMOUS EVEN AS IT EXPANDS.

YES, YOU **WILL** SEE OUR "WRETCHED ENTERTAINMENT" THROUGH TO ITS END. YOU AND YOUR SPECTRUM BRETHREN.

I SEE NO REASON FOR YOUR EFFORTS TO RESULT IN A **TOTAL** LOSS. HMM?

DO NOT LOOK AT ME. YOU LOOK, I LEAVE. WALK UP THE BLOCK, LEFT AT THE SERVICE ALLEY. GO.

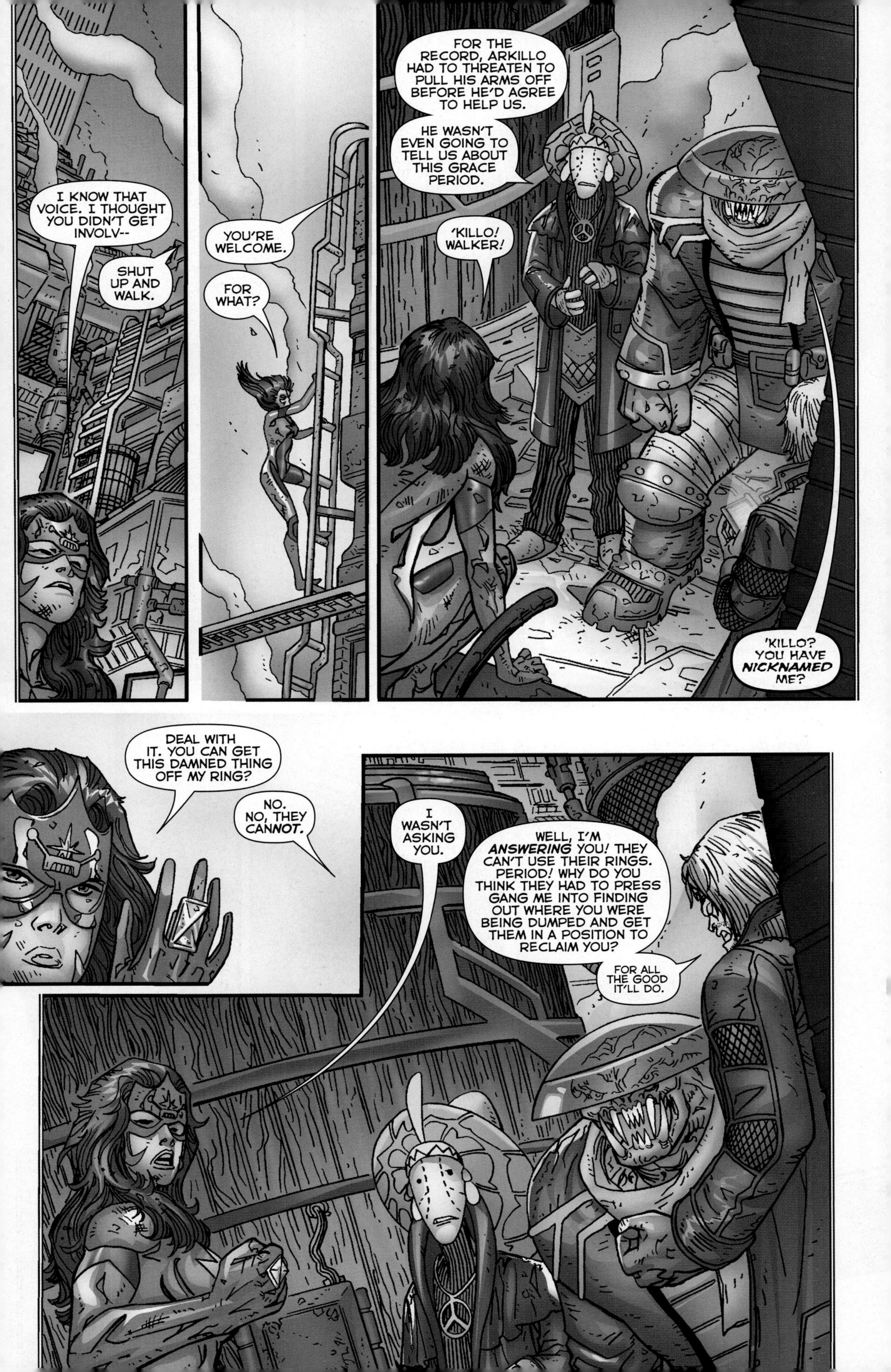
I KNOW THAT VOICE. I THOUGHT YOU DIDN'T GET INVOLV--
SHUT UP AND WALK.
YOU'RE WELCOME.
FOR WHAT?
FOR THE RECORD, ARKILLO HAD TO THREATEN TO PULL HIS ARMS OFF BEFORE HE'D AGREE TO HELP US.
HE WASN'T EVEN GOING TO TELL US ABOUT THIS GRACE PERIOD.
'KILLO! WALKER!
'KILLO? YOU HAVE **NICKNAMED** ME?
DEAL WITH IT. YOU CAN GET THIS DAMNED THING OFF MY RING?
NO. NO, THEY CAN*NOT.*
I WASN'T ASKING YOU.
WELL, I'M ***ANSWERING*** YOU! THEY CAN'T USE THEIR RINGS. PERIOD! WHY DO YOU THINK THEY HAD TO PRESS GANG ME INTO FINDING OUT WHERE YOU WERE BEING DUMPED AND GET THEM IN A POSITION TO RECLAIM YOU?
FOR ALL THE GOOD IT'LL DO.

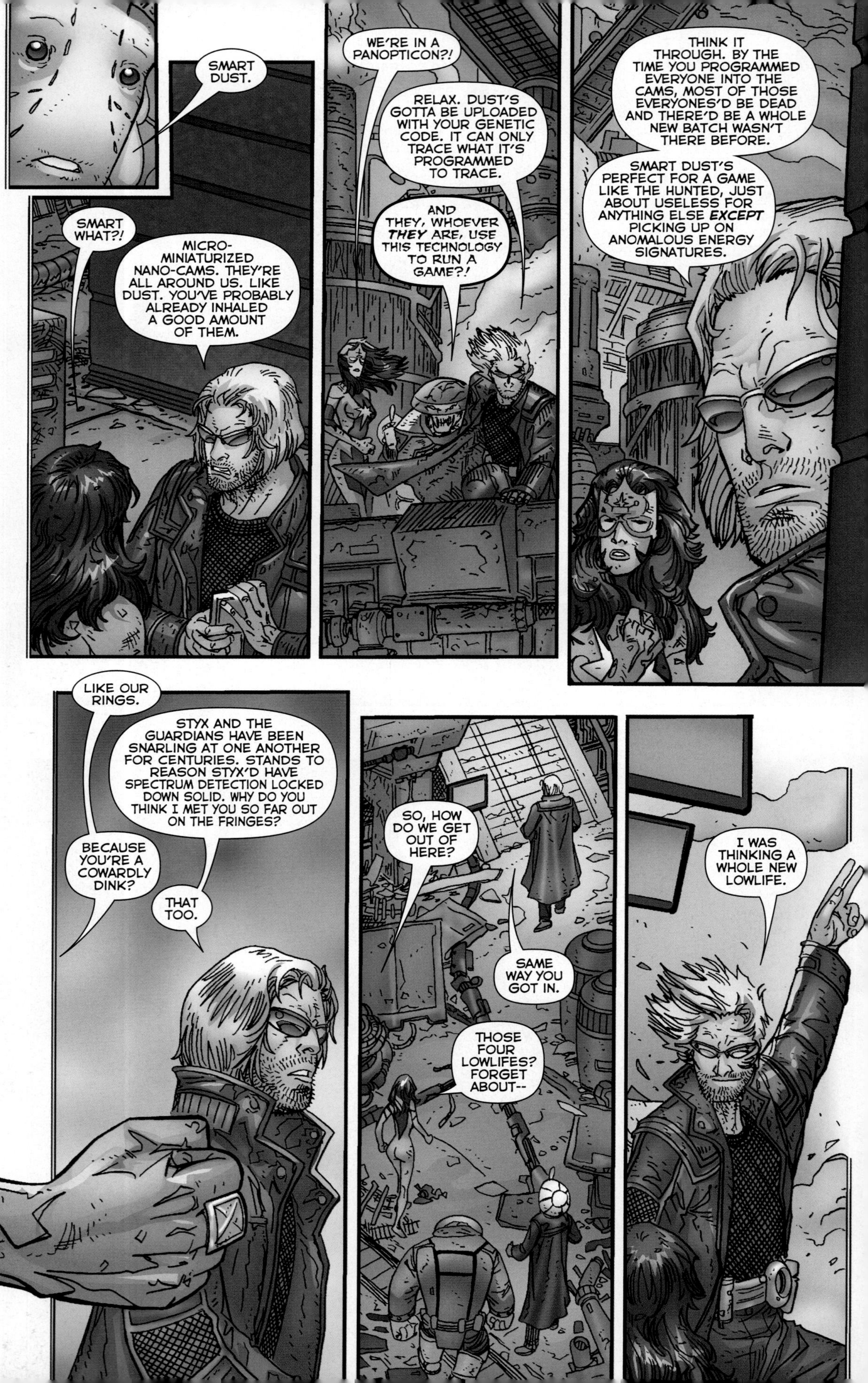
SMART DUST.
SMART WHAT?!
MICRO-MINIATURIZED NANO-CAMS. THEY'RE ALL AROUND US. LIKE DUST. YOU'VE PROBABLY ALREADY INHALED A GOOD AMOUNT OF THEM.
WE'RE IN A PANOPTICON?!
RELAX. DUST'S GOTTA BE UPLOADED WITH YOUR GENETIC CODE. IT CAN ONLY TRACE WHAT IT'S PROGRAMMED TO TRACE.
AND THEY, WHOEVER *THEY* ARE, USE THIS TECHNOLOGY TO RUN A GAME?!
THINK IT THROUGH. BY THE TIME YOU PROGRAMMED EVERYONE INTO THE CAMS, MOST OF THOSE EVERYONES'D BE DEAD AND THERE'D BE A WHOLE NEW BATCH WASN'T THERE BEFORE.
SMART DUST'S PERFECT FOR A GAME LIKE THE HUNTED, JUST ABOUT USELESS FOR ANYTHING ELSE ***EXCEPT*** PICKING UP ON ANOMALOUS ENERGY SIGNATURES.
LIKE OUR RINGS.
STYX AND THE GUARDIANS HAVE BEEN SNARLING AT ONE ANOTHER FOR CENTURIES. STANDS TO REASON STYX'D HAVE SPECTRUM DETECTION LOCKED DOWN SOLID. WHY DO YOU THINK I MET YOU SO FAR OUT ON THE FRINGES?
BECAUSE YOU'RE A COWARDLY DINK?
THAT TOO.
SO, HOW DO WE GET OUT OF HERE?
SAME WAY YOU GOT IN.
THOSE FOUR LOWLIFES? FORGET ABOUT--
I WAS THINKING A WHOLE NEW LOWLIFE.

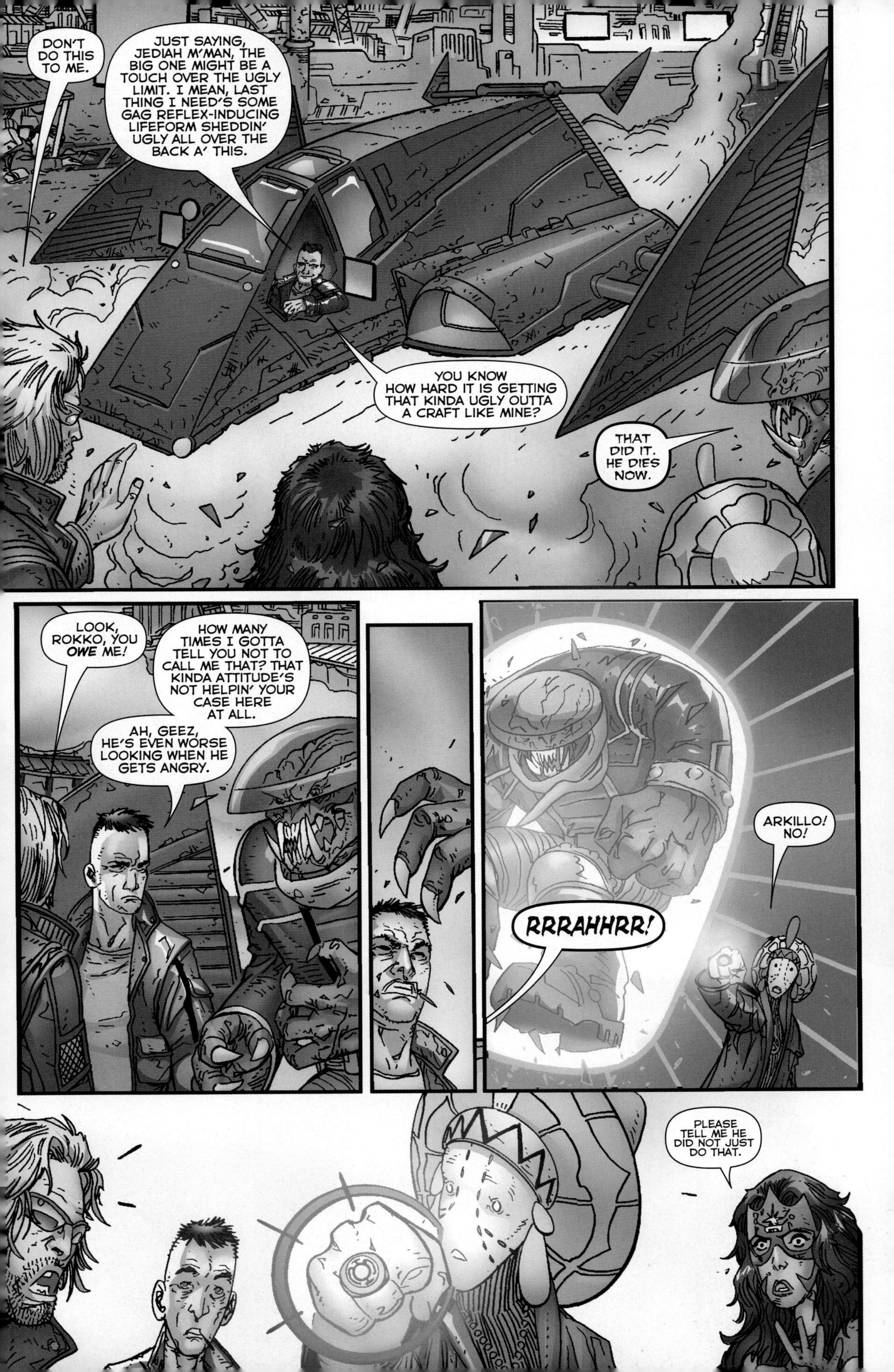
DON'T DO THIS TO ME.
JUST SAYING, JEDIAH M'MAN, THE BIG ONE MIGHT BE A TOUCH OVER THE UGLY LIMIT. I MEAN, LAST THING I NEED'S SOME GAG REFLEX-INDUCING LIFEFORM SHEDDIN' UGLY ALL OVER THE BACK A' THIS.
YOU KNOW HOW HARD IT IS GETTING THAT KINDA UGLY OUTTA A CRAFT LIKE MINE?
THAT DID IT. HE DIES NOW.
LOOK, ROKKO, YOU *OWE* ME!
HOW MANY TIMES I GOTTA TELL YOU NOT TO CALL ME THAT? THAT KINDA ATTITUDE'S NOT HELPIN' YOUR CASE HERE AT ALL.
AH, GEEZ, HE'S EVEN WORSE LOOKING WHEN HE GETS ANGRY.
RRRAHHRR!
ARKILLO! NO!
PLEASE TELL ME HE DID NOT JUST DO THAT.

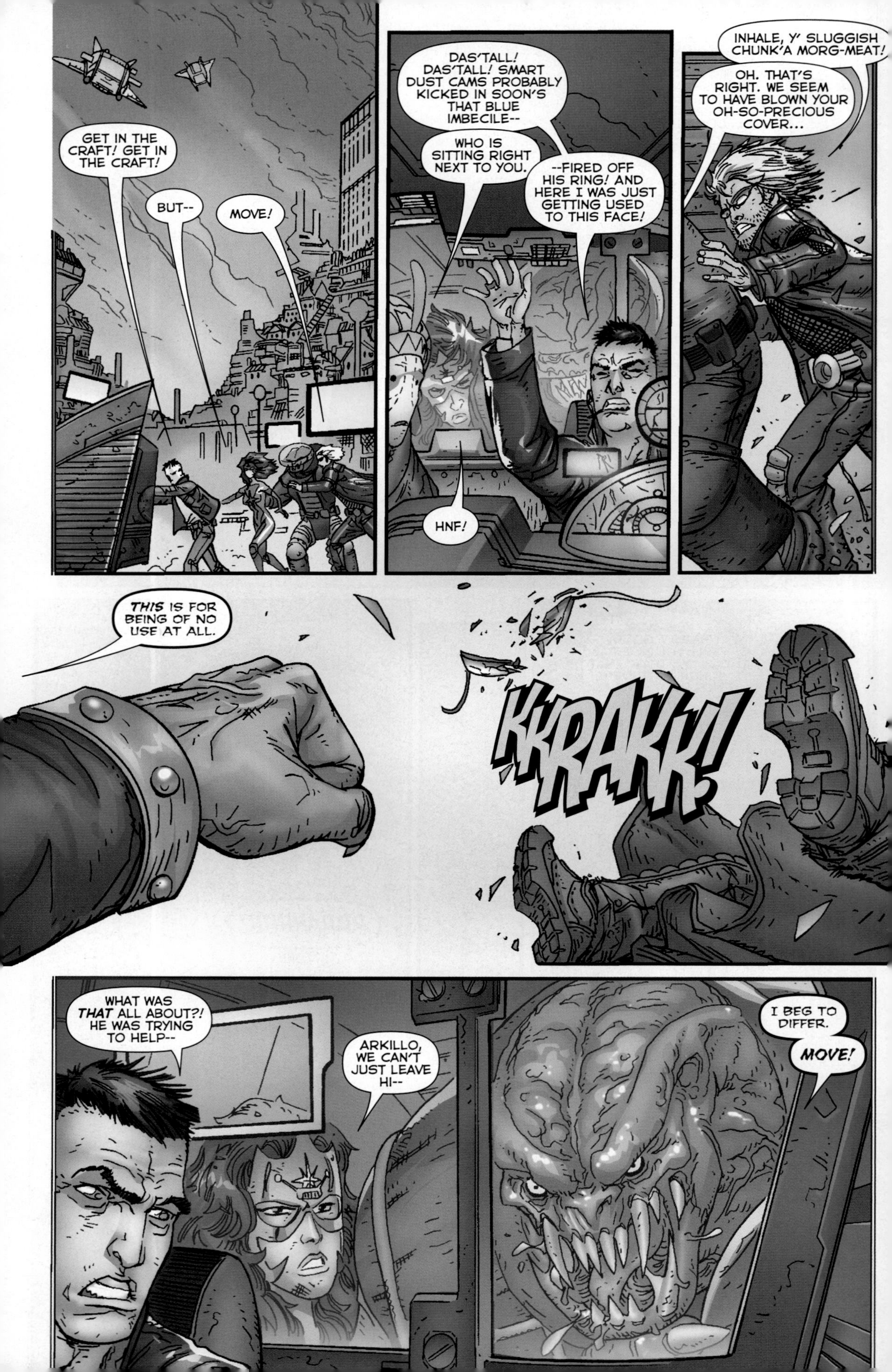
GET IN THE CRAFT! GET IN THE CRAFT!
BUT--
MOVE!
DAS'TALL! DAS'TALL! SMART DUST CAMS PROBABLY KICKED IN SOON'S THAT BLUE IMBECILE--
WHO IS SITTING RIGHT NEXT TO YOU.
--FIRED OFF HIS RING! AND HERE I WAS JUST GETTING USED TO THIS FACE!
HNF!
INHALE, Y' SLUGGISH CHUNK'A MORG-MEAT!
OH. THAT'S RIGHT. WE SEEM TO HAVE BLOWN YOUR OH-SO-PRECIOUS COVER...
THIS is for being of no use at all.
KKRAKK!
WHAT WAS THAT ALL ABOUT?! HE WAS TRYING TO HELP--
ARKILLO, WE CAN'T JUST LEAVE HI--
I BEG TO DIFFER.
MOVE!

THAT'S A RELIEF. AIRBORNE GETS TO DEAL WITH THE SPECTRUM WARRIORS.

MINUS ONE.

SCAN HIM.

HE'S A SPECTRUM SCUT, ALL RIGHT.

GREEN. WHICH ONES ARE THE GREEN ONES AGAIN?

IT MATTER?

NOT TO THIS ONE. NOT ANYMORE. BAG HIM BEFORE HE COMES TO. ANYONE GOT A DAMPER CAP WE CAN GET ON THAT RING?

RIGHT HERE... SOMEWHERE.

WHAT D'Y' FIGGER HE DID T' BE LEFT BEHIND?

"DON'T KNOW. DON'T CARE."

SUGAR-COATED GORE WHAMMIES! Start your day with a BANG! GlimmerNet / glm.brkfst/

CHT-UT-UT-UT-UT-UT-UT
CHT-UT-UT-UT-UT-UT-UT

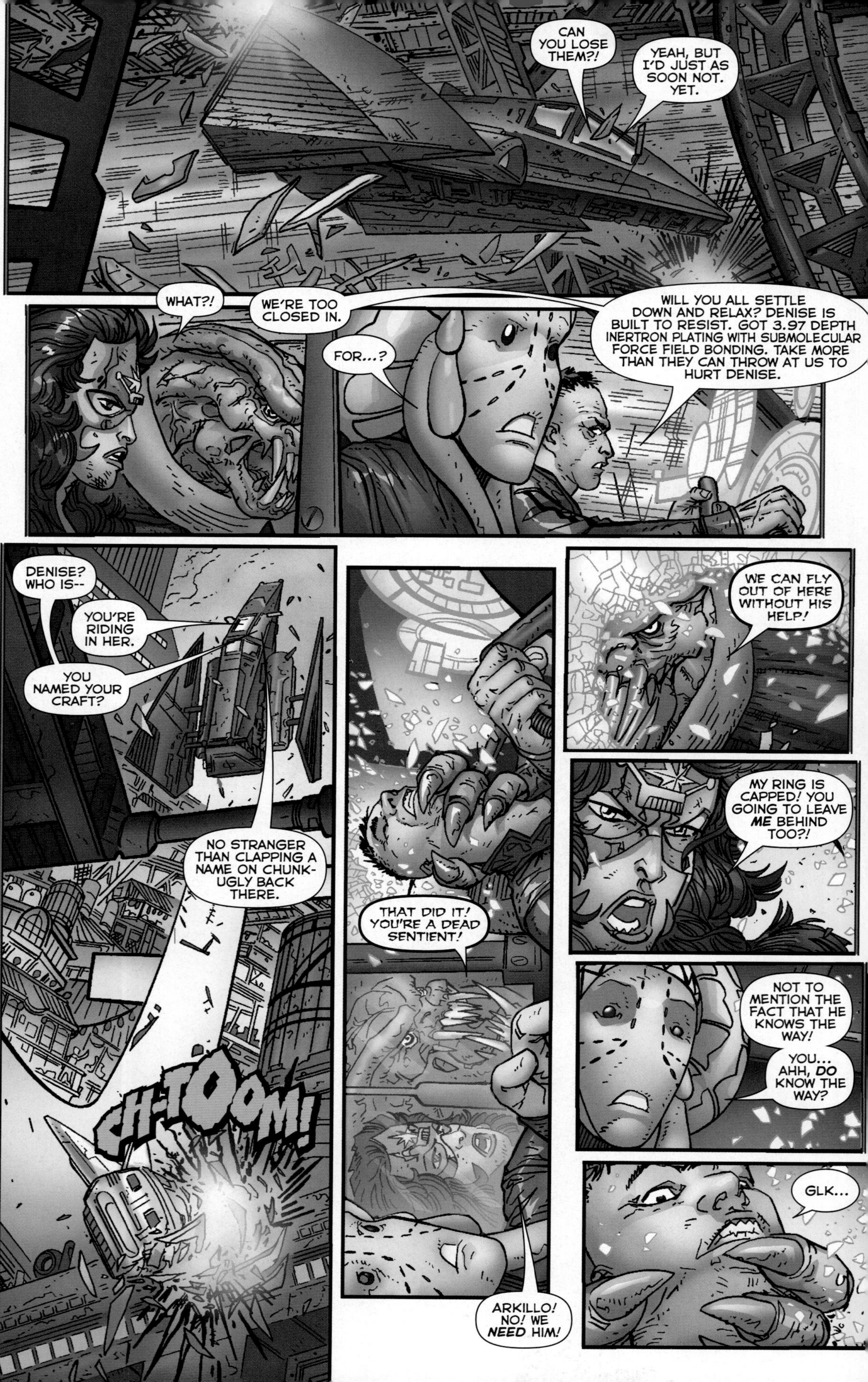
CAN YOU LOSE THEM?!
YEAH, BUT I'D JUST AS SOON NOT. YET.
WHAT?!
WE'RE TOO CLOSED IN.
FOR...?
WILL YOU ALL SETTLE DOWN AND RELAX? DENISE IS BUILT TO RESIST. GOT 3.97 DEPTH INERTRON PLATING WITH SUBMOLECULAR FORCE FIELD BONDING. TAKE MORE THAN THEY CAN THROW AT US TO HURT DENISE.
DENISE? WHO IS--
YOU'RE RIDING IN HER.
YOU NAMED YOUR CRAFT?
NO STRANGER THAN CLAPPING A NAME ON CHUNK-UGLY BACK THERE.
CH-TOOM!
THAT DID IT! YOU'RE A DEAD SENTIENT!
ARKILLO! NO! WE NEED HIM!
WE CAN FLY OUT OF HERE WITHOUT HIS HELP!
MY RING IS CAPPED! YOU GOING TO LEAVE ME BEHIND TOO?!
NOT TO MENTION THE FACT THAT HE KNOWS THE WAY!
YOU... AHH, DO KNOW THE WAY?
GLK...

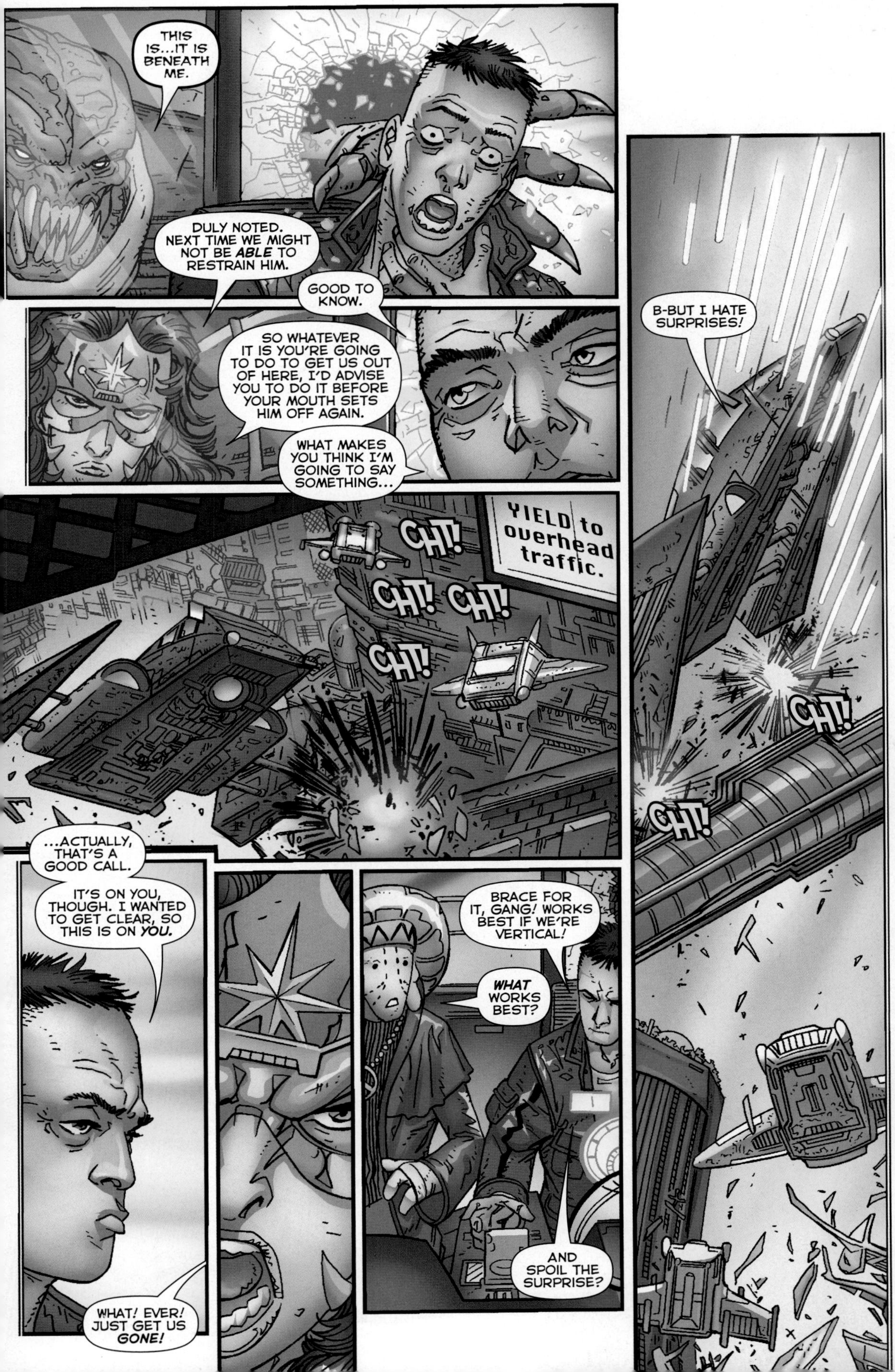
THIS IS...IT IS BENEATH ME.
DULY NOTED. NEXT TIME WE MIGHT NOT BE *ABLE* TO RESTRAIN HIM.
GOOD TO KNOW.
SO WHATEVER IT IS YOU'RE GOING TO DO TO GET US OUT OF HERE, I'D ADVISE YOU TO DO IT BEFORE YOUR MOUTH SETS HIM OFF AGAIN.
WHAT MAKES YOU THINK I'M GOING TO SAY SOMETHING...
B-BUT I HATE SURPRISES!
YIELD to overhead traffic.
CHT!
CHT! CHT!
CHT!
CHT!
CHT!
...ACTUALLY, THAT'S A GOOD CALL.
IT'S ON YOU, THOUGH. I WANTED TO GET CLEAR, SO THIS IS ON *YOU.*
WHAT! EVER! JUST GET US *GONE!*
BRACE FOR IT, GANG! WORKS BEST IF WE'RE VERTICAL!
WHAT WORKS BEST?
AND SPOIL THE SURPRISE?

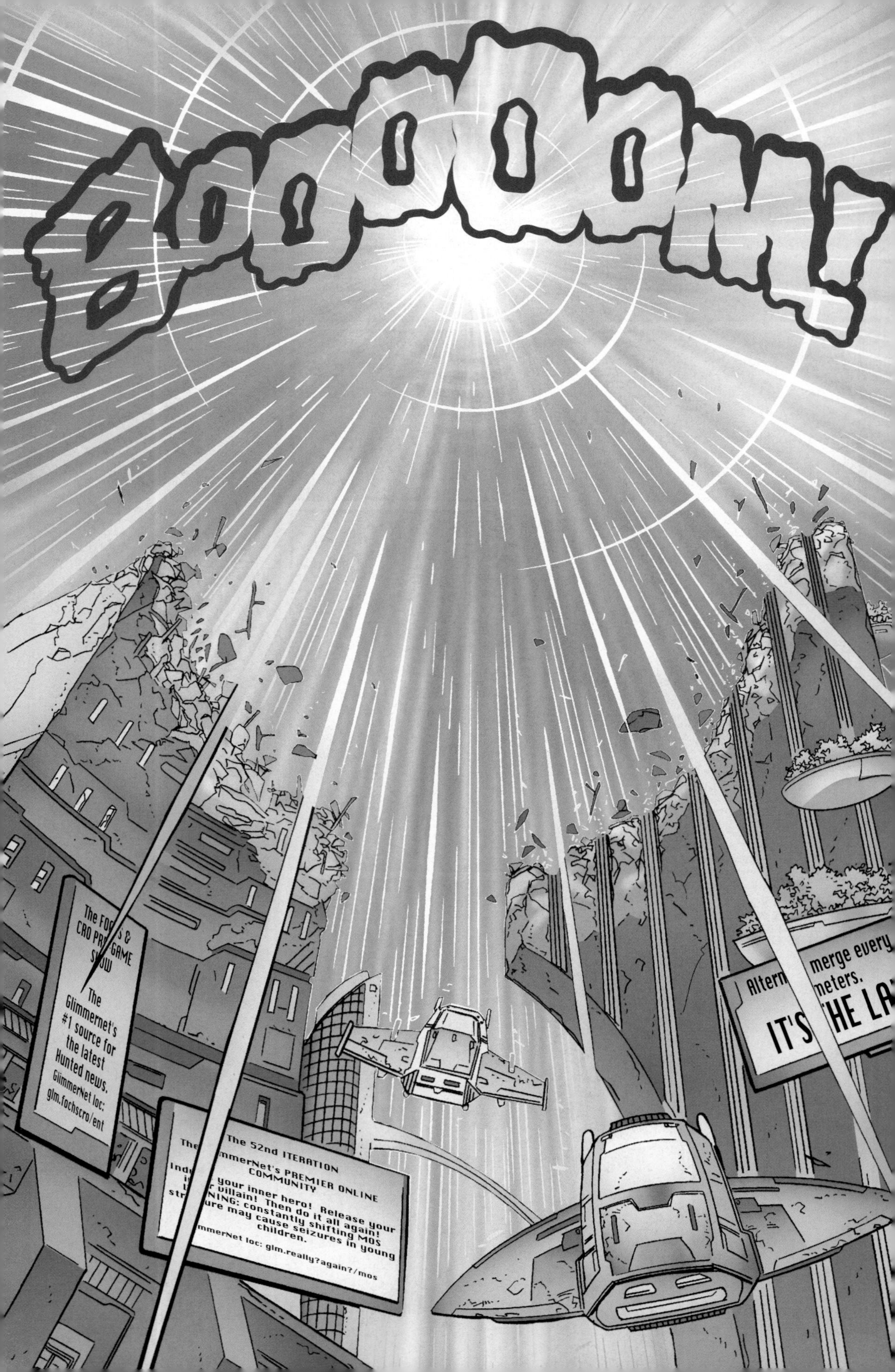
BOOOOOOM!
The FOC S & CRO PR GAME S OW
The Glimmernet's #1 source for the latest Hunted news. GlimmerNet loc: glm.fochscro/ent
The 52nd ITERATION
The immerNet's PREMIER ONLINE COMMUNITY
your inner hero! Release your villain! Then do it all again!
NING: constantly shifting MOS ure may cause seizures in young children.
mmerNet loc: glm.really?again?/mos
Altern merge every meters.
IT'S HE LA

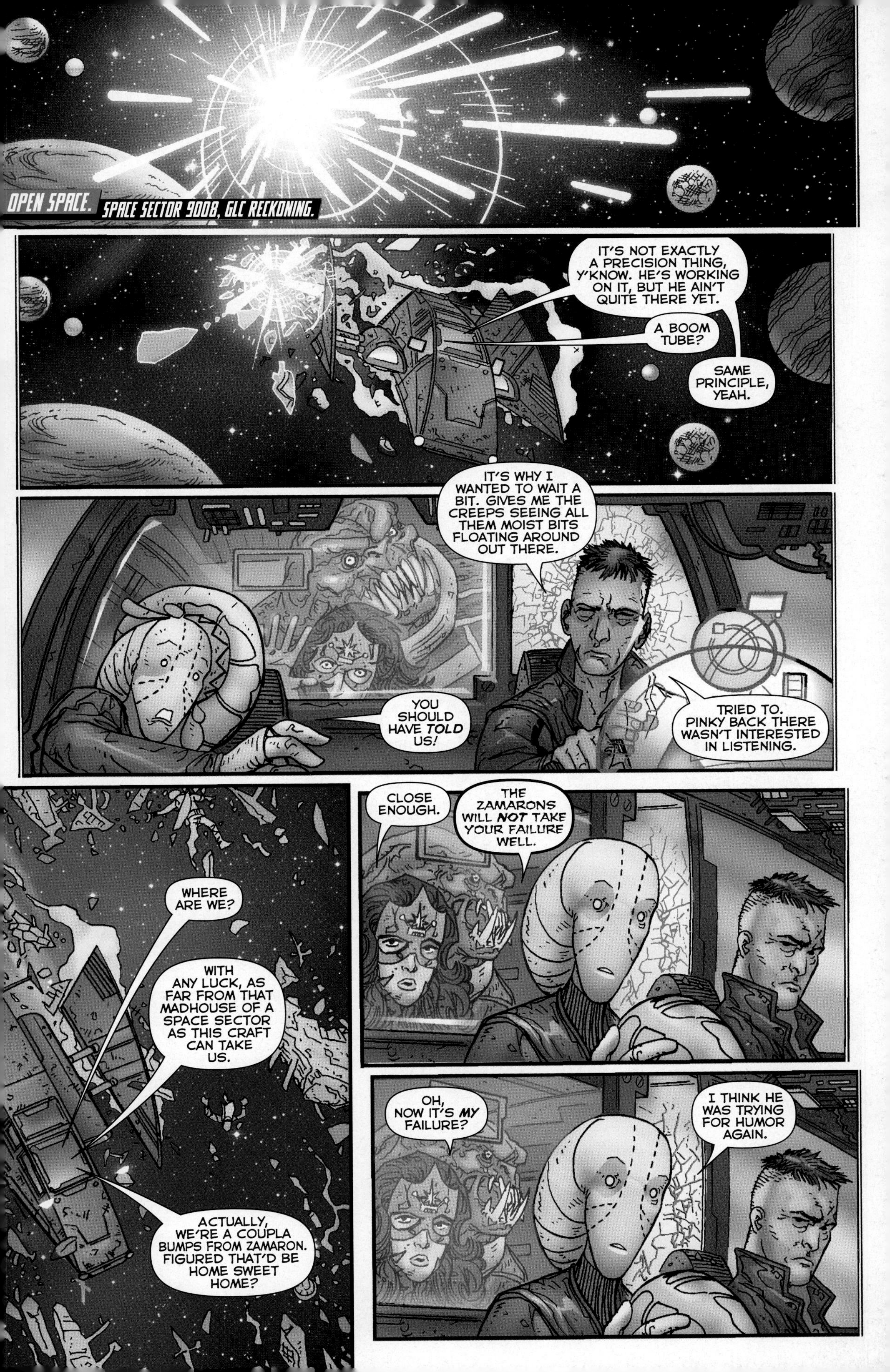
OPEN SPACE.
SPACE SECTOR 9008, GLC RECKONING.
IT'S NOT EXACTLY A PRECISION THING, Y'KNOW. HE'S WORKING ON IT, BUT HE AIN'T QUITE THERE YET.
A BOOM TUBE?
SAME PRINCIPLE, YEAH.
IT'S WHY I WANTED TO WAIT A BIT. GIVES ME THE CREEPS SEEING ALL THEM MOIST BITS FLOATING AROUND OUT THERE.
YOU SHOULD HAVE TOLD US!
TRIED TO. PINKY BACK THERE WASN'T INTERESTED IN LISTENING.
WHERE ARE WE?
WITH ANY LUCK, AS FAR FROM THAT MADHOUSE OF A SPACE SECTOR AS THIS CRAFT CAN TAKE US.
ACTUALLY, WE'RE A COUPLA BUMPS FROM ZAMARON. FIGURED THAT'D BE HOME SWEET HOME?
CLOSE ENOUGH.
THE ZAMARONS WILL NOT TAKE YOUR FAILURE WELL.
OH, NOW IT'S MY FAILURE?
I THINK HE WAS TRYING FOR HUMOR AGAIN.

I'M GOING TO ASSUME THE ZAMARONS ARE GOOD FOR MY FEE?

GRH...YOUR FEE BE DAMNED. WE CAN TAKE HER FROM HE--

I THINK HE STANDS A BETTER CHANCE OF SURVIVING THE APPROACH TO ZAMARON WITH US ON BOARD.

AND WHY SHOULD THIS CHOK'S WELL-BEING MATTER TO US?

HE DID GET US OUT.

YOU ARE SOOOOO WELCOME.

ARE YOU SURE YOU WANT TO PLACE HIM IN SUCH PERIL?

I'M IN PERIL?

YOU KEEP RUNNING YOUR MOUTH LIKE THAT...YES.

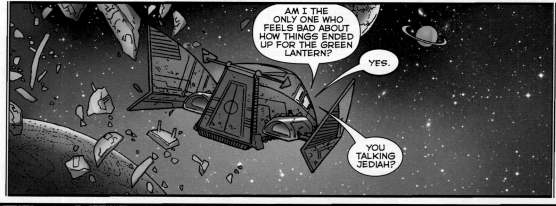

AM I THE ONLY ONE WHO FEELS BAD ABOUT HOW THINGS ENDED UP FOR THE GREEN LANTERN?

YES.

YOU TALKING JEDIAH?

DON'T YOU WORRY ABOUT HIM. HE'S LIKE A CAT. AHHH...YOU GUYS DO KNOW WHAT A CAT IS?

ALWAYS LANDS ON HIS FEET?

YOU GOT IT.

WELCOME TO THE HUNTED, THE GLIMMERNET'S MOST POPULAR STREAMING PROGRAM. YOU HAVE BEEN CONSCRIPTED TO SERVE AS A CONTESTANT. THIS IS NOT AN HONOR.
YOU HAVE BEEN CHOSEN BECAUSE YOU REPRESENT A THREAT TO THE TENEBRIAN DOMINION AND ITS AFFILIATED HOLDINGS. THE RULES ARE AS FOLLOWS.
YOU WILL BE ASSIGNED A BOUNTY, RELEASED FROM CUSTODY AND GRANTED A FULL PLANETARY ROTATION GRACE PERIOD, AFTER WHICH YOU WILL BE HUNTED BY ANYONE WHO CHOOSES TO HUNT YOU FOR WHATEVER REASON.
THE COMPETITION IS OPEN TO ALL REGISTERED CITIZENS OF THE TENEBRIAN DOMINION, REGARDLESS OF AGE. IF YOU ARE TAKEN DOWN BY A MINOR, THE BOUNTY WILL BE PLACED IN STATE TRUST UNTIL THE CHILD COMES OF AGE.
THE HUNT WILL CONTINUE UNTIL DEATH. THERE IS NO REPRIEVE. THERE ARE NO CONDITIONS UNDER WHICH THE HUNT, ONCE BEGUN, WILL BE SUSPENDED.
DELIBERATE FORFEITURE OF THE HUNT BY WAY OF SUICIDE OR A REFUSAL TO DEFEND ONESELF WILL RESULT IN THE CONTESTANT'S IMMEDIATE FAMILY AND / OR FRIENDS REPLACING THE CONTESTANT AS HUNTED.
COLLATERAL DAMAGE, WHETHER GENERATED BY HUNTED OR HUNTER, IS ACKNOWLEDGED AS BEING PART AND PARCEL OF THE GAME EXPERIENCE.
COLLATERAL DAMAGE IN SERVICE TO THE GAME WILL NOT BE CONSIDERED A PUNISHABLE OFFENSE. FAMILIES WILL RECEIVE THE STANDARD WRONGFUL DEATH BENEFITS PACKAGE SHOULD A LOVED ONE DIE DURING A LIVE FEED.
THE HUNTED IS THE SOLE BENEFICIARY OF ANY AND ALL PROCEEDS THAT RESULT FROM THE MERCHANDISING / EXPLOITATION OF YOUR IMAGE / LIFE EXPERIENCES IN PERPETUITY.
BY LISTENING TO THIS RECORDING, YOU AGREE TO THE TERMS AS STATED.
WE NOW RETURN YOU TO REALITY AS YOU PERCEIVE IT.

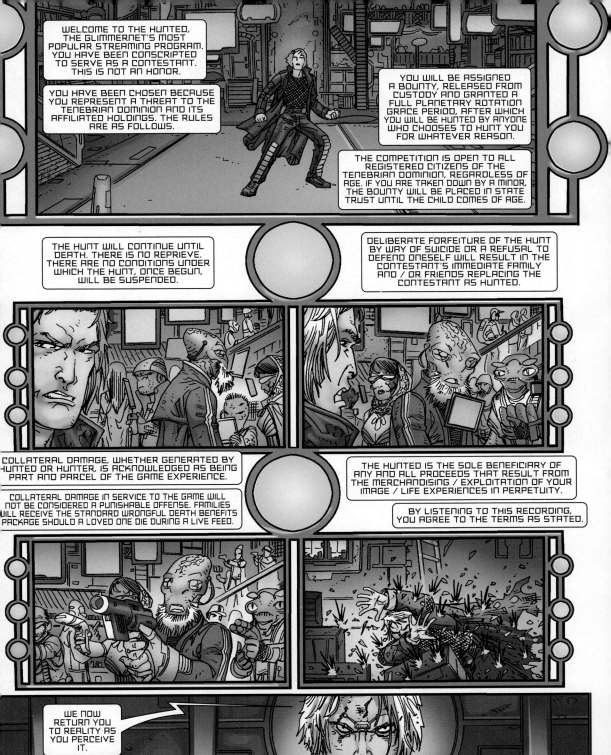

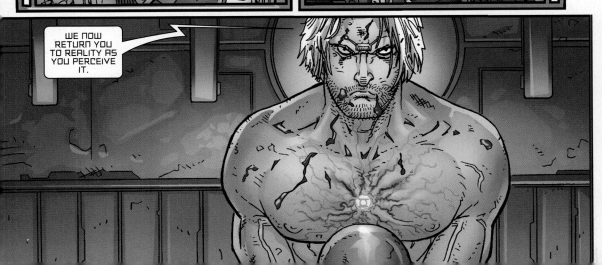

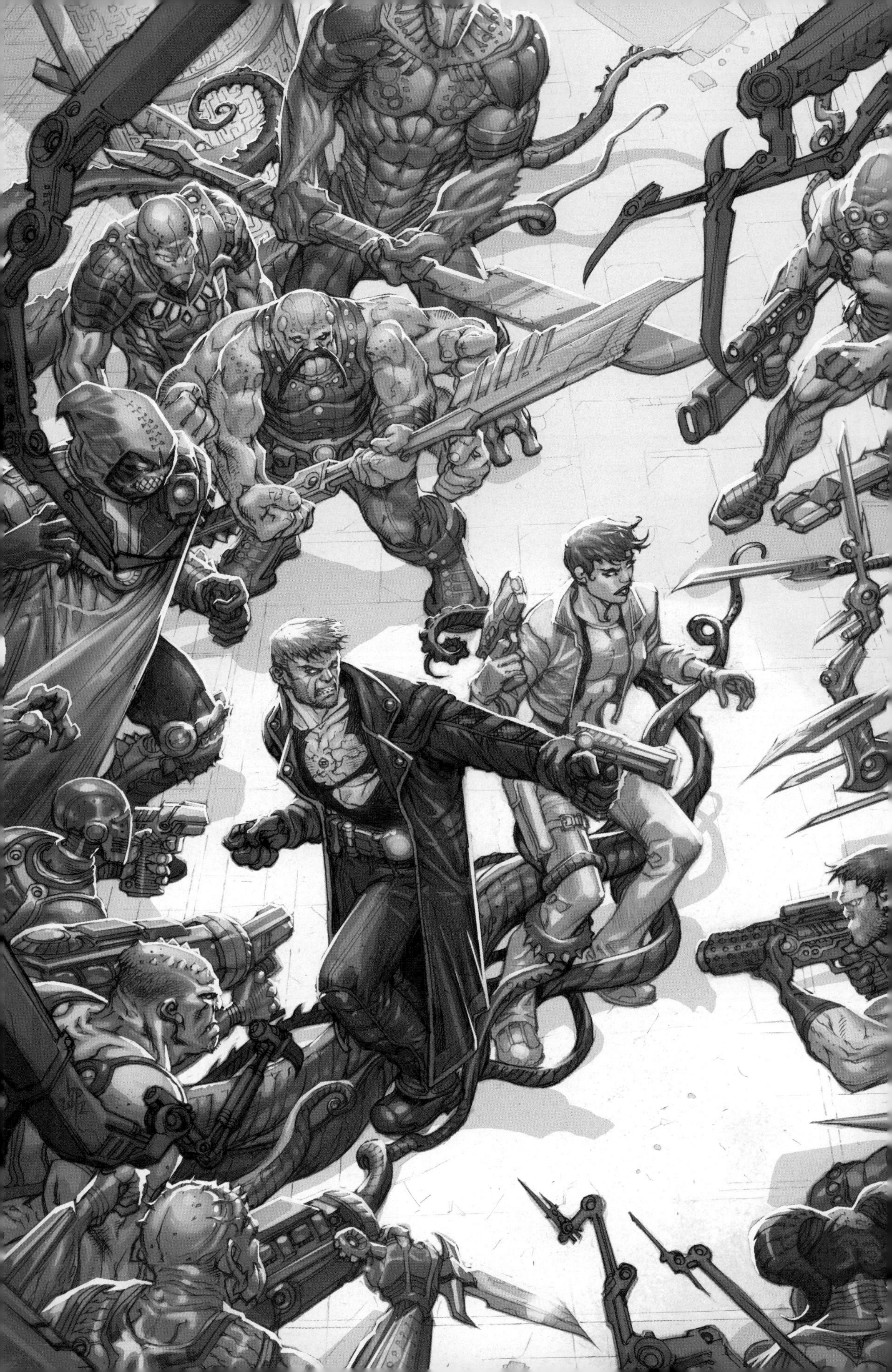

GLIMMERNET THE HUNTED

ACCESS *YOUR* TRUTH TODAY
FREQUENTLY ASKED QUESTIONS

WHAT IS THE HUNTED?
ROLL ME OVER! WHAT SEEPING PROTRUSION HAVE YOU BEEN LIVING UNDER!?
THE HUNTED IS ONLY THE SINGLE MOST WATCHED GLIMMERNET FEED IN...WELL, FOREVER! IT'S THE GAME EVERYONE CAN PLAY! I MEAN...REALLY? HOW CAN YOU NOT KNOW THIS!?
WHAT ARE THE RULES OF THE GAME?
THOUGHT YOU'D NEVER ASK! THE STARS OF THE HUNTED ARE THE HUNTED! AND YOU GET TO HUNT THEM! BY THE NUMBERS NOW...
ONE. THE HUNTED SHALL BE CHOSEN FROM THOSE WHOSE VERY EXISTENCE POSES A THREAT TO THE TENEBRIAN DOMINION.
I THINK THEY'RE TALKING, LIKE, TRAITORS AND CRIMINALS AND LIKE THAT.
TWO. THE HUNTED SHALL, UPON RELEASE, BE GIVEN A FULL PLANETARY ROTATION CYCLE GRACE PERIOD.
WHAT ARE THE RULES OF THE GAME? (cont'd)
SORRY, FOLKS, BUT IF YOU SPOT THE CONTESTANT BEFORE THAT TIME PERIOD HAS LAPSED, IT'S HANDS OFF. UNLESS, THAT IS, YOU DON'T MIND TAKING THE CONTESTANT'S PLACE.
HAH! THOUGHT NOT!
AND C. UPON EXPIRATION OF THE GRACE PERIOD, THE GAME SHALL COMMENCE AND ALL ESTABLISHED GAME RULES SHALL APPLY.
WHAT ARE THE RULES OF THE GAME? (cont'd)
WHICH MEANS ONCE THAT GRACE PERIOD EXPIRES, THE HUNT BEGINS AND ANYTHING GOES! BEST OF ALL, YOU'RE ALL INVITED TO PARTICIPATE.
UNLESS YOU'RE TOO SQUEAMISH FOR THAT, EVEN. IN WHICH CASE...GROW A SET, WHY DON'T YOU!
WE'RE TALKING TO THE DEATH HERE, SO IF YOU'RE SQUEAMISH, YOU MIGHT CONSIDER CONFINING YOURSELF TO SPECTATOR.
ARE THERE PRIZES?
ARE THERE EVER! BRING DOWN ONE OF THE HUNTED AND YOU GET THE BOUNTY. IT'S AS SIMPLE AS THAT.
BOUNTIES, OF COURSE, VARY DEPENDING ON THE CONTESTANT'S THREAT LEVEL; THE MORE DANGEROUS THE CONTESTANT, THE BIGGER THE PAYOUT. WELL D'UH!
ARE THERE PRIZES? (cont'd)
AND BESTEST OF ALL, THERE ARE, AT ANY GIVEN MOMENT, DOZENS OF HUNTED IN PLAY. SO WHAT ARE YOU WAITING FOR!?
KILL 'EM DEAD! KILL 'EM DEAD! GOOOOO GET'EM!
YAAAY!!

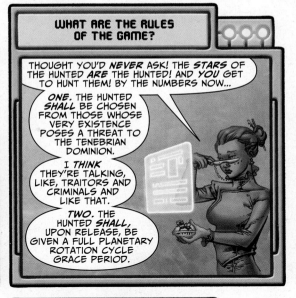

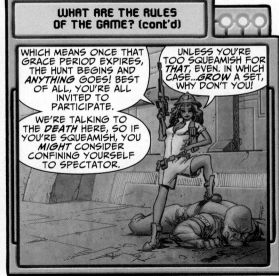

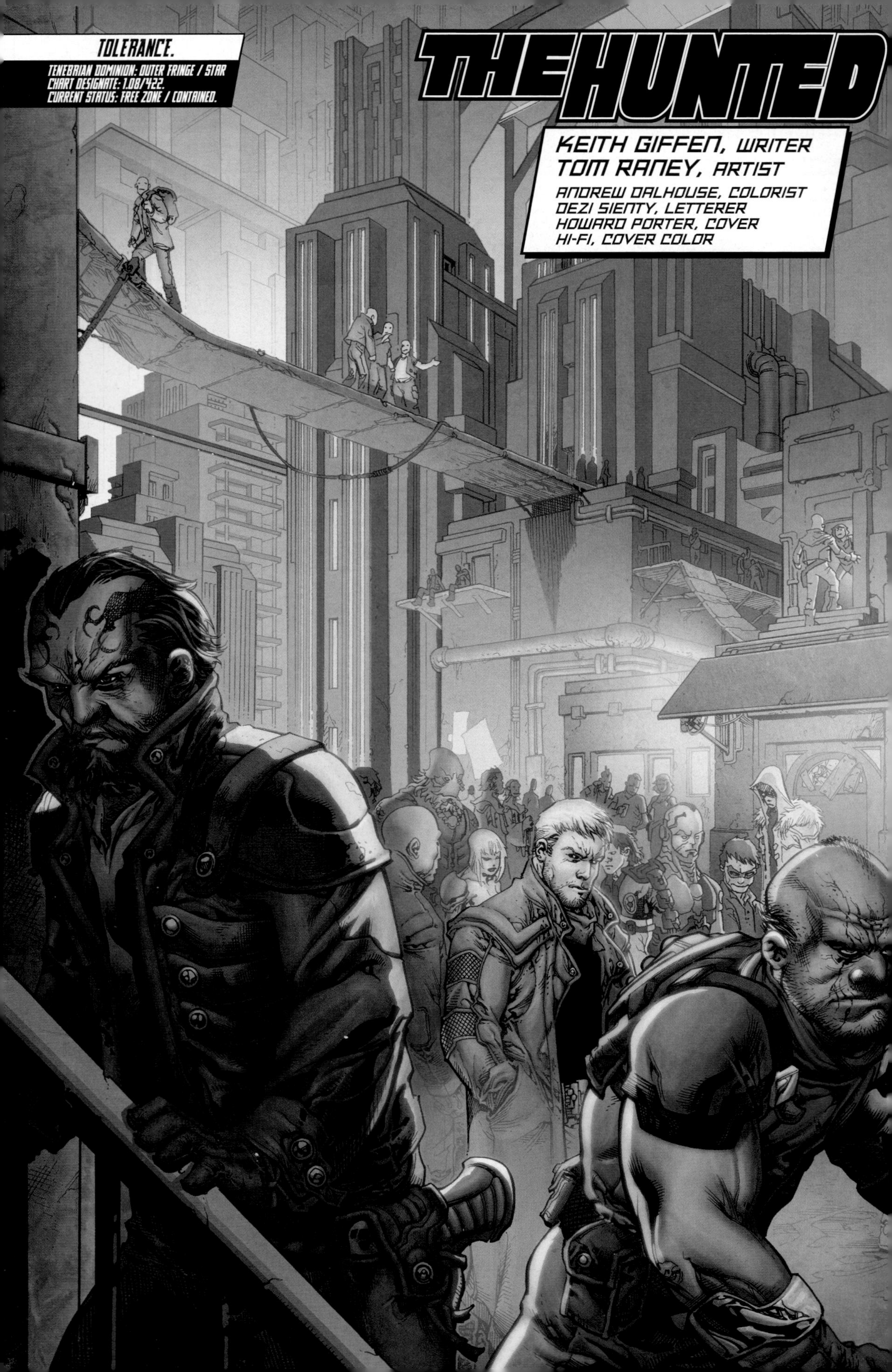
TOLERANCE.
TENEBRIAN DOMINION: OUTER FRINGE / STAR CHART DESIGNATE: 1.08/422.
CURRENT STATUS: FREE ZONE / CONTAINED.
THE HUNTED
KEITH GIFFEN, WRITER
TOM RANEY, ARTIST
ANDREW DALHOUSE, COLORIST
DEZI SIENTY, LETTERER
HOWARD PORTER, COVER
HI-FI, COVER COLOR

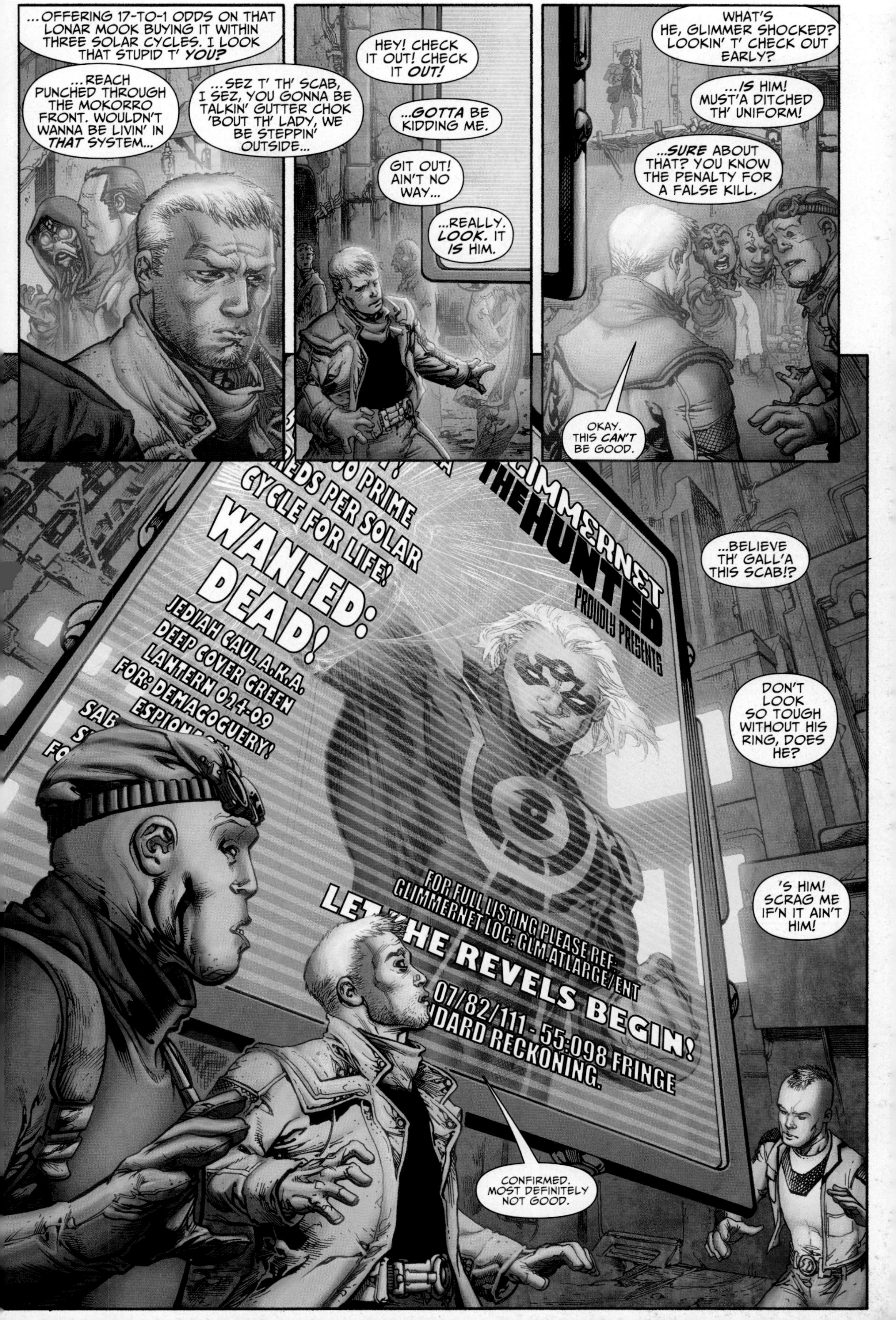
...OFFERING 17-TO-1 ODDS ON THAT LONAR MOOK BUYING IT WITHIN THREE SOLAR CYCLES. I LOOK THAT STUPID T' YOU?
...REACH PUNCHED THROUGH THE MOKORRO FRONT. WOULDN'T WANNA BE LIVIN' IN THAT SYSTEM...
...SEZ T' TH' SCAB, I SEZ, YOU GONNA BE TALKIN' GUTTER CHOK 'BOUT TH' LADY, WE BE STEPPIN' OUTSIDE...
HEY! CHECK IT OUT! CHECK IT OUT!
...GOTTA BE KIDDING ME.
GIT OUT! AIN'T NO WAY...
...REALLY. LOOK. IT IS HIM.
WHAT'S HE, GLIMMER SHOCKED? LOOKIN' T' CHECK OUT EARLY?
...IS HIM! MUST'A DITCHED TH' UNIFORM!
...SURE ABOUT THAT? YOU KNOW THE PENALTY FOR A FALSE KILL.
OKAY. THIS CAN'T BE GOOD.
GLIMMERNET
THE HUNTED
PROUDLY PRESENTS
PRIME
REDS PER SOLAR
CYCLE FOR LIFE!
WANTED
DEAD:
JEDIAH CAUL A.K.A.
DEEP COVER GREEN
LANTERN 024-09
FOR: DEMAGOGUERY!
ESPIONAGE
FOR FULL LISTING PLEASE REF:
GLIMMERNET LOC: GLM.ATLARGE/ENT
HE REVELS BEGIN!
07/82/111 - 55:098 FRINGE
DARD RECKONING.
...BELIEVE TH' GALL'A THIS SCAB!?
DON'T LOOK SO TOUGH WITHOUT HIS RING, DOES HE?
'S HIM! SCRAG ME IF'N IT AIN'T HIM!
CONFIRMED. MOST DEFINITELY NOT GOOD.

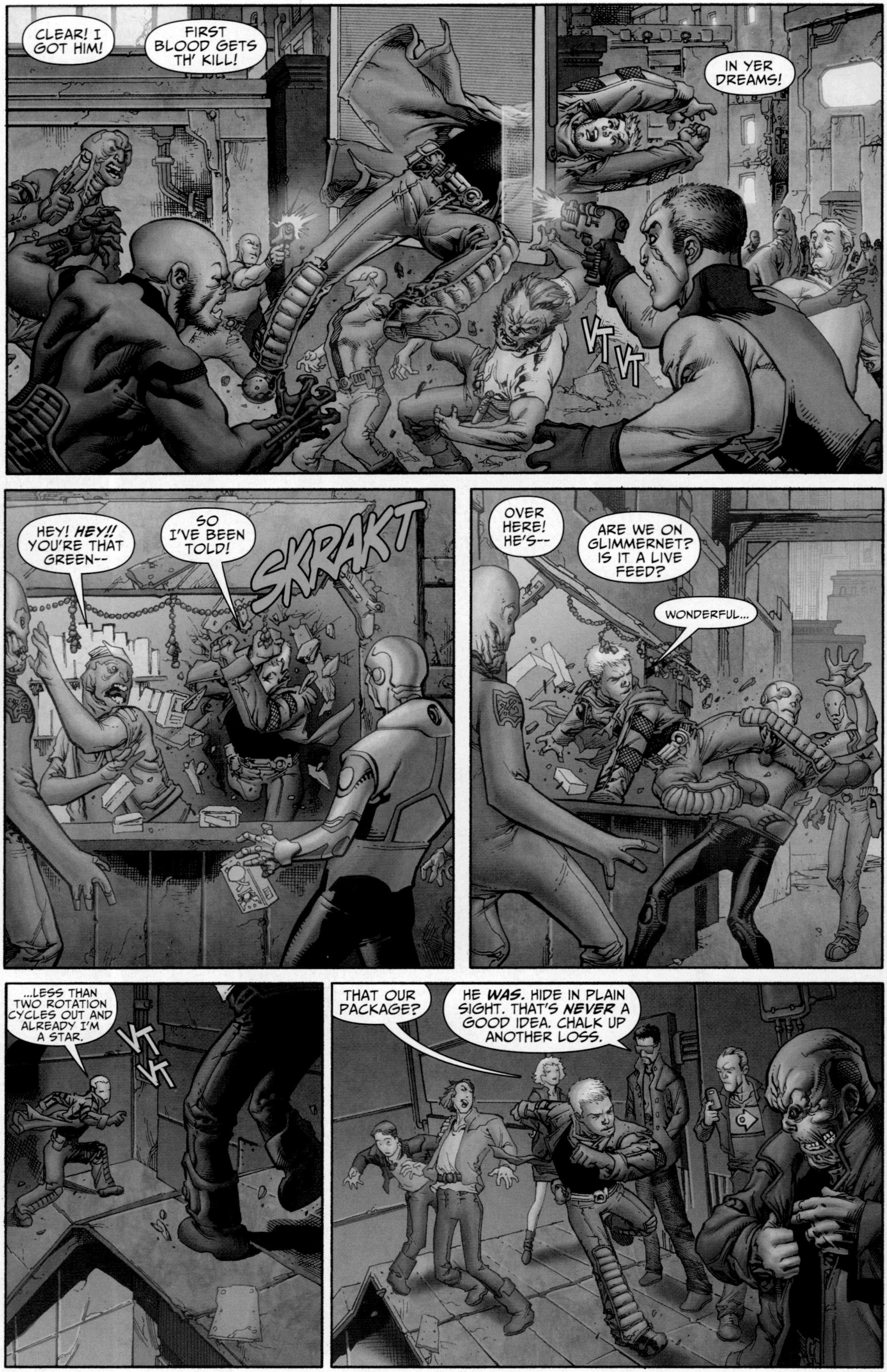

CLEAR! I GOT HIM!
FIRST BLOOD GETS TH' KILL!
IN YER DREAMS!
VT VT
HEY! **HEY!!** YOU'RE THAT GREEN--
SO I'VE BEEN TOLD!
SKRAKT
OVER HERE! HE'S--
ARE WE ON GLIMMERNET? IS IT A LIVE FEED?
WONDERFUL...
...LESS THAN TWO ROTATION CYCLES OUT AND ALREADY I'M A STAR.
VT VT
THAT OUR PACKAGE?
HE **WAS.** HIDE IN PLAIN SIGHT. THAT'S **NEVER** A GOOD IDEA. CHALK UP ANOTHER LOSS.

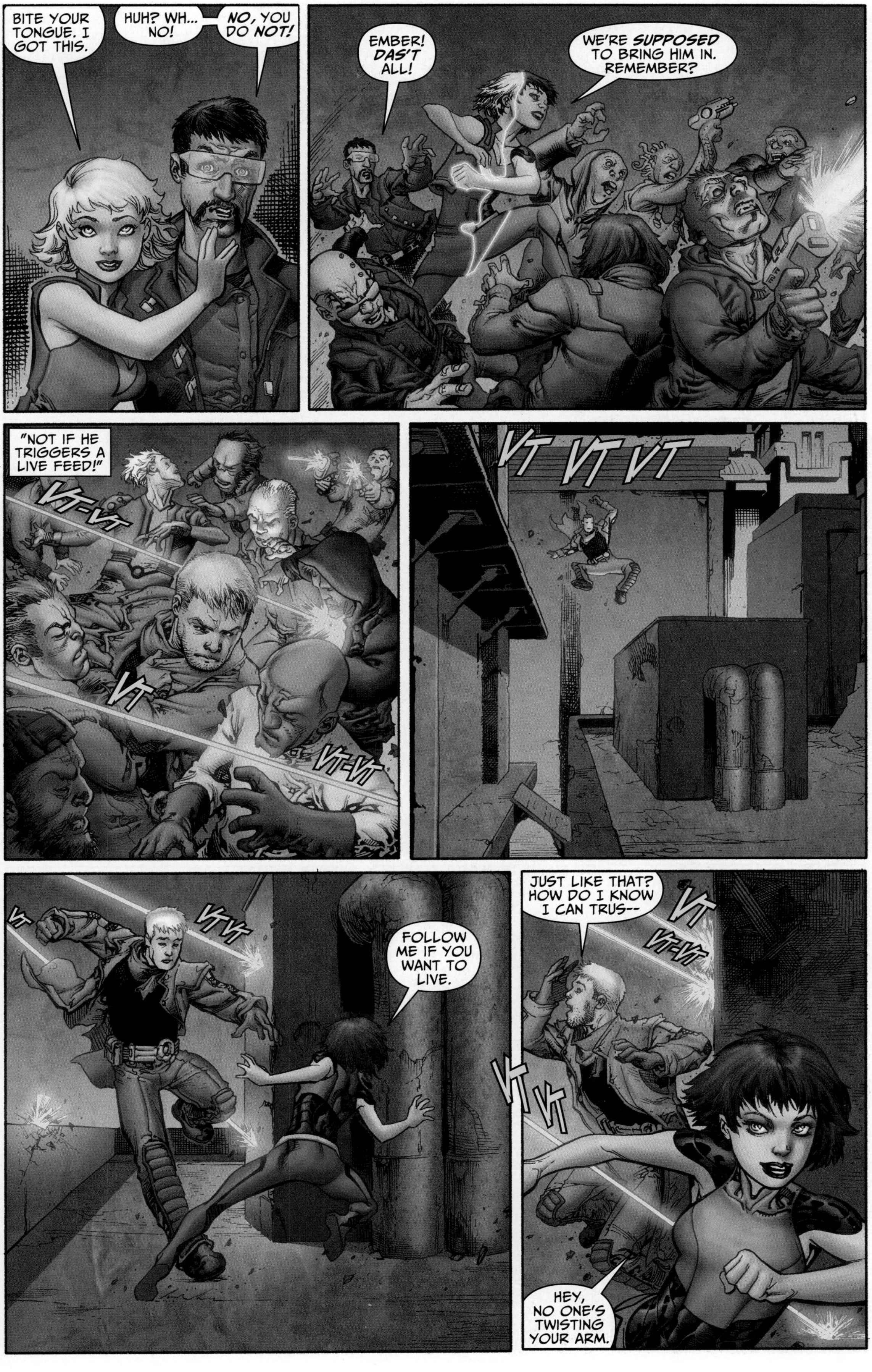
BITE YOUR TONGUE. I GOT THIS.
HUH? WH... NO!
NO, YOU DO NOT!
EMBER! DAS'T ALL!
WE'RE SUPPOSED TO BRING HIM IN. REMEMBER?
"NOT IF HE TRIGGERS A LIVE FEED!"
VT-VT
VT
VT-VT
VT VT VT
VT
VT-VT
FOLLOW ME IF YOU WANT TO LIVE.
JUST LIKE THAT? HOW DO I KNOW I CAN TRUS--
VT
VT-VT
VT
VT
HEY, NO ONE'S TWISTING YOUR ARM.

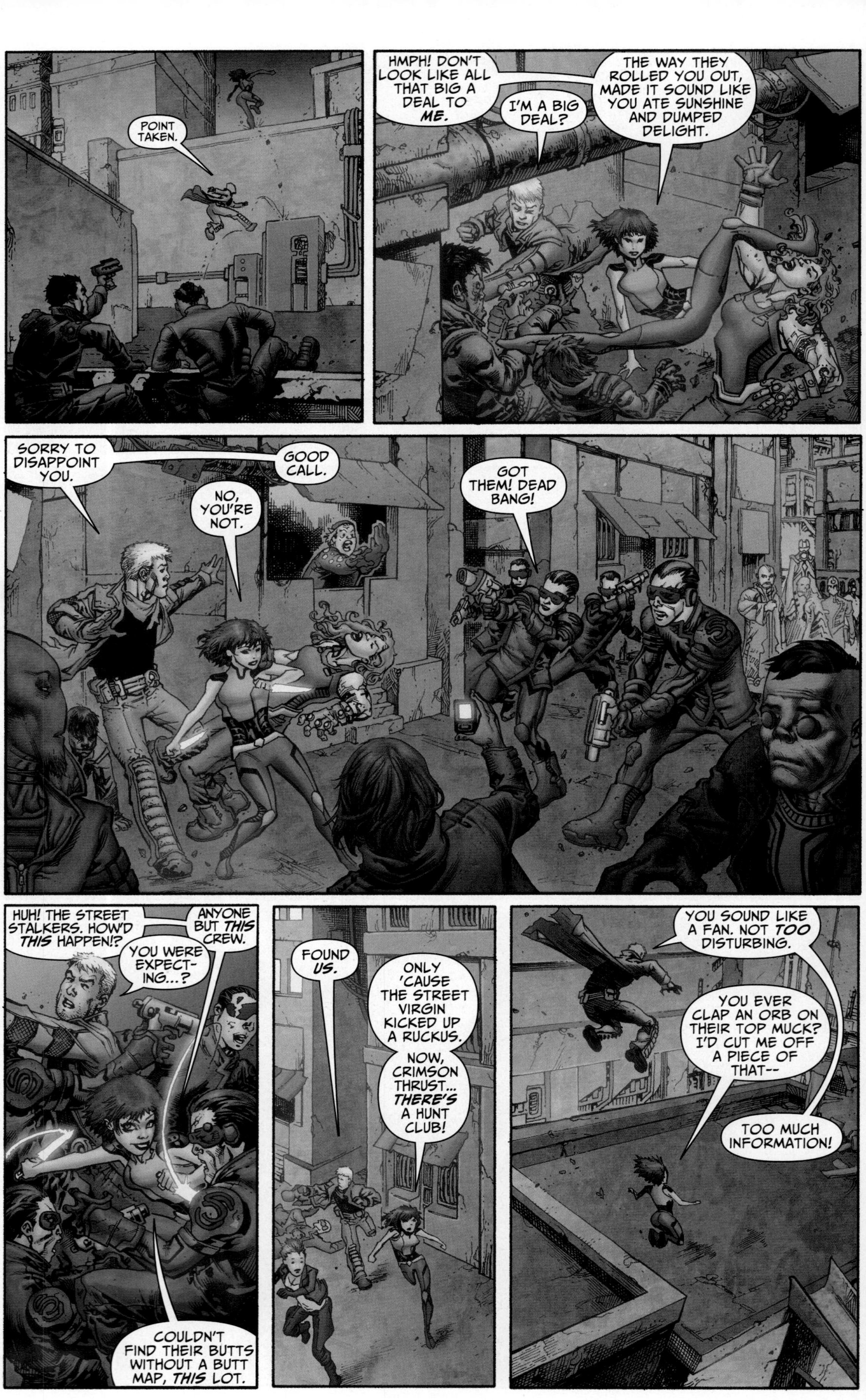

POINT TAKEN.
HMPH! DON'T LOOK LIKE ALL THAT BIG A DEAL TO *ME.*
I'M A BIG DEAL?
THE WAY THEY ROLLED YOU OUT, MADE IT SOUND LIKE YOU ATE SUNSHINE AND DUMPED DELIGHT.
SORRY TO DISAPPOINT YOU.
GOOD CALL.
NO, YOU'RE NOT.
GOT THEM! DEAD BANG!
HUH! THE STREET STALKERS. HOW'D *THIS* HAPPEN!?
ANYONE BUT *THIS* CREW.
YOU WERE EXPECTING...?
COULDN'T FIND THEIR BUTTS WITHOUT A BUTT MAP, *THIS* LOT.
FOUND *US.*
ONLY 'CAUSE THE STREET VIRGIN KICKED UP A RUCKUS.
NOW, CRIMSON THRUST... *THERE'S* A HUNT CLUB!
YOU SOUND LIKE A FAN. NOT *TOO* DISTURBING.
YOU EVER CLAP AN ORB ON THEIR TOP MUCK? I'D CUT ME OFF A PIECE OF THAT--
TOO MUCH INFORMATION!

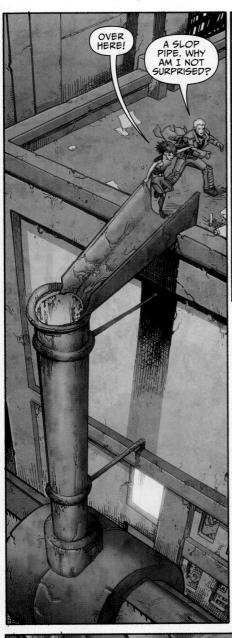

OVER HERE!

A SLOP PIPE. WHY AM I NOT SURPRISED?

WE PREFER "ESCAPE HATCH."

"WE"?

VT VT

VT VT

BIT LATE TO BE ASKING QUESTIONS, DON'CHA THINK?

GOOD POINT.

VT VT

VT VT

THRESHITALL! THEY HIT TH' WASTE PIPES, 'N' IT'S BYE-BYE BOUNTY!

STEADY! STEADY! GOT A MANUAL SLUICE! AIN'T GOIN' NOWHERES!

...TRUE YOU USED TO BE A GREEN LANTERN?

NOW? YOU WANT TO TALK ABOUT THAT NOW!?

CHEE...YOU ALWAYS THIS GROUCHY?

GRRRTTCHHH

UH-OH.

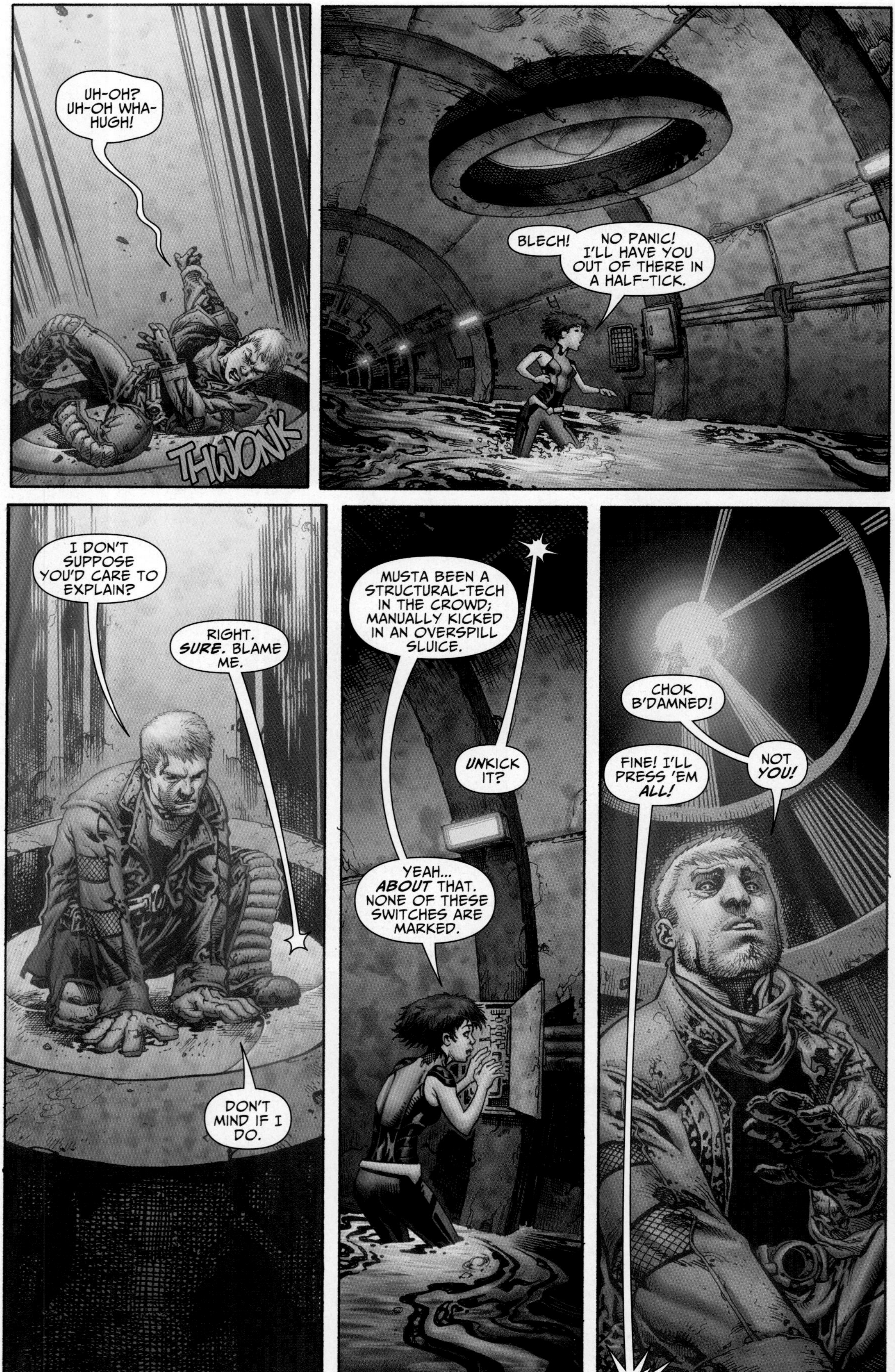
UH-OH? UH-OH WHA-HUGH!
THWONK
BLECH!
NO PANIC! I'LL HAVE YOU OUT OF THERE IN A HALF-TICK.
I DON'T SUPPOSE YOU'D CARE TO EXPLAIN?
RIGHT. SURE. BLAME ME.
DON'T MIND IF I DO.
MUSTA BEEN A STRUCTURAL-TECH IN THE CROWD; MANUALLY KICKED IN AN OVERSPILL SLUICE.
UNKICK IT?
YEAH... ABOUT THAT. NONE OF THESE SWITCHES ARE MARKED.
CHOK B'DAMNED!
NOT YOU!
FINE! I'LL PRESS 'EM ALL!

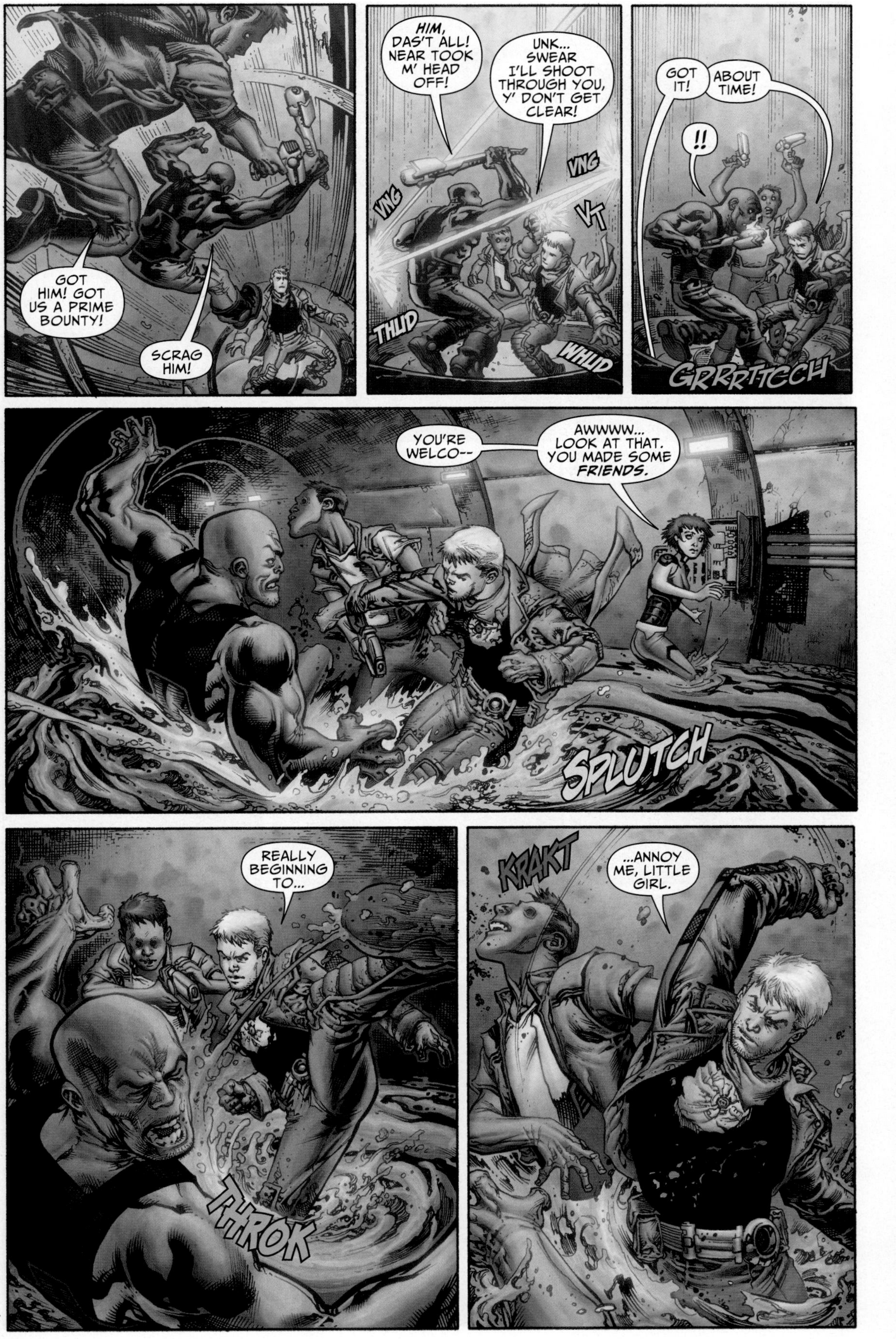
GOT HIM! GOT US A PRIME BOUNTY!
SCRAG HIM!
HIM, DAS'T ALL! NEAR TOOK M' HEAD OFF!
UNK... SWEAR I'LL SHOOT THROUGH YOU, Y' DON'T GET CLEAR!
VNG
VNG
VT
THUD
WHUD
GOT IT!
ABOUT TIME!
!!
GRRRTTCCH
YOU'RE WELCO--
AWWWW... LOOK AT THAT. YOU MADE SOME FRIENDS.
SPLUTCH
REALLY BEGINNING TO...
THROK
KRAKT
...ANNOY ME, LITTLE GIRL.

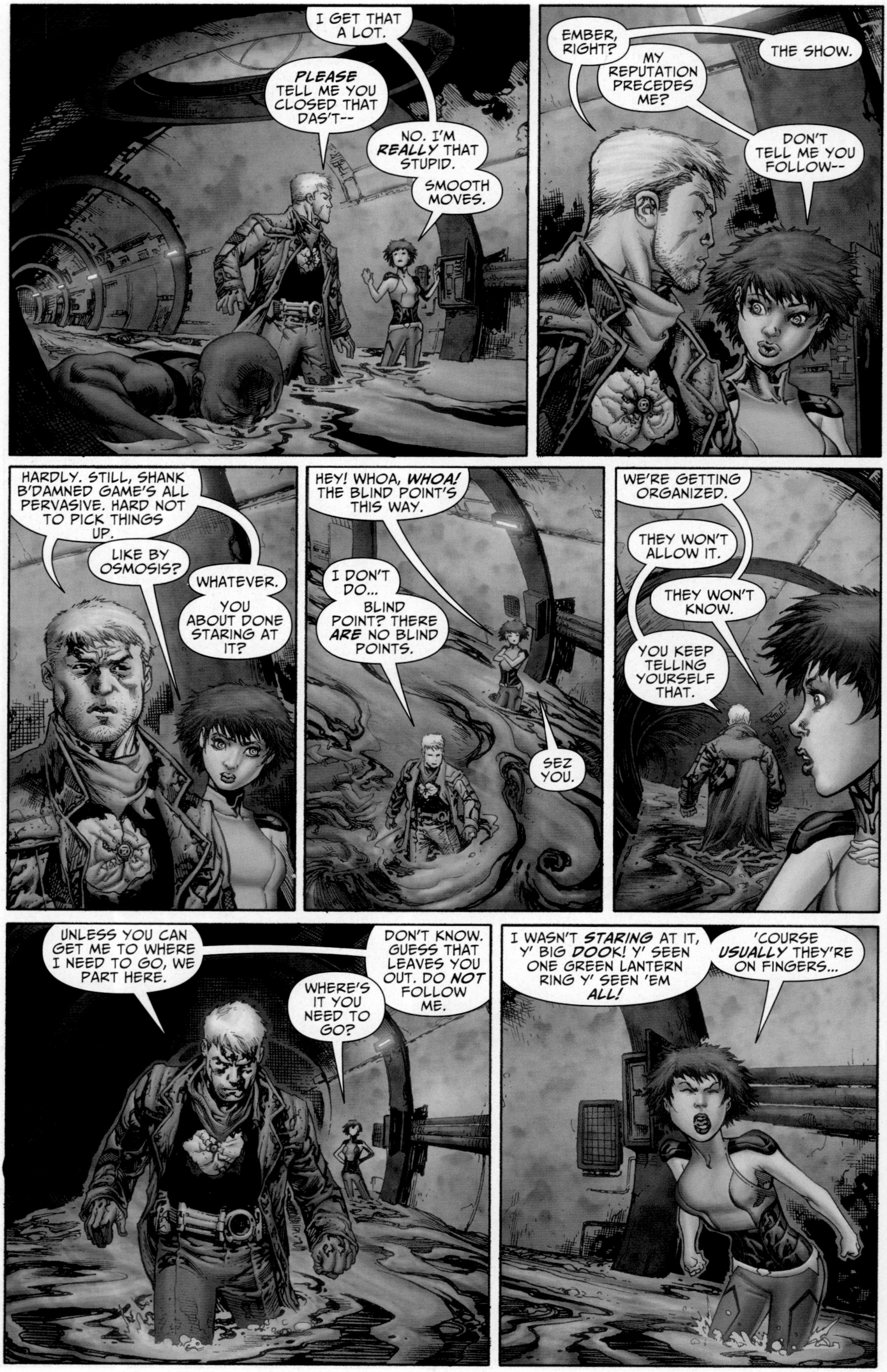
I GET THAT A LOT.
PLEASE TELL ME YOU CLOSED THAT DAS'T--
NO. I'M REALLY THAT STUPID.
SMOOTH MOVES.
EMBER, RIGHT?
MY REPUTATION PRECEDES ME?
THE SHOW.
DON'T TELL ME YOU FOLLOW--
HARDLY. STILL, SHANK B'DAMNED GAME'S ALL PERVASIVE. HARD NOT TO PICK THINGS UP.
LIKE BY OSMOSIS?
WHATEVER.
YOU ABOUT DONE STARING AT IT?
HEY! WHOA, WHOA! THE BLIND POINT'S THIS WAY.
I DON'T DO...
BLIND POINT? THERE ARE NO BLIND POINTS.
SEZ YOU.
WE'RE GETTING ORGANIZED.
THEY WON'T ALLOW IT.
THEY WON'T KNOW.
YOU KEEP TELLING YOURSELF THAT.
UNLESS YOU CAN GET ME TO WHERE I NEED TO GO, WE PART HERE.
WHERE'S IT YOU NEED TO GO?
DON'T KNOW. GUESS THAT LEAVES YOU OUT. DO NOT FOLLOW ME.
I WASN'T STARING AT IT, Y' BIG DOOK! Y' SEEN ONE GREEN LANTERN RING Y' SEEN 'EM ALL!
'COURSE USUALLY THEY'RE ON FINGERS...

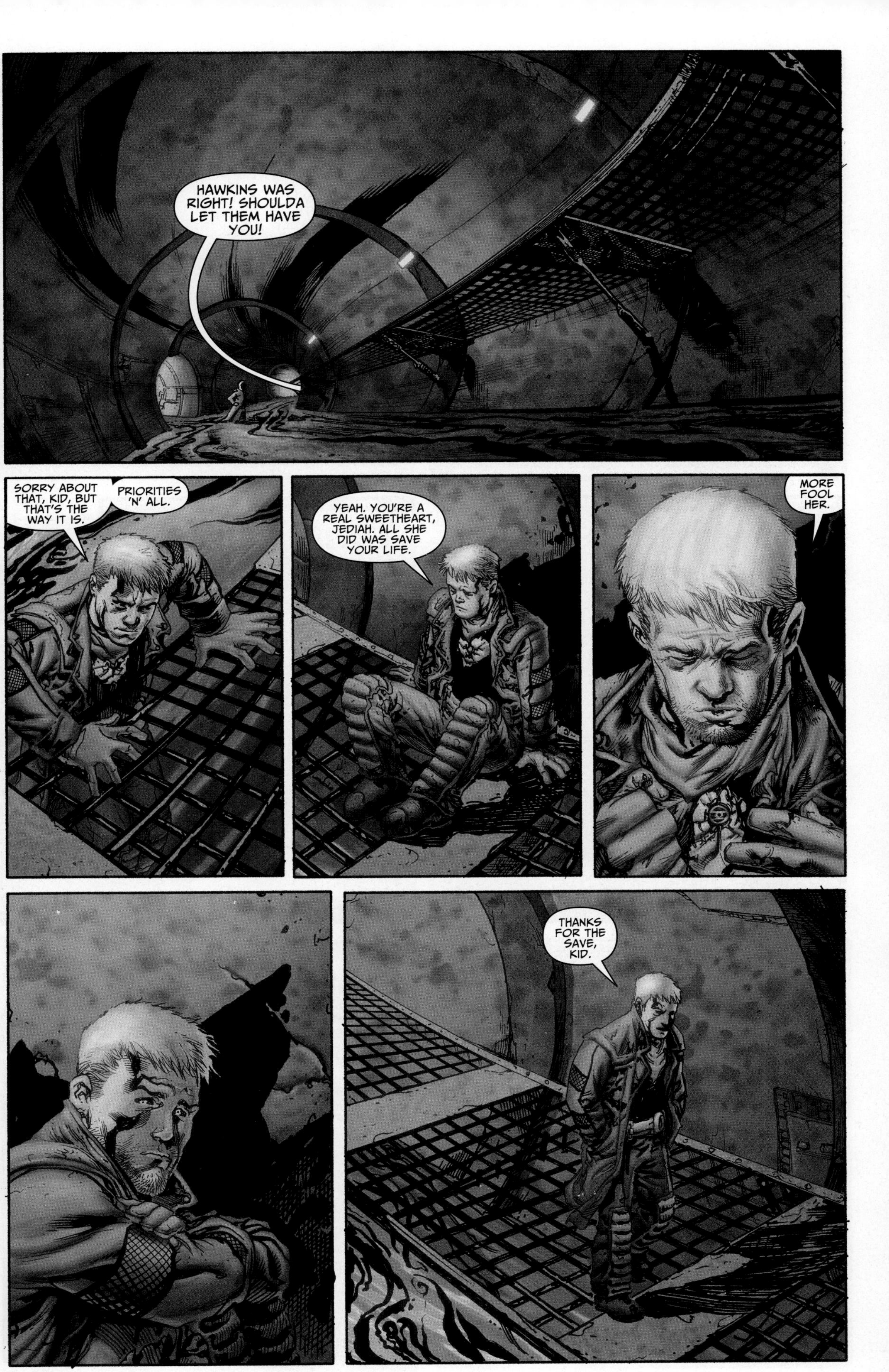
HAWKINS WAS RIGHT! SHOULDA LET THEM HAVE YOU!
SORRY ABOUT THAT, KID, BUT THAT'S THE WAY IT IS.
PRIORITIES 'N' ALL.
YEAH. YOU'RE A REAL SWEETHEART, JEDIAH. ALL SHE DID WAS SAVE YOUR LIFE.
MORE FOOL HER.
THANKS FOR THE SAVE, KID.

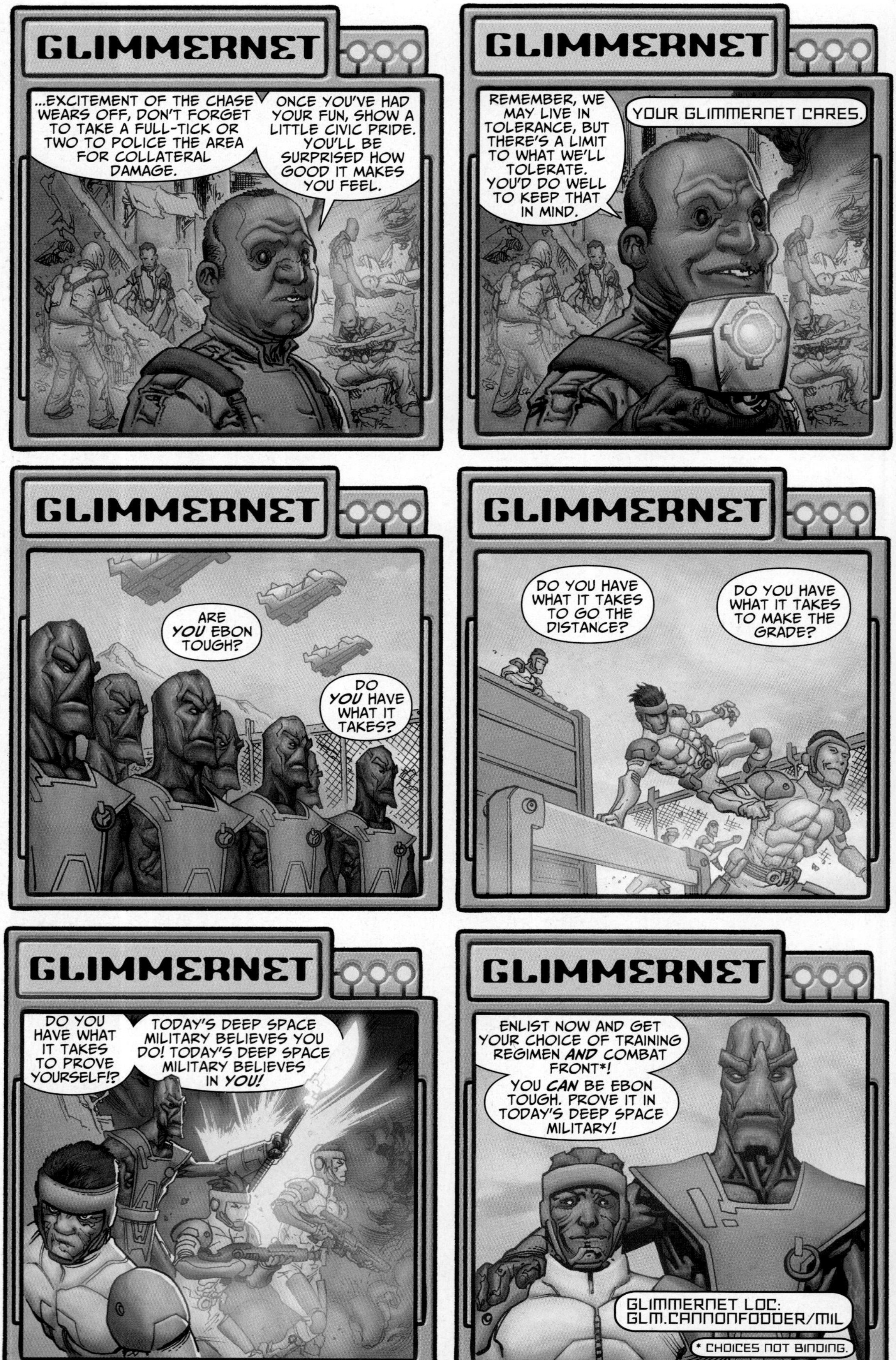
GLIMMERNET
...EXCITEMENT OF THE CHASE WEARS OFF, DON'T FORGET TO TAKE A FULL-TICK OR TWO TO POLICE THE AREA FOR COLLATERAL DAMAGE.
ONCE YOU'VE HAD YOUR FUN, SHOW A LITTLE CIVIC PRIDE. YOU'LL BE SURPRISED HOW GOOD IT MAKES YOU FEEL.
GLIMMERNET
REMEMBER, WE MAY LIVE IN TOLERANCE, BUT THERE'S A LIMIT TO WHAT WE'LL TOLERATE. YOU'D DO WELL TO KEEP THAT IN MIND.
YOUR GLIMMERNET CARES.
GLIMMERNET
ARE *YOU* EBON TOUGH?
DO *YOU* HAVE WHAT IT TAKES?
GLIMMERNET
DO YOU HAVE WHAT IT TAKES TO GO THE DISTANCE?
DO YOU HAVE WHAT IT TAKES TO MAKE THE GRADE?
GLIMMERNET
DO YOU HAVE WHAT IT TAKES TO PROVE YOURSELF!?
TODAY'S DEEP SPACE MILITARY BELIEVES YOU DO! TODAY'S DEEP SPACE MILITARY BELIEVES IN *YOU!*
GLIMMERNET
ENLIST NOW AND GET YOUR CHOICE OF TRAINING REGIMEN *AND* COMBAT FRONT*!
YOU *CAN* BE EBON TOUGH. PROVE IT IN TODAY'S DEEP SPACE MILITARY!
GLIMMERNET LOC: GLM.CANNONFODDER/MIL
* CHOICES NOT BINDING.

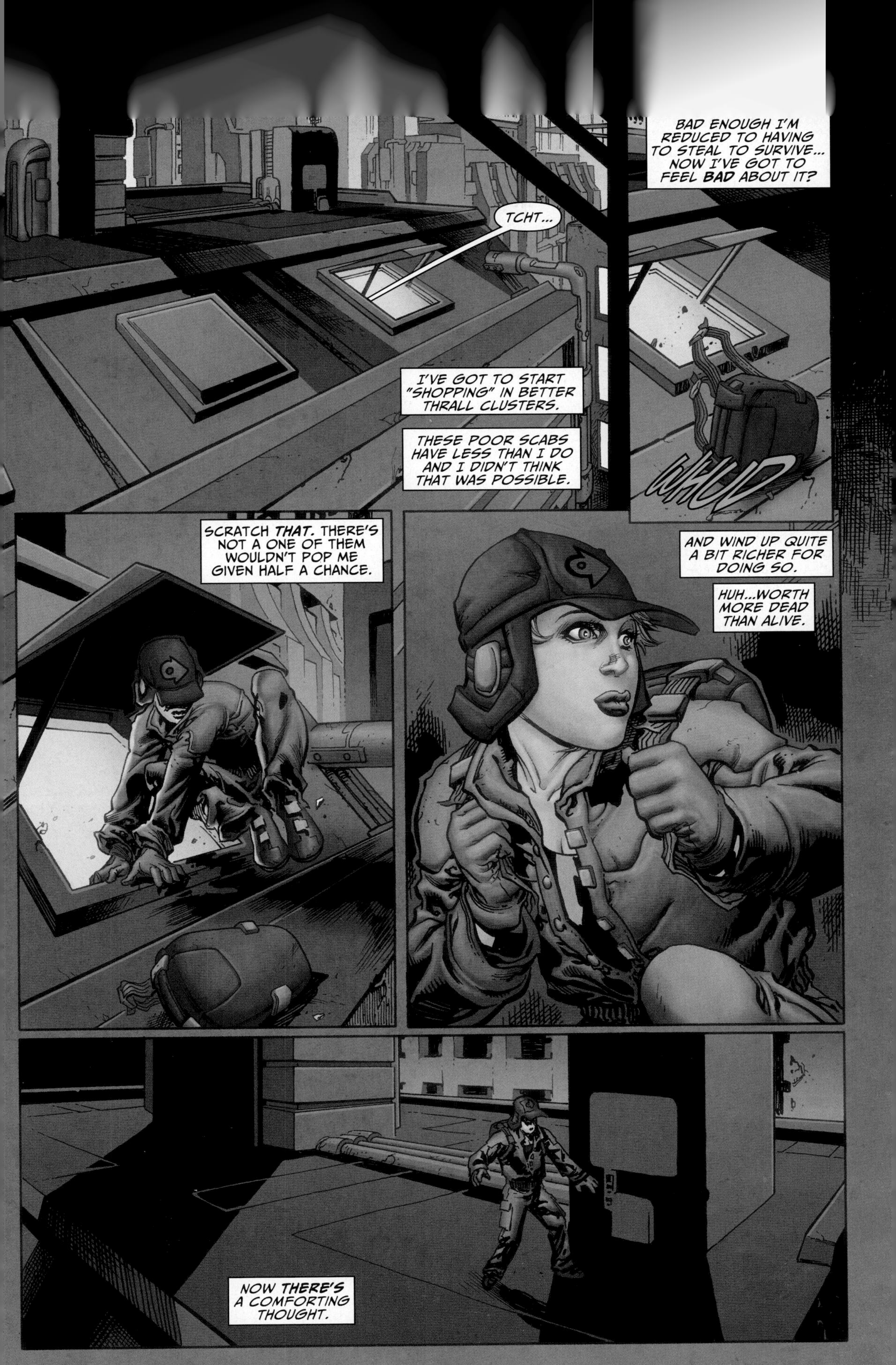
TCHT...
I'VE GOT TO START "SHOPPING" IN BETTER THRALL CLUSTERS.
THESE POOR SCABS HAVE LESS THAN I DO AND I DIDN'T THINK THAT WAS POSSIBLE.
BAD ENOUGH I'M REDUCED TO HAVING TO STEAL TO SURVIVE... NOW I'VE GOT TO FEEL BAD ABOUT IT?
WHUD
SCRATCH THAT. THERE'S NOT A ONE OF THEM WOULDN'T POP ME GIVEN HALF A CHANCE.
AND WIND UP QUITE A BIT RICHER FOR DOING SO.
HUH...WORTH MORE DEAD THAN ALIVE.
NOW THERE'S A COMFORTING THOUGHT.

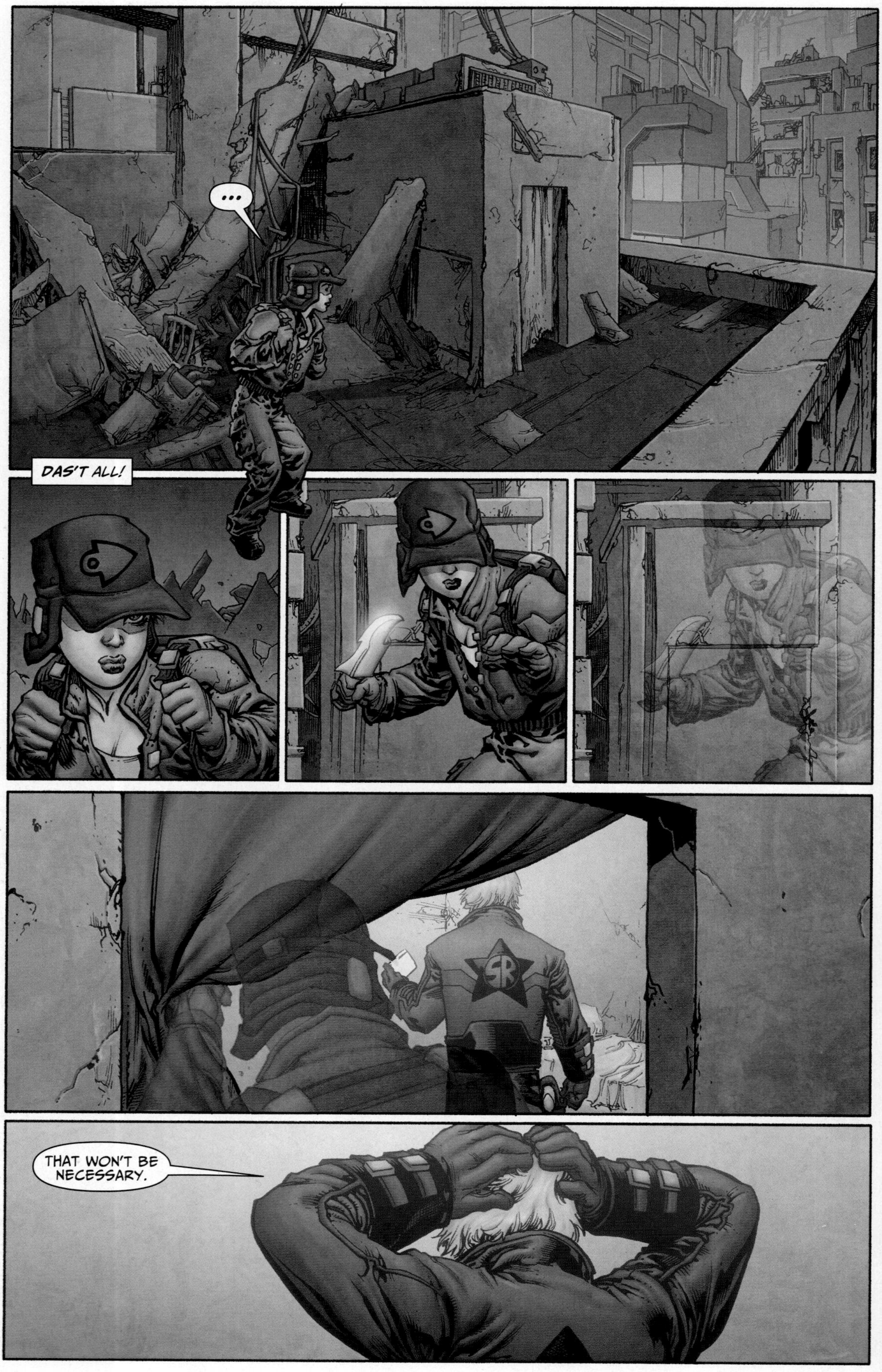
...
DAS'T ALL!
THAT WON'T BE NECESSARY.

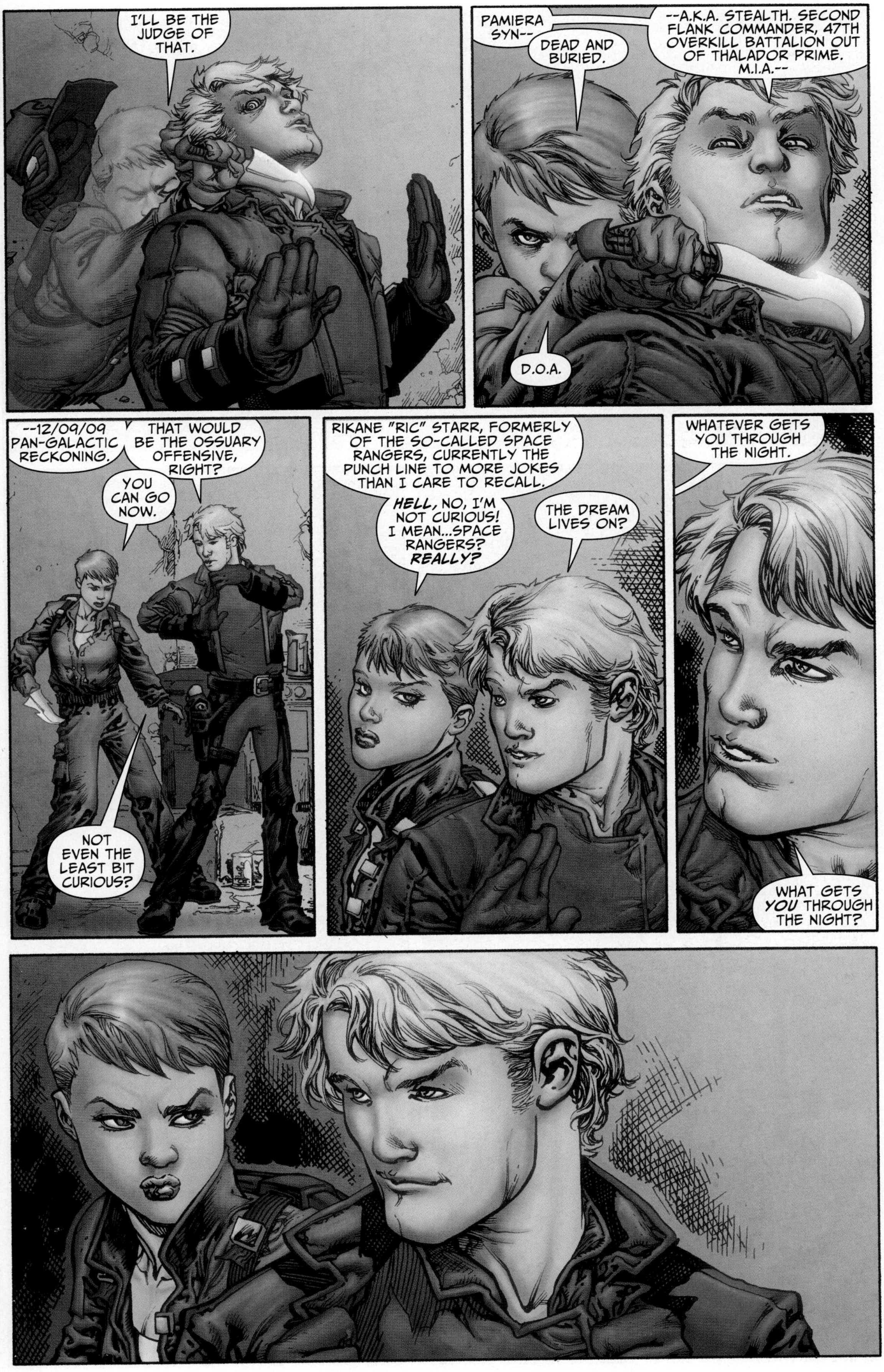

I'LL BE THE JUDGE OF THAT.
PAMIERA SYN--
--A.K.A. STEALTH. SECOND FLANK COMMANDER, 47TH OVERKILL BATTALION OUT OF THALADOR PRIME. M.I.A.--
DEAD AND BURIED.
D.O.A.
--12/09/09 PAN-GALACTIC RECKONING.
THAT WOULD BE THE OSSUARY OFFENSIVE, RIGHT?
YOU CAN GO NOW.
NOT EVEN THE LEAST BIT CURIOUS?
RIKANE "RIC" STARR, FORMERLY OF THE SO-CALLED SPACE RANGERS, CURRENTLY THE PUNCH LINE TO MORE JOKES THAN I CARE TO RECALL.
HELL, NO, I'M NOT CURIOUS! I MEAN...SPACE RANGERS? REALLY?
THE DREAM LIVES ON?
WHATEVER GETS YOU THROUGH THE NIGHT.
WHAT GETS YOU THROUGH THE NIGHT?

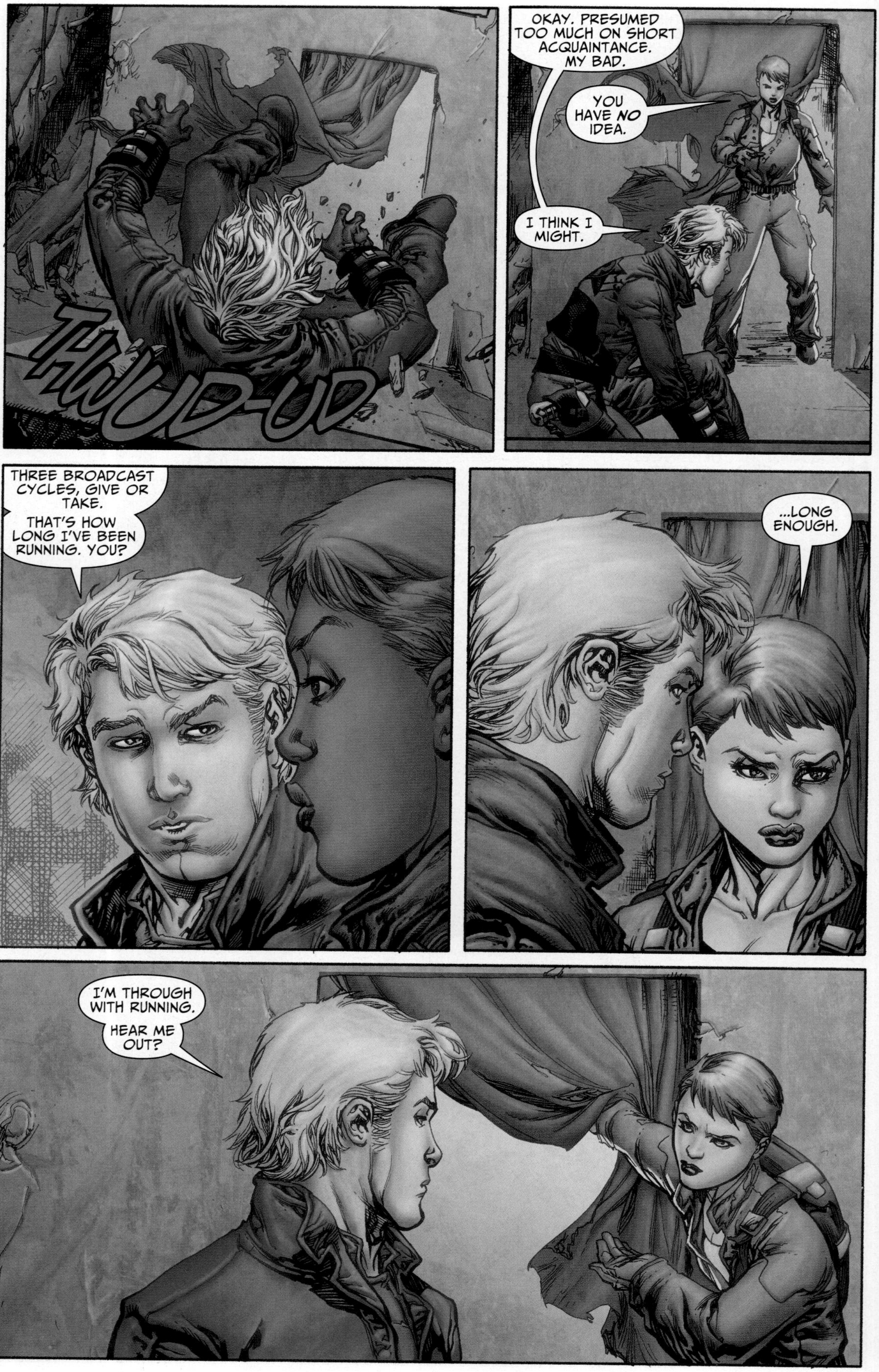
THUUD-UD
OKAY. PRESUMED TOO MUCH ON SHORT ACQUAINTANCE. MY BAD.
YOU HAVE NO IDEA.
I THINK I MIGHT.
THREE BROADCAST CYCLES, GIVE OR TAKE.
THAT'S HOW LONG I'VE BEEN RUNNING. YOU?
...LONG ENOUGH.
I'M THROUGH WITH RUNNING.
HEAR ME OUT?

A STAR IS BORN?

I SHOULD THINK SO. THE CAMERAS *LOVE* HIM. WE *ARE* DOLING HIM OUT?

AS WE SPEAK. HOLO-POSTERS, "LIMITED EDITION" LOGO GEAR--THE FULL MERCHANDISING BLITZ. WE'VE EVEN GOT A PROTEIN PATTY READY TO ROLL.

I'M *LOVING* IT! FROM DEEP COVER OPERATIVE TO CREDIT SPONGE FOR THE CAUSE.

SIGH... I WISH WE HAD SEEN MORE OF THE RING. THE MASSES DO *SO* RESPOND TO SYMBOLISM.

PERHAPS, IN HINDSIGHT, A MORE... *CONSISTENTLY* VISIBLE BRAND?

SECOND-GUESSING THE LADY STYX? MY, MY, YOU *ARE* A BRAVE ONE. OR IS THAT FOOLISH? I TEND TO CONFUSE THE TWO.

WH..? NO! I DIDN'T... I MEAN--

JEDIAH CAUL-- FORMER GREEN LANTERN, CURRENTLY HUNTED--SHOULD SERVE US WELL. PRELIMINARY GLIMMERNET RATINGS STAND AT 6.9 PERCENT UP SINCE HIS DROP INTO THE GAME.

PROBABILITY PROJECTIONS PREDICT A 3.09 PERCENT RATINGS INCREASE PER BROADCAST CYCLE AS LONG AS HE REMAINS AT LARGE.

HE IS THE ENEMY.

THEY ARE *ALL* THE ENEMY. IT IS WHY THEY ARE CHOSEN TO BE HUNTED.

OF COURSE.

ESCAPED! LIVE FEED TERMINATED.

STILL, IT *WILL* BE DIFFICULT TO TOP A DISGRACED GREEN LANTERN.

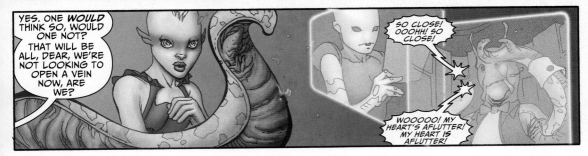

YES. ONE *WOULD* THINK SO, WOULD ONE NOT? THAT WILL BE ALL, DEAR, WE'RE NOT LOOKING TO OPEN A VEIN NOW, ARE WE?

SO CLOSE! OOOHH! SO CLOSE!

WOOOOO! MY HEART'S AFLUTTER! MY HEART IS AFLUTTER!

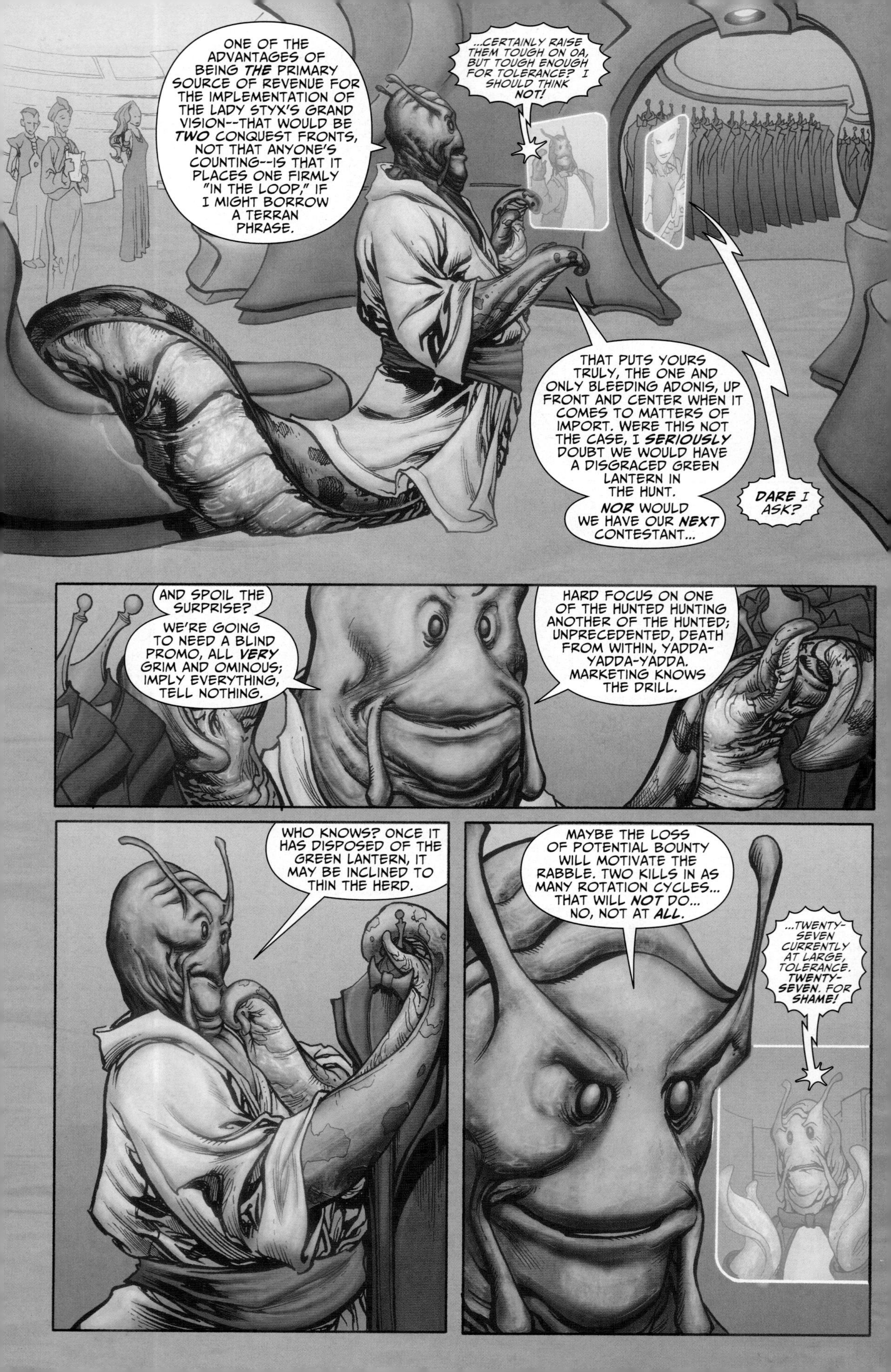
ONE OF THE ADVANTAGES OF BEING THE PRIMARY SOURCE OF REVENUE FOR THE IMPLEMENTATION OF THE LADY STYX'S GRAND VISION--THAT WOULD BE TWO CONQUEST FRONTS, NOT THAT ANYONE'S COUNTING--IS THAT IT PLACES ONE FIRMLY "IN THE LOOP," IF I MIGHT BORROW A TERRAN PHRASE.
...CERTAINLY RAISE THEM TOUGH ON OA, BUT TOUGH ENOUGH FOR TOLERANCE? I SHOULD THINK NOT!
THAT PUTS YOURS TRULY, THE ONE AND ONLY BLEEDING ADONIS, UP FRONT AND CENTER WHEN IT COMES TO MATTERS OF IMPORT. WERE THIS NOT THE CASE, I SERIOUSLY DOUBT WE WOULD HAVE A DISGRACED GREEN LANTERN IN THE HUNT.
NOR WOULD WE HAVE OUR NEXT CONTESTANT...
DARE I ASK?
AND SPOIL THE SURPRISE?
WE'RE GOING TO NEED A BLIND PROMO, ALL VERY GRIM AND OMINOUS; IMPLY EVERYTHING, TELL NOTHING.
HARD FOCUS ON ONE OF THE HUNTED HUNTING ANOTHER OF THE HUNTED; UNPRECEDENTED, DEATH FROM WITHIN, YADDA-YADDA-YADDA. MARKETING KNOWS THE DRILL.
WHO KNOWS? ONCE IT HAS DISPOSED OF THE GREEN LANTERN, IT MAY BE INCLINED TO THIN THE HERD.
MAYBE THE LOSS OF POTENTIAL BOUNTY WILL MOTIVATE THE RABBLE. TWO KILLS IN AS MANY ROTATION CYCLES... THAT WILL NOT DO... NO, NOT AT ALL.
...TWENTY-SEVEN CURRENTLY AT LARGE, TOLERANCE. TWENTY-SEVEN. FOR SHAME!

HOW DID YOU FIND ME?

I HAVE MY WAYS.

NEED AN ANSWER. IF YOU CAN FIND ME, ONE OF THEM CAN.

IT'S ONLY A MATTER OF TIME BEFORE *SOMEONE* DOES. DON'T KNOW IF YOU'VE NOTICED, BUT THEY OUTNUMBER US.

US? YOU *DO* PRESUME A LOT ON SHORT ACQUAINTANCE.

GOT TWENTY-SEVEN ACTIVE CONTESTANTS AT LAST COUNT.

YOU KEEP *COUNT?*

SOMEONE'S GOT TO.

WRONG. IT'S EVERY LIFE-FORM FOR ITSELF OUT THERE.

OH, AND FOR THE RECORD, THERE IS NO "US."

COLONEL T'MORRA CRACKED THEIR SMART DUST TRANSMISSION CRYPTOS. WE'VE BEEN CARVING OUT BLIND SPOTS EVER SINCE.

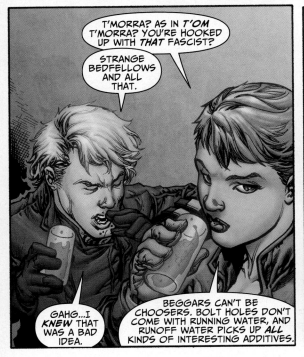

T'MORRA? AS IN *T'OM T'MORRA?* YOU'RE HOOKED UP WITH *THAT* FASCIST?

STRANGE BEDFELLOWS AND ALL THAT.

GAHG...I *KNEW* THAT WAS A BAD IDEA.

BEGGARS CAN'T BE CHOOSERS. BOLT HOLES DON'T COME WITH RUNNING WATER, AND RUNOFF WATER PICKS UP *ALL* KINDS OF INTERESTING ADDITIVES.

KEEPS ME ALIVE. THAT'S WHAT COUNTS.

NEVER HEARD OF *QUALITY* OF LIFE?

YOU STILL HAVEN'T ANSWERED MY QUESTION. HOW DID YOU FIND ME?

I DIDN'T.

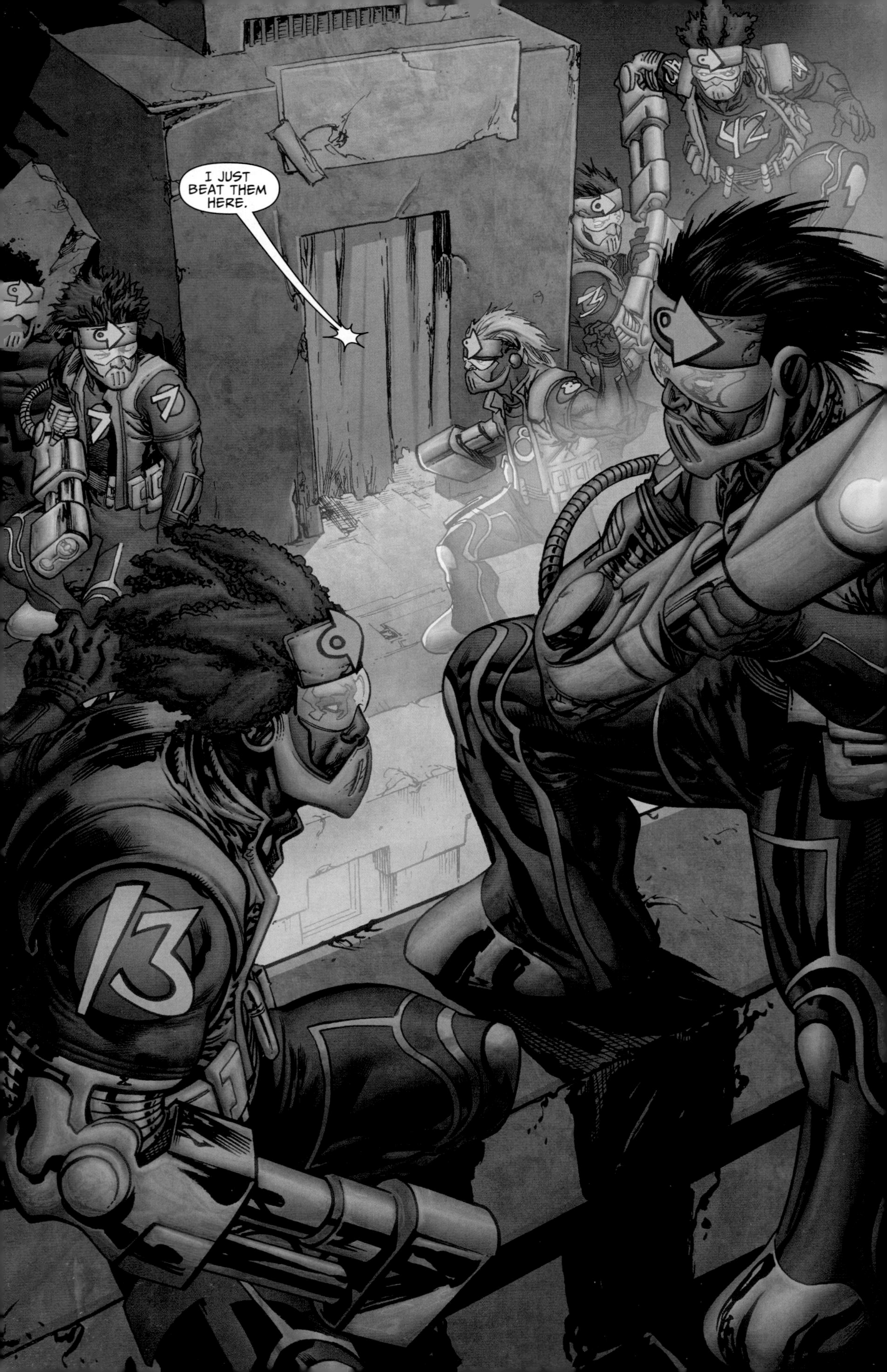
I JUST BEAT THEM HERE.

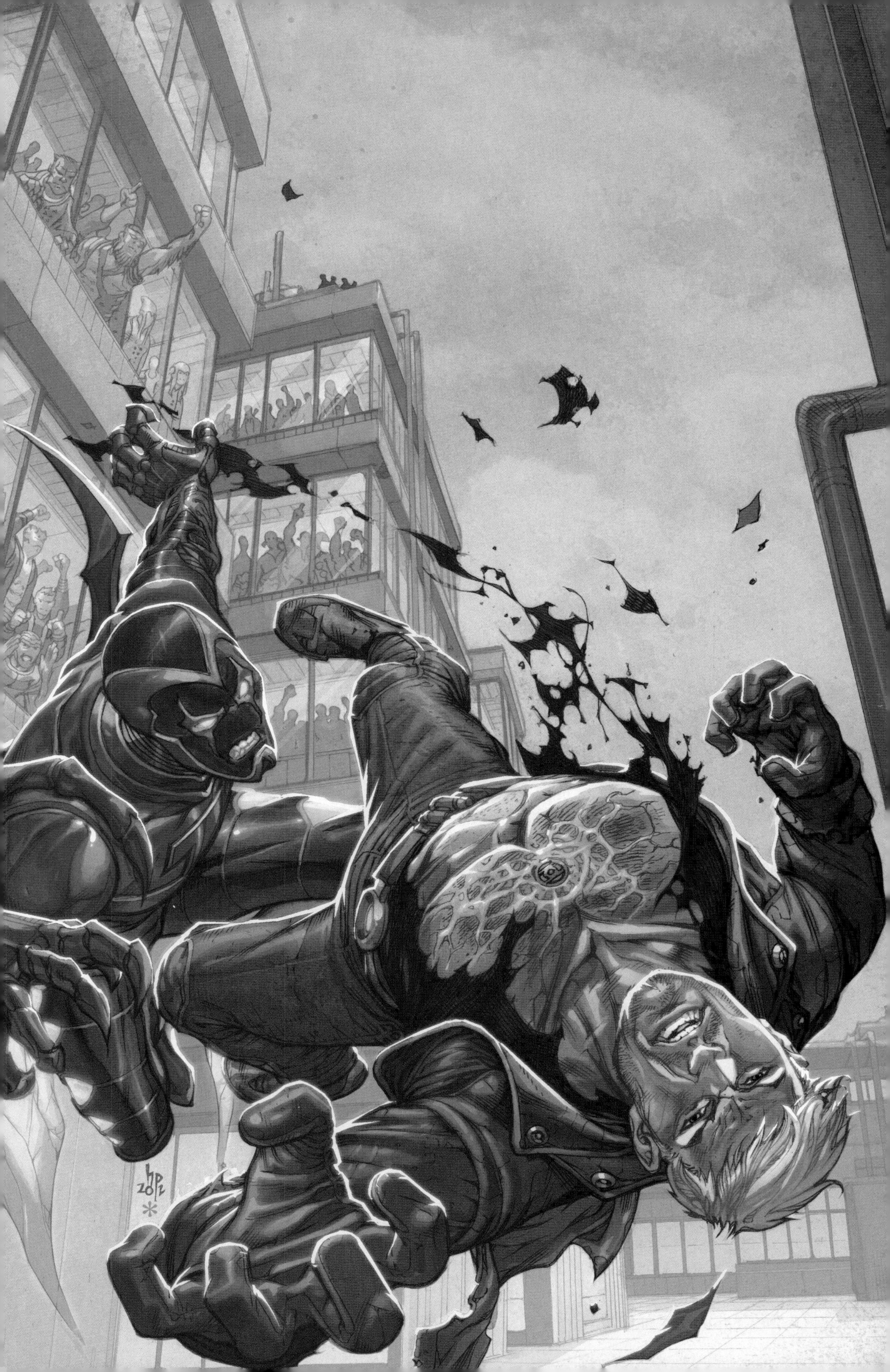

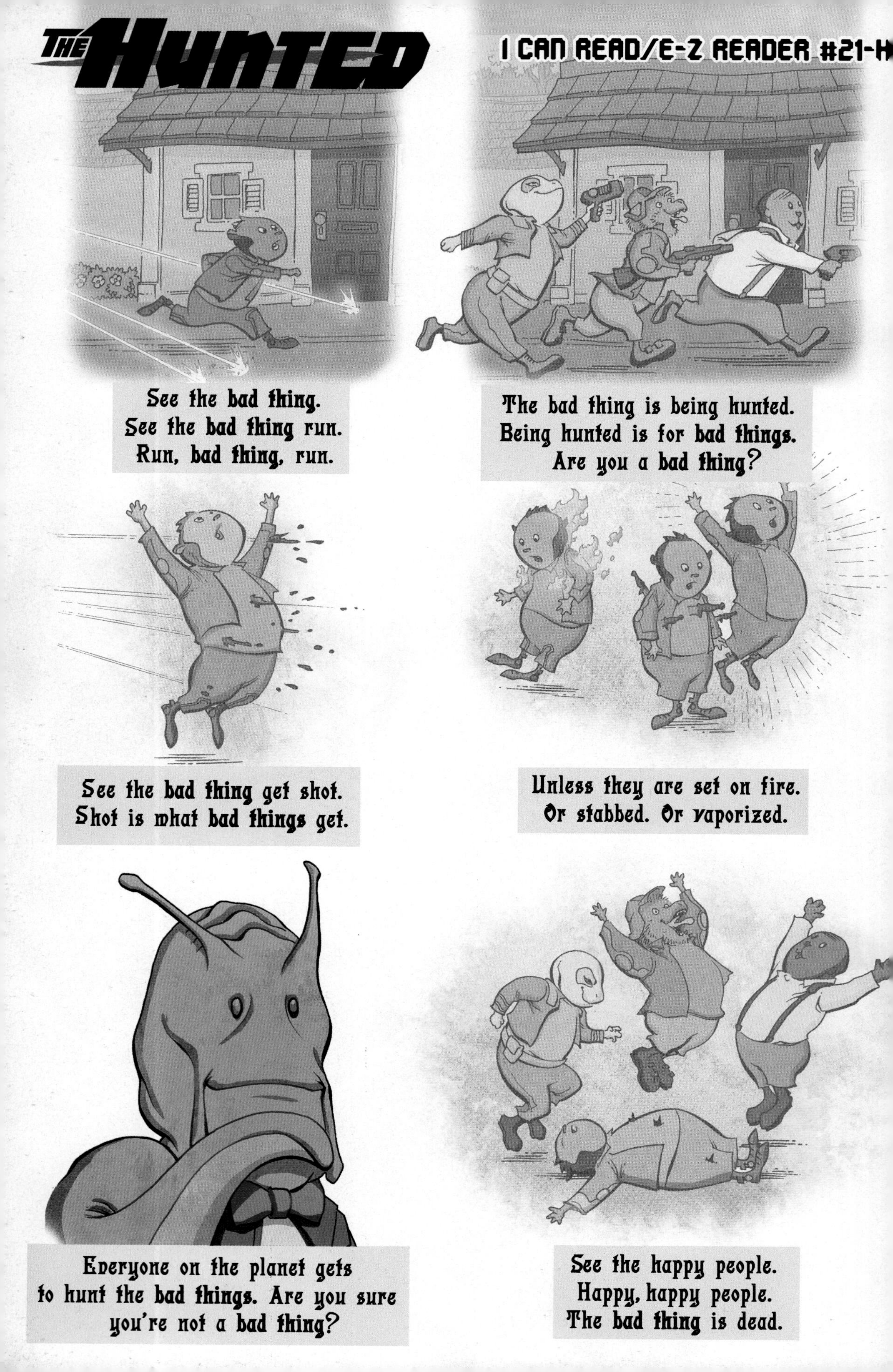
THE HUNTED
I CAN READ/E-Z READER #21-H
See the bad thing.
See the bad thing run.
Run, bad thing, run.
The bad thing is being hunted.
Being hunted is for bad things.
Are you a bad thing?
See the bad thing get shot.
Shot is what bad things get.
Unless they are set on fire.
Or stabbed. Or vaporized.
Everyone on the planet gets
to hunt the bad things. Are you sure
you're not a bad thing?
See the happy people.
Happy, happy people.
The bad thing is dead.

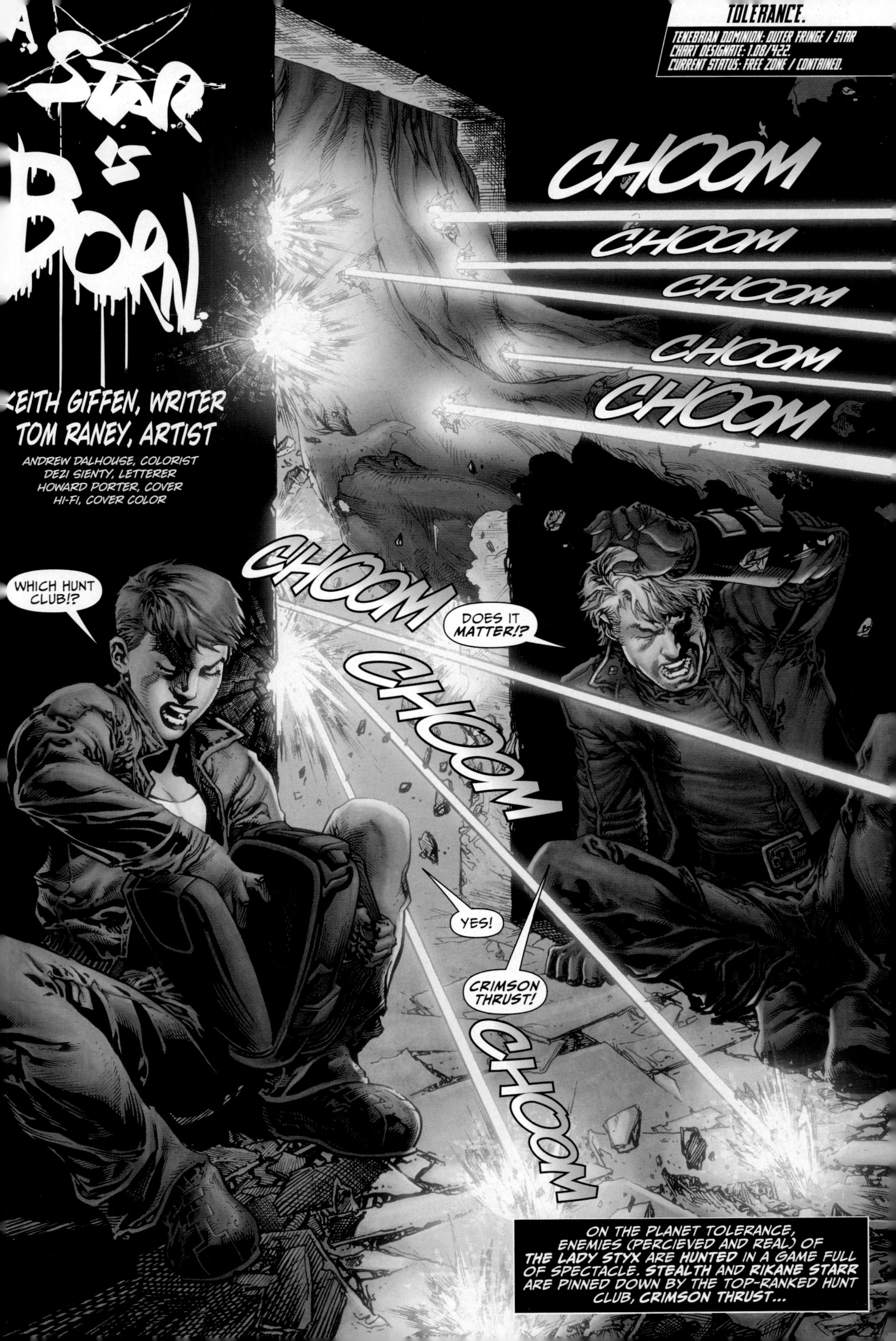
A STAR IS BORN
KEITH GIFFEN, WRITER
TOM RANEY, ARTIST
ANDREW DALHOUSE, COLORIST
DEZI SIENTY, LETTERER
HOWARD PORTER, COVER
HI-FI, COVER COLOR
TOLERANCE.
TENEBRIAN DOMINION: OUTER FRINGE / STAR
CHART DESIGNATE: 1.08/422.
CURRENT STATUS: FREE ZONE / CONTAINED.
CHOOM
CHOOM
CHOOM
CHOOM
CHOOM
CHOOM
WHICH HUNT CLUB!?
DOES IT MATTER!?
CHOOM
CHOOM
YES!
CRIMSON THRUST!
CHOOM
CHOOM
ON THE PLANET TOLERANCE, ENEMIES (PERCIEVED AND REAL) OF THE LADY STYX ARE HUNTED IN A GAME FULL OF SPECTACLE. STEALTH AND RIKANE STARR ARE PINNED DOWN BY THE TOP-RANKED HUNT CLUB, CRIMSON THRUST...

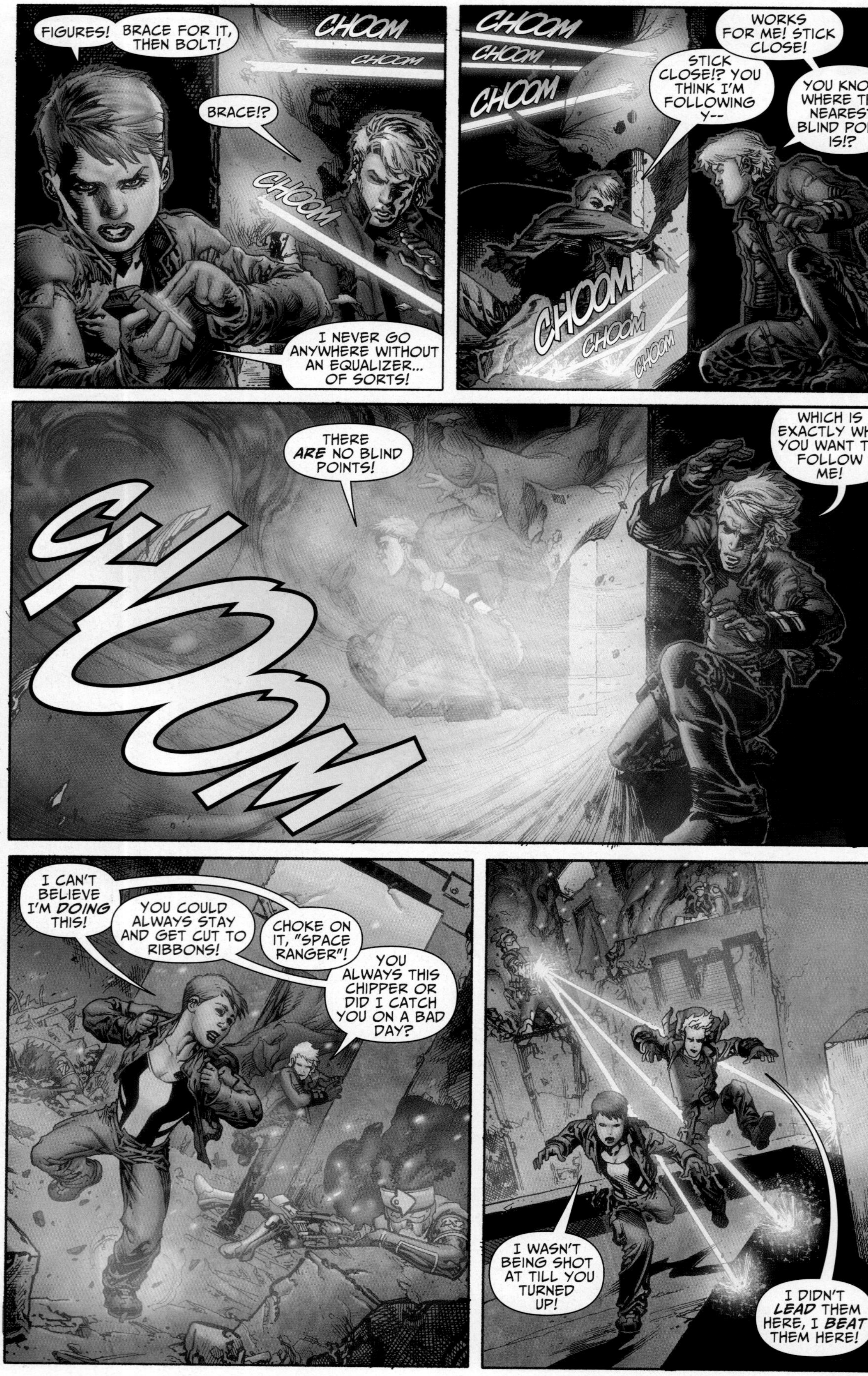
FIGURES!
BRACE FOR IT, THEN BOLT!
CHOOM
CHOOM
BRACE!?
CHOOM
I NEVER GO ANYWHERE WITHOUT AN EQUALIZER... OF SORTS!
CHOOM
CHOOM
CHOOM
WORKS FOR ME! STICK CLOSE!
STICK CLOSE!? YOU THINK I'M FOLLOWING Y--
YOU KNOW WHERE THE NEAREST BLIND POINT IS!?
CHOOM
CHOOM
CHOOM
CHOOM
THERE ARE NO BLIND POINTS!
WHICH IS EXACTLY WHY YOU WANT TO FOLLOW ME!
I CAN'T BELIEVE I'M DOING THIS!
YOU COULD ALWAYS STAY AND GET CUT TO RIBBONS!
CHOKE ON IT, "SPACE RANGER"!
YOU ALWAYS THIS CHIPPER OR DID I CATCH YOU ON A BAD DAY?
I WASN'T BEING SHOT AT TILL YOU TURNED UP!
I DIDN'T LEAD THEM HERE, I BEAT THEM HERE!

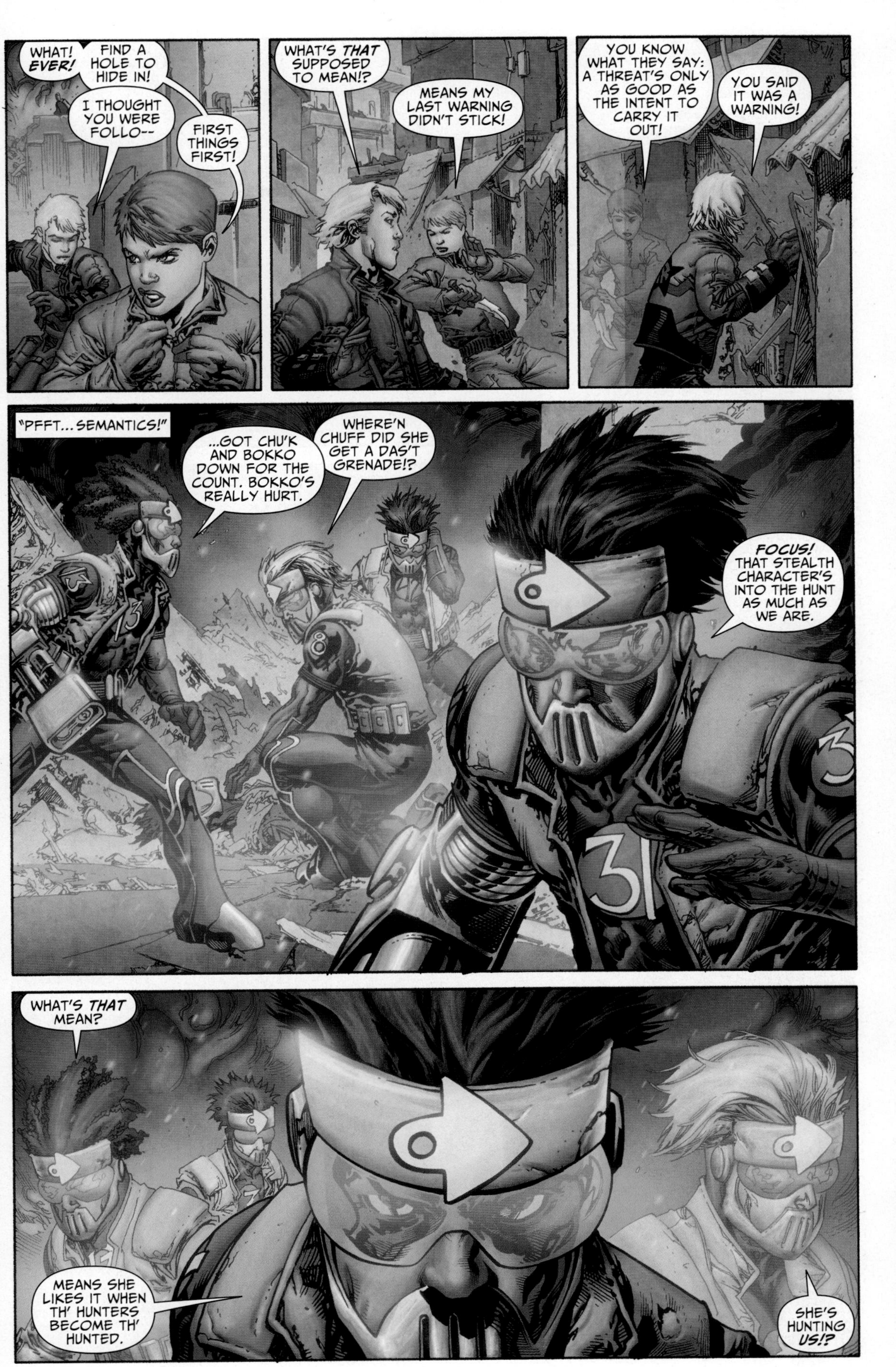
WHAT! EVER!
FIND A HOLE TO HIDE IN!
I THOUGHT YOU WERE FOLLO--
FIRST THINGS FIRST!
WHAT'S THAT SUPPOSED TO MEAN!?
MEANS MY LAST WARNING DIDN'T STICK!
YOU KNOW WHAT THEY SAY: A THREAT'S ONLY AS GOOD AS THE INTENT TO CARRY IT OUT!
YOU SAID IT WAS A WARNING!
"PFFT... SEMANTICS!"
...GOT CHU'K AND BOKKO DOWN FOR THE COUNT. BOKKO'S REALLY HURT.
WHERE'N CHUFF DID SHE GET A DAS'T GRENADE!?
FOCUS! THAT STEALTH CHARACTER'S INTO THE HUNT AS MUCH AS WE ARE.
WHAT'S THAT MEAN?
MEANS SHE LIKES IT WHEN TH' HUNTERS BECOME TH' HUNTED.
SHE'S HUNTING US!?

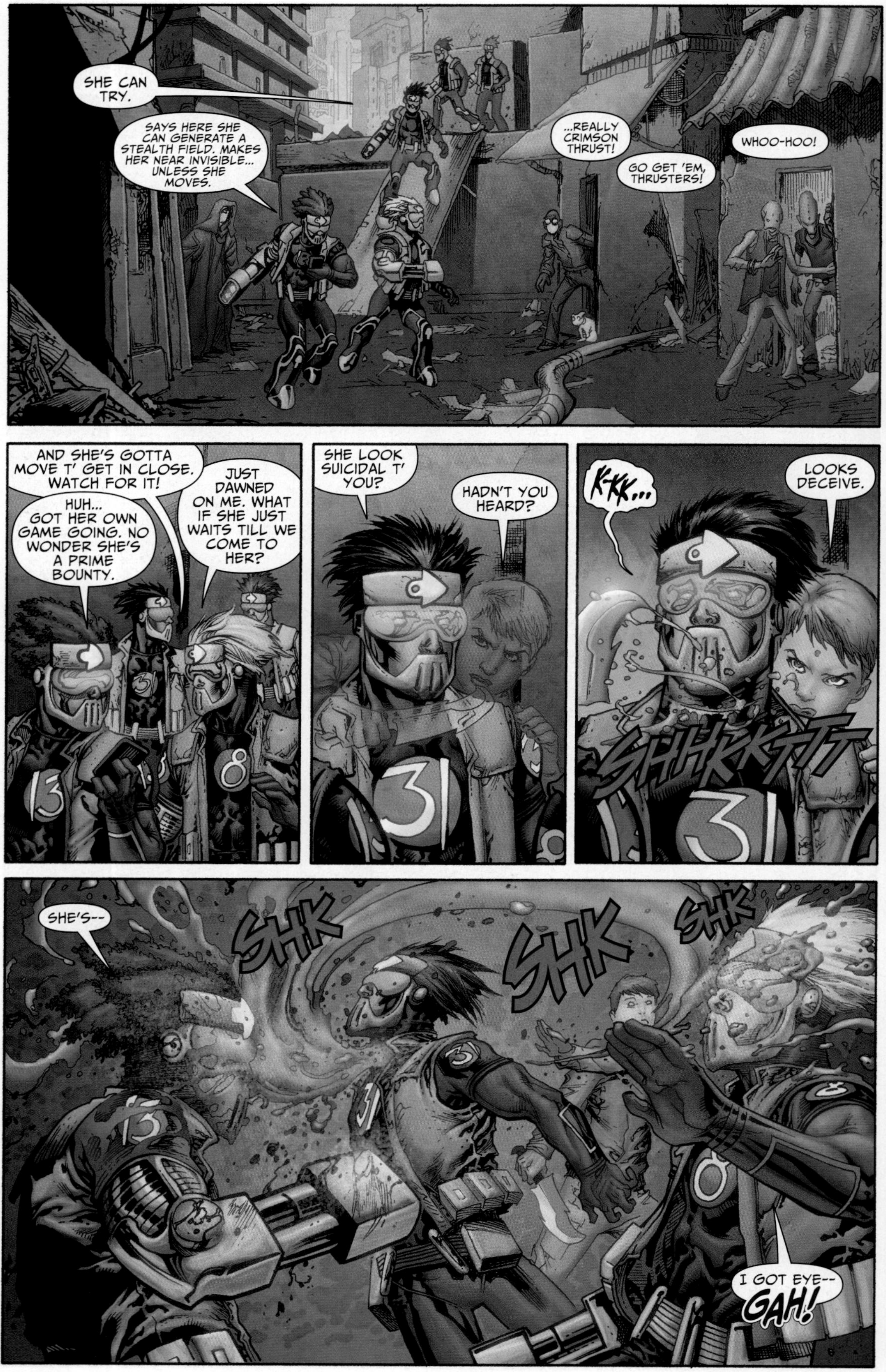
SHE CAN TRY.
SAYS HERE SHE CAN GENERATE A STEALTH FIELD. MAKES HER NEAR INVISIBLE... UNLESS SHE MOVES.
...REALLY CRIMSON THRUST!
GO GET 'EM, THRUSTERS!
WHOO-HOO!
AND SHE'S GOTTA MOVE T' GET IN CLOSE. WATCH FOR IT!
HUH... GOT HER OWN GAME GOING. NO WONDER SHE'S A PRIME BOUNTY.
JUST DAWNED ON ME. WHAT IF SHE JUST WAITS TILL WE COME TO HER?
SHE LOOK SUICIDAL T' YOU?
HADN'T YOU HEARD?
K-KK...
LOOKS DECEIVE.
SHHKKTTT
SHE'S--
SHK
SHK
SHK
I GOT EYE-- GAH!

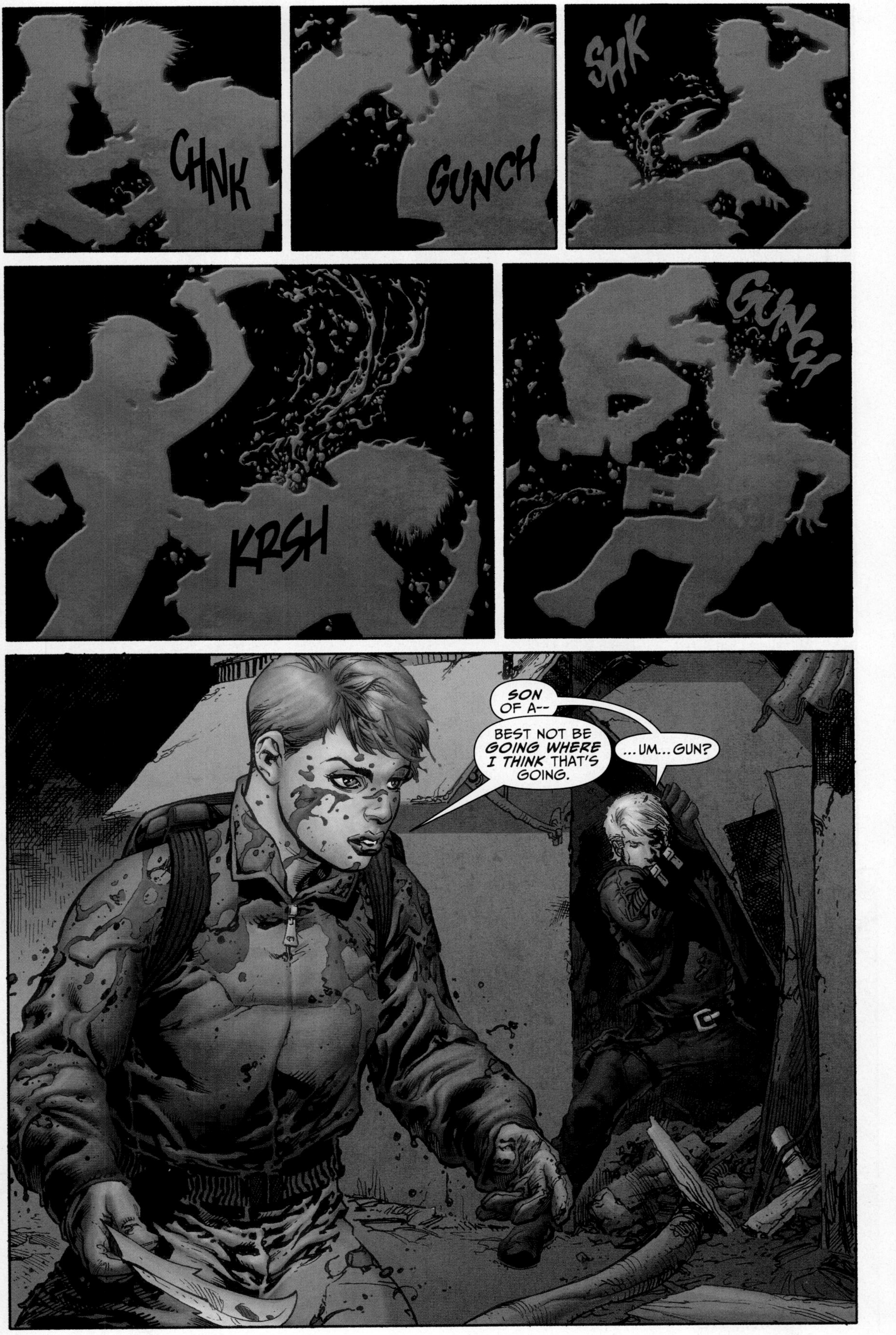
CHNK
GUNCH
SHK
KRSH
GUNCH
SON OF A--
BEST NOT BE GOING WHERE I THINK THAT'S GOING.
...UM...GUN?

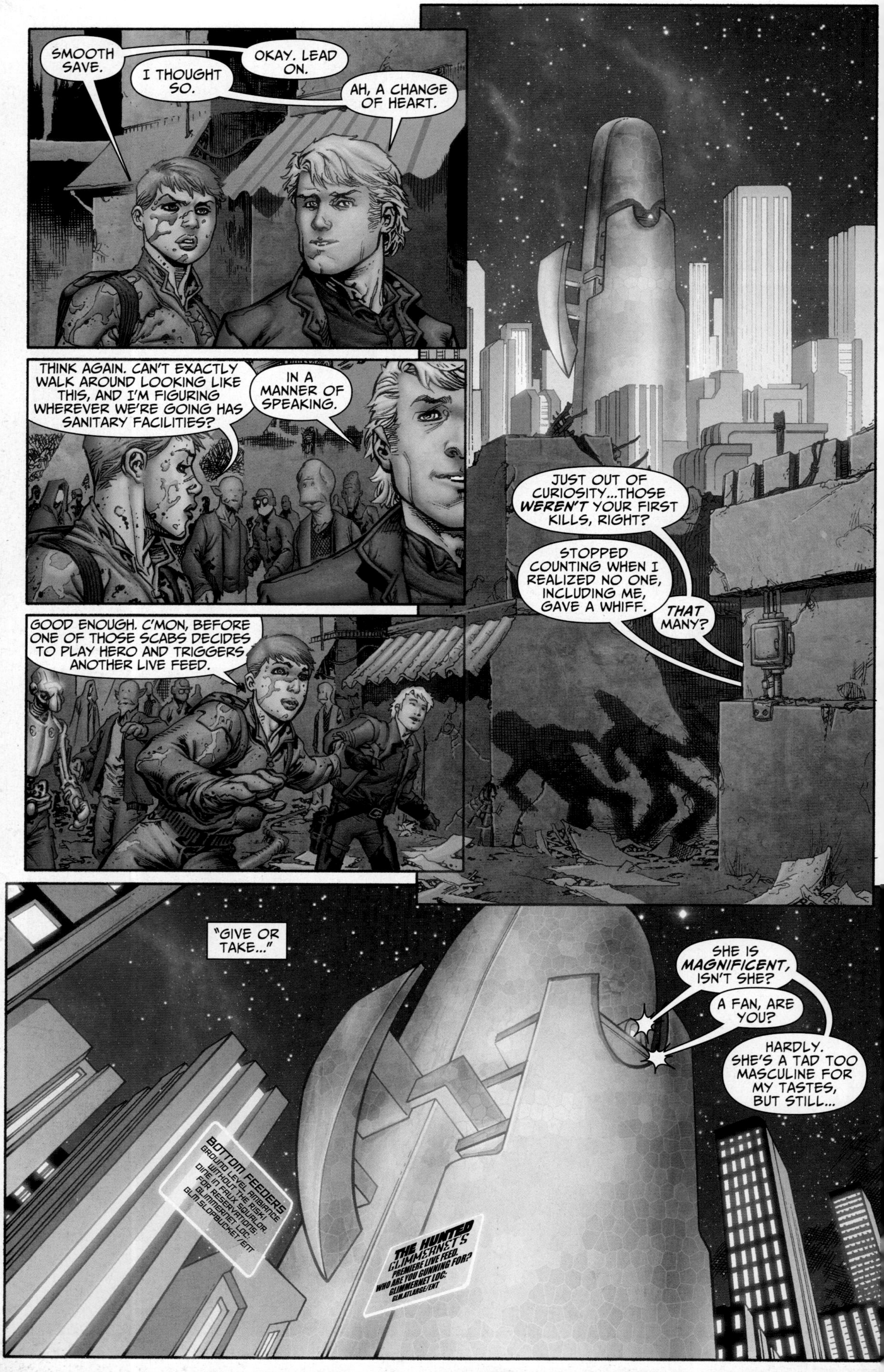
SMOOTH SAVE.
OKAY. LEAD ON.
I THOUGHT SO.
AH, A CHANGE OF HEART.
THINK AGAIN. CAN'T EXACTLY WALK AROUND LOOKING LIKE THIS, AND I'M FIGURING WHEREVER WE'RE GOING HAS SANITARY FACILITIES?
IN A MANNER OF SPEAKING.
GOOD ENOUGH. C'MON, BEFORE ONE OF THOSE SCABS DECIDES TO PLAY HERO AND TRIGGERS ANOTHER LIVE FEED.
JUST OUT OF CURIOSITY...THOSE *WEREN'T* YOUR FIRST KILLS, RIGHT?
STOPPED COUNTING WHEN I REALIZED NO ONE, INCLUDING ME, GAVE A WHIFF.
THAT MANY?
"GIVE OR TAKE..."
SHE IS *MAGNIFICENT*, ISN'T SHE?
A FAN, ARE YOU?
HARDLY. SHE'S A TAD TOO MASCULINE FOR MY TASTES, BUT STILL...
BOTTOM FEEDERS
GROUND LEVEL AMBIANCE WITHOUT THE RISK!
DINE IN FAUX SQUALOR.
FOR RESERVATIONS:
GLIMMERNET LOC:
GLM.SLOPBUCKET/ENT
THE HUNTED
GLIMMERNET'S PREMIERE LIVE FEED.
WHO ARE YOU GUNNING FOR?
GLIMMERNET LOC:
GLM.ATLARGE/ENT

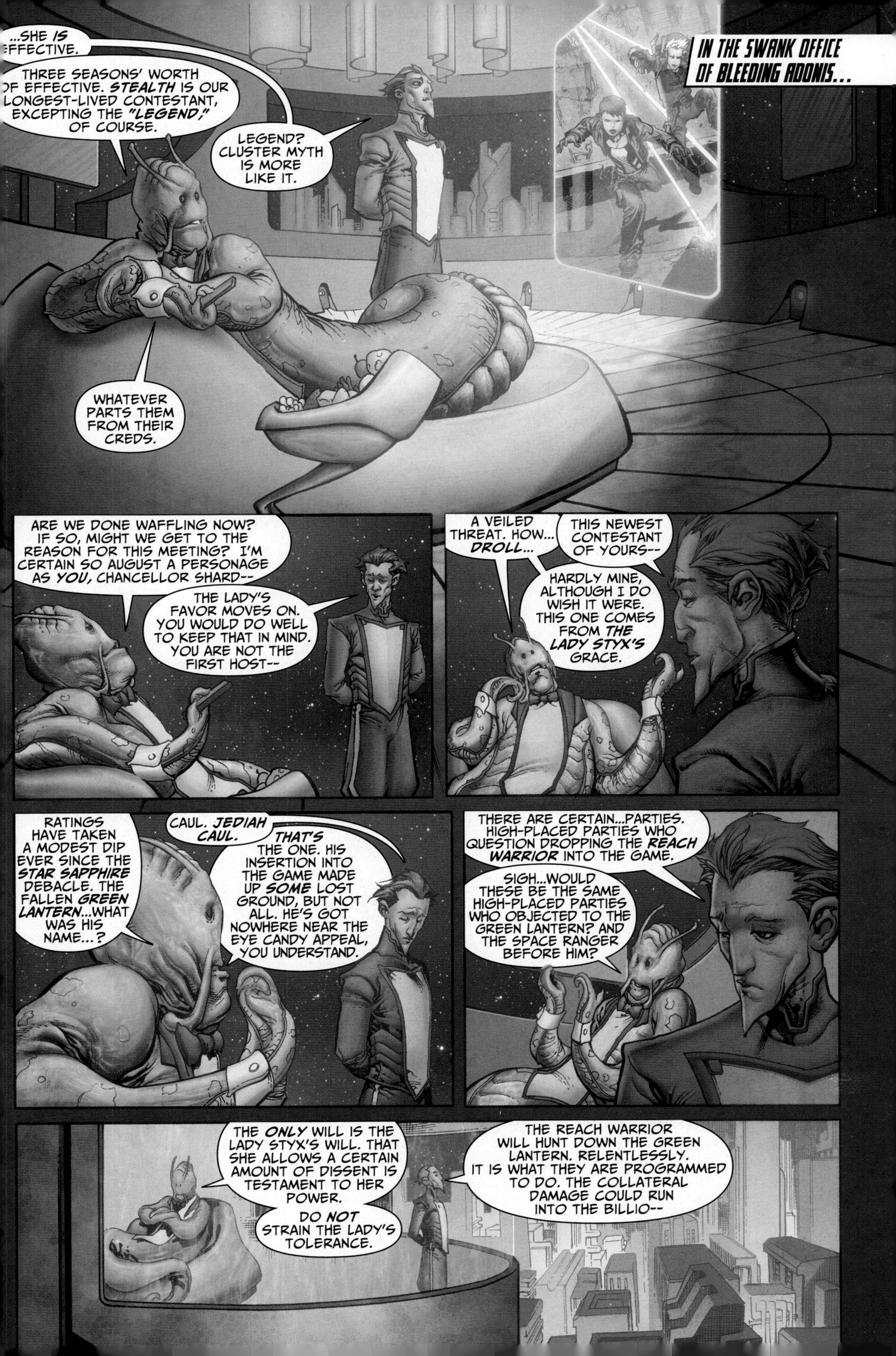
IN THE SWANK OFFICE OF BLEEDING ADONIS...
...SHE IS EFFECTIVE.
THREE SEASONS' WORTH OF EFFECTIVE. STEALTH IS OUR LONGEST-LIVED CONTESTANT, EXCEPTING THE "LEGEND," OF COURSE.
LEGEND? CLUSTER MYTH IS MORE LIKE IT.
WHATEVER PARTS THEM FROM THEIR CREDS.
ARE WE DONE WAFFLING NOW? IF SO, MIGHT WE GET TO THE REASON FOR THIS MEETING? I'M CERTAIN SO AUGUST A PERSONAGE AS YOU, CHANCELLOR SHARD--
THE LADY'S FAVOR MOVES ON. YOU WOULD DO WELL TO KEEP THAT IN MIND. YOU ARE NOT THE FIRST HOST--
A VEILED THREAT. HOW... DROLL...
THIS NEWEST CONTESTANT OF YOURS--
HARDLY MINE, ALTHOUGH I DO WISH IT WERE. THIS ONE COMES FROM THE LADY STYX'S GRACE.
RATINGS HAVE TAKEN A MODEST DIP EVER SINCE THE STAR SAPPHIRE DEBACLE. THE FALLEN GREEN LANTERN...WHAT WAS HIS NAME...?
CAUL. JEDIAH CAUL.
THAT'S THE ONE. HIS INSERTION INTO THE GAME MADE UP SOME LOST GROUND, BUT NOT ALL. HE'S GOT NOWHERE NEAR THE EYE CANDY APPEAL, YOU UNDERSTAND.
THERE ARE CERTAIN...PARTIES. HIGH-PLACED PARTIES WHO QUESTION DROPPING THE REACH WARRIOR INTO THE GAME.
SIGH...WOULD THESE BE THE SAME HIGH-PLACED PARTIES WHO OBJECTED TO THE GREEN LANTERN? AND THE SPACE RANGER BEFORE HIM?
THE REACH WARRIOR WILL HUNT DOWN THE GREEN LANTERN. RELENTLESSLY. IT IS WHAT THEY ARE PROGRAMMED TO DO. THE COLLATERAL DAMAGE COULD RUN INTO THE BILLIO--
THE ONLY WILL IS THE LADY STYX'S WILL. THAT SHE ALLOWS A CERTAIN AMOUNT OF DISSENT IS TESTAMENT TO HER POWER.
DO NOT STRAIN THE LADY'S TOLERANCE.

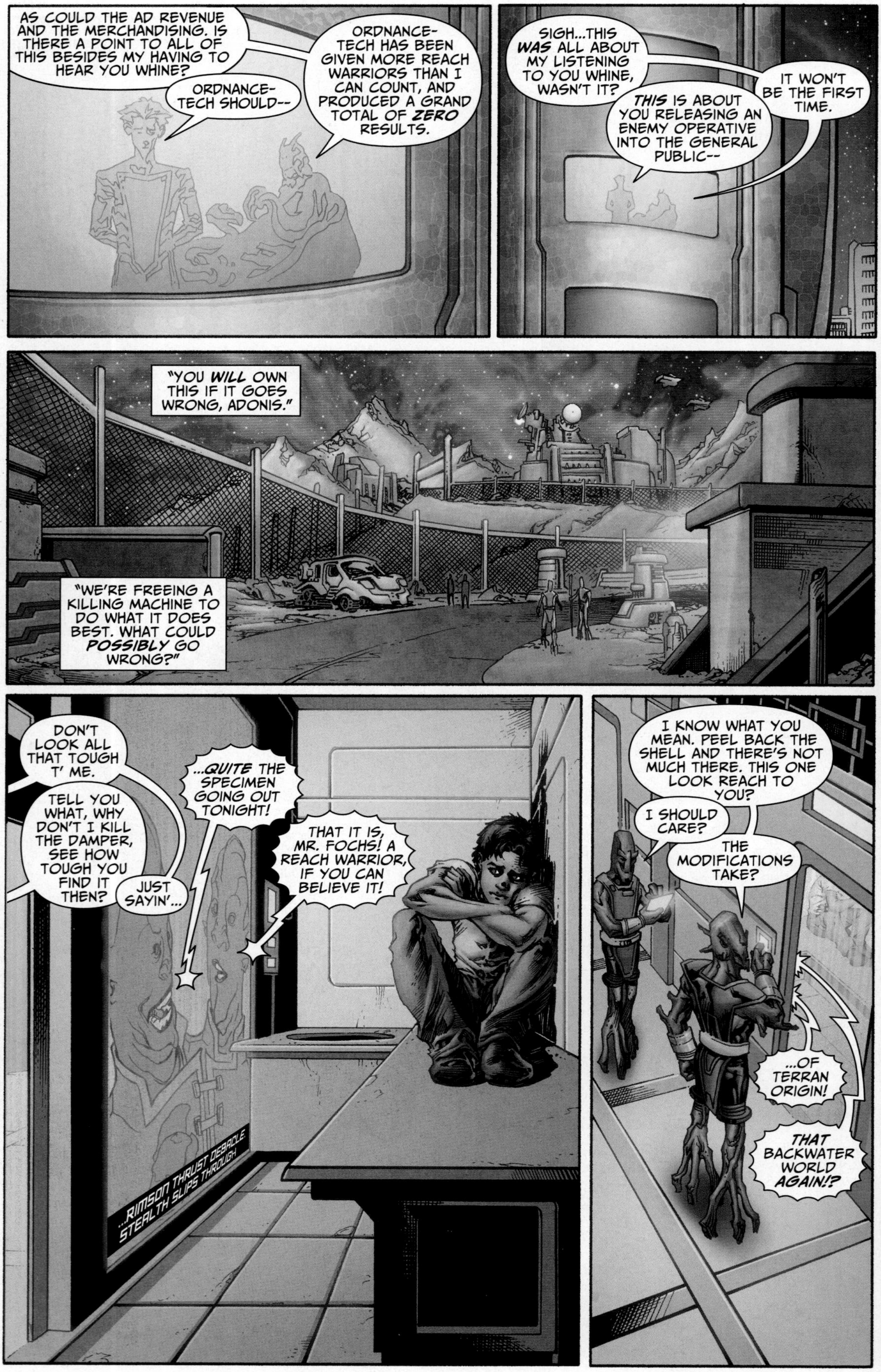

AS COULD THE AD REVENUE AND THE MERCHANDISING. IS THERE A POINT TO ALL OF THIS BESIDES MY HAVING TO HEAR YOU WHINE?
ORDNANCE-TECH SHOULD--
ORDNANCE-TECH HAS BEEN GIVEN MORE REACH WARRIORS THAN I CAN COUNT, AND PRODUCED A GRAND TOTAL OF ZERO RESULTS.
SIGH...THIS WAS ALL ABOUT MY LISTENING TO YOU WHINE, WASN'T IT?
IT WON'T BE THE FIRST TIME.
THIS IS ABOUT YOU RELEASING AN ENEMY OPERATIVE INTO THE GENERAL PUBLIC--
"YOU WILL OWN THIS IF IT GOES WRONG, ADONIS."
"WE'RE FREEING A KILLING MACHINE TO DO WHAT IT DOES BEST. WHAT COULD POSSIBLY GO WRONG?"
DON'T LOOK ALL THAT TOUGH T' ME.
TELL YOU WHAT, WHY DON'T I KILL THE DAMPER, SEE HOW TOUGH YOU FIND IT THEN?
JUST SAYIN'...
...QUITE THE SPECIMEN GOING OUT TONIGHT!
THAT IT IS, MR. FOCHS! A REACH WARRIOR, IF YOU CAN BELIEVE IT!
...RIMSON THRUST DEBACLE. STEALTH SLIPS THROUGH
I KNOW WHAT YOU MEAN. PEEL BACK THE SHELL AND THERE'S NOT MUCH THERE. THIS ONE LOOK REACH TO YOU?
I SHOULD CARE?
THE MODIFICATIONS TAKE?
...OF TERRAN ORIGIN!
THAT BACKWATER WORLD AGAIN!?

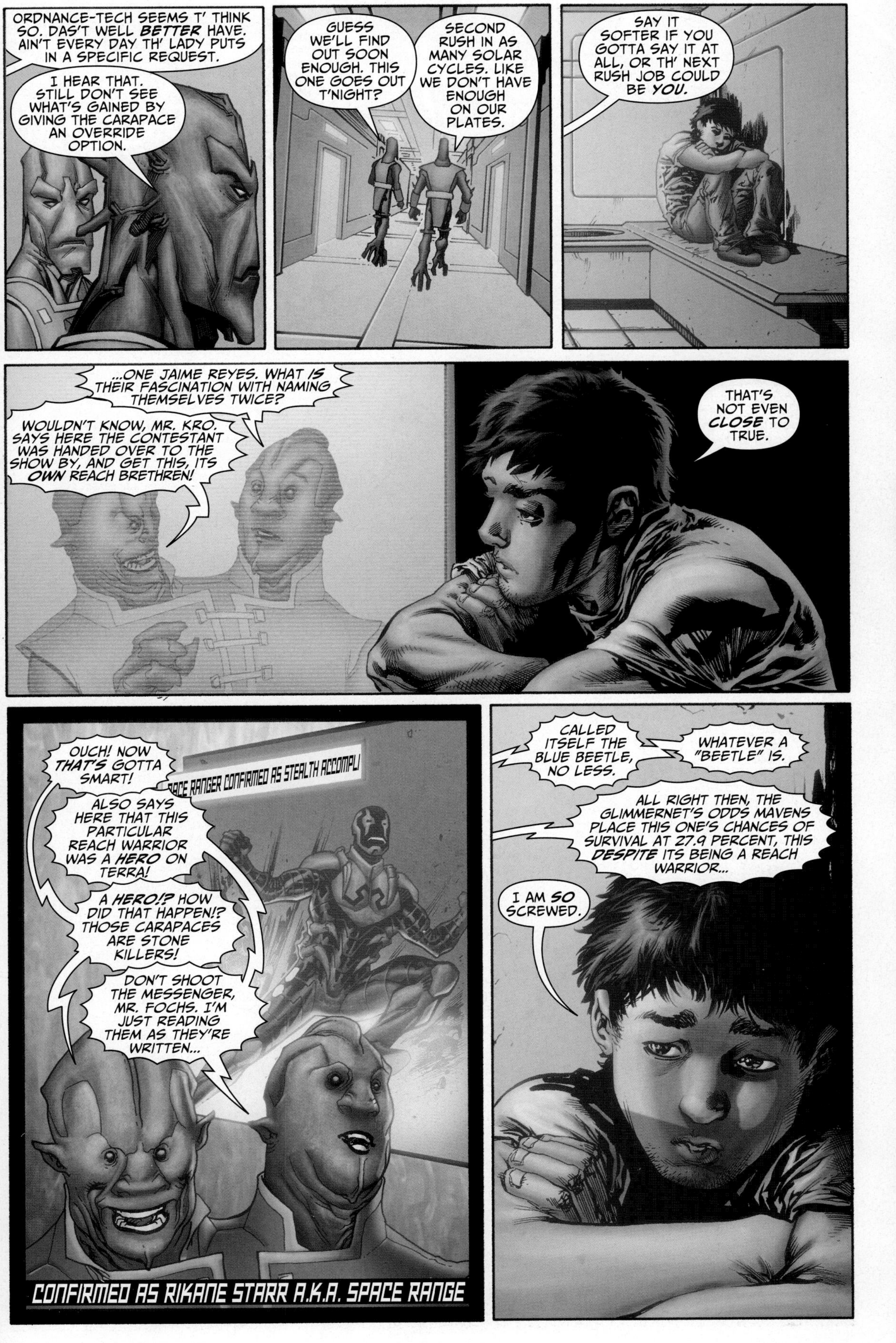
ORDNANCE-TECH SEEMS T' THINK SO. DAS'T WELL BETTER HAVE. AIN'T EVERY DAY TH' LADY PUTS IN A SPECIFIC REQUEST.
I HEAR THAT. STILL DON'T SEE WHAT'S GAINED BY GIVING THE CARAPACE AN OVERRIDE OPTION.
GUESS WE'LL FIND OUT SOON ENOUGH. THIS ONE GOES OUT T'NIGHT?
SECOND RUSH IN AS MANY SOLAR CYCLES. LIKE WE DON'T HAVE ENOUGH ON OUR PLATES.
SAY IT SOFTER IF YOU GOTTA SAY IT AT ALL, OR TH' NEXT RUSH JOB COULD BE YOU.
...ONE JAIME REYES. WHAT IS THEIR FASCINATION WITH NAMING THEMSELVES TWICE?
WOULDN'T KNOW, MR. KRO. SAYS HERE THE CONTESTANT WAS HANDED OVER TO THE SHOW BY, AND GET THIS, ITS OWN REACH BRETHREN!
THAT'S NOT EVEN CLOSE TO TRUE.
OUCH! NOW THAT'S GOTTA SMART!
PACE RANGER CONFIRMED AS STEALTH ACCOMPLI
ALSO SAYS HERE THAT THIS PARTICULAR REACH WARRIOR WAS A HERO ON TERRA!
A HERO!? HOW DID THAT HAPPEN!? THOSE CARAPACES ARE STONE KILLERS!
DON'T SHOOT THE MESSENGER, MR. FOCHS. I'M JUST READING THEM AS THEY'RE WRITTEN...
CONFIRMED AS RIKANE STARR A.K.A. SPACE RANGE
CALLED ITSELF THE BLUE BEETLE, NO LESS.
WHATEVER A "BEETLE" IS.
ALL RIGHT THEN, THE GLIMMERNET'S ODDS MAVENS PLACE THIS ONE'S CHANCES OF SURVIVAL AT 27.9 PERCENT, THIS DESPITE ITS BEING A REACH WARRIOR...
I AM SO SCREWED.

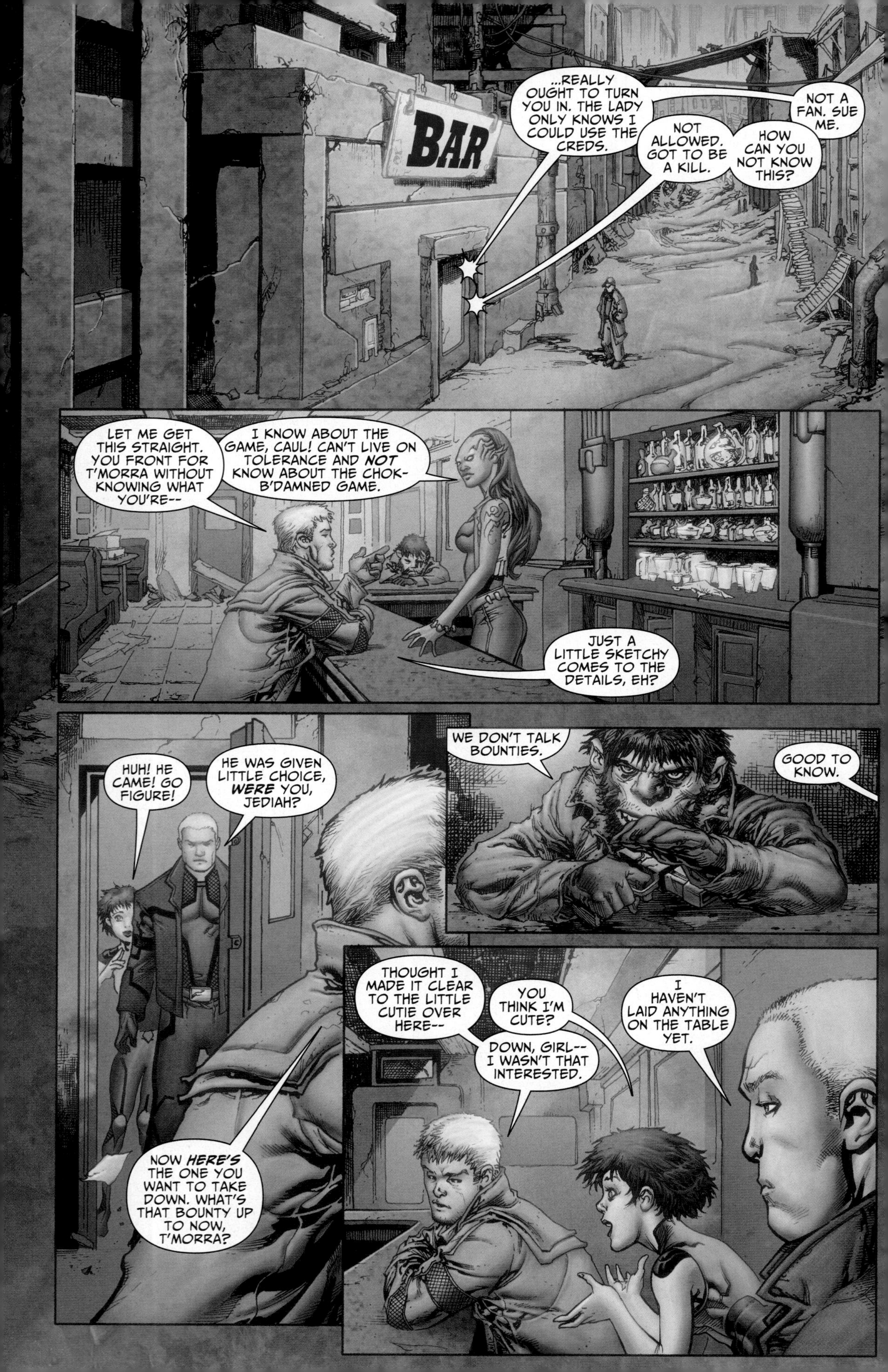
BAR
...REALLY OUGHT TO TURN YOU IN. THE LADY ONLY KNOWS I COULD USE THE CREDS.
NOT A FAN. SUE ME.
NOT ALLOWED. GOT TO BE A KILL.
HOW CAN YOU NOT KNOW THIS?
LET ME GET THIS STRAIGHT. YOU FRONT FOR T'MORRA WITHOUT KNOWING WHAT YOU'RE--
I KNOW ABOUT THE GAME, CAUL! CAN'T LIVE ON TOLERANCE AND ***NOT*** KNOW ABOUT THE CHOK-B'DAMNED GAME.
JUST A LITTLE SKETCHY COMES TO THE DETAILS, EH?
WE DON'T TALK BOUNTIES.
GOOD TO KNOW.
HUH! HE CAME! GO FIGURE!
HE WAS GIVEN LITTLE CHOICE, ***WERE*** YOU, JEDIAH?
NOW ***HERE'S*** THE ONE YOU WANT TO TAKE DOWN. WHAT'S THAT BOUNTY UP TO NOW, T'MORRA?
THOUGHT I MADE IT CLEAR TO THE LITTLE CUTIE OVER HERE--
YOU THINK I'M CUTE?
DOWN, GIRL-- I WASN'T THAT INTERESTED.
I HAVEN'T LAID ANYTHING ON THE TABLE YET.

DON'T MATTER. NOT INTERESTED.

YOU WERE RIGHT. HE *IS* A DINK.

SH! HE THINKS I'M CUTE.

THAT DESPERATE?

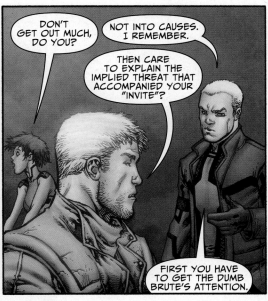

DON'T GET OUT MUCH, DO YOU?

NOT INTO CAUSES. I REMEMBER.

THEN CARE TO EXPLAIN THE IMPLIED THREAT THAT ACCOMPANIED YOUR "INVITE"?

FIRST YOU HAVE TO GET THE DUMB BRUTE'S ATTENTION.

THAT'S IT! I'M GONE!

A REACH WARRIOR WILL BE DROPPED INTO THE GAME TONIGHT.

YES, I'M SURE. NO, YOU MAY NOT KNOW HOW I CAME BY THIS INFORMATION.

YOU'RE WELCOME.

THE RING'S NOT CHARGED.

RESIDUAL ENERGY. YOU'RE LOUSY WITH IT. *ALL* OF YOU SPECTRUM WARRIORS ARE.

YOU *ARE* AWARE OF THE REACTION THE CARAPACE WILL HAVE ONCE IT--

IT'LL HUNT ME DOWN LIKE A SCENT-HOUND.

WOW. SUCKS TO BE YOU.

WHATEVER HAPPENED TO "HE THINKS I'M CUTE"?

I GOT A GOOD LOOK AT HIM.

EASY...IT'S NOT NICE TO SPEAK ILL OF THE DEAD.

I'M RIGHT HERE.

WE KNOW.

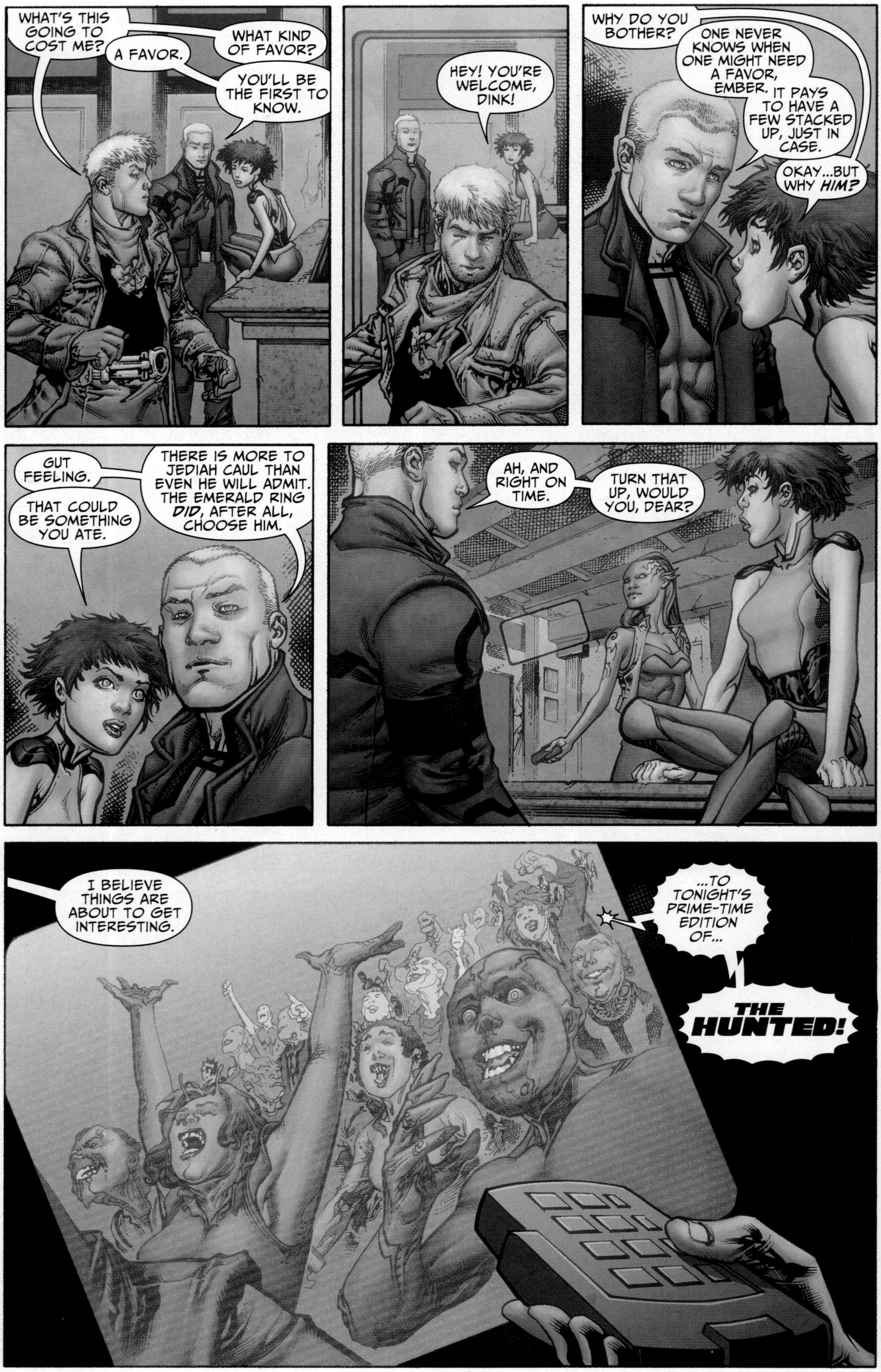
WHAT'S THIS GOING TO COST ME?
A FAVOR.
WHAT KIND OF FAVOR?
YOU'LL BE THE FIRST TO KNOW.
HEY! YOU'RE WELCOME, DINK!
WHY DO YOU BOTHER?
ONE NEVER KNOWS WHEN ONE MIGHT NEED A FAVOR, EMBER.
IT PAYS TO HAVE A FEW STACKED UP, JUST IN CASE.
OKAY...BUT WHY HIM?
GUT FEELING.
THAT COULD BE SOMETHING YOU ATE.
THERE IS MORE TO JEDIAH CAUL THAN EVEN HE WILL ADMIT. THE EMERALD RING DID, AFTER ALL, CHOOSE HIM.
AH, AND RIGHT ON TIME.
TURN THAT UP, WOULD YOU, DEAR?
I BELIEVE THINGS ARE ABOUT TO GET INTERESTING.
...TO TONIGHT'S PRIME-TIME EDITION OF...
THE HUNTED!

RECORD-BREAKING INITIAL BOUNTY APPLIED TO HUNTED CONTESTANTS

LET'S GET RIGHT DOWN TO IT, SHALL WE? ALL DAY LONG WE'VE BEEN TEASING YOU ABOUT TONIGHT'S CONTESTANT AND, I'VE GOT TO TELL YOU, THE SPECULATION HAS BEEN RUNNING *RAMPANT!*

SO, WITHOUT FURTHER ADO, LET ME PRESENT TO YOU THAT CONTESTANT, A PRIME BOUNTY STARTING OFF AT 30,000 CREDS...

LADY STYX DENIES THIRD ARMY RUMORS AS

...JAIME REYES, OUR VERY OWN *REACH* WARRIOR!

GIVE IT UP, SENTIENTS! GIVE IT UP FOR THE MOST NOTORIOUS CONTESTANT IN THE HUNTED'S HISTORY! LET HIM KNOW HOW MUCH YOU LOOK FORWARD TO HUNTING HIM DOWN!

JAIME REYES, MASCS AND FEMS! GIVE! IT! UP!

ECONOMIC GROWTH INDICATORS SHOW SLUGGISH FOURTH QUARTER

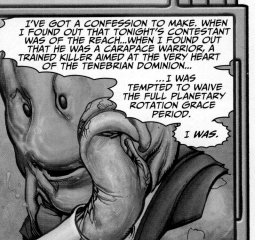

I'VE GOT A CONFESSION TO MAKE. WHEN I FOUND OUT THAT TONIGHT'S CONTESTANT WAS OF THE REACH...WHEN I FOUND OUT THAT HE WAS A CARAPACE WARRIOR, A TRAINED KILLER AIMED AT THE VERY HEART OF THE TENEBRIAN DOMINION...

...I WAS TEMPTED TO WAIVE THE FULL PLANETARY ROTATION GRACE PERIOD.

I *WAS*.

WHEN I THINK OF THE ATROCITIES COMMITTED BY THIS KIND, THE INNOCENTS SLAUGHTERED FOR THE "GLORY" OF *THEIR* CORRUPT EMPIRE...

OH, YES. I *WAS* TEMPTED.

TELL ME, REACH SCUM, WERE OUR POSITIONS REVERSED, WOULD YOU GIVE IN TO TEMPTATION? *WOULD* YOU!?

I-I...

SILENCE IS THE SOUL'S CONFESSION! YOU HEARD! THE BEAST KNOWS NEITHER PITY NOR COMPASSION!

WH-WHAT...?

ONE FULL PLANETARY ROTATION, REACH SCUM! THEN... OH, *THEN* THERE WILL BE A RECKONING!

SENTIENTS, I GIVE YOU JAIME REYES! LET THE REVELS BEGIN!

GOD IN HEAVEN, WHAT HAVE I FALLEN INTO?

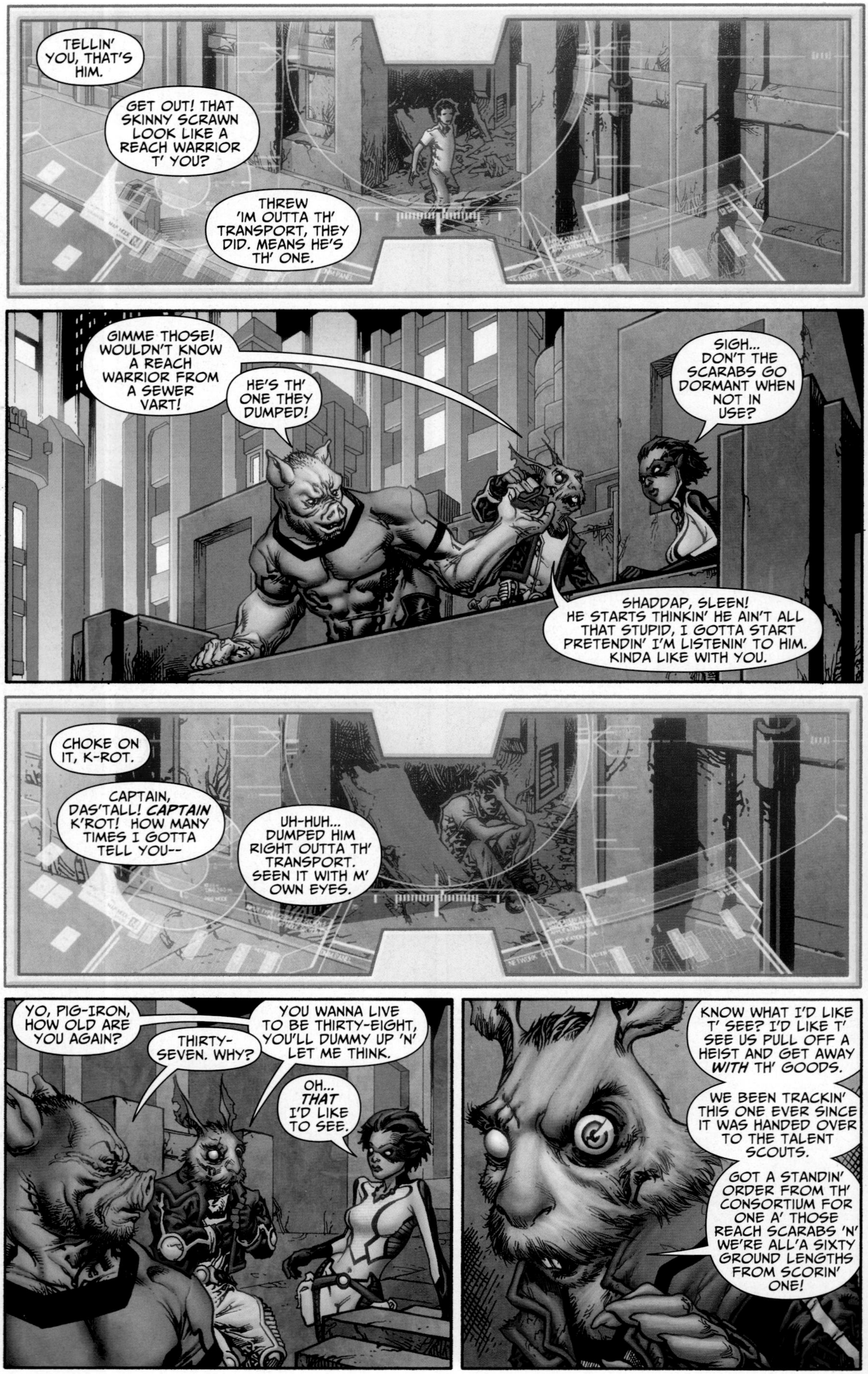
TELLIN' YOU, THAT'S HIM.
GET OUT! THAT SKINNY SCRAWN LOOK LIKE A REACH WARRIOR T' YOU?
THREW 'IM OUTTA TH' TRANSPORT, THEY DID. MEANS HE'S TH' ONE.
GIMME THOSE! WOULDN'T KNOW A REACH WARRIOR FROM A SEWER VART!
HE'S TH' ONE THEY DUMPED!
SIGH... DON'T THE SCARABS GO DORMANT WHEN NOT IN USE?
SHADDAP, SLEEN! HE STARTS THINKIN' HE AIN'T ALL THAT STUPID, I GOTTA START PRETENDIN' I'M LISTENIN' TO HIM. KINDA LIKE WITH YOU.
CHOKE ON IT, K-ROT.
CAPTAIN, DAS'TALL! *CAPTAIN* K'ROT! HOW MANY TIMES I GOTTA TELL YOU--
UH-HUH... DUMPED HIM RIGHT OUTTA TH' TRANSPORT. SEEN IT WITH M' OWN EYES.
YO, PIG-IRON, HOW OLD ARE YOU AGAIN?
THIRTY-SEVEN. WHY?
YOU WANNA LIVE TO BE THIRTY-EIGHT, YOU'LL DUMMY UP 'N' LET ME THINK.
OH... *THAT* I'D LIKE TO SEE.
KNOW WHAT I'D LIKE T' SEE? I'D LIKE T' SEE US PULL OFF A HEIST AND GET AWAY ***WITH*** TH' GOODS.
WE BEEN TRACKIN' THIS ONE EVER SINCE IT WAS HANDED OVER TO THE TALENT SCOUTS.
GOT A STANDIN' ORDER FROM TH' CONSORTIUM FOR ONE A' THOSE REACH SCARABS 'N' WE'RE ALL'A SIXTY GROUND LENGTHS FROM SCORIN' ONE!

"NOW DUMMY TH' CHOK UP 'N' LEMME *THINK!*"

OKAY...OKAY. ONE STEP AT A TIME. I'M JAIME REYES. I LIVE IN EL PASO WITH MY PARENTS AND LITTLE SISTER. I'M ALSO THE BLUE BEETLE, A KINDA, SORTA SUPERHERO, THANKS TO THE SCARAB IMBEDDED IN MY SPINE.

RIGHT. SO FAR SO GOOD.

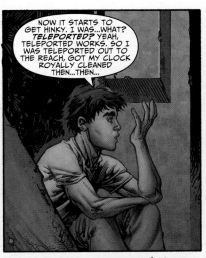

NOW IT STARTS TO GET HINKY. I WAS...WHAT? *TELEPORTED?* YEAH, TELEPORTED WORKS. SO I WAS TELEPORTED OUT TO THE REACH, GOT MY CLOCK ROYALLY CLEANED THEN...THEN...

THEN I WIND UP HERE...WHEREVER HERE IS. ON A SHOW OF SOME KIND THAT SEEMS TO REVOLVE AROUND PEOPLE WINNING A PRIZE FOR KILLING ME.

WELL, SURE... *THAT* MAKES SENSE...

CLOK

HA! HO! TAKE THAT! AND THAT!

THUK WHUK

THOK THOK

K'RO... SORRY. *CAPTAIN* K'ROT, OH GREAT AND BENEVOLENT LEADER? I THINK HE'S UNCONSCIOUS.

OH. RIGHT. YEAH. UNCONSCIOUS. SO... WHERE'S TH' CHOK-BUKKIN' SCARAB?

THEY USUALLY BURROW INTO THE HOST FORM'S BODY.

GONNA HAVE TO DIG IT OUT, EH? WORKS FOR...

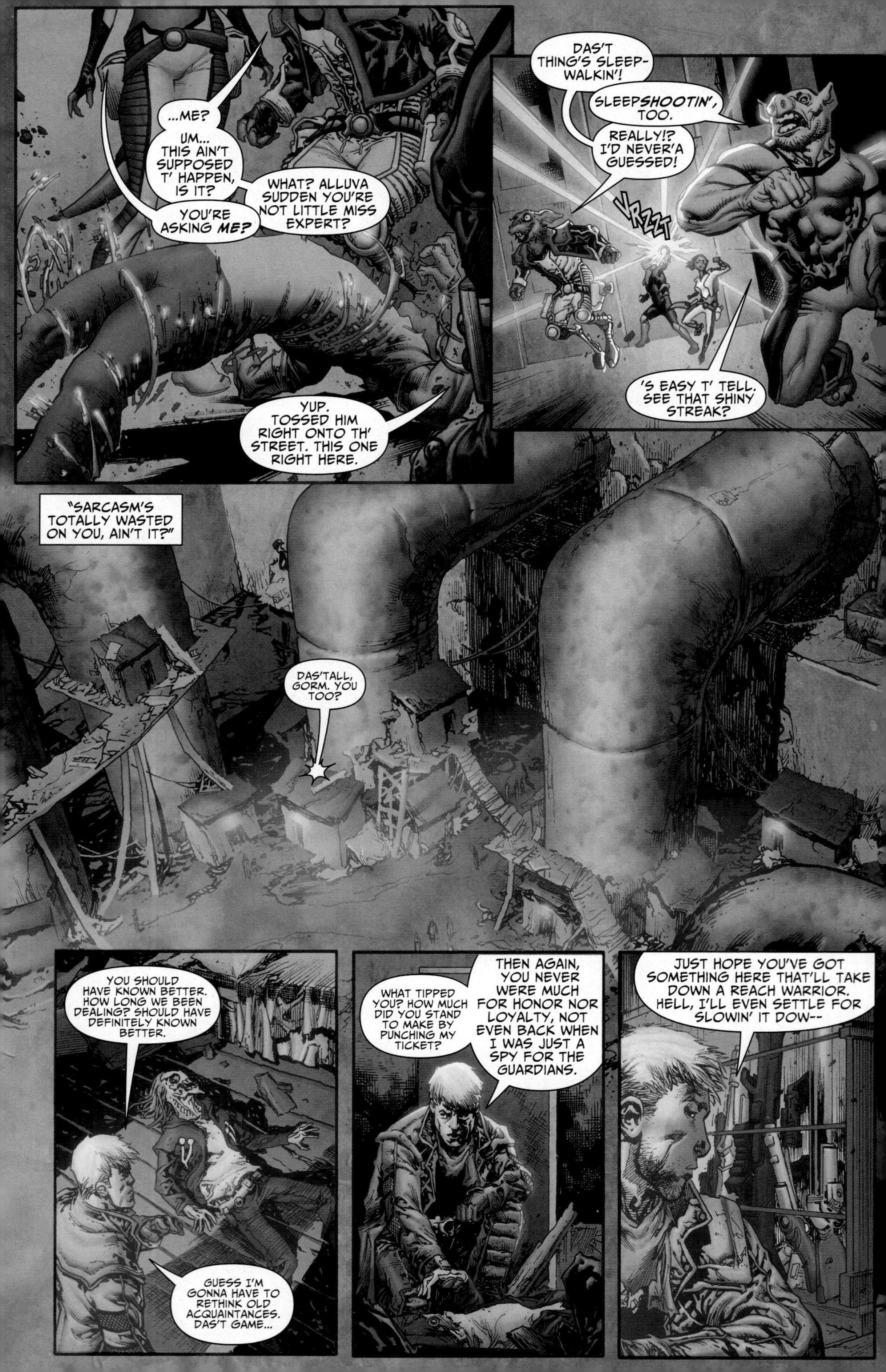
...ME?
UM... THIS AIN'T SUPPOSED T' HAPPEN, IS IT?
YOU'RE ASKING ME?
WHAT? ALLUVA SUDDEN YOU'RE NOT LITTLE MISS EXPERT?
YUP. TOSSED HIM RIGHT ONTO TH' STREET. THIS ONE RIGHT HERE.
DAS'T THING'S SLEEP-WALKIN'!
SLEEPSHOOTIN', TOO.
REALLY!? I'D NEVER'A GUESSED!
VRZZT
'S EASY T' TELL. SEE THAT SHINY STREAK?
"SARCASM'S TOTALLY WASTED ON YOU, AIN'T IT?"
DAS'TALL, GORM. YOU TOO?
YOU SHOULD HAVE KNOWN BETTER. HOW LONG WE BEEN DEALING? SHOULD HAVE DEFINITELY KNOWN BETTER.
GUESS I'M GONNA HAVE TO RETHINK OLD ACQUAINTANCES. DAS'T GAME...
WHAT TIPPED YOU? HOW MUCH DID YOU STAND TO MAKE BY PUNCHING MY TICKET?
THEN AGAIN, YOU NEVER WERE MUCH FOR HONOR NOR LOYALTY, NOT EVEN BACK WHEN I WAS JUST A SPY FOR THE GUARDIANS.
JUST HOPE YOU'VE GOT SOMETHING HERE THAT'LL TAKE DOWN A REACH WARRIOR. HELL, I'LL EVEN SETTLE FOR SLOWIN' IT DOW--

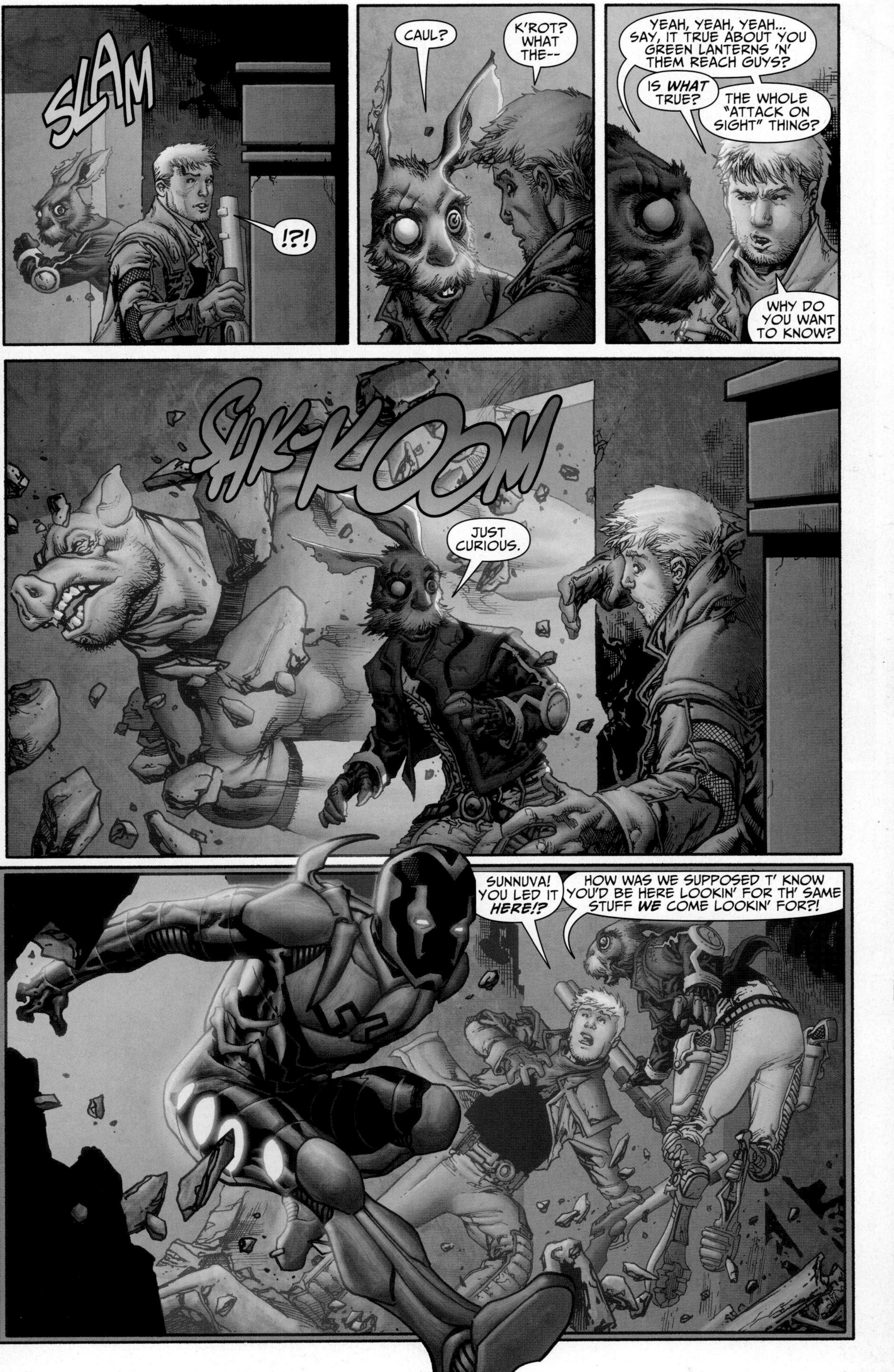
SLAM
!?!
CAUL?
K'ROT? WHAT THE--
YEAH, YEAH, YEAH... SAY, IT TRUE ABOUT YOU GREEN LANTERNS 'N' THEM REACH GUYS?
IS *WHAT* TRUE?
THE WHOLE "ATTACK ON SIGHT" THING?
WHY DO YOU WANT TO KNOW?
SHK-KOOM
JUST CURIOUS.
SUNNUVA! YOU LED IT *HERE!?*
HOW WAS WE SUPPOSED T' KNOW YOU'D BE HERE LOOKIN' FOR TH' SAME STUFF *WE* COME LOOKIN' FOR?!

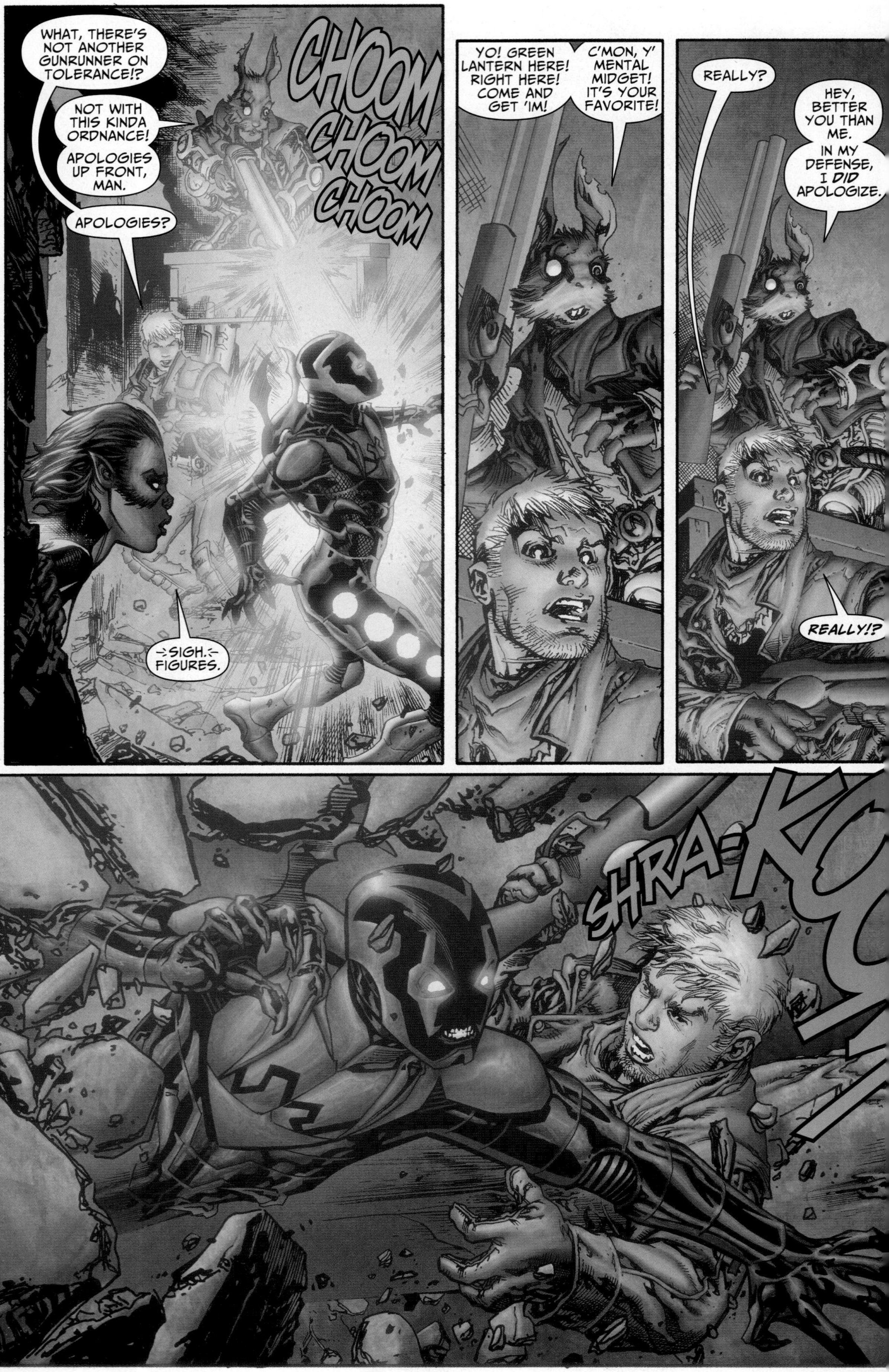

WHAT, THERE'S NOT ANOTHER GUNRUNNER ON TOLERANCE!?
NOT WITH THIS KINDA ORDNANCE!
APOLOGIES UP FRONT, MAN.
APOLOGIES?
CHOOM CHOOM CHOOM
-SIGH.- FIGURES.
YO! GREEN LANTERN HERE! RIGHT HERE! COME AND GET 'IM!
C'MON, Y' MENTAL MIDGET! IT'S YOUR FAVORITE!
REALLY?
HEY, BETTER YOU THAN ME.
IN MY DEFENSE, I *DID* APOLOGIZE.
REALLY!?
SHRA-KO

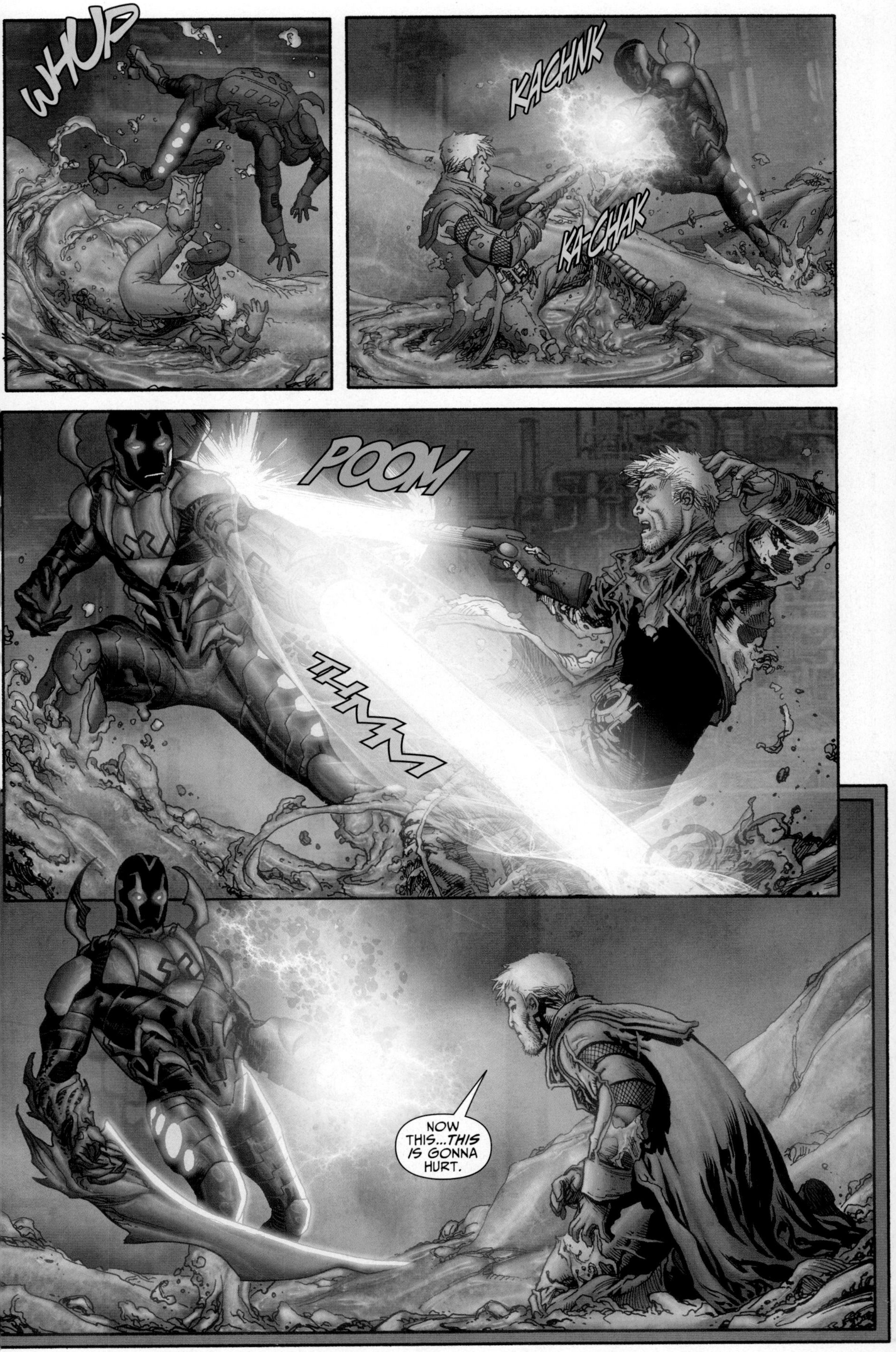
WHUP
KACHNK
KA-CHAK
POOM
THMMM
NOW THIS...THIS IS GONNA HURT.

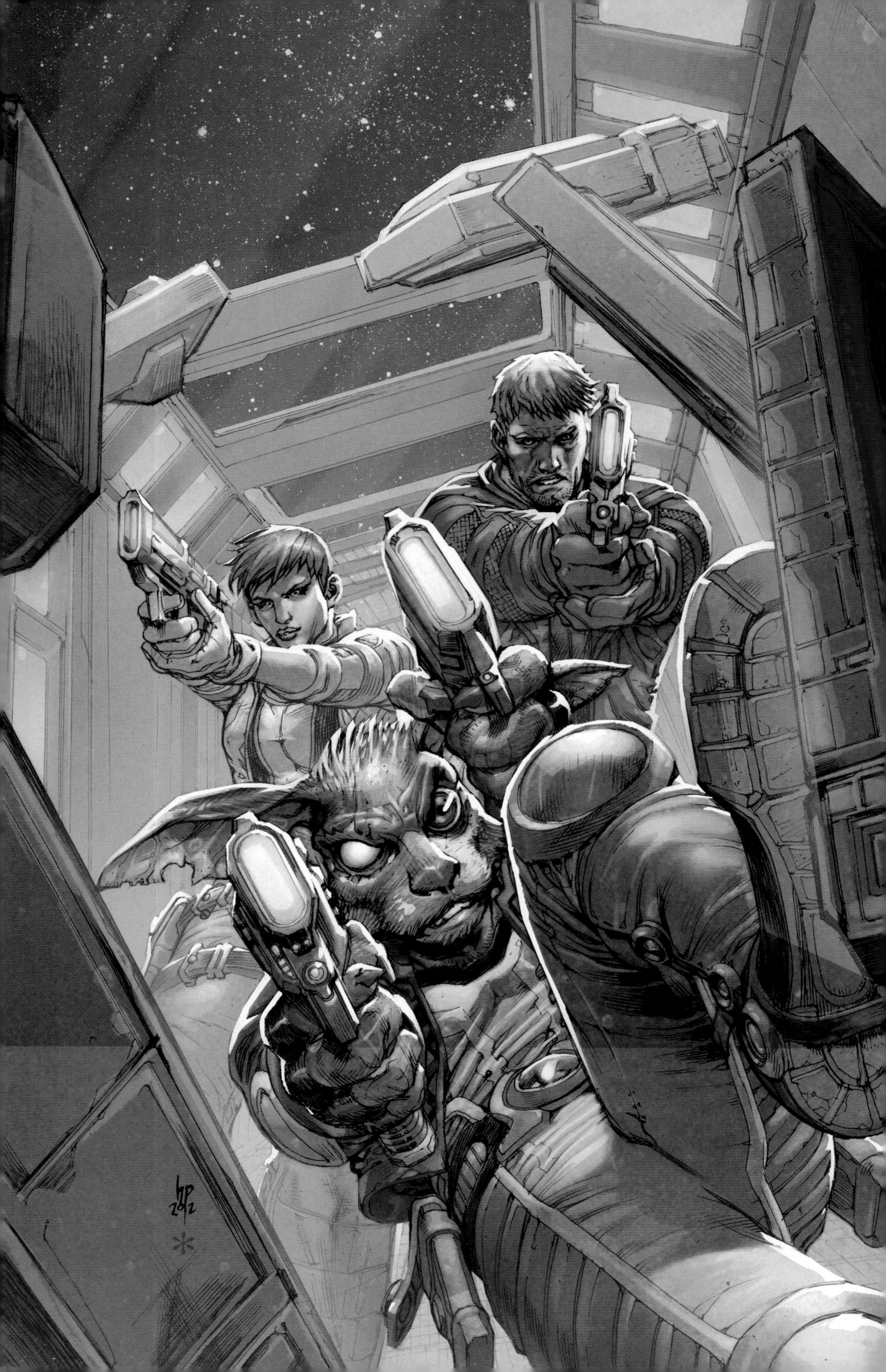

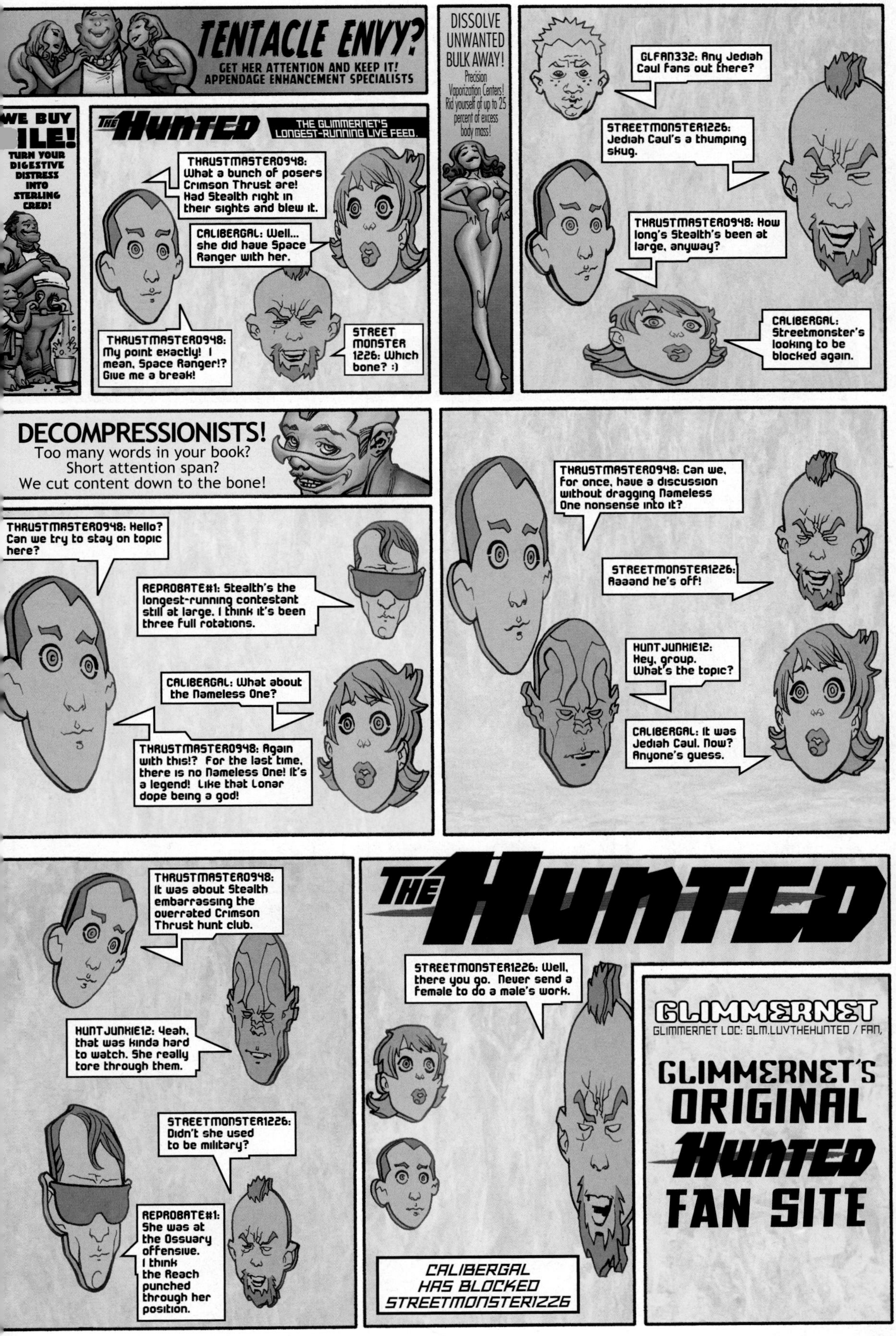
TENTACLE ENVY?
GET HER ATTENTION AND KEEP IT! APPENDAGE ENHANCEMENT SPECIALISTS
DISSOLVE UNWANTED BULK AWAY!
Precision Vaporization Centers! Rid yourself of up to 25 percent of excess body mass!
GLFAN332: Any Jediah Caul fans out there?
STREETMONSTER1226: Jediah Caul's a thumping skug.
THRUSTMASTER0948: How long's Stealth's been at large, anyway?
CALIBERGAL: Streetmonster's looking to be blocked again.
WE BUY ...ILE! TURN YOUR DIGESTIVE DISTRESS INTO STERLING CRED!
THE HUNTED
THE GLIMMERNET'S LONGEST-RUNNING LIVE FEED.
THRUSTMASTER0948: What a bunch of posers Crimson Thrust are! Had Stealth right in their sights and blew it.
CALIBERGAL: Well... she did have Space Ranger with her.
THRUSTMASTER0948: My point exactly! I mean, Space Ranger!? Give me a break!
STREET MONSTER 1226: Which bone? :)
DECOMPRESSIONISTS!
Too many words in your book? Short attention span? We cut content down to the bone!
THRUSTMASTER0948: Hello? Can we try to stay on topic here?
REPROBATE#1: Stealth's the longest-running contestant still at large. I think it's been three full rotations.
CALIBERGAL: What about the Nameless One?
THRUSTMASTER0948: Again with this!? For the last time, there is no Nameless One! It's a legend! Like that Lonar dope being a god!
THRUSTMASTER0948: Can we, for once, have a discussion without dragging Nameless One nonsense into it?
STREETMONSTER1226: Aaaand he's off!
HUNTJUNKIE12: Hey, group. What's the topic?
CALIBERGAL: It was Jediah Caul. Now? Anyone's guess.
THRUSTMASTER0948: It was about Stealth embarrassing the overrated Crimson Thrust hunt club.
HUNTJUNKIE12: Yeah, that was kinda hard to watch. She really tore through them.
STREETMONSTER1226: Didn't she used to be military?
REPROBATE#1: She was at the Ossuary offensive. I think the Reach punched through her position.
THE HUNTED
STREETMONSTER1226: Well, there you go. Never send a female to do a male's work.
CALIBERGAL HAS BLOCKED STREETMONSTER1226
GLIMMERNET
GLIMMERNET LOC: GLM.LUVTHEHUNTED / FAN,
GLIMMERNET'S ORIGINAL Hunted FAN SITE

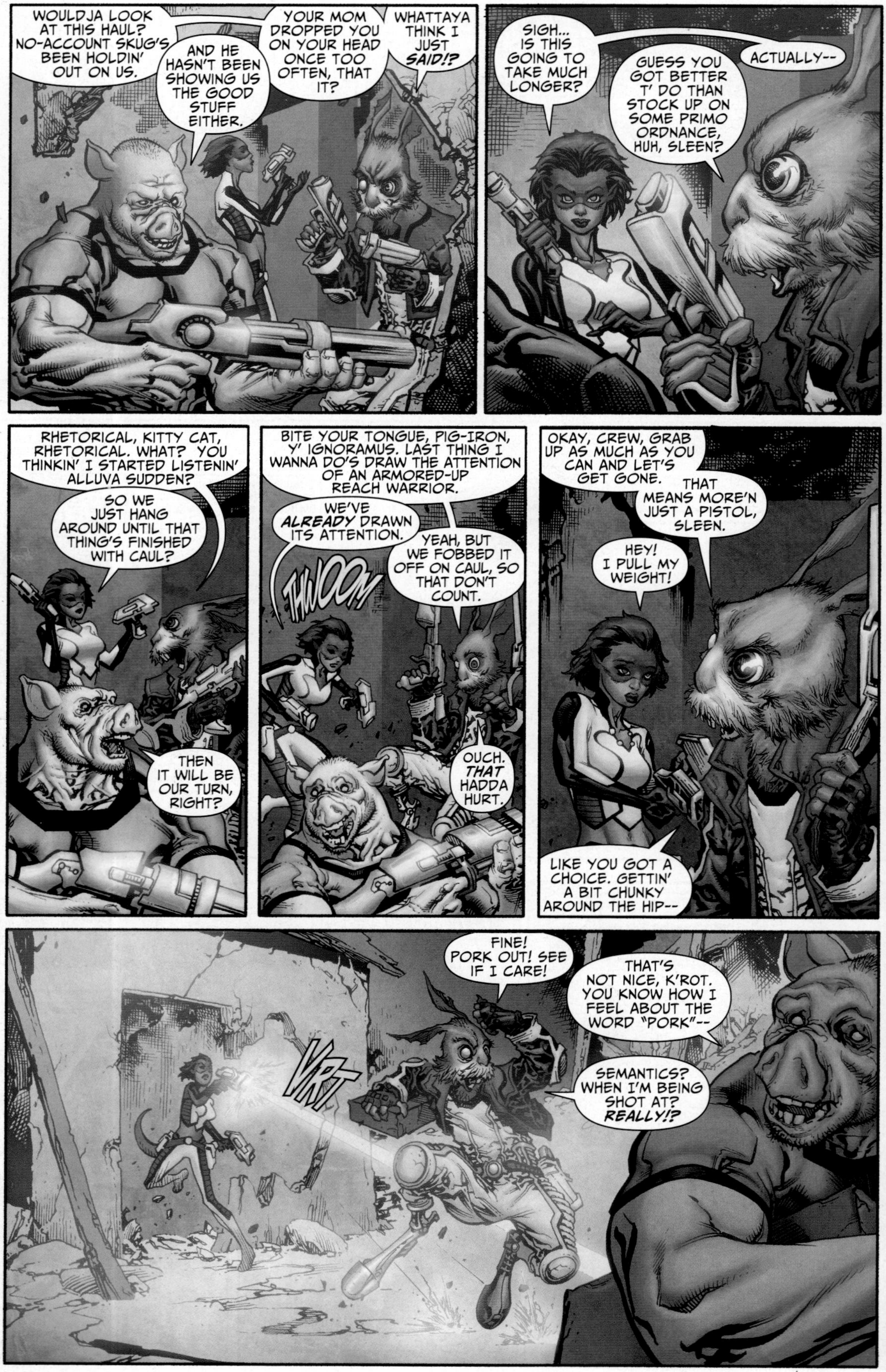

WOULDJA LOOK AT THIS HAUL? NO-ACCOUNT SKUG'S BEEN HOLDIN' OUT ON US.
AND HE HASN'T BEEN SHOWING US THE GOOD STUFF EITHER.
YOUR MOM DROPPED YOU ON YOUR HEAD ONCE TOO OFTEN, THAT IT?
WHATTAYA THINK I JUST SAID!?
SIGH... IS THIS GOING TO TAKE MUCH LONGER?
ACTUALLY--
GUESS YOU GOT BETTER T' DO THAN STOCK UP ON SOME PRIMO ORDNANCE, HUH, SLEEN?
RHETORICAL, KITTY CAT, RHETORICAL. WHAT? YOU THINKIN' I STARTED LISTENIN' ALLUVA SUDDEN?
SO WE JUST HANG AROUND UNTIL THAT THING'S FINISHED WITH CAUL?
THEN IT WILL BE OUR TURN, RIGHT?
BITE YOUR TONGUE, PIG-IRON, Y' IGNORAMUS. LAST THING I WANNA DO'S DRAW THE ATTENTION OF AN ARMORED-UP REACH WARRIOR.
WE'VE ALREADY DRAWN ITS ATTENTION.
YEAH, BUT WE FOBBED IT OFF ON CAUL, SO THAT DON'T COUNT.
THWOOM
OUCH. THAT HADDA HURT.
OKAY, CREW, GRAB UP AS MUCH AS YOU CAN AND LET'S GET GONE.
THAT MEANS MORE'N JUST A PISTOL, SLEEN.
HEY! I PULL MY WEIGHT!
LIKE YOU GOT A CHOICE. GETTIN' A BIT CHUNKY AROUND THE HIP--
FINE! PORK OUT! SEE IF I CARE!
THAT'S NOT NICE, K'ROT. YOU KNOW HOW I FEEL ABOUT THE WORD "PORK"--
VRT
SEMANTICS? WHEN I'M BEING SHOT AT? REALLY!?

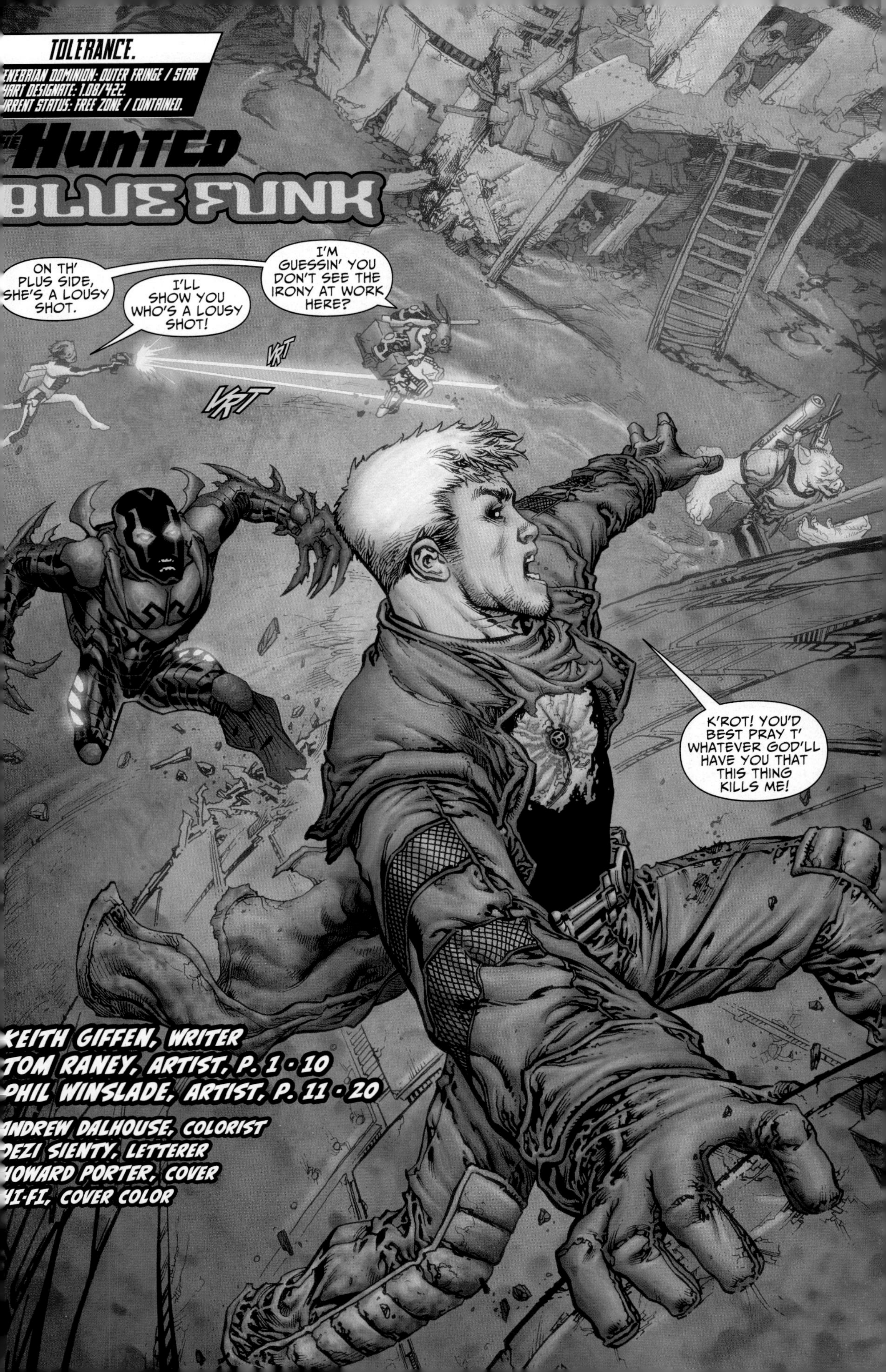
TOLERANCE.
ENEBRIAN DOMINION: OUTER FRINGE / STAR
HART DESIGNATE: 1.08/422.
URRENT STATUS: FREE ZONE / CONTAINED.
THE HUNTED
BLUE FUNK
ON TH' PLUS SIDE, SHE'S A LOUSY SHOT.
I'M GUESSIN' YOU DON'T SEE THE IRONY AT WORK HERE?
I'LL SHOW YOU WHO'S A LOUSY SHOT!
VRT
VRT
K'ROT! YOU'D BEST PRAY T' WHATEVER GOD'LL HAVE YOU THAT THIS THING KILLS ME!
KEITH GIFFEN, WRITER
TOM RANEY, ARTIST, P. 1 - 10
PHIL WINSLADE, ARTIST, P. 11 - 20
ANDREW DALHOUSE, COLORIST
DEZI SIENTY, LETTERER
HOWARD PORTER, COVER
HI-FI, COVER COLOR

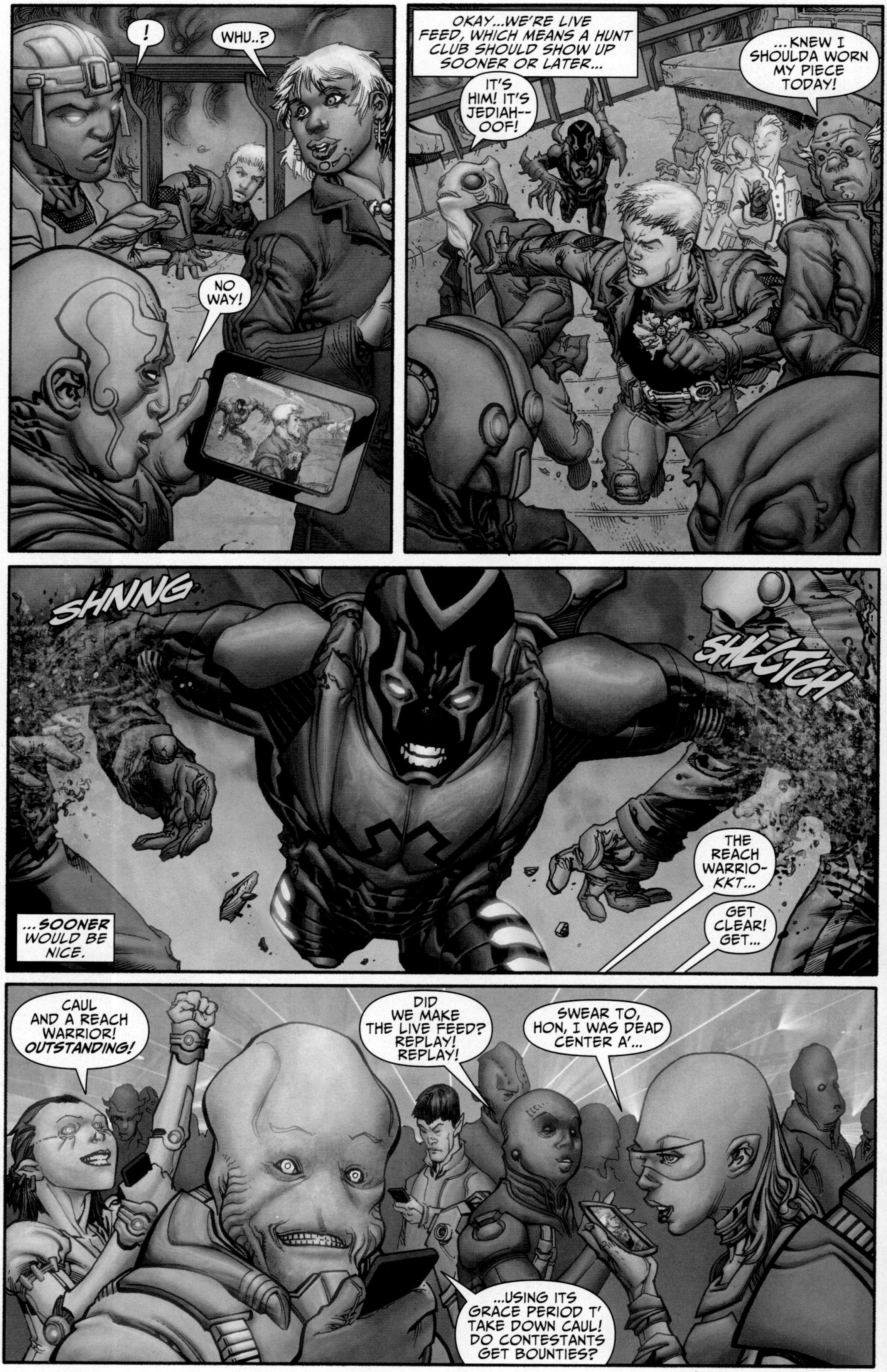
!
WHU..?
NO WAY!
OKAY...WE'RE LIVE FEED, WHICH MEANS A HUNT CLUB SHOULD SHOW UP SOONER OR LATER...
IT'S HIM! IT'S JEDIAH-- OOF!
...KNEW I SHOULDA WORN MY PIECE TODAY!
SHNNG
SHLCTCH
THE REACH WARRIO-KKT...
GET CLEAR! GET...
...SOONER WOULD BE NICE.
CAUL AND A REACH WARRIOR! OUTSTANDING!
DID WE MAKE THE LIVE FEED? REPLAY! REPLAY!
SWEAR TO, HON, I WAS DEAD CENTER A'...
...USING ITS GRACE PERIOD T' TAKE DOWN CAUL! DO CONTESTANTS GET BOUNTIES?

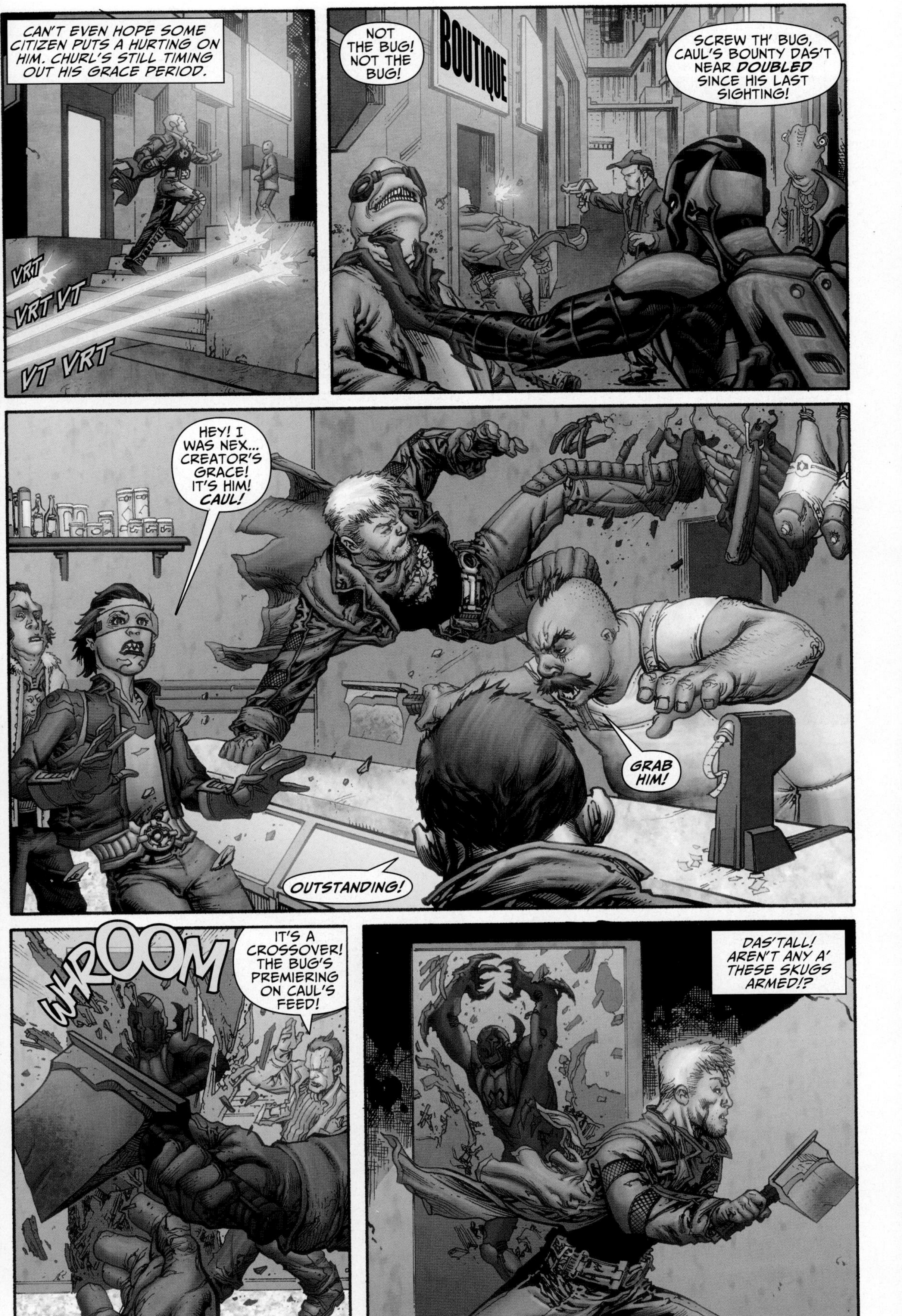
CAN'T EVEN HOPE SOME CITIZEN PUTS A HURTING ON HIM. CHURL'S STILL TIMING OUT HIS GRACE PERIOD.
VRT
VRT VT
VT VRT
NOT THE BUG! NOT THE BUG!
BOUTIQUE
SCREW TH' BUG, CAUL'S BOUNTY DAS'T NEAR DOUBLED SINCE HIS LAST SIGHTING!
HEY! I WAS NEX... CREATOR'S GRACE! IT'S HIM! CAUL!
GRAB HIM!
OUTSTANDING!
WHROOM
IT'S A CROSSOVER! THE BUG'S PREMIERING ON CAUL'S FEED!
DAS'TALL! AREN'T ANY A' THESE SKUGS ARMED!?

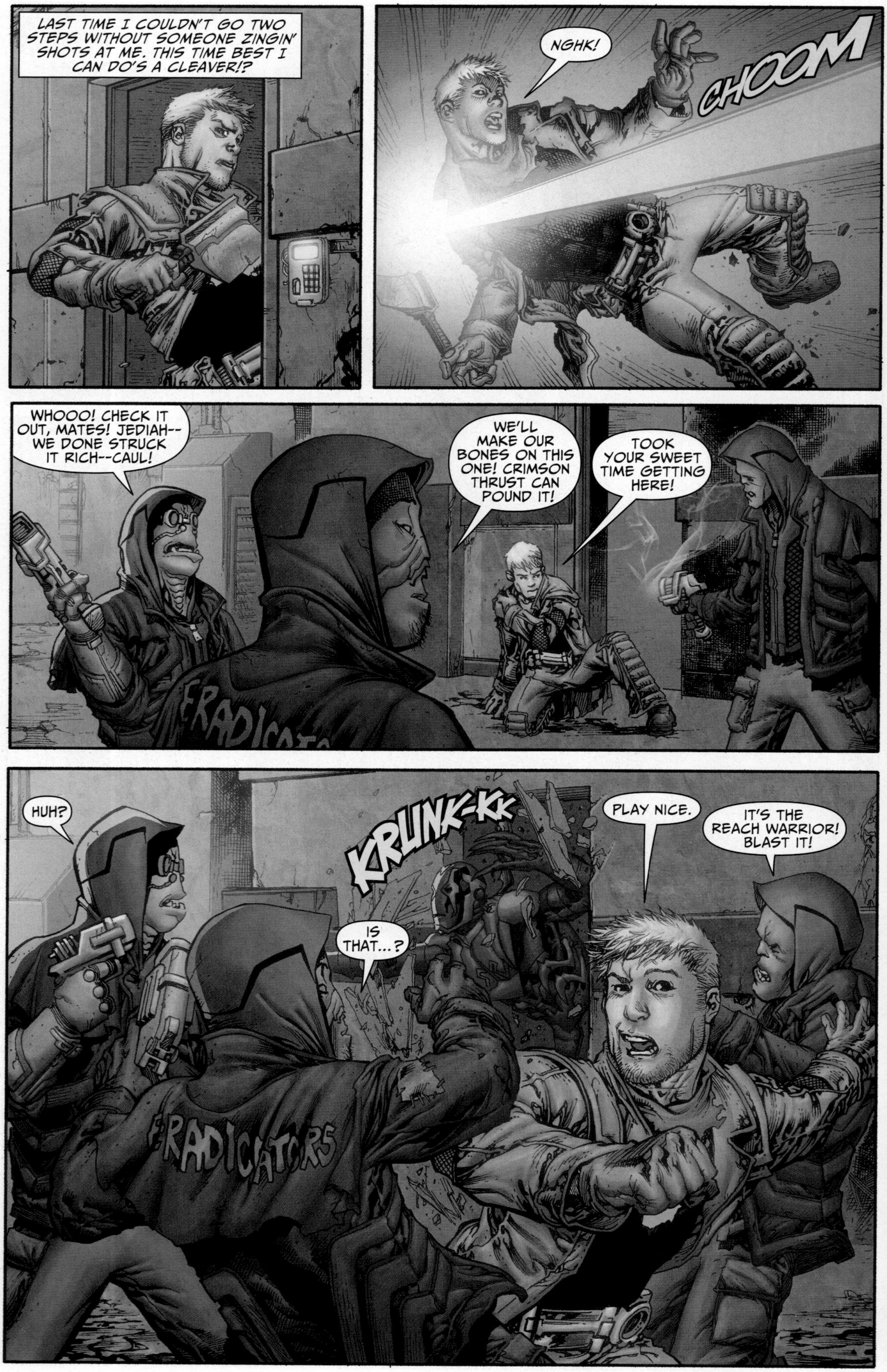
LAST TIME I COULDN'T GO TWO STEPS WITHOUT SOMEONE ZINGIN' SHOTS AT ME. THIS TIME BEST I CAN DO'S A CLEAVER!?
NGHK!
CHOOM
WHOOO! CHECK IT OUT, MATES! JEDIAH-- WE DONE STRUCK IT RICH--CAUL!
WE'LL MAKE OUR BONES ON THIS ONE! CRIMSON THRUST CAN POUND IT!
TOOK YOUR SWEET TIME GETTING HERE!
HUH?
KRUNK-KK
IS THAT...?
PLAY NICE.
IT'S THE REACH WARRIOR! BLAST IT!
ERADICATORS

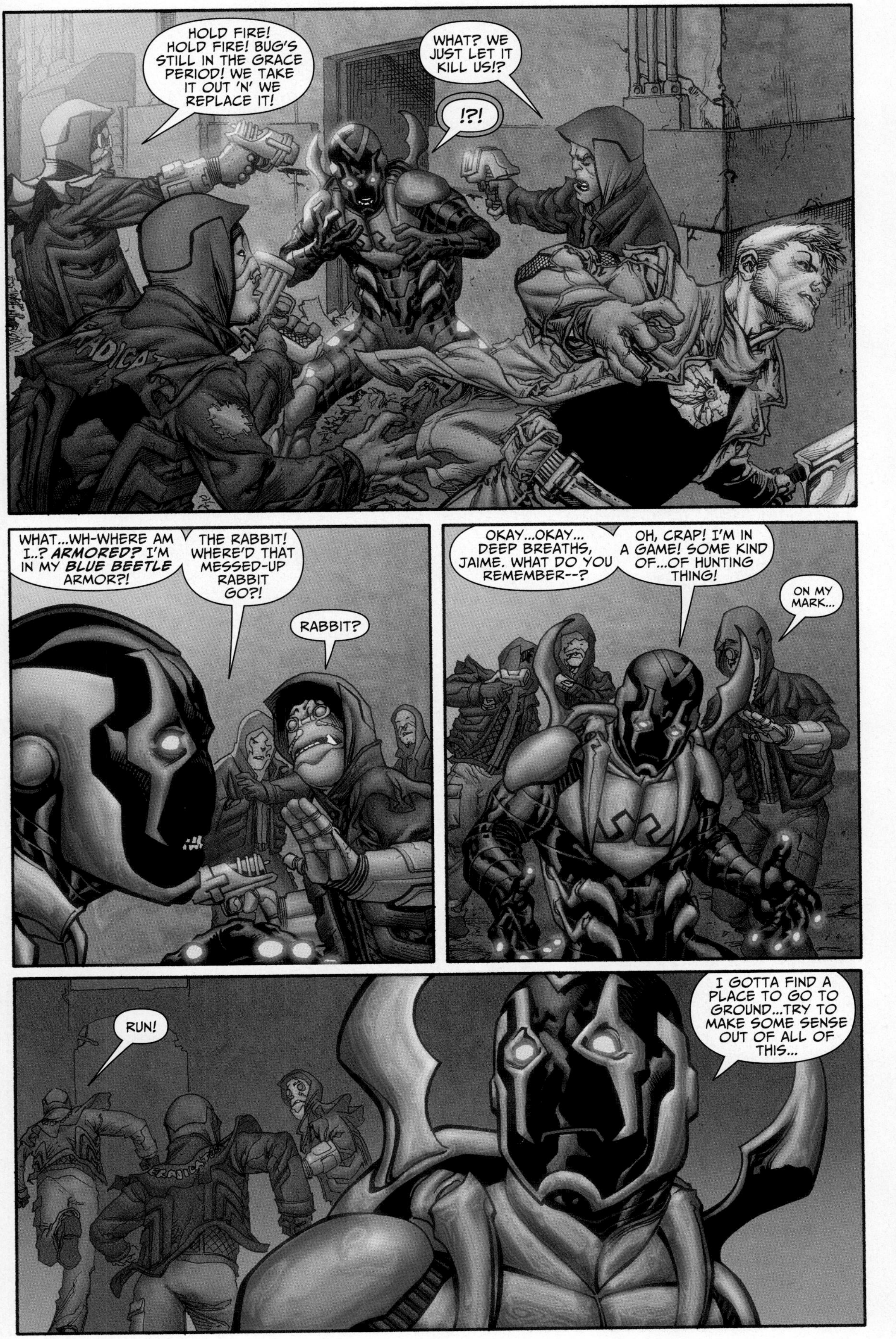
HOLD FIRE! HOLD FIRE! BUG'S STILL IN THE GRACE PERIOD! WE TAKE IT OUT 'N' WE REPLACE IT!
WHAT? WE JUST LET IT KILL US!?
!?!
WHAT...WH-WHERE AM I..? ARMORED? I'M IN MY BLUE BEETLE ARMOR?!
THE RABBIT! WHERE'D THAT MESSED-UP RABBIT GO?!
RABBIT?
OKAY...OKAY... DEEP BREATHS, JAIME. WHAT DO YOU REMEMBER--?
OH, CRAP! I'M IN A GAME! SOME KIND OF...OF HUNTING THING!
ON MY MARK...
RUN!
I GOTTA FIND A PLACE TO GO TO GROUND...TRY TO MAKE SOME SENSE OUT OF ALL OF THIS...

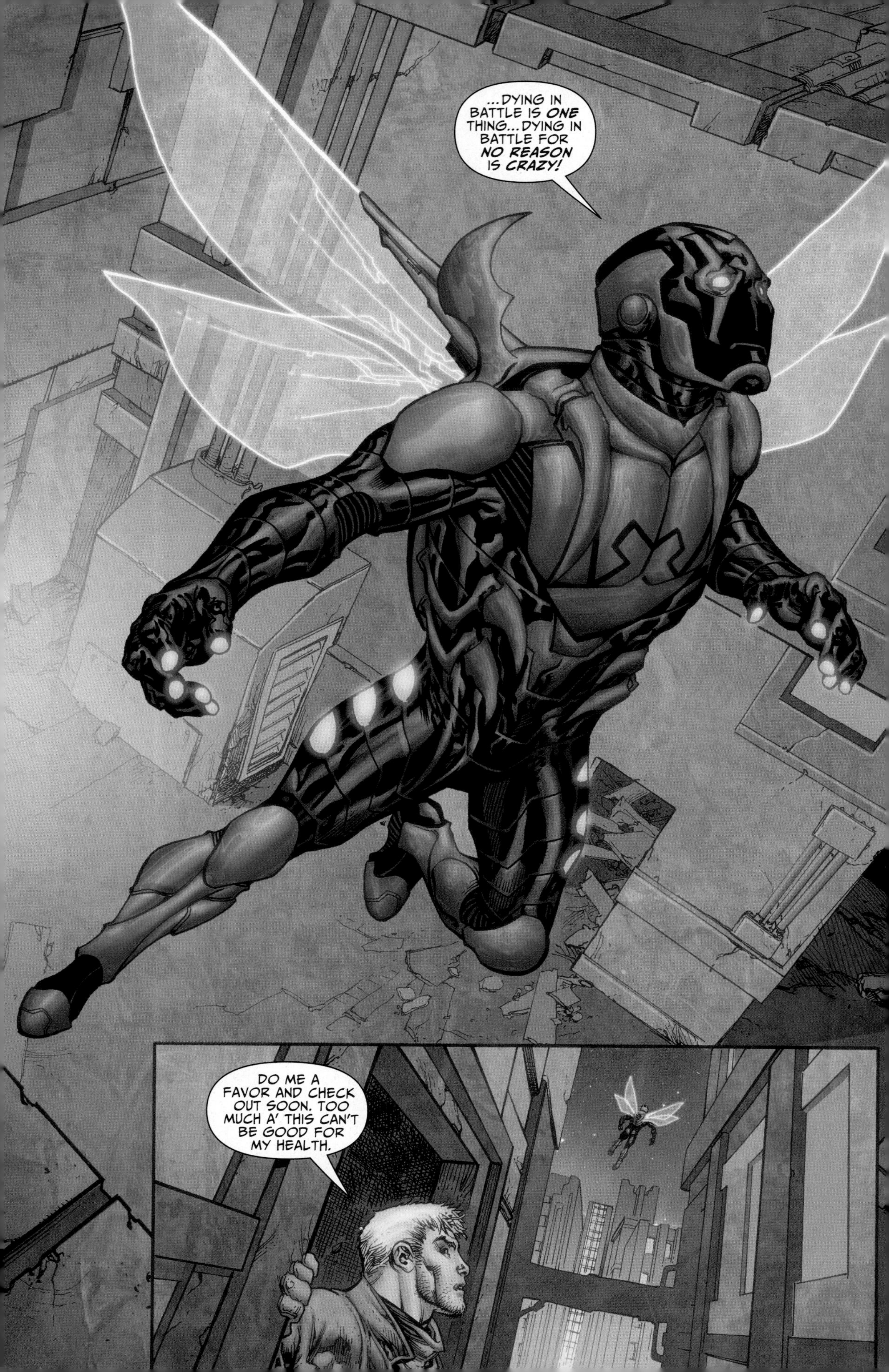
...DYING IN BATTLE IS ONE THING...DYING IN BATTLE FOR NO REASON IS CRAZY!
DO ME A FAVOR AND CHECK OUT SOON. TOO MUCH A' THIS CAN'T BE GOOD FOR MY HEALTH.

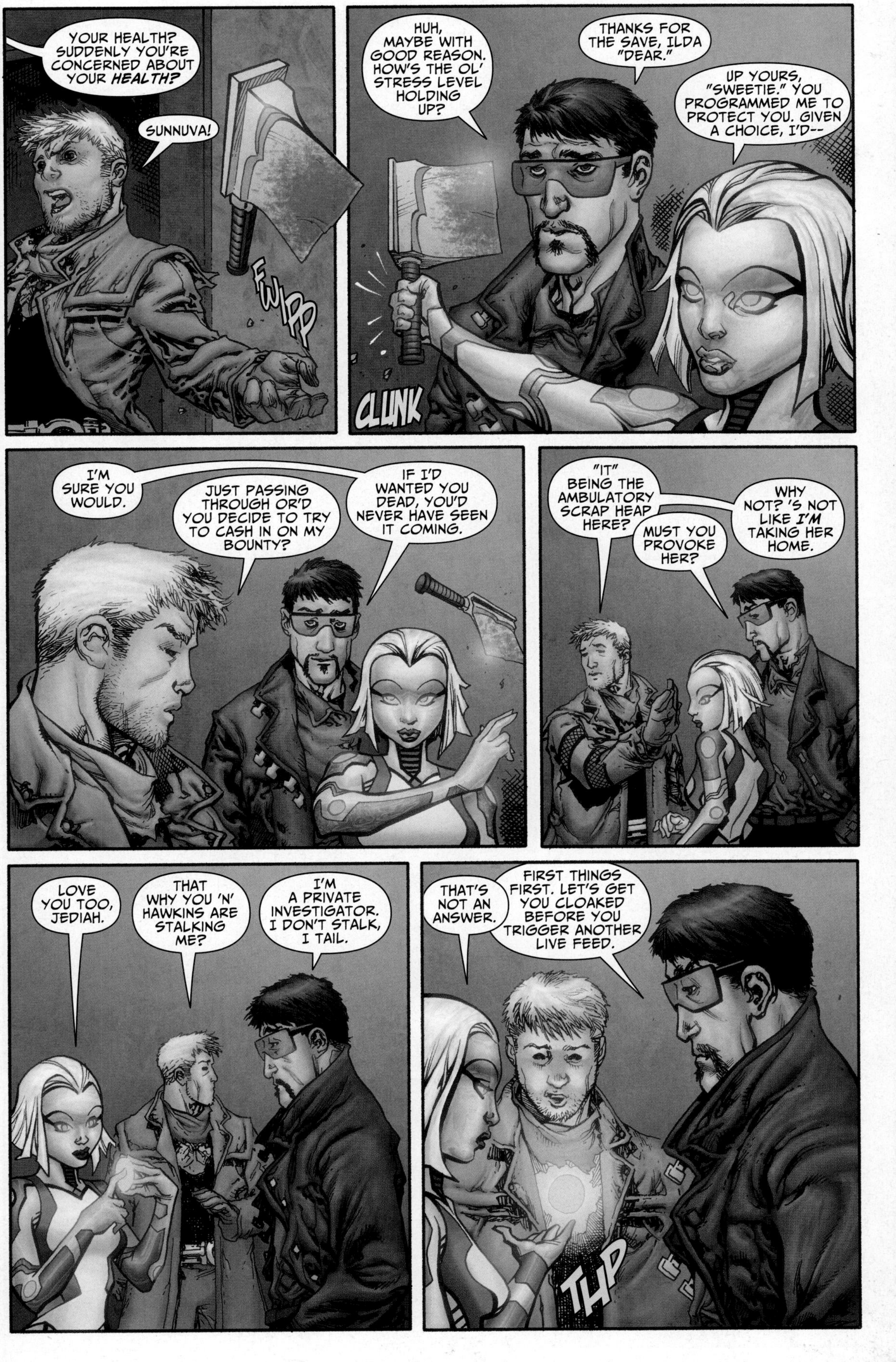

YOUR HEALTH? SUDDENLY YOU'RE CONCERNED ABOUT YOUR ***HEALTH?***
SUNNUVA!
FWIPP
HUH, MAYBE WITH GOOD REASON. HOW'S THE OL' STRESS LEVEL HOLDING UP?
THANKS FOR THE SAVE, ILDA "DEAR."
UP YOURS, "SWEETIE." YOU PROGRAMMED ME TO PROTECT YOU. GIVEN A CHOICE, I'D--
CLUNK
I'M SURE YOU WOULD.
JUST PASSING THROUGH OR'D YOU DECIDE TO TRY TO CASH IN ON MY BOUNTY?
IF I'D WANTED YOU DEAD, YOU'D NEVER HAVE SEEN IT COMING.
"IT" BEING THE AMBULATORY SCRAP HEAP HERE?
MUST YOU PROVOKE HER?
WHY NOT? 'S NOT LIKE ***I'M*** TAKING HER HOME.
LOVE YOU TOO, JEDIAH.
THAT WHY YOU 'N' HAWKINS ARE STALKING ME?
I'M A PRIVATE INVESTIGATOR. I DON'T STALK, I TAIL.
THAT'S NOT AN ANSWER.
FIRST THINGS FIRST. LET'S GET YOU CLOAKED BEFORE YOU TRIGGER ANOTHER LIVE FEED.
THP

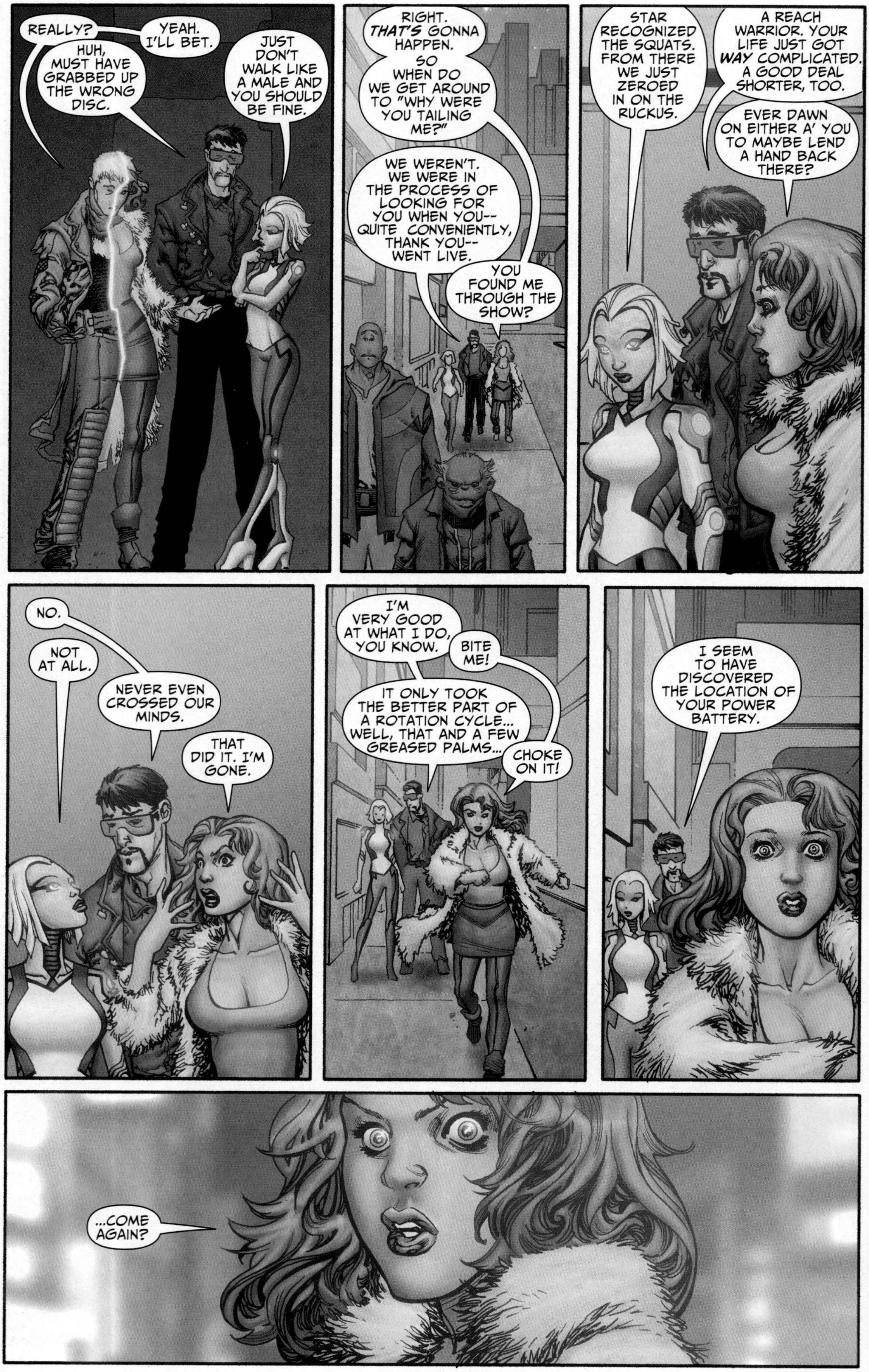
REALLY?
YEAH. I'LL BET.
HUH, MUST HAVE GRABBED UP THE WRONG DISC.
JUST DON'T WALK LIKE A MALE AND YOU SHOULD BE FINE.
RIGHT. *THAT'S* GONNA HAPPEN.
SO WHEN DO WE GET AROUND TO "WHY WERE YOU TAILING ME?"
WE WEREN'T. WE WERE IN THE PROCESS OF LOOKING FOR YOU WHEN YOU-- QUITE CONVENIENTLY, THANK YOU-- WENT LIVE.
YOU FOUND ME THROUGH THE SHOW?
STAR RECOGNIZED THE SQUATS. FROM THERE WE JUST ZEROED IN ON THE RUCKUS.
A REACH WARRIOR. YOUR LIFE JUST GOT *WAY* COMPLICATED. A GOOD DEAL SHORTER, TOO.
EVER DAWN ON EITHER A' YOU TO MAYBE LEND A HAND BACK THERE?
NO.
NOT AT ALL.
NEVER EVEN CROSSED OUR MINDS.
THAT DID IT. I'M GONE.
I'M VERY GOOD AT WHAT I DO, YOU KNOW.
BITE ME!
IT ONLY TOOK THE BETTER PART OF A ROTATION CYCLE... WELL, THAT AND A FEW GREASED PALMS...
CHOKE ON IT!
I SEEM TO HAVE DISCOVERED THE LOCATION OF YOUR POWER BATTERY.
...COME AGAIN?

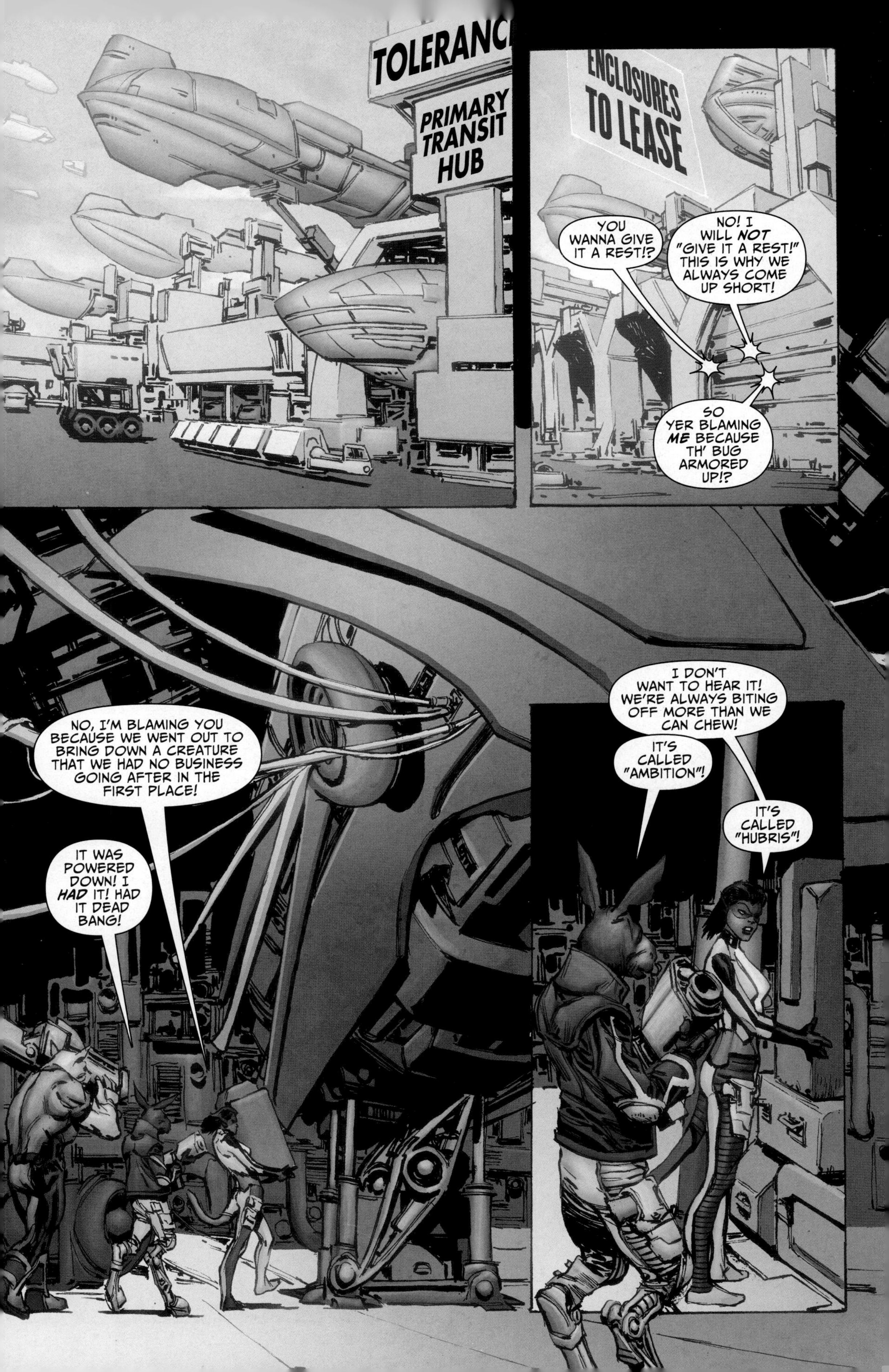
TOLERANC
PRIMARY TRANSIT HUB
ENCLOSURES TO LEASE
YOU WANNA GIVE IT A REST!?
NO! I WILL NOT "GIVE IT A REST!" THIS IS WHY WE ALWAYS COME UP SHORT!
SO YER BLAMING ME BECAUSE TH' BUG ARMORED UP!?
NO, I'M BLAMING YOU BECAUSE WE WENT OUT TO BRING DOWN A CREATURE THAT WE HAD NO BUSINESS GOING AFTER IN THE FIRST PLACE!
IT WAS POWERED DOWN! I HAD IT! HAD IT DEAD BANG!
I DON'T WANT TO HEAR IT! WE'RE ALWAYS BITING OFF MORE THAN WE CAN CHEW!
IT'S CALLED "AMBITION"!
IT'S CALLED "HUBRIS"!

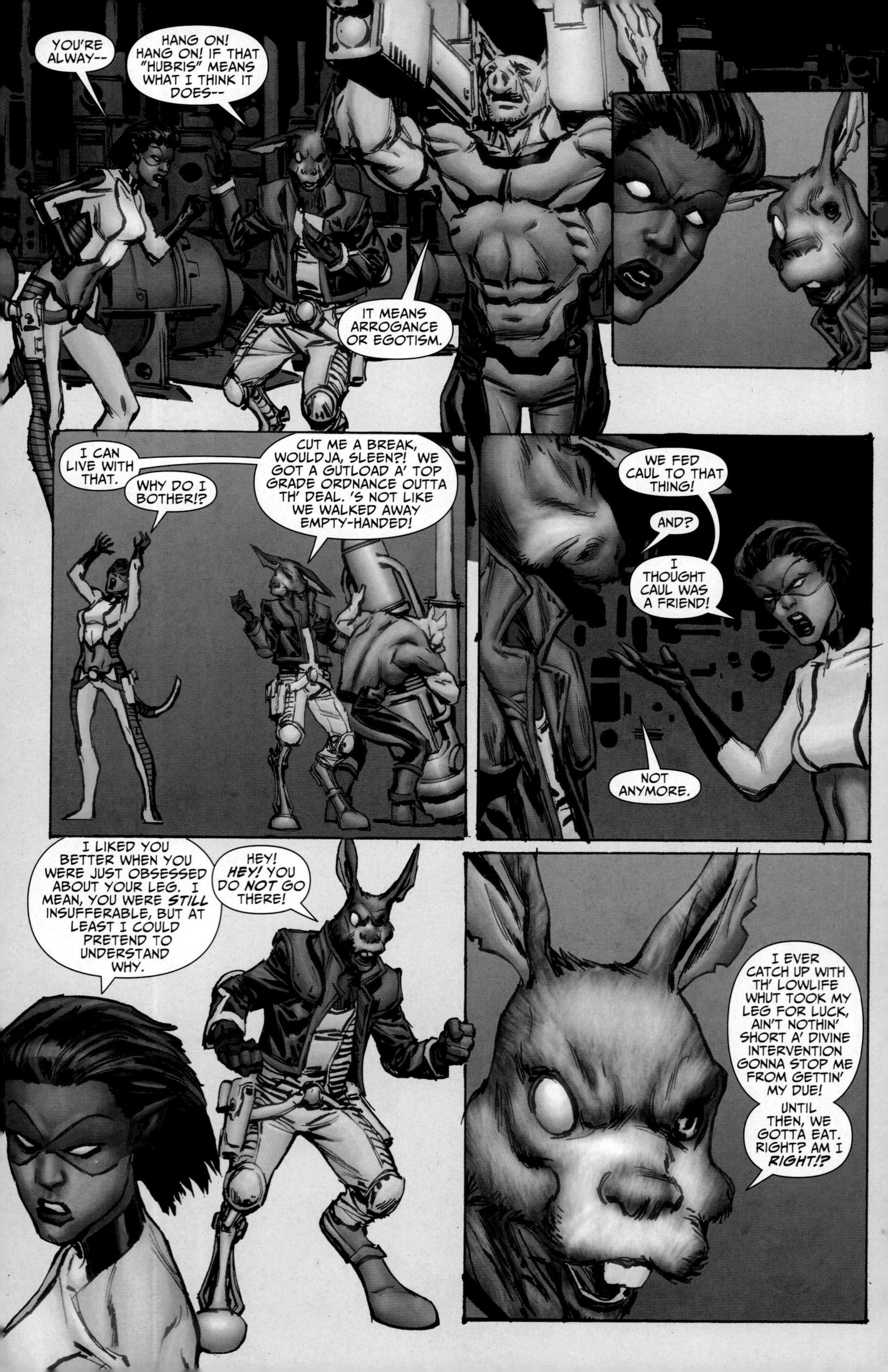
YOU'RE ALWAY--
HANG ON! HANG ON! IF THAT "HUBRIS" MEANS WHAT I THINK IT DOES--
IT MEANS ARROGANCE OR EGOTISM.
I CAN LIVE WITH THAT.
WHY DO I BOTHER!?
CUT ME A BREAK, WOULDJA, SLEEN?! WE GOT A GUTLOAD A' TOP GRADE ORDNANCE OUTTA TH' DEAL. 'S NOT LIKE WE WALKED AWAY EMPTY-HANDED!
WE FED CAUL TO THAT THING!
AND?
I THOUGHT CAUL WAS A FRIEND!
NOT ANYMORE.
I LIKED YOU BETTER WHEN YOU WERE JUST OBSESSED ABOUT YOUR LEG. I MEAN, YOU WERE STILL INSUFFERABLE, BUT AT LEAST I COULD PRETEND TO UNDERSTAND WHY.
HEY! HEY! YOU DO NOT GO THERE!
I EVER CATCH UP WITH TH' LOWLIFE WHUT TOOK MY LEG FOR LUCK, AIN'T NOTHIN' SHORT A' DIVINE INTERVENTION GONNA STOP ME FROM GETTIN' MY DUE!
UNTIL THEN, WE GOTTA EAT. RIGHT? AM I RIGHT!?

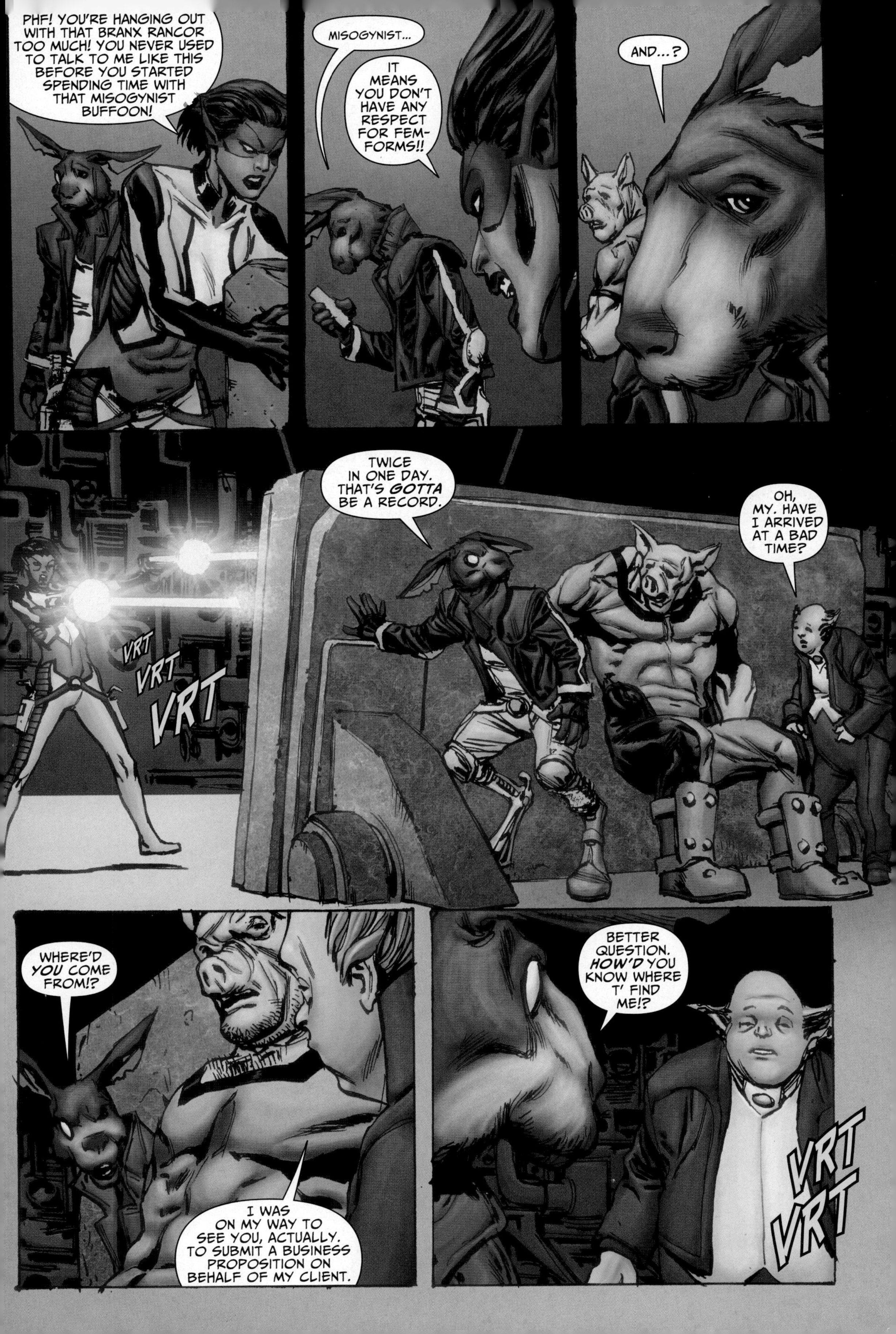
PHF! YOU'RE HANGING OUT WITH THAT BRANX RANCOR TOO MUCH! YOU NEVER USED TO TALK TO ME LIKE THIS BEFORE YOU STARTED SPENDING TIME WITH THAT MISOGYNIST BUFFOON!
MISOGYNIST...
IT MEANS YOU DON'T HAVE ANY RESPECT FOR FEM-FORMS!!
AND...?
TWICE IN ONE DAY. THAT'S GOTTA BE A RECORD.
VRT
VRT
VRT
OH, MY. HAVE I ARRIVED AT A BAD TIME?
WHERE'D YOU COME FROM!?
I WAS ON MY WAY TO SEE YOU, ACTUALLY. TO SUBMIT A BUSINESS PROPOSITION ON BEHALF OF MY CLIENT.
BETTER QUESTION. HOW'D YOU KNOW WHERE T' FIND ME!?
VRT
VRT

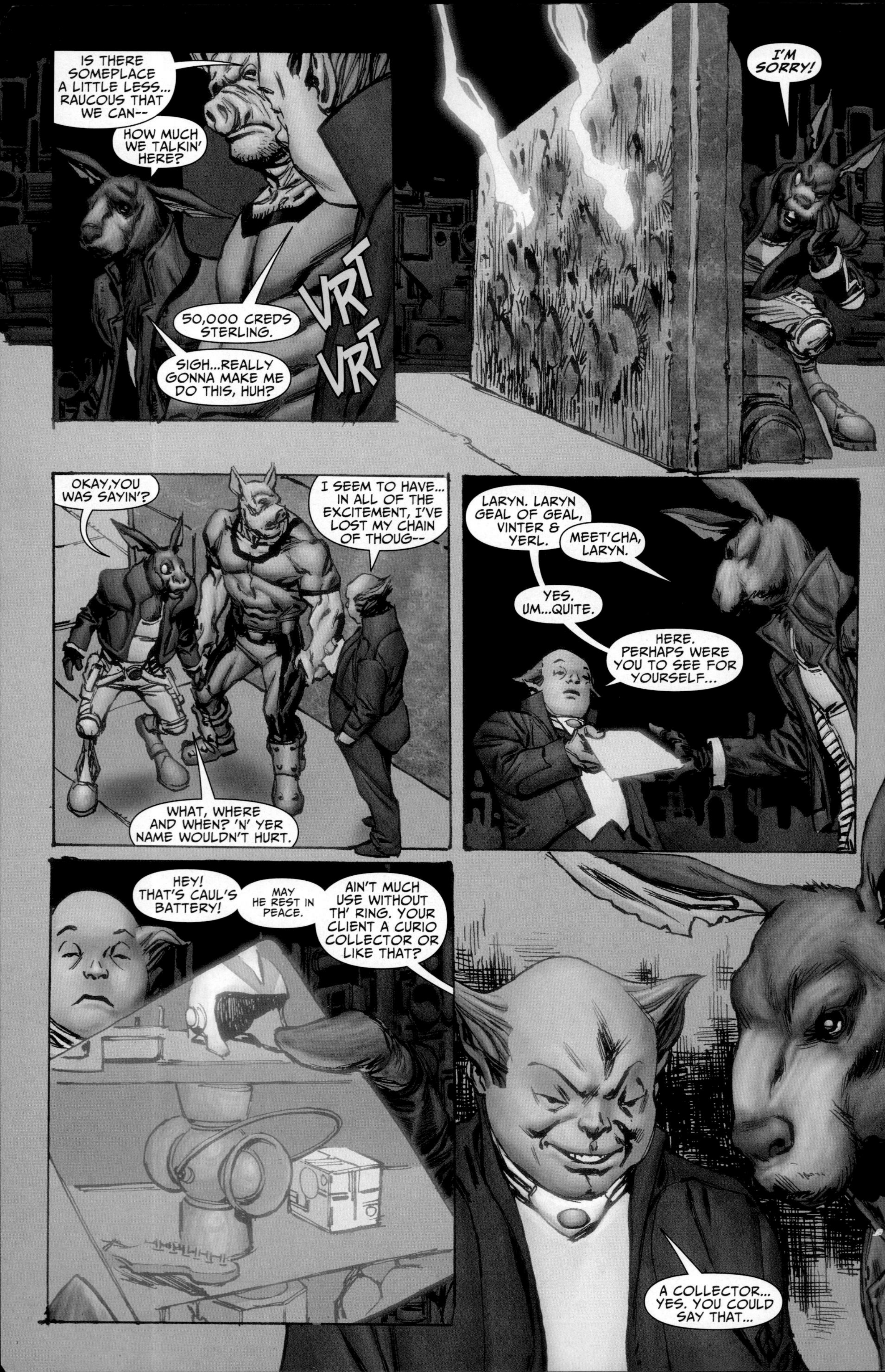
IS THERE SOMEPLACE A LITTLE LESS... RAUCOUS THAT WE CAN--
HOW MUCH WE TALKIN' HERE?
50,000 CREDS STERLING.
SIGH...REALLY GONNA MAKE ME DO THIS, HUH?
VRT VRT
I'M SORRY!
OKAY,YOU WAS SAYIN'?
I SEEM TO HAVE... IN ALL OF THE EXCITEMENT, I'VE LOST MY CHAIN OF THOUG--
WHAT, WHERE AND WHEN? 'N' YER NAME WOULDN'T HURT.
LARYN. LARYN GEAL OF GEAL, VINTER & YERL.
MEET'CHA, LARYN.
YES. UM...QUITE.
HERE. PERHAPS WERE YOU TO SEE FOR YOURSELF...
HEY! THAT'S CAUL'S BATTERY!
MAY HE REST IN PEACE.
AIN'T MUCH USE WITHOUT TH' RING. YOUR CLIENT A CURIO COLLECTOR OR LIKE THAT?
A COLLECTOR... YES. YOU COULD SAY THAT...

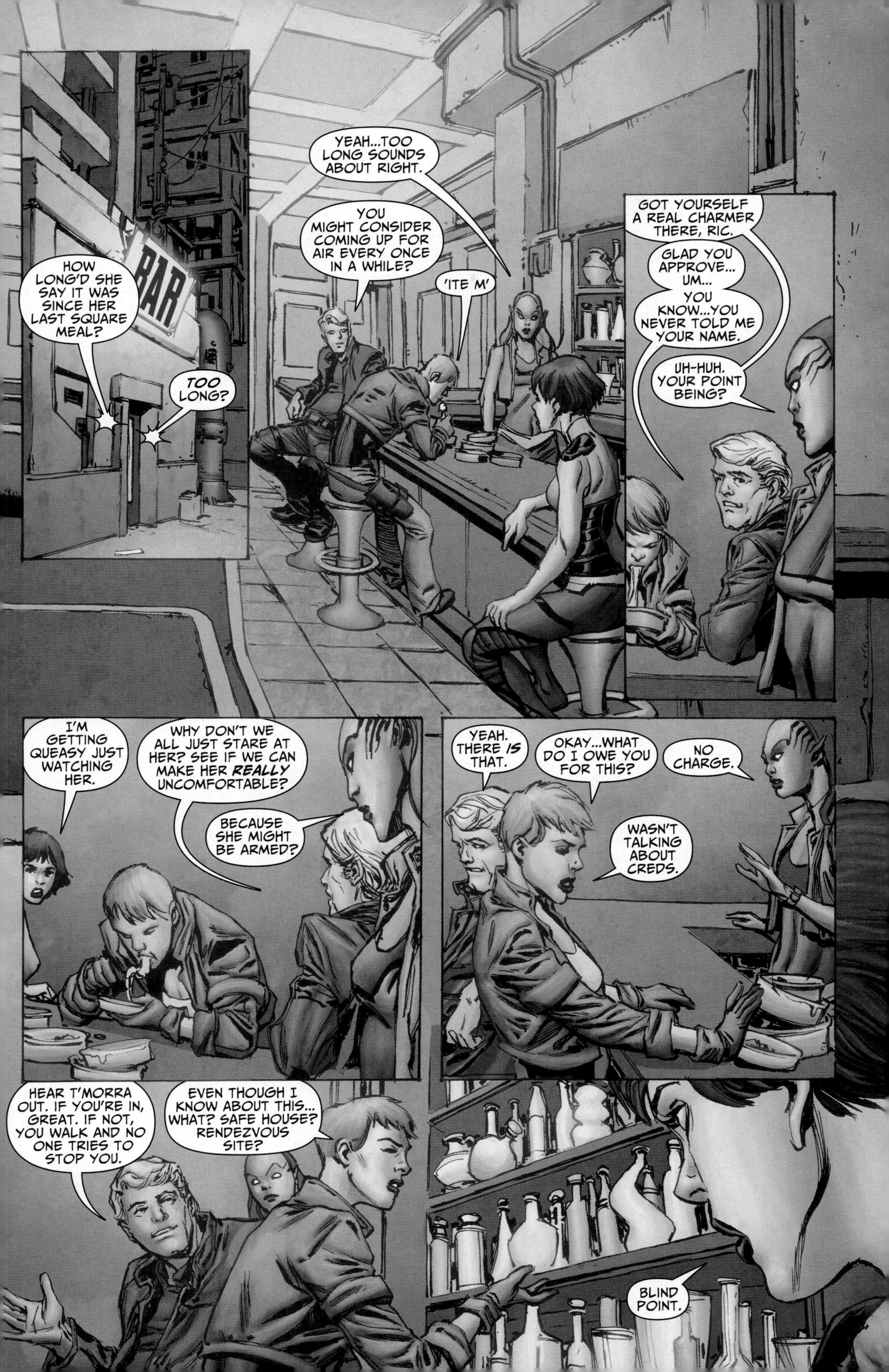

HOW LONG'D SHE SAY IT WAS SINCE HER LAST SQUARE MEAL?
TOO LONG?
BAR
YEAH...TOO LONG SOUNDS ABOUT RIGHT.
YOU MIGHT CONSIDER COMING UP FOR AIR EVERY ONCE IN A WHILE?
'ITE M'
GOT YOURSELF A REAL CHARMER THERE, RIC.
GLAD YOU APPROVE... UM...
YOU KNOW...YOU NEVER TOLD ME YOUR NAME.
UH-HUH. YOUR POINT BEING?
I'M GETTING QUEASY JUST WATCHING HER.
WHY DON'T WE ALL JUST STARE AT HER? SEE IF WE CAN MAKE HER REALLY UNCOMFORTABLE?
BECAUSE SHE MIGHT BE ARMED?
YEAH. THERE IS THAT.
OKAY...WHAT DO I OWE YOU FOR THIS?
NO CHARGE.
WASN'T TALKING ABOUT CREDS.
HEAR T'MORRA OUT. IF YOU'RE IN, GREAT. IF NOT, YOU WALK AND NO ONE TRIES TO STOP YOU.
EVEN THOUGH I KNOW ABOUT THIS... WHAT? SAFE HOUSE? RENDEZVOUS SITE?
BLIND POINT.

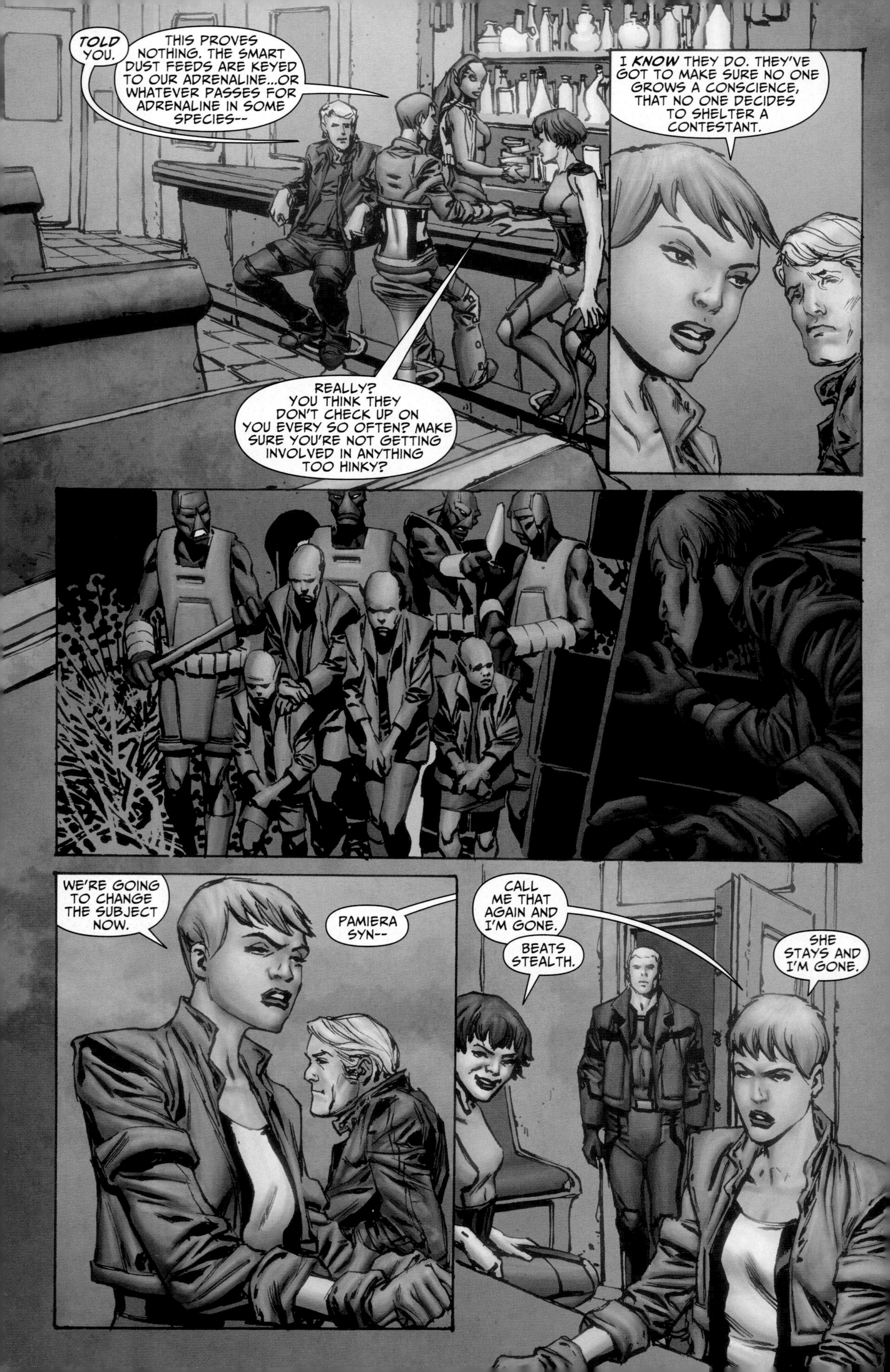

TOLD YOU.
THIS PROVES NOTHING. THE SMART DUST FEEDS ARE KEYED TO OUR ADRENALINE...OR WHATEVER PASSES FOR ADRENALINE IN SOME SPECIES--
REALLY? YOU THINK THEY DON'T CHECK UP ON YOU EVERY SO OFTEN? MAKE SURE YOU'RE NOT GETTING INVOLVED IN ANYTHING TOO HINKY?
I KNOW THEY DO. THEY'VE GOT TO MAKE SURE NO ONE GROWS A CONSCIENCE, THAT NO ONE DECIDES TO SHELTER A CONTESTANT.
WE'RE GOING TO CHANGE THE SUBJECT NOW.
PAMIERA SYN--
CALL ME THAT AGAIN AND I'M GONE.
BEATS STEALTH.
SHE STAYS AND I'M GONE.

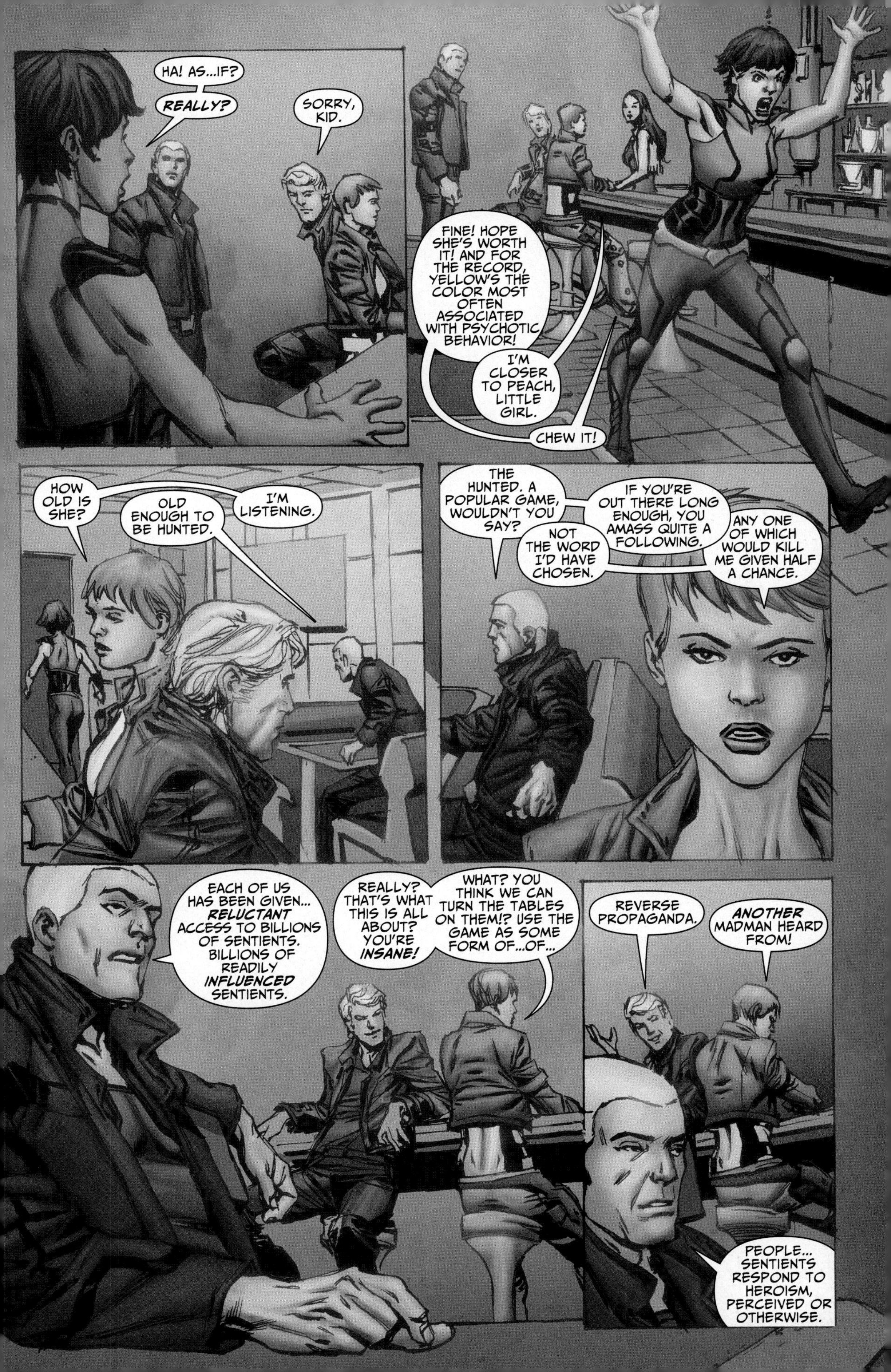

HA! AS...IF?
REALLY?
SORRY, KID.
FINE! HOPE SHE'S WORTH IT! AND FOR THE RECORD, YELLOW'S THE COLOR MOST OFTEN ASSOCIATED WITH PSYCHOTIC BEHAVIOR!
I'M CLOSER TO PEACH, LITTLE GIRL.
CHEW IT!
HOW OLD IS SHE?
I'M LISTENING.
OLD ENOUGH TO BE HUNTED.
THE HUNTED. A POPULAR GAME, WOULDN'T YOU SAY?
NOT THE WORD I'D HAVE CHOSEN.
IF YOU'RE OUT THERE LONG ENOUGH, YOU AMASS QUITE A FOLLOWING.
ANY ONE OF WHICH WOULD KILL ME GIVEN HALF A CHANCE.
EACH OF US HAS BEEN GIVEN... *RELUCTANT* ACCESS TO BILLIONS OF SENTIENTS. BILLIONS OF READILY *INFLUENCED* SENTIENTS.
REALLY? THAT'S WHAT THIS IS ALL ABOUT? YOU'RE *INSANE!*
WHAT? YOU THINK WE CAN TURN THE TABLES ON THEM!? USE THE GAME AS SOME FORM OF...OF...
REVERSE PROPAGANDA.
ANOTHER MADMAN HEARD FROM!
PEOPLE... SENTIENTS RESPOND TO HEROISM, PERCEIVED OR OTHERWISE.

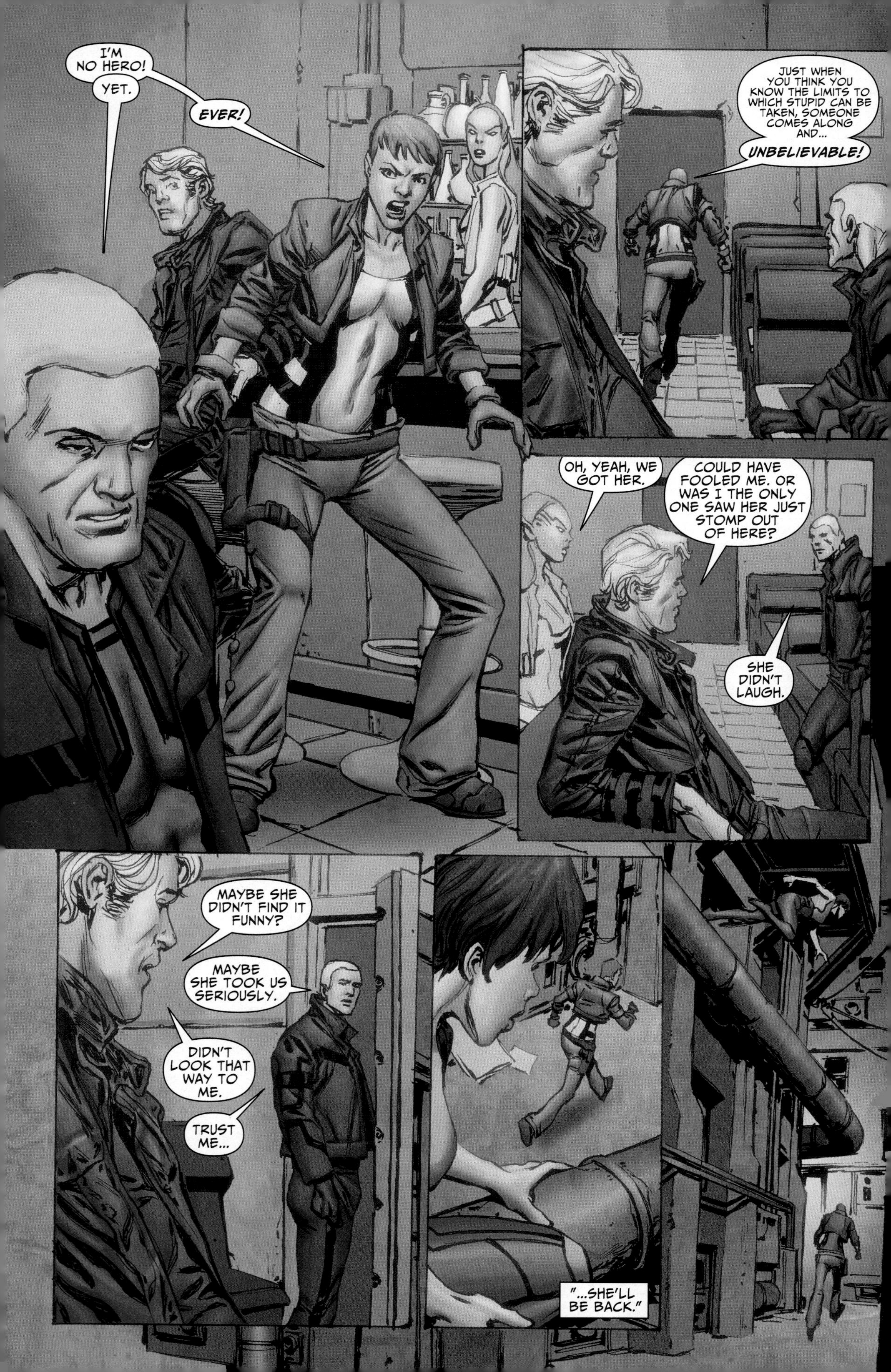
I'M NO HERO!
YET.
EVER!
JUST WHEN YOU THINK YOU KNOW THE LIMITS TO WHICH STUPID CAN BE TAKEN, SOMEONE COMES ALONG AND...
UNBELIEVABLE!
OH, YEAH, WE GOT HER.
COULD HAVE FOOLED ME. OR WAS I THE ONLY ONE SAW HER JUST STOMP OUT OF HERE?
SHE DIDN'T LAUGH.
MAYBE SHE DIDN'T FIND IT FUNNY?
MAYBE SHE TOOK US SERIOUSLY.
DIDN'T LOOK THAT WAY TO ME.
TRUST ME...
"...SHE'LL BE BACK."

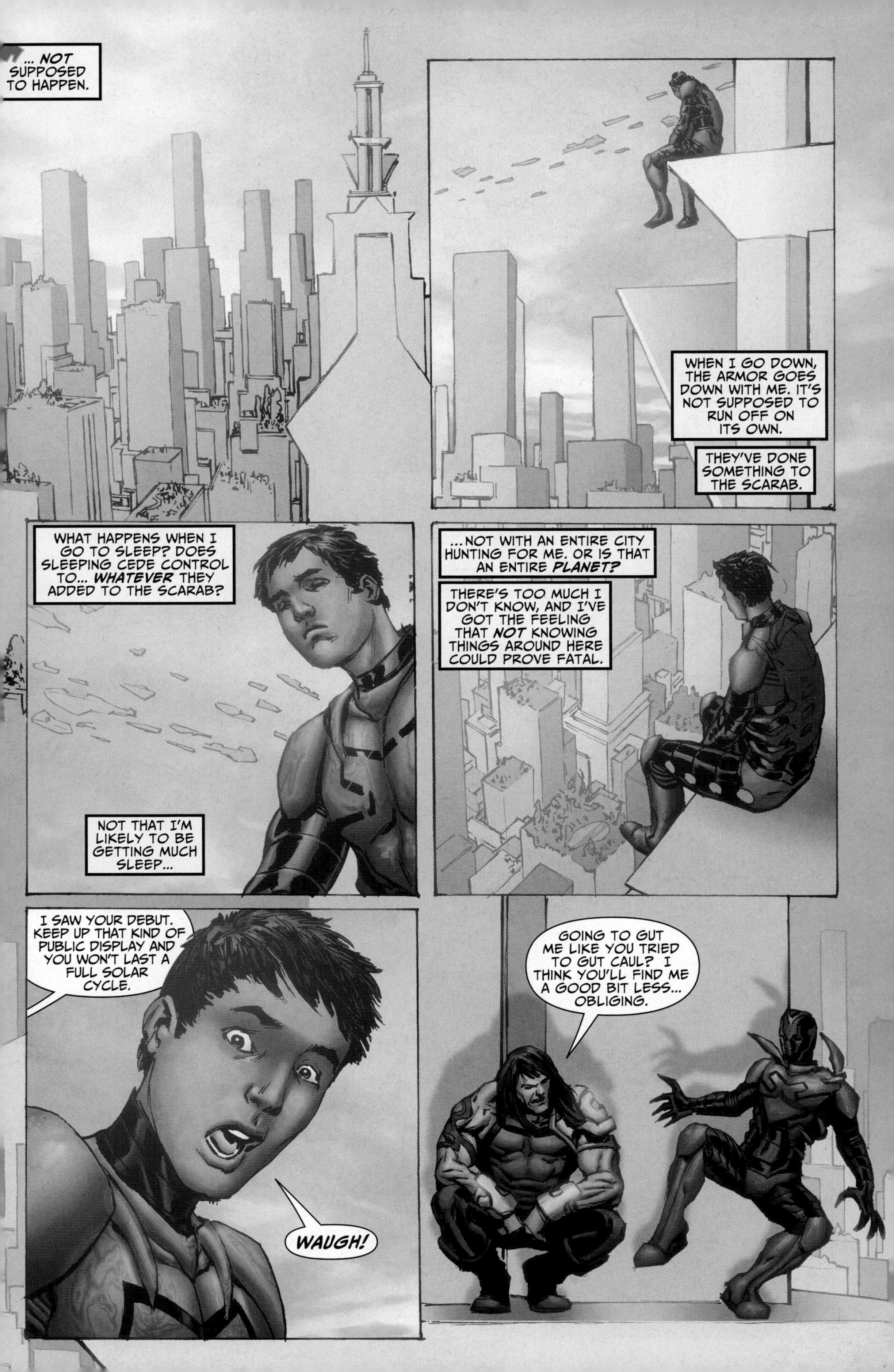
... NOT SUPPOSED TO HAPPEN.
WHEN I GO DOWN, THE ARMOR GOES DOWN WITH ME. IT'S NOT SUPPOSED TO RUN OFF ON ITS OWN.
THEY'VE DONE SOMETHING TO THE SCARAB.
WHAT HAPPENS WHEN I GO TO SLEEP? DOES SLEEPING CEDE CONTROL TO... WHATEVER THEY ADDED TO THE SCARAB?
NOT THAT I'M LIKELY TO BE GETTING MUCH SLEEP...
...NOT WITH AN ENTIRE CITY HUNTING FOR ME. OR IS THAT AN ENTIRE PLANET?
THERE'S TOO MUCH I DON'T KNOW, AND I'VE GOT THE FEELING THAT NOT KNOWING THINGS AROUND HERE COULD PROVE FATAL.
I SAW YOUR DEBUT. KEEP UP THAT KIND OF PUBLIC DISPLAY AND YOU WON'T LAST A FULL SOLAR CYCLE.
WAUGH!
GOING TO GUT ME LIKE YOU TRIED TO GUT CAUL? I THINK YOU'LL FIND ME A GOOD BIT LESS... OBLIGING.

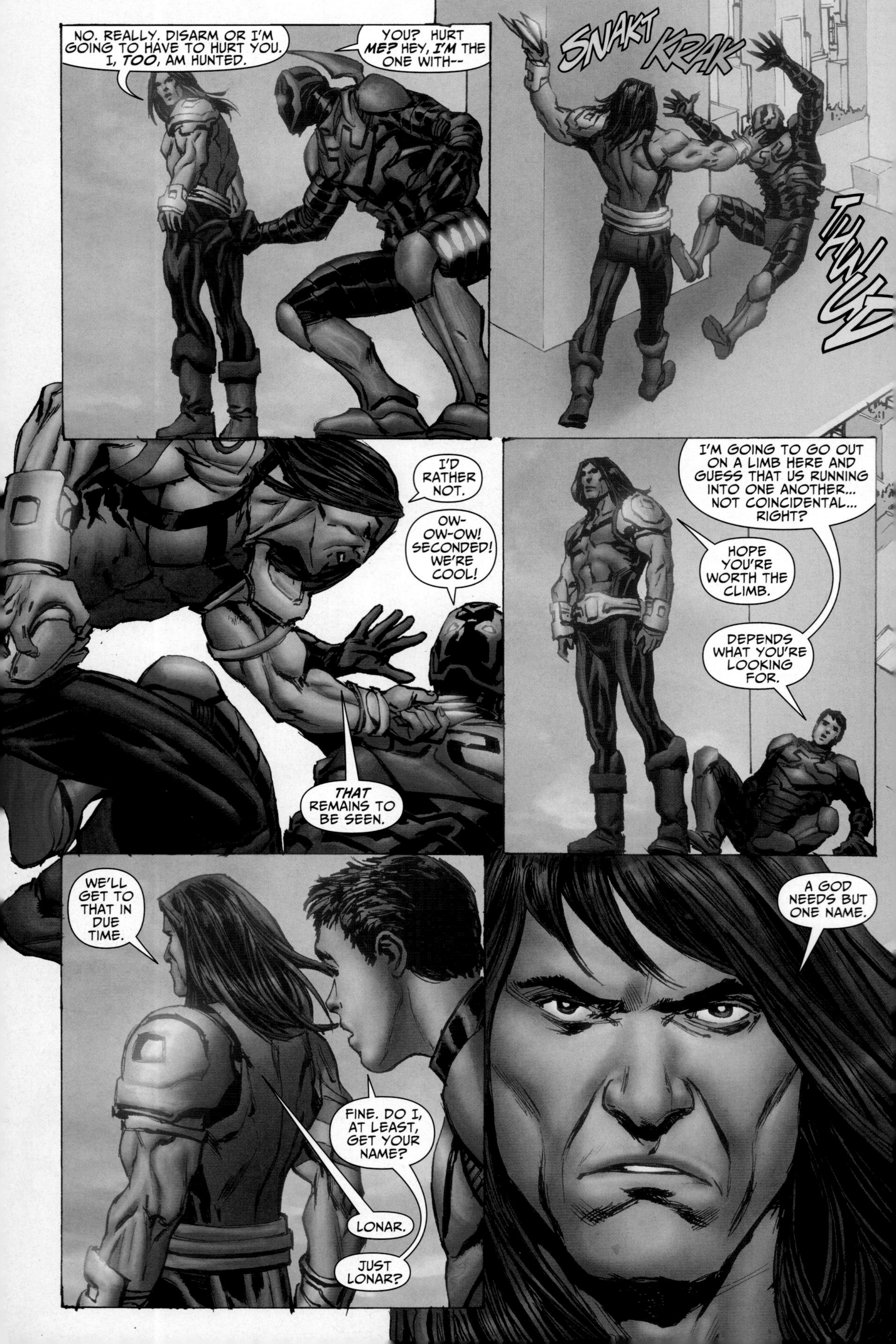
NO. REALLY. DISARM OR I'M GOING TO HAVE TO HURT YOU. I, *TOO*, AM HUNTED.
YOU? HURT *ME?* HEY, *I'M* THE ONE WITH--
SNAKT
KRAK
THWUMP
I'D RATHER NOT.
OW-OW-OW! SECONDED! WE'RE COOL!
THAT REMAINS TO BE SEEN.
I'M GOING TO GO OUT ON A LIMB HERE AND GUESS THAT US RUNNING INTO ONE ANOTHER... NOT COINCIDENTAL... RIGHT?
HOPE YOU'RE WORTH THE CLIMB.
DEPENDS WHAT YOU'RE LOOKING FOR.
WE'LL GET TO THAT IN DUE TIME.
FINE. DO I, AT LEAST, GET YOUR NAME?
LONAR.
JUST LONAR?
A GOD NEEDS BUT ONE NAME.

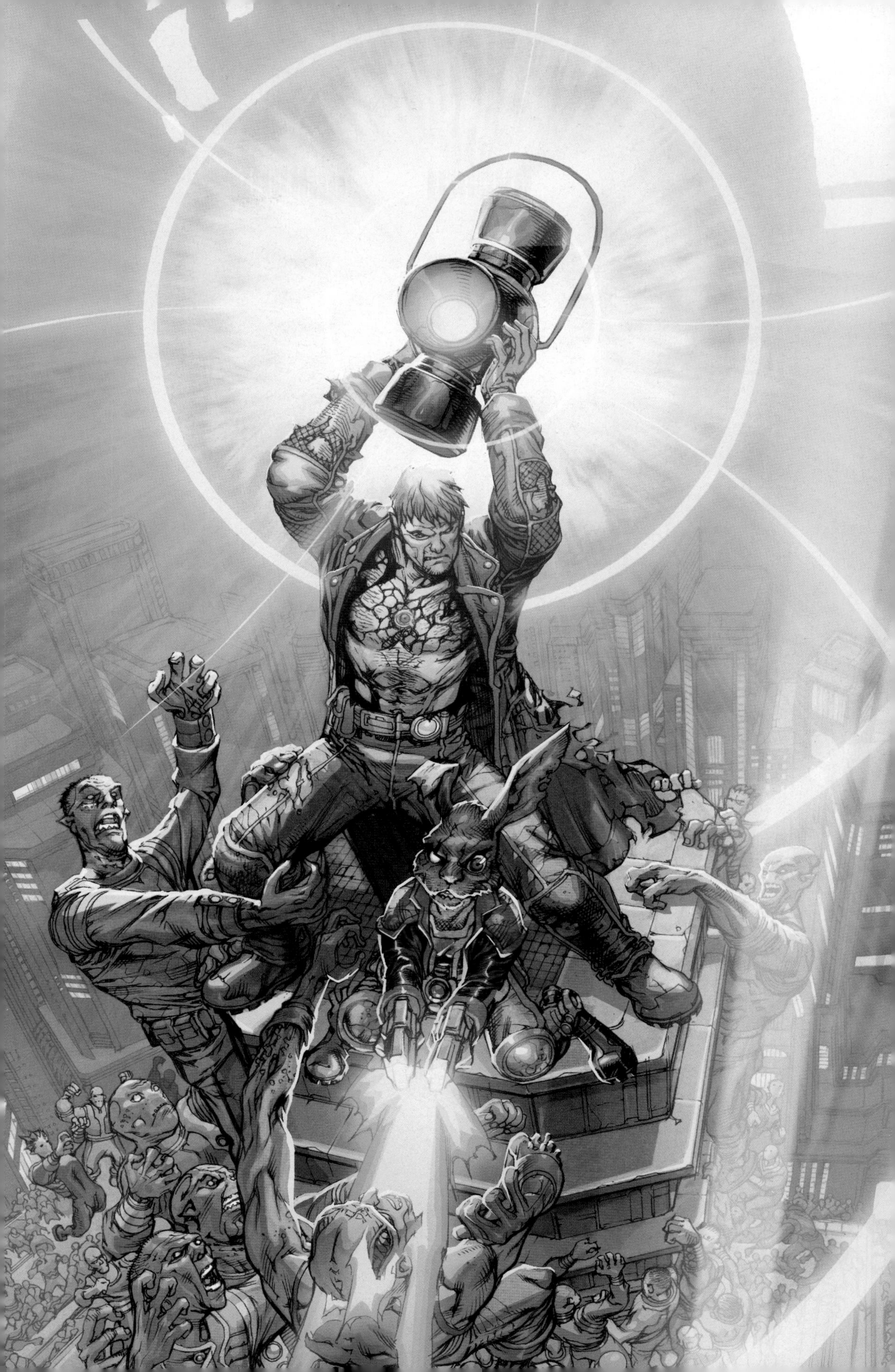

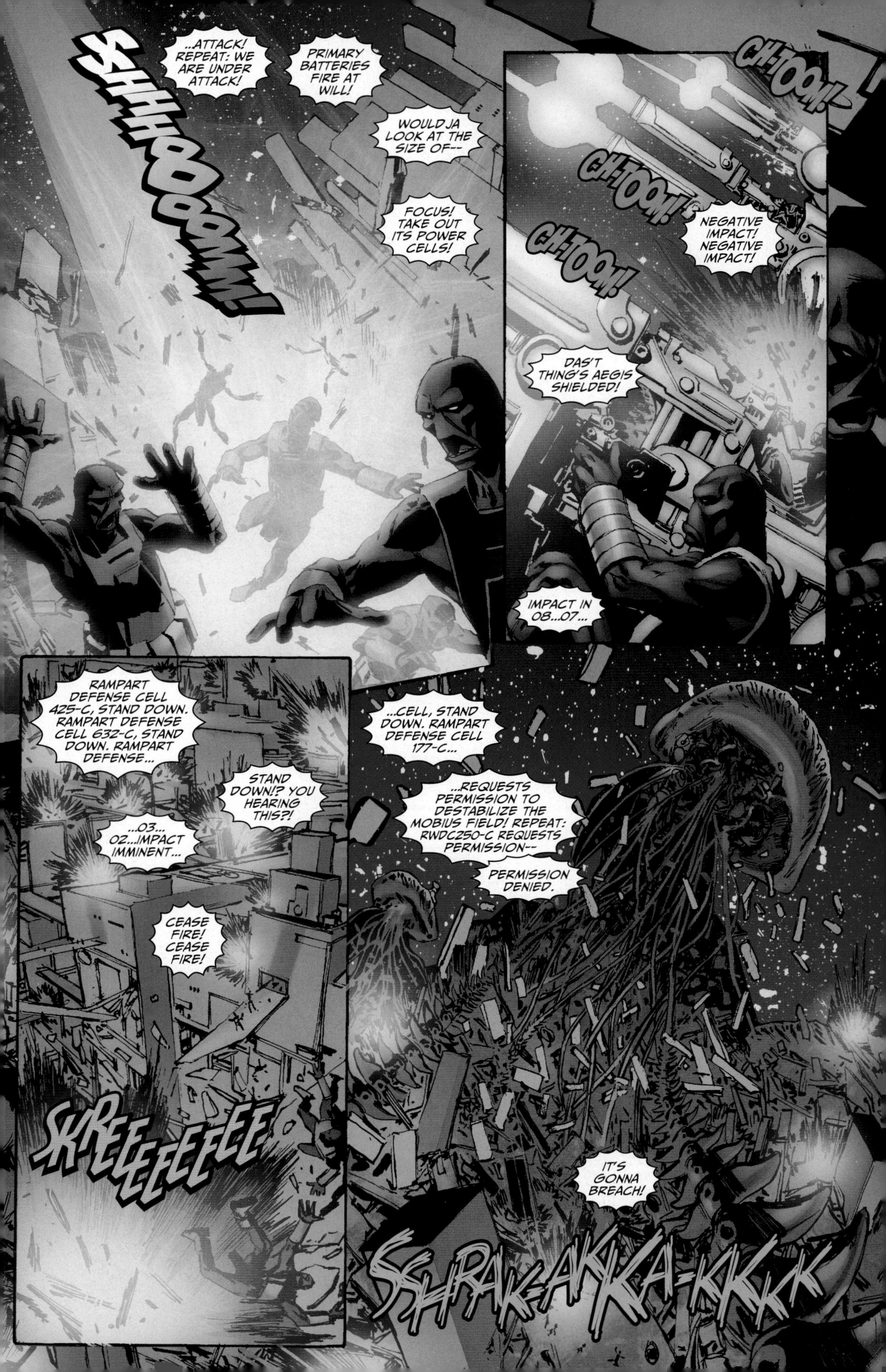
SSHHHOOOOMM!
...ATTACK! REPEAT: WE ARE UNDER ATTACK!
PRIMARY BATTERIES FIRE AT WILL!
WOULD JA LOOK AT THE SIZE OF--
FOCUS! TAKE OUT ITS POWER CELLS!
CH-TOOM!
CH-TOOM!
CH-TOOM!
NEGATIVE IMPACT! NEGATIVE IMPACT!
DAS'T THING'S AEGIS SHIELDED!
IMPACT IN 08...07...
RAMPART DEFENSE CELL 425-C, STAND DOWN. RAMPART DEFENSE CELL 632-C, STAND DOWN. RAMPART DEFENSE...
STAND DOWN!? YOU HEARING THIS?!
...03... 02...IMPACT IMMINENT...
CEASE FIRE! CEASE FIRE!
SKREEEEEEEE
...CELL, STAND DOWN. RAMPART DEFENSE CELL 177-C...
...REQUESTS PERMISSION TO DESTABILIZE THE MOBIUS FIELD! REPEAT: RWDC250-C REQUESTS PERMISSION--
PERMISSION DENIED.
IT'S GONNA BREACH!
SSHRAK-AKKA-KKKK

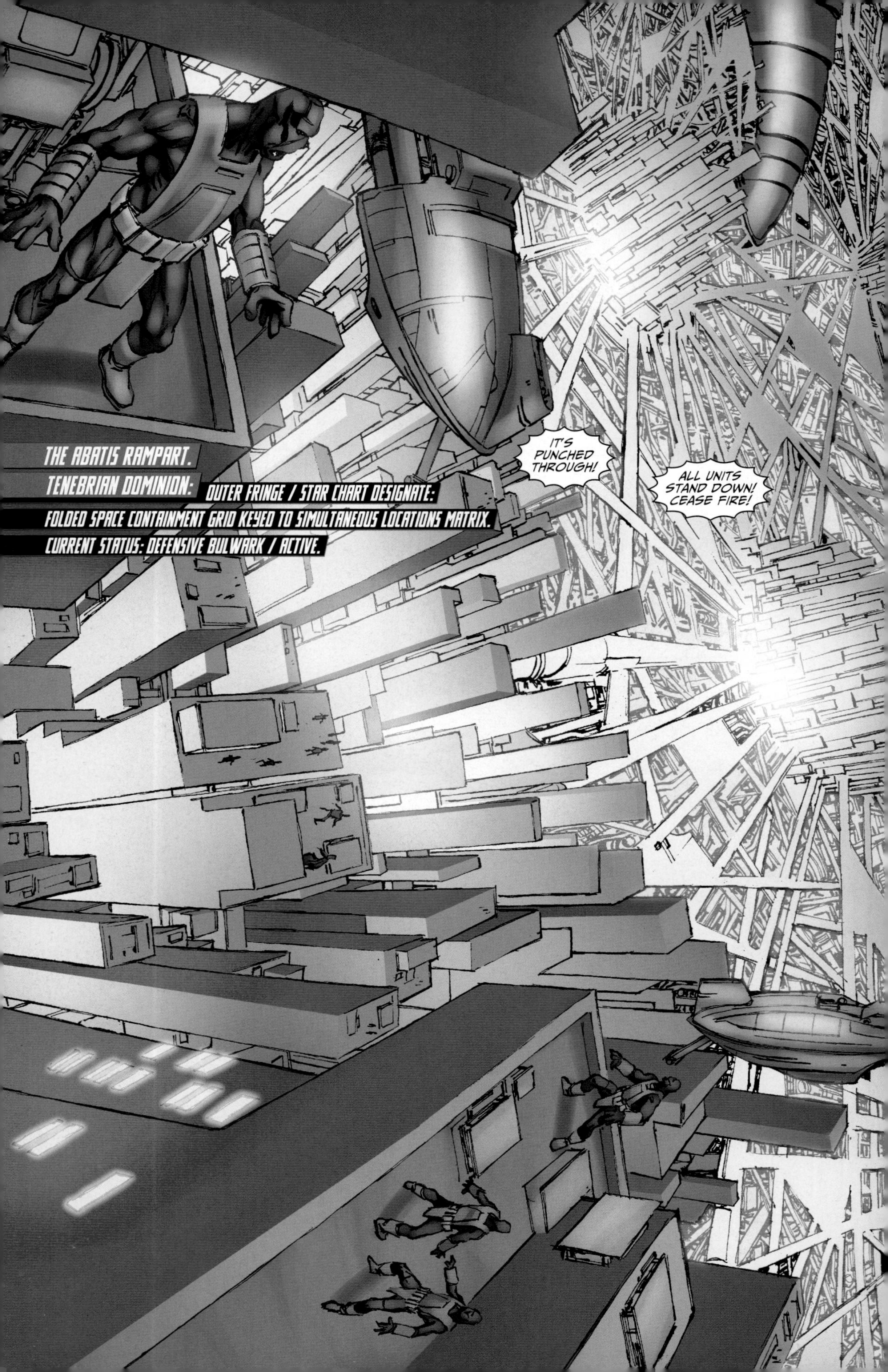
THE ABATIS RAMPART.
TENEBRIAN DOMINION: OUTER FRINGE / STAR CHART DESIGNATE:
FOLDED SPACE CONTAINMENT GRID KEYED TO SIMULTANEOUS LOCATIONS MATRIX.
CURRENT STATUS: DEFENSIVE BULWARK / ACTIVE.
IT'S PUNCHED THROUGH!
ALL UNITS STAND DOWN! CEASE FIRE!

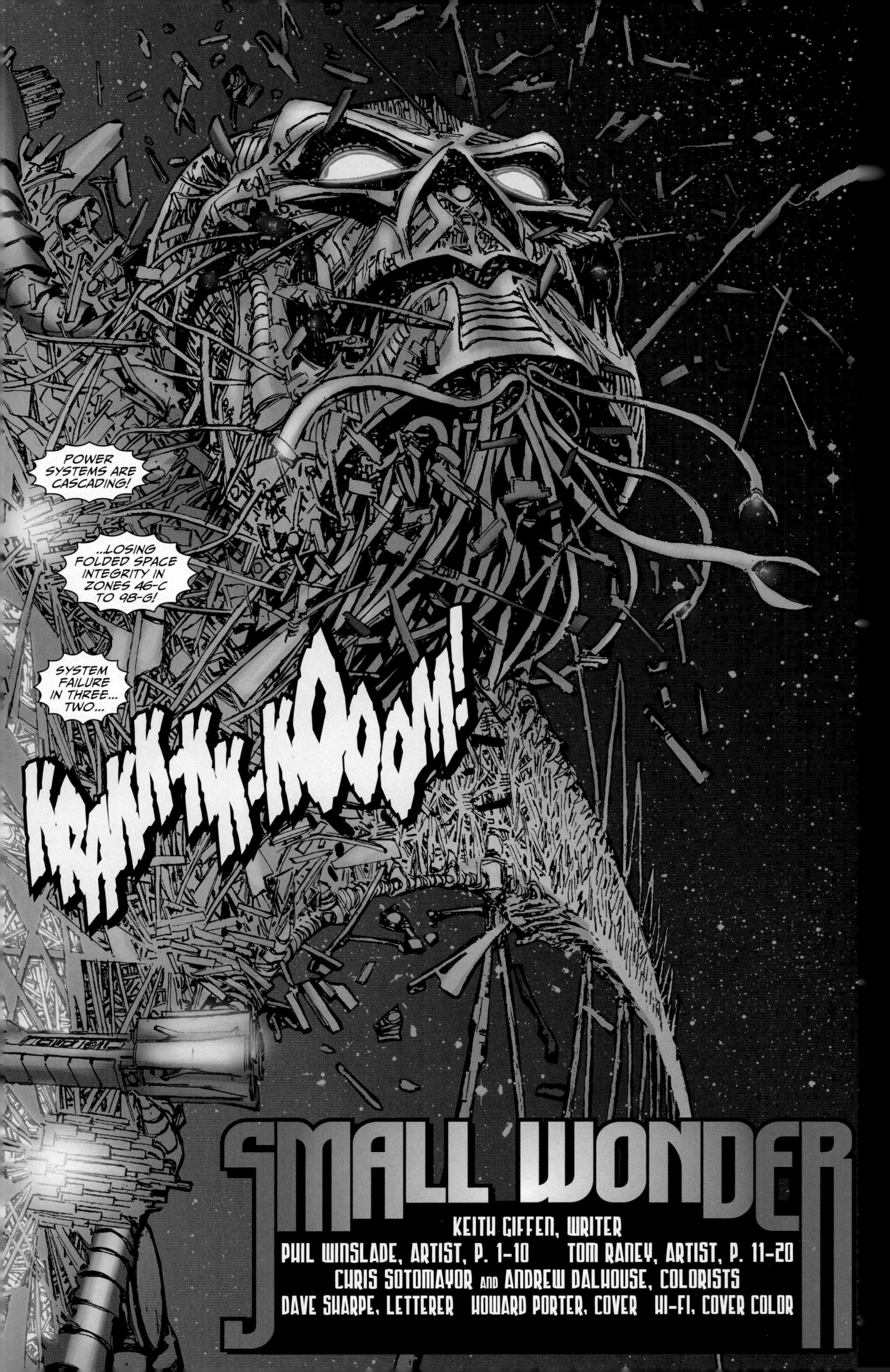
POWER SYSTEMS ARE CASCADING!
...LOSING FOLDED SPACE INTEGRITY IN ZONES 46-C TO 98-G!
SYSTEM FAILURE IN THREE... TWO...
KRAKK-KK-KOOOM!
SMALL WONDER
KEITH GIFFEN, WRITER
PHIL WINSLADE, ARTIST, P. 1-10 TOM RANEY, ARTIST, P. 11-20
CHRIS SOTOMAYOR AND ANDREW DALHOUSE, COLORISTS
DAVE SHARPE, LETTERER HOWARD PORTER, COVER HI-FI, COVER COLOR

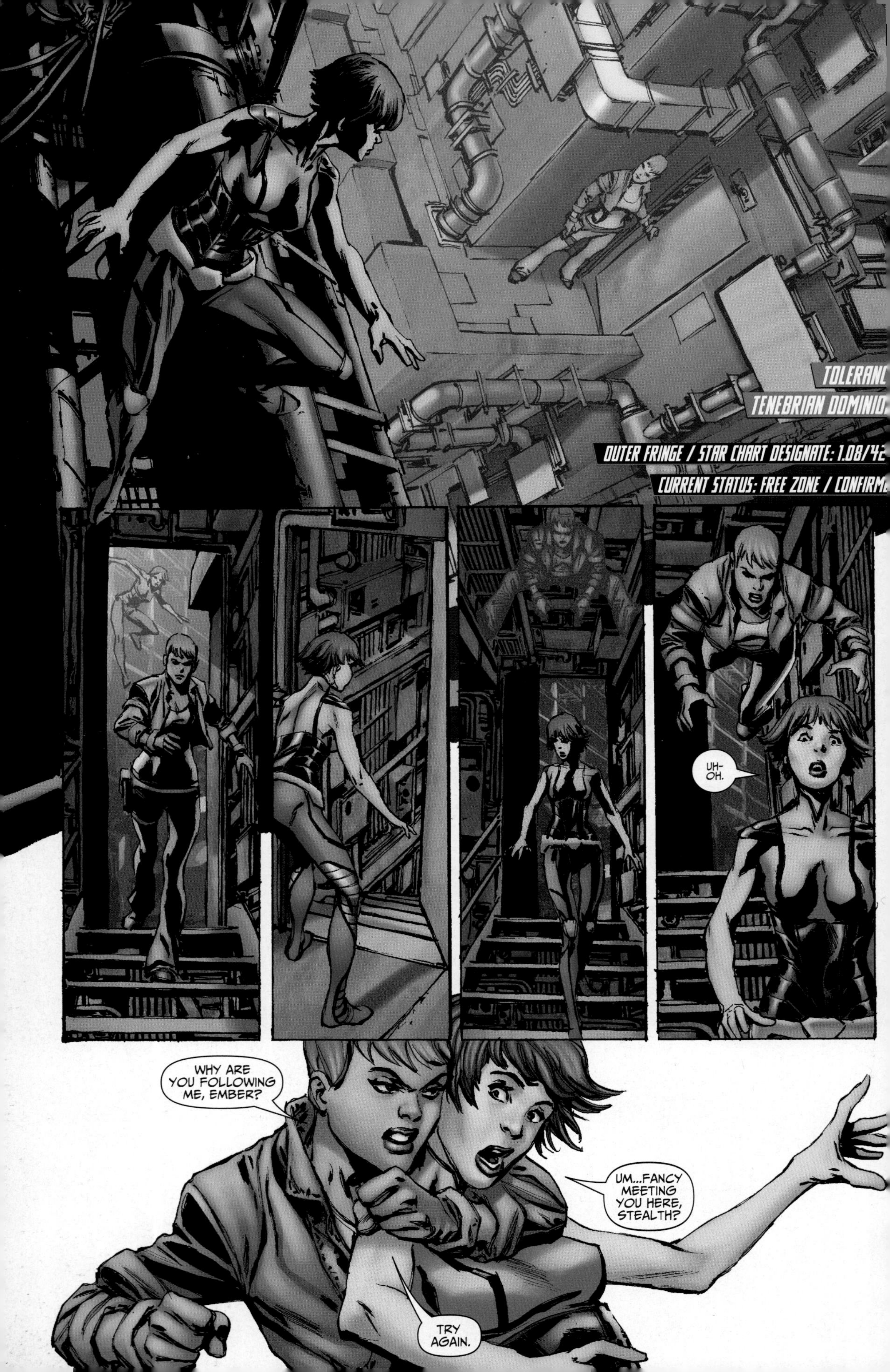

TOLERANC
TENEBRIAN DOMINIO
OUTER FRINGE / STAR CHART DESIGNATE: 1.08/42
CURRENT STATUS: FREE ZONE / CONFIRM
UH-OH.
WHY ARE YOU FOLLOWING ME, EMBER?
UM...FANCY MEETING YOU HERE, STEALTH?
TRY AGAIN.

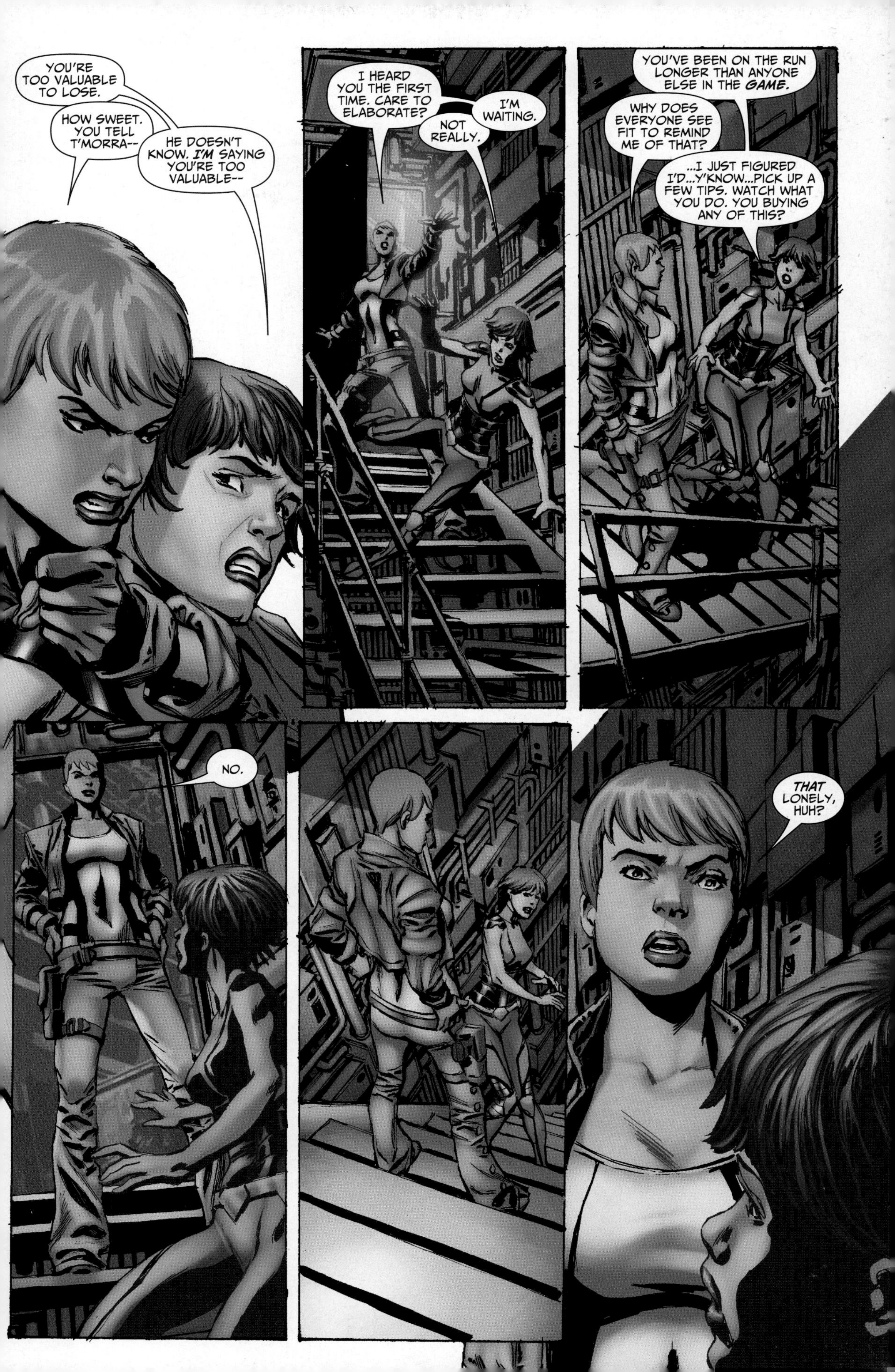
YOU'RE TOO VALUABLE TO LOSE.
HOW SWEET. YOU TELL T'MORRA--
HE DOESN'T KNOW. I'M SAYING YOU'RE TOO VALUABLE--
I HEARD YOU THE FIRST TIME. CARE TO ELABORATE?
NOT REALLY.
I'M WAITING.
YOU'VE BEEN ON THE RUN LONGER THAN ANYONE ELSE IN THE GAME.
WHY DOES EVERYONE SEE FIT TO REMIND ME OF THAT?
...I JUST FIGURED I'D...Y'KNOW...PICK UP A FEW TIPS. WATCH WHAT YOU DO. YOU BUYING ANY OF THIS?
NO.
THAT LONELY, HUH?

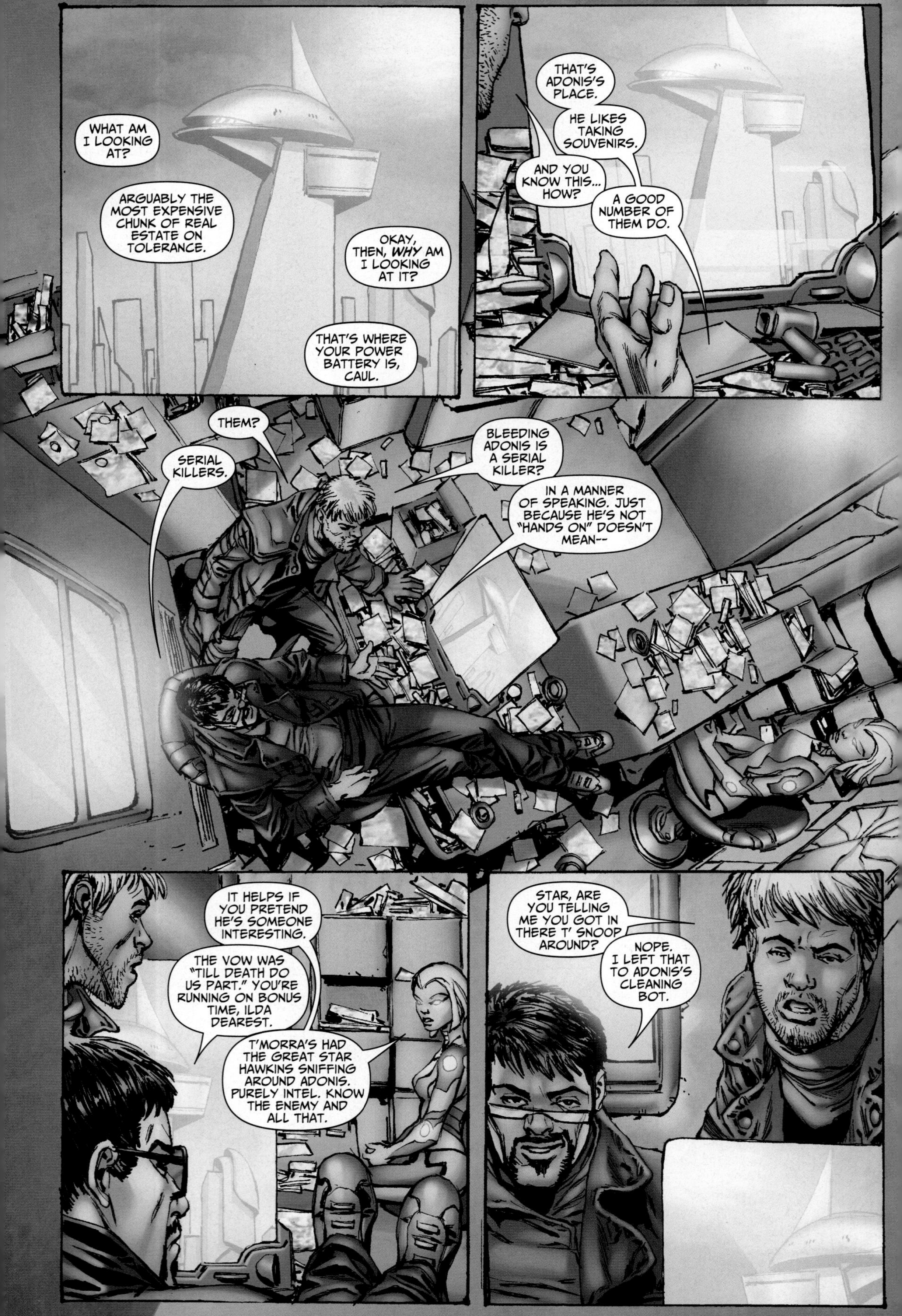
WHAT AM I LOOKING AT?
ARGUABLY THE MOST EXPENSIVE CHUNK OF REAL ESTATE ON TOLERANCE.
OKAY, THEN, WHY AM I LOOKING AT IT?
THAT'S WHERE YOUR POWER BATTERY IS, CAUL.
THAT'S ADONIS'S PLACE.
HE LIKES TAKING SOUVENIRS.
AND YOU KNOW THIS... HOW?
A GOOD NUMBER OF THEM DO.
THEM?
SERIAL KILLERS.
BLEEDING ADONIS IS A SERIAL KILLER?
IN A MANNER OF SPEAKING. JUST BECAUSE HE'S NOT "HANDS ON" DOESN'T MEAN--
IT HELPS IF YOU PRETEND HE'S SOMEONE INTERESTING.
THE VOW WAS "TILL DEATH DO US PART." YOU'RE RUNNING ON BONUS TIME, ILDA DEAREST.
T'MORRA'S HAD THE GREAT STAR HAWKINS SNIFFING AROUND ADONIS. PURELY INTEL. KNOW THE ENEMY AND ALL THAT.
STAR, ARE YOU TELLING ME YOU GOT IN THERE T' SNOOP AROUND?
NOPE. I LEFT THAT TO ADONIS'S CLEANING BOT.

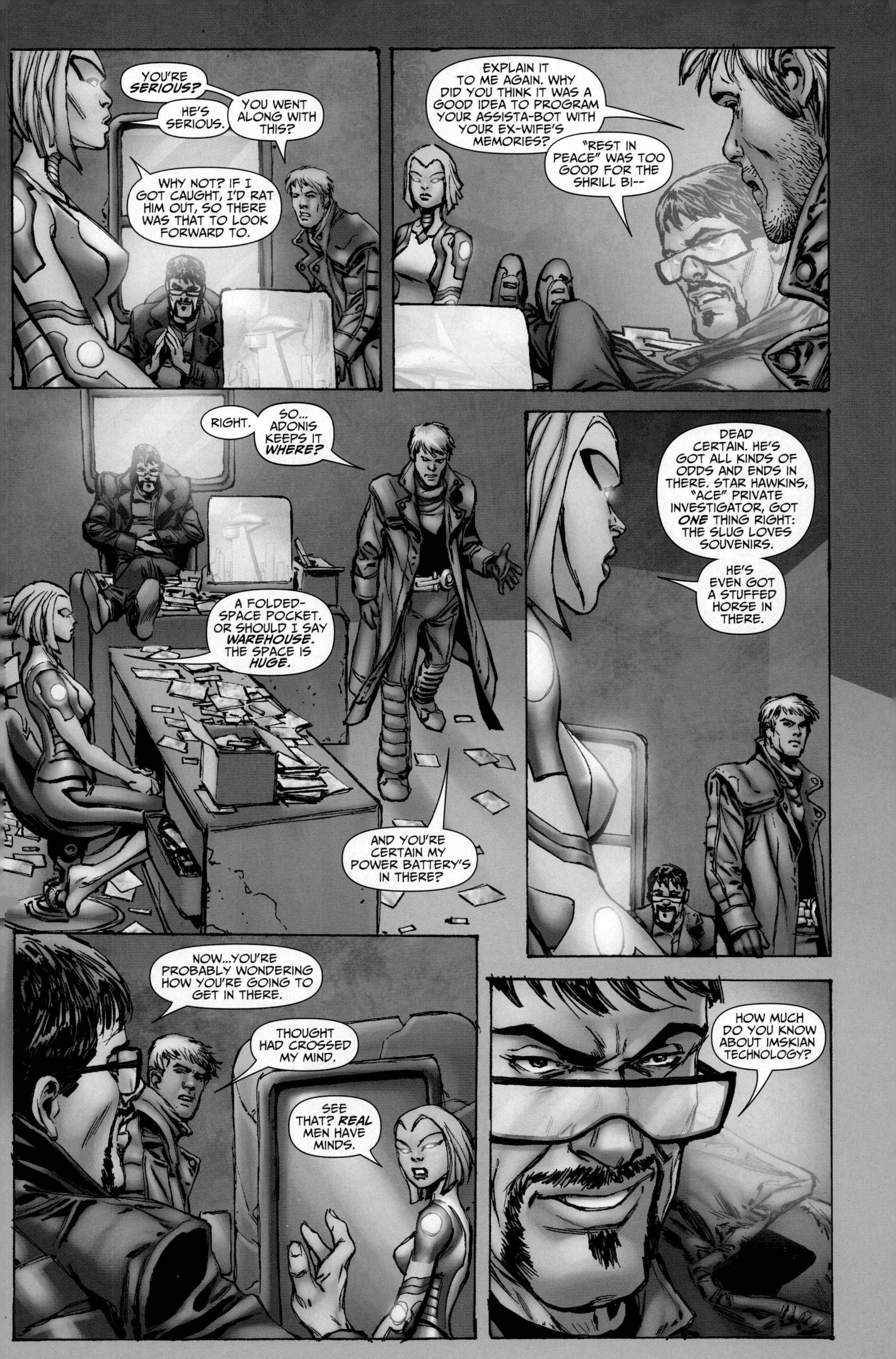
YOU'RE SERIOUS?
HE'S SERIOUS.
YOU WENT ALONG WITH THIS?
WHY NOT? IF I GOT CAUGHT, I'D RAT HIM OUT, SO THERE WAS THAT TO LOOK FORWARD TO.
EXPLAIN IT TO ME AGAIN. WHY DID YOU THINK IT WAS A GOOD IDEA TO PROGRAM YOUR ASSISTA-BOT WITH YOUR EX-WIFE'S MEMORIES?
"REST IN PEACE" WAS TOO GOOD FOR THE SHRILL BI--
RIGHT.
SO... ADONIS KEEPS IT WHERE?
A FOLDED-SPACE POCKET. OR SHOULD I SAY WAREHOUSE. THE SPACE IS HUGE.
AND YOU'RE CERTAIN MY POWER BATTERY'S IN THERE?
DEAD CERTAIN. HE'S GOT ALL KINDS OF ODDS AND ENDS IN THERE. STAR HAWKINS, "ACE" PRIVATE INVESTIGATOR, GOT ONE THING RIGHT: THE SLUG LOVES SOUVENIRS.
HE'S EVEN GOT A STUFFED HORSE IN THERE.
NOW...YOU'RE PROBABLY WONDERING HOW YOU'RE GOING TO GET IN THERE.
THOUGHT HAD CROSSED MY MIND.
SEE THAT? REAL MEN HAVE MINDS.
HOW MUCH DO YOU KNOW ABOUT IMSKIAN TECHNOLOGY?

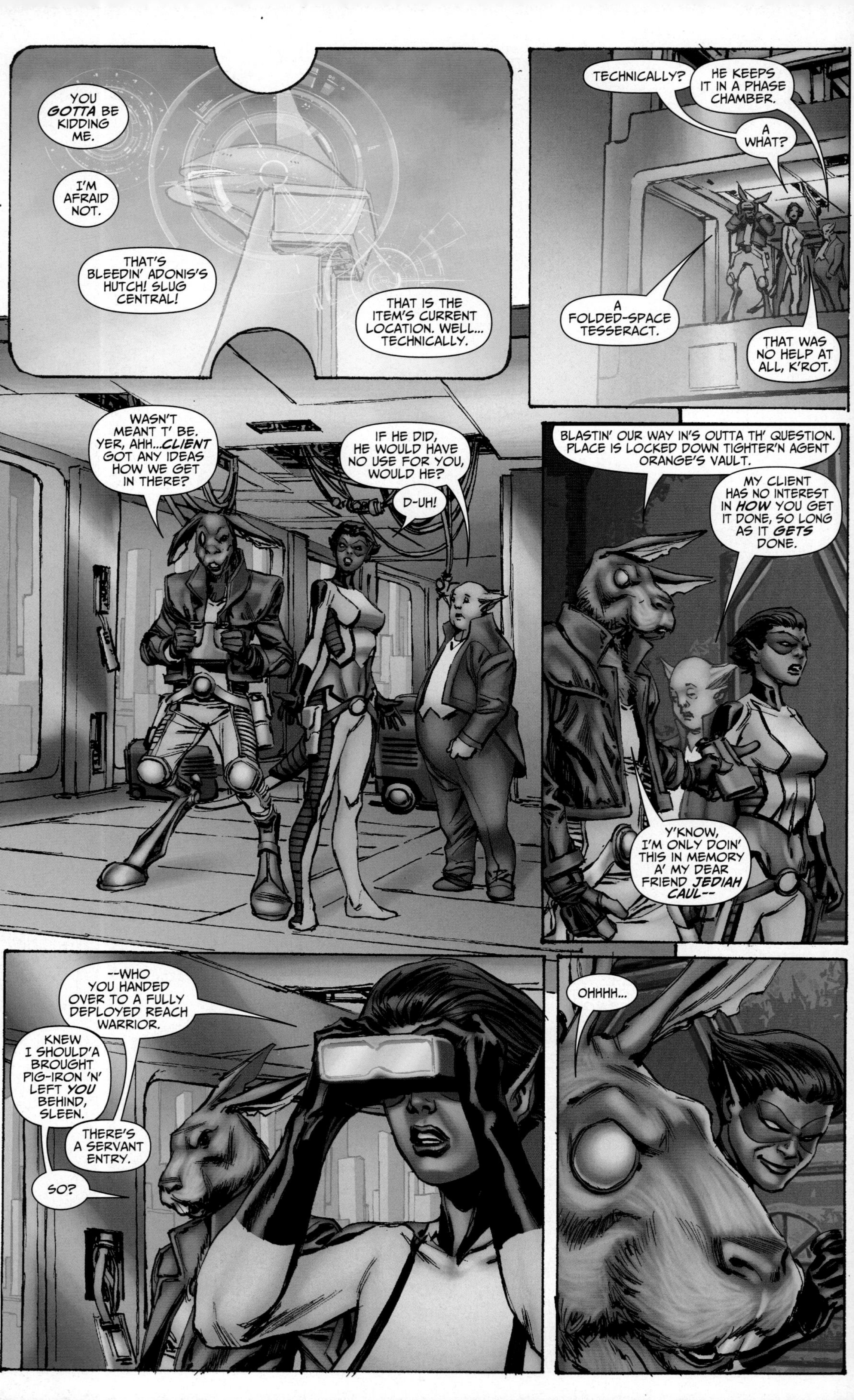
YOU *GOTTA* BE KIDDING ME.
I'M AFRAID NOT.
THAT'S BLEEDIN' ADONIS'S HUTCH! SLUG CENTRAL!
THAT IS THE ITEM'S CURRENT LOCATION. WELL... TECHNICALLY.
TECHNICALLY?
HE KEEPS IT IN A PHASE CHAMBER.
A WHAT?
A FOLDED-SPACE TESSERACT.
THAT WAS NO HELP AT ALL, K'ROT.
WASN'T MEANT T' BE. YER, AHH...*CLIENT* GOT ANY IDEAS HOW WE GET IN THERE?
IF HE DID, HE WOULD HAVE NO USE FOR YOU, WOULD HE?
D-UH!
BLASTIN' OUR WAY IN'S OUTTA TH' QUESTION. PLACE IS LOCKED DOWN TIGHTER'N AGENT ORANGE'S VAULT.
MY CLIENT HAS NO INTEREST IN *HOW* YOU GET IT DONE, SO LONG AS IT *GETS* DONE.
Y'KNOW, I'M ONLY DOIN' THIS IN MEMORY A' MY DEAR FRIEND *JEDIAH CAUL*--
--WHO YOU HANDED OVER TO A FULLY DEPLOYED REACH WARRIOR.
KNEW I SHOULD'A BROUGHT PIG-IRON 'N' LEFT *YOU* BEHIND, SLEEN.
THERE'S A SERVANT ENTRY.
SO?
OHHHH...

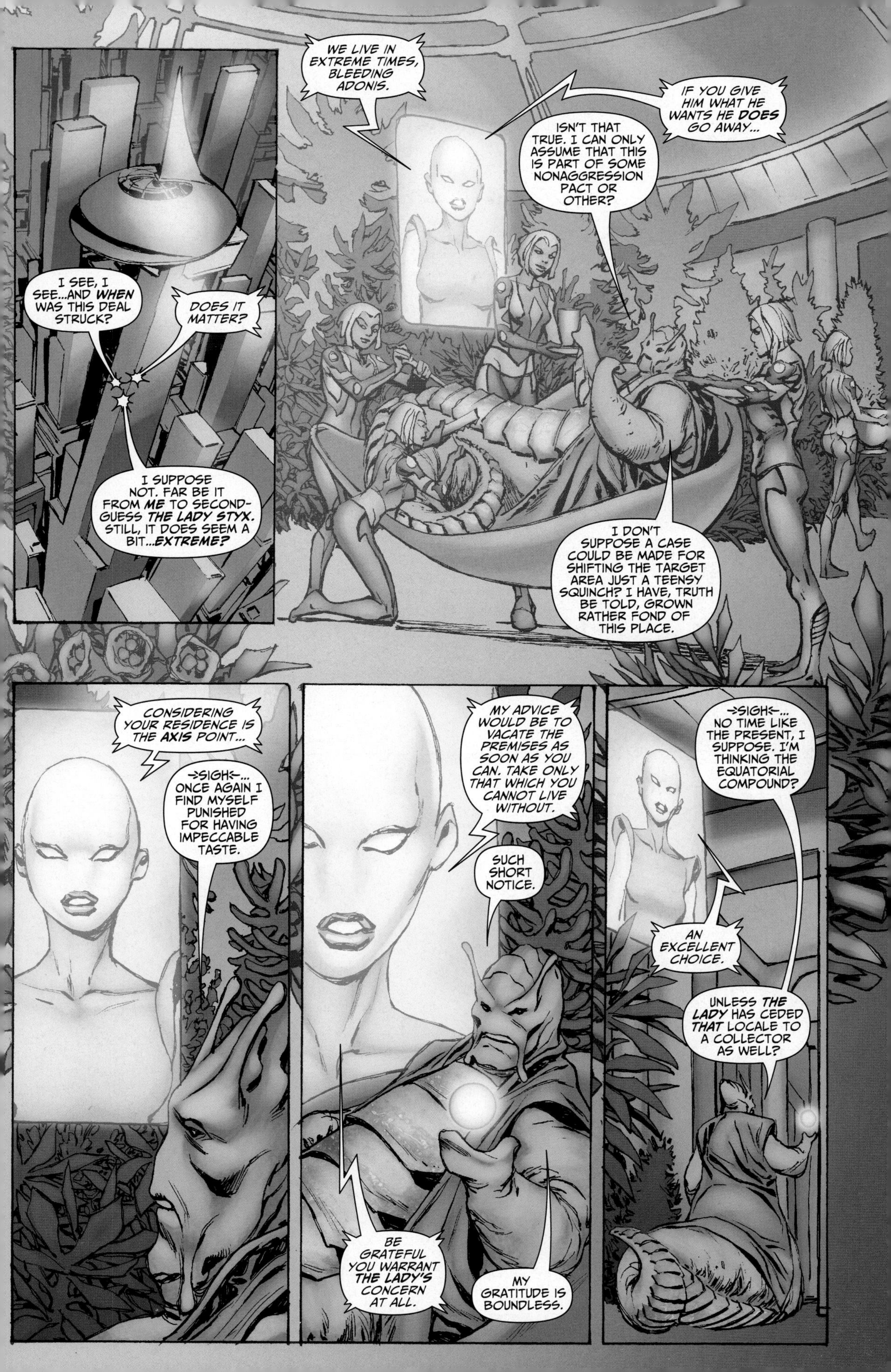

I SEE, I SEE...AND WHEN WAS THIS DEAL STRUCK?
DOES IT MATTER?
I SUPPOSE NOT. FAR BE IT FROM ME TO SECOND-GUESS THE LADY STYX. STILL, IT DOES SEEM A BIT...EXTREME?
WE LIVE IN EXTREME TIMES, BLEEDING ADONIS.
ISN'T THAT TRUE. I CAN ONLY ASSUME THAT THIS IS PART OF SOME NONAGGRESSION PACT OR OTHER?
IF YOU GIVE HIM WHAT HE WANTS HE DOES GO AWAY...
I DON'T SUPPOSE A CASE COULD BE MADE FOR SHIFTING THE TARGET AREA JUST A TEENSY SQUINCH? I HAVE, TRUTH BE TOLD, GROWN RATHER FOND OF THIS PLACE.
CONSIDERING YOUR RESIDENCE IS THE AXIS POINT...
>SIGH<... ONCE AGAIN I FIND MYSELF PUNISHED FOR HAVING IMPECCABLE TASTE.
MY ADVICE WOULD BE TO VACATE THE PREMISES AS SOON AS YOU CAN. TAKE ONLY THAT WHICH YOU CANNOT LIVE WITHOUT.
SUCH SHORT NOTICE.
BE GRATEFUL YOU WARRANT THE LADY'S CONCERN AT ALL.
MY GRATITUDE IS BOUNDLESS.
>SIGH<... NO TIME LIKE THE PRESENT, I SUPPOSE. I'M THINKING THE EQUATORIAL COMPOUND?
AN EXCELLENT CHOICE.
UNLESS THE LADY HAS CEDED THAT LOCALE TO A COLLECTOR AS WELL?

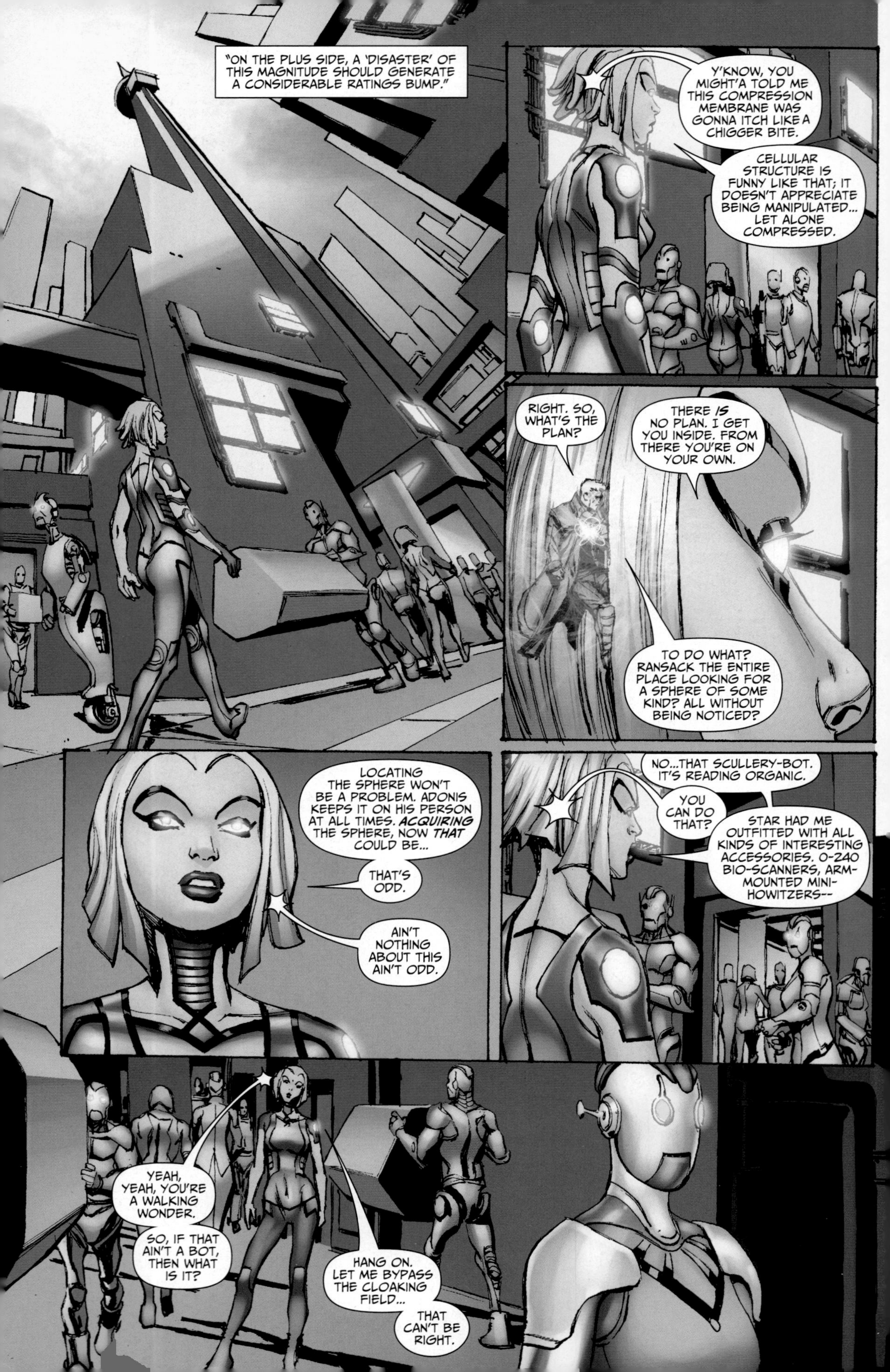
"ON THE PLUS SIDE, A 'DISASTER' OF THIS MAGNITUDE SHOULD GENERATE A CONSIDERABLE RATINGS BUMP."
Y'KNOW, YOU MIGHT'A TOLD ME THIS COMPRESSION MEMBRANE WAS GONNA ITCH LIKE A CHIGGER BITE.
CELLULAR STRUCTURE IS FUNNY LIKE THAT; IT DOESN'T APPRECIATE BEING MANIPULATED... LET ALONE COMPRESSED.
RIGHT. SO, WHAT'S THE PLAN?
THERE *IS* NO PLAN. I GET YOU INSIDE. FROM THERE YOU'RE ON YOUR OWN.
TO DO WHAT? RANSACK THE ENTIRE PLACE LOOKING FOR A SPHERE OF SOME KIND? ALL WITHOUT BEING NOTICED?
LOCATING THE SPHERE WON'T BE A PROBLEM. ADONIS KEEPS IT ON HIS PERSON AT ALL TIMES. *ACQUIRING* THE SPHERE, NOW *THAT* COULD BE...
THAT'S ODD.
AIN'T NOTHING ABOUT THIS AIN'T ODD.
NO...THAT SCULLERY-BOT. IT'S READING ORGANIC.
YOU CAN DO THAT?
STAR HAD ME OUTFITTED WITH ALL KINDS OF INTERESTING ACCESSORIES. O-240 BIO-SCANNERS, ARM-MOUNTED MINI-HOWITZERS--
YEAH, YEAH, YOU'RE A WALKING WONDER.
SO, IF THAT AIN'T A BOT, THEN WHAT IS IT?
HANG ON. LET ME BYPASS THE CLOAKING FIELD...
THAT CAN'T BE RIGHT.

HOW 'BOUT LETTING ME BE THE JUDGE A' THAT?

IT'S READING AS AN OUTSIZED LEPORIDAE OF THE FAMILY LAGOMORPHA.

TRANSLATED?

A GIANT RABBIT.

K'ROT!

COME AGAIN?

GET ME IN CLOSE! I GOT ME A SCORE TO SETTLE!

NOW?!

YOU TWO PLAY NICE NOW.

HAH?

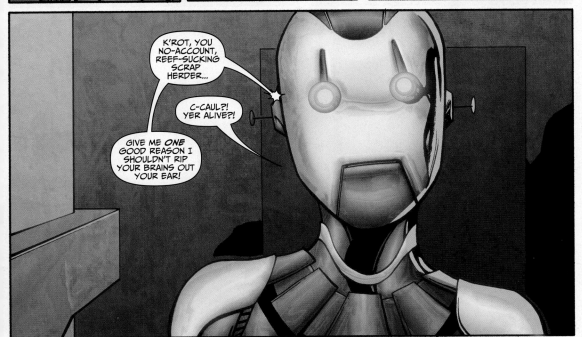

K'ROT, YOU NO-ACCOUNT, REEF-SUCKING SCRAP HERDER...

C-CAUL?! YER ALIVE?!

GIVE ME ONE GOOD REASON I SHOULDN'T RIP YOUR BRAINS OUT YOUR EAR!

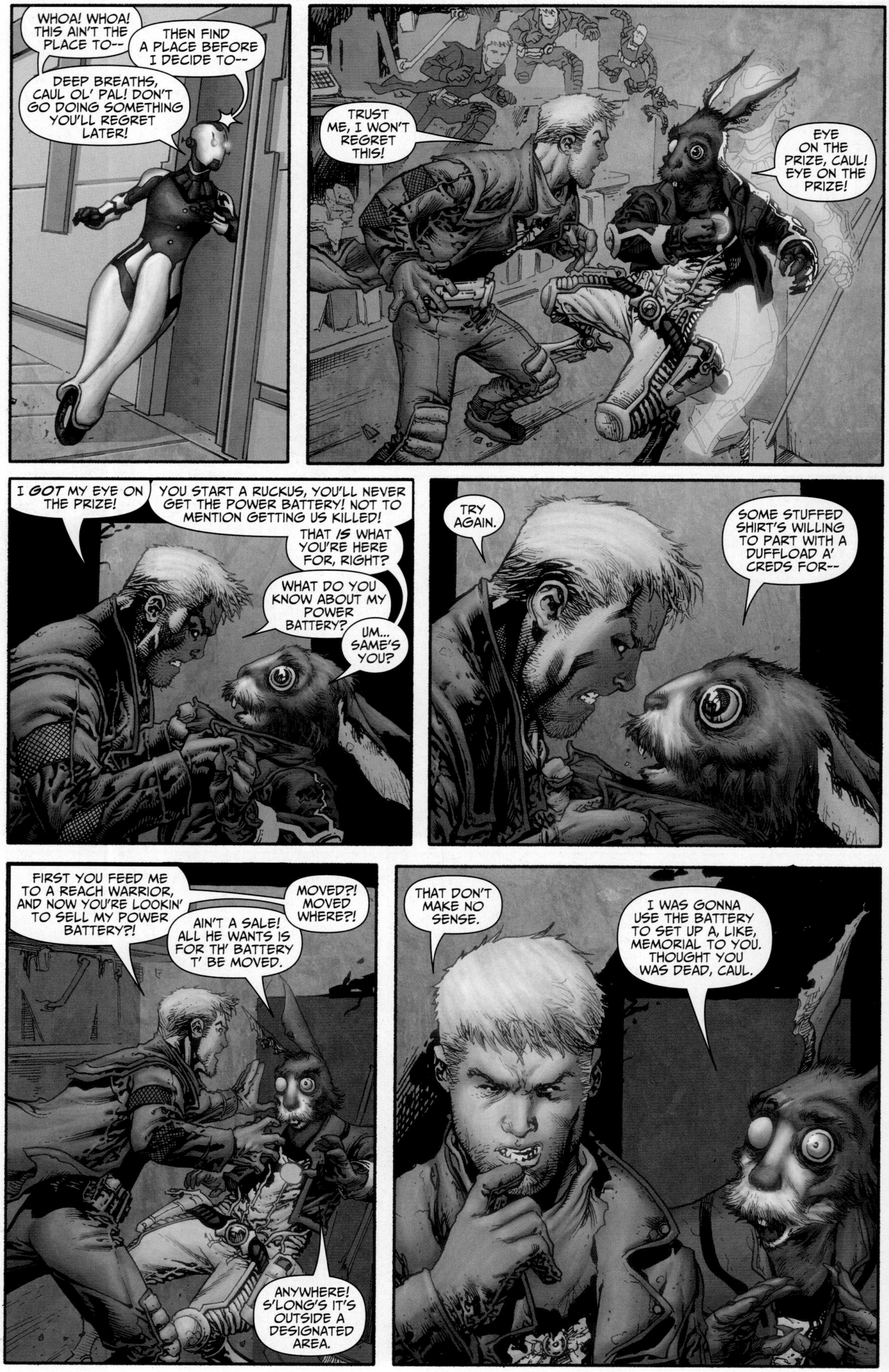
WHOA! WHOA! THIS AIN'T THE PLACE TO--
THEN FIND A PLACE BEFORE I DECIDE TO--
DEEP BREATHS, CAUL OL' PAL! DON'T GO DOING SOMETHING YOU'LL REGRET LATER!
TRUST ME, I WON'T REGRET THIS!
EYE ON THE PRIZE, CAUL! EYE ON THE PRIZE!
I GOT MY EYE ON THE PRIZE!
YOU START A RUCKUS, YOU'LL NEVER GET THE POWER BATTERY! NOT TO MENTION GETTING US KILLED!
THAT IS WHAT YOU'RE HERE FOR, RIGHT?
WHAT DO YOU KNOW ABOUT MY POWER BATTERY?
UM... SAME'S YOU?
TRY AGAIN.
SOME STUFFED SHIRT'S WILLING TO PART WITH A DUFFLOAD A' CREDS FOR--
FIRST YOU FEED ME TO A REACH WARRIOR, AND NOW YOU'RE LOOKIN' TO SELL MY POWER BATTERY?!
AIN'T A SALE! ALL HE WANTS IS FOR TH' BATTERY T' BE MOVED.
MOVED?! MOVED WHERE?!
ANYWHERE! S'LONG'S IT'S OUTSIDE A DESIGNATED AREA.
THAT DON'T MAKE NO SENSE.
I WAS GONNA USE THE BATTERY TO SET UP A, LIKE, MEMORIAL TO YOU. THOUGHT YOU WAS DEAD, CAUL.

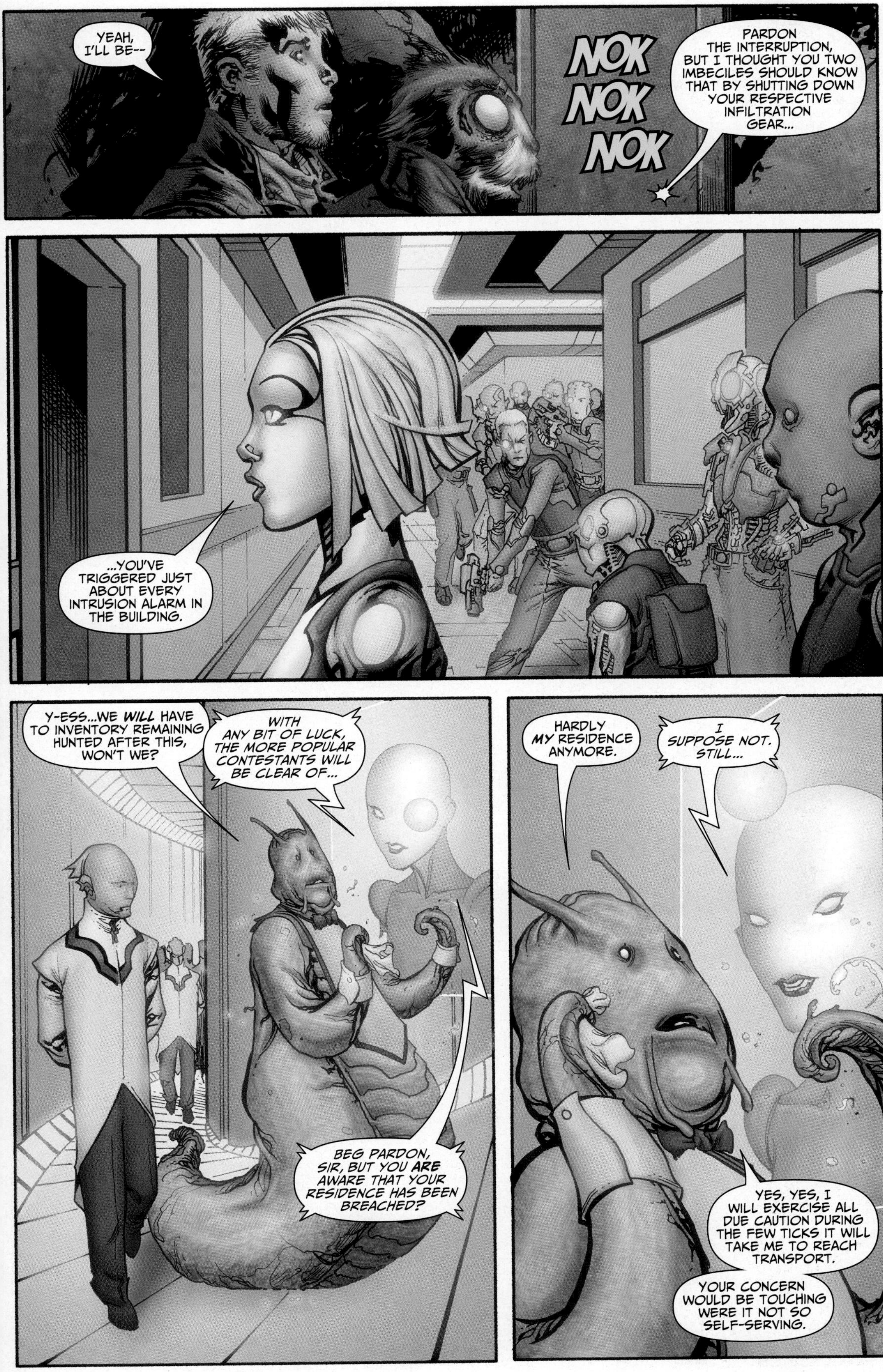
YEAH, I'LL BE--
NOK NOK NOK
PARDON THE INTERRUPTION, BUT I THOUGHT YOU TWO IMBECILES SHOULD KNOW THAT BY SHUTTING DOWN YOUR RESPECTIVE INFILTRATION GEAR...
...YOU'VE TRIGGERED JUST ABOUT EVERY INTRUSION ALARM IN THE BUILDING.
Y-ESS...WE WILL HAVE TO INVENTORY REMAINING HUNTED AFTER THIS, WON'T WE?
WITH ANY BIT OF LUCK, THE MORE POPULAR CONTESTANTS WILL BE CLEAR OF...
BEG PARDON, SIR, BUT YOU ARE AWARE THAT YOUR RESIDENCE HAS BEEN BREACHED?
HARDLY MY RESIDENCE ANYMORE.
I SUPPOSE NOT. STILL...
YES, YES, I WILL EXERCISE ALL DUE CAUTION DURING THE FEW TICKS IT WILL TAKE ME TO REACH TRANSPORT.
YOUR CONCERN WOULD BE TOUCHING WERE IT NOT SO SELF-SERVING.

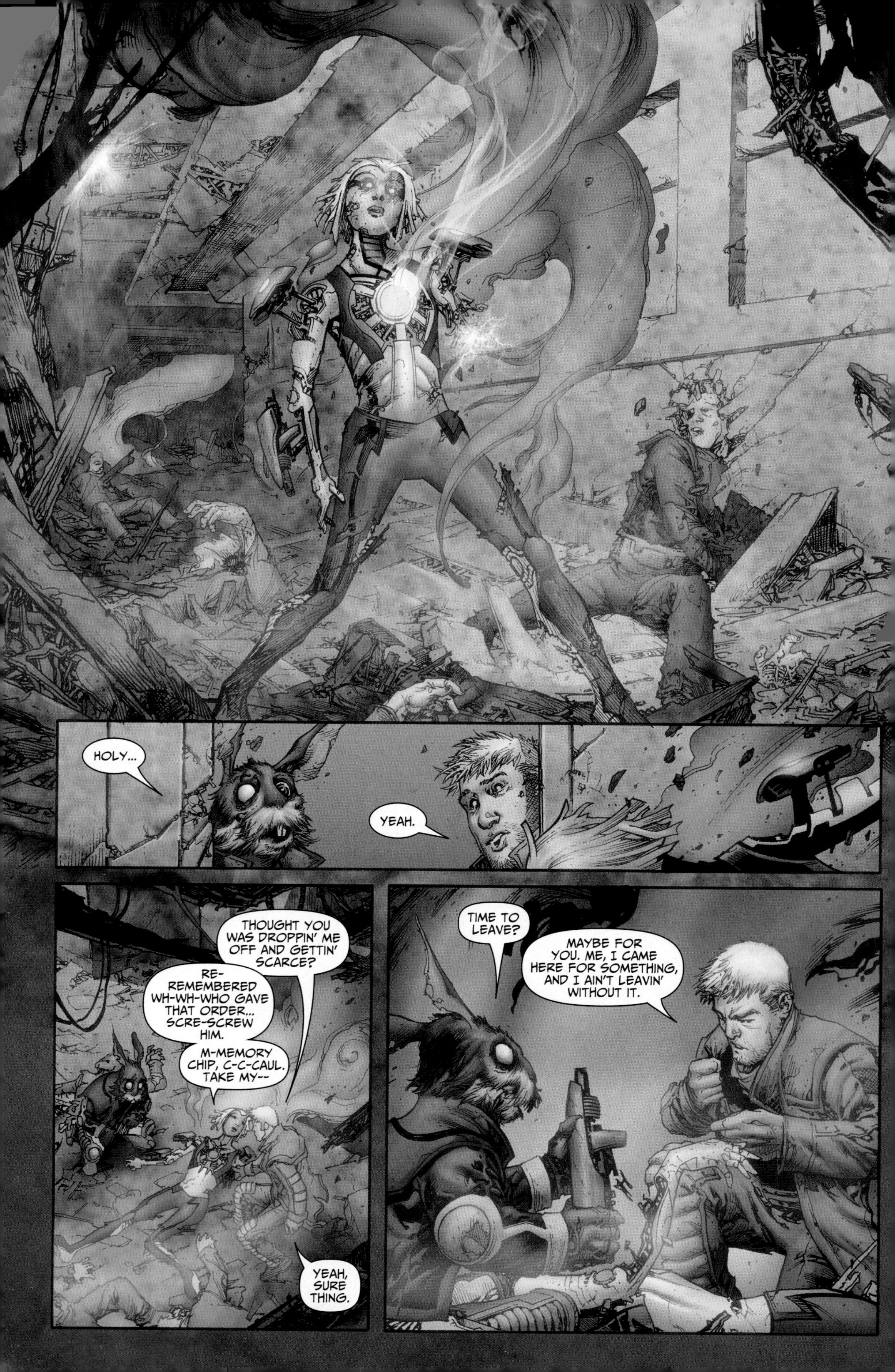
HOLY...
YEAH.
THOUGHT YOU WAS DROPPIN' ME OFF AND GETTIN' SCARCE?
RE-REMEMBERED WH-WH-WHO GAVE THAT ORDER... SCRE-SCREW HIM.
M-MEMORY CHIP, C-C-CAUL. TAKE MY--
YEAH, SURE THING.
TIME TO LEAVE?
MAYBE FOR YOU. ME, I CAME HERE FOR SOMETHING, AND I AIN'T LEAVIN' WITHOUT IT.

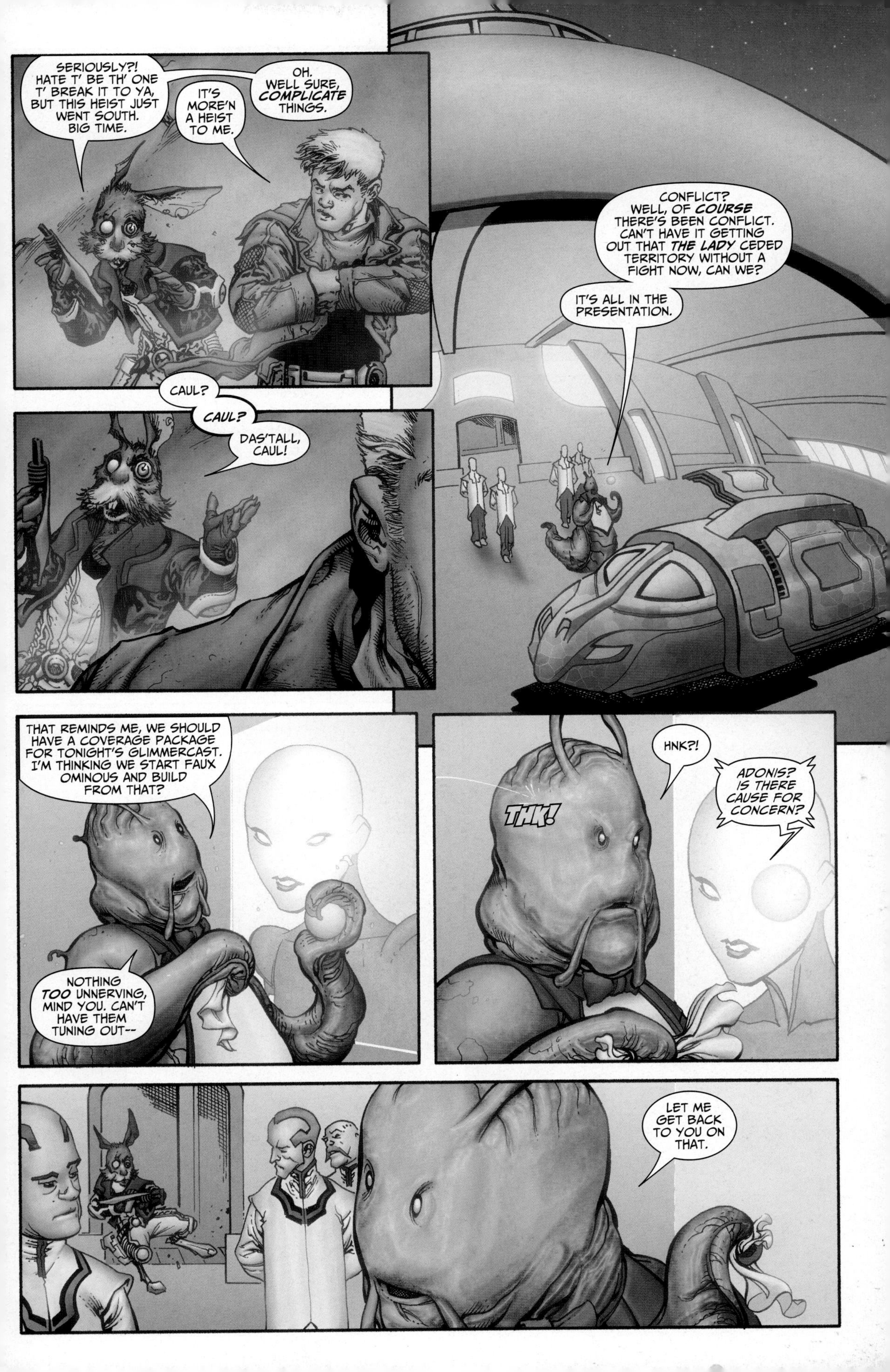
SERIOUSLY?! HATE T' BE TH' ONE T' BREAK IT TO YA, BUT THIS HEIST JUST WENT SOUTH. BIG TIME.
IT'S MORE'N A HEIST TO ME.
OH. WELL SURE, COMPLICATE THINGS.
CONFLICT? WELL, OF COURSE THERE'S BEEN CONFLICT. CAN'T HAVE IT GETTING OUT THAT THE LADY CEDED TERRITORY WITHOUT A FIGHT NOW, CAN WE?
IT'S ALL IN THE PRESENTATION.
CAUL?
CAUL?
DAS'TALL, CAUL!
THAT REMINDS ME, WE SHOULD HAVE A COVERAGE PACKAGE FOR TONIGHT'S GLIMMERCAST. I'M THINKING WE START FAUX OMINOUS AND BUILD FROM THAT?
NOTHING TOO UNNERVING, MIND YOU. CAN'T HAVE THEM TUNING OUT--
THK!
HNK?!
ADONIS? IS THERE CAUSE FOR CONCERN?
LET ME GET BACK TO YOU ON THAT.

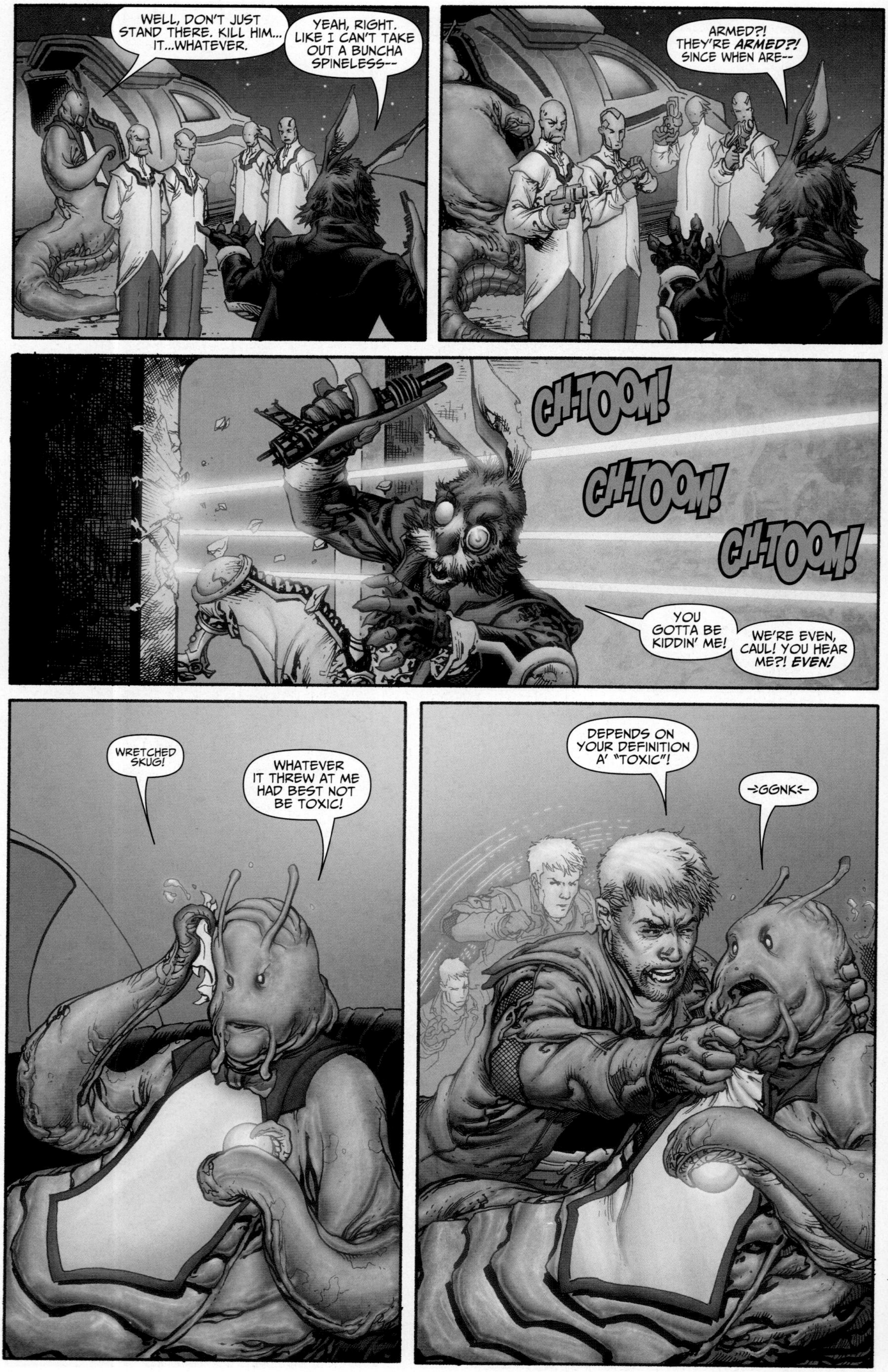
WELL, DON'T JUST STAND THERE. KILL HIM... IT...WHATEVER.
YEAH, RIGHT. LIKE I CAN'T TAKE OUT A BUNCHA SPINELESS--
ARMED?! THEY'RE ARMED?! SINCE WHEN ARE--
CH-TOOM!
CH-TOOM!
CH-TOOM!
YOU GOTTA BE KIDDIN' ME!
WE'RE EVEN, CAUL! YOU HEAR ME?! EVEN!
WRETCHED SKUG!
WHATEVER IT THREW AT ME HAD BEST NOT BE TOXIC!
DEPENDS ON YOUR DEFINITION A' "TOXIC"!
GGNK

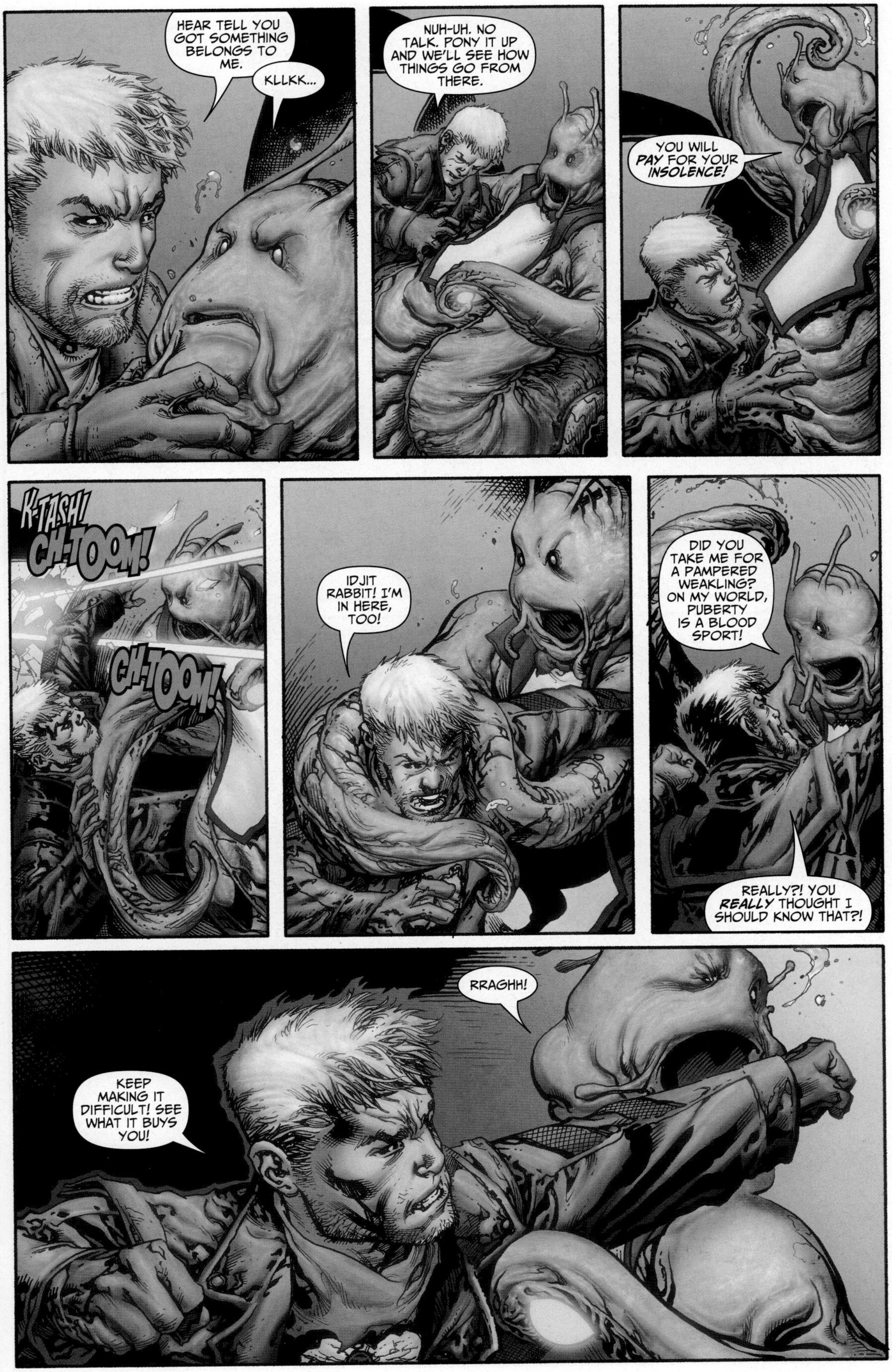
HEAR TELL YOU GOT SOMETHING BELONGS TO ME.
KLLKK...
NUH-UH. NO TALK. PONY IT UP AND WE'LL SEE HOW THINGS GO FROM THERE.
YOU WILL PAY FOR YOUR INSOLENCE!
K-TASH!
CH-TOOM!
CH-TOOM!
IDJIT RABBIT! I'M IN HERE, TOO!
DID YOU TAKE ME FOR A PAMPERED WEAKLING? ON MY WORLD, PUBERTY IS A BLOOD SPORT!
REALLY?! YOU REALLY THOUGHT I SHOULD KNOW THAT?!
RRAGHH!
KEEP MAKING IT DIFFICULT! SEE WHAT IT BUYS YOU!

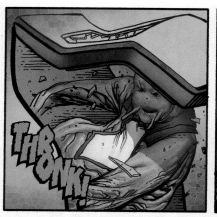

THRONK!

JUST CONSIDER TH A "SUCKS T' B YOU" DAY.

THWUD!

MY POWER BATTERY, SLUG. YOU CAN HAND IT OVER, OR I CAN TAKE IT FROM YOUR DEAD BODY.

NOT PLANNING ON KILLING ME? NOT PLANNING ON KILLING THE AUTHOR OF YOUR MISERY? IS *THAT* WHAT YOU WANT ME TO BELIEVE?

LIKE I COULD GIVE A WHIFF WHAT YOU...

...BELIEVE?

AH, YES. THEN THERE'S THE MATTER OF YOUR TIMING. I REALLY WAS HOPING TO BE WELL CLEAR OF THIS.

THIS? WHAT DO YOU MEAN BY THIS?!

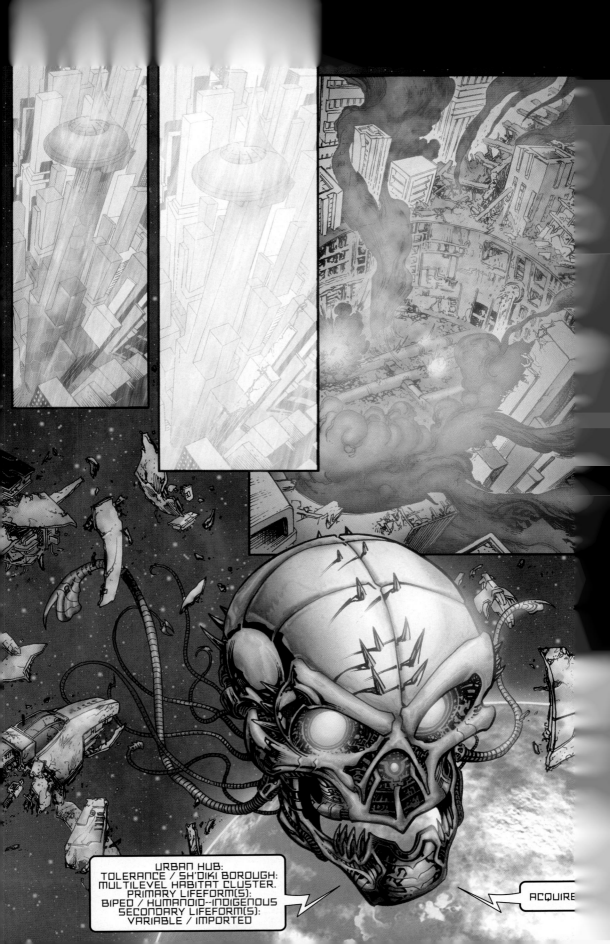

URBAN HUB:
TOLERANCE / SH'DIKI BOROUGH:
MULTILEVEL HABITAT CLUSTER.
PRIMARY LIFEFORM(S):
BIPED / HUMANOID--INDIGENOUS
SECONDARY LIFEFORM(S):
VARIABLE / IMPORTED

ACQUIRE

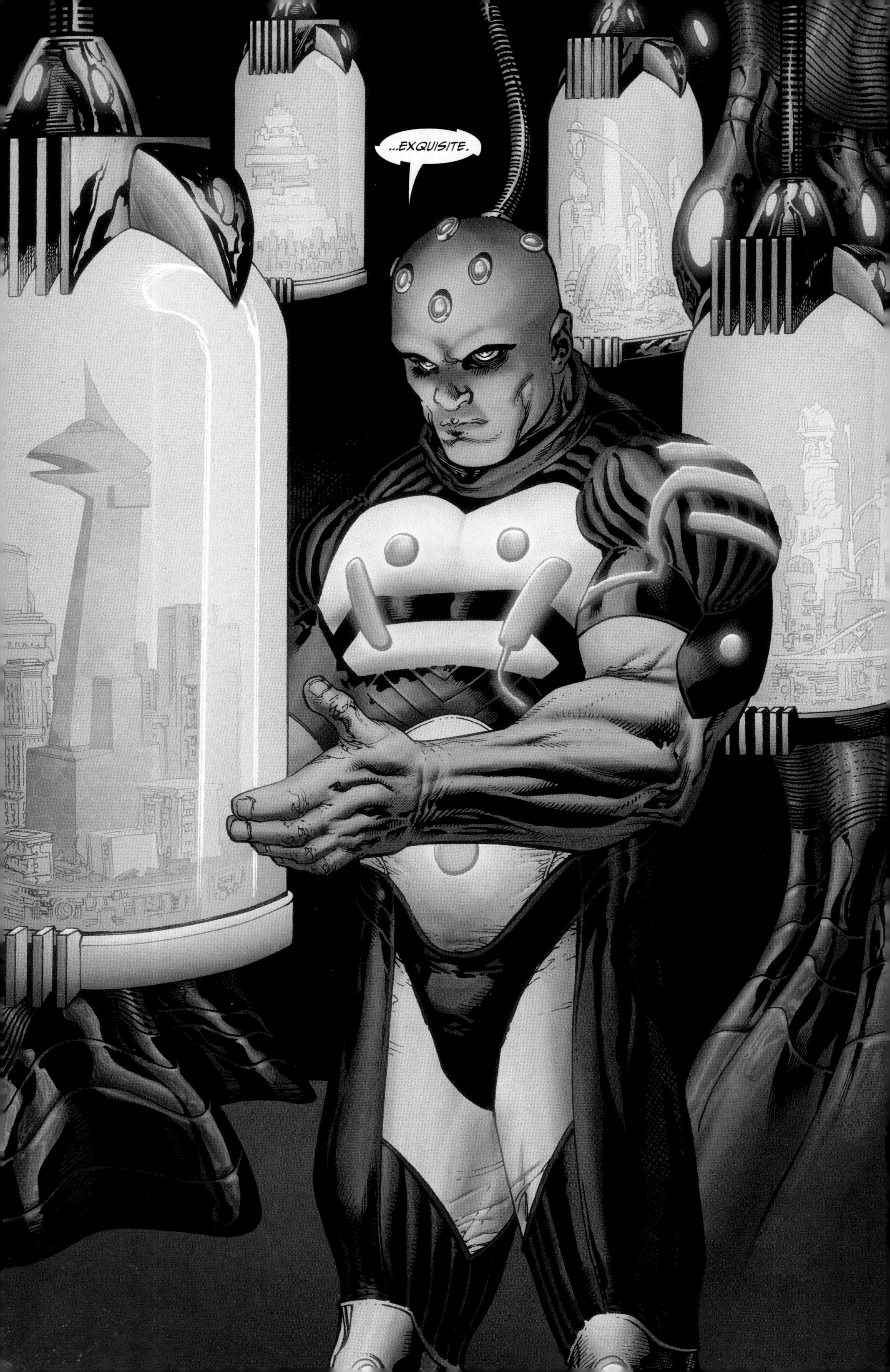
...EXQUISITE.

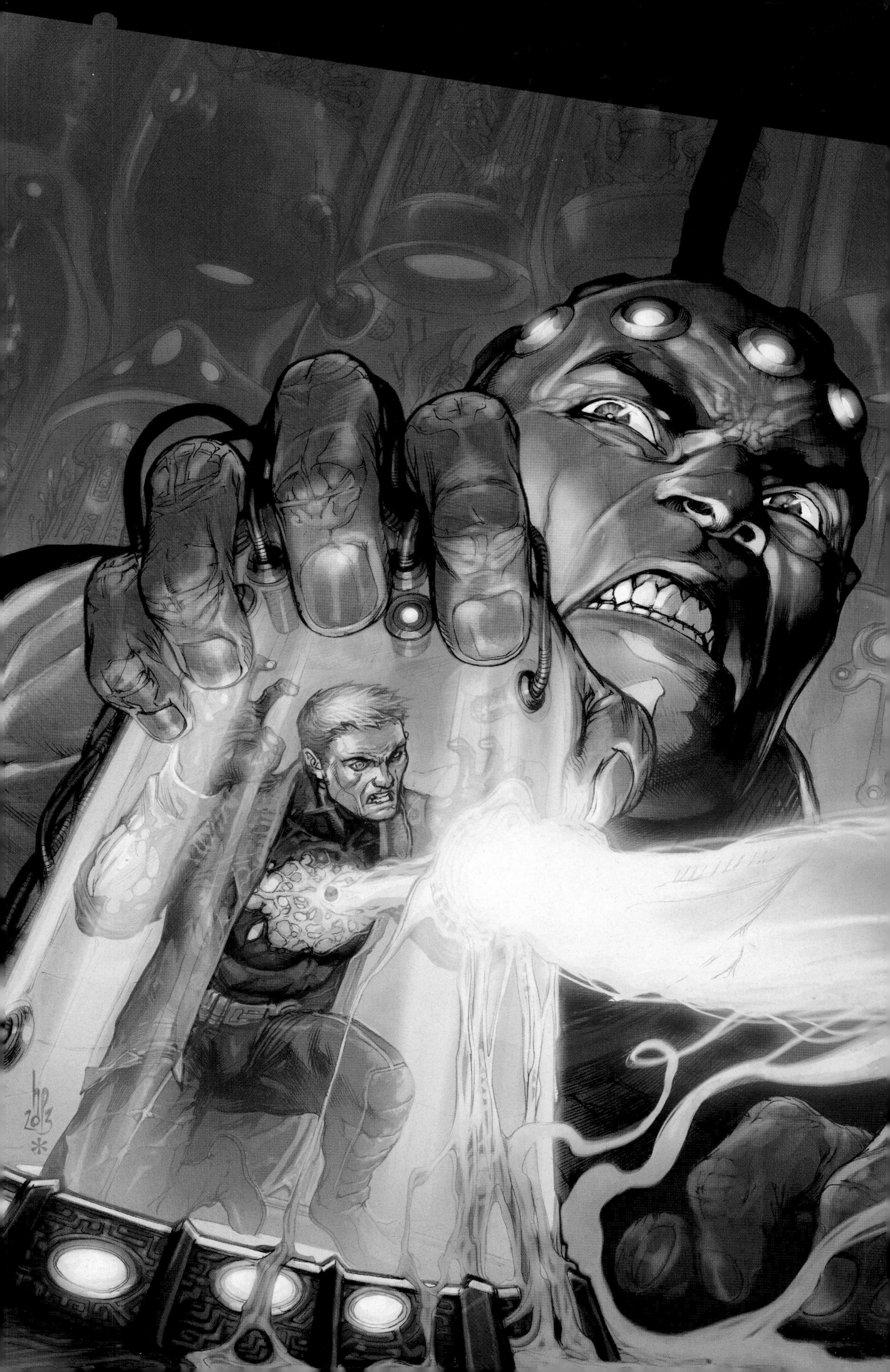

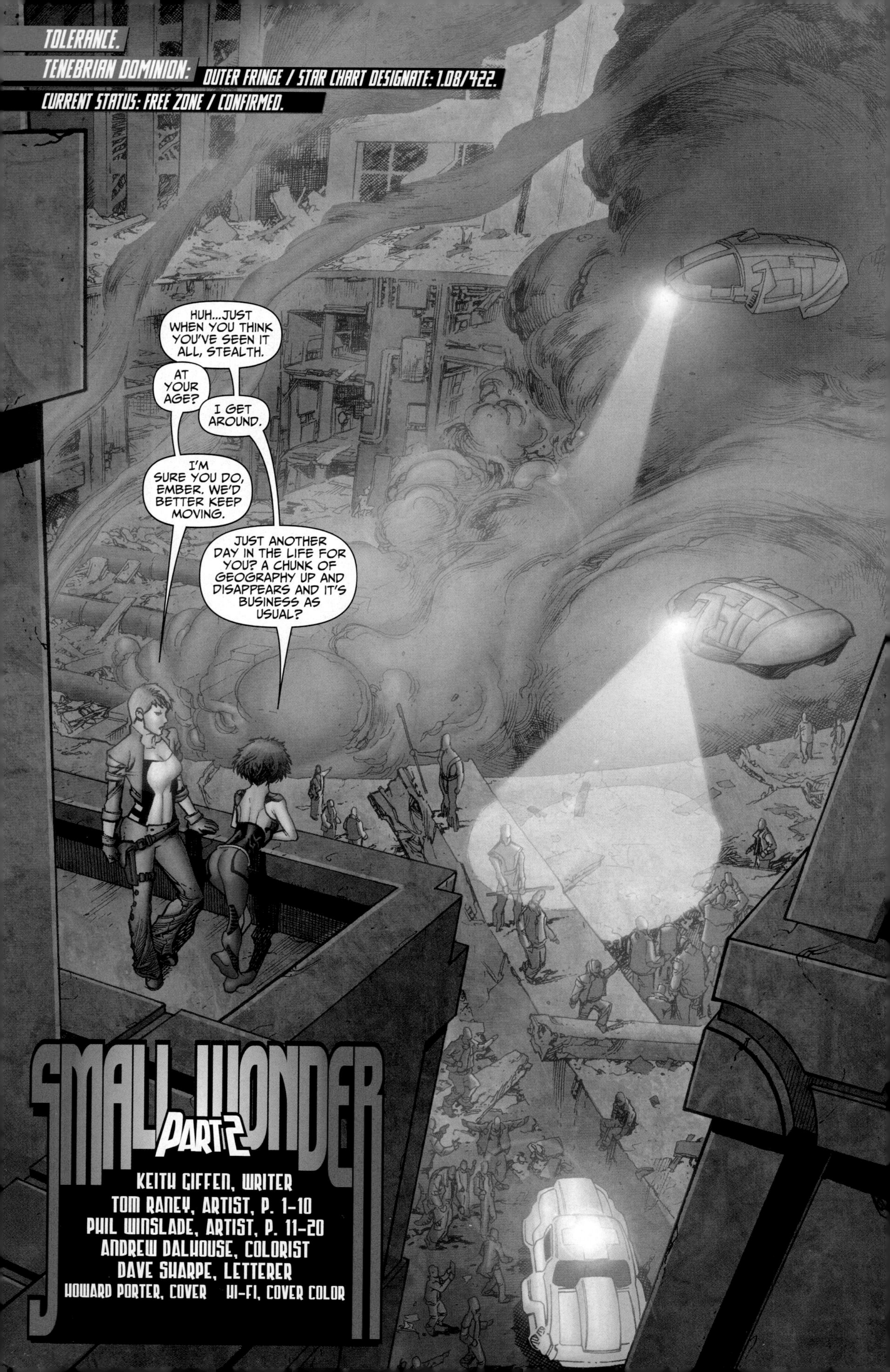

TOLERANCE.
TENEBRIAN DOMINION: OUTER FRINGE / STAR CHART DESIGNATE: 1.08/422.
CURRENT STATUS: FREE ZONE / CONFIRMED.
HUH...JUST WHEN YOU THINK YOU'VE SEEN IT ALL, STEALTH.
AT YOUR AGE?
I GET AROUND.
I'M SURE YOU DO, EMBER. WE'D BETTER KEEP MOVING.
JUST ANOTHER DAY IN THE LIFE FOR YOU? A CHUNK OF GEOGRAPHY UP AND DISAPPEARS AND IT'S BUSINESS AS USUAL?
SMALL WONDER
PART 2
KEITH GIFFEN, WRITER
TOM RANEY, ARTIST, P. 1-10
PHIL WINSLADE, ARTIST, P. 11-20
ANDREW DALHOUSE, COLORIST
DAVE SHARPE, LETTERER
HOWARD PORTER, COVER HI-FI, COVER COLOR

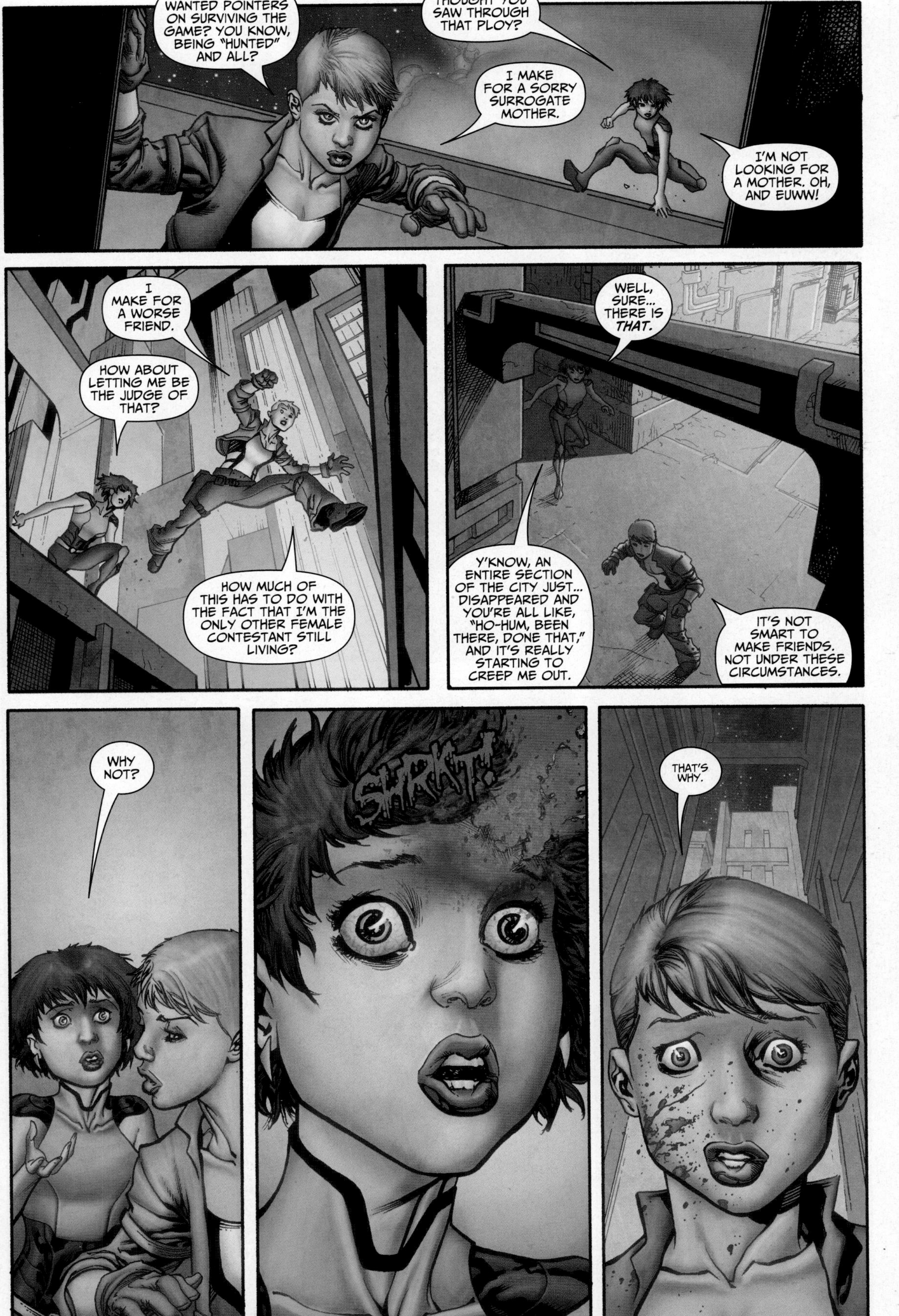
THOUGHT YOU WANTED POINTERS ON SURVIVING THE GAME? YOU KNOW, BEING "HUNTED" AND ALL?
THOUGHT YOU SAW THROUGH THAT PLOY?
I MAKE FOR A SORRY SURROGATE MOTHER.
I'M NOT LOOKING FOR A MOTHER. OH, AND EUWW!
I MAKE FOR A WORSE FRIEND.
HOW ABOUT LETTING ME BE THE JUDGE OF THAT?
HOW MUCH OF THIS HAS TO DO WITH THE FACT THAT I'M THE ONLY OTHER FEMALE CONTESTANT STILL LIVING?
WELL, SURE... THERE IS *THAT.*
Y'KNOW, AN ENTIRE SECTION OF THE CITY JUST... DISAPPEARED AND YOU'RE ALL LIKE, "HO-HUM, BEEN THERE, DONE THAT," AND IT'S REALLY STARTING TO CREEP ME OUT.
IT'S NOT SMART TO MAKE FRIENDS. NOT UNDER THESE CIRCUMSTANCES.
WHY NOT?
SHRKT!
THAT'S WHY.

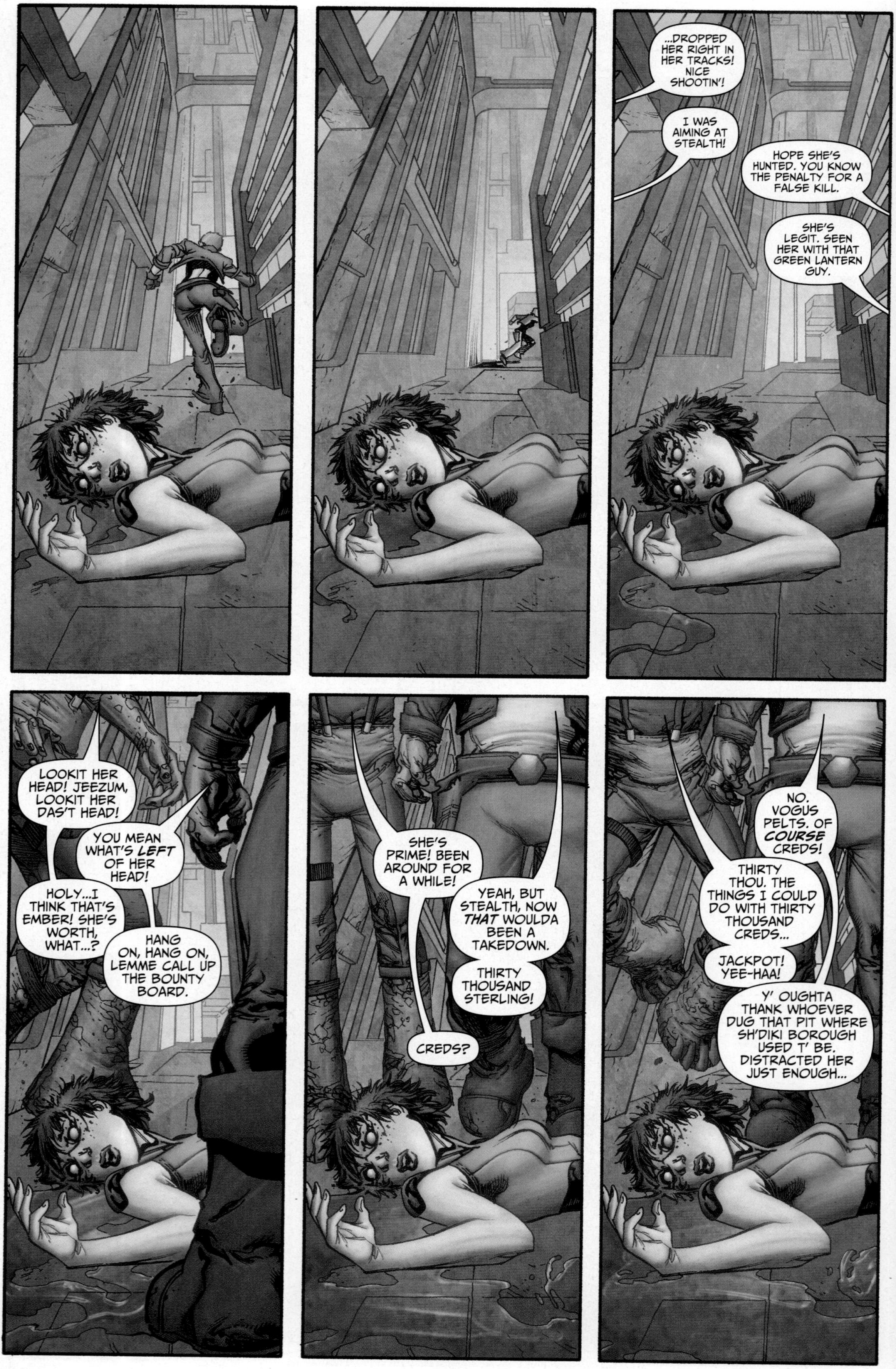
...DROPPED HER RIGHT IN HER TRACKS! NICE SHOOTIN'!
I WAS AIMING AT STEALTH!
HOPE SHE'S HUNTED. YOU KNOW THE PENALTY FOR A FALSE KILL.
SHE'S LEGIT. SEEN HER WITH THAT GREEN LANTERN GUY.
LOOKIT HER HEAD! JEEZUM, LOOKIT HER DAS'T HEAD!
YOU MEAN WHAT'S *LEFT* OF HER HEAD!
HOLY...I THINK THAT'S EMBER! SHE'S WORTH, WHAT...?
HANG ON, HANG ON, LEMME CALL UP THE BOUNTY BOARD.
SHE'S PRIME! BEEN AROUND FOR A WHILE!
YEAH, BUT STEALTH, NOW *THAT* WOULDA BEEN A TAKEDOWN.
THIRTY THOUSAND STERLING!
CREDS?
NO. VOGUS PELTS. OF *COURSE* CREDS!
THIRTY THOU. THE THINGS I COULD DO WITH THIRTY THOUSAND CREDS...
JACKPOT! YEE-HAA!
Y' OUGHTA THANK WHOEVER DUG THAT PIT WHERE SH'DIKI BOROUGH USED T' BE. DISTRACTED HER JUST ENOUGH...

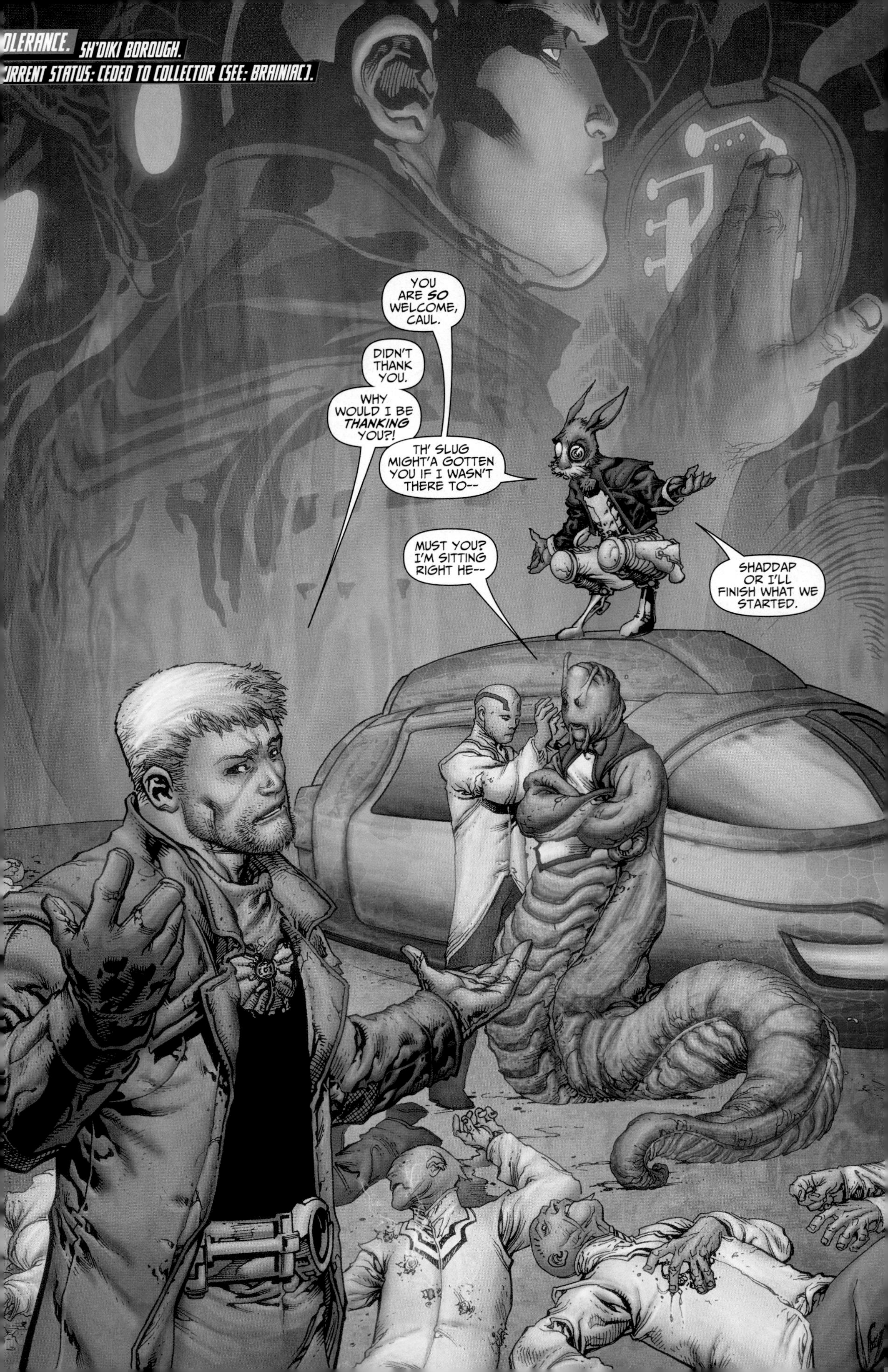
OLERANCE. SH'DIKI BOROUGH.
URRENT STATUS: CEDED TO COLLECTOR (SEE: BRAINIAC).
YOU ARE *SO* WELCOME, CAUL.
DIDN'T THANK YOU.
WHY WOULD I BE *THANKING* YOU?!
TH' SLUG MIGHT'A GOTTEN YOU IF I WASN'T THERE TO--
MUST YOU? I'M SITTING RIGHT HE--
SHADDAP OR I'LL FINISH WHAT WE STARTED.

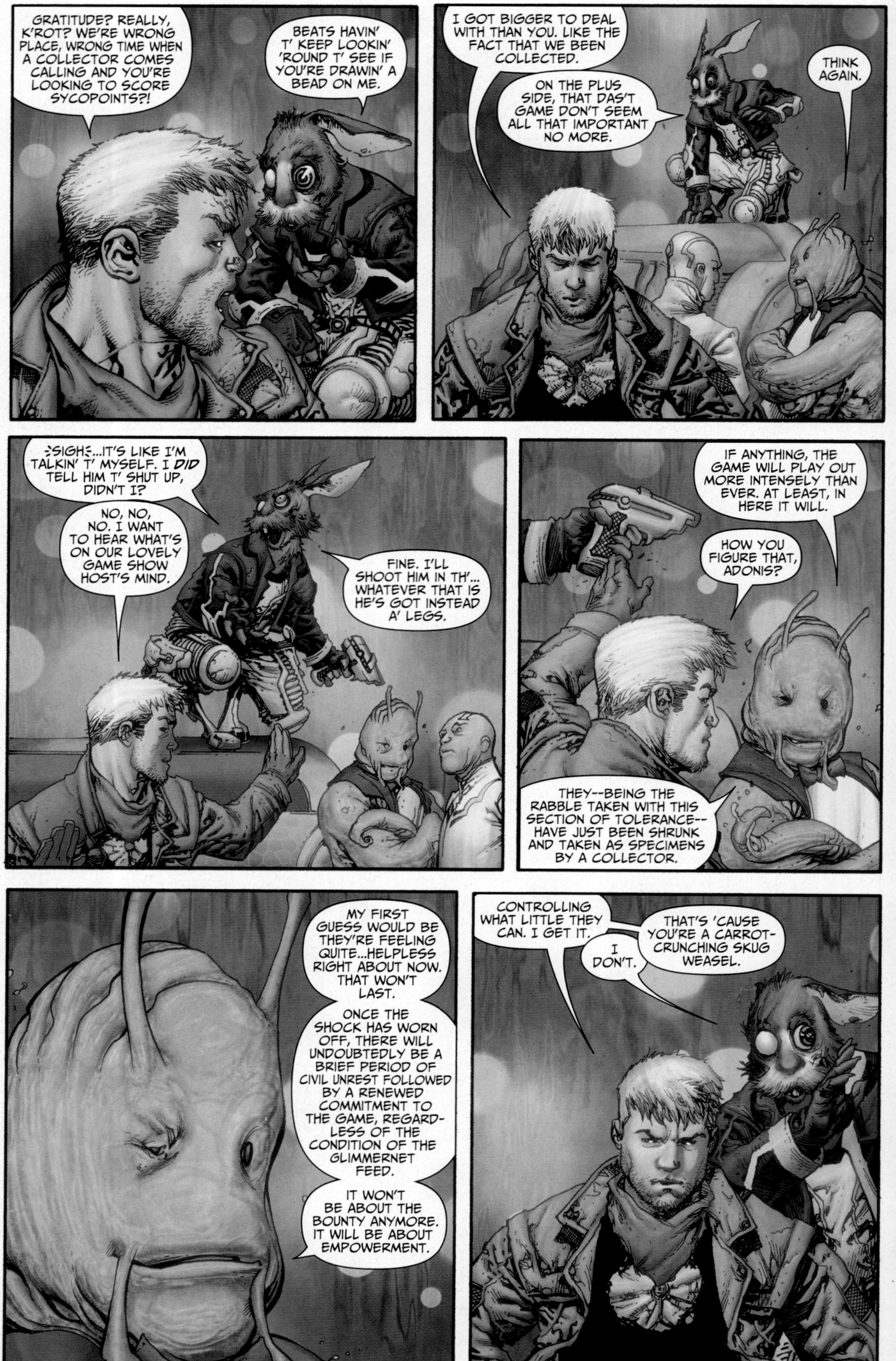
GRATITUDE? REALLY, K'ROT? WE'RE WRONG PLACE, WRONG TIME WHEN A COLLECTOR COMES CALLING AND YOU'RE LOOKING TO SCORE SYCOPOINTS?!
BEATS HAVIN' T' KEEP LOOKIN' 'ROUND T' SEE IF YOU'RE DRAWIN' A BEAD ON ME.
I GOT BIGGER TO DEAL WITH THAN YOU. LIKE THE FACT THAT WE BEEN COLLECTED.
ON THE PLUS SIDE, THAT DAS'T GAME DON'T SEEM ALL THAT IMPORTANT NO MORE.
THINK AGAIN.
SIGH...IT'S LIKE I'M TALKIN' T' MYSELF. I DID TELL HIM T' SHUT UP, DIDN'T I?
NO, NO, NO. I WANT TO HEAR WHAT'S ON OUR LOVELY GAME SHOW HOST'S MIND.
FINE. I'LL SHOOT HIM IN TH'... WHATEVER THAT IS HE'S GOT INSTEAD A' LEGS.
IF ANYTHING, THE GAME WILL PLAY OUT MORE INTENSELY THAN EVER. AT LEAST, IN HERE IT WILL.
HOW YOU FIGURE THAT, ADONIS?
THEY--BEING THE RABBLE TAKEN WITH THIS SECTION OF TOLERANCE--HAVE JUST BEEN SHRUNK AND TAKEN AS SPECIMENS BY A COLLECTOR.
MY FIRST GUESS WOULD BE THEY'RE FEELING QUITE...HELPLESS RIGHT ABOUT NOW. THAT WON'T LAST.
ONCE THE SHOCK HAS WORN OFF, THERE WILL UNDOUBTEDLY BE A BRIEF PERIOD OF CIVIL UNREST FOLLOWED BY A RENEWED COMMITMENT TO THE GAME, REGARDLESS OF THE CONDITION OF THE GLIMMERNET FEED.
IT WON'T BE ABOUT THE BOUNTY ANYMORE. IT WILL BE ABOUT EMPOWERMENT.
CONTROLLING WHAT LITTLE THEY CAN. I GET IT.
THAT'S 'CAUSE YOU'RE A CARROT-CRUNCHING SKUG WEASEL.
I DON'T.

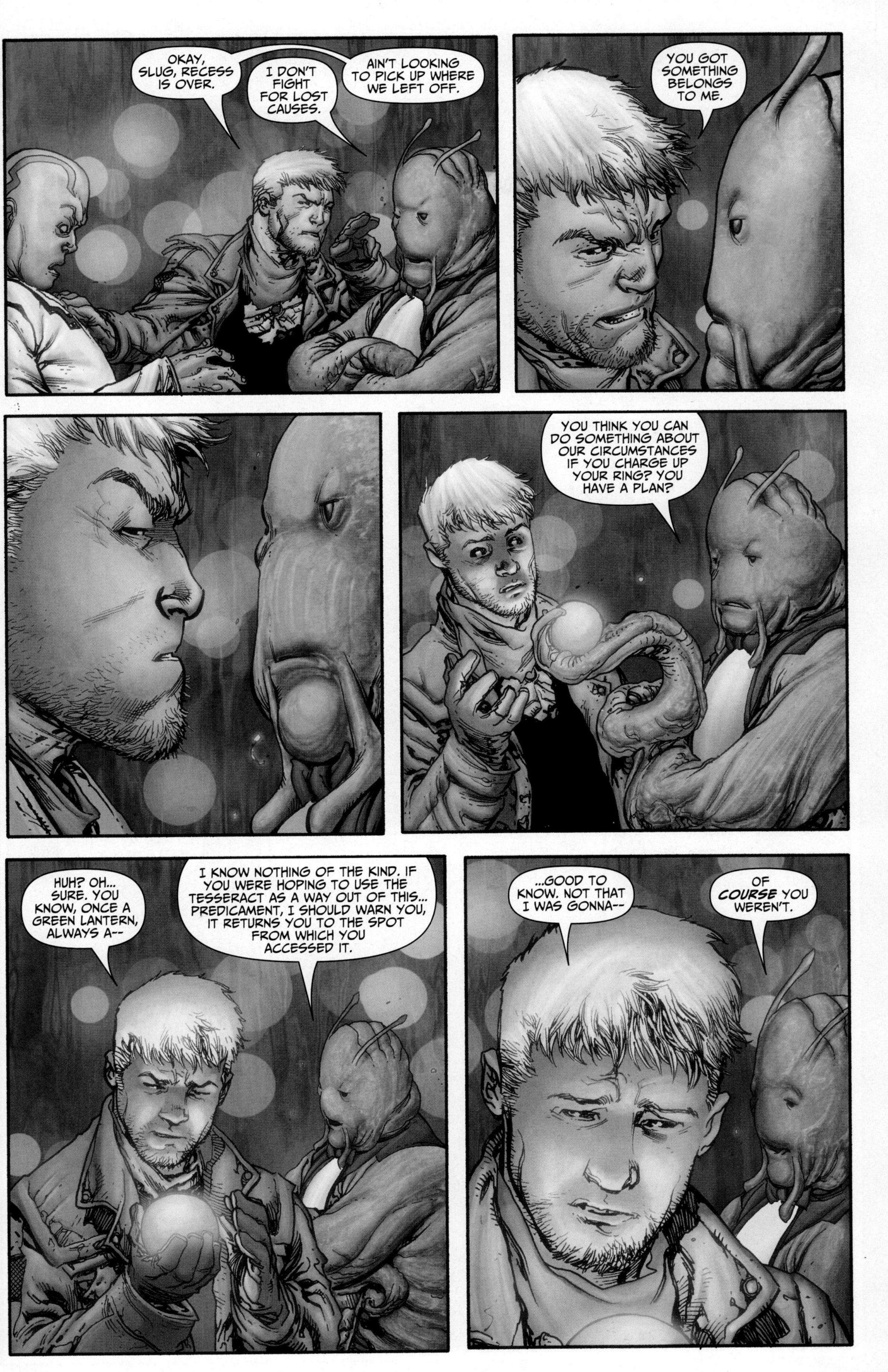
OKAY, SLUG, RECESS IS OVER.
I DON'T FIGHT FOR LOST CAUSES.
AIN'T LOOKING TO PICK UP WHERE WE LEFT OFF.
YOU GOT SOMETHING BELONGS TO ME.
YOU THINK YOU CAN DO SOMETHING ABOUT OUR CIRCUMSTANCES IF YOU CHARGE UP YOUR RING? YOU HAVE A PLAN?
HUH? OH... SURE. YOU KNOW, ONCE A GREEN LANTERN, ALWAYS A--
I KNOW NOTHING OF THE KIND. IF YOU WERE HOPING TO USE THE TESSERACT AS A WAY OUT OF THIS... PREDICAMENT, I SHOULD WARN YOU, IT RETURNS YOU TO THE SPOT FROM WHICH YOU ACCESSED IT.
...GOOD TO KNOW. NOT THAT I WAS GONNA--
OF *COURSE* YOU WEREN'T.

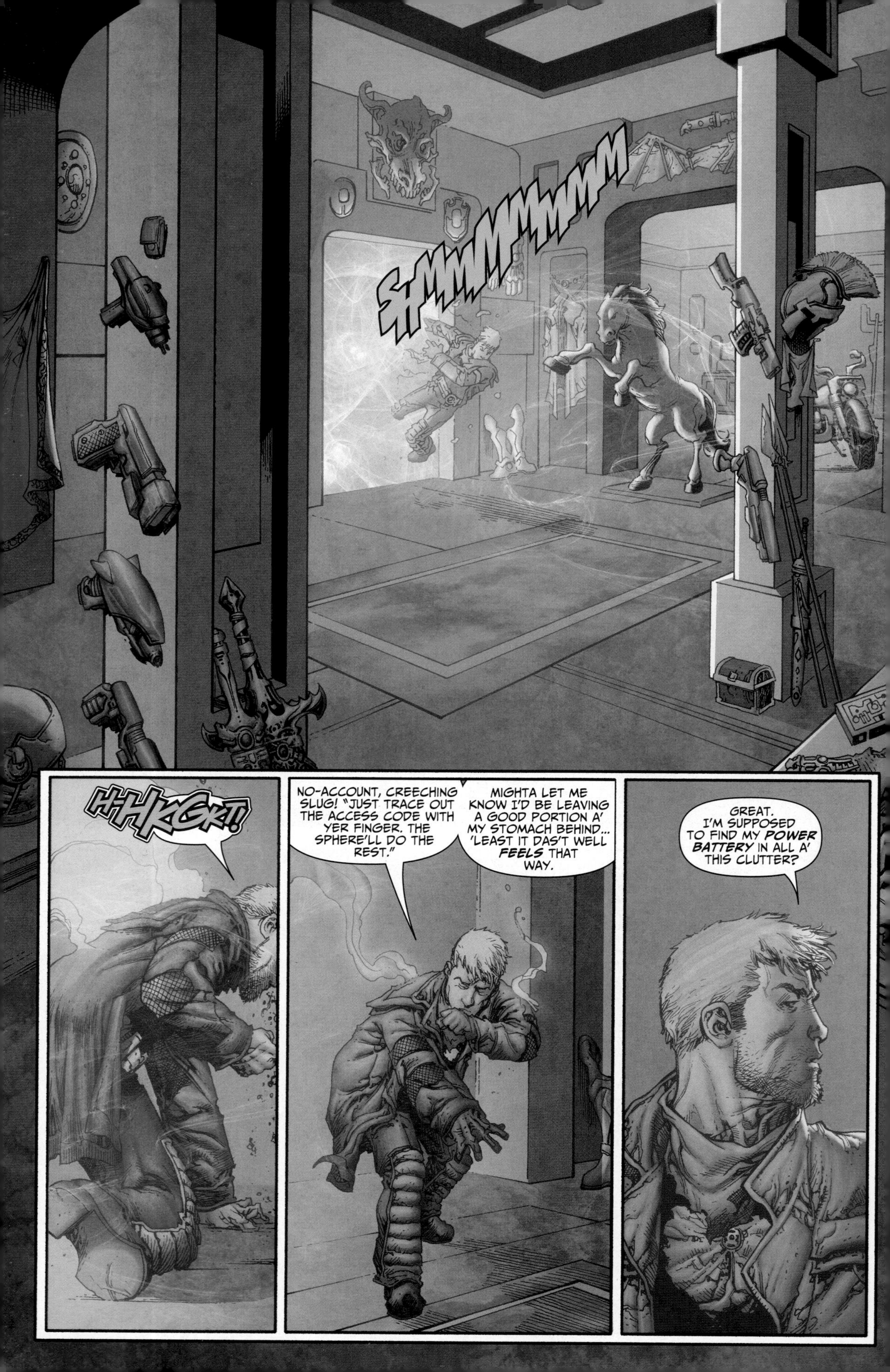
SHMMMMMMMMMMM
H-HKGKT!
NO-ACCOUNT, CREECHING SLUG! "JUST TRACE OUT THE ACCESS CODE WITH YER FINGER. THE SPHERE'LL DO THE REST."
MIGHTA LET ME KNOW I'D BE LEAVING A GOOD PORTION A' MY STOMACH BEHIND... 'LEAST IT DAS'T WELL FEELS THAT WAY.
GREAT. I'M SUPPOSED TO FIND MY POWER BATTERY IN ALL A' THIS CLUTTER?

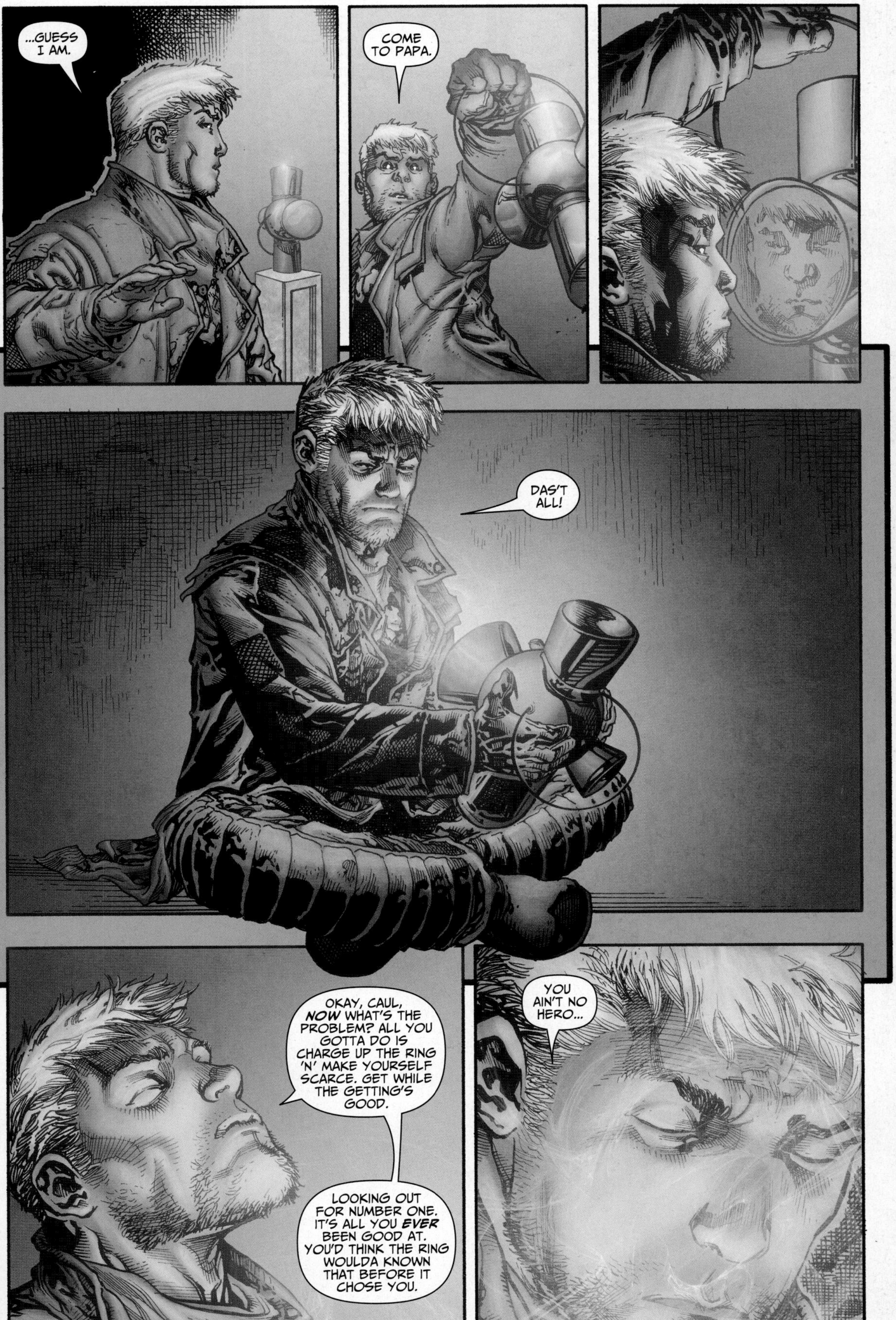
...GUESS I AM.
COME TO PAPA.
DAS'T ALL!
OKAY, CAUL, *NOW* WHAT'S THE PROBLEM? ALL YOU GOTTA DO IS CHARGE UP THE RING 'N' MAKE YOURSELF SCARCE. GET WHILE THE GETTING'S GOOD.
LOOKING OUT FOR NUMBER ONE. IT'S ALL YOU *EVER* BEEN GOOD AT. YOU'D THINK THE RING WOULDA KNOWN THAT BEFORE IT CHOSE YOU.
YOU AIN'T NO HERO...

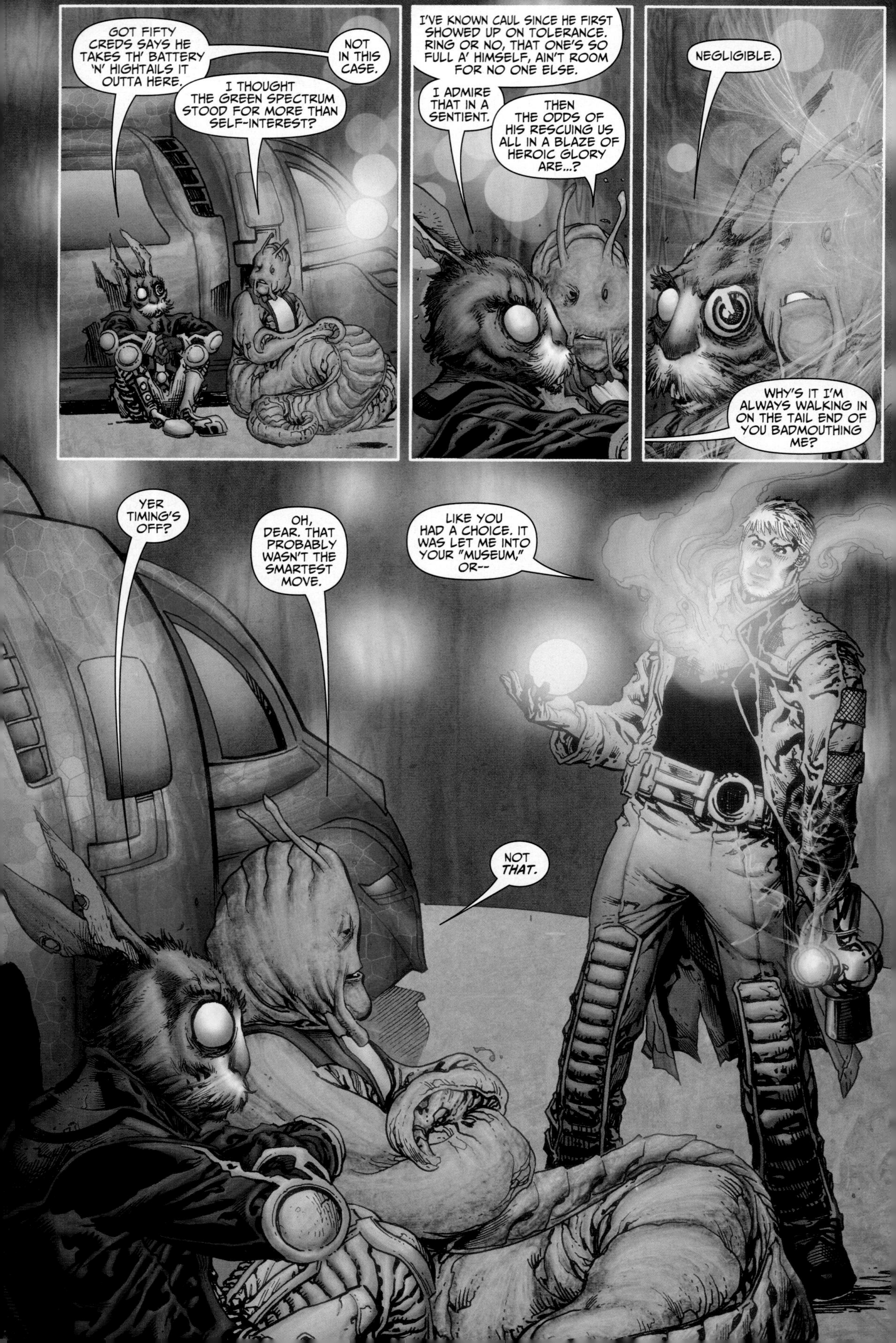
GOT FIFTY CREDS SAYS HE TAKES TH' BATTERY 'N' HIGHTAILS IT OUTTA HERE.
NOT IN THIS CASE.
I THOUGHT THE GREEN SPECTRUM STOOD FOR MORE THAN SELF-INTEREST?
I'VE KNOWN CAUL SINCE HE FIRST SHOWED UP ON TOLERANCE. RING OR NO, THAT ONE'S SO FULL A' HIMSELF, AIN'T ROOM FOR NO ONE ELSE.
I ADMIRE THAT IN A SENTIENT.
THEN THE ODDS OF HIS RESCUING US ALL IN A BLAZE OF HEROIC GLORY ARE...?
NEGLIGIBLE.
WHY'S IT I'M ALWAYS WALKING IN ON THE TAIL END OF YOU BADMOUTHING ME?
YER TIMING'S OFF?
OH, DEAR. THAT PROBABLY WASN'T THE SMARTEST MOVE.
LIKE YOU HAD A CHOICE. IT WAS LET ME INTO YOUR "MUSEUM," OR--
NOT *THAT.*

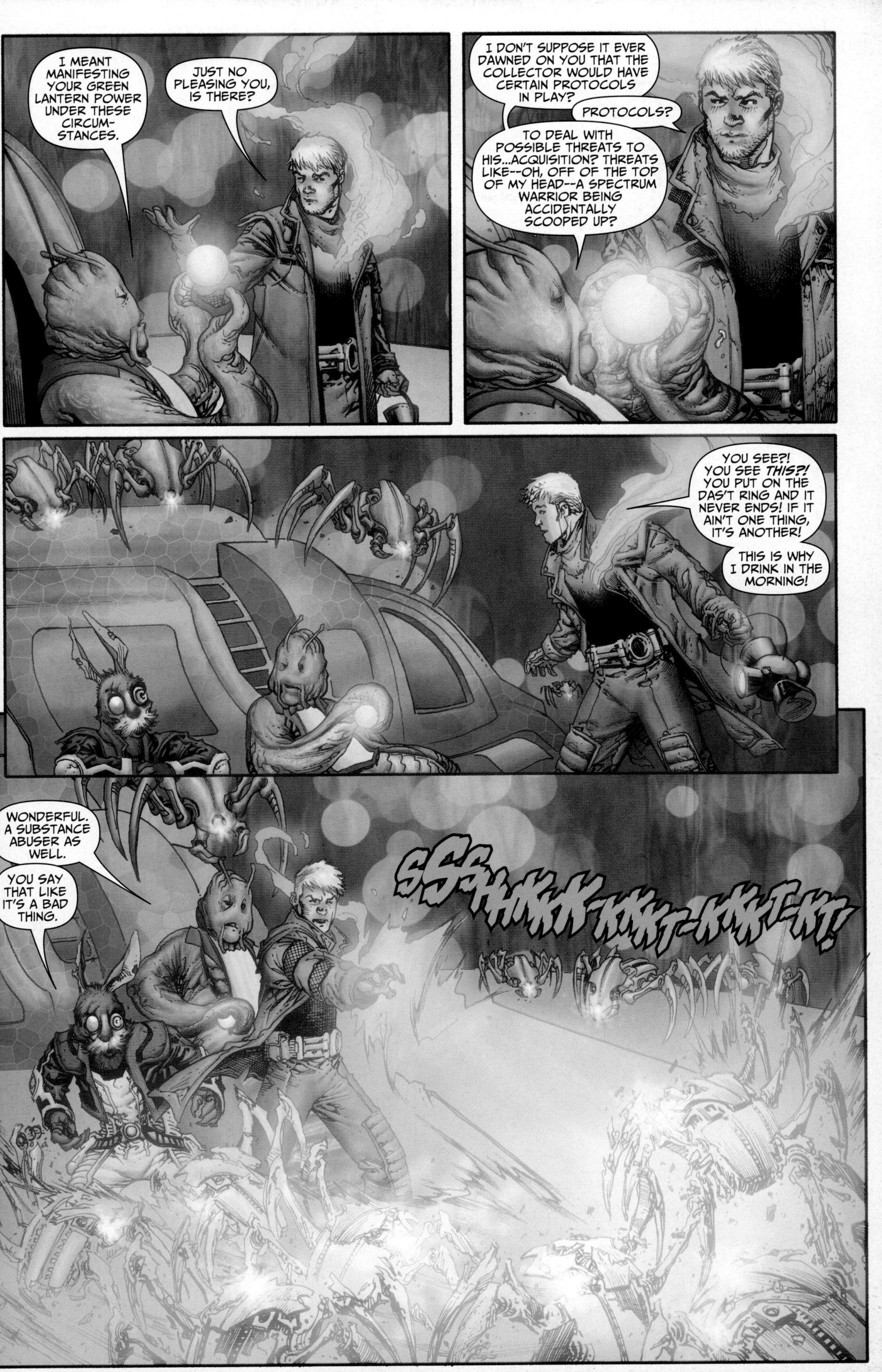
I MEANT MANIFESTING YOUR GREEN LANTERN POWER UNDER THESE CIRCUM-STANCES.
JUST NO PLEASING YOU, IS THERE?
I DON'T SUPPOSE IT EVER DAWNED ON YOU THAT THE COLLECTOR WOULD HAVE CERTAIN PROTOCOLS IN PLAY?
PROTOCOLS?
TO DEAL WITH POSSIBLE THREATS TO HIS...ACQUISITION? THREATS LIKE--OH, OFF OF THE TOP OF MY HEAD--A SPECTRUM WARRIOR BEING ACCIDENTALLY SCOOPED UP?
YOU SEE?! YOU SEE *THIS?!* YOU PUT ON THE DAS'T RING AND IT NEVER ENDS! IF IT AIN'T ONE THING, IT'S ANOTHER!
THIS IS WHY I DRINK IN THE MORNING!
WONDERFUL. A SUBSTANCE ABUSER AS WELL.
YOU SAY THAT LIKE IT'S A BAD THING.
SSSHKKK-KKKT-KKKT-KT!

:SIGH:... INTOLERABLE. I SHOULD KNOW BETTER THAN TO RELY ON OUTSIDE PROVIDERS.

ACCESS THE LARYN GEAL CREATURE'S CEREBRAL IMPLANT.

ACCESSING.

DETONATE.

AFFIRMATIVE.

PFT!

IS THE MEMBRANE AT RISK?

VARIABLE. A DELIBERATE EFFORT TO BREACH CONTAINMENT HAS A LESS THAN FIFTEEN PERCENT CHANCE OF SUCCESS.

DEPENDENT ON THE EXTENT OF THE WILLPOWER EXERTED?

COLLATERAL DAMAGE?

NOT A CONCERN THE MEMBRANE CAN WITHSTAND PRESSURE UP TO FOUR THOUSAND TIMES THAT OF--

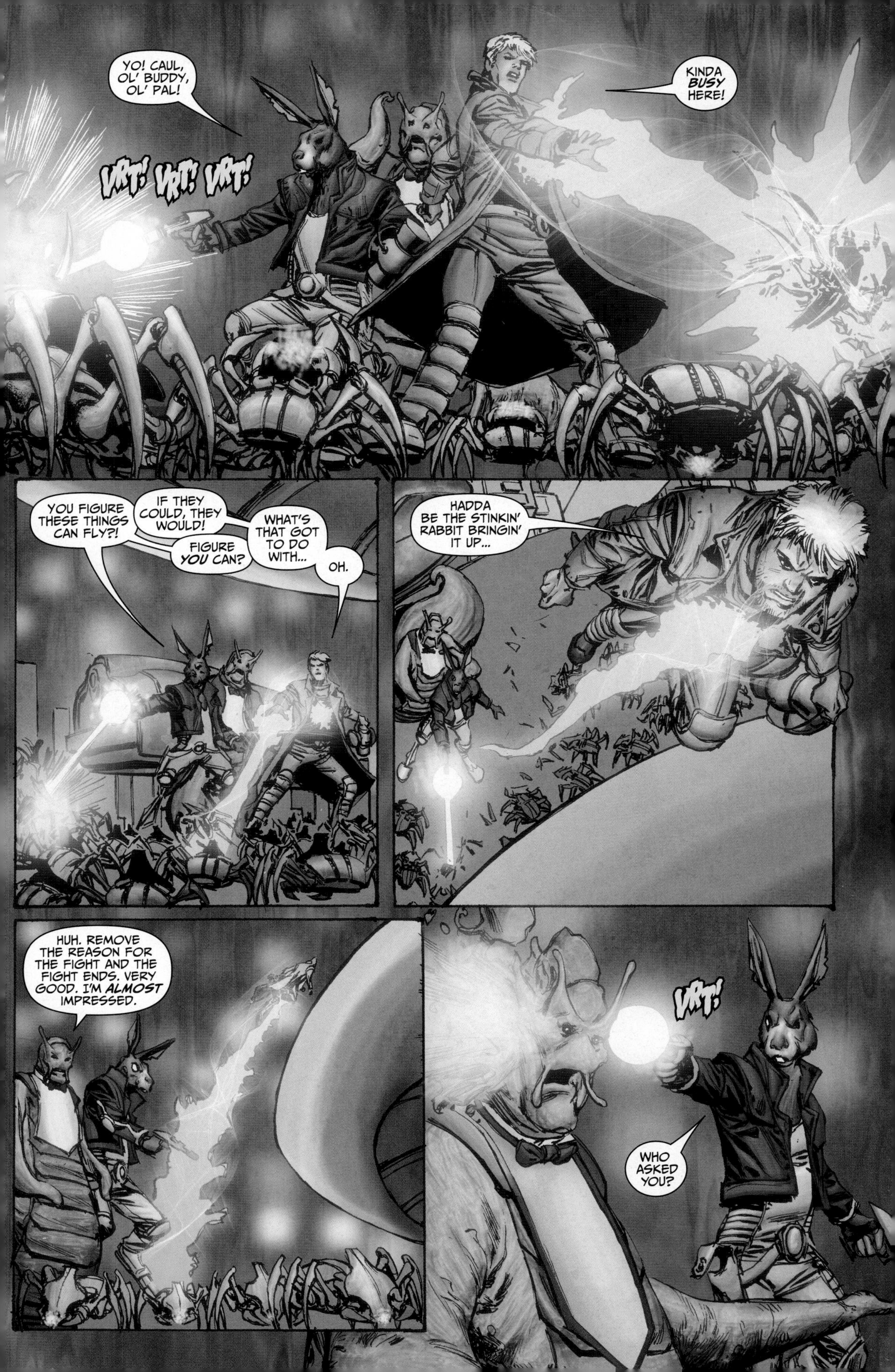
YO! CAUL, OL' BUDDY, OL' PAL!
KINDA BUSY HERE!
VRT! VRT! VRT!
YOU FIGURE THESE THINGS CAN FLY?!
IF THEY COULD, THEY WOULD!
FIGURE YOU CAN?
WHAT'S THAT GOT TO DO WITH...
OH.
HADDA BE THE STINKIN' RABBIT BRINGIN' IT UP...
HUH. REMOVE THE REASON FOR THE FIGHT AND THE FIGHT ENDS. VERY GOOD. I'M ALMOST IMPRESSED.
VRT!
WHO ASKED YOU?

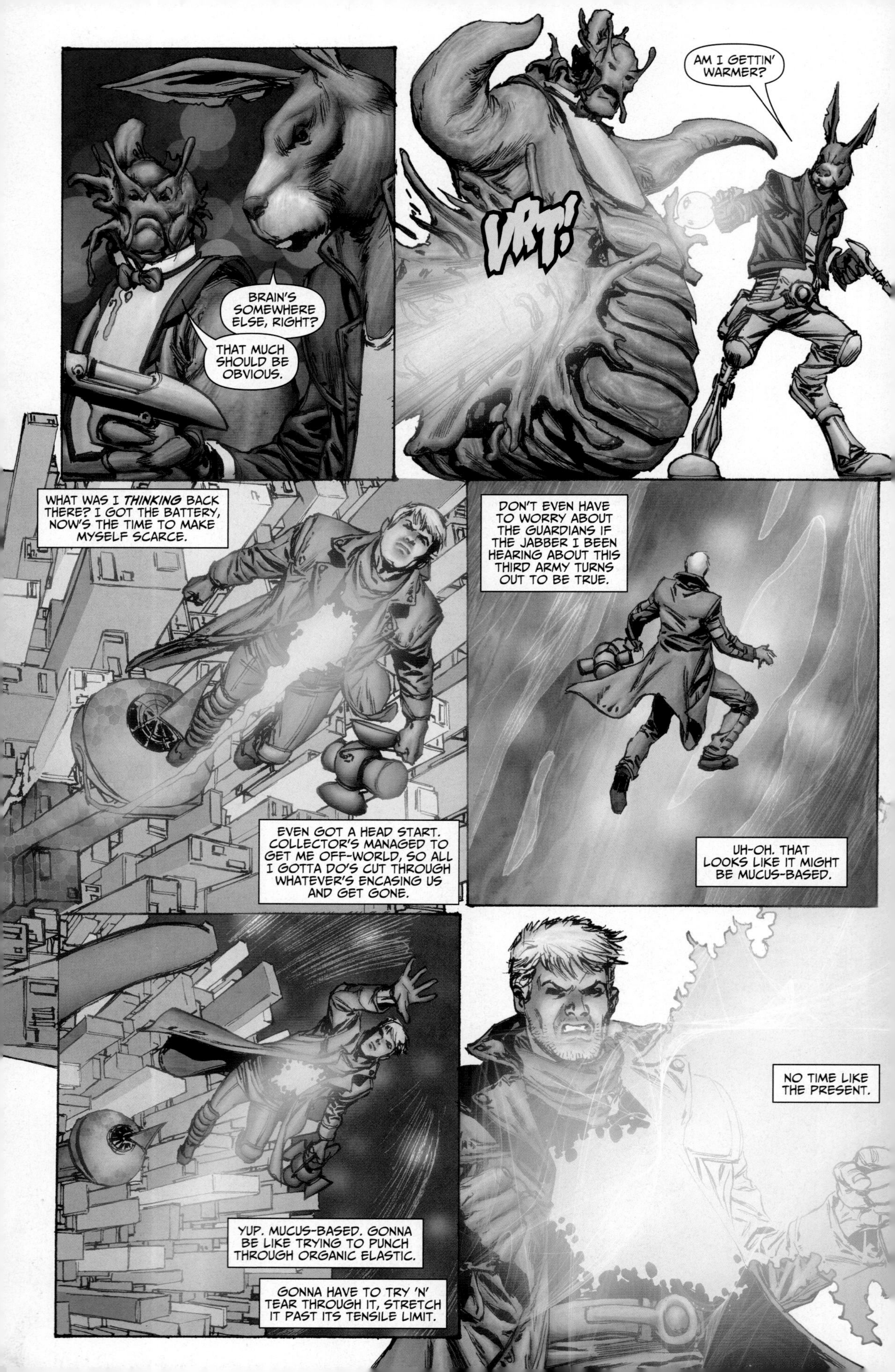

BRAIN'S SOMEWHERE ELSE, RIGHT?
THAT MUCH SHOULD BE OBVIOUS.
VRT!
AM I GETTIN' WARMER?
WHAT WAS I *THINKING* BACK THERE? I GOT THE BATTERY, NOW'S THE TIME TO MAKE MYSELF SCARCE.
EVEN GOT A HEAD START. COLLECTOR'S MANAGED TO GET ME OFF-WORLD, SO ALL I GOTTA DO'S CUT THROUGH WHATEVER'S ENCASING US AND GET GONE.
DON'T EVEN HAVE TO WORRY ABOUT THE GUARDIANS IF THE JABBER I BEEN HEARING ABOUT THIS THIRD ARMY TURNS OUT TO BE TRUE.
UH-OH. THAT LOOKS LIKE IT MIGHT BE MUCUS-BASED.
YUP. MUCUS-BASED. GONNA BE LIKE TRYING TO PUNCH THROUGH ORGANIC ELASTIC.
GONNA HAVE TO TRY 'N' TEAR THROUGH IT, STRETCH IT PAST ITS TENSILE LIMIT.
NO TIME LIKE THE PRESENT.

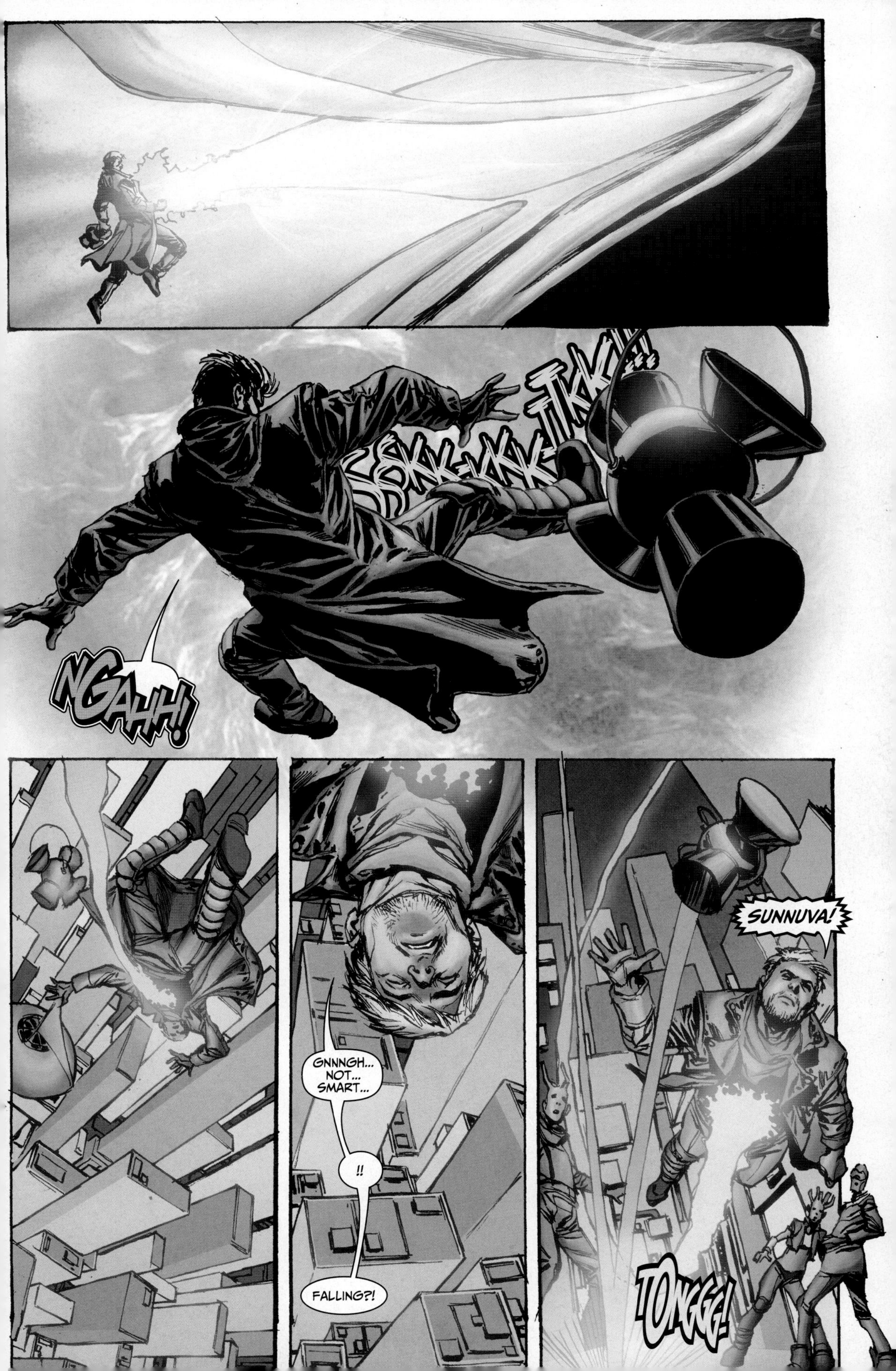
TKKK!!
NGAHH!
GNNNGH... NOT... SMART...
!!
FALLING?!
SUNNUVA!
TONGGG!

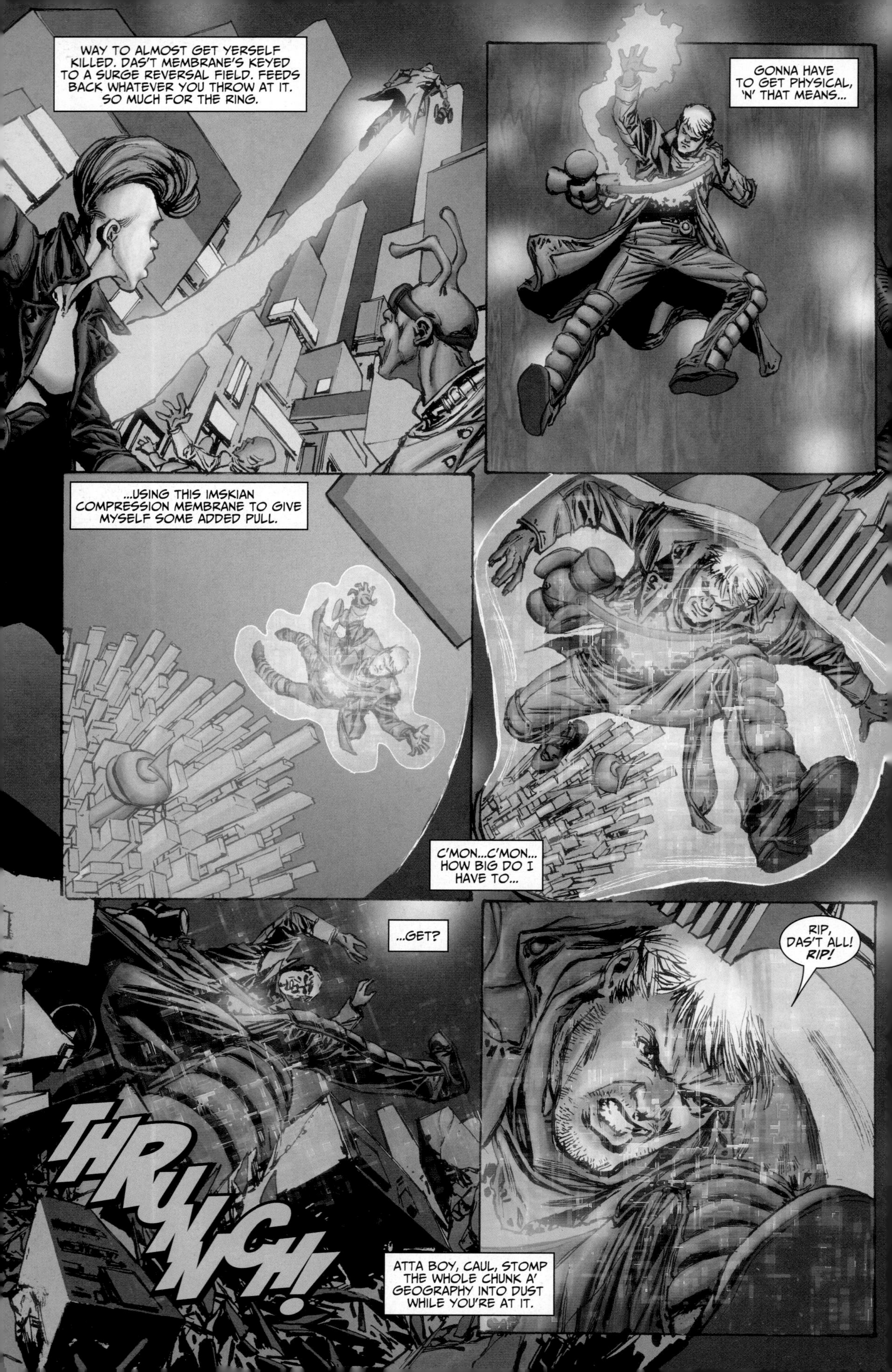
WAY TO ALMOST GET YERSELF KILLED. DAS'T MEMBRANE'S KEYED TO A SURGE REVERSAL FIELD. FEEDS BACK WHATEVER YOU THROW AT IT. SO MUCH FOR THE RING.
GONNA HAVE TO GET PHYSICAL, 'N' THAT MEANS...
...USING THIS IMSKIAN COMPRESSION MEMBRANE TO GIVE MYSELF SOME ADDED PULL.
C'MON...C'MON... HOW BIG DO I HAVE TO...
...GET?
THRUNCH!
RIP, DAS'T ALL! RIP!
ATTA BOY, CAUL, STOMP THE WHOLE CHUNK A' GEOGRAPHY INTO DUST WHILE YOU'RE AT IT.

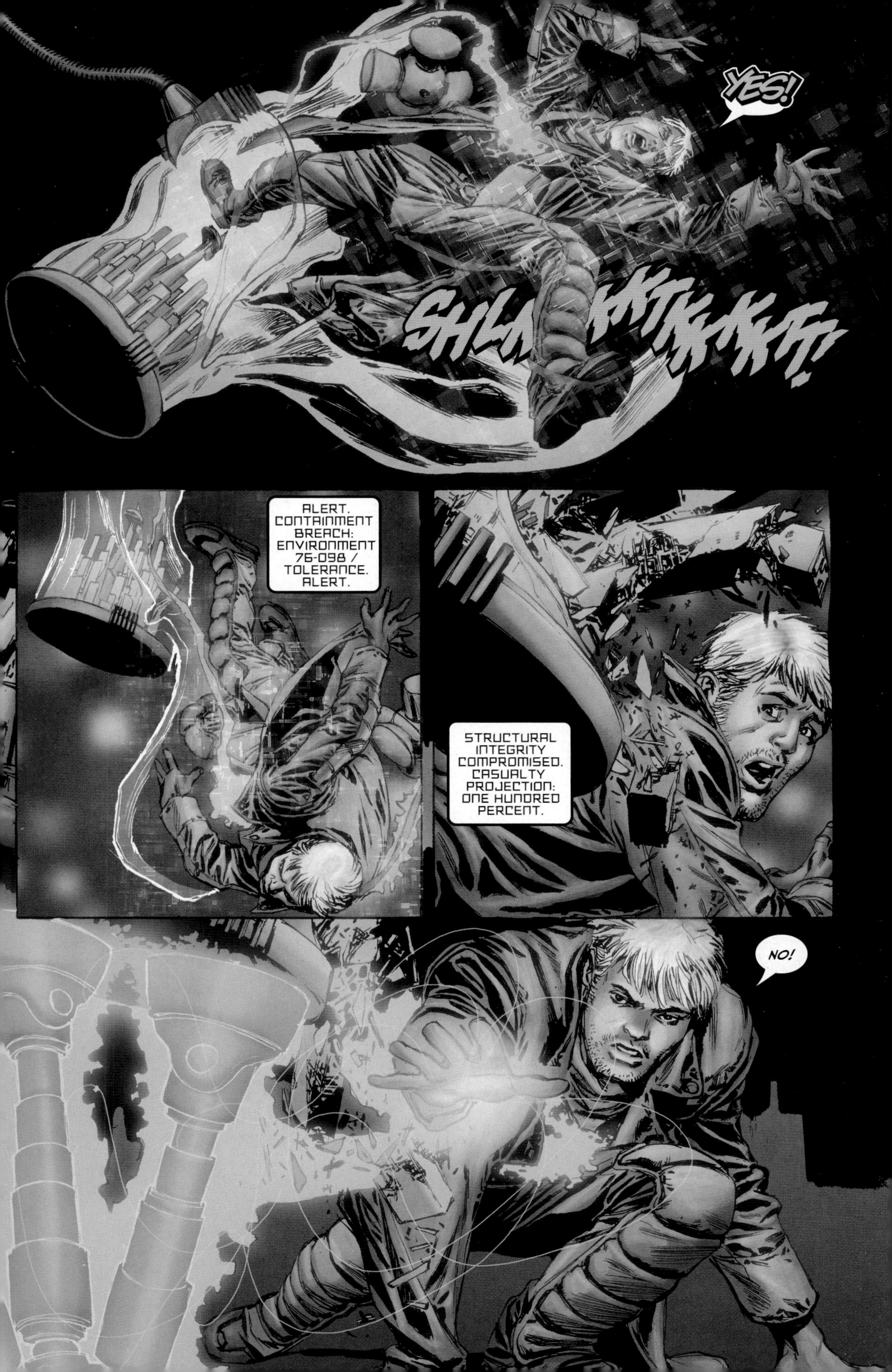
YES!
ALERT. CONTAINMENT BREACH: ENVIRONMENT 76-098 / TOLERANCE. ALERT.
STRUCTURAL INTEGRITY COMPROMISED. CASUALTY PROJECTION: ONE HUNDRED PERCENT.
NO!

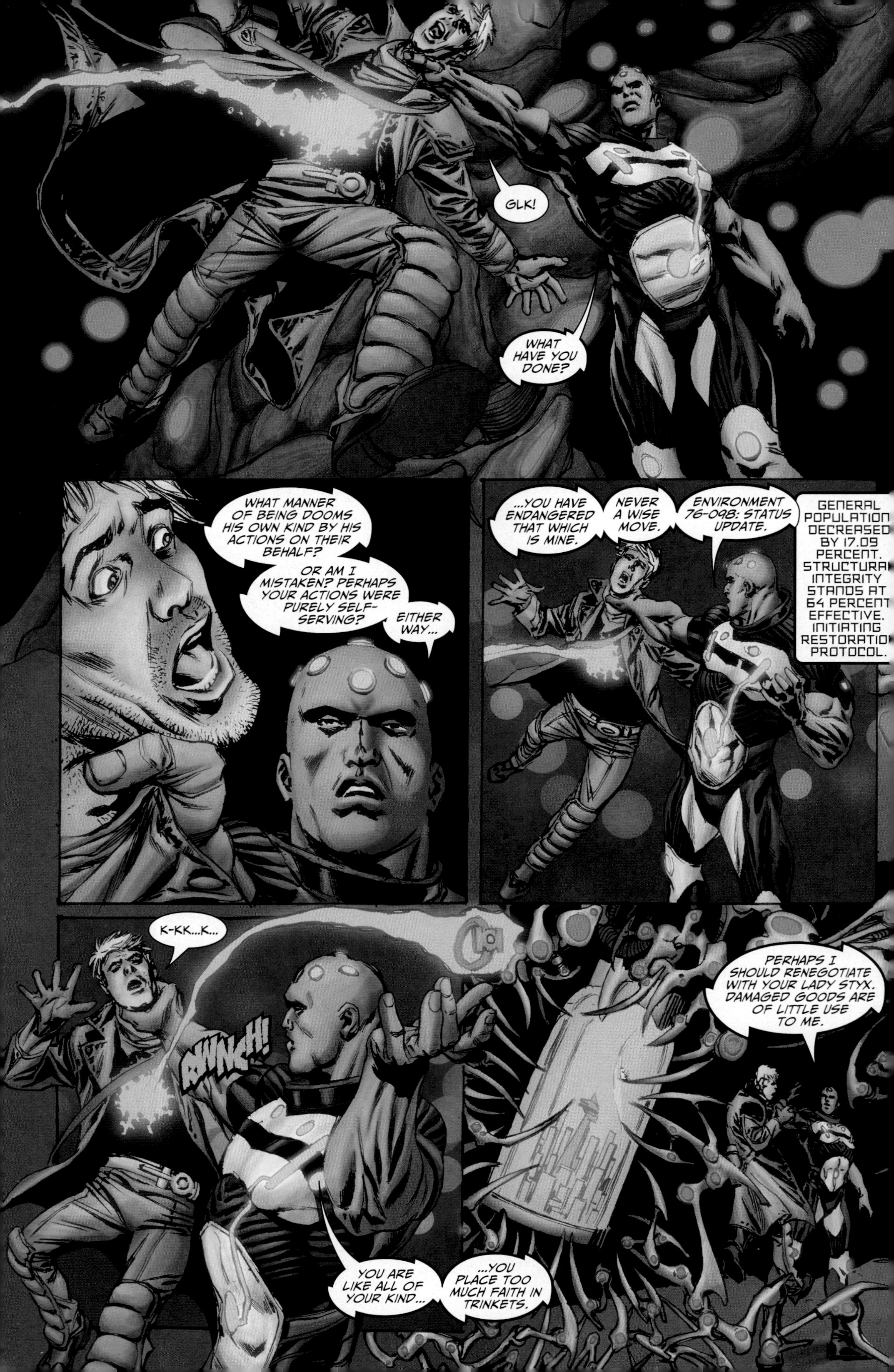
GLK!
WHAT HAVE YOU DONE?
WHAT MANNER OF BEING DOOMS HIS OWN KIND BY HIS ACTIONS ON THEIR BEHALF?
OR AM I MISTAKEN? PERHAPS YOUR ACTIONS WERE PURELY SELF-SERVING?
EITHER WAY...
...YOU HAVE ENDANGERED THAT WHICH IS MINE.
NEVER A WISE MOVE.
ENVIRONMENT 76-098: STATUS UPDATE.
GENERAL POPULATION DECREASED BY 17.09 PERCENT. STRUCTURAL INTEGRITY STANDS AT 64 PERCENT EFFECTIVE. INITIATING RESTORATION PROTOCOL.
K-KK...K...
BWNCH!
YOU ARE LIKE ALL OF YOUR KIND...
...YOU PLACE TOO MUCH FAITH IN TRINKETS.
PERHAPS I SHOULD RENEGOTIATE WITH YOUR LADY STYX. DAMAGED GOODS ARE OF LITTLE USE TO ME.

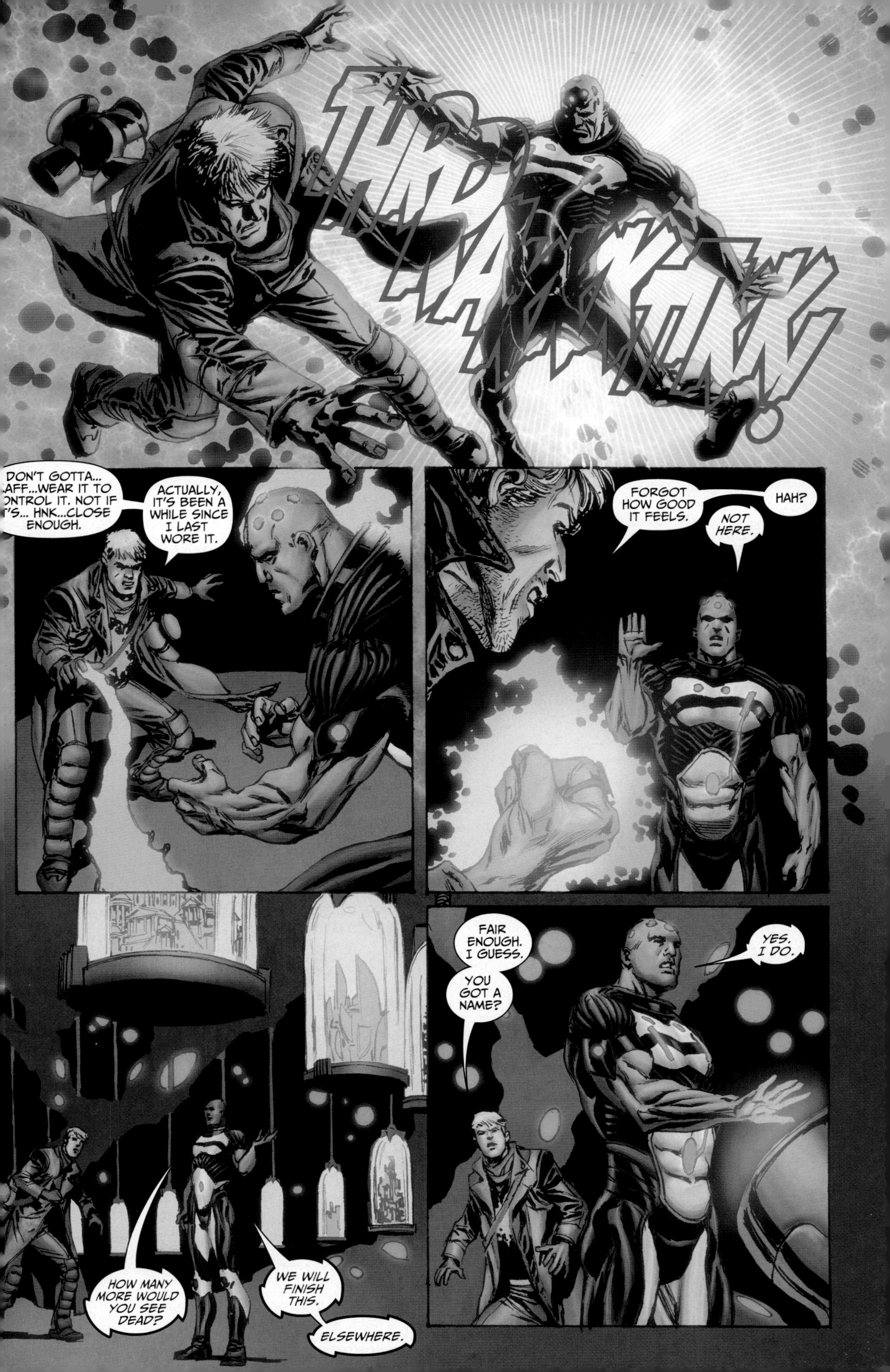
THRAKATHUNK!
DON'T GOTTA... ...AFF...WEAR IT TO ...ONTROL IT. NOT IF ...T'S... HNK...CLOSE ENOUGH.
ACTUALLY, IT'S BEEN A WHILE SINCE I LAST WORE IT.
FORGOT HOW GOOD IT FEELS.
HAH?
NOT HERE.
HOW MANY MORE WOULD YOU SEE DEAD?
WE WILL FINISH THIS.
ELSEWHERE.
FAIR ENOUGH. I GUESS.
YOU GOT A NAME?
YES. I DO.

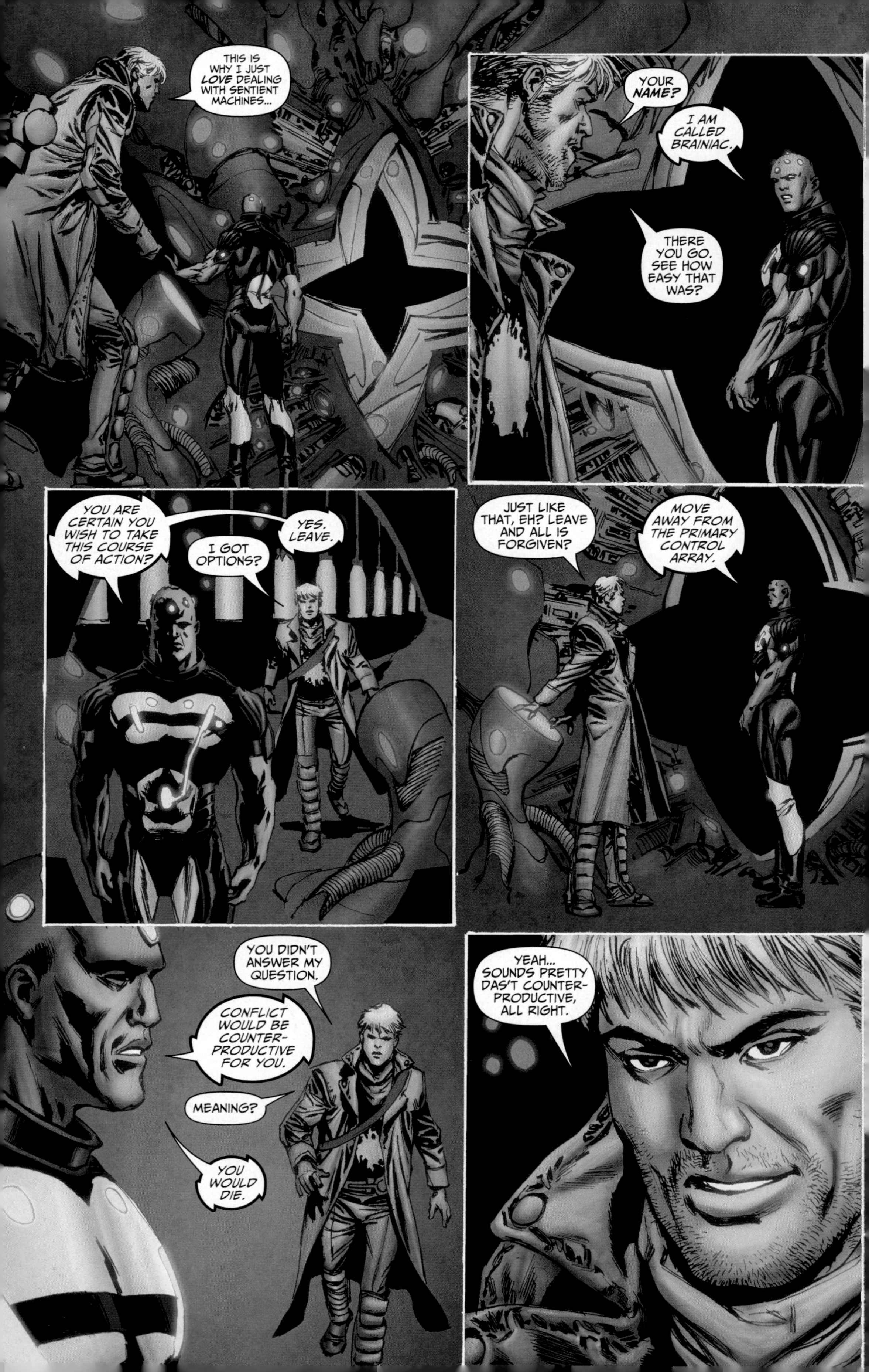
THIS IS WHY I JUST LOVE DEALING WITH SENTIENT MACHINES...
YOUR NAME?
I AM CALLED BRAINIAC.
THERE YOU GO. SEE HOW EASY THAT WAS?
YOU ARE CERTAIN YOU WISH TO TAKE THIS COURSE OF ACTION?
I GOT OPTIONS?
YES. LEAVE.
JUST LIKE THAT, EH? LEAVE AND ALL IS FORGIVEN?
MOVE AWAY FROM THE PRIMARY CONTROL ARRAY.
YOU DIDN'T ANSWER MY QUESTION.
CONFLICT WOULD BE COUNTER-PRODUCTIVE FOR YOU.
MEANING?
YOU WOULD DIE.
YEAH... SOUNDS PRETTY DAS'T COUNTER-PRODUCTIVE, ALL RIGHT.

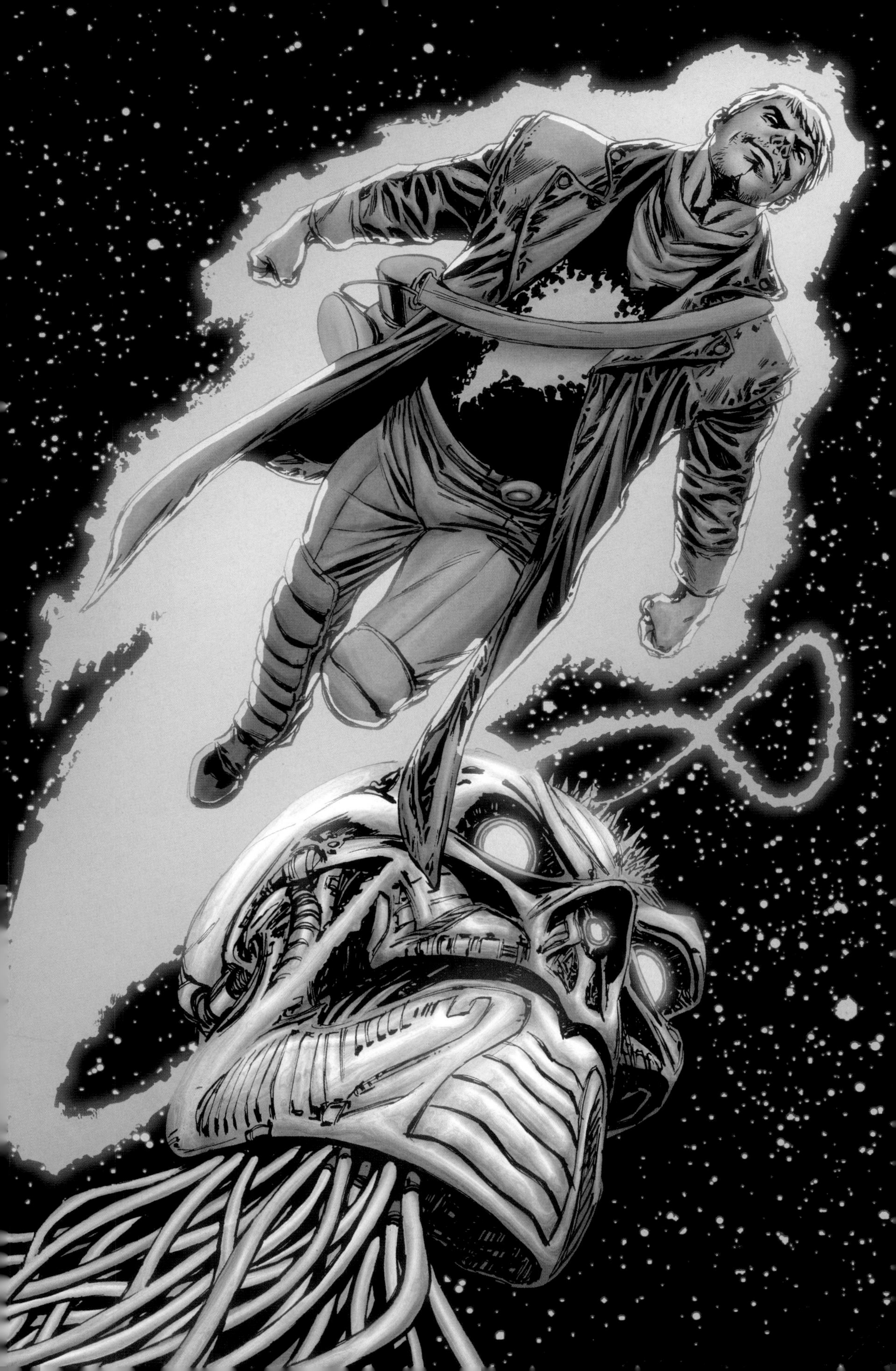

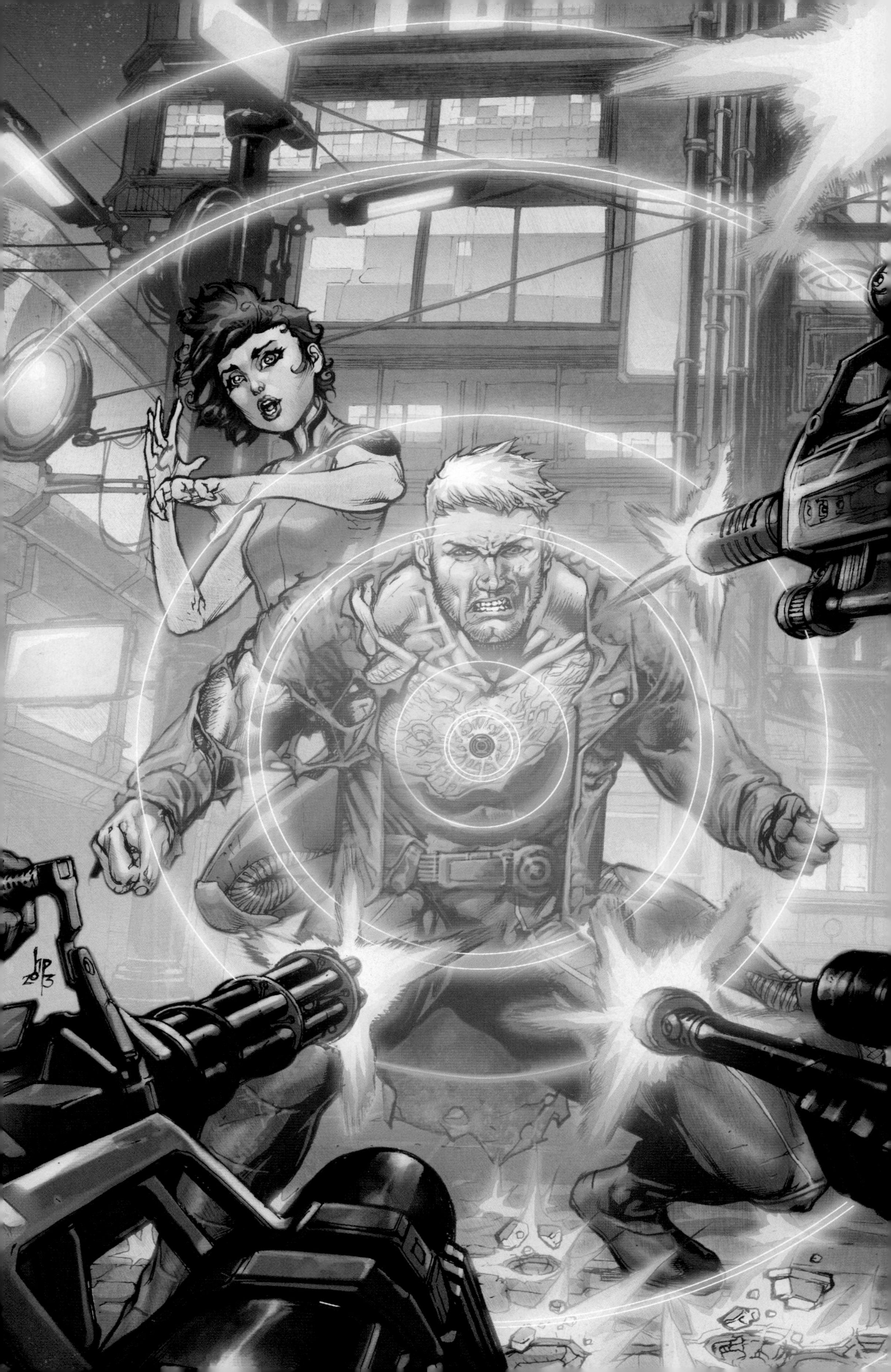

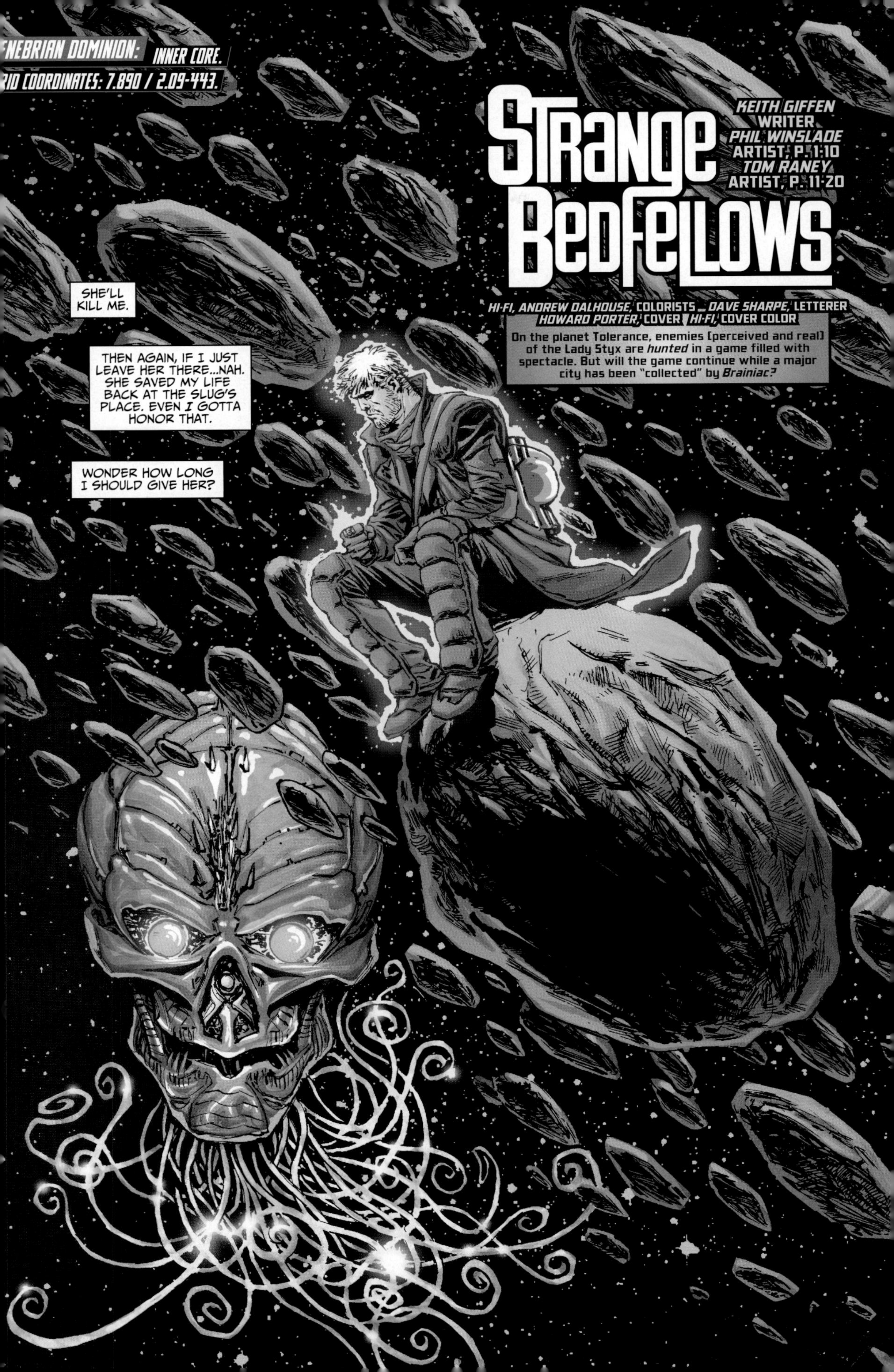

FNEBRIAN DOMINION: INNER CORE.
RID COORDINATES: 7.890 / 2.09-443.
STRANGE BEDFELLOWS
KEITH GIFFEN WRITER
PHIL WINSLADE ARTIST, P. 1-10
TOM RANEY ARTIST, P. 11-20
HI-FI, ANDREW DALHOUSE, COLORISTS _ DAVE SHARPE, LETTERER
HOWARD PORTER, COVER HI-FI, COVER COLOR
On the planet Tolerance, enemies [perceived and real] of the Lady Styx are hunted in a game filled with spectacle. But will the game continue while a major city has been "collected" by Brainiac?
SHE'LL KILL ME.
THEN AGAIN, IF I JUST LEAVE HER THERE...NAH. SHE SAVED MY LIFE BACK AT THE SLUG'S PLACE. EVEN I GOTTA HONOR THAT.
WONDER HOW LONG I SHOULD GIVE HER?

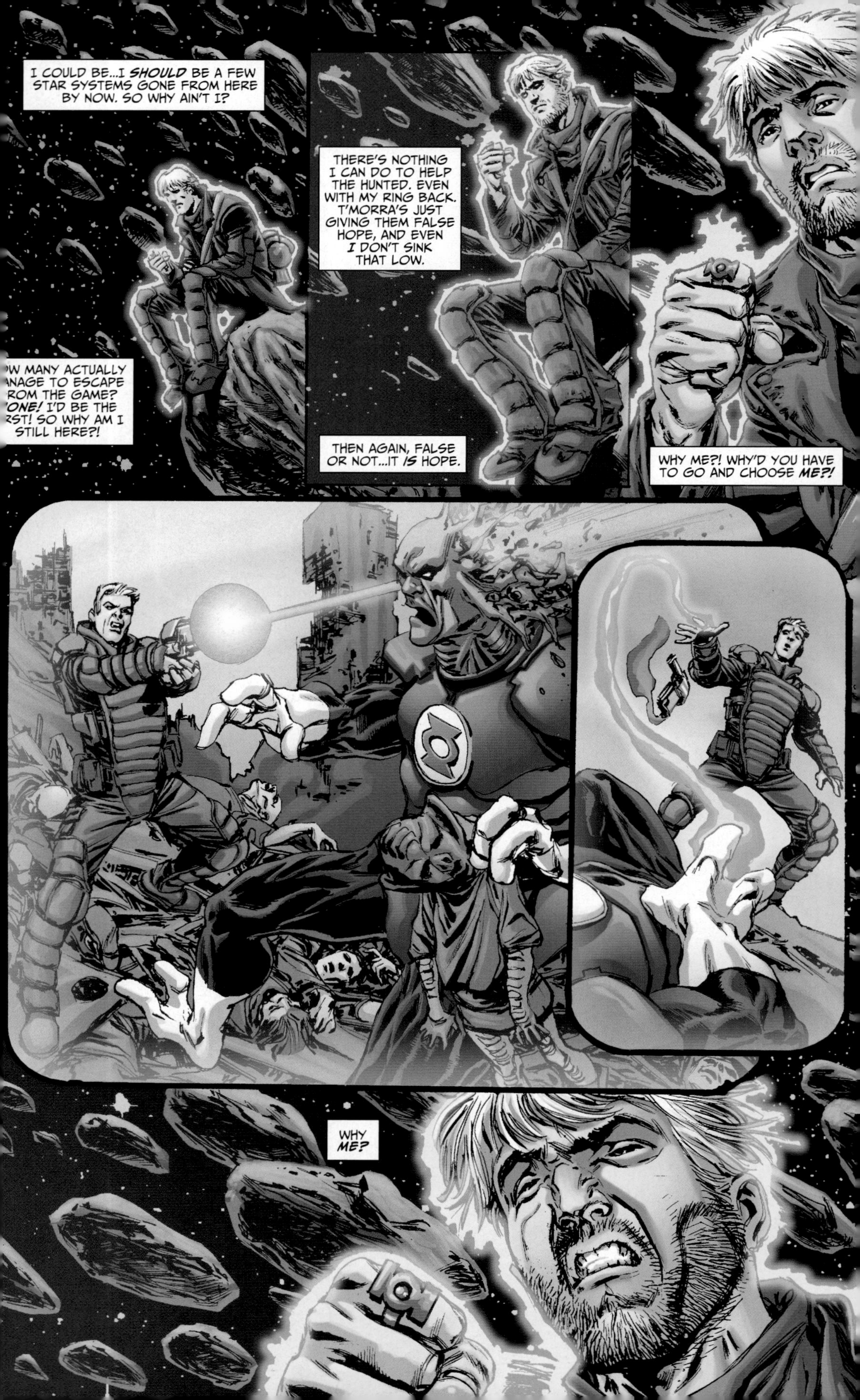
I COULD BE...I SHOULD BE A FEW STAR SYSTEMS GONE FROM HERE BY NOW. SO WHY AIN'T I?
OW MANY ACTUALLY ANAGE TO ESCAPE ROM THE GAME? ONE! I'D BE THE RST! SO WHY AM I STILL HERE?!
THERE'S NOTHING I CAN DO TO HELP THE HUNTED. EVEN WITH MY RING BACK. T'MORRA'S JUST GIVING THEM FALSE HOPE, AND EVEN I DON'T SINK THAT LOW.
THEN AGAIN, FALSE OR NOT...IT IS HOPE.
WHY ME?! WHY'D YOU HAVE TO GO AND CHOOSE ME?!
WHY ME?

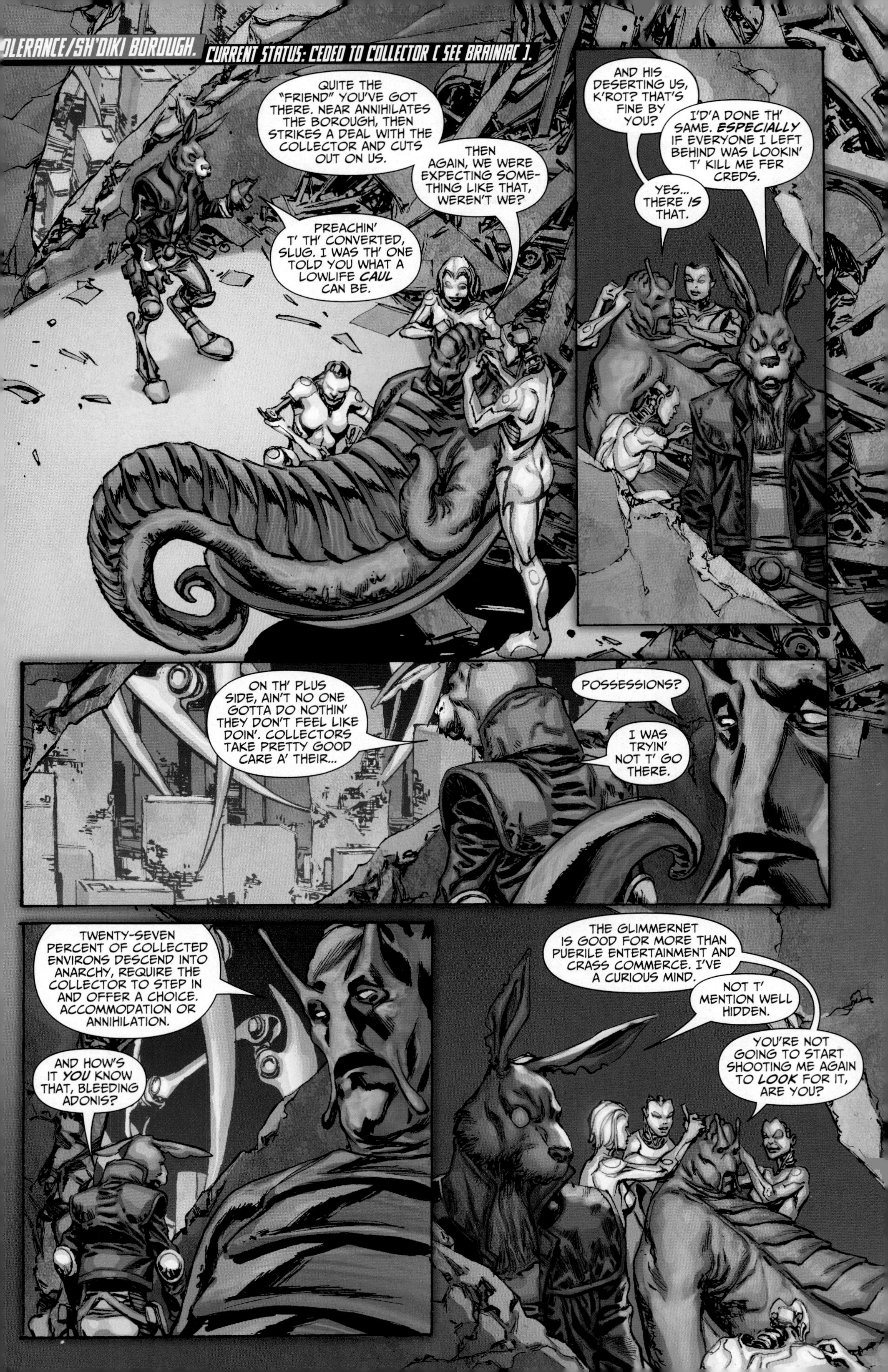
OLERANCE/SH'DIKI BOROUGH.
CURRENT STATUS: CEDED TO COLLECTOR [SEE BRAINIAC].
QUITE THE "FRIEND" YOU'VE GOT THERE. NEAR ANNIHILATES THE BOROUGH, THEN STRIKES A DEAL WITH THE COLLECTOR AND CUTS OUT ON US.
THEN AGAIN, WE WERE EXPECTING SOMETHING LIKE THAT, WEREN'T WE?
PREACHIN' T' TH' CONVERTED, SLUG. I WAS TH' ONE TOLD YOU WHAT A LOWLIFE CAUL CAN BE.
AND HIS DESERTING US, K'ROT? THAT'S FINE BY YOU?
I'D'A DONE TH' SAME. ESPECIALLY IF EVERYONE I LEFT BEHIND WAS LOOKIN' T' KILL ME FER CREDS.
YES... THERE IS THAT.
ON TH' PLUS SIDE, AIN'T NO ONE GOTTA DO NOTHIN' THEY DON'T FEEL LIKE DOIN'. COLLECTORS TAKE PRETTY GOOD CARE A' THEIR...
POSSESSIONS?
I WAS TRYIN' NOT T' GO THERE.
TWENTY-SEVEN PERCENT OF COLLECTED ENVIRONS DESCEND INTO ANARCHY, REQUIRE THE COLLECTOR TO STEP IN AND OFFER A CHOICE. ACCOMMODATION OR ANNIHILATION.
AND HOW'S IT YOU KNOW THAT, BLEEDING ADONIS?
THE GLIMMERNET IS GOOD FOR MORE THAN PUERILE ENTERTAINMENT AND CRASS COMMERCE. I'VE A CURIOUS MIND.
NOT T' MENTION WELL HIDDEN.
YOU'RE NOT GOING TO START SHOOTING ME AGAIN TO LOOK FOR IT, ARE YOU?

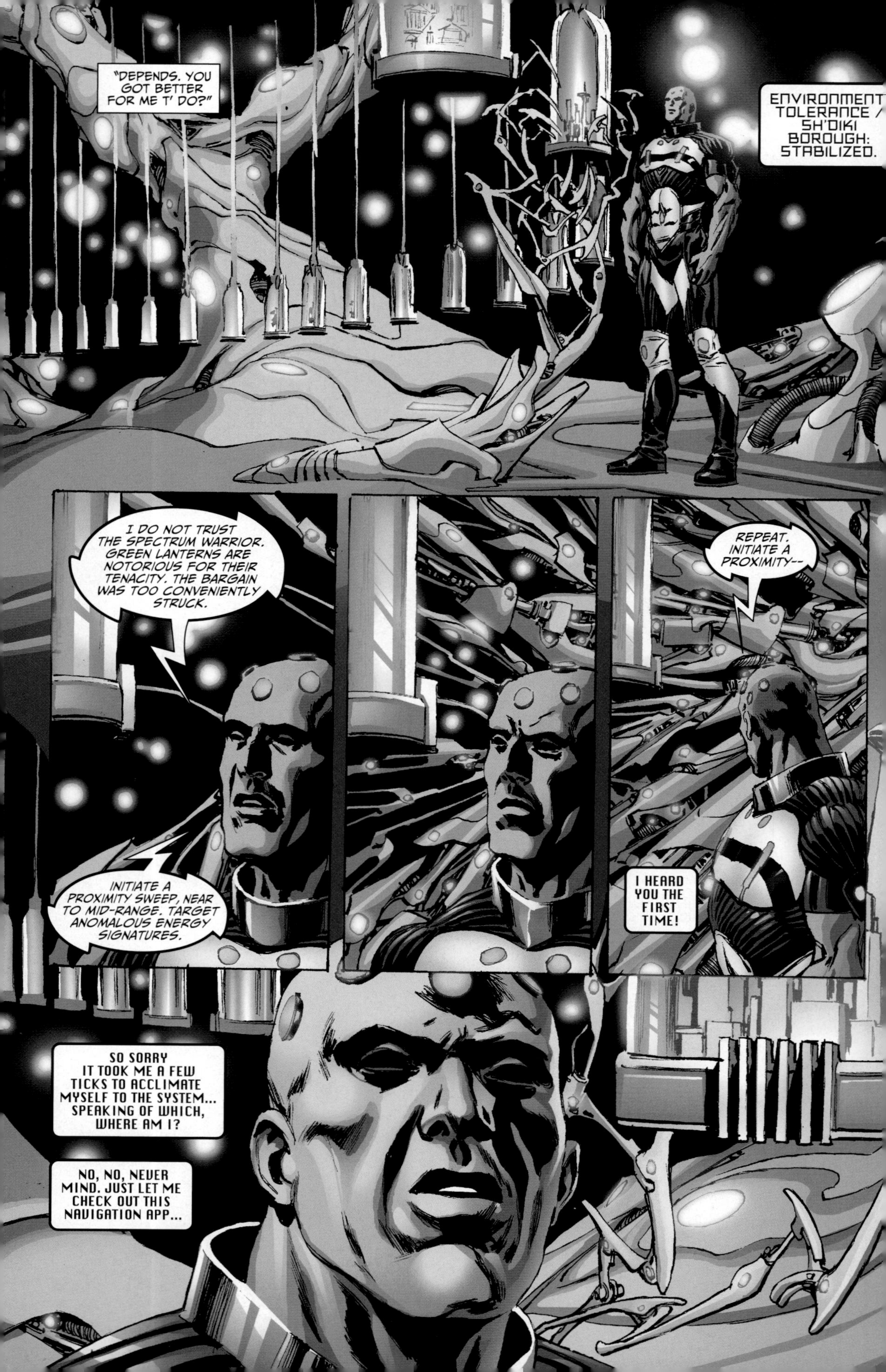
"DEPENDS. YOU GOT BETTER FOR ME T' DO?"
ENVIRONMENT TOLERANCE / SH'DIKI BOROUGH: STABILIZED.
I DO NOT TRUST THE SPECTRUM WARRIOR. GREEN LANTERNS ARE NOTORIOUS FOR THEIR TENACITY. THE BARGAIN WAS TOO CONVENIENTLY STRUCK.
INITIATE A PROXIMITY SWEEP, NEAR TO MID-RANGE. TARGET ANOMALOUS ENERGY SIGNATURES.
REPEAT. INITIATE A PROXIMITY--
I HEARD YOU THE FIRST TIME!
SO SORRY IT TOOK ME A FEW TICKS TO ACCLIMATE MYSELF TO THE SYSTEM... SPEAKING OF WHICH, WHERE AM I?
NO, NO, NEVER MIND. JUST LET ME CHECK OUT THIS NAVIGATION APP...

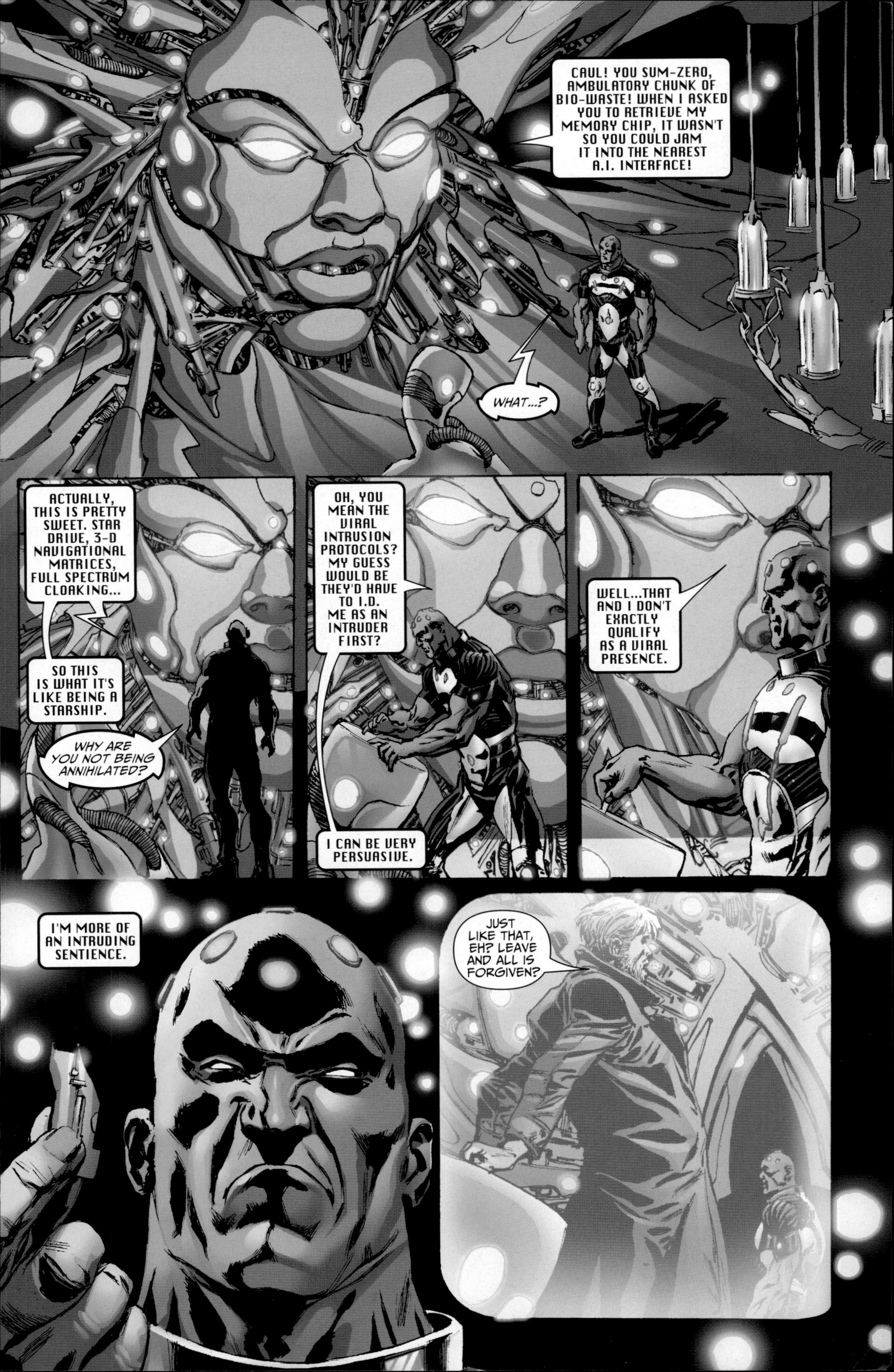
CAUL! YOU SUM-ZERO, AMBULATORY CHUNK OF BIO-WASTE! WHEN I ASKED YOU TO RETRIEVE MY MEMORY CHIP, IT WASN'T SO YOU COULD JAM IT INTO THE NEAREST A.I. INTERFACE!
WHAT...?
ACTUALLY, THIS IS PRETTY SWEET. STAR DRIVE, 3-D NAVIGATIONAL MATRICES, FULL SPECTRUM CLOAKING...
SO THIS IS WHAT IT'S LIKE BEING A STARSHIP.
WHY ARE YOU NOT BEING ANNIHILATED?
OH, YOU MEAN THE VIRAL INTRUSION PROTOCOLS? MY GUESS WOULD BE THEY'D HAVE TO I.D. ME AS AN INTRUDER FIRST?
I CAN BE VERY PERSUASIVE.
WELL...THAT AND I DON'T EXACTLY QUALIFY AS A VIRAL PRESENCE.
I'M MORE OF AN INTRUDING SENTIENCE.
JUST LIKE THAT, EH? LEAVE AND ALL IS FORGIVEN?

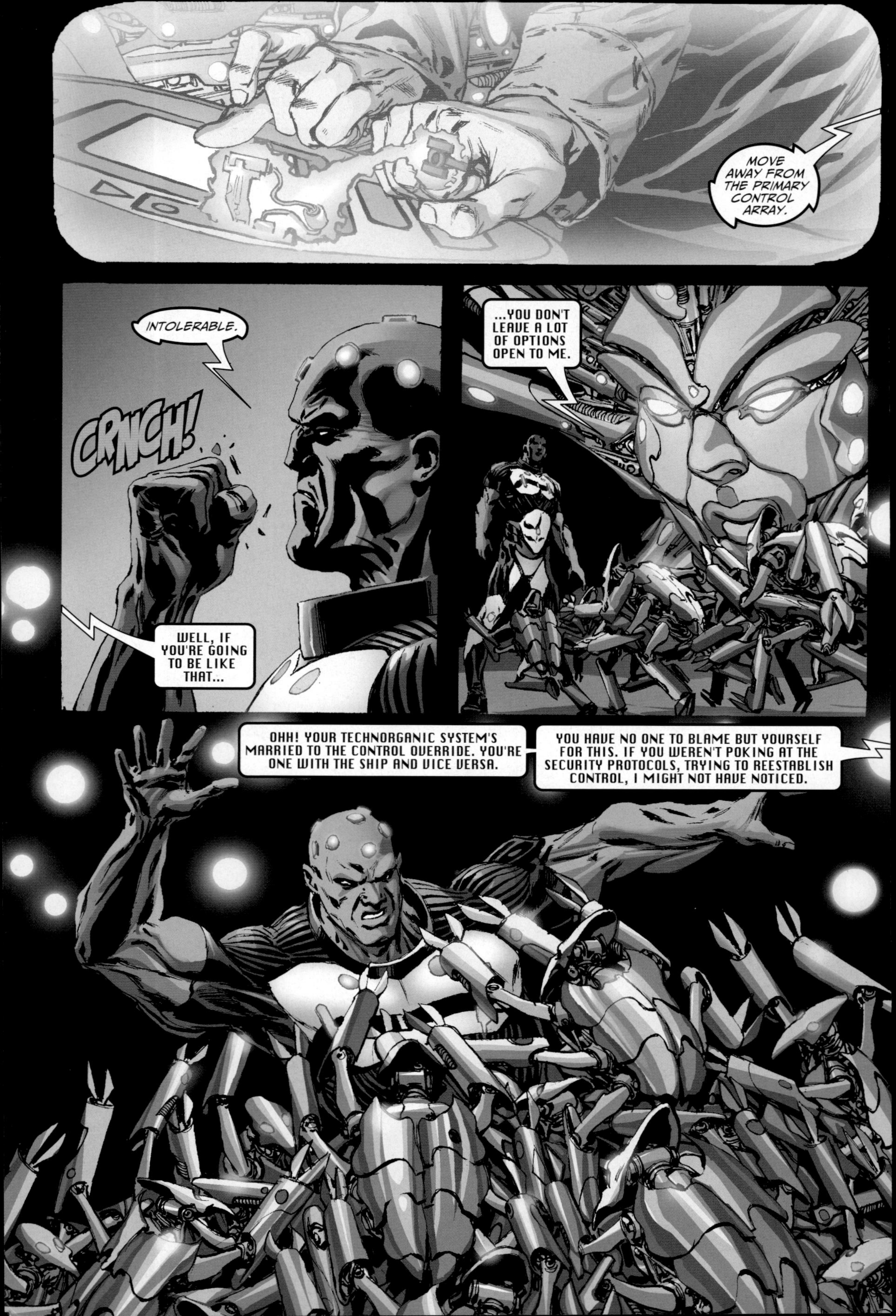
MOVE AWAY FROM THE PRIMARY CONTROL ARRAY.
INTOLERABLE.
CRNCH!
WELL, IF YOU'RE GOING TO BE LIKE THAT...
...YOU DON'T LEAVE A LOT OF OPTIONS OPEN TO ME.
OHH! YOUR TECHNORGANIC SYSTEM'S MARRIED TO THE CONTROL OVERRIDE. YOU'RE ONE WITH THE SHIP AND VICE VERSA.
YOU HAVE NO ONE TO BLAME BUT YOURSELF FOR THIS. IF YOU WEREN'T POKING AT THE SECURITY PROTOCOLS, TRYING TO REESTABLISH CONTROL, I MIGHT NOT HAVE NOTICED.

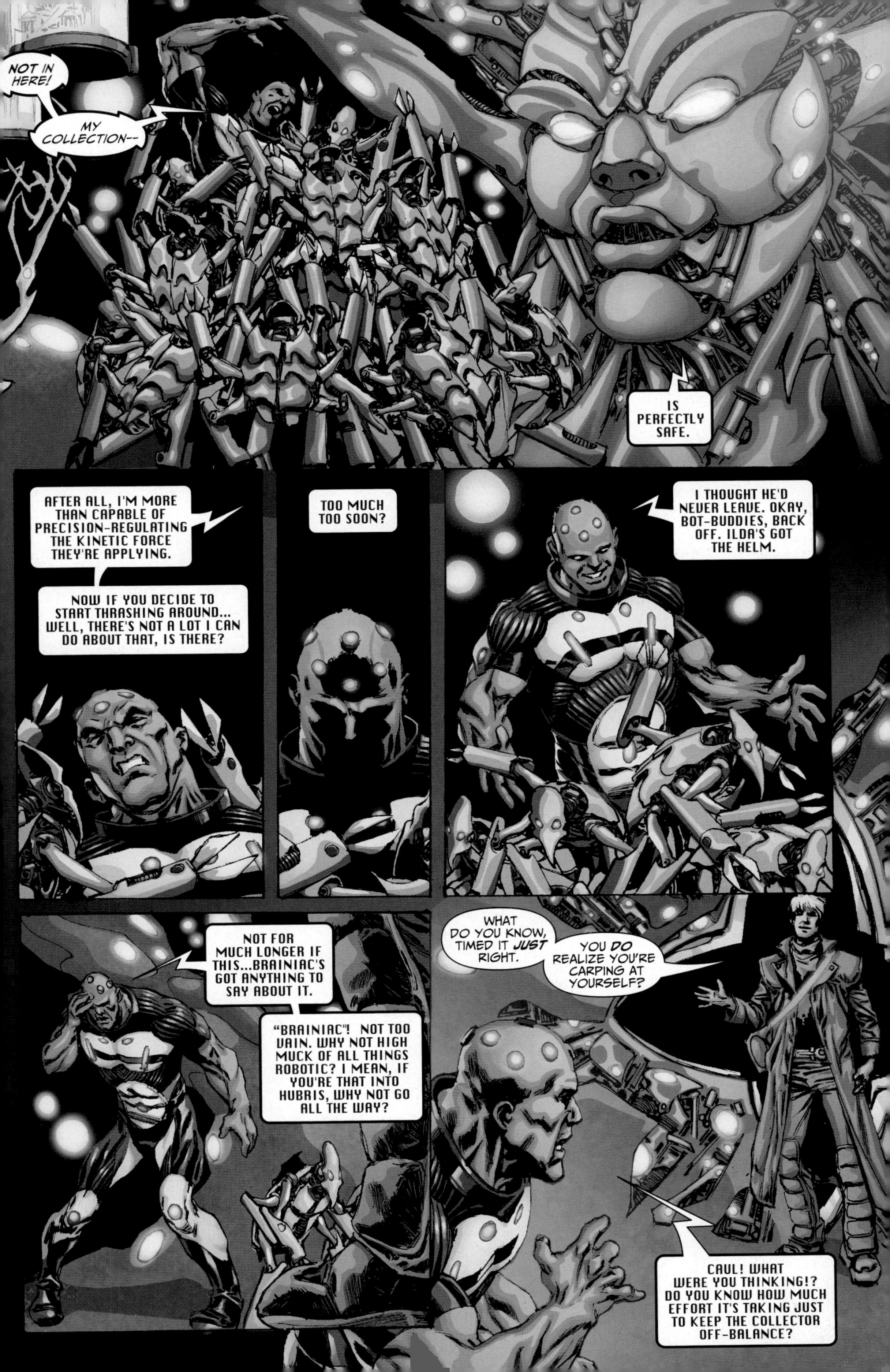
NOT IN HERE!
MY COLLECTION--
IS PERFECTLY SAFE.
AFTER ALL, I'M MORE THAN CAPABLE OF PRECISION-REGULATING THE KINETIC FORCE THEY'RE APPLYING.
NOW IF YOU DECIDE TO START THRASHING AROUND... WELL, THERE'S NOT A LOT I CAN DO ABOUT THAT, IS THERE?
TOO MUCH TOO SOON?
I THOUGHT HE'D NEVER LEAVE. OKAY, BOT-BUDDIES, BACK OFF. ILDA'S GOT THE HELM.
NOT FOR MUCH LONGER IF THIS...BRAINIAC'S GOT ANYTHING TO SAY ABOUT IT.
"BRAINIAC"! NOT TOO VAIN. WHY NOT HIGH MUCK OF ALL THINGS ROBOTIC? I MEAN, IF YOU'RE THAT INTO HUBRIS, WHY NOT GO ALL THE WAY?
WHAT DO YOU KNOW, TIMED IT JUST RIGHT.
YOU DO REALIZE YOU'RE CARPING AT YOURSELF?
CAUL! WHAT WERE YOU THINKING!? DO YOU KNOW HOW MUCH EFFORT IT'S TAKING JUST TO KEEP THE COLLECTOR OFF-BALANCE?

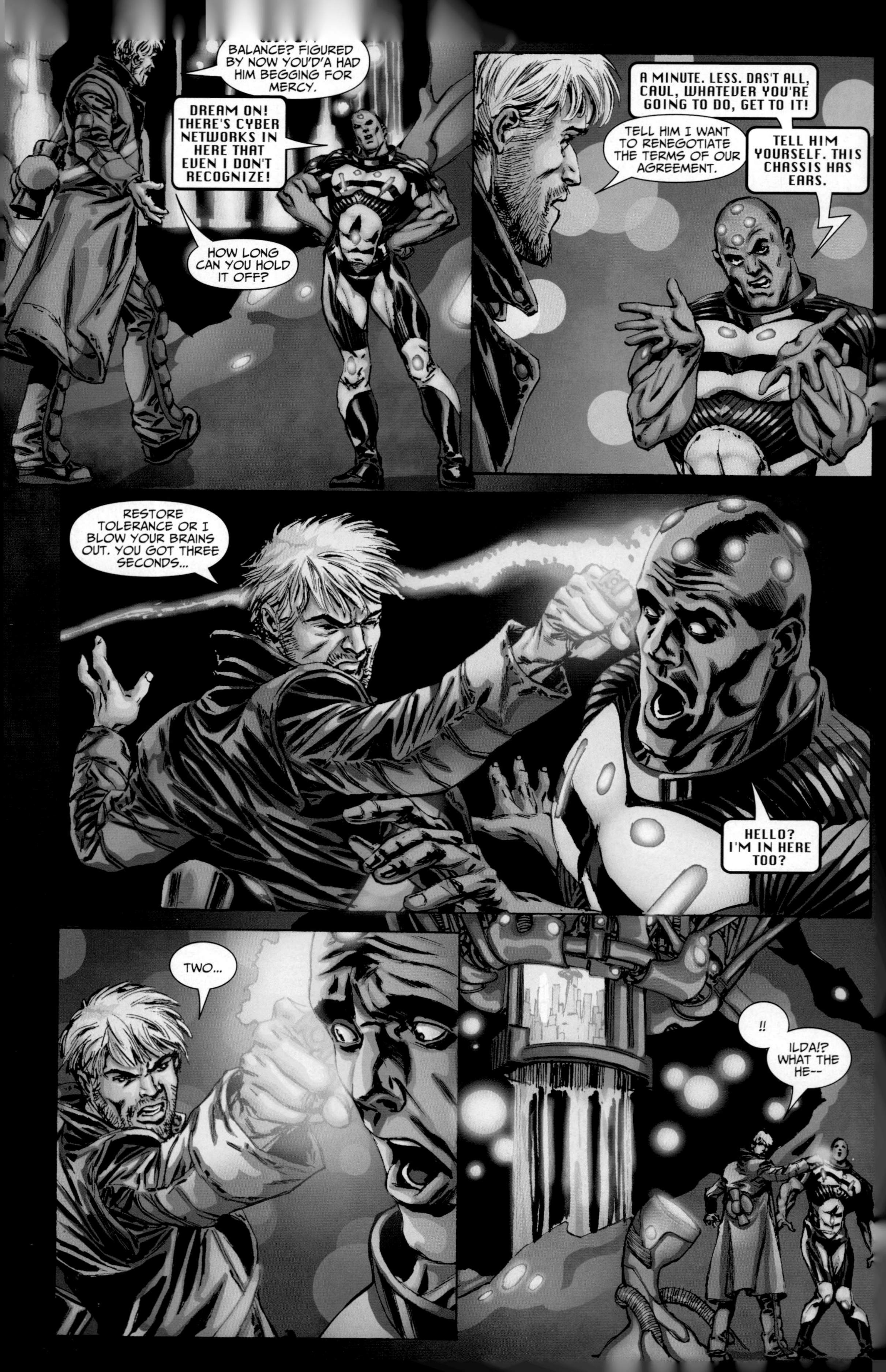
BALANCE? FIGURED BY NOW YOU'D'A HAD HIM BEGGING FOR MERCY.
DREAM ON! THERE'S CYBER NETWORKS IN HERE THAT EVEN I DON'T RECOGNIZE!
HOW LONG CAN YOU HOLD IT OFF?
A MINUTE. LESS. DAS'T ALL, CAUL, WHATEVER YOU'RE GOING TO DO, GET TO IT!
TELL HIM I WANT TO RENEGOTIATE THE TERMS OF OUR AGREEMENT.
TELL HIM YOURSELF. THIS CHASSIS HAS EARS.
RESTORE TOLERANCE OR I BLOW YOUR BRAINS OUT. YOU GOT THREE SECONDS...
HELLO? I'M IN HERE TOO?
TWO...
!!
ILDA!? WHAT THE HE--

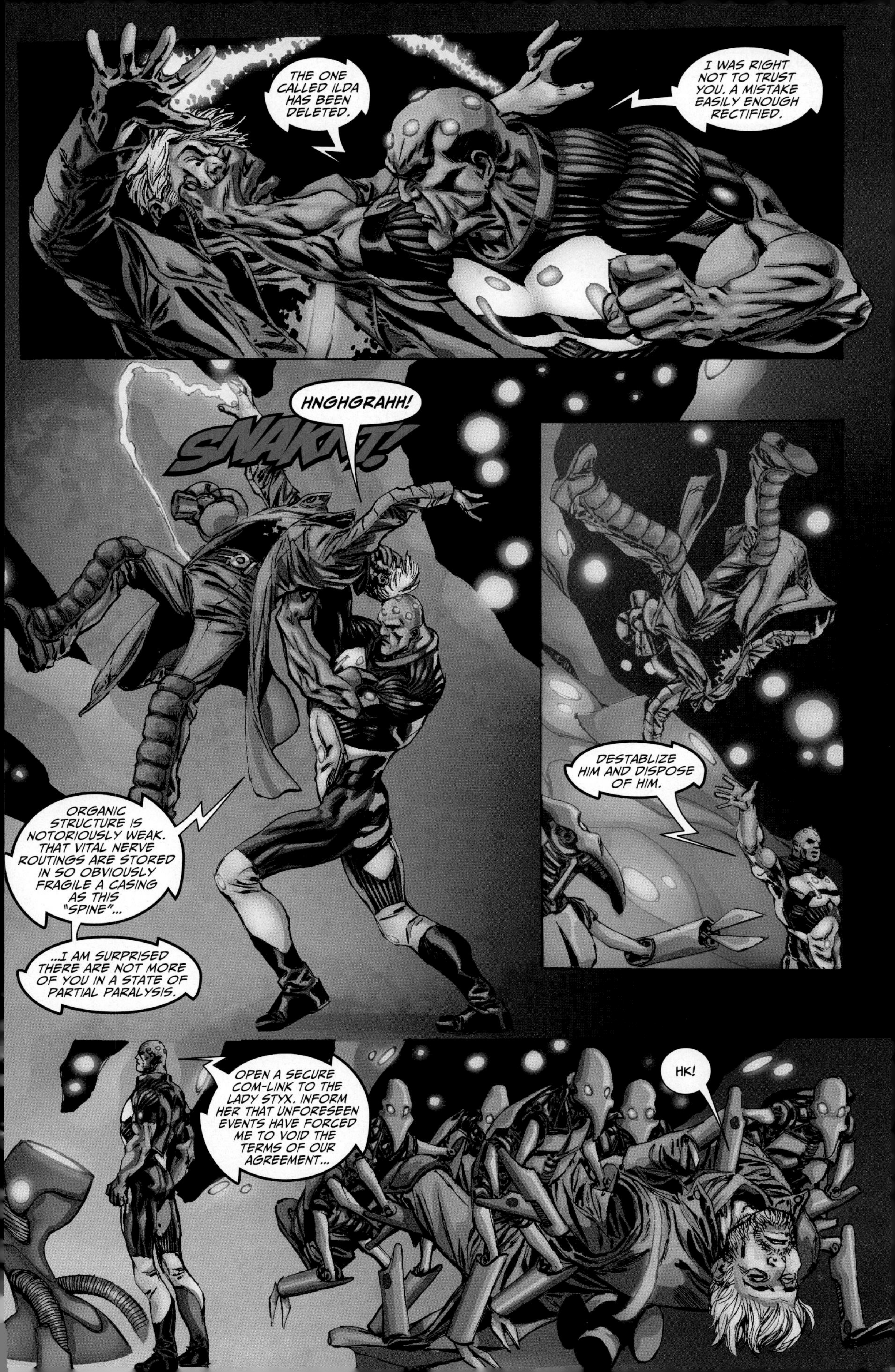
THE ONE CALLED ILDA HAS BEEN DELETED.
I WAS RIGHT NOT TO TRUST YOU. A MISTAKE EASILY ENOUGH RECTIFIED.
HNGHGRAHH!
SNAKT!
ORGANIC STRUCTURE IS NOTORIOUSLY WEAK. THAT VITAL NERVE ROUTINGS ARE STORED IN SO OBVIOUSLY FRAGILE A CASING AS THIS "SPINE"...
...I AM SURPRISED THERE ARE NOT MORE OF YOU IN A STATE OF PARTIAL PARALYSIS.
DESTABLIZE HIM AND DISPOSE OF HIM.
OPEN A SECURE COM-LINK TO THE LADY STYX. INFORM HER THAT UNFORESEEN EVENTS HAVE FORCED ME TO VOID THE TERMS OF OUR AGREEMENT...
HK!

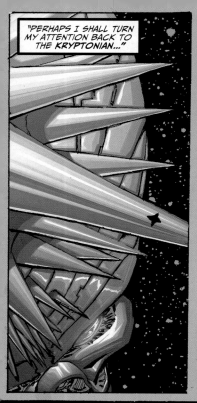

"PERHAPS I SHALL TURN MY ATTENTION BACK TO THE *KRYPTONIAN*..."

MY BACK...SCUG-SWILLING FECAL WART BROKE MY DA'S'T BACK!

PARALYZED ME FROM THE NECK DOWN...

OKAY...NOW *THAT* I CAN DO SOMETHING ABOUT...HOPEFULLY TEMPORARILY.

THAT CHUNK OF TOLERANCE ON THE OTHER HAND... THOSE FOLKS ARE DEADER'N'...

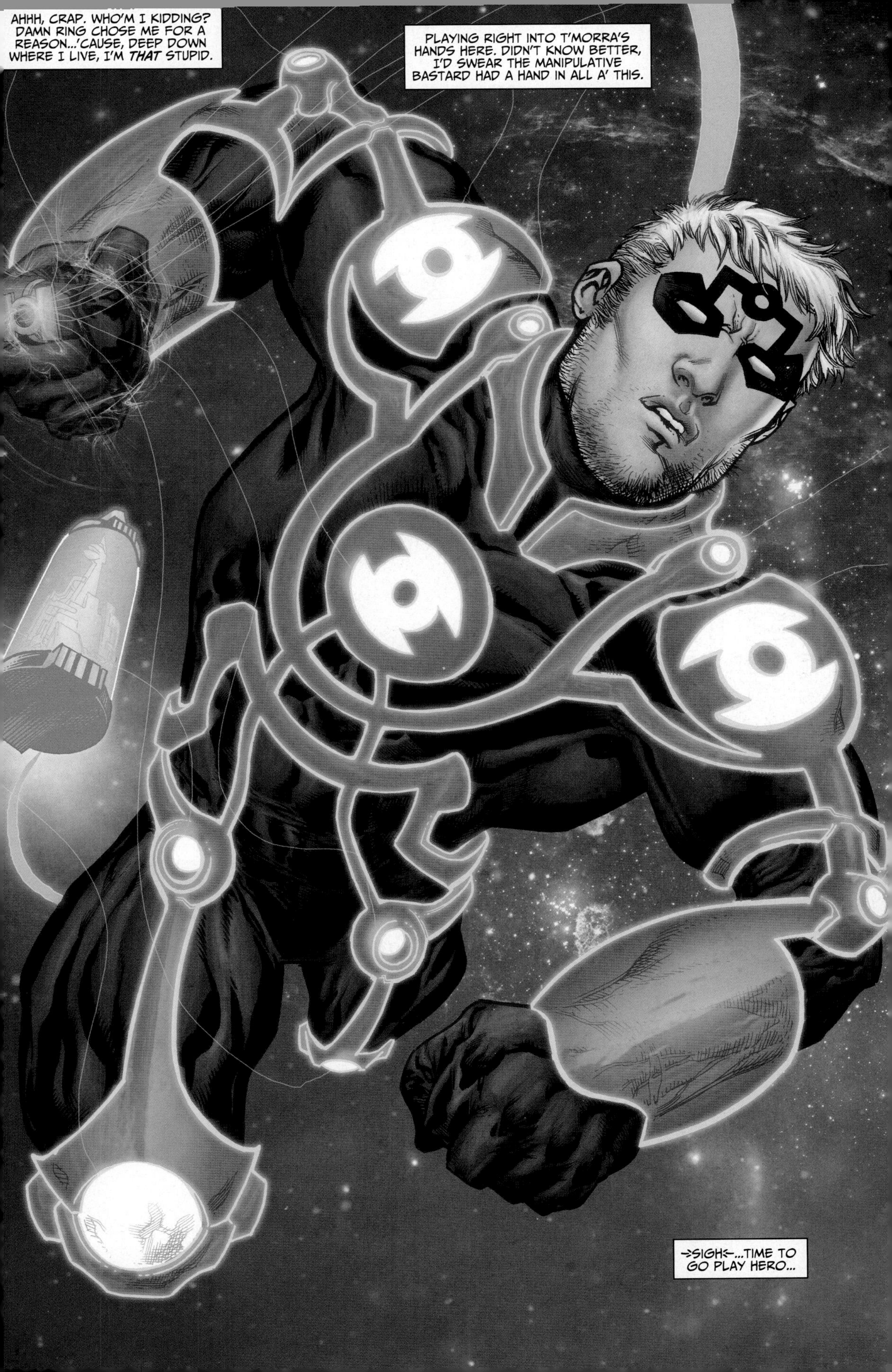
AHHH, CRAP. WHO'M I KIDDING? DAMN RING CHOSE ME FOR A REASON...'CAUSE, DEEP DOWN WHERE I LIVE, I'M *THAT* STUPID.
PLAYING RIGHT INTO T'MORRA'S HANDS HERE. DIDN'T KNOW BETTER, I'D SWEAR THE MANIPULATIVE BASTARD HAD A HAND IN ALL A' THIS.
>SIGH<...TIME TO GO PLAY HERO...

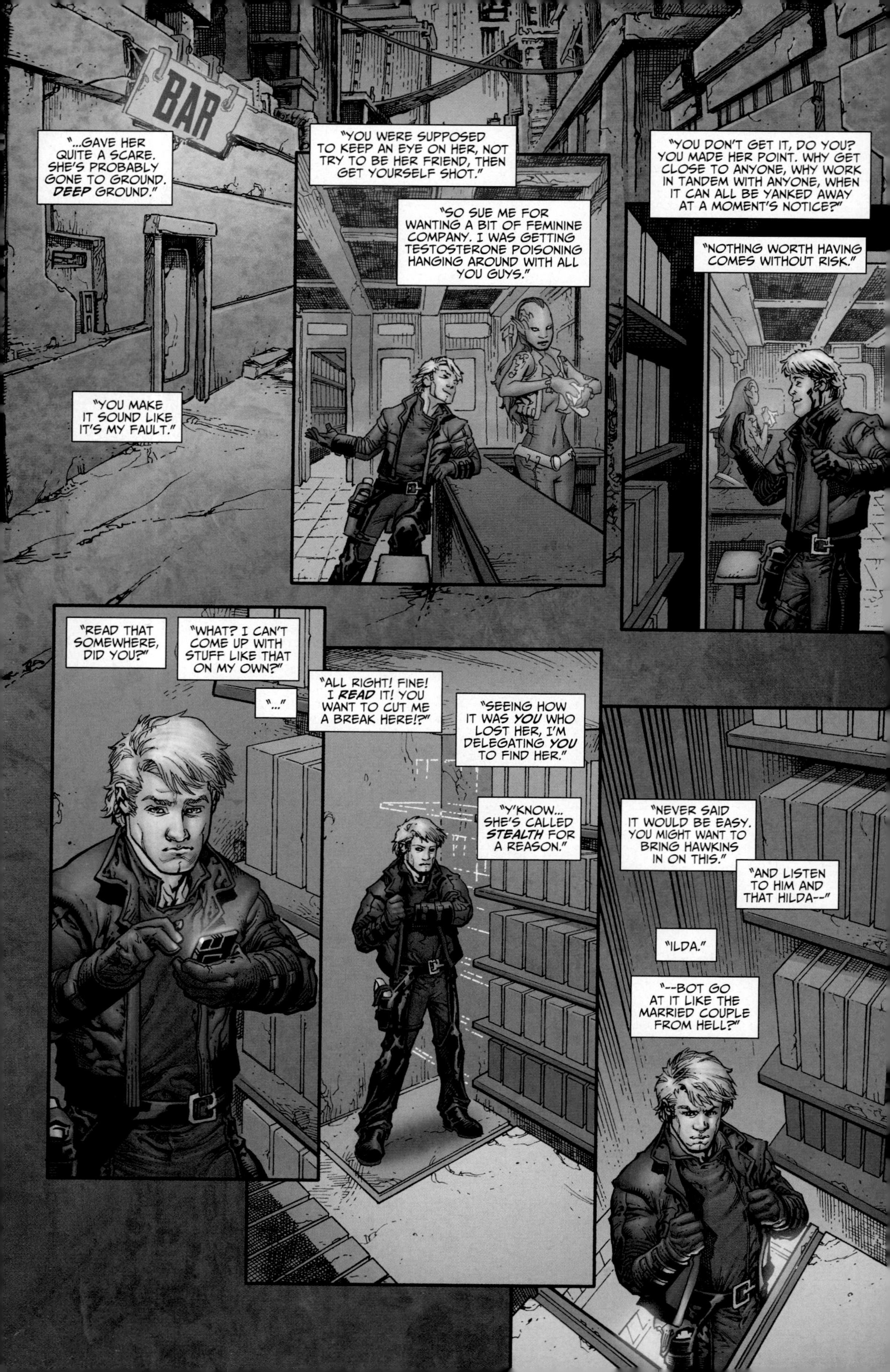
BAR
"...GAVE HER QUITE A SCARE. SHE'S PROBABLY GONE TO GROUND. DEEP GROUND."
"YOU MAKE IT SOUND LIKE IT'S MY FAULT."
"YOU WERE SUPPOSED TO KEEP AN EYE ON HER, NOT TRY TO BE HER FRIEND, THEN GET YOURSELF SHOT."
"SO SUE ME FOR WANTING A BIT OF FEMININE COMPANY. I WAS GETTING TESTOSTERONE POISONING HANGING AROUND WITH ALL YOU GUYS."
"YOU DON'T GET IT, DO YOU? YOU MADE HER POINT. WHY GET CLOSE TO ANYONE, WHY WORK IN TANDEM WITH ANYONE, WHEN IT CAN ALL BE YANKED AWAY AT A MOMENT'S NOTICE?"
"NOTHING WORTH HAVING COMES WITHOUT RISK."
"READ THAT SOMEWHERE, DID YOU?"
"WHAT? I CAN'T COME UP WITH STUFF LIKE THAT ON MY OWN?"
"..."
"ALL RIGHT! FINE! I READ IT! YOU WANT TO CUT ME A BREAK HERE!?"
"SEEING HOW IT WAS YOU WHO LOST HER, I'M DELEGATING YOU TO FIND HER."
"Y'KNOW... SHE'S CALLED STEALTH FOR A REASON."
"NEVER SAID IT WOULD BE EASY. YOU MIGHT WANT TO BRING HAWKINS IN ON THIS."
"AND LISTEN TO HIM AND THAT HILDA--"
"ILDA."
"--BOT GO AT IT LIKE THE MARRIED COUPLE FROM HELL?"

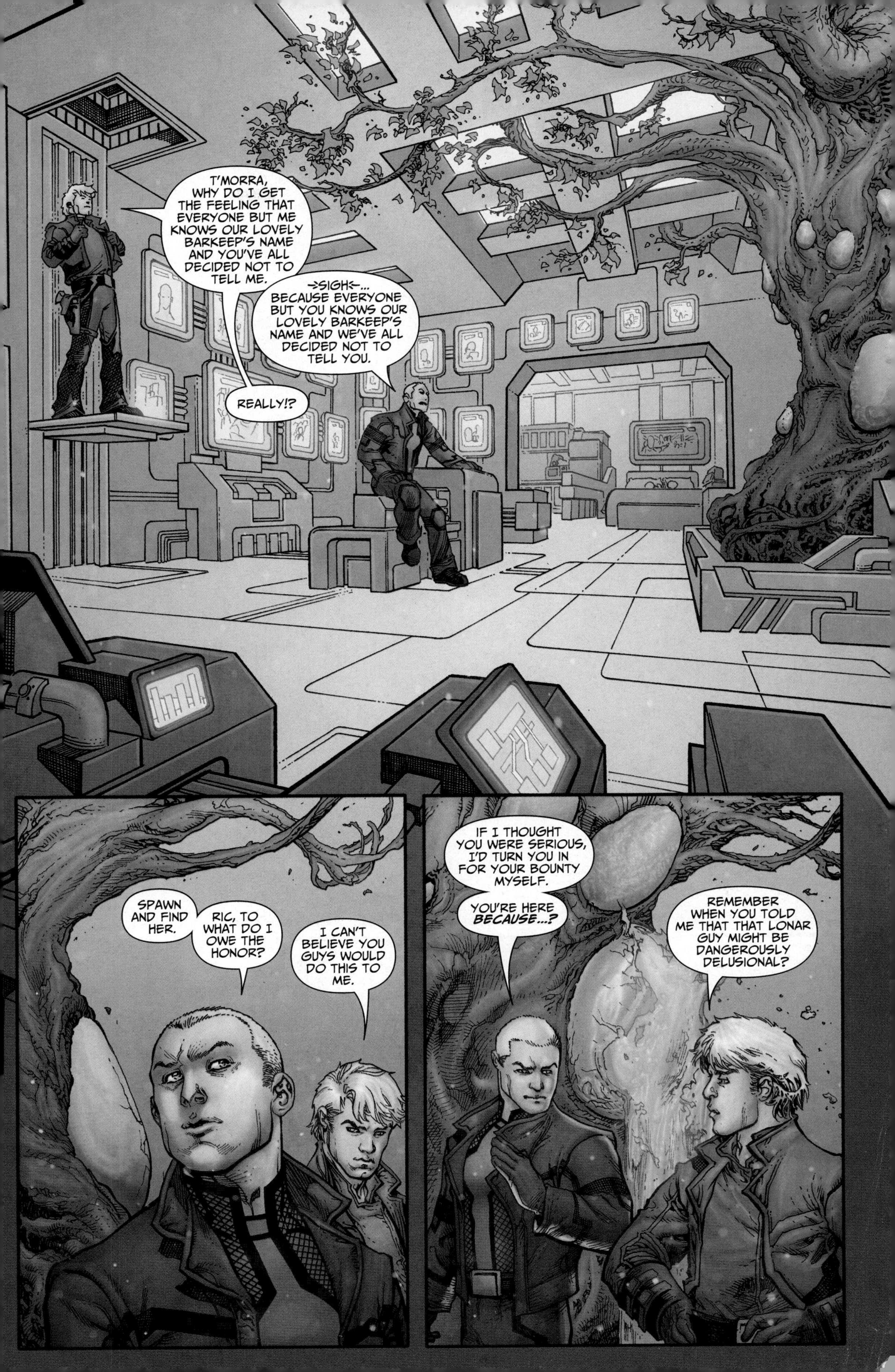
T'MORRA, WHY DO I GET THE FEELING THAT EVERYONE BUT ME KNOWS OUR LOVELY BARKEEP'S NAME AND YOU'VE ALL DECIDED NOT TO TELL ME.
>SIGH<... BECAUSE EVERYONE BUT YOU KNOWS OUR LOVELY BARKEEP'S NAME AND WE'VE ALL DECIDED NOT TO TELL YOU.
REALLY!?
SPAWN AND FIND HER.
RIC, TO WHAT DO I OWE THE HONOR?
I CAN'T BELIEVE YOU GUYS WOULD DO THIS TO ME.
IF I THOUGHT YOU WERE SERIOUS, I'D TURN YOU IN FOR YOUR BOUNTY MYSELF.
YOU'RE HERE *BECAUSE...?*
REMEMBER WHEN YOU TOLD ME THAT THAT LONAR GUY MIGHT BE DANGEROUSLY DELUSIONAL?

HE BELIEVES HIMSELF A GOD. NEED I SAY MORE?

YEAH, WELL, SCUTTLEBUTT HAS IT THAT HE'S HOOKED UP WITH THE REACH WARRIOR, THAT "BLUE BEETLE."

HE'S GOING TO FIND HIMSELF DISAPPOINTED.

HOW'S THAT? I MEAN, ASSUMING IT'S TRUE 'N' ALL.

KAFF!

'SCUSE ME WHILE I CATCH A QUICK RINSE.

HEY, RIC.

WELCOME BACK, EMBER.

HOW MANY TIMES THAT MAKE IT THAT SHE'S GOTTEN POPPED? THREE? FOUR? MUST DRIVE BOUNTY PAYOUT TO DISTRACTION.

SHE'S DEAD. SHE'S BACK. SHE'S DEAD. SHE'S--

CAN WE STICK TO THE TOPIC AT HAND?

...INTERRUPT...

WE INTERRUPT ...

...INTERRUPT THIS PROGRAM...

...INTERRUPT THIS...

...LIVE FEED INTERRUPTION...

OKAY. FINE. SO WHY'S LONAR GOING TO BE DISAPPOINTED?

...INTERRUPT...

...INTERRUPT THIS PROGRAM...

...LATER.

LATER!? BUT YOU JUST SAID--

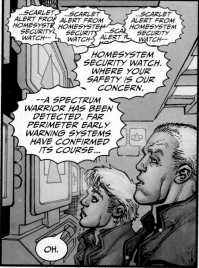

...SCARLET ALERT FROM HOMESYSTEM SECURITY WATCH--

...SCARLET ALERT FROM HOMESYSTEM SECURITY WATCH--

...SCARLET ALERT FROM HOMESYSTEM SECURITY WATCH--

...SCARLET ALERT F

...SCARLET ALERT FR

HOMESYSTEM SECURITY WATCH. WHERE YOUR SAFETY IS OUR CONCERN.

--A SPECTRUM WARRIOR HAS BEEN DETECTED. FAR PERIMETER EARLY WARNING SYSTEMS HAVE CONFIRMED ITS COURSE...

OH.

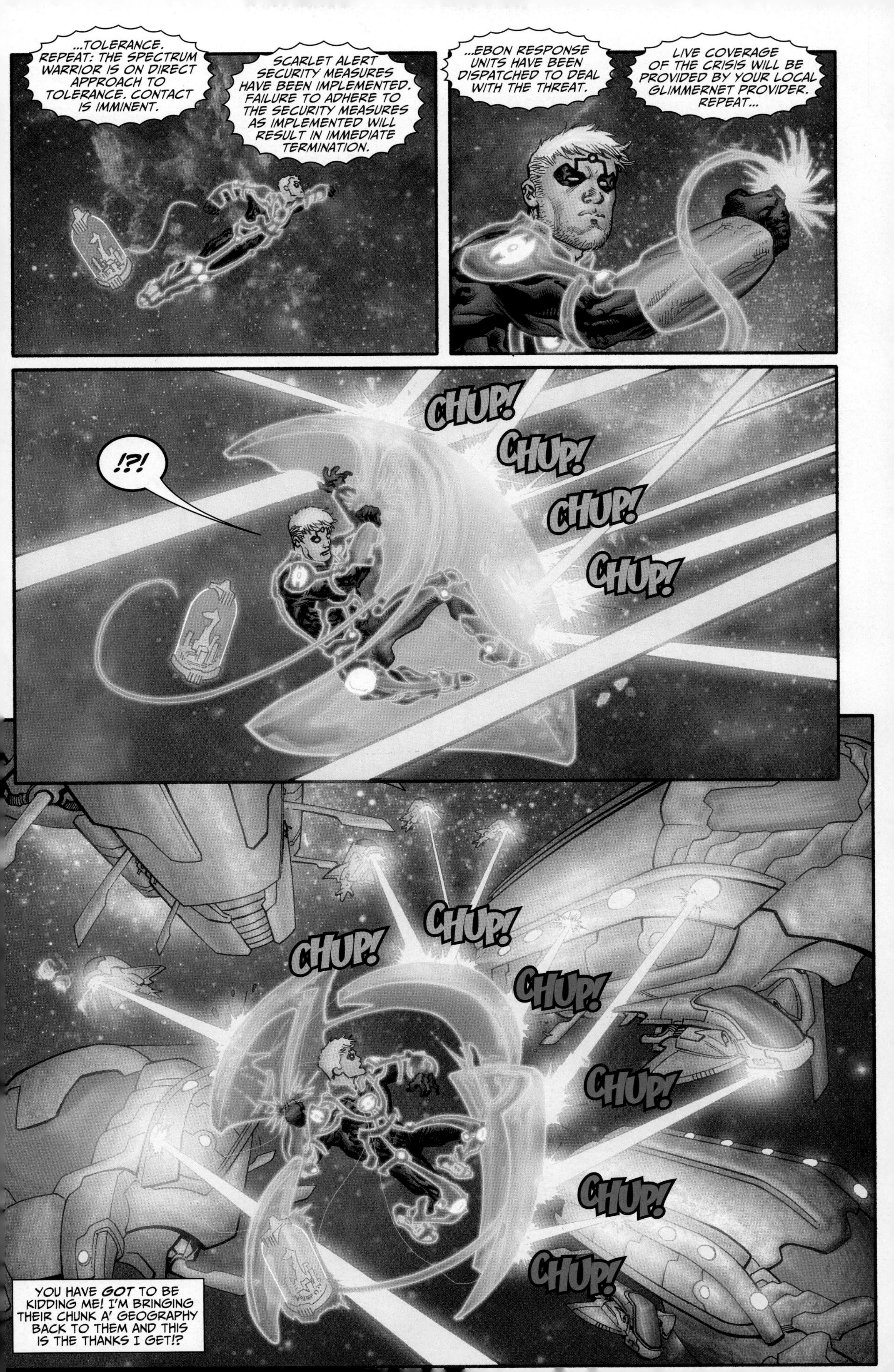

...TOLERANCE. REPEAT: THE SPECTRUM WARRIOR IS ON DIRECT APPROACH TO TOLERANCE. CONTACT IS IMMINENT.
SCARLET ALERT SECURITY MEASURES HAVE BEEN IMPLEMENTED. FAILURE TO ADHERE TO THE SECURITY MEASURES AS IMPLEMENTED WILL RESULT IN IMMEDIATE TERMINATION.
...EBON RESPONSE UNITS HAVE BEEN DISPATCHED TO DEAL WITH THE THREAT.
LIVE COVERAGE OF THE CRISIS WILL BE PROVIDED BY YOUR LOCAL GLIMMERNET PROVIDER. REPEAT...
CHUP!
CHUP!
CHUP!
CHUP!
!?!
CHUP!
CHUP!
CHUP!
CHUP!
CHUP!
CHUP!
YOU HAVE *GOT* TO BE KIDDING ME! I'M BRINGING THEIR CHUNK A' GEOGRAPHY BACK TO THEM AND THIS IS THE THANKS I GET!?

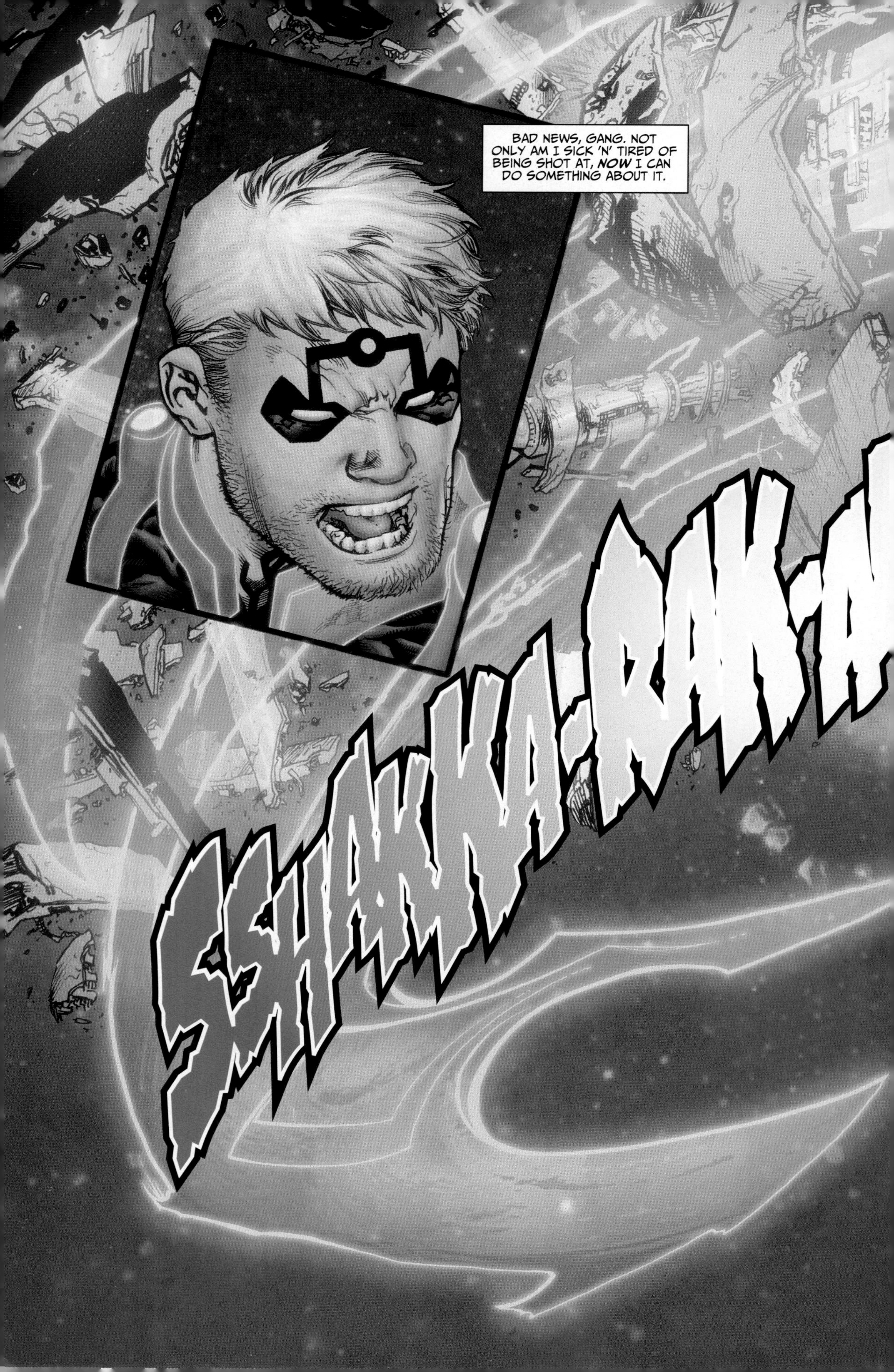
BAD NEWS, GANG. NOT ONLY AM I SICK 'N' TIRED OF BEING SHOT AT, *NOW* I CAN DO SOMETHING ABOUT IT.
S-SHAKKA-RAK-A

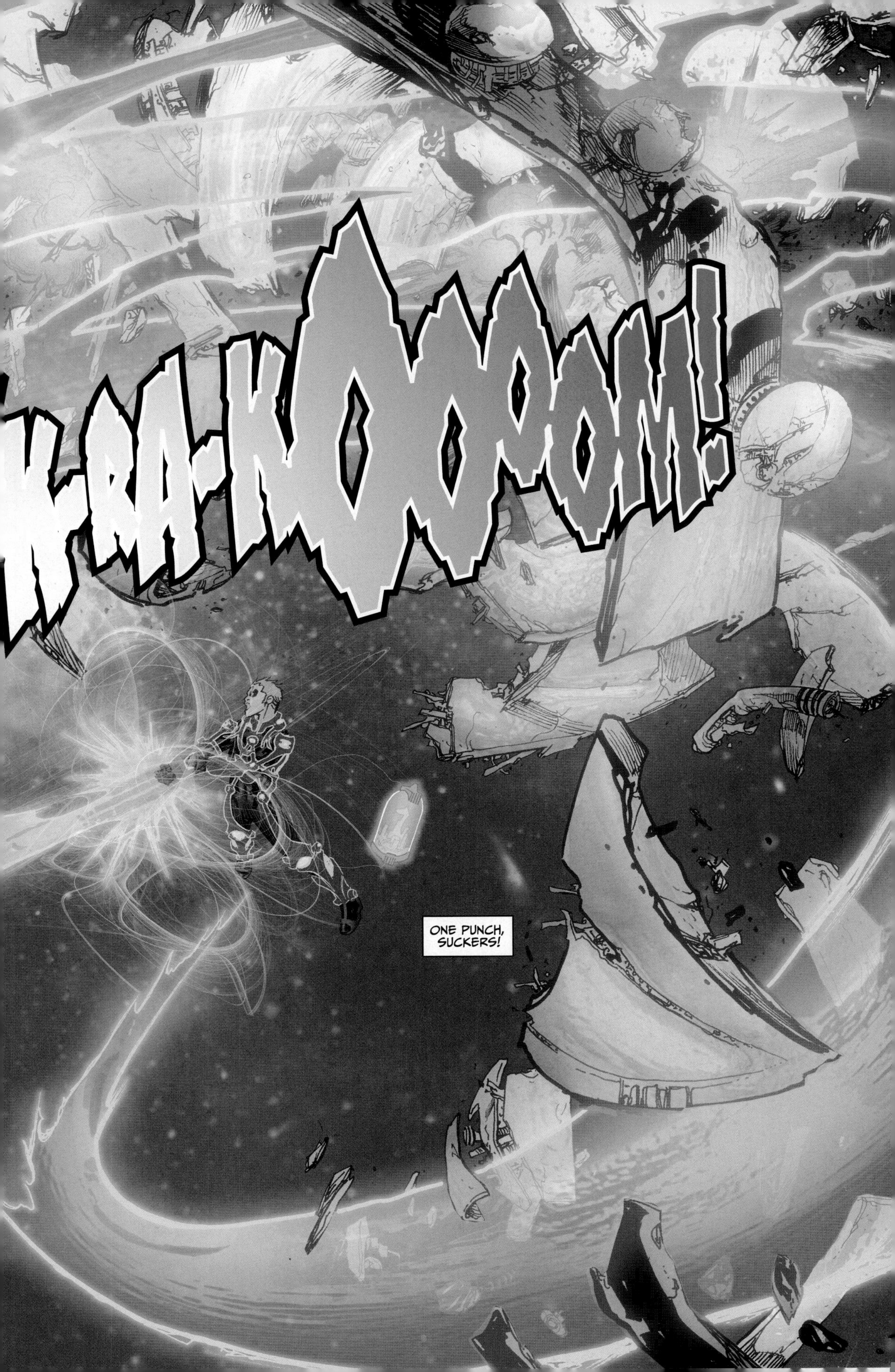

K-RA-KOOOOM!
ONE PUNCH, SUCKERS!

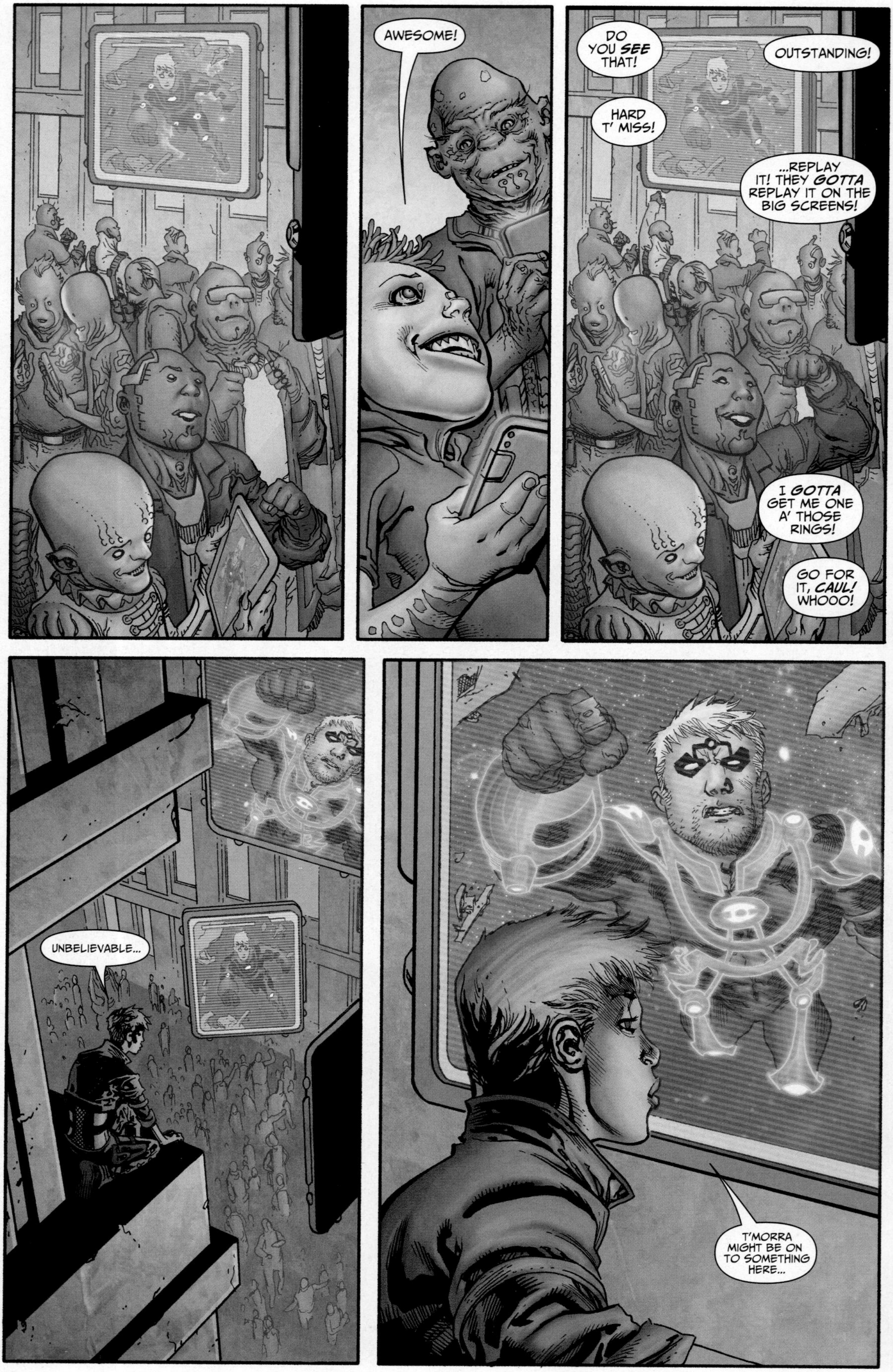
AWESOME!
DO YOU SEE THAT!
HARD T' MISS!
OUTSTANDING!
...REPLAY IT! THEY GOTTA REPLAY IT ON THE BIG SCREENS!
I GOTTA GET ME ONE A' THOSE RINGS!
GO FOR IT, CAUL! WHOOO!
UNBELIEVABLE...
T'MORRA MIGHT BE ON TO SOMETHING HERE...

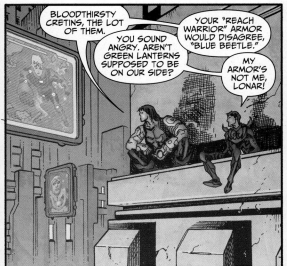

BLOODTHIRSTY CRETINS, THE LOT OF THEM.

YOU SOUND ANGRY. AREN'T GREEN LANTERNS SUPPOSED TO BE ON OUR SIDE?

YOUR "REACH WARRIOR" ARMOR WOULD DISAGREE, "BLUE BEETLE."

MY ARMOR'S NOT ME, LONAR!

SO YOU SAY.

OKAY! THAT'S IT! YOU'VE BEEN TALKING IN RIDDLES SINCE WE FIRST "MET" AND I'M SICK AND TIRED OF IT!

THE WHOLE "GOD" THING? THAT I CAN DEAL WITH. MY MOM'S SECOND COUSIN THOUGHT SHE WAS A ROTTWEILER. CRAZY I CAN HANDLE.

BUT MIND GAMES!? I'M OUT OF HERE!

THANKS FOR THE LOWDOWN ON THIS GAME OR COMPETITION OR WHATEVER IT IS, BUT I GOTTA START FOCUSING ON FINDING MY WAY--

I CAN GET YOU HOME. I CAN ALSO REMOVE THE REACH MAGGOT.

THE SCARAB?

I PREFER MAGGOT.

YOU HELP ME, I HELP YOU.

AND-- JUST FOR THE SAKE OF ARGUMENT--IF I DON'T WANT TO HELP YOU DO WHATEVER?

I CAN'T HAVE YOU RUNNING AROUND FREE ONCE YOU KNOW.

WHAT? YOU GOING TO KILL ME TO ENSURE MY SILENCE?

HELLO? LONAR?

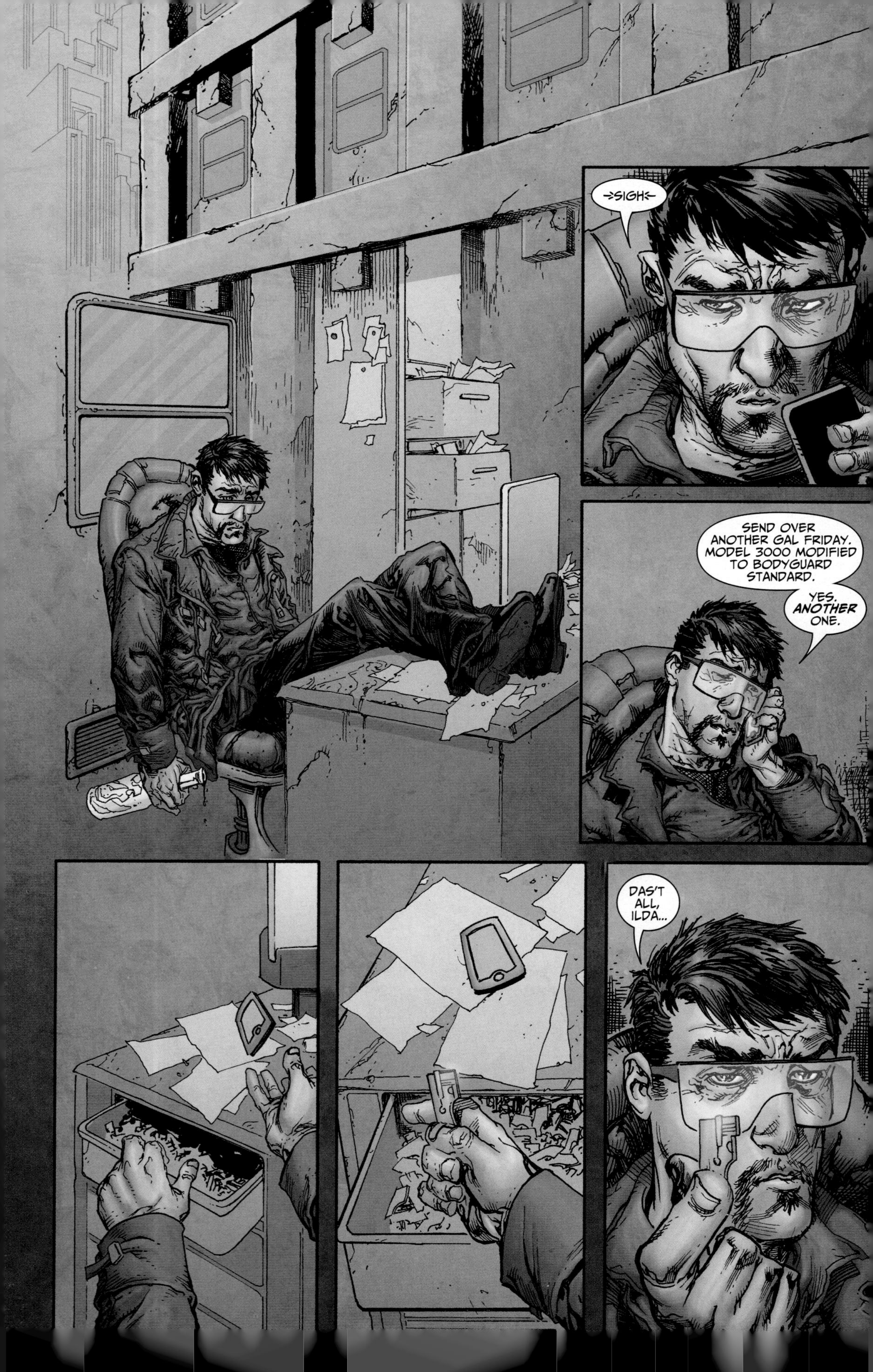

-SIGH-
SEND OVER ANOTHER GAL FRIDAY. MODEL 3000 MODIFIED TO BODYGUARD STANDARD.
YES. ANOTHER ONE.
DAS'T ALL, ILDA...

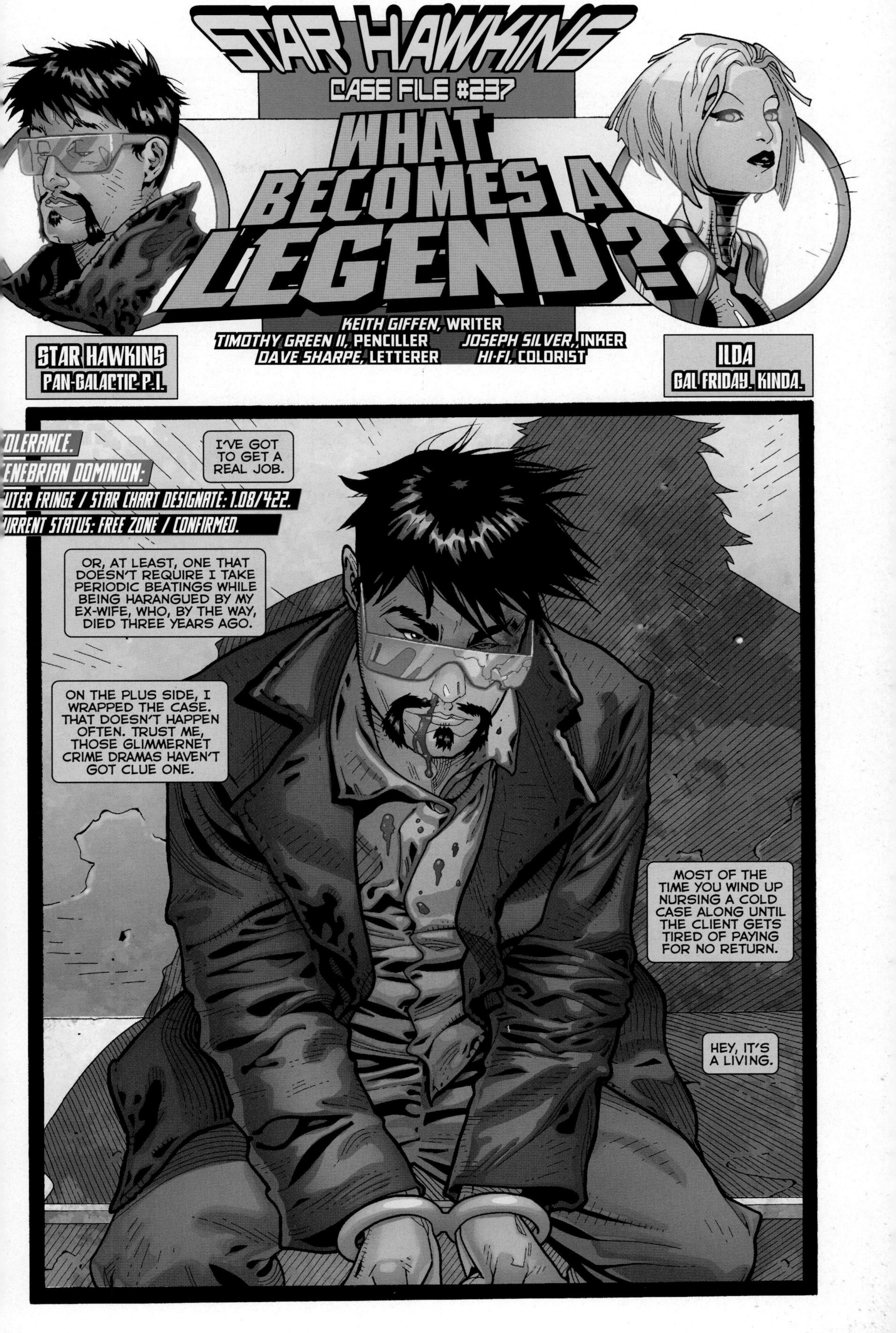
STAR HAWKINS
CASE FILE #237
WHAT BECOMES A LEGEND?
KEITH GIFFEN, WRITER
TIMOTHY GREEN II, PENCILLER
JOSEPH SILVER, INKER
DAVE SHARPE, LETTERER
HI-FI, COLORIST
STAR HAWKINS
PAN-GALACTIC P.I.
ILDA
GAL FRIDAY. KINDA.
OLERANCE.
ENEBRIAN DOMINION:
UTER FRINGE / STAR CHART DESIGNATE: 1.08/422.
URRENT STATUS: FREE ZONE / CONFIRMED.
I'VE GOT TO GET A REAL JOB.
OR, AT LEAST, ONE THAT DOESN'T REQUIRE I TAKE PERIODIC BEATINGS WHILE BEING HARANGUED BY MY EX-WIFE, WHO, BY THE WAY, DIED THREE YEARS AGO.
ON THE PLUS SIDE, I WRAPPED THE CASE. THAT DOESN'T HAPPEN OFTEN. TRUST ME, THOSE GLIMMERNET CRIME DRAMAS HAVEN'T GOT CLUE ONE.
MOST OF THE TIME YOU WIND UP NURSING A COLD CASE ALONG UNTIL THE CLIENT GETS TIRED OF PAYING FOR NO RETURN.
HEY, IT'S A LIVING.

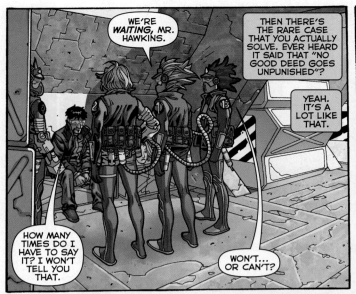

WE'RE *WAITING*, MR. HAWKINS.

THEN THERE'S THE RARE CASE THAT YOU ACTUALLY SOLVE. EVER HEARD IT SAID THAT "NO GOOD DEED GOES UNPUNISHED"?

YEAH. IT'S A LOT LIKE THAT.

HOW MANY TIMES DO I HAVE TO SAY IT? I WON'T TELL YOU THAT.

WON'T... OR CAN'T?

WHAT?

THAT MADE, LIKE, NO SENSE AT ALL.

AND WHAT IF HE *DON'T* KNOW WHO HIRED HIM?

DO YOU KNOW WHO HIRED YOU?

YES, I DO.

THIS BRAIN TRUST CALLS THEMSELVES CRIMSON THRUST. THEY'RE THE PREMIER HUNT CLUB ON TOLERANCE...

...OR IN TOLERANCE OR HOWEVER YOU PUT IT WHEN AN ENTIRE POPULATION CAN'T DECIDE WHETHER IT'S THE PLANET'S NAME OR A CITY'S NAME OR JUST A STATE OF MIND.

IF HE DIDN'T KNOW, HE'D BE FRONT-LOADING THAT! INSTEAD A' TELLING US HE *WON'T* TELL, HE'D BE TELLING US HE *CAN'T!*

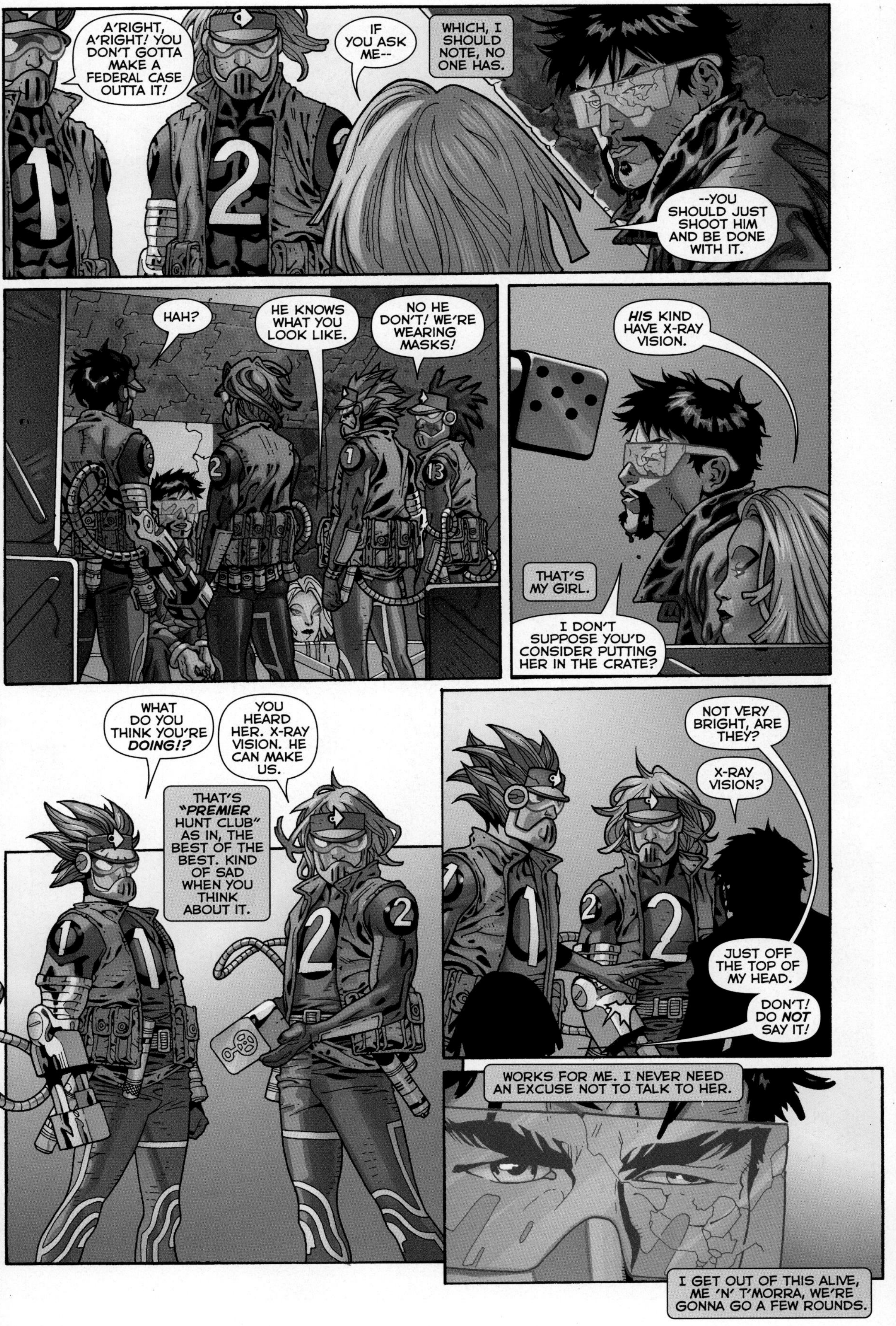

A'RIGHT, A'RIGHT! YOU DON'T GOTTA MAKE A FEDERAL CASE OUTTA IT!
IF YOU ASK ME--
WHICH, I SHOULD NOTE, NO ONE HAS.
--YOU SHOULD JUST SHOOT HIM AND BE DONE WITH IT.
HAH?
HE KNOWS WHAT YOU LOOK LIKE.
NO HE DON'T! WE'RE WEARING MASKS!
HIS KIND HAVE X-RAY VISION.
THAT'S MY GIRL.
I DON'T SUPPOSE YOU'D CONSIDER PUTTING HER IN THE CRATE?
WHAT DO YOU THINK YOU'RE DOING!?
YOU HEARD HER. X-RAY VISION. HE CAN MAKE US.
THAT'S "PREMIER HUNT CLUB" AS IN, THE BEST OF THE BEST. KIND OF SAD WHEN YOU THINK ABOUT IT.
NOT VERY BRIGHT, ARE THEY?
X-RAY VISION?
JUST OFF THE TOP OF MY HEAD.
DON'T! DO NOT SAY IT!
WORKS FOR ME. I NEVER NEED AN EXCUSE NOT TO TALK TO HER.
I GET OUT OF THIS ALIVE, ME 'N' T'MORRA, WE'RE GONNA GO A FEW ROUNDS.

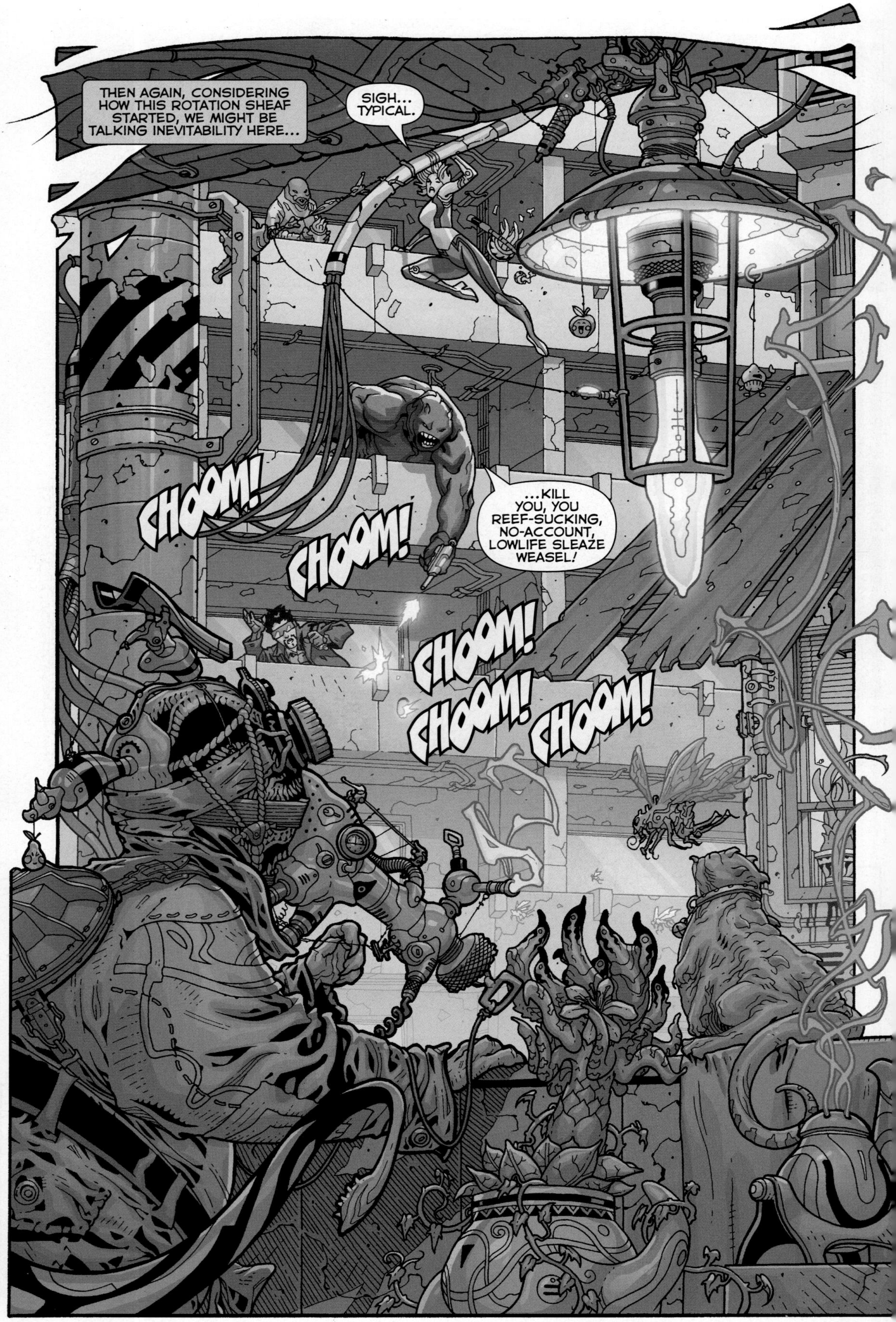
THEN AGAIN, CONSIDERING HOW THIS ROTATION SHEAF STARTED, WE MIGHT BE TALKING INEVITABILITY HERE...
SIGH... TYPICAL.
CHOOM!
CHOOM!
...KILL YOU, YOU REEF-SUCKING, NO-ACCOUNT, LOWLIFE SLEAZE WEASEL!
CHOOM!
CHOOM!
CHOOM!

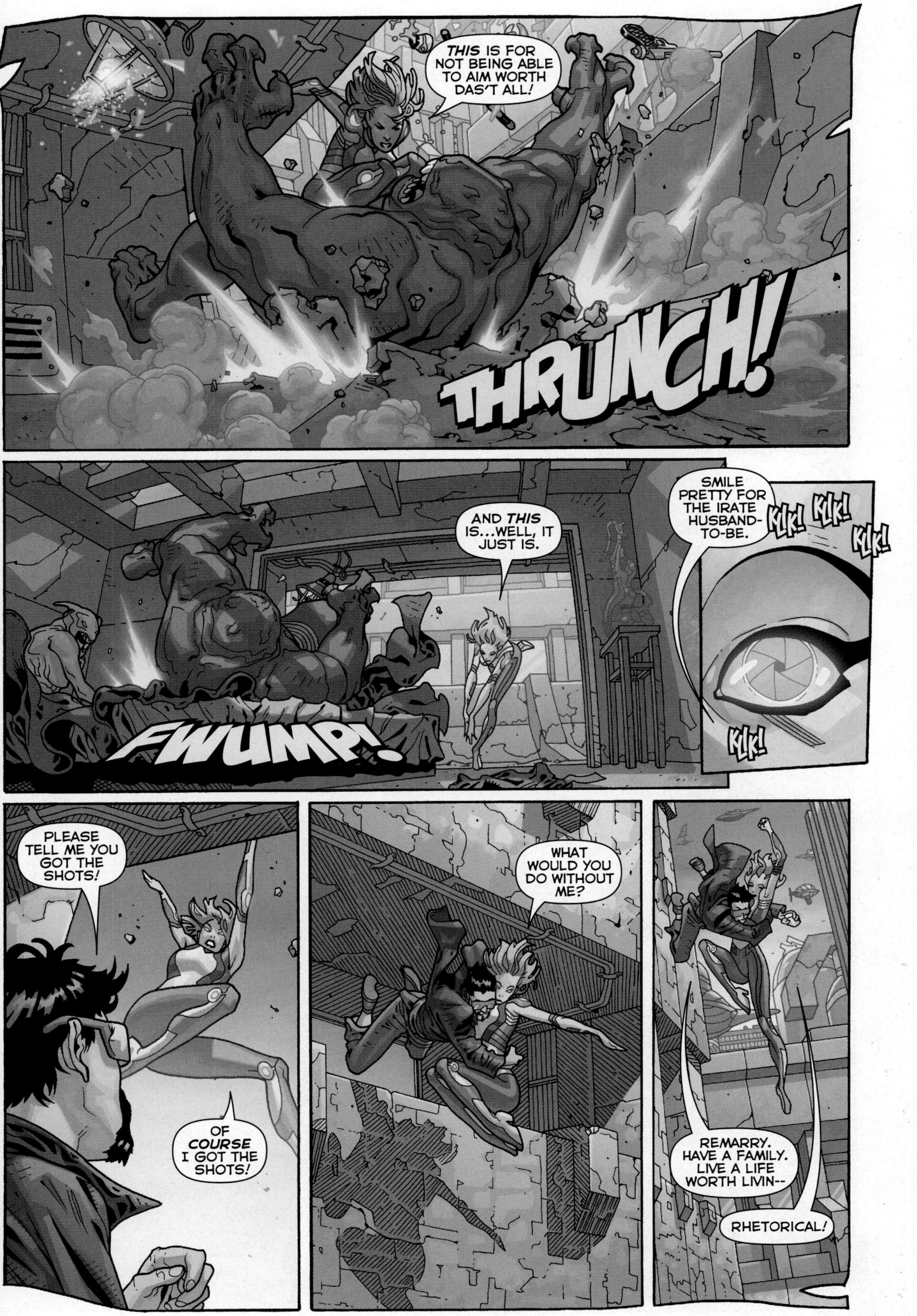
THIS IS FOR NOT BEING ABLE TO AIM WORTH DAS'T ALL!
THRUNCH!
AND THIS IS...WELL, IT JUST IS.
FWUMP!
SMILE PRETTY FOR THE IRATE HUSBAND-TO-BE.
KLIK! KLIK! KLIK!
KLIK!
PLEASE TELL ME YOU GOT THE SHOTS!
OF COURSE I GOT THE SHOTS!
WHAT WOULD YOU DO WITHOUT ME?
REMARRY. HAVE A FAMILY. LIVE A LIFE WORTH LIVIN--
RHETORICAL!

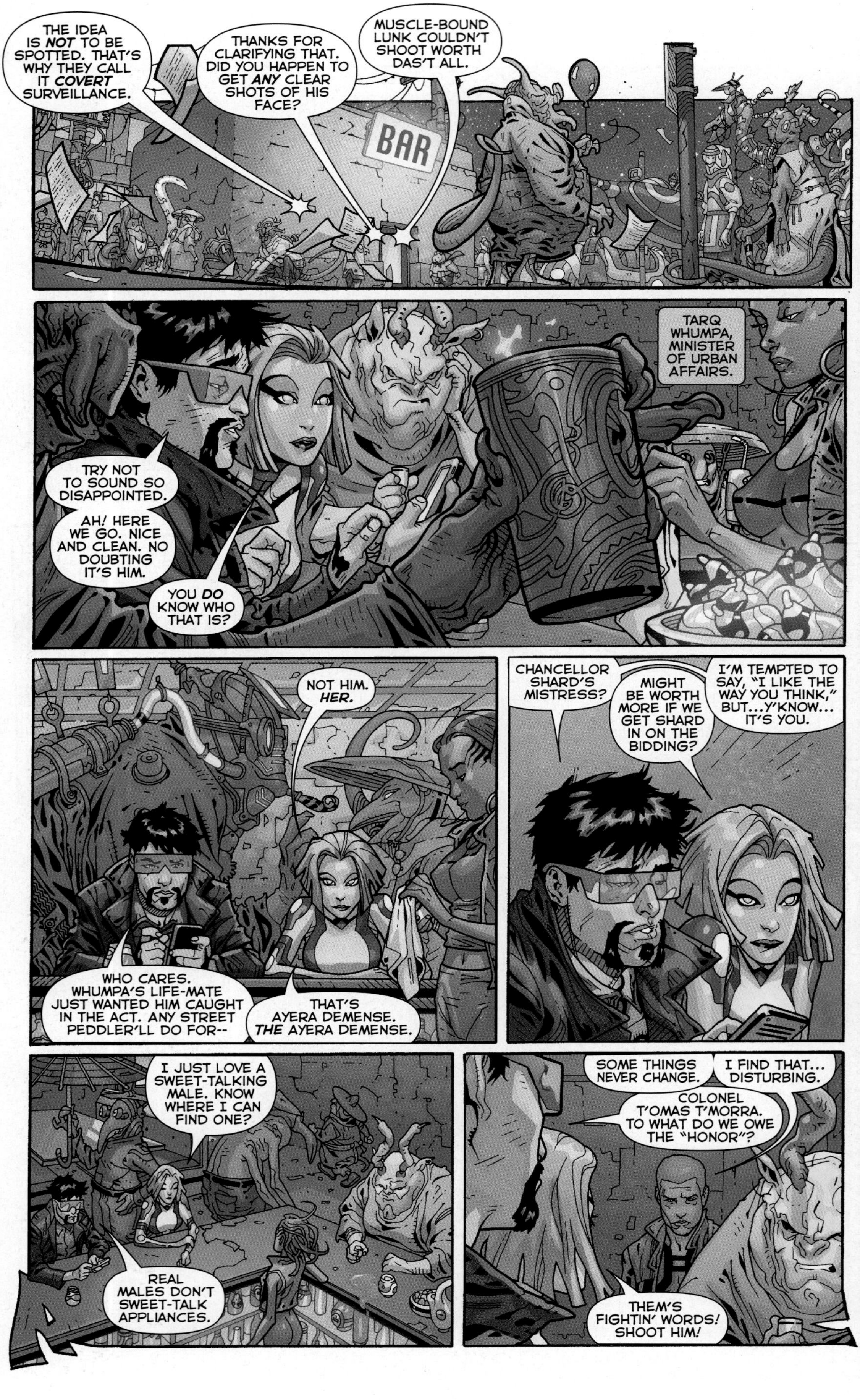
THE IDEA IS NOT TO BE SPOTTED. THAT'S WHY THEY CALL IT COVERT SURVEILLANCE.
THANKS FOR CLARIFYING THAT. DID YOU HAPPEN TO GET ANY CLEAR SHOTS OF HIS FACE?
MUSCLE-BOUND LUNK COULDN'T SHOOT WORTH DAS'T ALL.
BAR
TARQ WHUMPA, MINISTER OF URBAN AFFAIRS.
TRY NOT TO SOUND SO DISAPPOINTED.
AH! HERE WE GO. NICE AND CLEAN. NO DOUBTING IT'S HIM.
YOU DO KNOW WHO THAT IS?
NOT HIM. HER.
WHO CARES. WHUMPA'S LIFE-MATE JUST WANTED HIM CAUGHT IN THE ACT. ANY STREET PEDDLER'LL DO FOR--
THAT'S AYERA DEMENSE. THE AYERA DEMENSE.
CHANCELLOR SHARD'S MISTRESS?
MIGHT BE WORTH MORE IF WE GET SHARD IN ON THE BIDDING?
I'M TEMPTED TO SAY, "I LIKE THE WAY YOU THINK," BUT...Y'KNOW... IT'S YOU.
I JUST LOVE A SWEET-TALKING MALE. KNOW WHERE I CAN FIND ONE?
REAL MALES DON'T SWEET-TALK APPLIANCES.
SOME THINGS NEVER CHANGE.
I FIND THAT... DISTURBING.
COLONEL T'OMAS T'MORRA. TO WHAT DO WE OWE THE "HONOR"?
THEM'S FIGHTIN' WORDS! SHOOT HIM!

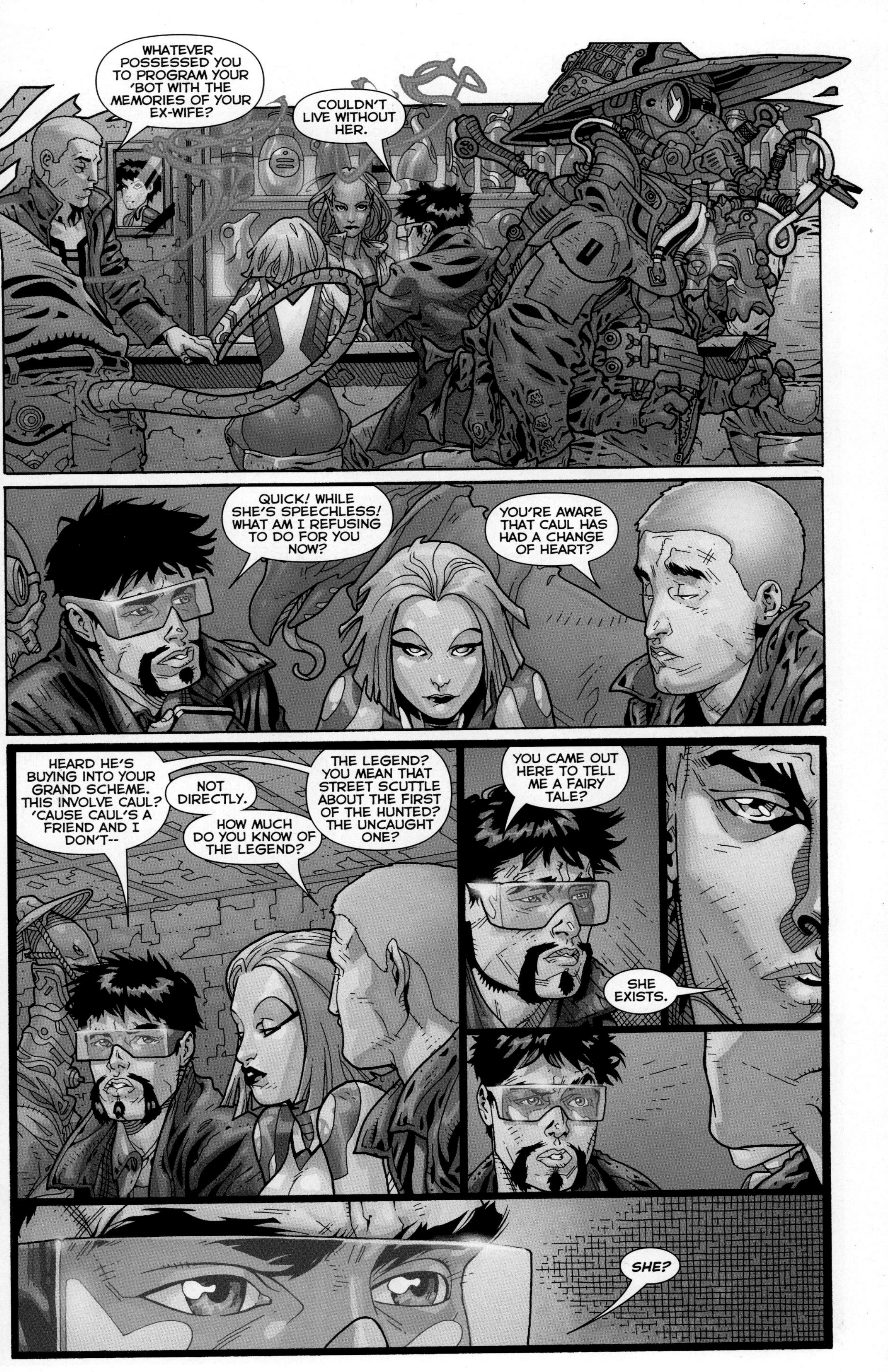
WHATEVER POSSESSED YOU TO PROGRAM YOUR 'BOT WITH THE MEMORIES OF YOUR EX-WIFE?
COULDN'T LIVE WITHOUT HER.
QUICK! WHILE SHE'S SPEECHLESS! WHAT AM I REFUSING TO DO FOR YOU NOW?
YOU'RE AWARE THAT CAUL HAS HAD A CHANGE OF HEART?
HEARD HE'S BUYING INTO YOUR GRAND SCHEME. THIS INVOLVE CAUL? 'CAUSE CAUL'S A FRIEND AND I DON'T--
NOT DIRECTLY.
HOW MUCH DO YOU KNOW OF THE LEGEND?
THE LEGEND? YOU MEAN THAT STREET SCUTTLE ABOUT THE FIRST OF THE HUNTED? THE UNCAUGHT ONE?
YOU CAME OUT HERE TO TELL ME A FAIRY TALE?
SHE EXISTS.
SHE?

YEAH. *SHE.* YOU GOT A PROBLEM WITH THAT?

ONE OF MANY. I DON'T SUPPOSE YOU'D BE UP FOR SLITTING HIS THROAT? YOU KNOW, SISTER-HOOD AND ALL?

THERE A REASON YOU KEEP TALKING ABOUT IT AND NOT DOING IT?

I'M NOT A COMPLETE IDIOT--

THAT'S OPEN FOR DEBATE.

I HAD HER FITTED WITH A RESTRAINT PROTOCOL. SHE'S INCAPABLE OF--

FULFILLING HER HEART'S DESIRE.

--DELIBERATELY INJURING ME OR ALLOWING ME TO BE HURT.

YOU TWO OUGHT TO TAKE THIS SHOW ON THE ROAD.

IF I MIGHT CONTINUE?

YOU WANT ME TO TRACK DOWN THIS LEGEND AND BRING HER TO YOU SO YOU CAN USE HER TO FUEL THIS WHOLE "HUNTED AS PROPAGANDA TOOL" THING YOU'VE COOKED UP.

NEVER MIND THAT SHE'S MANAGED TO KEEP HERSELF HIDDEN AWAY SINCE THE DA'S[?] SHOW DEBUTED.

I'M SITTING ON A POTENTIAL CRED BONANZA HERE. CHANCELLOR SHARD'S MISTRES[?] SHACKED UP WI[?] THE MINISTER O[?] URBAN AFFAIRS[?] AND YOU WANT M[?] TO PUT IT ON HO[?] TO GO TRAIPSIN[?] OFF ON ONE O[?] YOUR SNIPE HUNTS?

I THINK I CAN TAKE IT FROM HERE.

YOU KNOW HOW MUCH CERTAIN PARTIES WILL PAY TO KEEP THESE PICS OFF THE GLIMMERNET?

CHOOM!

FOOF!

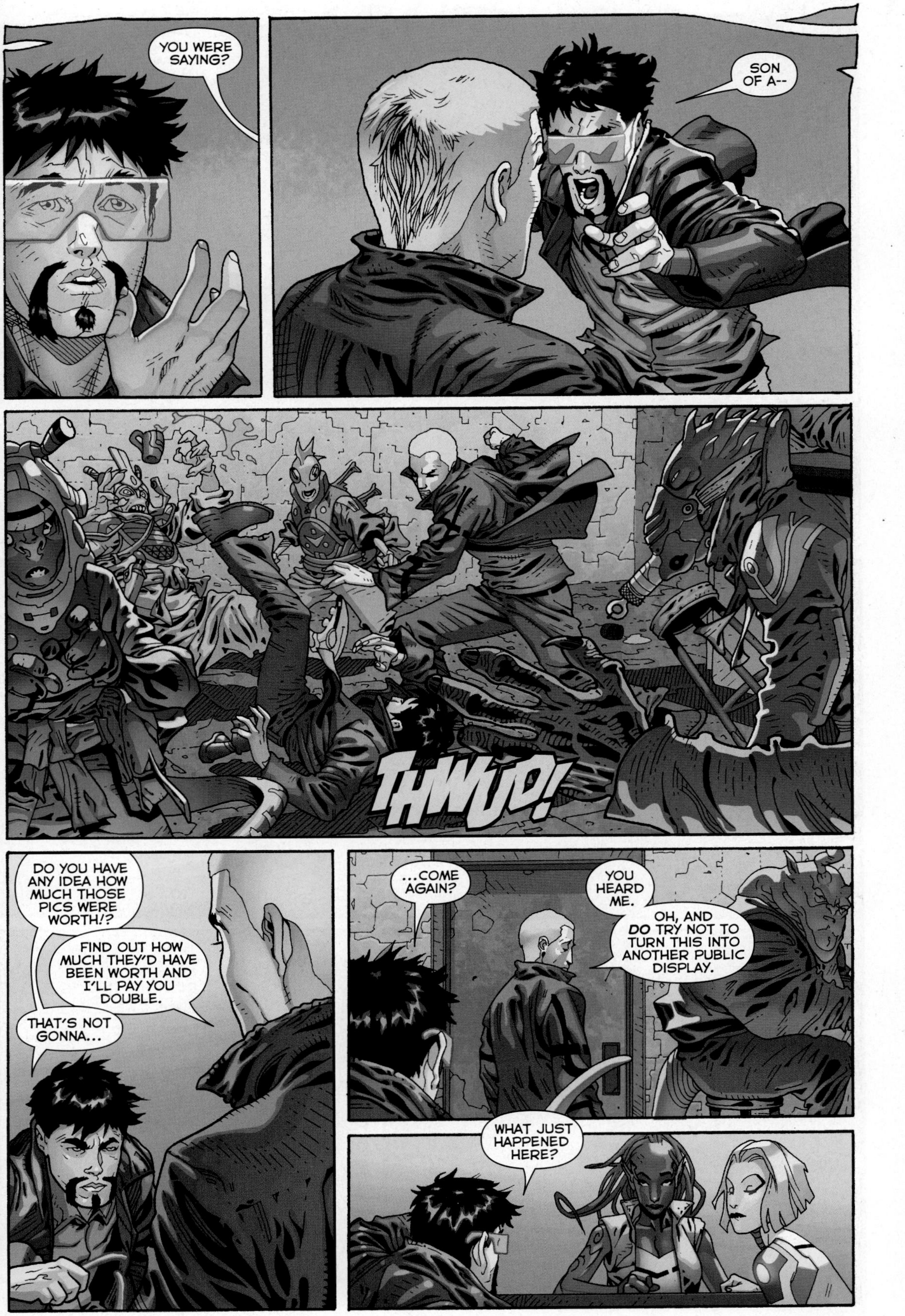
YOU WERE SAYING?
SON OF A--
THWUD!
DO YOU HAVE ANY IDEA HOW MUCH THOSE PICS WERE WORTH!?
FIND OUT HOW MUCH THEY'D HAVE BEEN WORTH AND I'LL PAY YOU DOUBLE.
THAT'S NOT GONNA...
...COME AGAIN?
YOU HEARD ME.
OH, AND *DO* TRY NOT TO TURN THIS INTO ANOTHER PUBLIC DISPLAY.
WHAT JUST HAPPENED HERE?

...TALKING TO YOU. HEY! HEY!

HMN?

WHAT WAS *THAT* ALL ABOUT? 'S LIKE HE ZONED OUT ON US--

HE *WHAT?*

HE LIKES TO NARRATE HIS LIFE TO HIMSELF.

FOR THE RECORD, I DO *NOT* NARRATE MY LIFE TO MYSELF...

YOU SHOULD PUT HIM OUT OF HIS MISERY. HE'S OBVIOUSLY BRAIN DAMAGED.

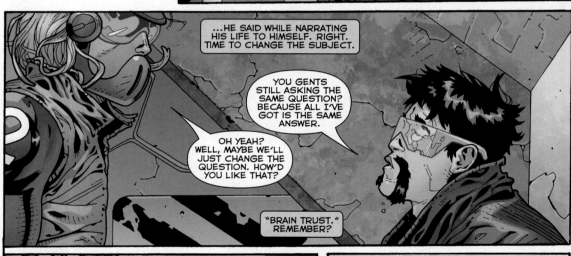

...HE SAID WHILE NARRATING HIS LIFE TO HIMSELF. RIGHT. TIME TO CHANGE THE SUBJECT.

YOU GENTS STILL ASKING THE SAME QUESTION? BECAUSE ALL I'VE GOT IS THE SAME ANSWER.

OH YEAH? WELL, MAYBE WE'LL JUST CHANGE THE QUESTION. HOW'D YOU LIKE THAT?

"BRAIN TRUST." REMEMBER?

SHE WANTS A FACE-TO-FACE WITH HIM.

SHE *DOES* REALIZE SHE'S COURTING DISAPPOINT-MENT?

DIDN'T EXPECT *THAT,* ANY MORE THAN I EXPECTED CRIMSON THRUST TO BE RUNNING INTERFERENCE FOR HER.

THE LEGEND WANTS TO MEET ME. WONDERFUL. CONSIDERING MY LUCK WITH WOMEN...

SEE THAT? HE'S DOING IT AGAIN.

...I AM SO DEAD.

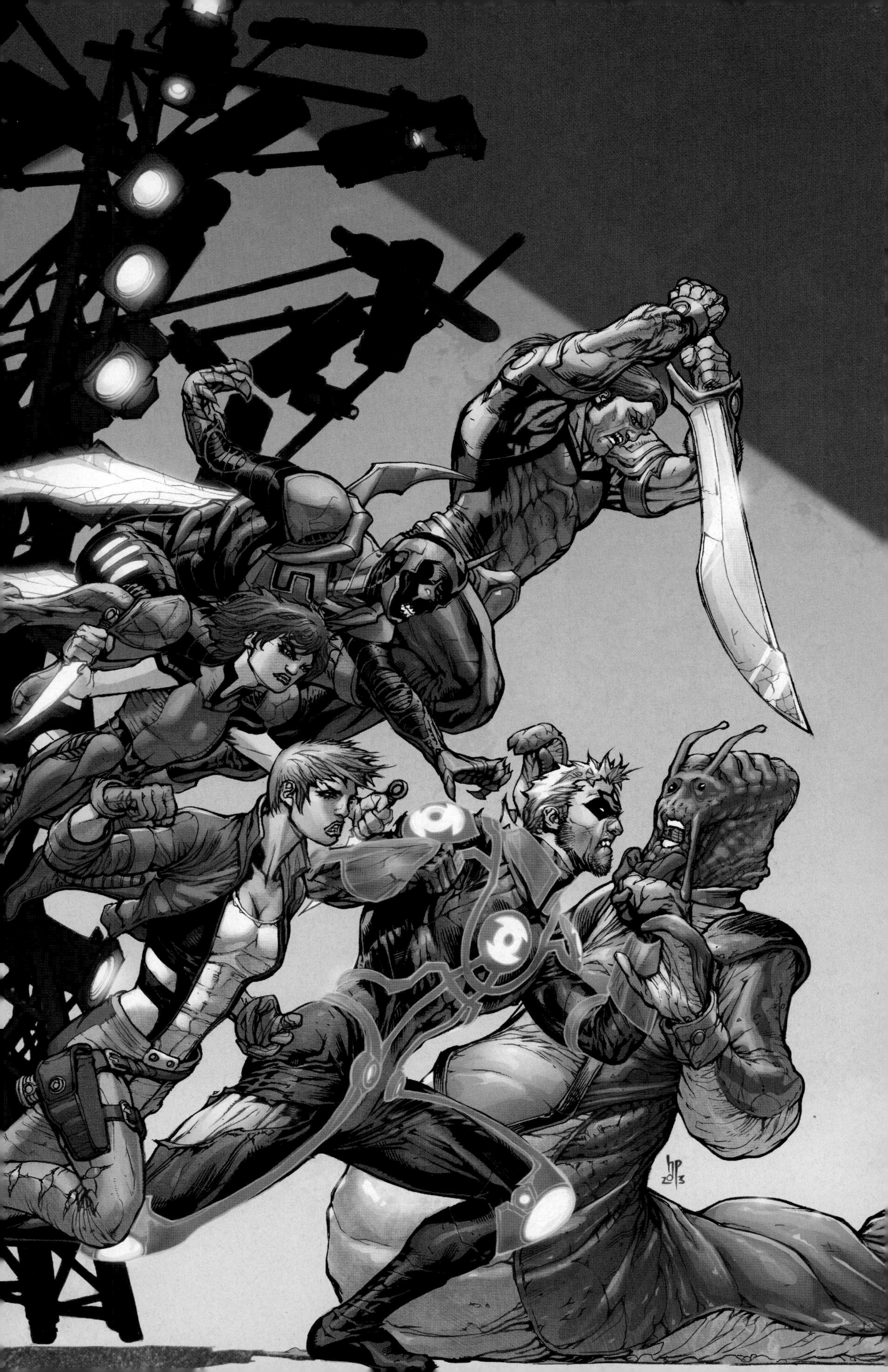

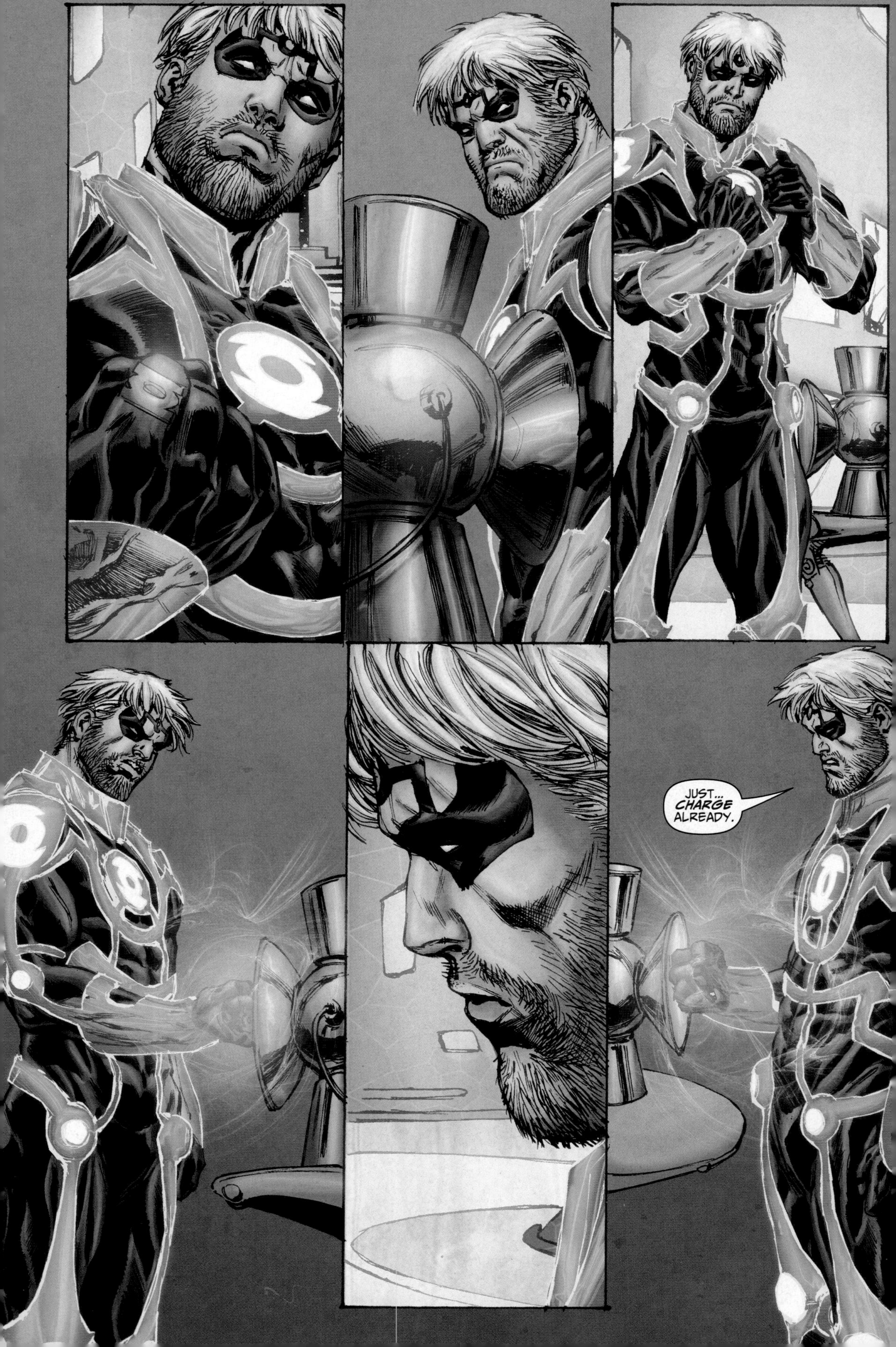
JUST... CHARGE ALREADY.

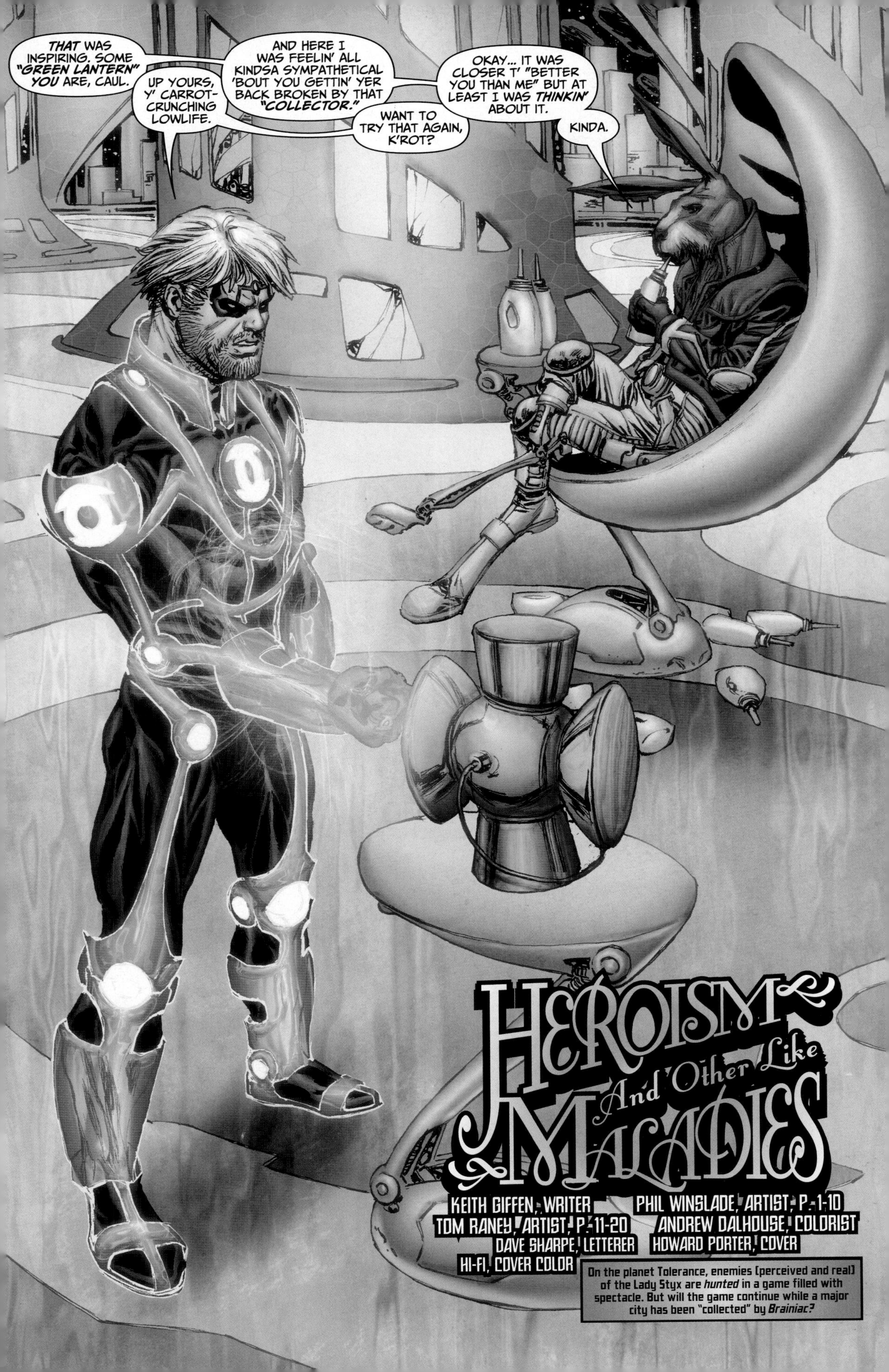
THAT WAS INSPIRING. SOME "GREEN LANTERN" YOU ARE, CAUL.
AND HERE I WAS FEELIN' ALL KINDSA SYMPATHETICAL 'BOUT YOU GETTIN' YER BACK BROKEN BY THAT "COLLECTOR."
UP YOURS, Y' CARROT-CRUNCHING LOWLIFE.
WANT TO TRY THAT AGAIN, K'ROT?
OKAY... IT WAS CLOSER T' "BETTER YOU THAN ME" BUT AT LEAST I WAS THINKIN' ABOUT IT.
KINDA.
HEROISM And Other Like MALADIES
KEITH GIFFEN, WRITER
PHIL WINSLADE, ARTIST, P. 1-10
TOM RANEY, ARTIST, P. 11-20
ANDREW DALHOUSE, COLORIST
DAVE SHARPE, LETTERER
HOWARD PORTER, COVER
HI-FI, COVER COLOR
On the planet Tolerance, enemies (perceived and real) of the Lady Styx are hunted in a game filled with spectacle. But will the game continue while a major city has been "collected" by Brainiac?

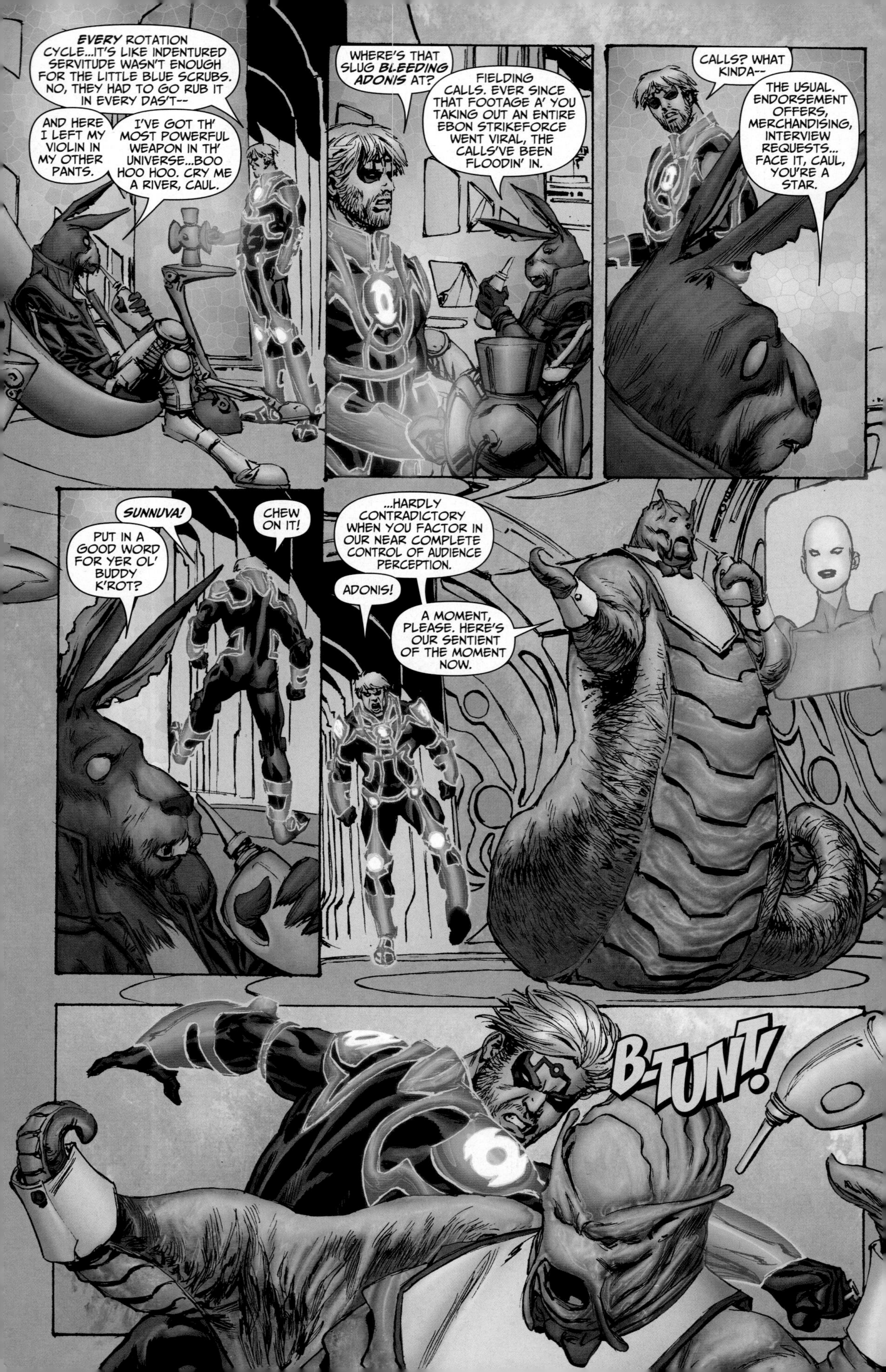
EVERY ROTATION CYCLE...IT'S LIKE INDENTURED SERVITUDE WASN'T ENOUGH FOR THE LITTLE BLUE SCRUBS. NO, THEY HAD TO GO RUB IT IN EVERY DAS'T--
AND HERE I LEFT MY VIOLIN IN MY OTHER PANTS.
I'VE GOT TH' MOST POWERFUL WEAPON IN TH' UNIVERSE...BOO HOO HOO. CRY ME A RIVER, CAUL.
WHERE'S THAT SLUG BLEEDING ADONIS AT?
FIELDING CALLS. EVER SINCE THAT FOOTAGE A' YOU TAKING OUT AN ENTIRE EBON STRIKEFORCE WENT VIRAL, THE CALLS'VE BEEN FLOODIN' IN.
CALLS? WHAT KINDA--
THE USUAL. ENDORSEMENT OFFERS, MERCHANDISING, INTERVIEW REQUESTS... FACE IT, CAUL, YOU'RE A STAR.
SUNNUVA!
PUT IN A GOOD WORD FOR YER OL' BUDDY K'ROT?
CHEW ON IT!
...HARDLY CONTRADICTORY WHEN YOU FACTOR IN OUR NEAR COMPLETE CONTROL OF AUDIENCE PERCEPTION.
ADONIS!
A MOMENT, PLEASE. HERE'S OUR SENTIENT OF THE MOMENT NOW.
B-TUNT!

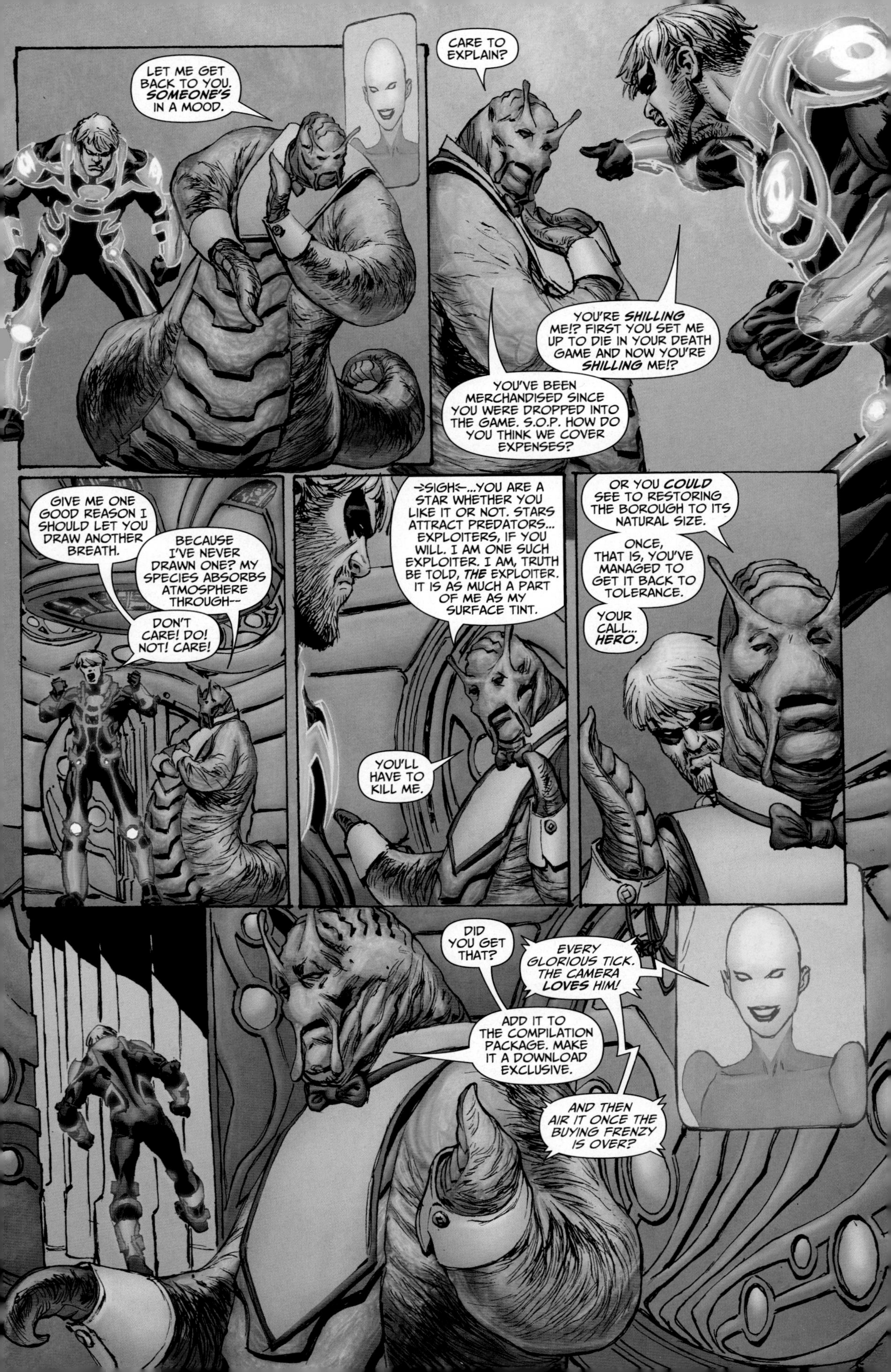
LET ME GET BACK TO YOU. SOMEONE'S IN A MOOD.
CARE TO EXPLAIN?
YOU'RE SHILLING ME!? FIRST YOU SET ME UP TO DIE IN YOUR DEATH GAME AND NOW YOU'RE SHILLING ME!?
YOU'VE BEEN MERCHANDISED SINCE YOU WERE DROPPED INTO THE GAME. S.O.P. HOW DO YOU THINK WE COVER EXPENSES?
GIVE ME ONE GOOD REASON I SHOULD LET YOU DRAW ANOTHER BREATH.
BECAUSE I'VE NEVER DRAWN ONE? MY SPECIES ABSORBS ATMOSPHERE THROUGH--
DON'T CARE! DO! NOT! CARE!
>SIGH<...YOU ARE A STAR WHETHER YOU LIKE IT OR NOT. STARS ATTRACT PREDATORS... EXPLOITERS, IF YOU WILL. I AM ONE SUCH EXPLOITER. I AM, TRUTH BE TOLD, THE EXPLOITER. IT IS AS MUCH A PART OF ME AS MY SURFACE TINT.
YOU'LL HAVE TO KILL ME.
OR YOU COULD SEE TO RESTORING THE BOROUGH TO ITS NATURAL SIZE.
ONCE, THAT IS, YOU'VE MANAGED TO GET IT BACK TO TOLERANCE.
YOUR CALL... HERO.
DID YOU GET THAT?
EVERY GLORIOUS TICK. THE CAMERA LOVES HIM!
ADD IT TO THE COMPILATION PACKAGE. MAKE IT A DOWNLOAD EXCLUSIVE.
AND THEN AIR IT ONCE THE BUYING FRENZY IS OVER?

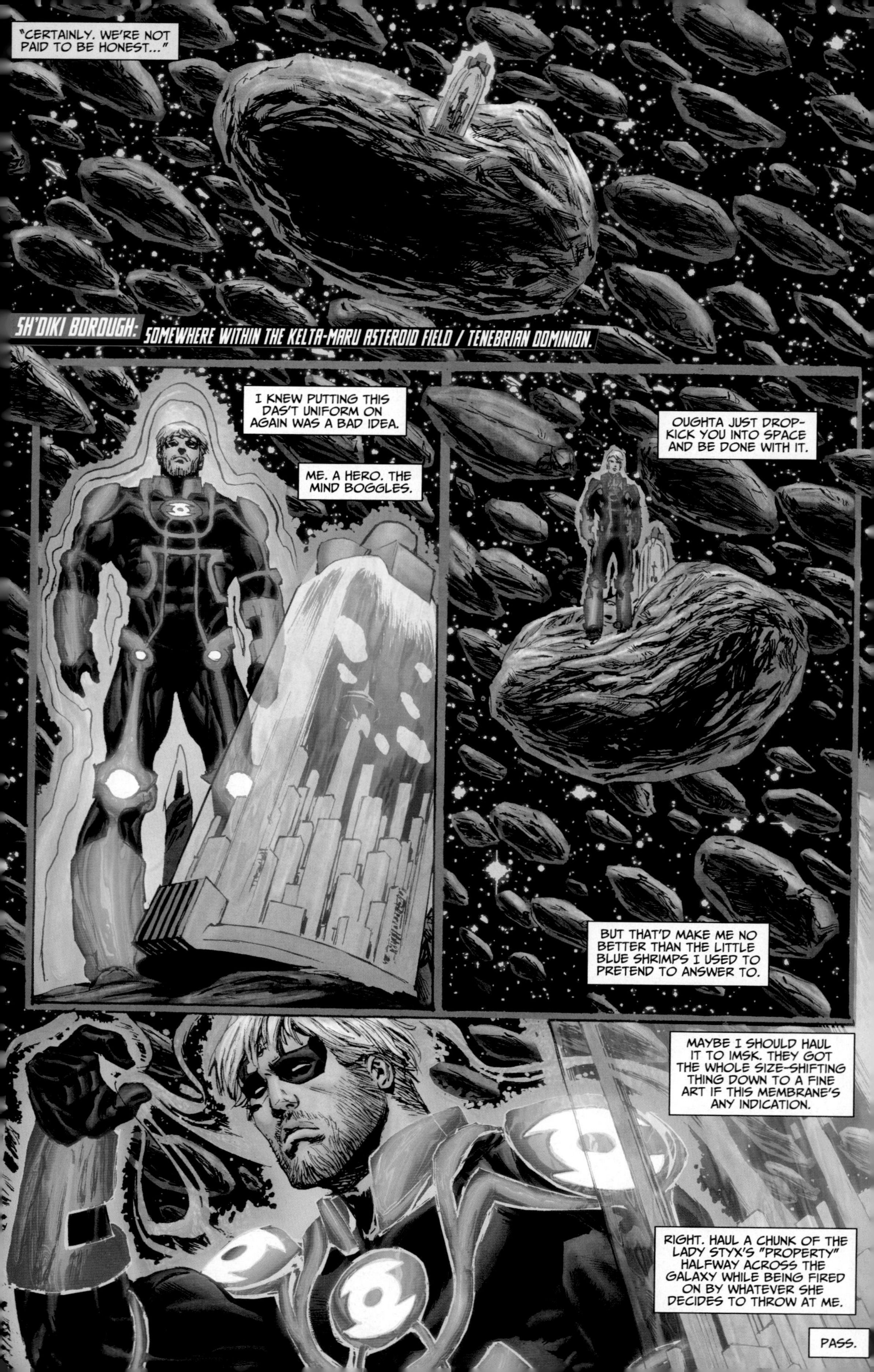
"CERTAINLY. WE'RE NOT PAID TO BE HONEST..."
SH'DIKI BOROUGH: SOMEWHERE WITHIN THE KELTA-MARU ASTEROID FIELD / TENEBRIAN DOMINION.
I KNEW PUTTING THIS DAS'T UNIFORM ON AGAIN WAS A BAD IDEA.
ME. A HERO. THE MIND BOGGLES.
OUGHTA JUST DROP-KICK YOU INTO SPACE AND BE DONE WITH IT.
BUT THAT'D MAKE ME NO BETTER THAN THE LITTLE BLUE SHRIMPS I USED TO PRETEND TO ANSWER TO.
MAYBE I SHOULD HAUL IT TO IMSK. THEY GOT THE WHOLE SIZE-SHIFTING THING DOWN TO A FINE ART IF THIS MEMBRANE'S ANY INDICATION.
RIGHT. HAUL A CHUNK OF THE LADY STYX'S "PROPERTY" HALFWAY ACROSS THE GALAXY WHILE BEING FIRED ON BY WHATEVER SHE DECIDES TO THROW AT ME.
PASS.

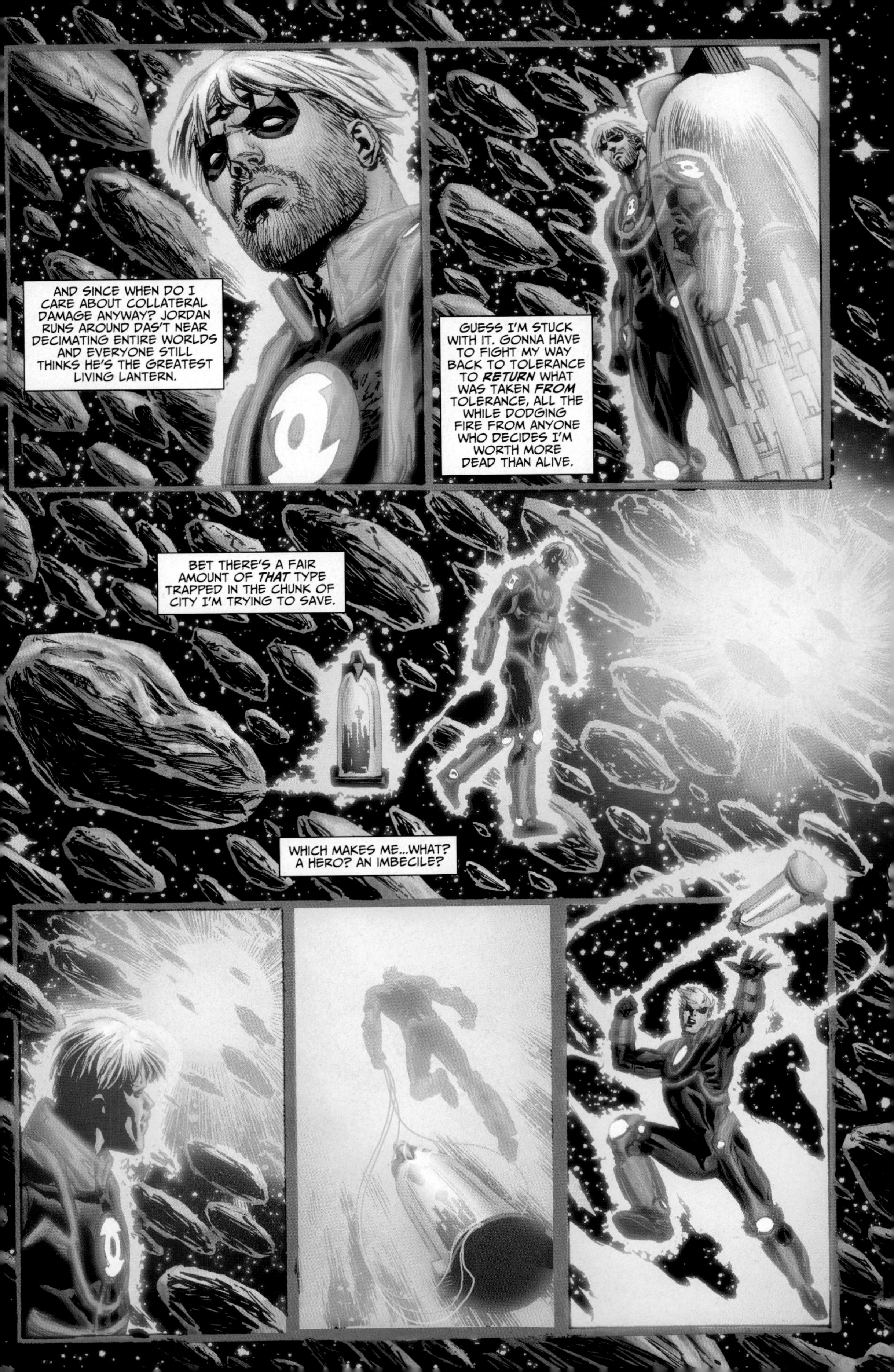
AND SINCE WHEN DO I CARE ABOUT COLLATERAL DAMAGE ANYWAY? JORDAN RUNS AROUND DAS'T NEAR DECIMATING ENTIRE WORLDS AND EVERYONE STILL THINKS HE'S THE GREATEST LIVING LANTERN.
GUESS I'M STUCK WITH IT. GONNA HAVE TO FIGHT MY WAY BACK TO TOLERANCE TO *RETURN* WHAT WAS TAKEN *FROM* TOLERANCE, ALL THE WHILE DODGING FIRE FROM ANYONE WHO DECIDES I'M WORTH MORE DEAD THAN ALIVE.
BET THERE'S A FAIR AMOUNT OF *THAT* TYPE TRAPPED IN THE CHUNK OF CITY I'M TRYING TO SAVE.
WHICH MAKES ME...WHAT? A HERO? AN IMBECILE?

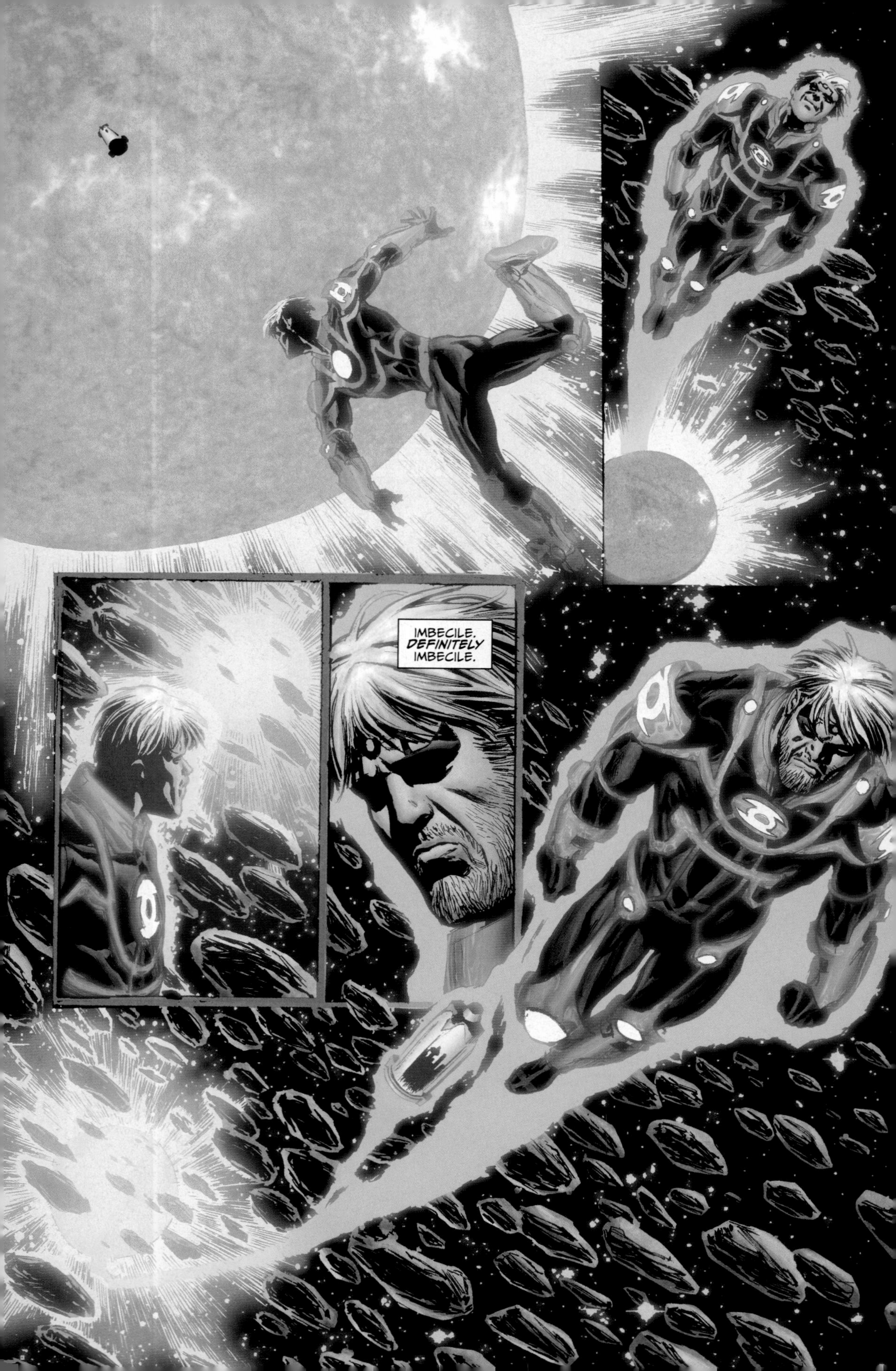
IMBECILE. DEFINITELY IMBECILE.

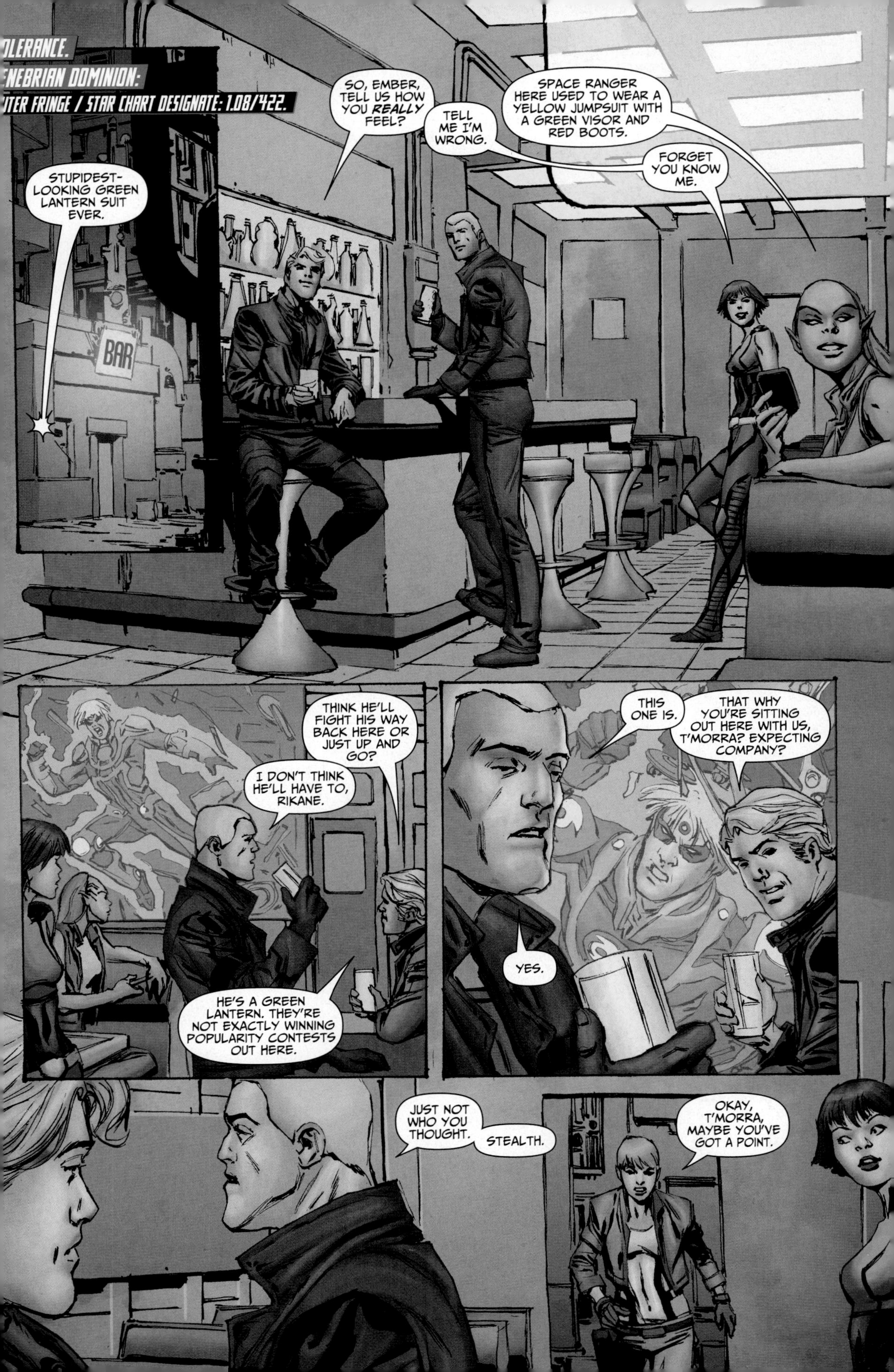
OLERANCE.
ENEBRIAN DOMINION:
UTER FRINGE / STAR CHART DESIGNATE: 1.08/422.
STUPIDEST-LOOKING GREEN LANTERN SUIT EVER.
SO, EMBER, TELL US HOW YOU REALLY FEEL?
TELL ME I'M WRONG.
SPACE RANGER HERE USED TO WEAR A YELLOW JUMPSUIT WITH A GREEN VISOR AND RED BOOTS.
FORGET YOU KNOW ME.
BAR
THINK HE'LL FIGHT HIS WAY BACK HERE OR JUST UP AND GO?
I DON'T THINK HE'LL HAVE TO, RIKANE.
HE'S A GREEN LANTERN. THEY'RE NOT EXACTLY WINNING POPULARITY CONTESTS OUT HERE.
THIS ONE IS.
THAT WHY YOU'RE SITTING OUT HERE WITH US, T'MORRA? EXPECTING COMPANY?
YES.
JUST NOT WHO YOU THOUGHT.
STEALTH.
OKAY, T'MORRA, MAYBE YOU'VE GOT A POINT.

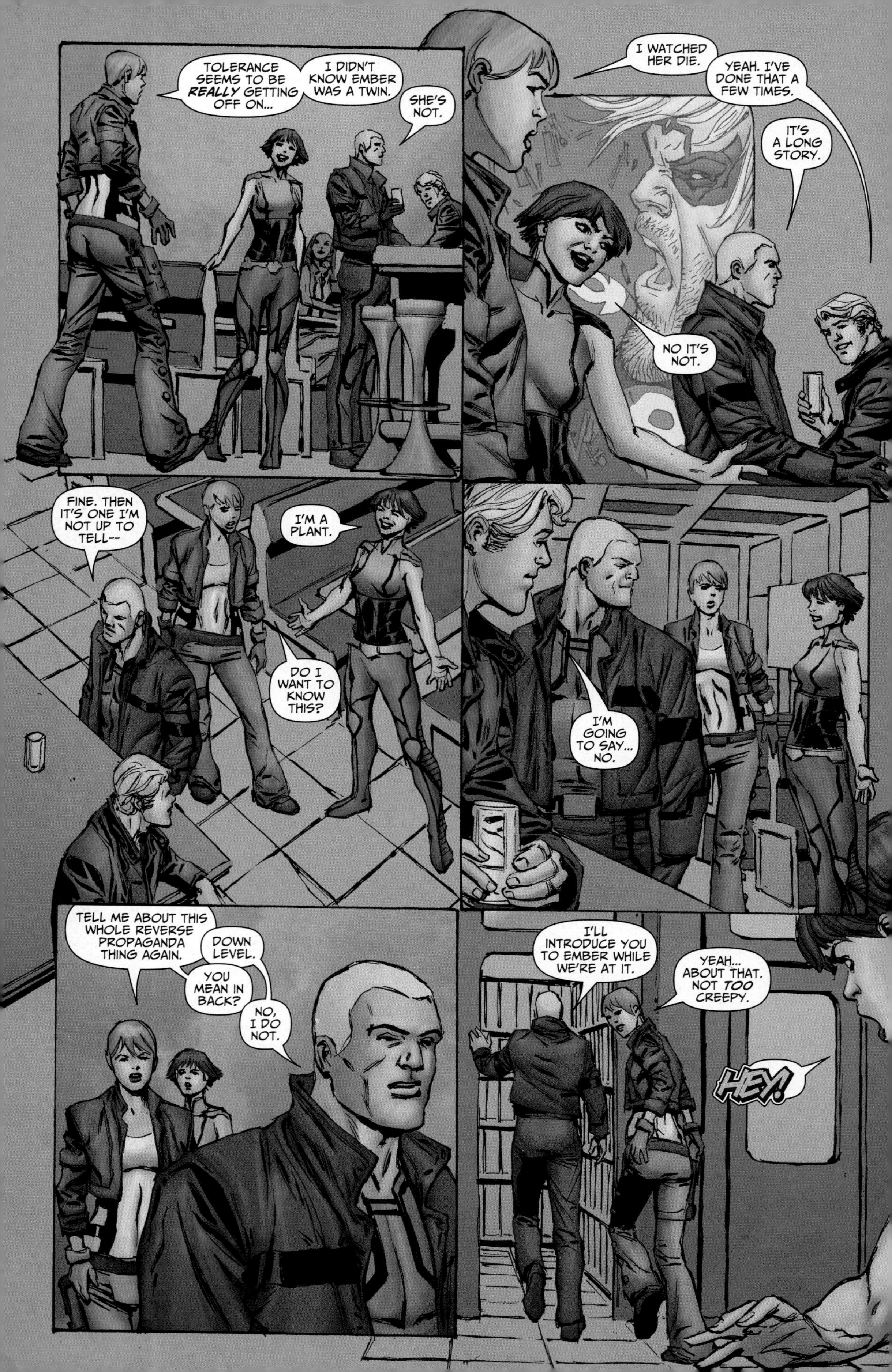
TOLERANCE SEEMS TO BE *REALLY* GETTING OFF ON...
I DIDN'T KNOW EMBER WAS A TWIN.
SHE'S NOT.
I WATCHED HER DIE.
YEAH. I'VE DONE THAT A FEW TIMES.
IT'S A LONG STORY.
NO IT'S NOT.
FINE. THEN IT'S ONE I'M NOT UP TO TELL--
I'M A PLANT.
DO I WANT TO KNOW THIS?
I'M GOING TO SAY... NO.
TELL ME ABOUT THIS WHOLE REVERSE PROPAGANDA THING AGAIN.
DOWN LEVEL.
YOU MEAN IN BACK?
NO, I DO NOT.
I'LL INTRODUCE YOU TO EMBER WHILE WE'RE AT IT.
YEAH... ABOUT THAT. NOT *TOO* CREEPY.
HEY!

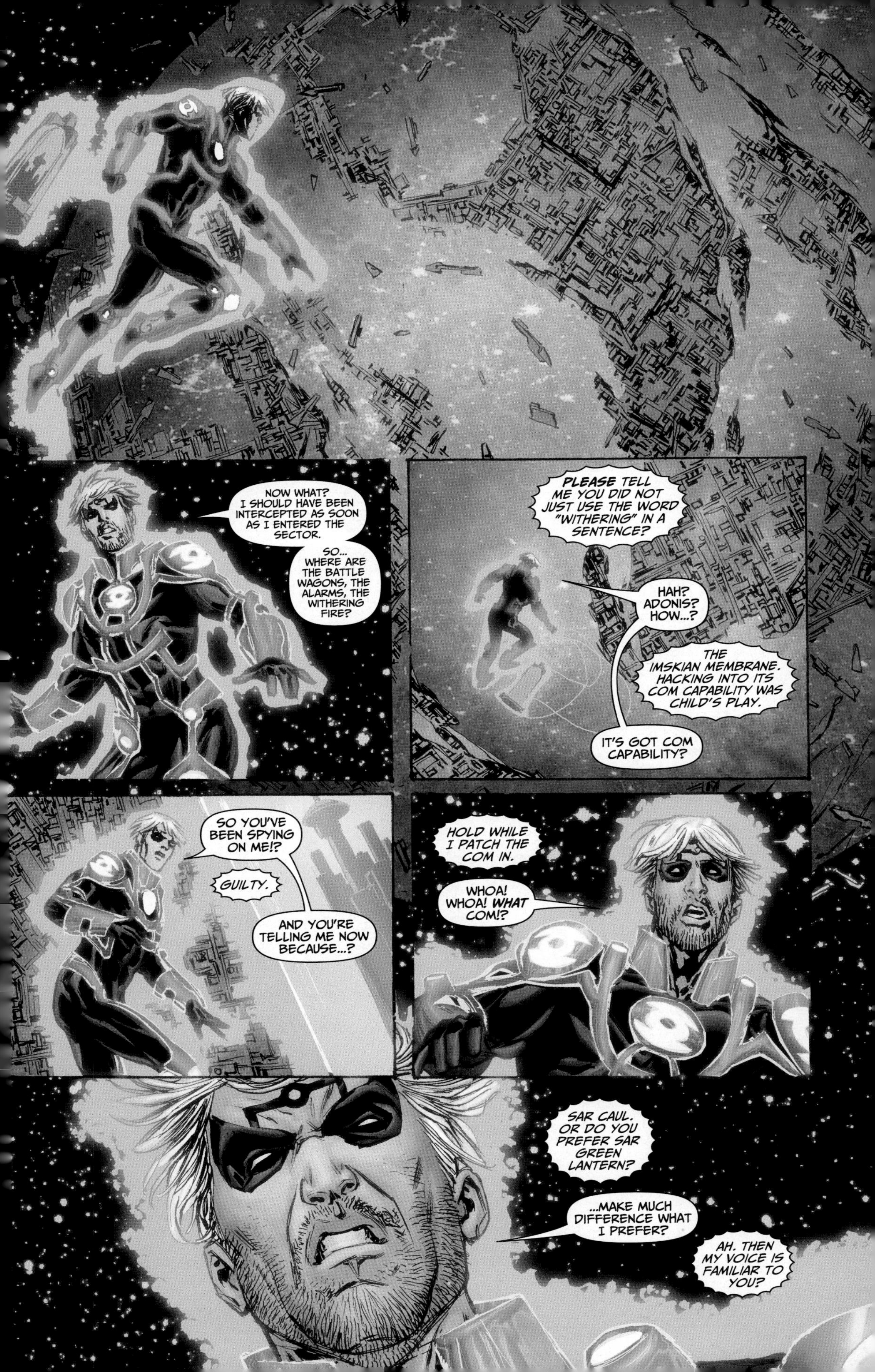
NOW WHAT? I SHOULD HAVE BEEN INTERCEPTED AS SOON AS I ENTERED THE SECTOR.
SO... WHERE ARE THE BATTLE WAGONS, THE ALARMS, THE WITHERING FIRE?
PLEASE TELL ME YOU DID NOT JUST USE THE WORD "WITHERING" IN A SENTENCE?
HAH? ADONIS? HOW...?
THE IMSKIAN MEMBRANE. HACKING INTO ITS COM CAPABILITY WAS CHILD'S PLAY.
IT'S GOT COM CAPABILITY?
SO YOU'VE BEEN SPYING ON ME!?
GUILTY.
AND YOU'RE TELLING ME NOW BECAUSE...?
HOLD WHILE I PATCH THE COM IN.
WHOA! WHOA! WHAT COM!?
SAR CAUL. OR DO YOU PREFER SAR GREEN LANTERN?
...MAKE MUCH DIFFERENCE WHAT I PREFER?
AH. THEN MY VOICE IS FAMILIAR TO YOU?

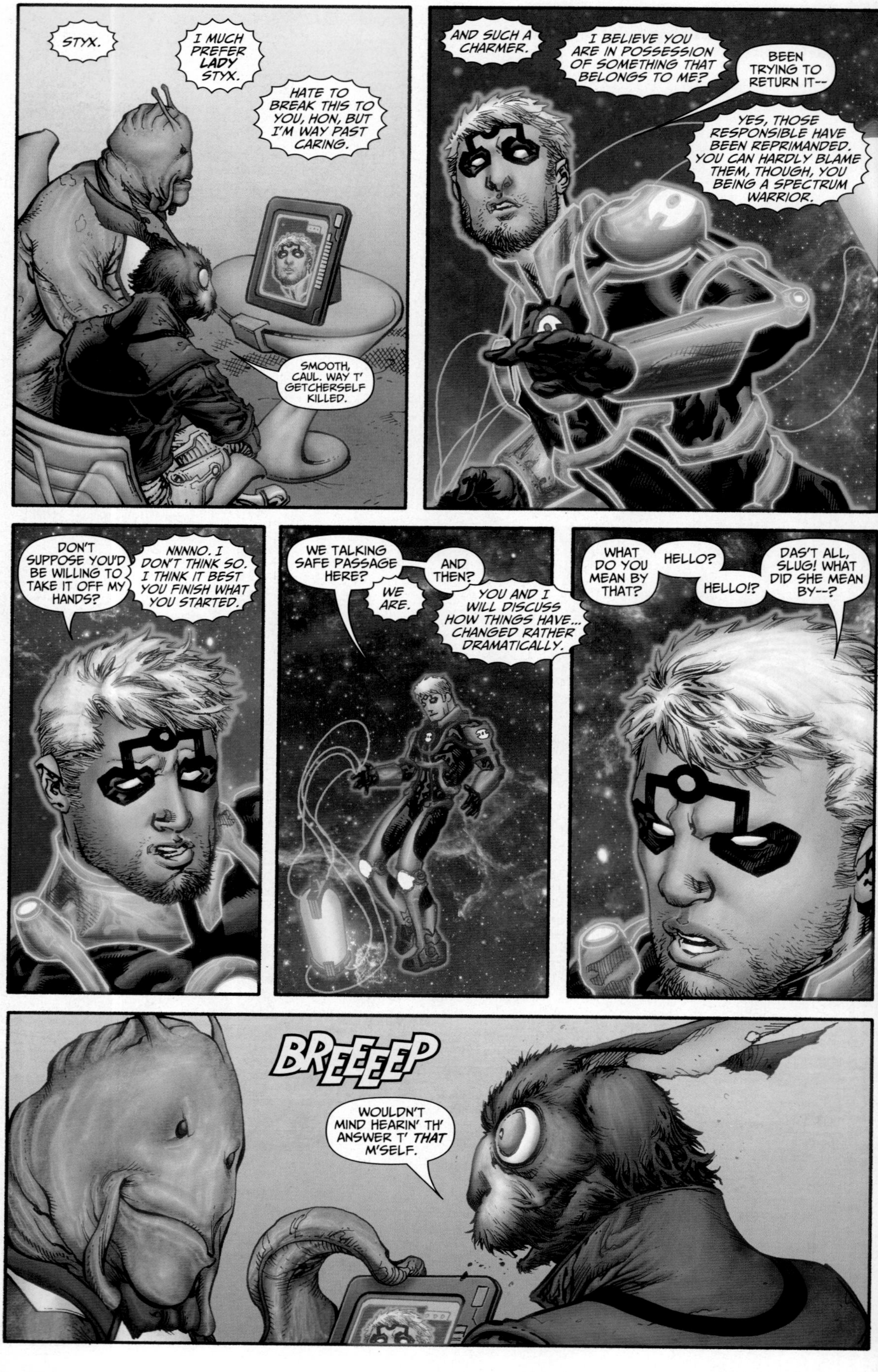
STYX.
I MUCH PREFER LADY STYX.
HATE TO BREAK THIS TO YOU, HON, BUT I'M WAY PAST CARING.
SMOOTH, CAUL. WAY T' GETCHERSELF KILLED.
AND SUCH A CHARMER.
I BELIEVE YOU ARE IN POSSESSION OF SOMETHING THAT BELONGS TO ME?
BEEN TRYING TO RETURN IT--
YES, THOSE RESPONSIBLE HAVE BEEN REPRIMANDED. YOU CAN HARDLY BLAME THEM, THOUGH, YOU BEING A SPECTRUM WARRIOR.
DON'T SUPPOSE YOU'D BE WILLING TO TAKE IT OFF MY HANDS?
NNNNO. I DON'T THINK SO. I THINK IT BEST YOU FINISH WHAT YOU STARTED.
WE TALKING SAFE PASSAGE HERE?
WE ARE.
AND THEN?
YOU AND I WILL DISCUSS HOW THINGS HAVE... CHANGED RATHER DRAMATICALLY.
WHAT DO YOU MEAN BY THAT?
HELLO?
HELLO!?
DAS'T ALL, SLUG! WHAT DID SHE MEAN BY--?
BREEEEP
WOULDN'T MIND HEARIN' TH' ANSWER T' THAT M'SELF.

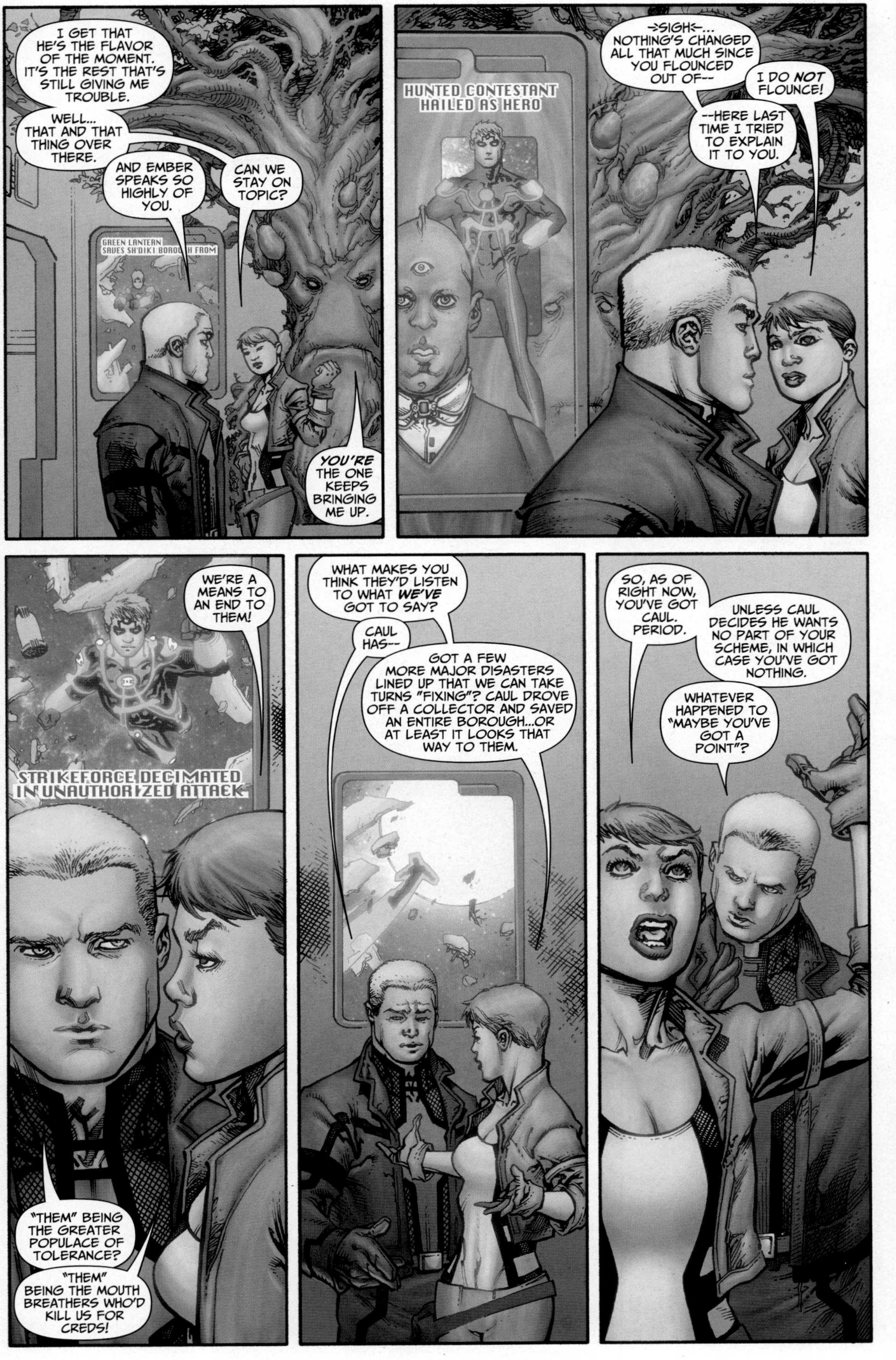
I GET THAT HE'S THE FLAVOR OF THE MOMENT. IT'S THE REST THAT'S STILL GIVING ME TROUBLE.
WELL... THAT AND THAT THING OVER THERE.
AND EMBER SPEAKS SO HIGHLY OF YOU.
CAN WE STAY ON TOPIC?
YOU'RE THE ONE KEEPS BRINGING ME UP.
GREEN LANTERN SAVES SH'DIKI BOROUGH FROM
HUNTED CONTESTANT HAILED AS HERO
>SIGH<... NOTHING'S CHANGED ALL THAT MUCH SINCE YOU FLOUNCED OUT OF--
I DO NOT FLOUNCE!
--HERE LAST TIME I TRIED TO EXPLAIN IT TO YOU.
WE'RE A MEANS TO AN END TO THEM!
STRIKEFORCE DECIMATED IN UNAUTHORIZED ATTACK
"THEM" BEING THE GREATER POPULACE OF TOLERANCE?
"THEM" BEING THE MOUTH BREATHERS WHO'D KILL US FOR CREDS!
WHAT MAKES YOU THINK THEY'D LISTEN TO WHAT WE'VE GOT TO SAY?
CAUL HAS--
GOT A FEW MORE MAJOR DISASTERS LINED UP THAT WE CAN TAKE TURNS "FIXING"? CAUL DROVE OFF A COLLECTOR AND SAVED AN ENTIRE BOROUGH...OR AT LEAST IT LOOKS THAT WAY TO THEM.
SO, AS OF RIGHT NOW, YOU'VE GOT CAUL. PERIOD.
UNLESS CAUL DECIDES HE WANTS NO PART OF YOUR SCHEME, IN WHICH CASE YOU'VE GOT NOTHING.
WHATEVER HAPPENED TO "MAYBE YOU'VE GOT A POINT"?

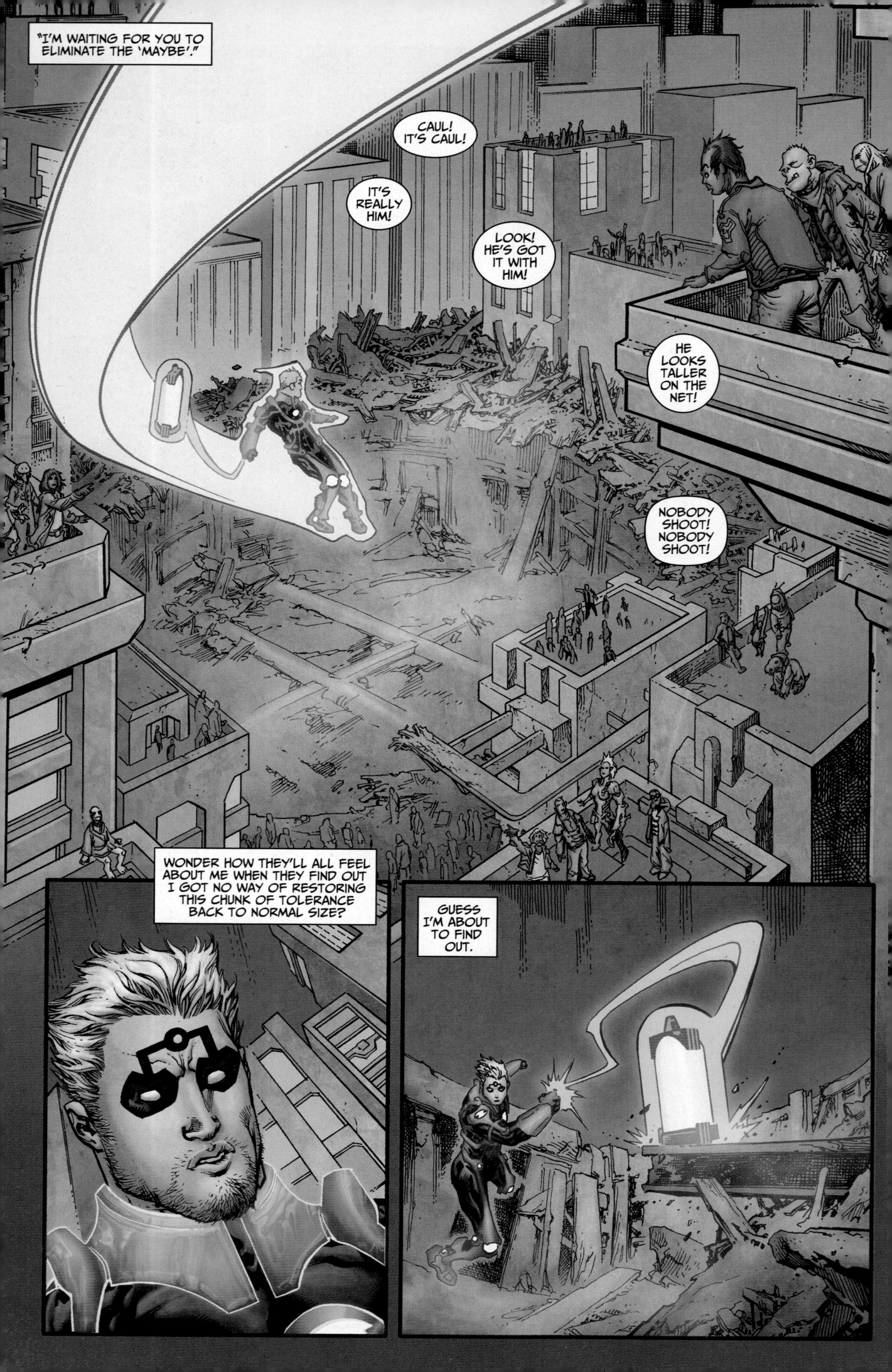
"I'M WAITING FOR YOU TO ELIMINATE THE 'MAYBE'."
CAUL! IT'S CAUL!
IT'S REALLY HIM!
LOOK! HE'S GOT IT WITH HIM!
HE LOOKS TALLER ON THE NET!
NOBODY SHOOT! NOBODY SHOOT!
WONDER HOW THEY'LL ALL FEEL ABOUT ME WHEN THEY FIND OUT I GOT NO WAY OF RESTORING THIS CHUNK OF TOLERANCE BACK TO NORMAL SIZE?
GUESS I'M ABOUT TO FIND OUT.

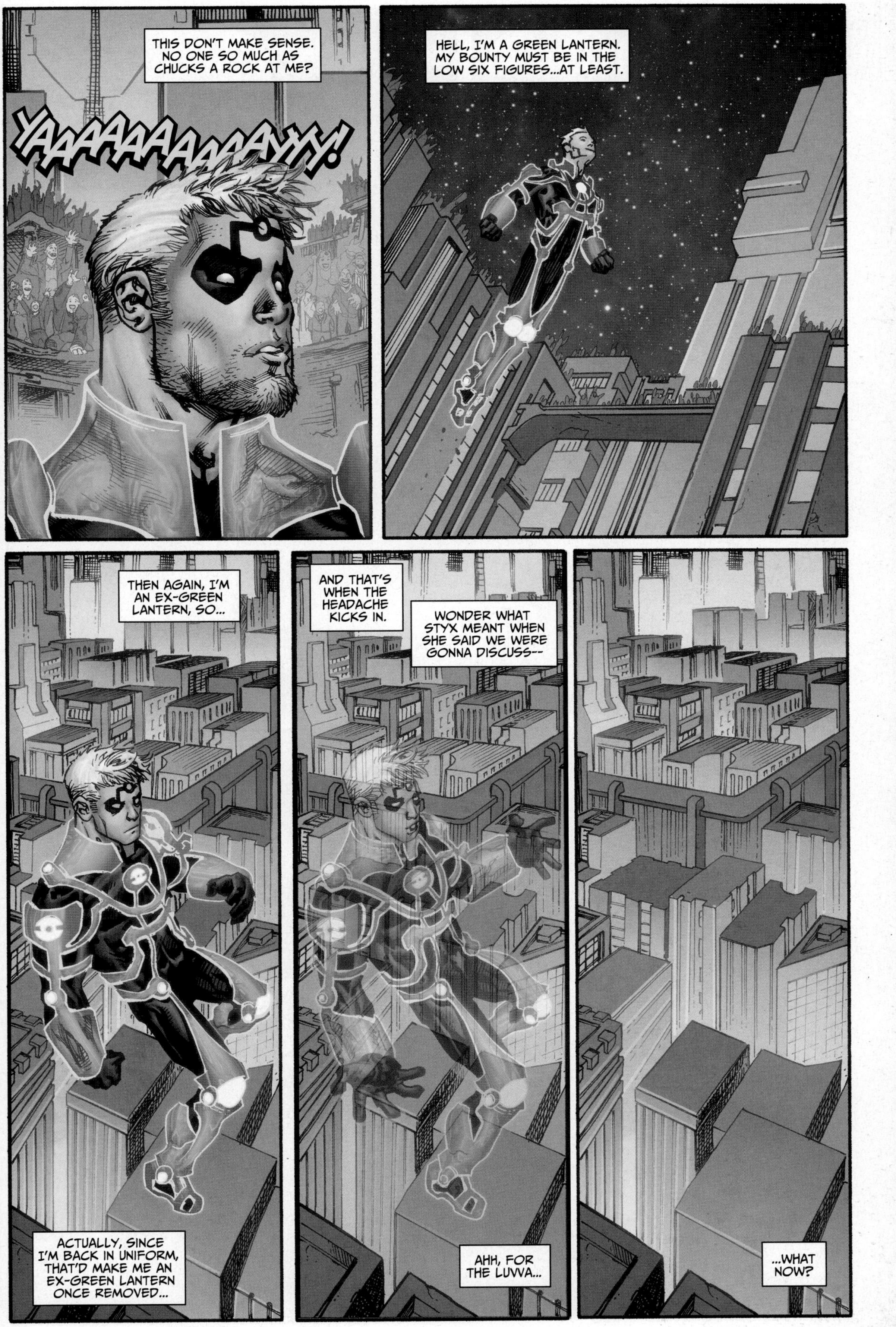
THIS DON'T MAKE SENSE. NO ONE SO MUCH AS CHUCKS A ROCK AT ME?
YAAAAAAAAAAYYY!
HELL, I'M A GREEN LANTERN. MY BOUNTY MUST BE IN THE LOW SIX FIGURES...AT LEAST.
THEN AGAIN, I'M AN EX-GREEN LANTERN, SO...
ACTUALLY, SINCE I'M BACK IN UNIFORM, THAT'D MAKE ME AN EX-GREEN LANTERN ONCE REMOVED...
AND THAT'S WHEN THE HEADACHE KICKS IN.
WONDER WHAT STYX MEANT WHEN SHE SAID WE WERE GONNA DISCUSS--
AHH, FOR THE LUVVA...
...WHAT NOW?

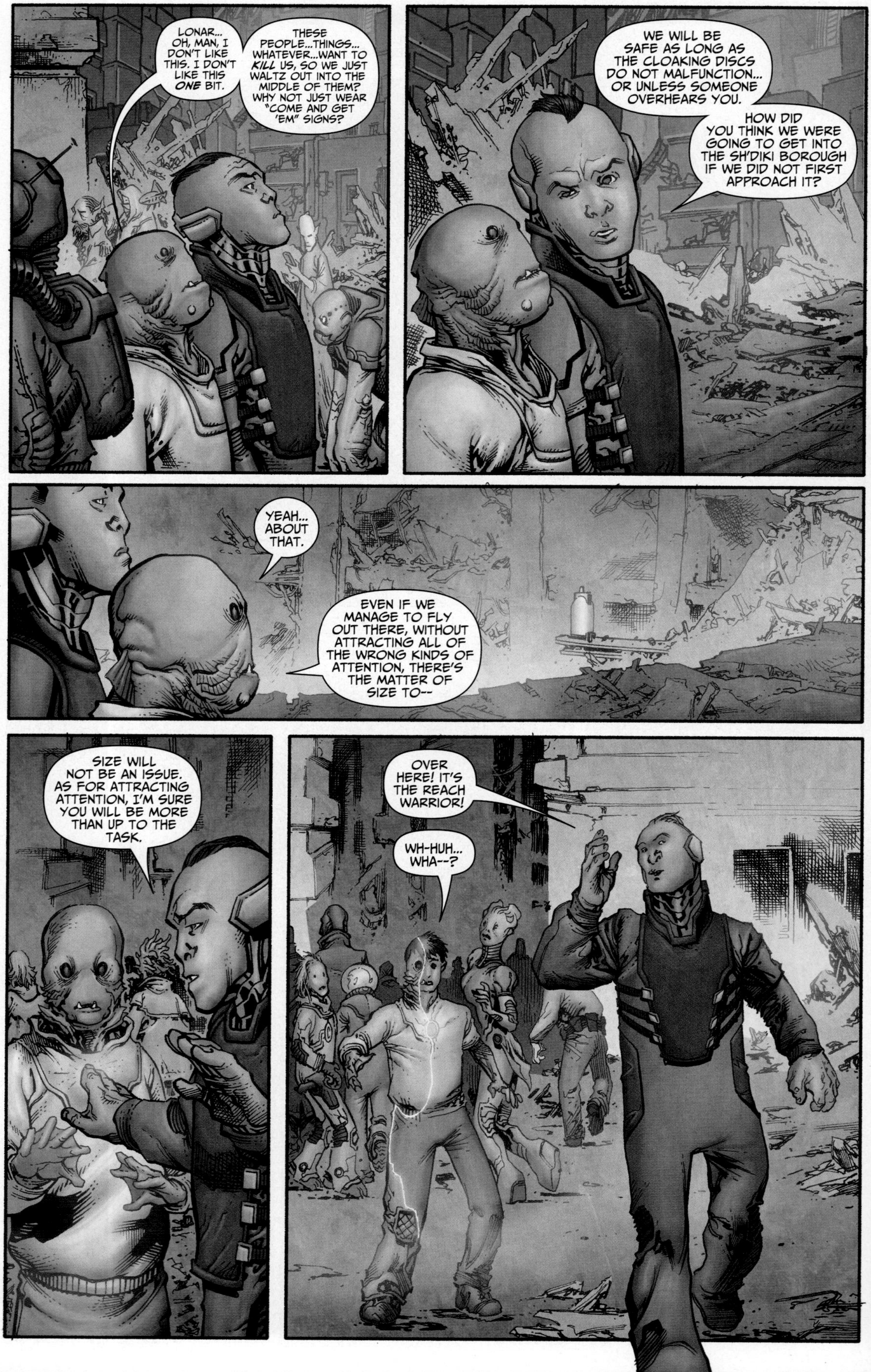
LONAR... OH, MAN, I DON'T LIKE THIS. I DON'T LIKE THIS ONE BIT.
THESE PEOPLE...THINGS... WHATEVER...WANT TO KILL US, SO WE JUST WALTZ OUT INTO THE MIDDLE OF THEM? WHY NOT JUST WEAR "COME AND GET 'EM" SIGNS?
WE WILL BE SAFE AS LONG AS THE CLOAKING DISCS DO NOT MALFUNCTION... OR UNLESS SOMEONE OVERHEARS YOU.
HOW DID YOU THINK WE WERE GOING TO GET INTO THE SH'DIKI BOROUGH IF WE DID NOT FIRST APPROACH IT?
YEAH... ABOUT THAT.
EVEN IF WE MANAGE TO FLY OUT THERE, WITHOUT ATTRACTING ALL OF THE WRONG KINDS OF ATTENTION, THERE'S THE MATTER OF SIZE TO--
SIZE WILL NOT BE AN ISSUE. AS FOR ATTRACTING ATTENTION, I'M SURE YOU WILL BE MORE THAN UP TO THE TASK.
OVER HERE! IT'S THE REACH WARRIOR!
WH-HUH... WHA--?

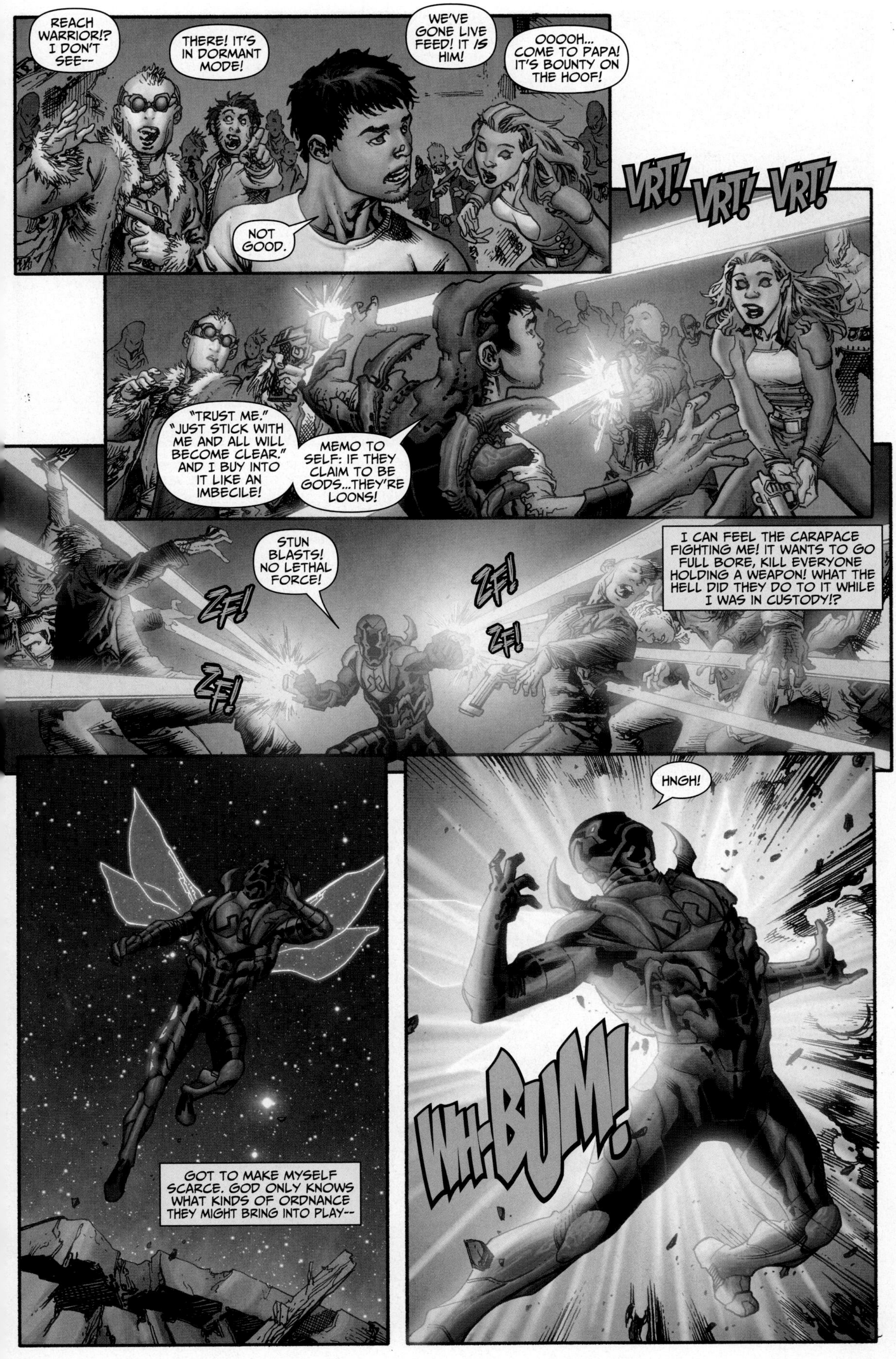
REACH WARRIOR!? I DON'T SEE--
THERE! IT'S IN DORMANT MODE!
WE'VE GONE LIVE FEED! IT IS HIM!
OOOOH... COME TO PAPA! IT'S BOUNTY ON THE HOOF!
NOT GOOD.
VRT! VRT! VRT!
"TRUST ME." "JUST STICK WITH ME AND ALL WILL BECOME CLEAR." AND I BUY INTO IT LIKE AN IMBECILE!
MEMO TO SELF: IF THEY CLAIM TO BE GODS...THEY'RE LOONS!
STUN BLASTS! NO LETHAL FORCE!
I CAN FEEL THE CARAPACE FIGHTING ME! IT WANTS TO GO FULL BORE, KILL EVERYONE HOLDING A WEAPON! WHAT THE HELL DID THEY DO TO IT WHILE I WAS IN CUSTODY!?
ZF!
ZF!
ZF!
ZF!
GOT TO MAKE MYSELF SCARCE. GOD ONLY KNOWS WHAT KINDS OF ORDNANCE THEY MIGHT BRING INTO PLAY--
HNGH!
WH-BUM!

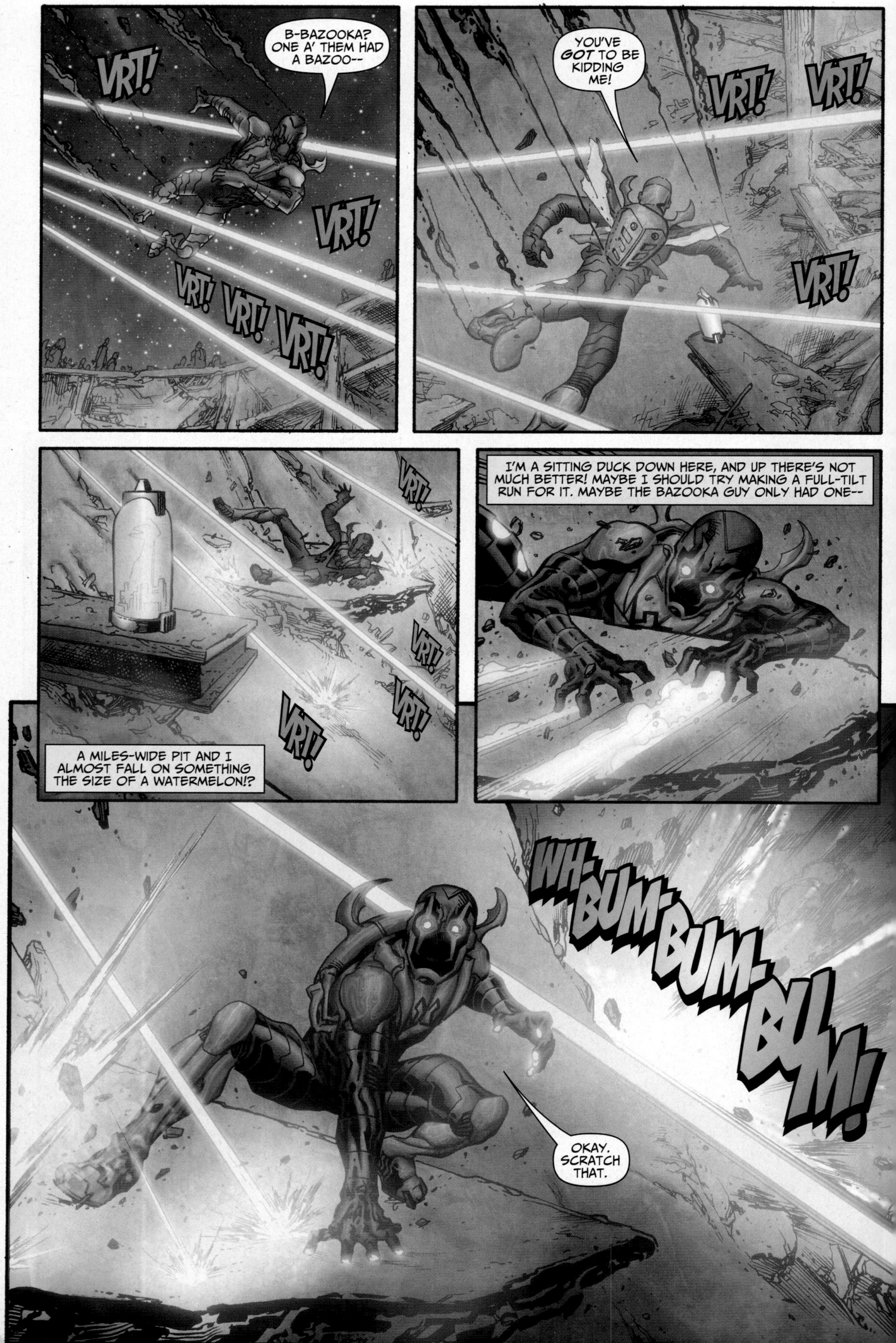

B-BAZOOKA? ONE A' THEM HAD A BAZOO--
VRT!
VRT!
VRT! VRT! VRT!
YOU'VE GOT TO BE KIDDING ME!
VRT! VRT!
VRT!
VRT!
VRT!
VRT!
VRT!
A MILES-WIDE PIT AND I ALMOST FALL ON SOMETHING THE SIZE OF A WATERMELON!?
I'M A SITTING DUCK DOWN HERE, AND UP THERE'S NOT MUCH BETTER! MAYBE I SHOULD TRY MAKING A FULL-TILT RUN FOR IT. MAYBE THE BAZOOKA GUY ONLY HAD ONE--
WH-BUM-BUM-BUM-BUM!
OKAY. SCRATCH THAT.

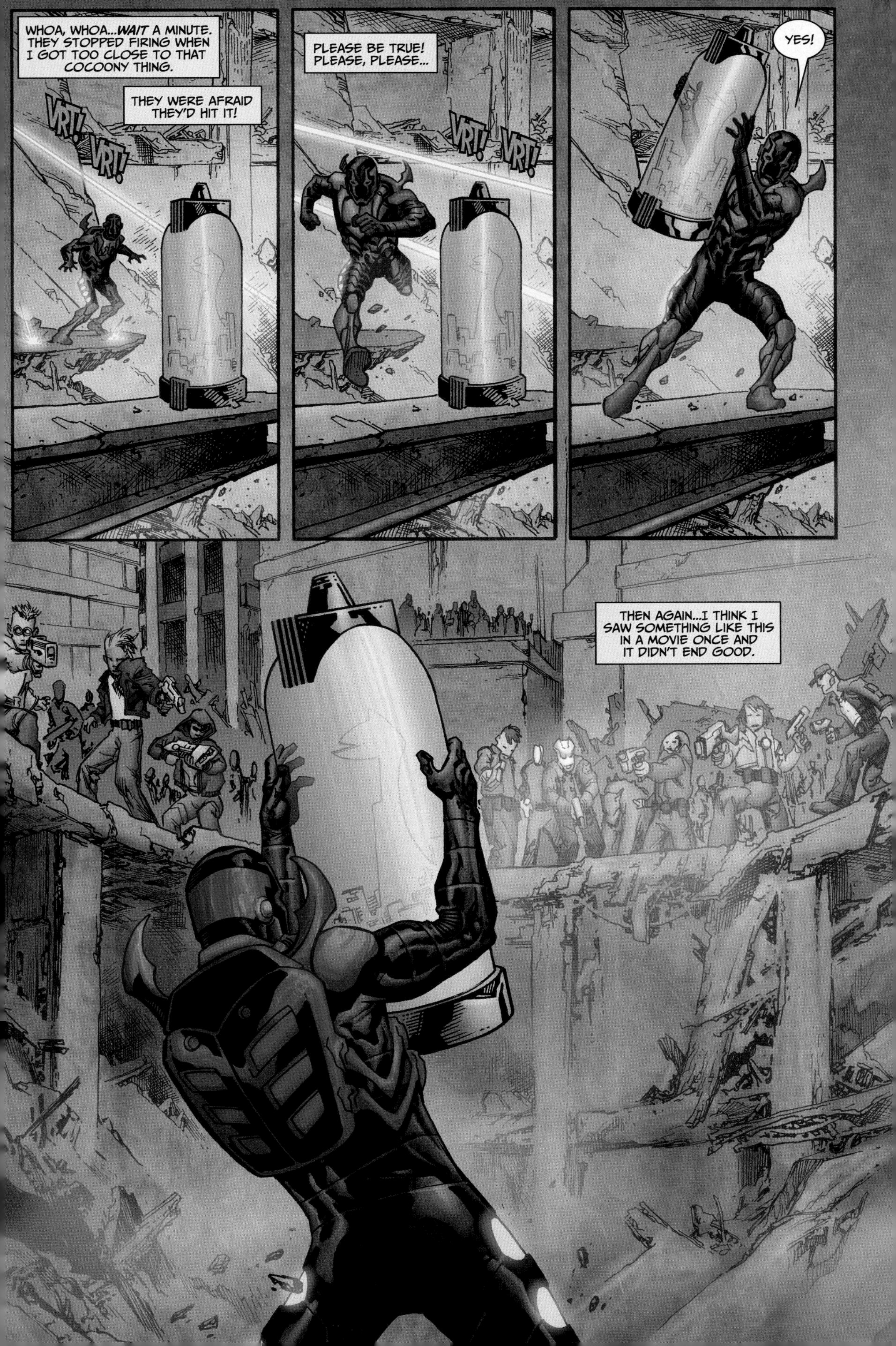
WHOA, WHOA...WAIT A MINUTE. THEY STOPPED FIRING WHEN I GOT TOO CLOSE TO THAT COCOONY THING.
THEY WERE AFRAID THEY'D HIT IT!
VRT! VRT!
PLEASE BE TRUE! PLEASE, PLEASE...
VRT! VRT!
YES!
THEN AGAIN...I THINK I SAW SOMETHING LIKE THIS IN A MOVIE ONCE AND IT DIDN'T END GOOD.

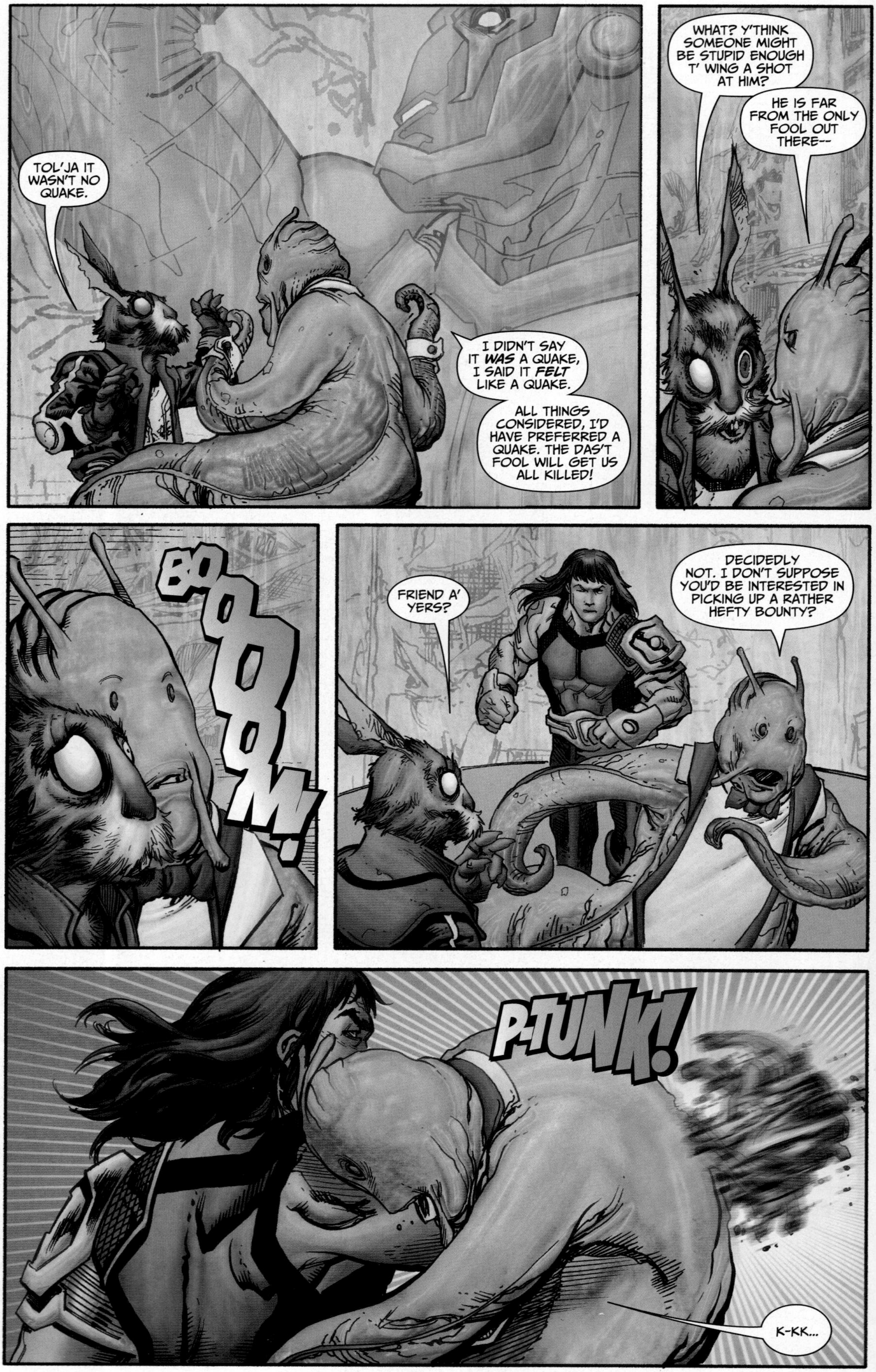
TOL'JA IT WASN'T NO QUAKE.
I DIDN'T SAY IT *WAS* A QUAKE, I SAID IT *FELT* LIKE A QUAKE.
ALL THINGS CONSIDERED, I'D HAVE PREFERRED A QUAKE. THE DAS'T FOOL WILL GET US ALL KILLED!
WHAT? Y'THINK SOMEONE MIGHT BE STUPID ENOUGH T' WING A SHOT AT HIM?
HE IS FAR FROM THE ONLY FOOL OUT THERE--
BOOOOOOM!
FRIEND A' YERS?
DECIDEDLY NOT. I DON'T SUPPOSE YOU'D BE INTERESTED IN PICKING UP A RATHER HEFTY BOUNTY?
P-TUNK!
K-KK...

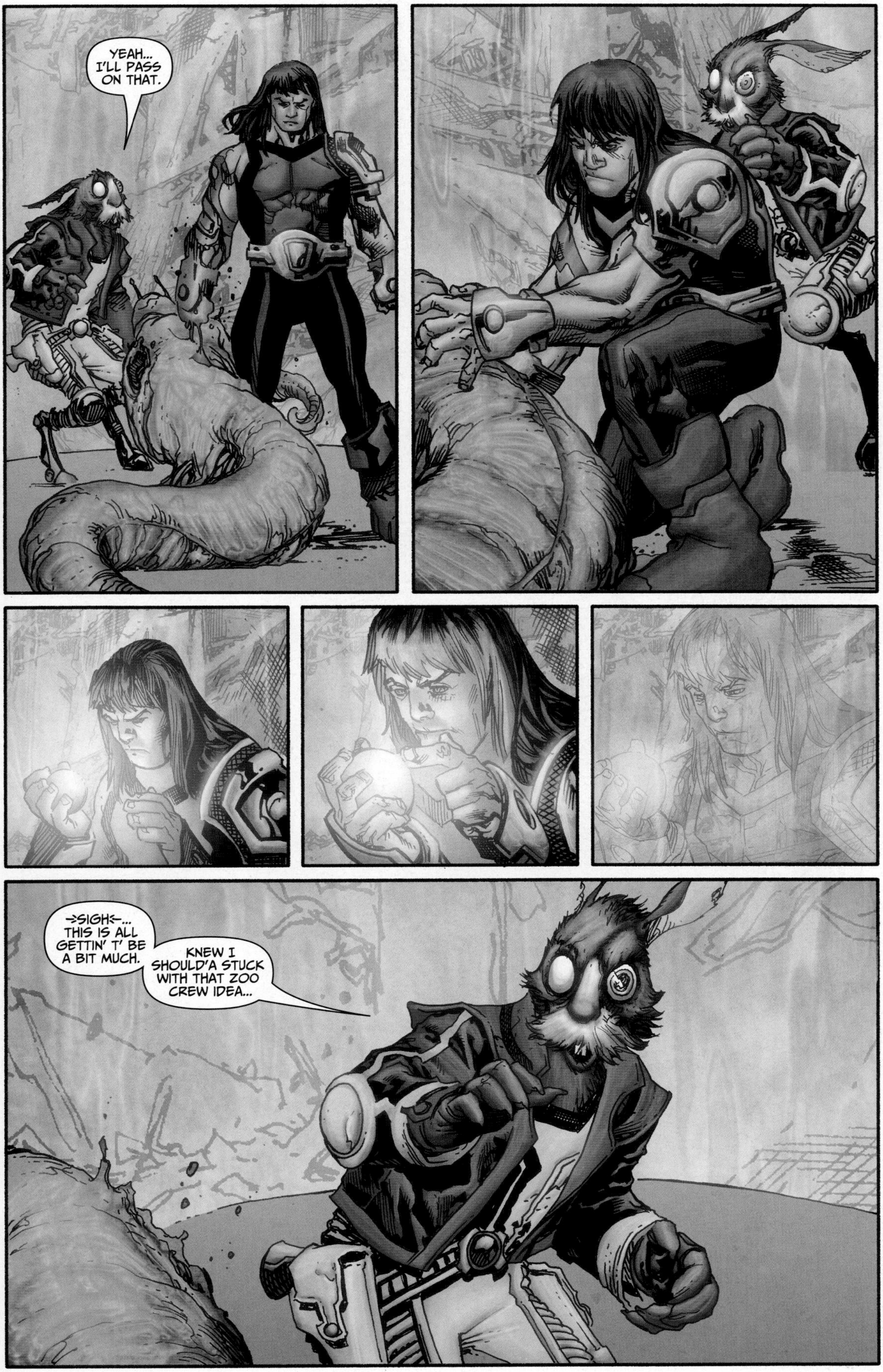
YEAH... I'LL PASS ON THAT.
>SIGH<... THIS IS ALL GETTIN' T' BE A BIT MUCH.
KNEW I SHOULD'A STUCK WITH THAT ZOO CREW IDEA...

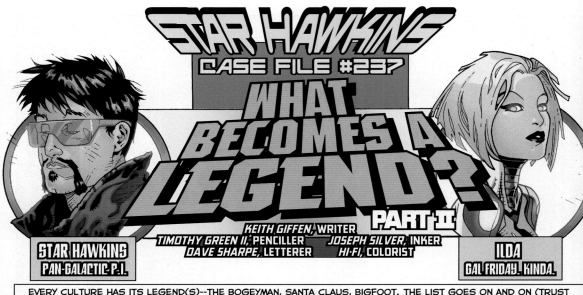

STAR HAWKINS

CASE FILE #237

WHAT BECOMES A LEGEND?

PART II

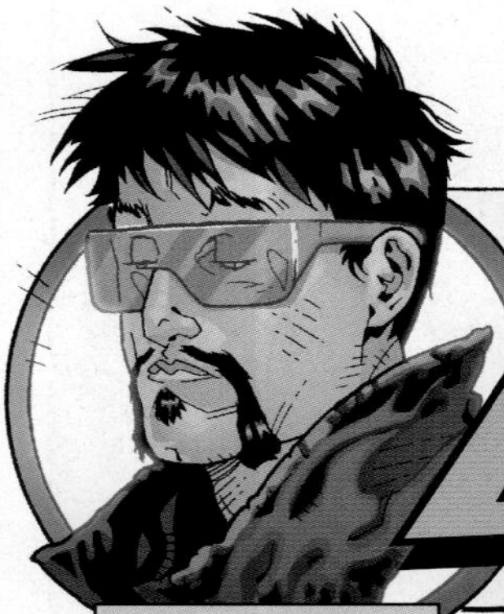

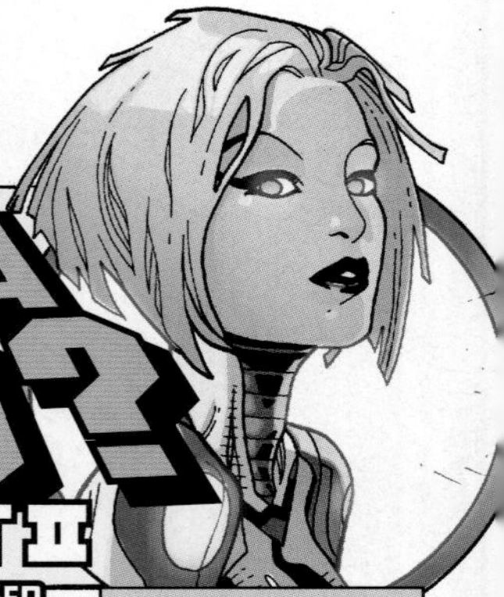

KEITH GIFFEN, WRITER
TIMOTHY GREEN II, PENCILLER
JOSEPH SILVER, INKER
DAVE SHARPE, LETTERER
HI-FI, COLORIST

STAR HAWKINS
PAN-GALACTIC P.I.

ILDA
GAL FRIDAY. KINDA.

EVERY CULTURE HAS ITS LEGEND(S)--THE BOGEYMAN, SANTA CLAUS, BIGFOOT. THE LIST GOES ON AND ON (TRUST US, IT GOES ON AND ON AND ON...I MEAN, HOW GULLIBLE *ARE* WE?). ON TOLERANCE, THE LEGEND OF CHOICE IS THE ONE ABOUT THE LONGEST-RUNNING HUNTED CONTESTANT. SOME SAY HE'S THE FIRST EVER CONTESTANT, OTHERS CLAIM SHE'S HIDING IN PLAIN SIGHT, WALKING AMONG THEM AS ONE OF THEM. STILL OTHERS SWEAR IT'S LONG SINCE SLIPPED FROM THE GAME, HAVING FOUND A WAY OFF TOLERANCE; THE FIRST EVER CONTESTANT TO ESCAPE. PAN-GALACTIC PRIVATE INVESTIGATOR STAR HAWKINS HAS BEEN CHARGED WITH THE TASK OF DISCOVERING WHETHER OR NOT THIS LEGENDARY CONTESTANT EXISTS.

SHE DOES.

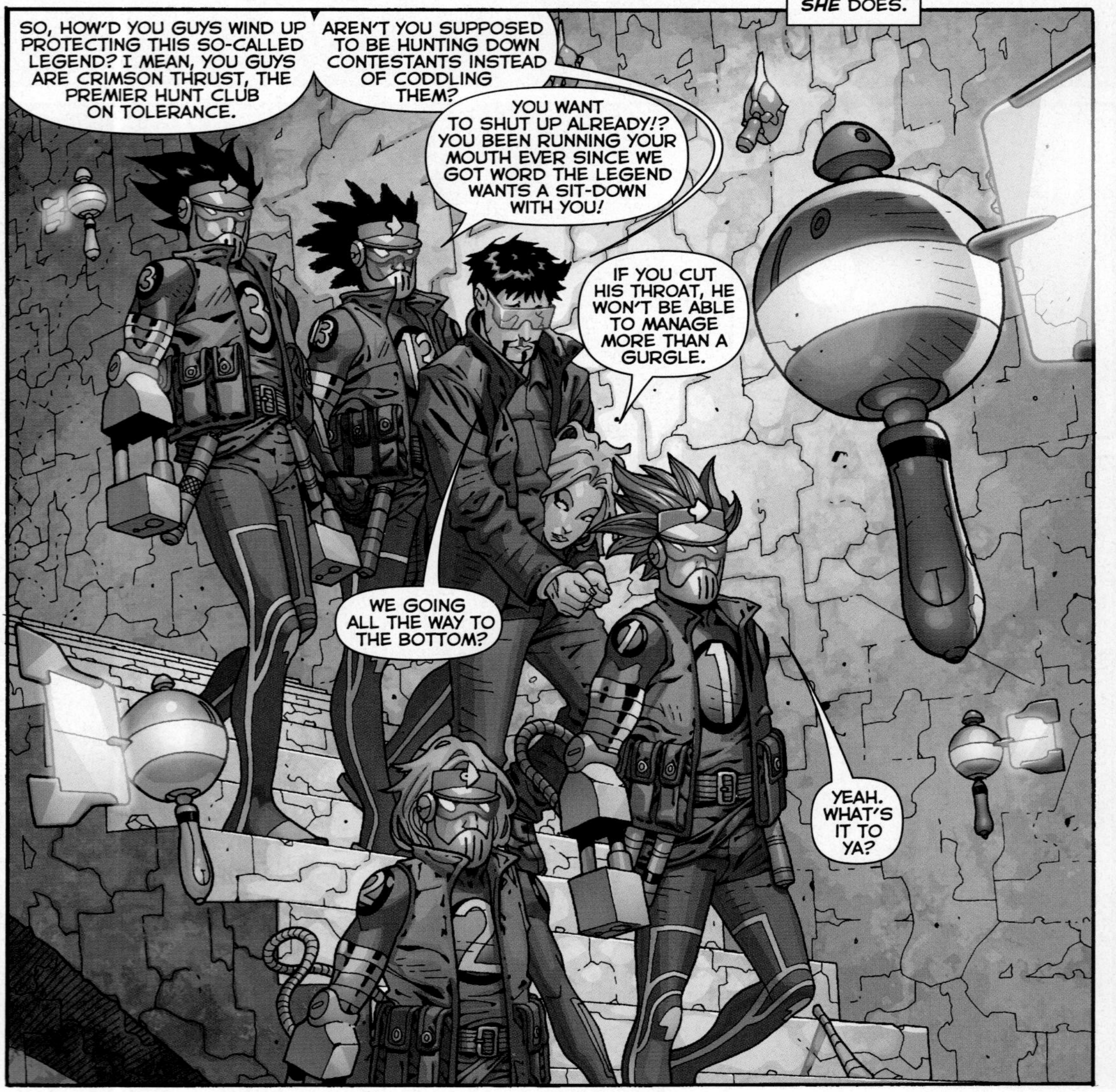

SO, HOW'D YOU GUYS WIND UP PROTECTING THIS SO-CALLED LEGEND? I MEAN, YOU GUYS ARE CRIMSON THRUST, THE PREMIER HUNT CLUB ON TOLERANCE.
AREN'T YOU SUPPOSED TO BE HUNTING DOWN CONTESTANTS INSTEAD OF CODDLING THEM?
YOU WANT TO SHUT UP ALREADY!? YOU BEEN RUNNING YOUR MOUTH EVER SINCE WE GOT WORD THE LEGEND WANTS A SIT-DOWN WITH YOU!
IF YOU CUT HIS THROAT, HE WON'T BE ABLE TO MANAGE MORE THAN A GURGLE.
WE GOING ALL THE WAY TO THE BOTTOM?
YEAH. WHAT'S IT TO YA?

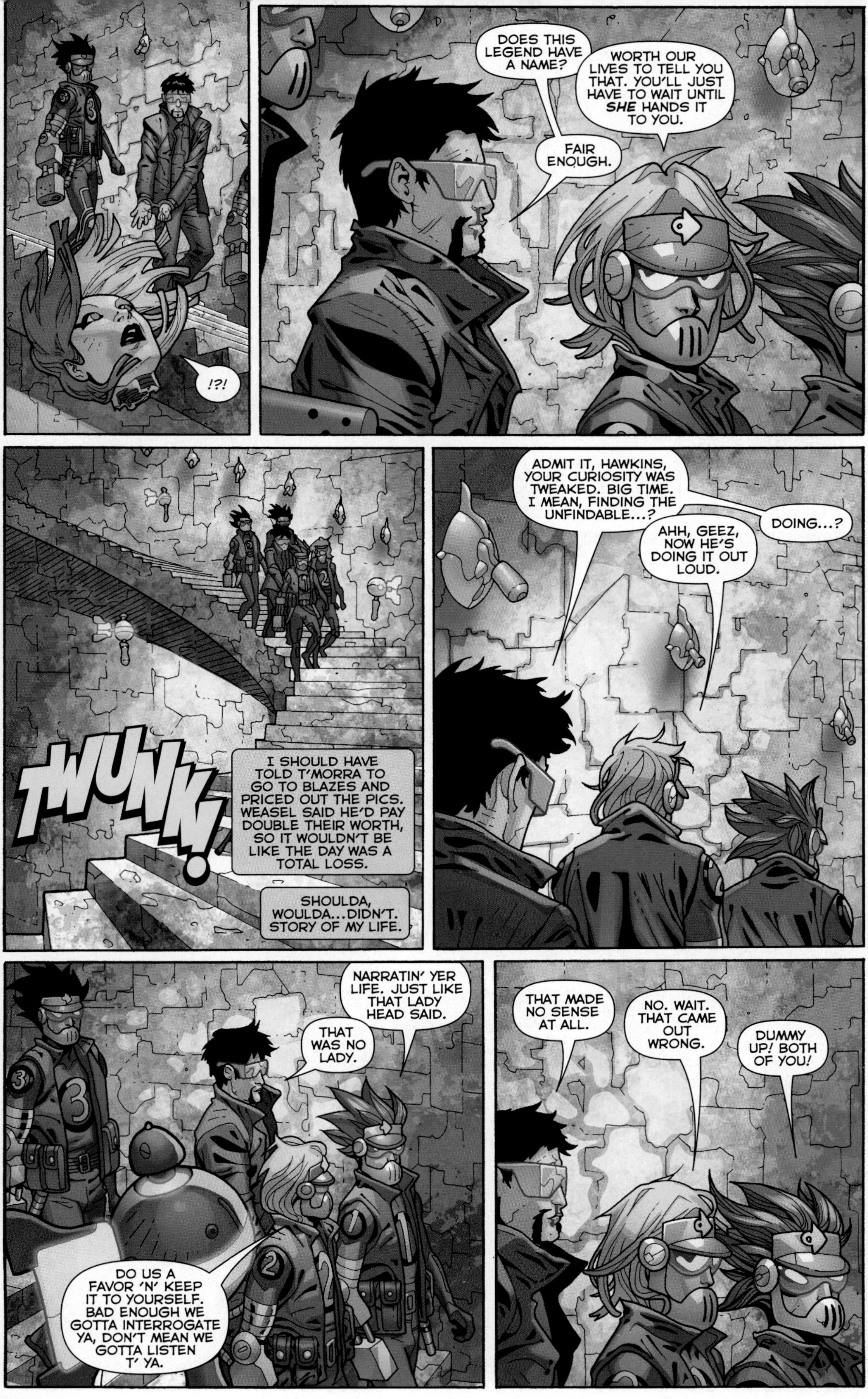
!?!
DOES THIS LEGEND HAVE A NAME?
WORTH OUR LIVES TO TELL YOU THAT. YOU'LL JUST HAVE TO WAIT UNTIL SHE HANDS IT TO YOU.
FAIR ENOUGH.
THWUNK!
I SHOULD HAVE TOLD T'MORRA TO GO TO BLAZES AND PRICED OUT THE PICS. WEASEL SAID HE'D PAY DOUBLE THEIR WORTH, SO IT WOULDN'T BE LIKE THE DAY WAS A TOTAL LOSS.
SHOULDA, WOULDA...DIDN'T. STORY OF MY LIFE.
ADMIT IT, HAWKINS, YOUR CURIOSITY WAS TWEAKED. BIG TIME. I MEAN, FINDING THE UNFINDABLE...?
DOING...?
AHH, GEEZ, NOW HE'S DOING IT OUT LOUD.
NARRATIN' YER LIFE. JUST LIKE THAT LADY HEAD SAID.
THAT WAS NO LADY.
DO US A FAVOR 'N' KEEP IT TO YOURSELF. BAD ENOUGH WE GOTTA INTERROGATE YA, DON'T MEAN WE GOTTA LISTEN T' YA.
THAT MADE NO SENSE AT ALL.
NO. WAIT. THAT CAME OUT WRONG.
DUMMY UP! BOTH OF YOU!

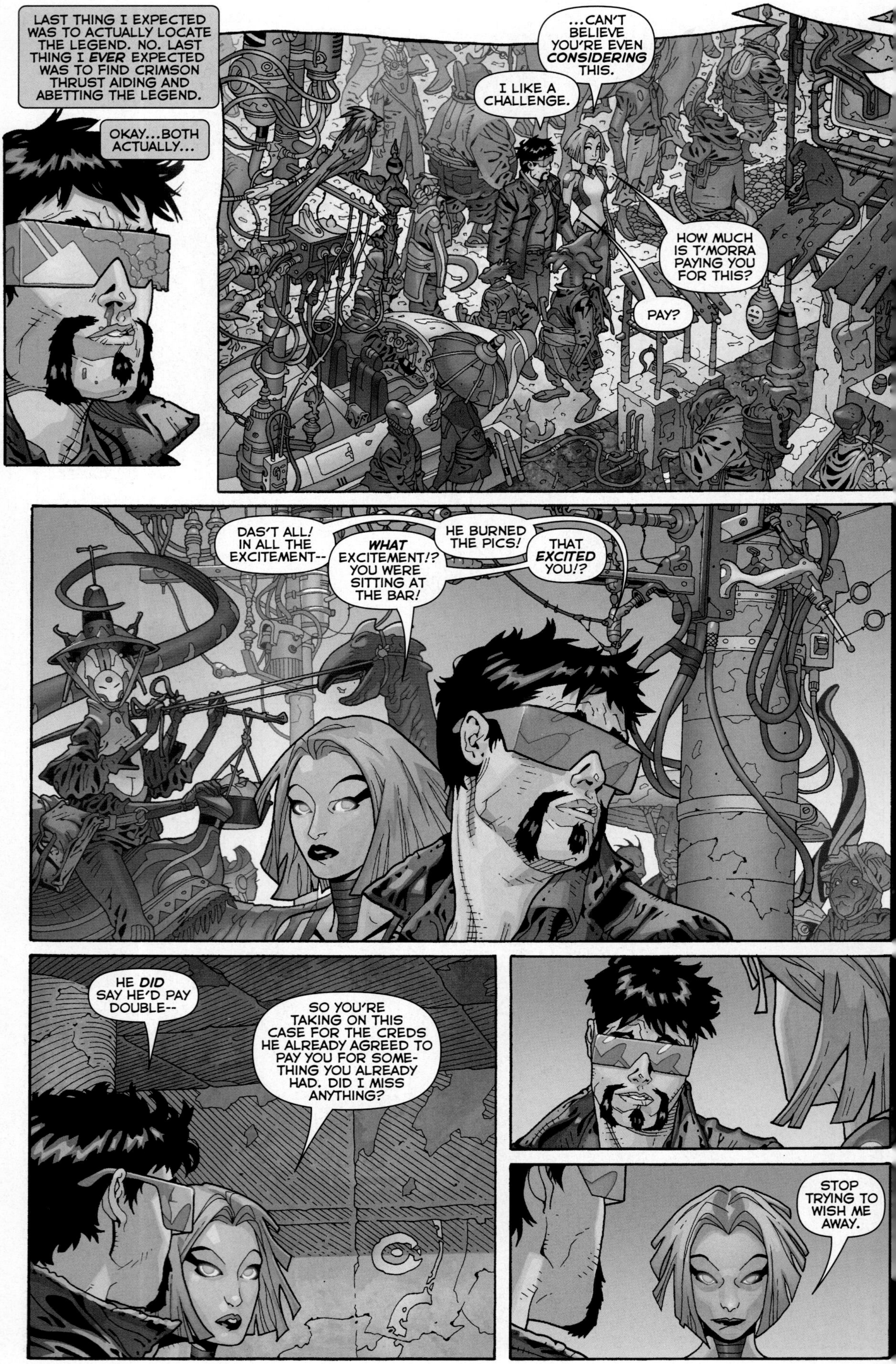
LAST THING I EXPECTED WAS TO ACTUALLY LOCATE THE LEGEND. NO. LAST THING I *EVER* EXPECTED WAS TO FIND CRIMSON THRUST AIDING AND ABETTING THE LEGEND.
OKAY...BOTH ACTUALLY...
...CAN'T BELIEVE YOU'RE EVEN *CONSIDERING* THIS.
I LIKE A CHALLENGE.
HOW MUCH IS T'MORRA PAYING YOU FOR THIS?
PAY?
DAS'T ALL! IN ALL THE EXCITEMENT--
HE BURNED THE PICS!
WHAT EXCITEMENT!? YOU WERE SITTING AT THE BAR!
THAT *EXCITED* YOU!?
HE *DID* SAY HE'D PAY DOUBLE--
SO YOU'RE TAKING ON THIS CASE FOR THE CREDS HE ALREADY AGREED TO PAY YOU FOR SOMETHING YOU ALREADY HAD. DID I MISS ANYTHING?
STOP TRYING TO WISH ME AWAY.

RIGHT... SO WHAT DO WE KNOW ABOUT THIS LEGEND?

HANG ON. LET ME DO A GLIMMERNET SEARCH.

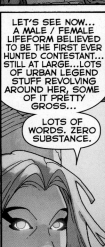

LET'S SEE NOW... A MALE / FEMALE LIFEFORM BELIEVED TO BE THE FIRST EVER HUNTED CONTESTANT... STILL AT LARGE...LOTS OF URBAN LEGEND STUFF REVOLVING AROUND HER, SOME OF IT PRETTY GROSS...

LOTS OF WORDS. ZERO SUBSTANCE.

BEEN THERE. DONE THAT.

WAS THAT A CRACK?

CONTRARY TO WHAT YOU MAY BELIEVE, NOT EVERYTHING IS ABOUT YOU.

WAS IT?

CONSUMING, YES. ENJOYING? NOT SO MUCH.

YOU ARE AWARE THAT I'VE GOT GLIMMERNET ACCESS TO EVERY INSULT EVER? THAT YOU'RE HOPELESSLY OUTCLASSED?

I SHOULD BE IMPRESSED? MY TOASTER TOASTS BREAD BETTER THAN I DO. I'M SUPPOSED TO SURRENDER TO ITS SUPERIOR ABILITY?

OF COURSE IT WAS. SO'S THIS...

CARE FOR AN ESPRESSOCHINO?

I AM CAPABLE OF CONSUMING--

CAN WE PLEASE JUST GET ON WITH THIS? THE SOONER YOU FAIL, THE SOONER I CAN--

WHAT MAKES YOU SO SURE I'M GOING TO FAIL?

OUR WEDDING NIGHT.

...OUCH.

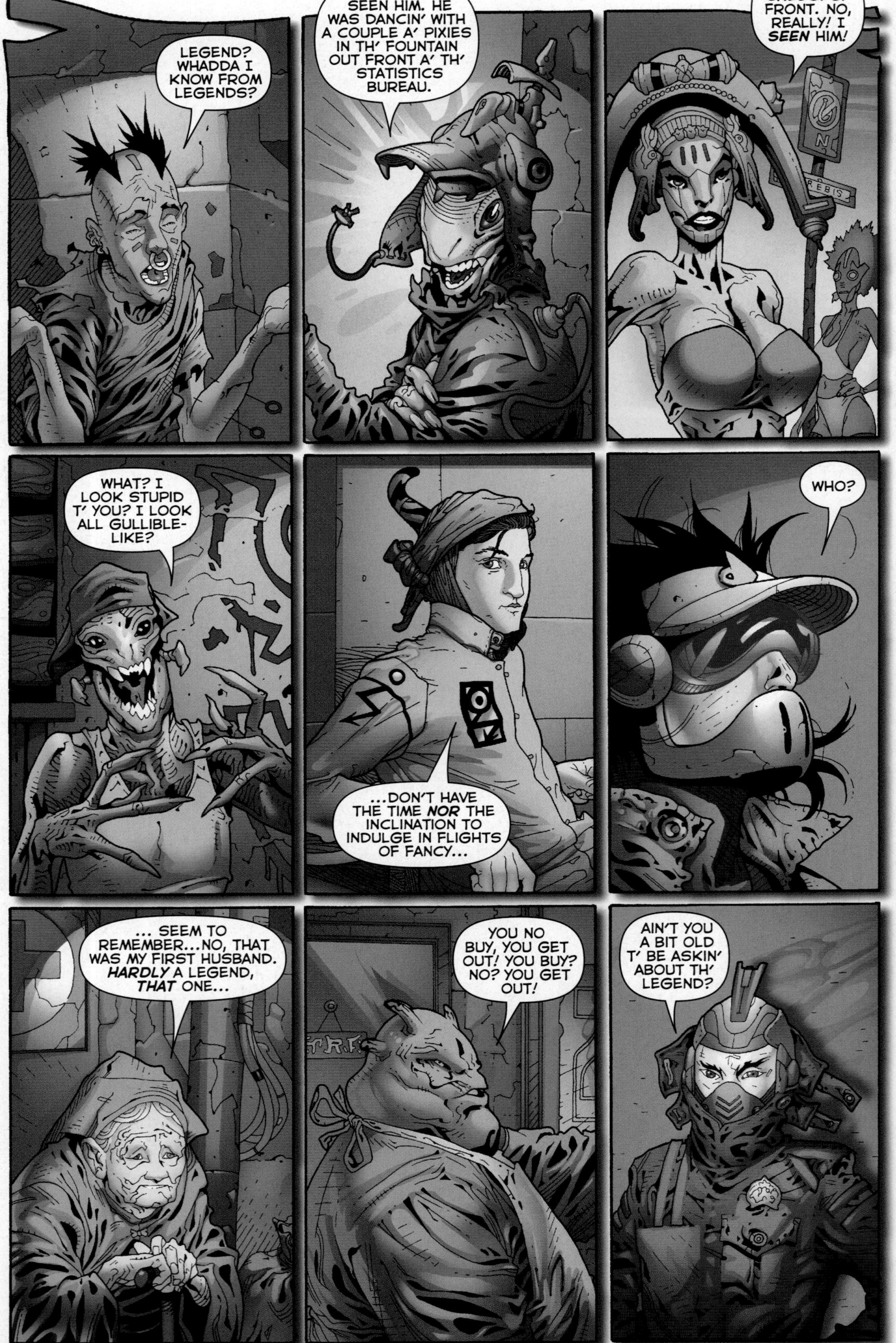
LEGEND? WHADDA I KNOW FROM LEGENDS?
YEAH, I SEEN HIM. HE WAS DANCIN' WITH A COUPLE A' PIXIES IN TH' FOUNTAIN OUT FRONT A' TH' STATISTICS BUREAU.
TWENNY CREDS. UP FRONT. NO, REALLY! I SEEN HIM!
WHAT? I LOOK STUPID T' YOU? I LOOK ALL GULLIBLE-LIKE?
...DON'T HAVE THE TIME NOR THE INCLINATION TO INDULGE IN FLIGHTS OF FANCY...
WHO?
... SEEM TO REMEMBER...NO, THAT WAS MY FIRST HUSBAND. HARDLY A LEGEND, THAT ONE...
YOU NO BUY, YOU GET OUT! YOU BUY? NO? YOU GET OUT!
AIN'T YOU A BIT OLD T' BE ASKIN' ABOUT TH' LEGEND?

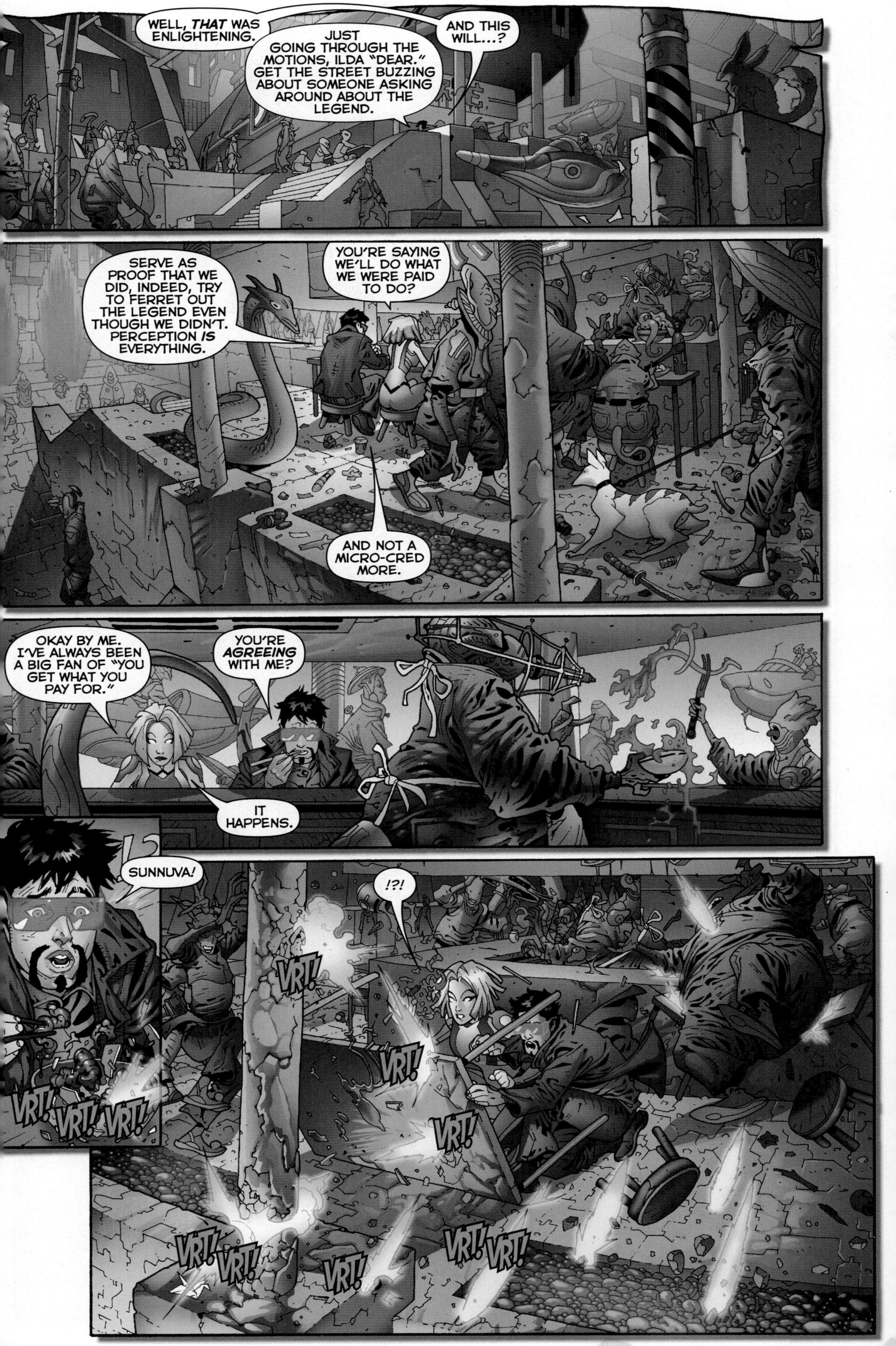

WELL, *THAT* WAS ENLIGHTENING.
AND THIS WILL...?
JUST GOING THROUGH THE MOTIONS, ILDA "DEAR." GET THE STREET BUZZING ABOUT SOMEONE ASKING AROUND ABOUT THE LEGEND.
SERVE AS PROOF THAT WE DID, INDEED, TRY TO FERRET OUT THE LEGEND EVEN THOUGH WE DIDN'T. PERCEPTION *IS* EVERYTHING.
YOU'RE SAYING WE'LL DO WHAT WE WERE PAID TO DO?
AND NOT A MICRO-CRED MORE.
OKAY BY ME. I'VE ALWAYS BEEN A BIG FAN OF "YOU GET WHAT YOU PAY FOR."
YOU'RE *AGREEING* WITH ME?
IT HAPPENS.
SUNNUVA!
VRT! VRT! VRT!
!?!
VRT!
VRT!
VRT!
VRT! VRT!
VRT!
VRT! VRT!

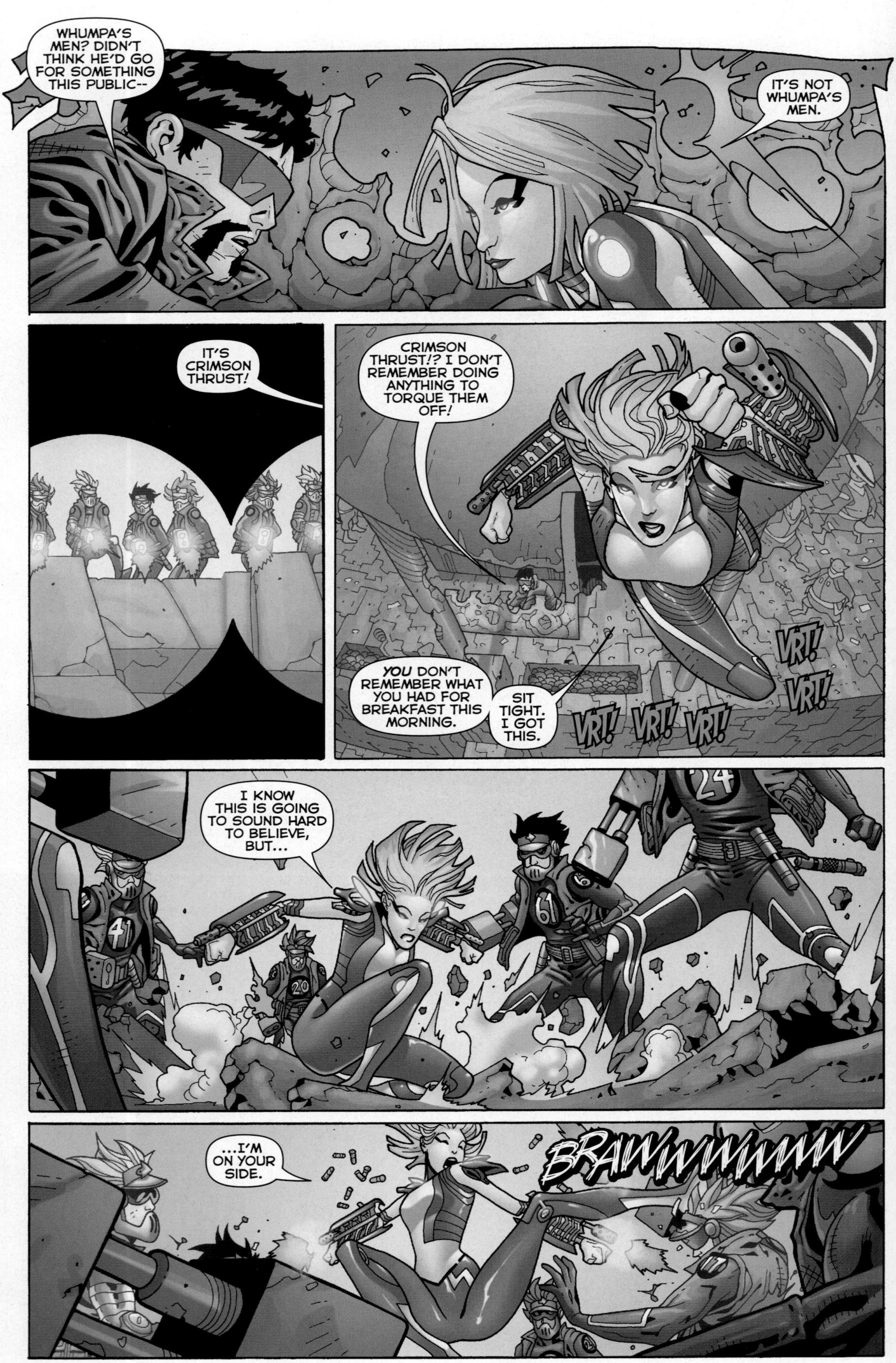
WHUMPA'S MEN? DIDN'T THINK HE'D GO FOR SOMETHING THIS PUBLIC--
IT'S NOT WHUMPA'S MEN.
IT'S CRIMSON THRUST!
CRIMSON THRUST!? I DON'T REMEMBER DOING ANYTHING TO TORQUE THEM OFF!
YOU DON'T REMEMBER WHAT YOU HAD FOR BREAKFAST THIS MORNING.
SIT TIGHT. I GOT THIS.
VRT! VRT! VRT! VRT! VRT!
I KNOW THIS IS GOING TO SOUND HARD TO BELIEVE, BUT...
...I'M ON YOUR SIDE.
BRAWWWWWW

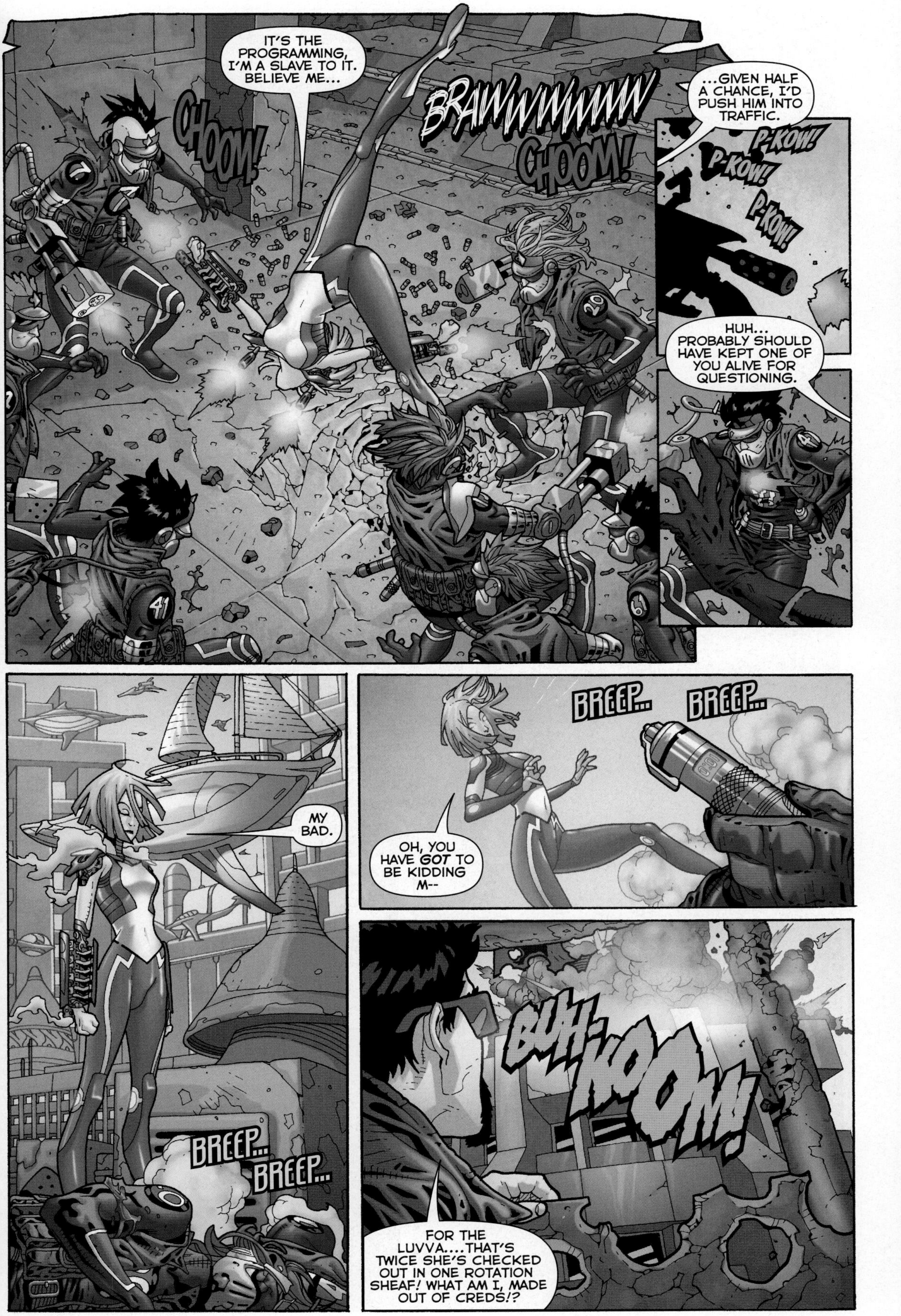

IT'S THE PROGRAMMING, I'M A SLAVE TO IT. BELIEVE ME...
CHOOM!
BRAWWWWWW
CHOOM!
...GIVEN HALF A CHANCE, I'D PUSH HIM INTO TRAFFIC.
P-KOW!
P-KOW!
P-KOW!
HUH... PROBABLY SHOULD HAVE KEPT ONE OF YOU ALIVE FOR QUESTIONING.
MY BAD.
BREEP...
BREEP...
BREEP...
BREEP...
OH, YOU HAVE *GOT* TO BE KIDDING M--
BUH-KOOM!
FOR THE LUVVA....THAT'S TWICE SHE'S CHECKED OUT IN ONE ROTATION SHEAF! WHAT AM I, MADE OUT OF CREDS!?

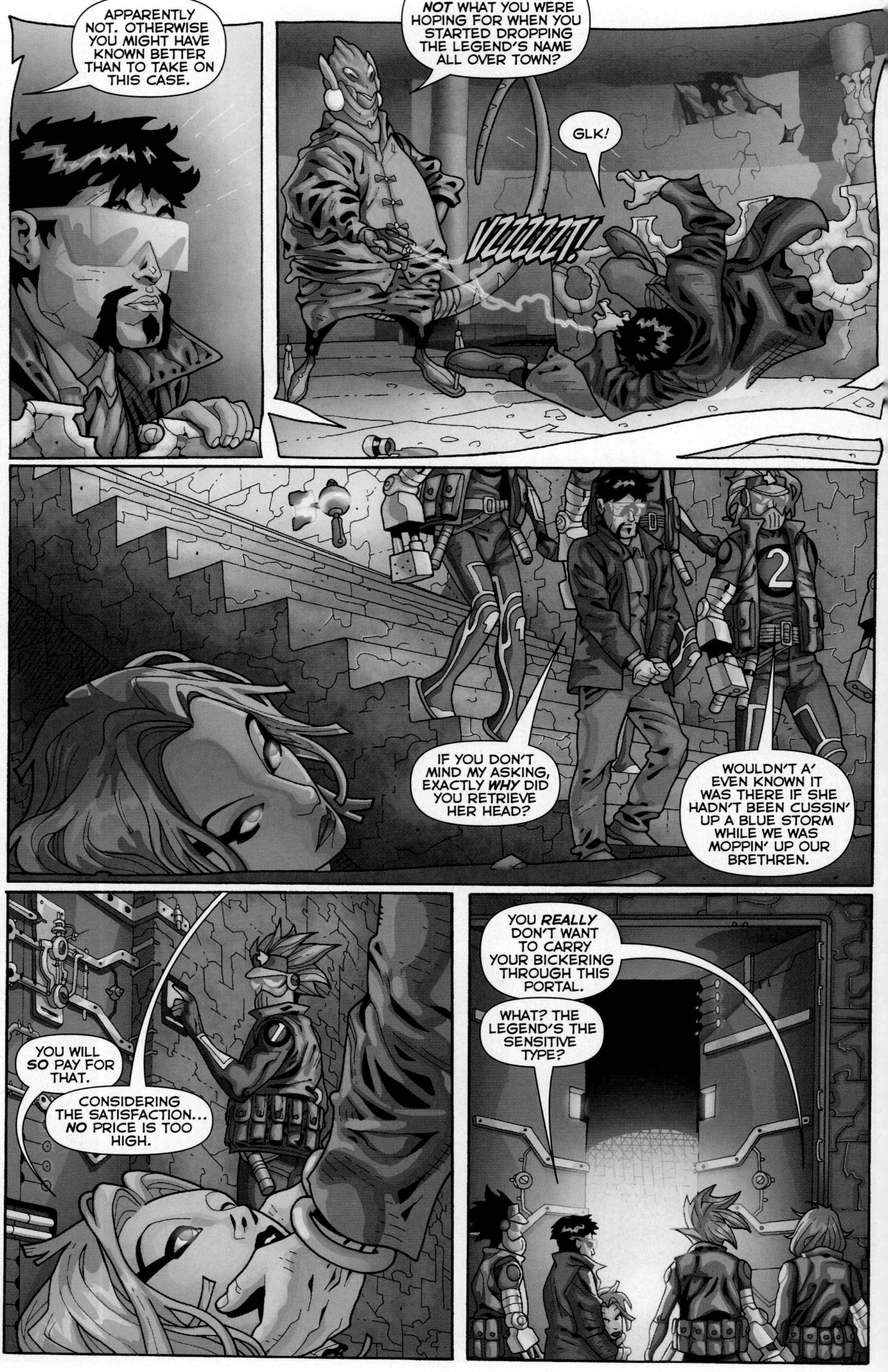
APPARENTLY NOT. OTHERWISE YOU MIGHT HAVE KNOWN BETTER THAN TO TAKE ON THIS CASE.
I CAN ONLY ASSUME THIS IS NOT WHAT YOU WERE HOPING FOR WHEN YOU STARTED DROPPING THE LEGEND'S NAME ALL OVER TOWN?
GLK!
VZZZZZT!
IF YOU DON'T MIND MY ASKING, EXACTLY WHY DID YOU RETRIEVE HER HEAD?
WOULDN'T A' EVEN KNOWN IT WAS THERE IF SHE HADN'T BEEN CUSSIN' UP A BLUE STORM WHILE WE WAS MOPPIN' UP OUR BRETHREN.
YOU WILL SO PAY FOR THAT.
CONSIDERING THE SATISFACTION... NO PRICE IS TOO HIGH.
YOU REALLY DON'T WANT TO CARRY YOUR BICKERING THROUGH THIS PORTAL.
WHAT? THE LEGEND'S THE SENSITIVE TYPE?

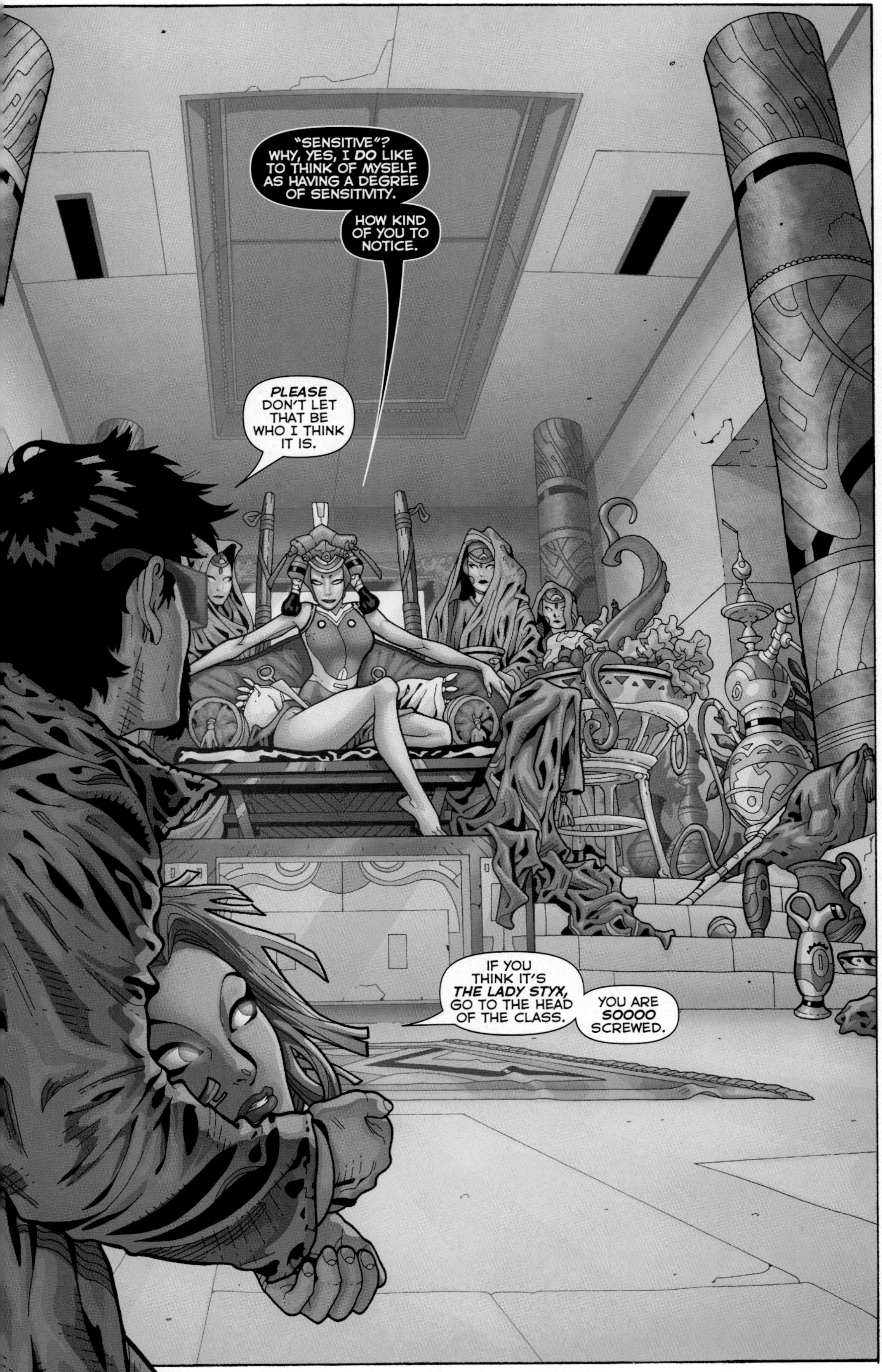
"SENSITIVE"? WHY, YES, I *DO* LIKE TO THINK OF MYSELF AS HAVING A DEGREE OF SENSITIVITY.
HOW KIND OF YOU TO NOTICE.
PLEASE DON'T LET THAT BE WHO I THINK IT IS.
IF YOU THINK IT'S ***THE LADY STYX,*** GO TO THE HEAD OF THE CLASS.
YOU ARE *SOOOO* SCREWED.

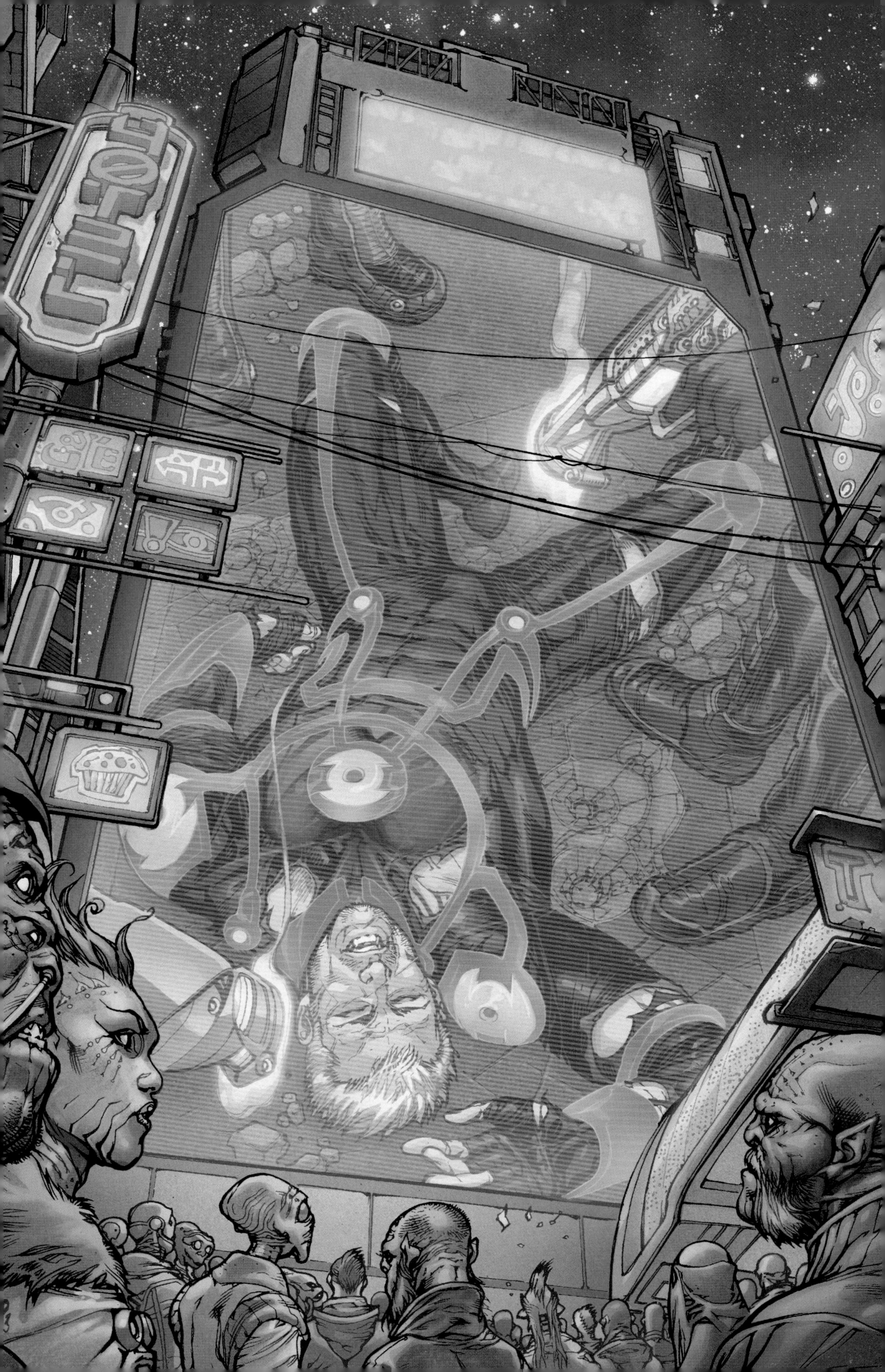

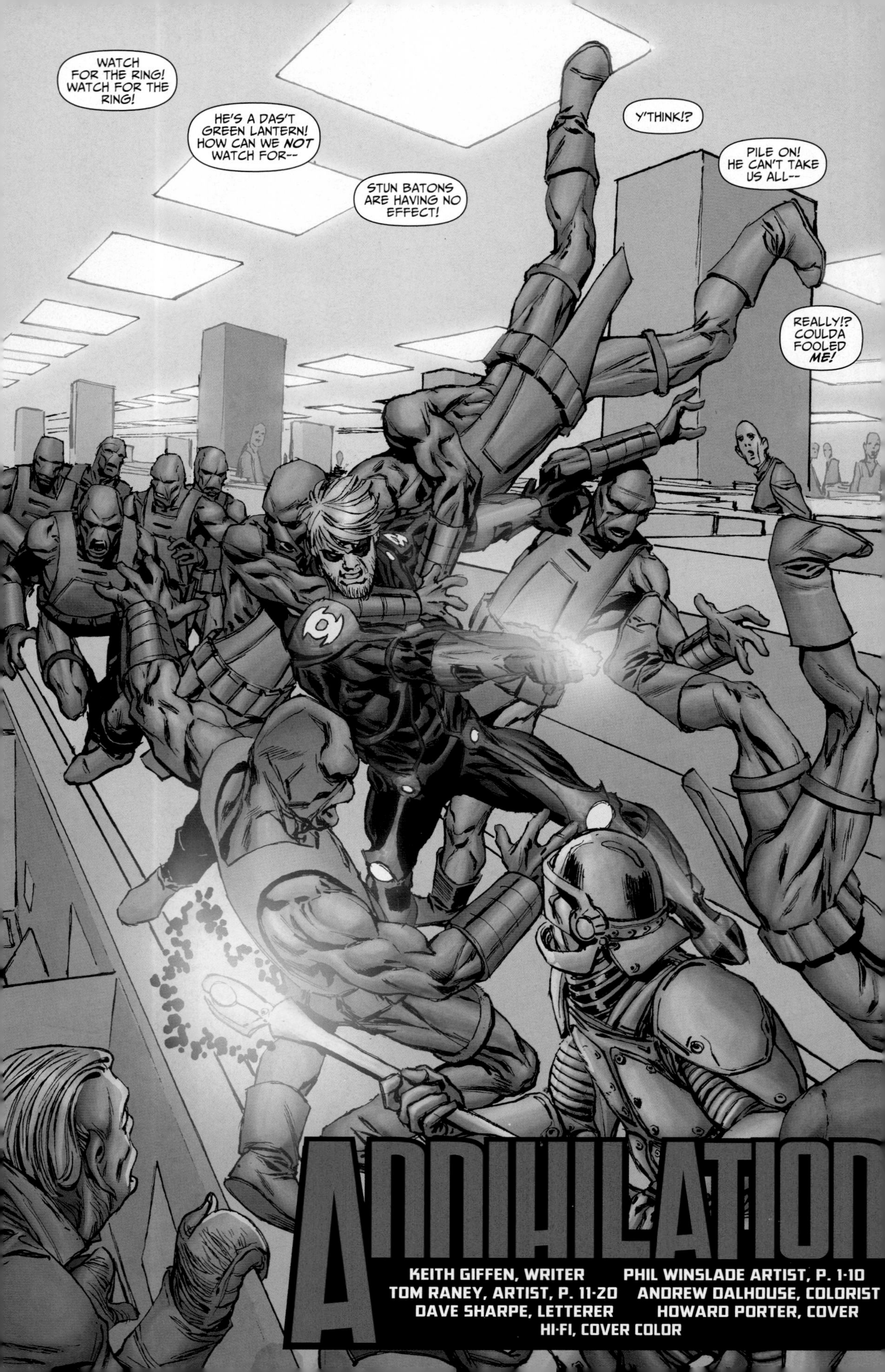
WATCH FOR THE RING! WATCH FOR THE RING!
HE'S A DAS'T GREEN LANTERN! HOW CAN WE *NOT* WATCH FOR--
STUN BATONS ARE HAVING NO EFFECT!
Y'THINK!?
PILE ON! HE CAN'T TAKE US ALL--
REALLY!? COULDA FOOLED *ME!*
ANNIHILATION
KEITH GIFFEN, WRITER
PHIL WINSLADE ARTIST, P. 1-10
TOM RANEY, ARTIST, P. 11-20
ANDREW DALHOUSE, COLORIST
DAVE SHARPE, LETTERER
HOWARD PORTER, COVER
HI-FI, COVER COLOR

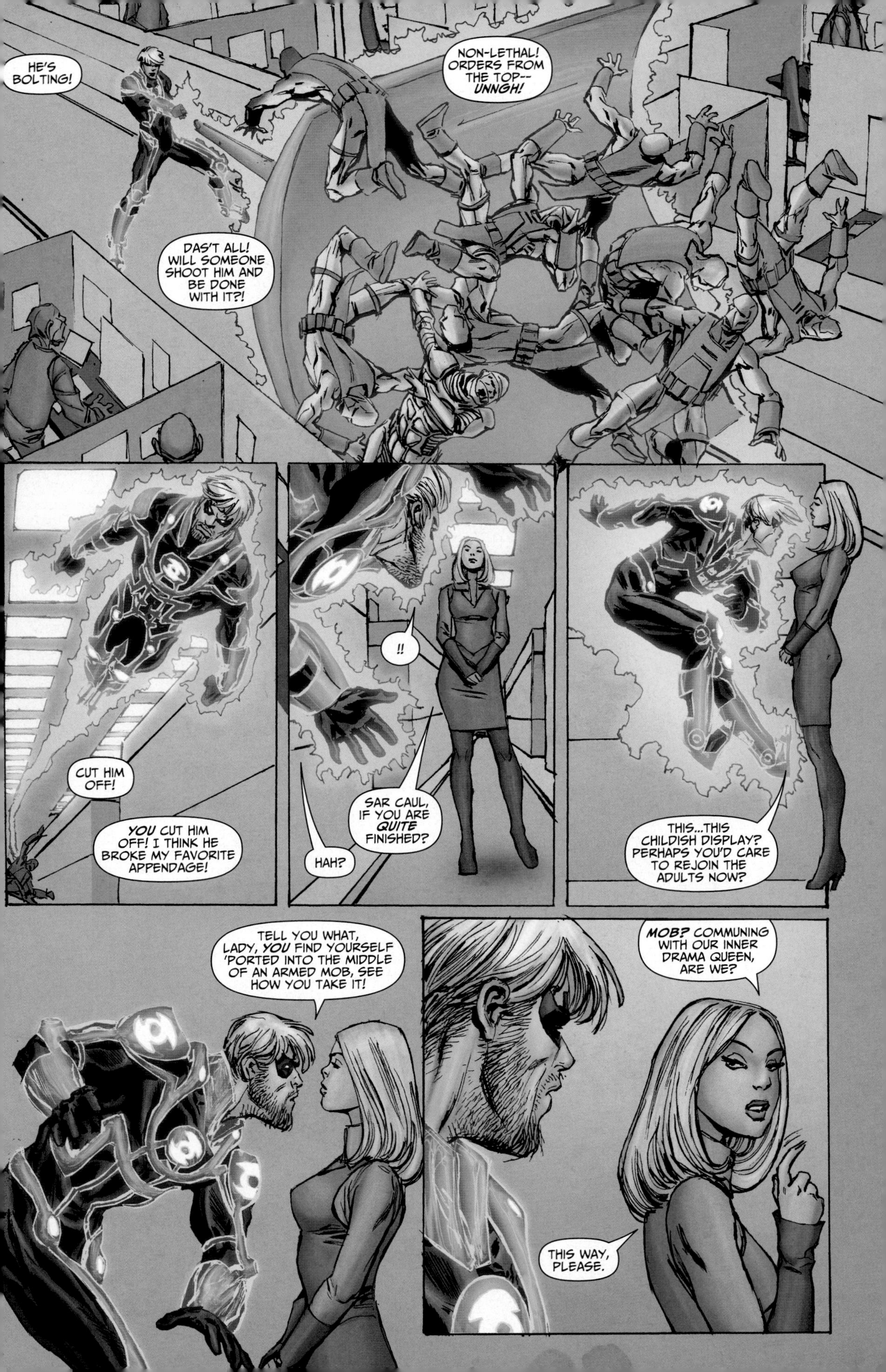
HE'S BOLTING!
NON-LETHAL! ORDERS FROM THE TOP-- UNNGH!
DAS'T ALL! WILL SOMEONE SHOOT HIM AND BE DONE WITH IT?!
CUT HIM OFF!
YOU CUT HIM OFF! I THINK HE BROKE MY FAVORITE APPENDAGE!
!!
SAR CAUL, IF YOU ARE QUITE FINISHED?
HAH?
THIS...THIS CHILDISH DISPLAY? PERHAPS YOU'D CARE TO REJOIN THE ADULTS NOW?
TELL YOU WHAT, LADY, YOU FIND YOURSELF 'PORTED INTO THE MIDDLE OF AN ARMED MOB, SEE HOW YOU TAKE IT!
MOB? COMMUNING WITH OUR INNER DRAMA QUEEN, ARE WE?
THIS WAY, PLEASE.

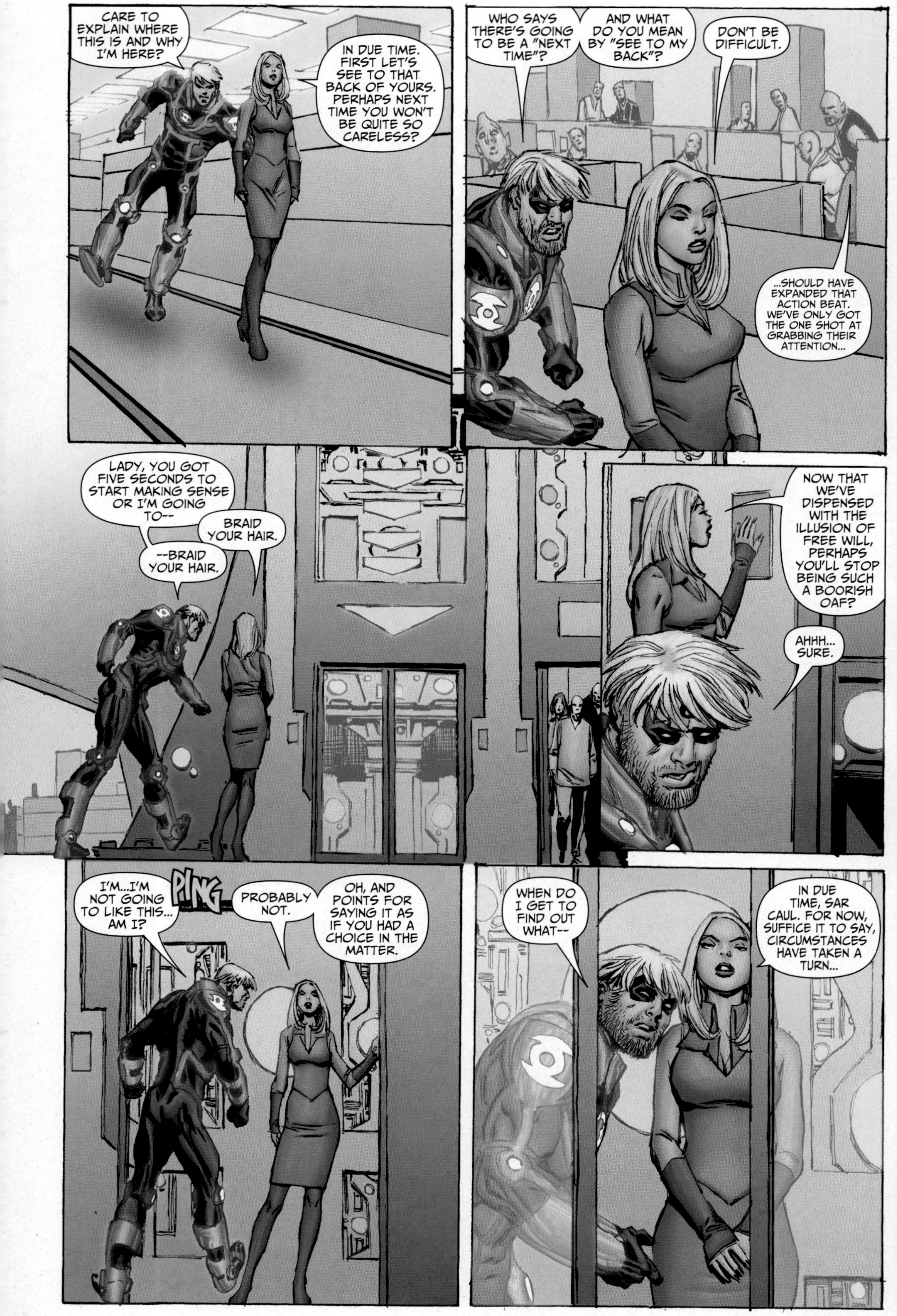
CARE TO EXPLAIN WHERE THIS IS AND WHY I'M HERE?
IN DUE TIME. FIRST LET'S BACK OF YOURS. PERHAPS NEXT TIME YOU WON'T BE QUITE SO CARELESS?
WHO SAYS THERE'S GOING TO BE A "NEXT TIME"?
AND WHAT DO YOU MEAN BY "SEE TO MY BACK"?
DON'T BE DIFFICULT.
...SHOULD HAVE EXPANDED THAT ACTION BEAT. WE'VE ONLY GOT THE ONE SHOT AT GRABBING THEIR ATTENTION...
LADY, YOU GOT FIVE SECONDS TO START MAKING SENSE OR I'M GOING TO--
BRAID YOUR HAIR.
--BRAID YOUR HAIR.
NOW THAT WE'VE DISPENSED WITH THE ILLUSION OF FREE WILL, PERHAPS YOU'LL STOP BEING SUCH A BOORISH OAF?
AHHH... SURE.
I'M...I'M NOT GOING TO LIKE THIS... AM I?
PING
PROBABLY NOT.
OH, AND POINTS FOR SAYING IT AS IF YOU HAD A CHOICE IN THE MATTER.
WHEN DO I GET TO FIND OUT WHAT--
IN DUE TIME, SAR CAUL. FOR NOW, SUFFICE IT TO SAY, CIRCUMSTANCES HAVE TAKEN A TURN...

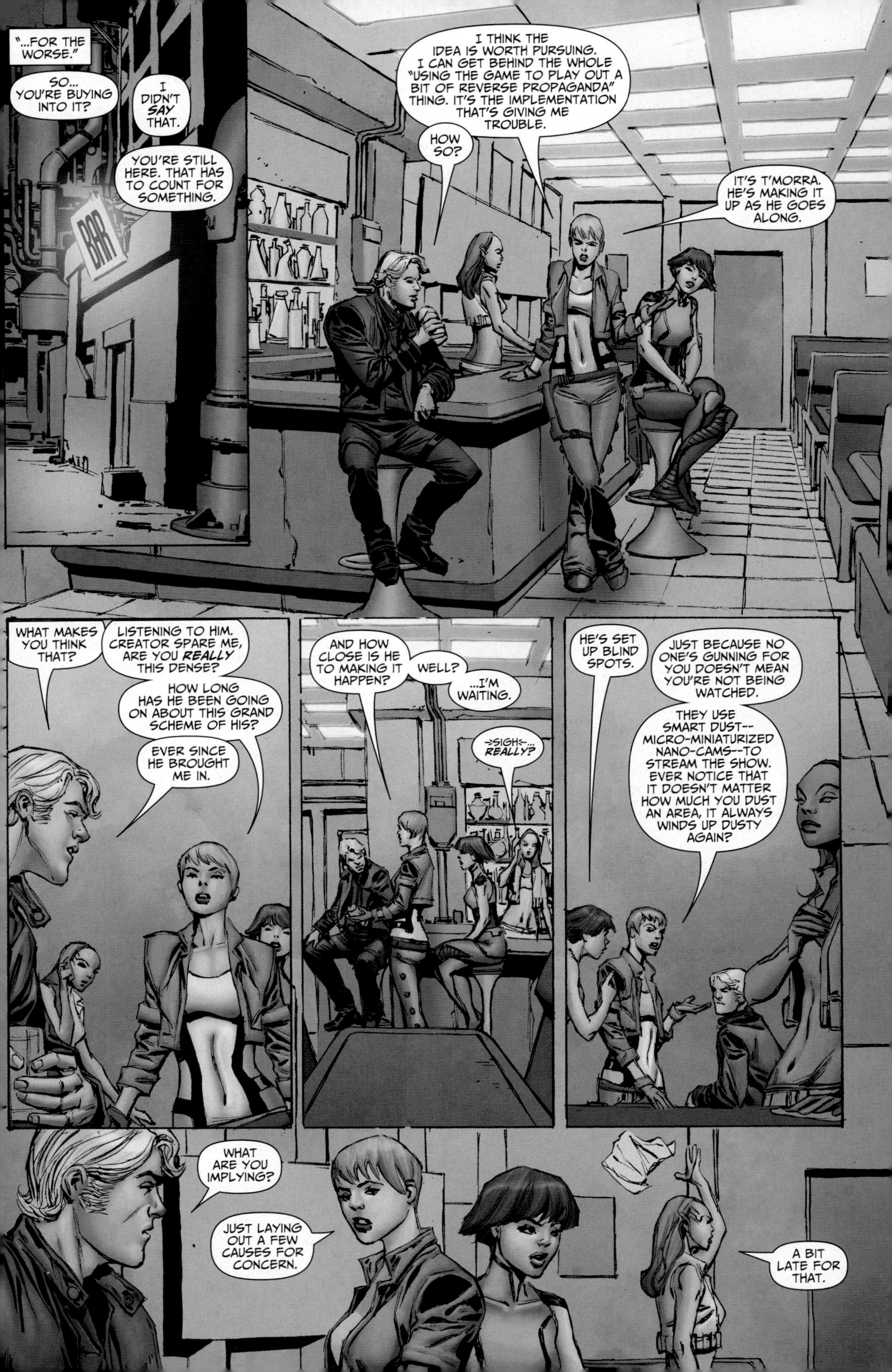

"...FOR THE WORSE."
SO... YOU'RE BUYING INTO IT?
I DIDN'T *SAY* THAT.
YOU'RE STILL HERE. THAT HAS TO COUNT FOR SOMETHING.
BAR
I THINK THE IDEA IS WORTH PURSUING. I CAN GET BEHIND THE WHOLE "USING THE GAME TO PLAY OUT A BIT OF REVERSE PROPAGANDA" THING. IT'S THE IMPLEMENTATION THAT'S GIVING ME TROUBLE.
HOW SO?
IT'S T'MORRA. HE'S MAKING IT UP AS HE GOES ALONG.
WHAT MAKES YOU THINK THAT?
LISTENING TO HIM. CREATOR SPARE ME, ARE YOU *REALLY* THIS DENSE?
HOW LONG HAS HE BEEN GOING ON ABOUT THIS GRAND SCHEME OF HIS?
EVER SINCE HE BROUGHT ME IN.
AND HOW CLOSE IS HE TO MAKING IT HAPPEN?
WELL?
...I'M WAITING.
>SIGH<... *REALLY?*
HE'S SET UP BLIND SPOTS.
JUST BECAUSE NO ONE'S GUNNING FOR YOU DOESN'T MEAN YOU'RE NOT BEING WATCHED.
THEY USE SMART DUST-- MICRO-MINIATURIZED NANO-CAMS--TO STREAM THE SHOW. EVER NOTICE THAT IT DOESN'T MATTER HOW MUCH YOU DUST AN AREA, IT ALWAYS WINDS UP DUSTY AGAIN?
WHAT ARE YOU IMPLYING?
JUST LAYING OUT A FEW CAUSES FOR CONCERN.
A BIT LATE FOR THAT.

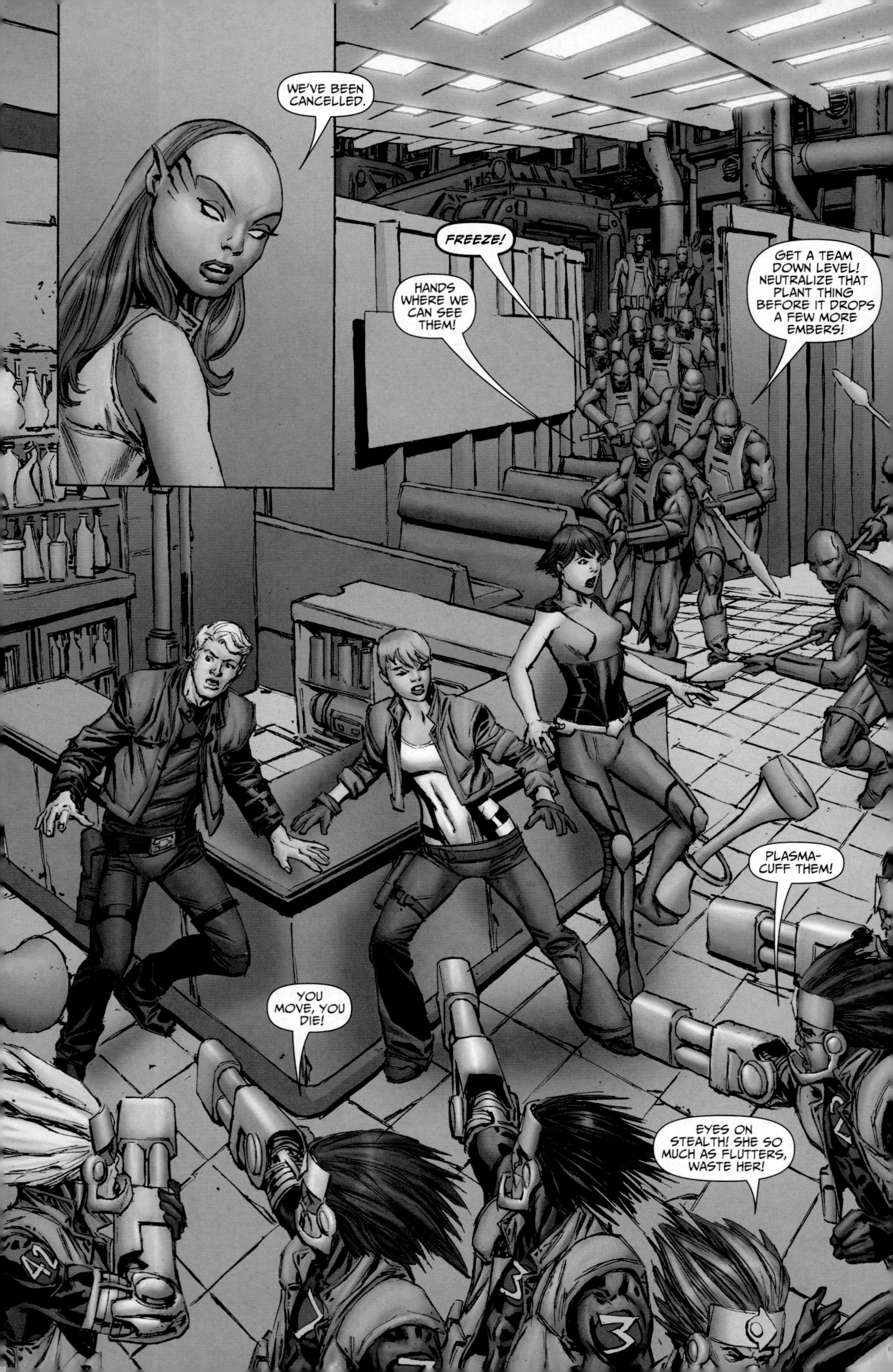
WE'VE BEEN CANCELLED.
FREEZE!
HANDS WHERE WE CAN SEE THEM!
GET A TEAM DOWN LEVEL! NEUTRALIZE THAT PLANT THING BEFORE IT DROPS A FEW MORE EMBERS!
PLASMA-CUFF THEM!
YOU MOVE, YOU DIE!
EYES ON STEALTH! SHE SO MUCH AS FLUTTERS, WASTE HER!

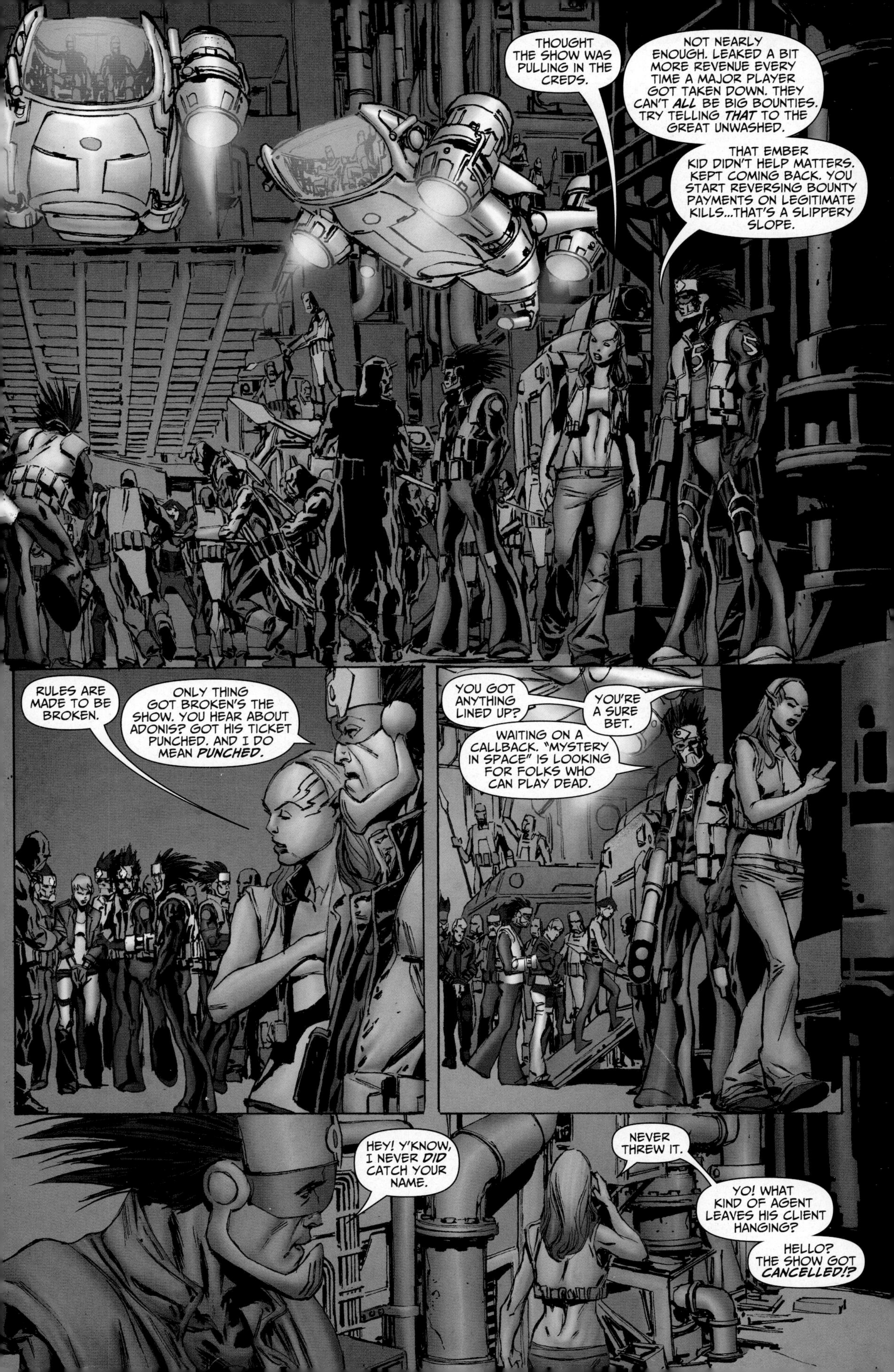
THOUGHT THE SHOW WAS PULLING IN THE CREDS.
NOT NEARLY ENOUGH. LEAKED A BIT MORE REVENUE EVERY TIME A MAJOR PLAYER GOT TAKEN DOWN. THEY CAN'T ALL BE BIG BOUNTIES. TRY TELLING THAT TO THE GREAT UNWASHED.
THAT EMBER KID DIDN'T HELP MATTERS. KEPT COMING BACK. YOU START REVERSING BOUNTY PAYMENTS ON LEGITIMATE KILLS...THAT'S A SLIPPERY SLOPE.
RULES ARE MADE TO BE BROKEN.
ONLY THING GOT BROKEN'S THE SHOW. YOU HEAR ABOUT ADONIS? GOT HIS TICKET PUNCHED. AND I DO MEAN PUNCHED.
YOU GOT ANYTHING LINED UP?
YOU'RE A SURE BET.
WAITING ON A CALLBACK. "MYSTERY IN SPACE" IS LOOKING FOR FOLKS WHO CAN PLAY DEAD.
HEY! Y'KNOW, I NEVER DID CATCH YOUR NAME.
NEVER THREW IT.
YO! WHAT KIND OF AGENT LEAVES HIS CLIENT HANGING?
HELLO? THE SHOW GOT CANCELLED!?

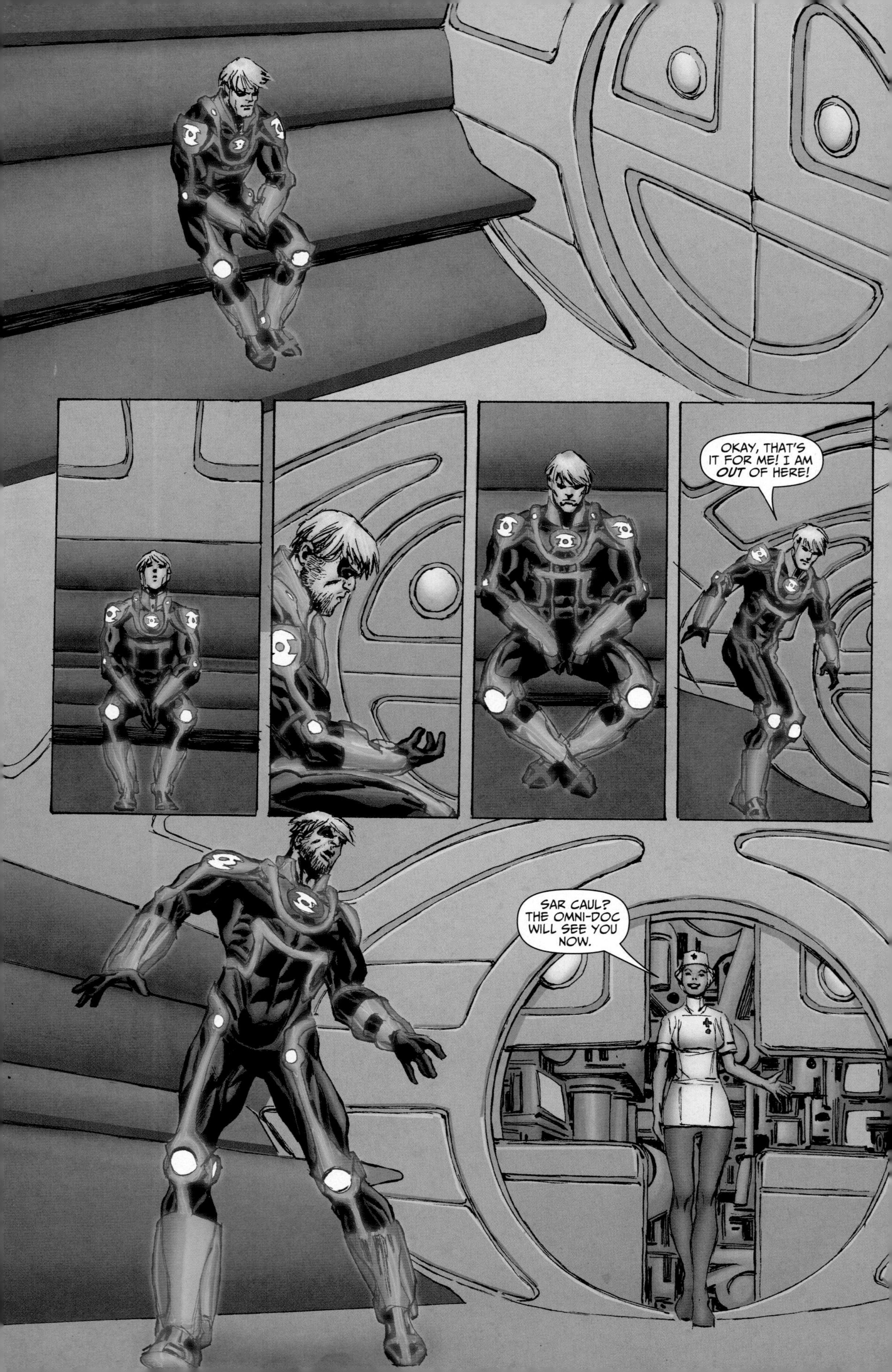
OKAY, THAT'S IT FOR ME! I AM *OUT* OF HERE!
SAR CAUL? THE OMNI-DOC WILL SEE YOU NOW.

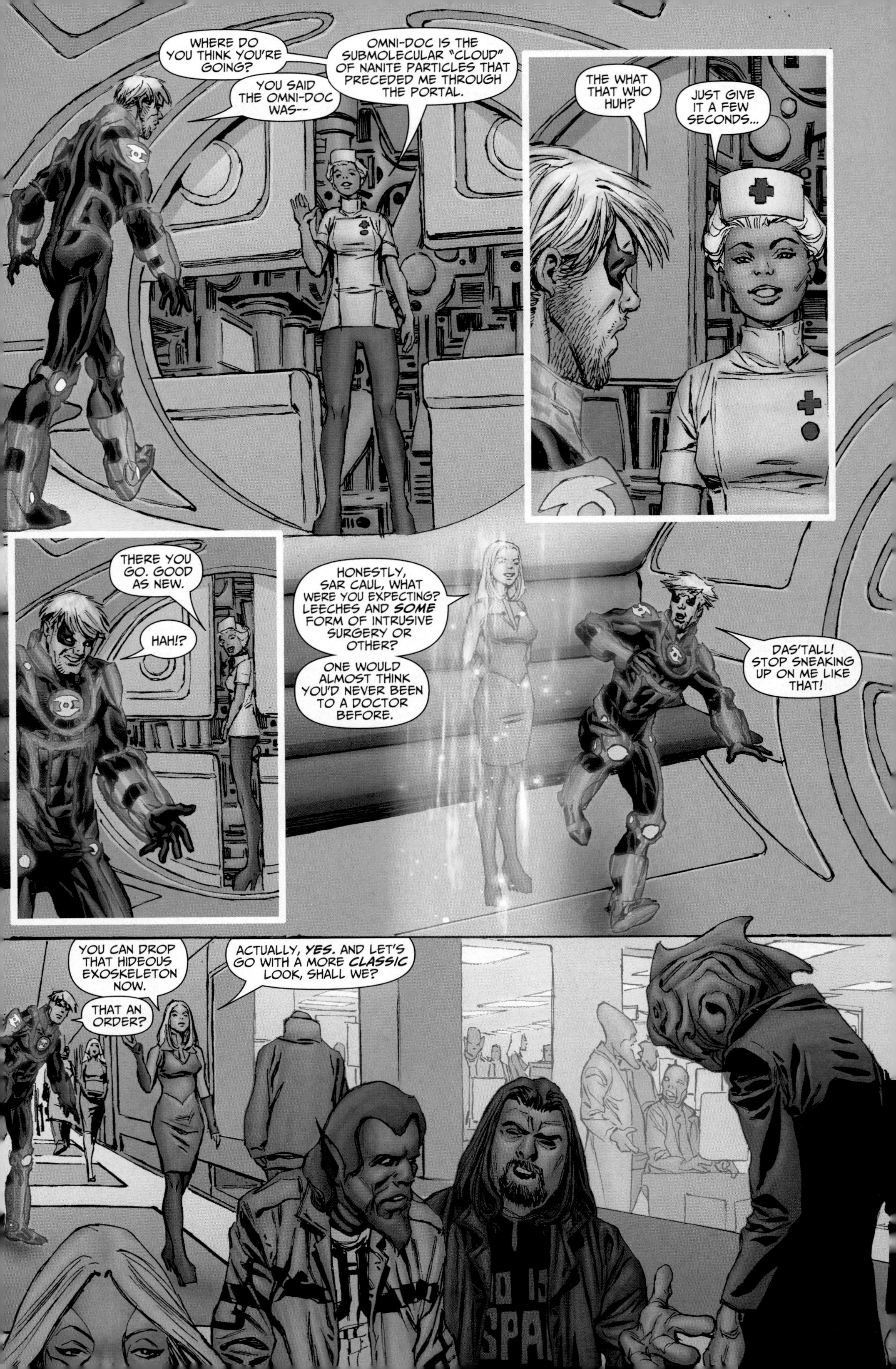
WHERE DO YOU THINK YOU'RE GOING?
YOU SAID THE OMNI-DOC WAS--
OMNI-DOC IS THE SUBMOLECULAR "CLOUD" OF NANITE PARTICLES THAT PRECEDED ME THROUGH THE PORTAL.
THE WHAT THAT WHO HUH?
JUST GIVE IT A FEW SECONDS...
THERE YOU GO. GOOD AS NEW.
HAH!?
HONESTLY, SAR CAUL, WHAT WERE YOU EXPECTING? LEECHES AND SOME FORM OF INTRUSIVE SURGERY OR OTHER?
ONE WOULD ALMOST THINK YOU'D NEVER BEEN TO A DOCTOR BEFORE.
DAS'TALL! STOP SNEAKING UP ON ME LIKE THAT!
YOU CAN DROP THAT HIDEOUS EXOSKELETON NOW.
THAT AN ORDER?
ACTUALLY, YES. AND LET'S GO WITH A MORE CLASSIC LOOK, SHALL WE?

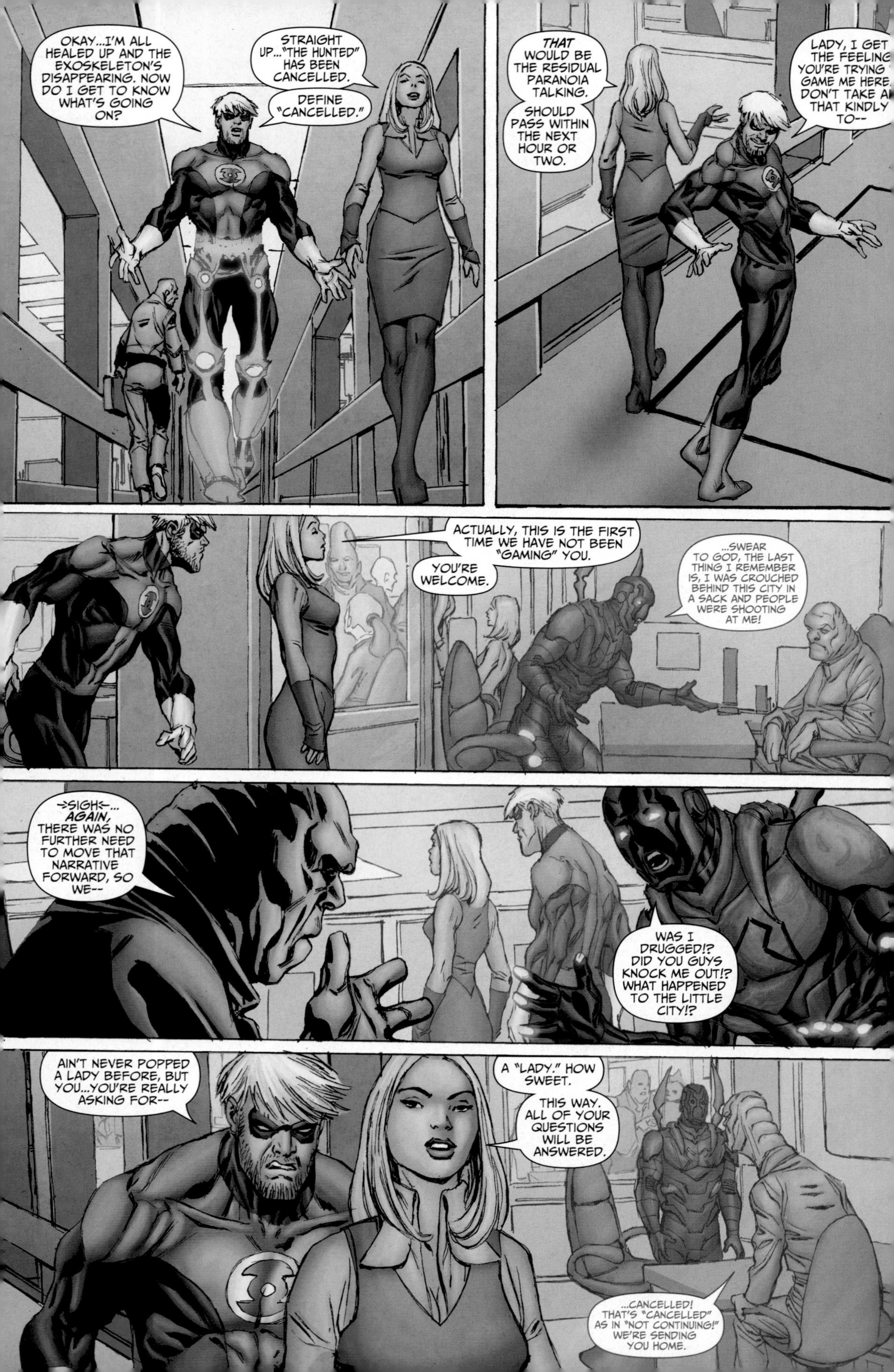
OKAY...I'M ALL HEALED UP AND THE EXOSKELETON'S DISAPPEARING. NOW DO I GET TO KNOW WHAT'S GOING ON?
STRAIGHT UP..."THE HUNTED" HAS BEEN CANCELLED.
DEFINE "CANCELLED."
THAT WOULD BE THE RESIDUAL PARANOIA TALKING.
SHOULD PASS WITHIN THE NEXT HOUR OR TWO.
LADY, I GET THE FEELING YOU'RE TRYING GAME ME HERE. DON'T TAKE A THAT KINDLY TO--
ACTUALLY, THIS IS THE FIRST TIME WE HAVE NOT BEEN "GAMING" YOU.
YOU'RE WELCOME.
...SWEAR TO GOD, THE LAST THING I REMEMBER IS, I WAS CROUCHED BEHIND THIS CITY IN A SACK AND PEOPLE WERE SHOOTING AT ME!
>SIGH<... *AGAIN,* THERE WAS NO FURTHER NEED TO MOVE THAT NARRATIVE FORWARD, SO WE--
WAS I DRUGGED!? DID YOU GUYS KNOCK ME OUT!? WHAT HAPPENED TO THE LITTLE CITY!?
AIN'T NEVER POPPED A LADY BEFORE, BUT YOU...YOU'RE REALLY ASKING FOR--
A "LADY." HOW SWEET.
THIS WAY. ALL OF YOUR QUESTIONS WILL BE ANSWERED.
...CANCELLED! THAT'S "CANCELLED" AS IN "NOT CONTINUING!" WE'RE SENDING YOU HOME.

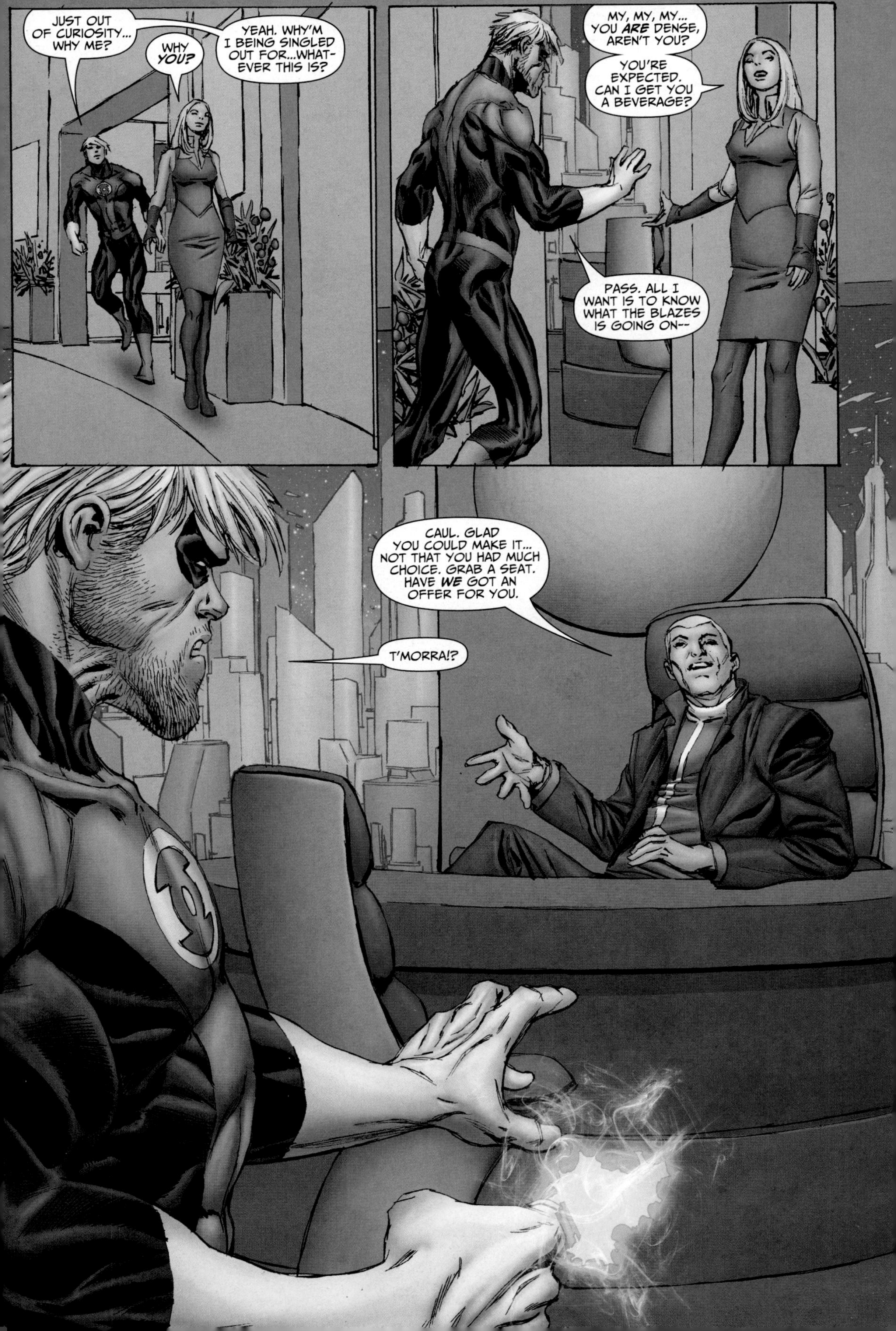
JUST OUT OF CURIOSITY... WHY ME?
WHY YOU?
YEAH. WHY'M I BEING SINGLED OUT FOR...WHAT-EVER THIS IS?
MY, MY, MY... YOU ARE DENSE, AREN'T YOU?
YOU'RE EXPECTED. CAN I GET YOU A BEVERAGE?
PASS. ALL I WANT IS TO KNOW WHAT THE BLAZES IS GOING ON--
CAUL. GLAD YOU COULD MAKE IT... NOT THAT YOU HAD MUCH CHOICE. GRAB A SEAT. HAVE WE GOT AN OFFER FOR YOU.
T'MORRA!?

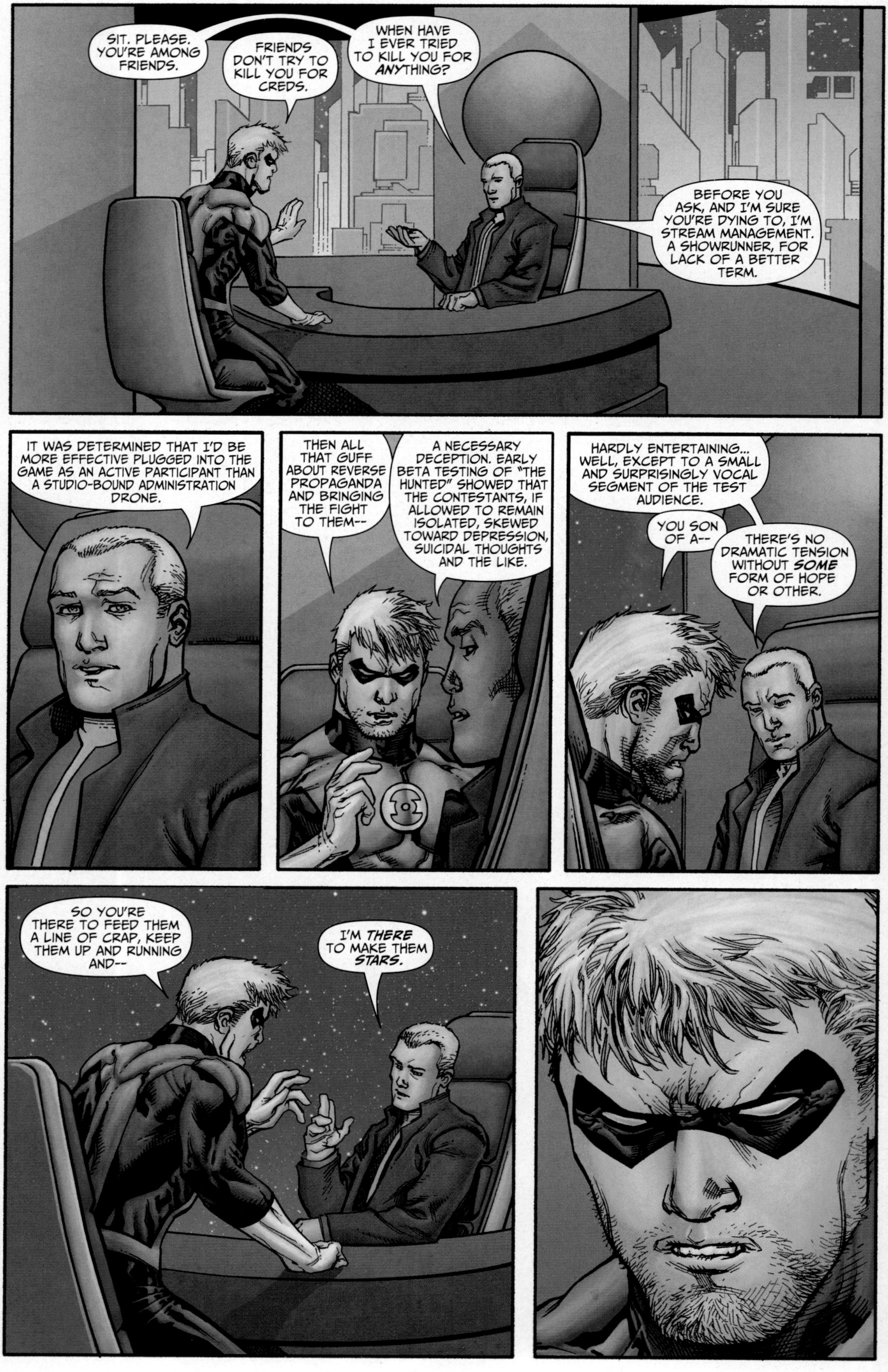
SIT. PLEASE. YOU'RE AMONG FRIENDS.
FRIENDS DON'T TRY TO KILL YOU FOR CREDS.
WHEN HAVE I EVER TRIED TO KILL YOU FOR ANYTHING?
BEFORE YOU ASK, AND I'M SURE YOU'RE DYING TO, I'M STREAM MANAGEMENT. A SHOWRUNNER, FOR LACK OF A BETTER TERM.
IT WAS DETERMINED THAT I'D BE MORE EFFECTIVE PLUGGED INTO THE GAME AS AN ACTIVE PARTICIPANT THAN A STUDIO-BOUND ADMINISTRATION DRONE.
THEN ALL THAT GUFF ABOUT REVERSE PROPAGANDA AND BRINGING THE FIGHT TO THEM--
A NECESSARY DECEPTION. EARLY BETA TESTING OF "THE HUNTED" SHOWED THAT THE CONTESTANTS, IF ALLOWED TO REMAIN ISOLATED, SKEWED TOWARD DEPRESSION, SUICIDAL THOUGHTS AND THE LIKE.
HARDLY ENTERTAINING... WELL, EXCEPT TO A SMALL AND SURPRISINGLY VOCAL SEGMENT OF THE TEST AUDIENCE.
YOU SON OF A--
THERE'S NO DRAMATIC TENSION WITHOUT SOME FORM OF HOPE OR OTHER.
SO YOU'RE THERE TO FEED THEM A LINE OF CRAP, KEEP THEM UP AND RUNNING AND--
I'M THERE TO MAKE THEM STARS.

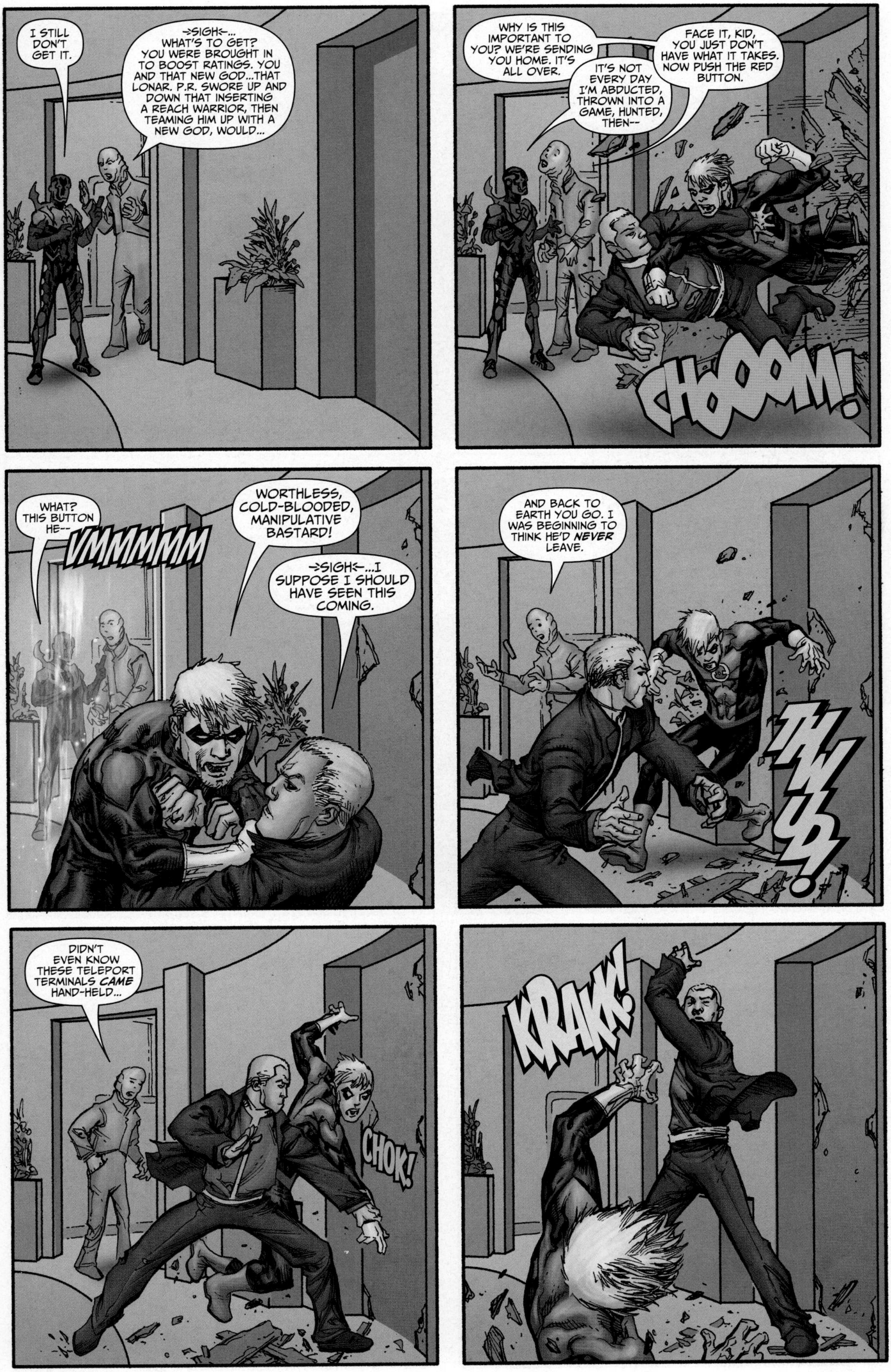
I STILL DON'T GET IT.
>SIGH<... WHAT'S TO GET? YOU WERE BROUGHT IN TO BOOST RATINGS. YOU AND THAT NEW GOD...THAT LONAR. P.R. SWORE UP AND DOWN THAT INSERTING A REACH WARRIOR, THEN TEAMING HIM UP WITH A NEW GOD, WOULD...
WHY IS THIS IMPORTANT TO YOU? WE'RE SENDING YOU HOME. IT'S ALL OVER.
IT'S NOT EVERY DAY I'M ABDUCTED, THROWN INTO A GAME, HUNTED, THEN--
FACE IT, KID, YOU JUST DON'T HAVE WHAT IT TAKES. NOW PUSH THE RED BUTTON.
CHOOOM!
WHAT? THIS BUTTON HE--
VMMMMM
WORTHLESS, COLD-BLOODED, MANIPULATIVE BASTARD!
>SIGH<...I SUPPOSE I SHOULD HAVE SEEN THIS COMING.
AND BACK TO EARTH YOU GO. I WAS BEGINNING TO THINK HE'D NEVER LEAVE.
THWUD!
DIDN'T EVEN KNOW THESE TELEPORT TERMINALS CAME HAND-HELD...
CHOK!
KRAKK!

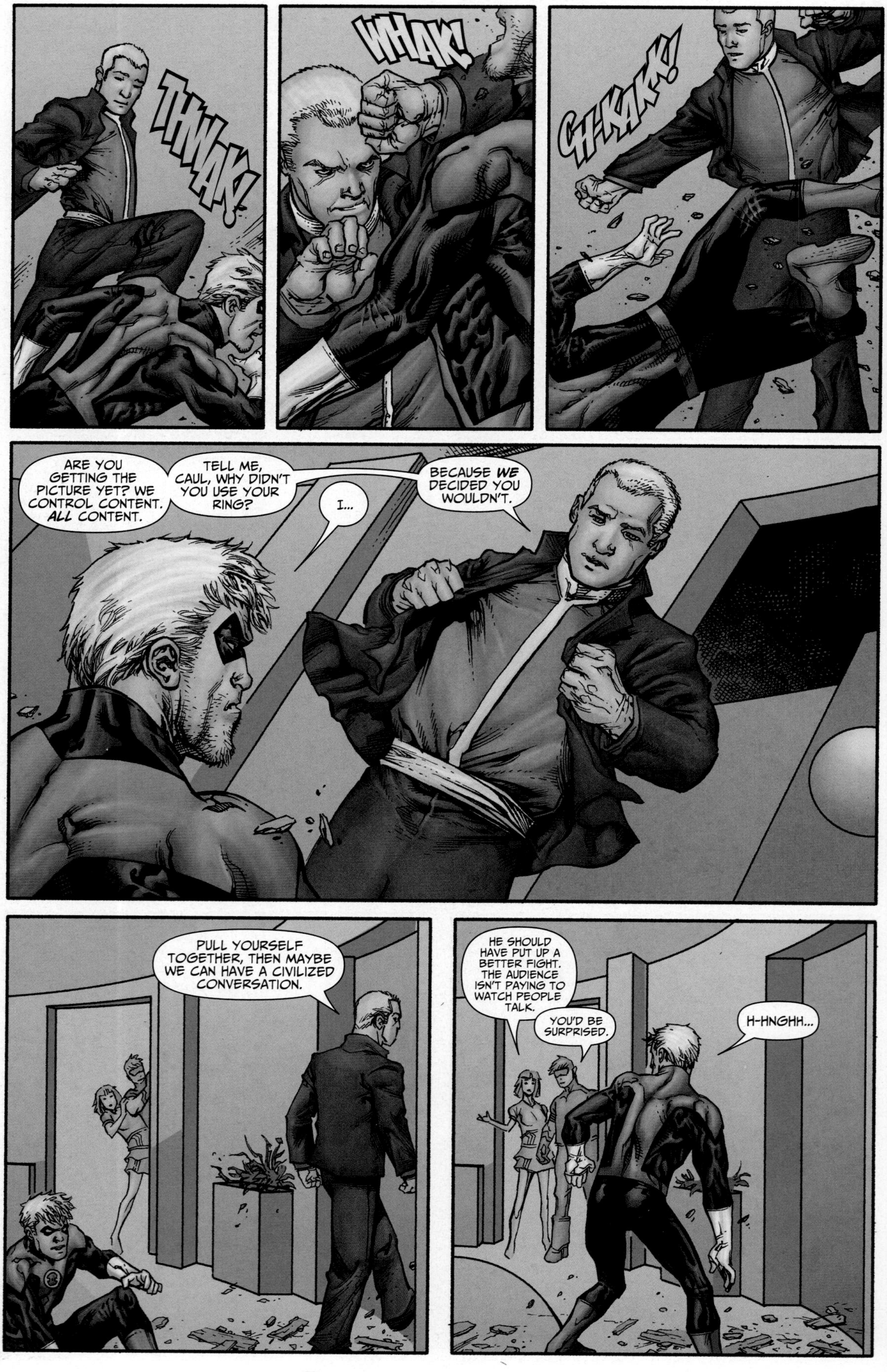
THWAK!
WHAK!
CH-KAKK!
ARE YOU GETTING THE PICTURE YET? WE CONTROL CONTENT. ALL CONTENT.
TELL ME, CAUL, WHY DIDN'T YOU USE YOUR RING?
I...
BECAUSE WE DECIDED YOU WOULDN'T.
PULL YOURSELF TOGETHER, THEN MAYBE WE CAN HAVE A CIVILIZED CONVERSATION.
HE SHOULD HAVE PUT UP A BETTER FIGHT. THE AUDIENCE ISN'T PAYING TO WATCH PEOPLE TALK.
YOU'D BE SURPRISED.
H-HNGHH...

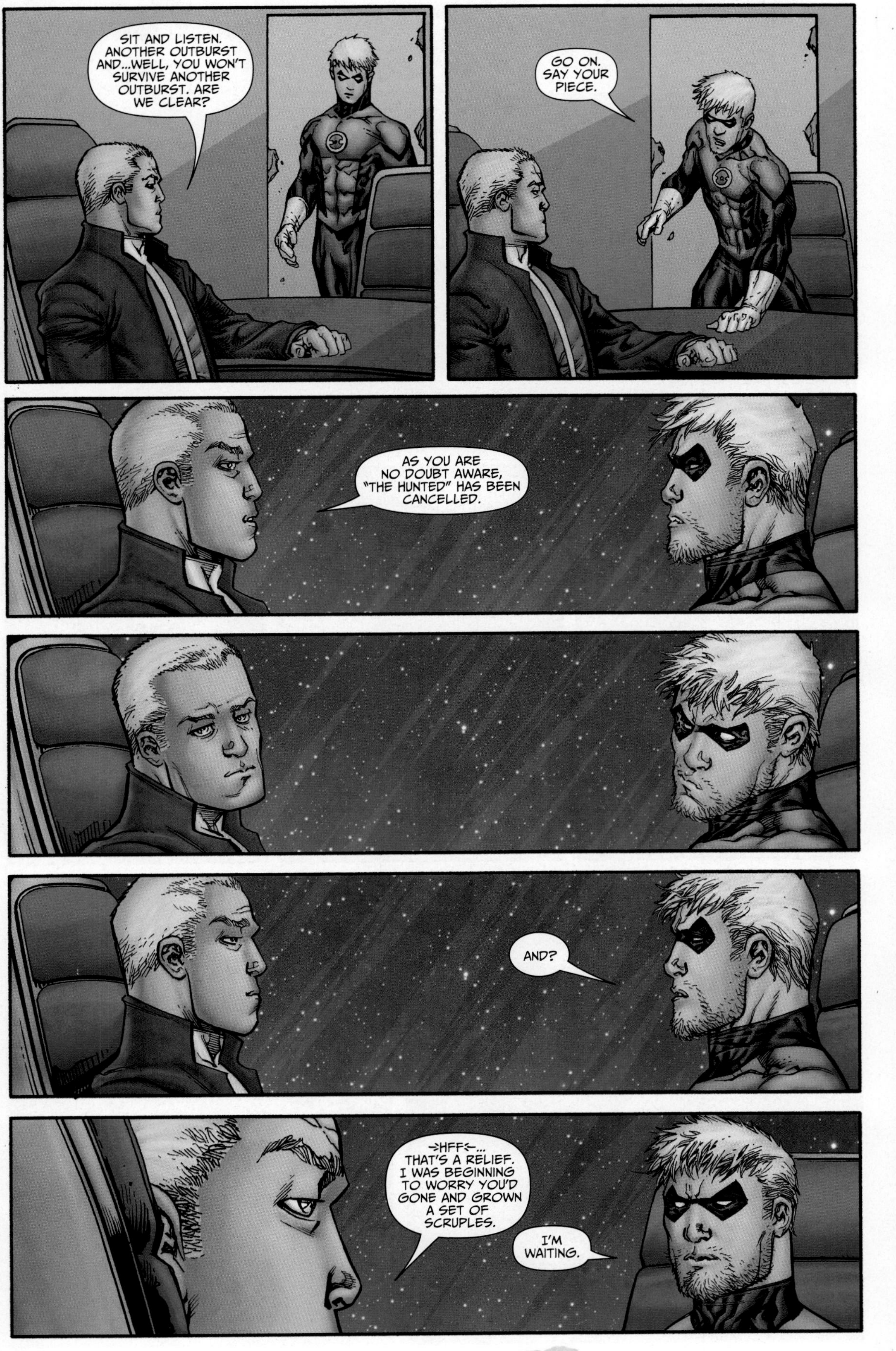
SIT AND LISTEN. ANOTHER OUTBURST AND...WELL, YOU WON'T SURVIVE ANOTHER OUTBURST. ARE WE CLEAR?
GO ON. SAY YOUR PIECE.
AS YOU ARE NO DOUBT AWARE, "THE HUNTED" HAS BEEN CANCELLED.
AND?
HFF... THAT'S A RELIEF. I WAS BEGINNING TO WORRY YOU'D GONE AND GROWN A SET OF SCRUPLES.
I'M WAITING.

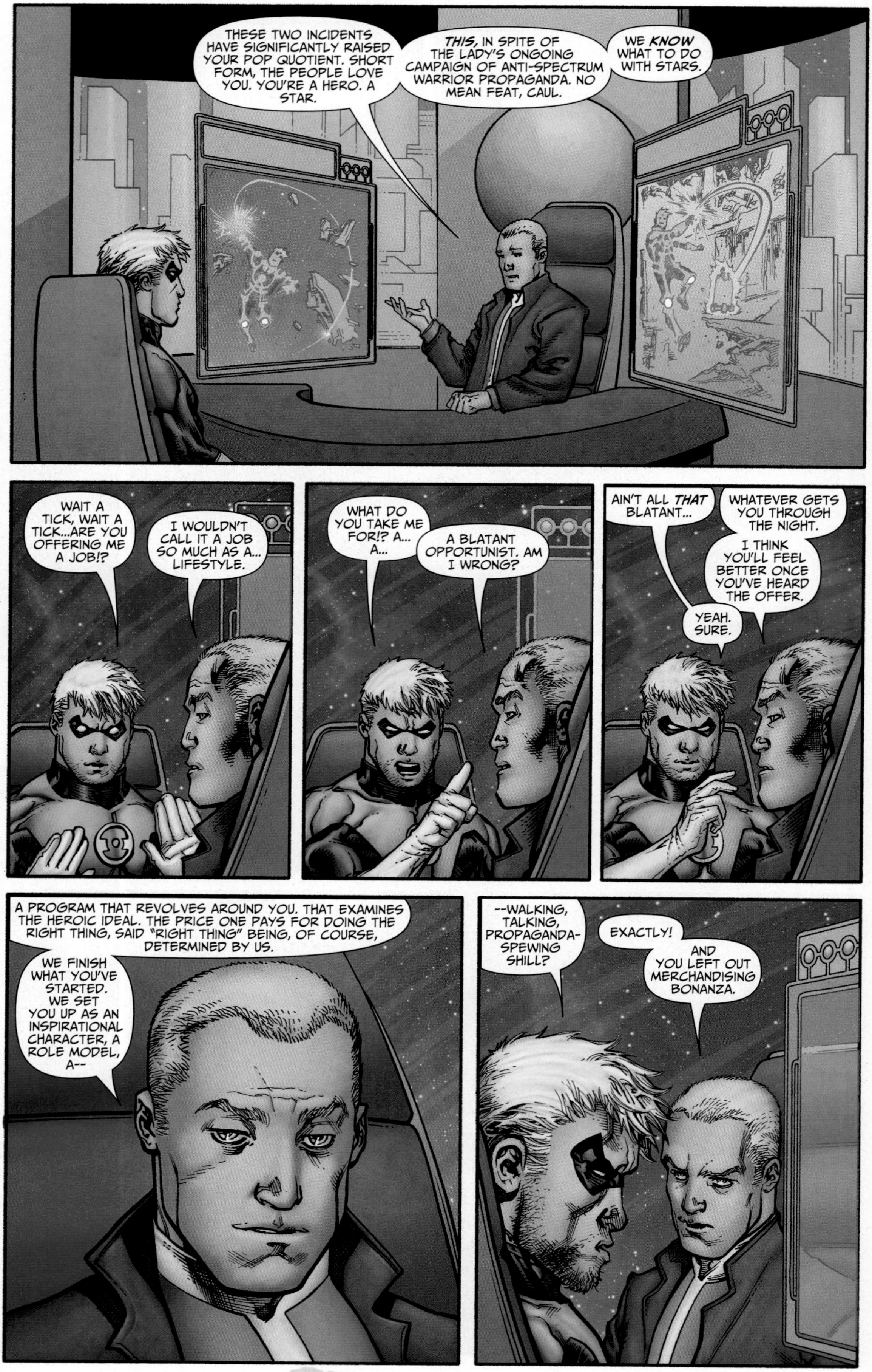
THESE TWO INCIDENTS HAVE SIGNIFICANTLY RAISED YOUR POP QUOTIENT. SHORT FORM, THE PEOPLE LOVE YOU. YOU'RE A HERO. A STAR.
THIS, IN SPITE OF THE LADY'S ONGOING CAMPAIGN OF ANTI-SPECTRUM WARRIOR PROPAGANDA. NO MEAN FEAT, CAUL.
WE *KNOW* WHAT TO DO WITH STARS.
WAIT A TICK, WAIT A TICK...ARE YOU OFFERING ME A JOB!?
I WOULDN'T CALL IT A JOB SO MUCH AS A... LIFESTYLE.
WHAT DO YOU TAKE ME FOR!? A... A...
A BLATANT OPPORTUNIST. AM I WRONG?
AIN'T ALL *THAT* BLATANT...
WHATEVER GETS YOU THROUGH THE NIGHT.
I THINK YOU'LL FEEL BETTER ONCE YOU'VE HEARD THE OFFER.
YEAH. SURE.
A PROGRAM THAT REVOLVES AROUND YOU. THAT EXAMINES THE HEROIC IDEAL. THE PRICE ONE PAYS FOR DOING THE RIGHT THING, SAID "RIGHT THING" BEING, OF COURSE, DETERMINED BY US.
WE FINISH WHAT YOU'VE STARTED. WE SET YOU UP AS AN INSPIRATIONAL CHARACTER, A ROLE MODEL, A--
--WALKING, TALKING, PROPAGANDA-SPEWING SHILL?
EXACTLY!
AND YOU LEFT OUT MERCHANDISING BONANZA.

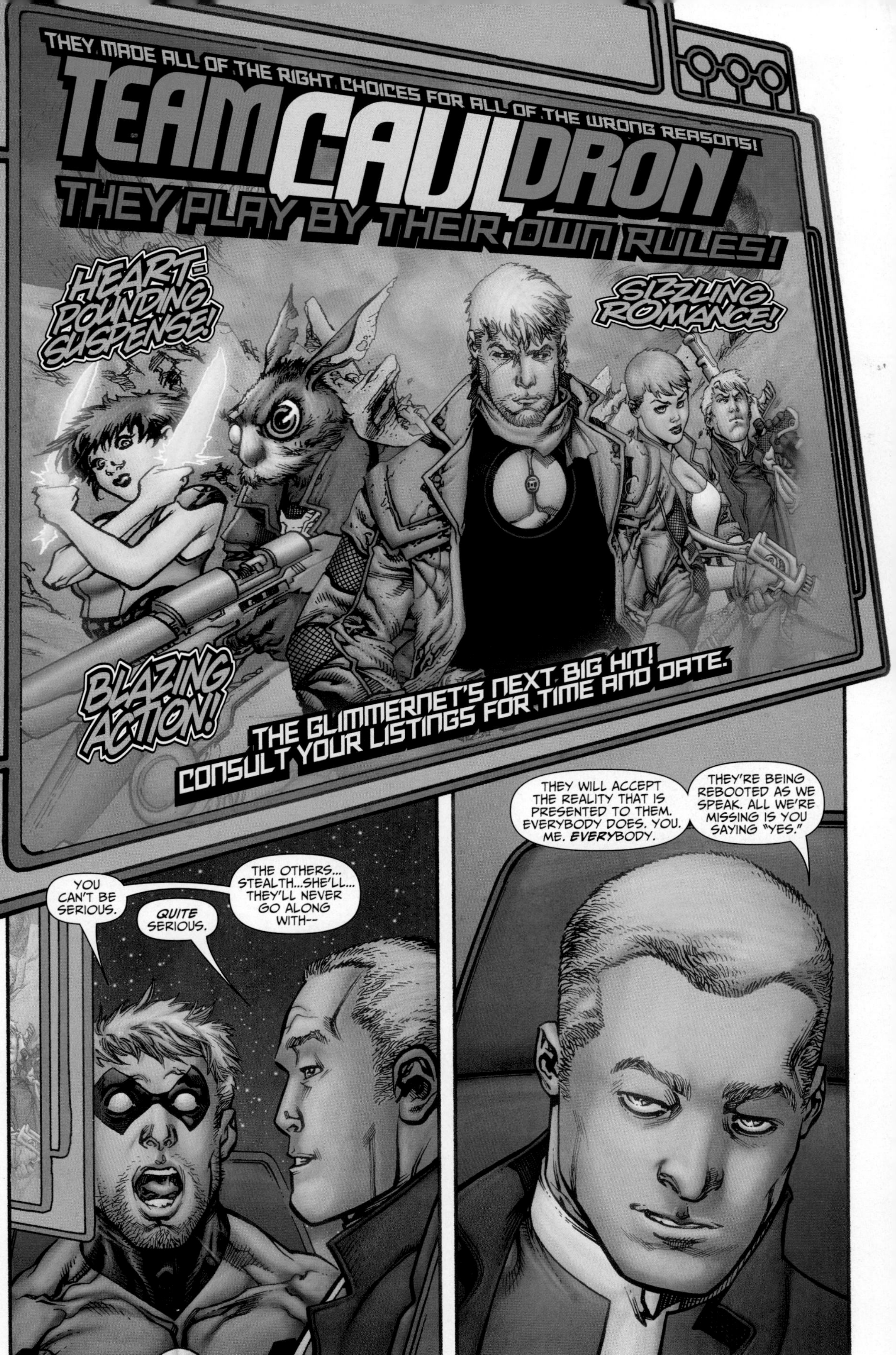
THEY MADE ALL OF THE RIGHT CHOICES FOR ALL OF THE WRONG REASONS!
TEAM CAULDRON
THEY PLAY BY THEIR OWN RULES!
HEART-POUNDING SUSPENSE!
SIZZLING ROMANCE!
BLAZING ACTION!
THE GLIMMERNET'S NEXT BIG HIT! CONSULT YOUR LISTINGS FOR TIME AND DATE.
YOU CAN'T BE SERIOUS.
QUITE SERIOUS.
THE OTHERS... STEALTH...SHE'LL... THEY'LL NEVER GO ALONG WITH--
THEY WILL ACCEPT THE REALITY THAT IS PRESENTED TO THEM. EVERYBODY DOES. YOU. ME. EVERYBODY.
THEY'RE BEING REBOOTED AS WE SPEAK. ALL WE'RE MISSING IS YOU SAYING "YES."

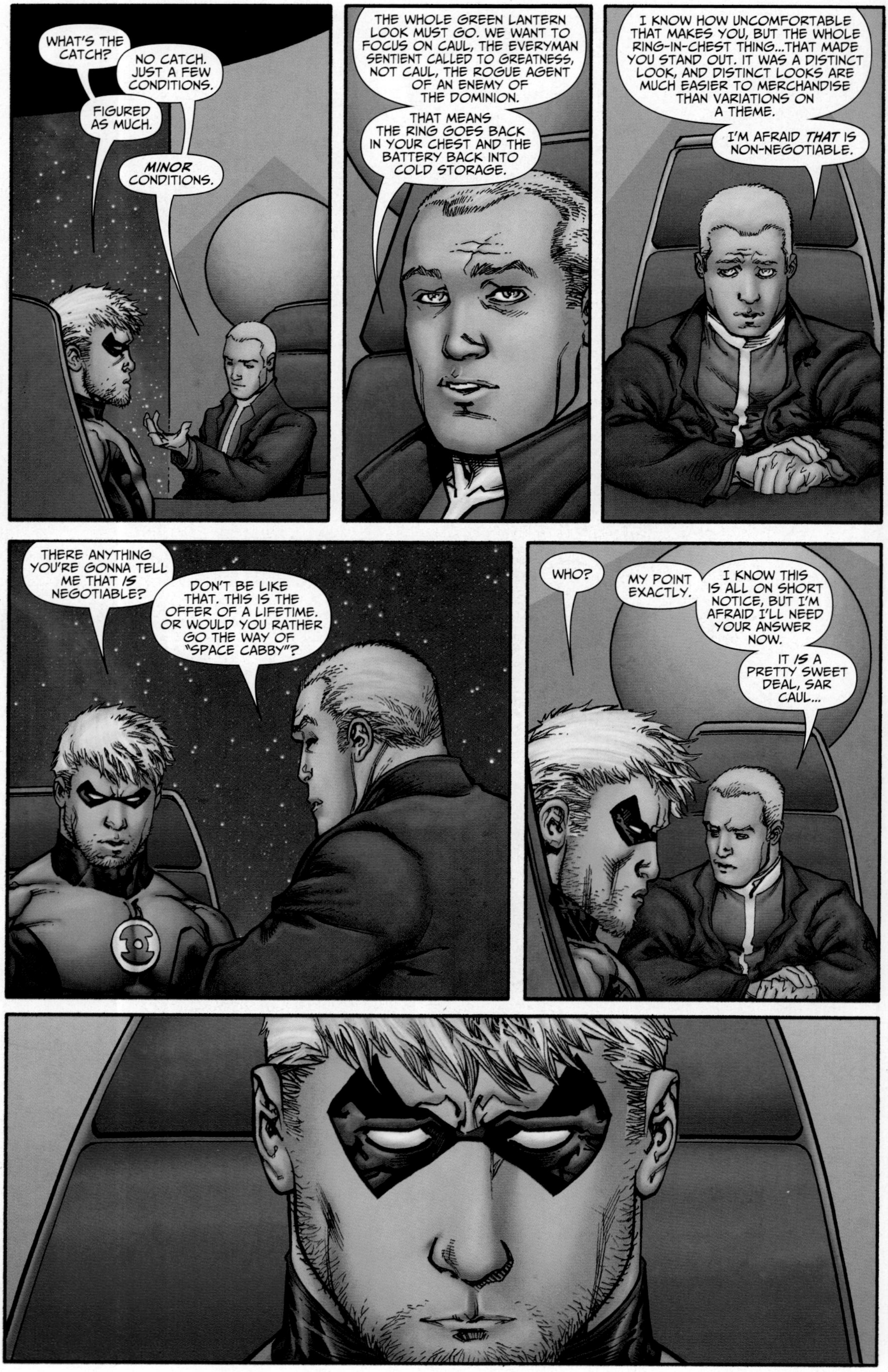
WHAT'S THE CATCH?
NO CATCH. JUST A FEW CONDITIONS.
FIGURED AS MUCH.
MINOR CONDITIONS.
THE WHOLE GREEN LANTERN LOOK MUST GO. WE WANT TO FOCUS ON CAUL, THE EVERYMAN SENTIENT CALLED TO GREATNESS, NOT CAUL, THE ROGUE AGENT OF AN ENEMY OF THE DOMINION.
THAT MEANS THE RING GOES BACK IN YOUR CHEST AND THE BATTERY BACK INTO COLD STORAGE.
I KNOW HOW UNCOMFORTABLE THAT MAKES YOU, BUT THE WHOLE RING-IN-CHEST THING...THAT MADE YOU STAND OUT. IT WAS A DISTINCT LOOK, AND DISTINCT LOOKS ARE MUCH EASIER TO MERCHANDISE THAN VARIATIONS ON A THEME.
I'M AFRAID THAT IS NON-NEGOTIABLE.
THERE ANYTHING YOU'RE GONNA TELL ME THAT IS NEGOTIABLE?
DON'T BE LIKE THAT. THIS IS THE OFFER OF A LIFETIME. OR WOULD YOU RATHER GO THE WAY OF "SPACE CABBY"?
WHO?
MY POINT EXACTLY.
I KNOW THIS IS ALL ON SHORT NOTICE, BUT I'M AFRAID I'LL NEED YOUR ANSWER NOW.
IT IS A PRETTY SWEET DEAL, SAR CAUL...

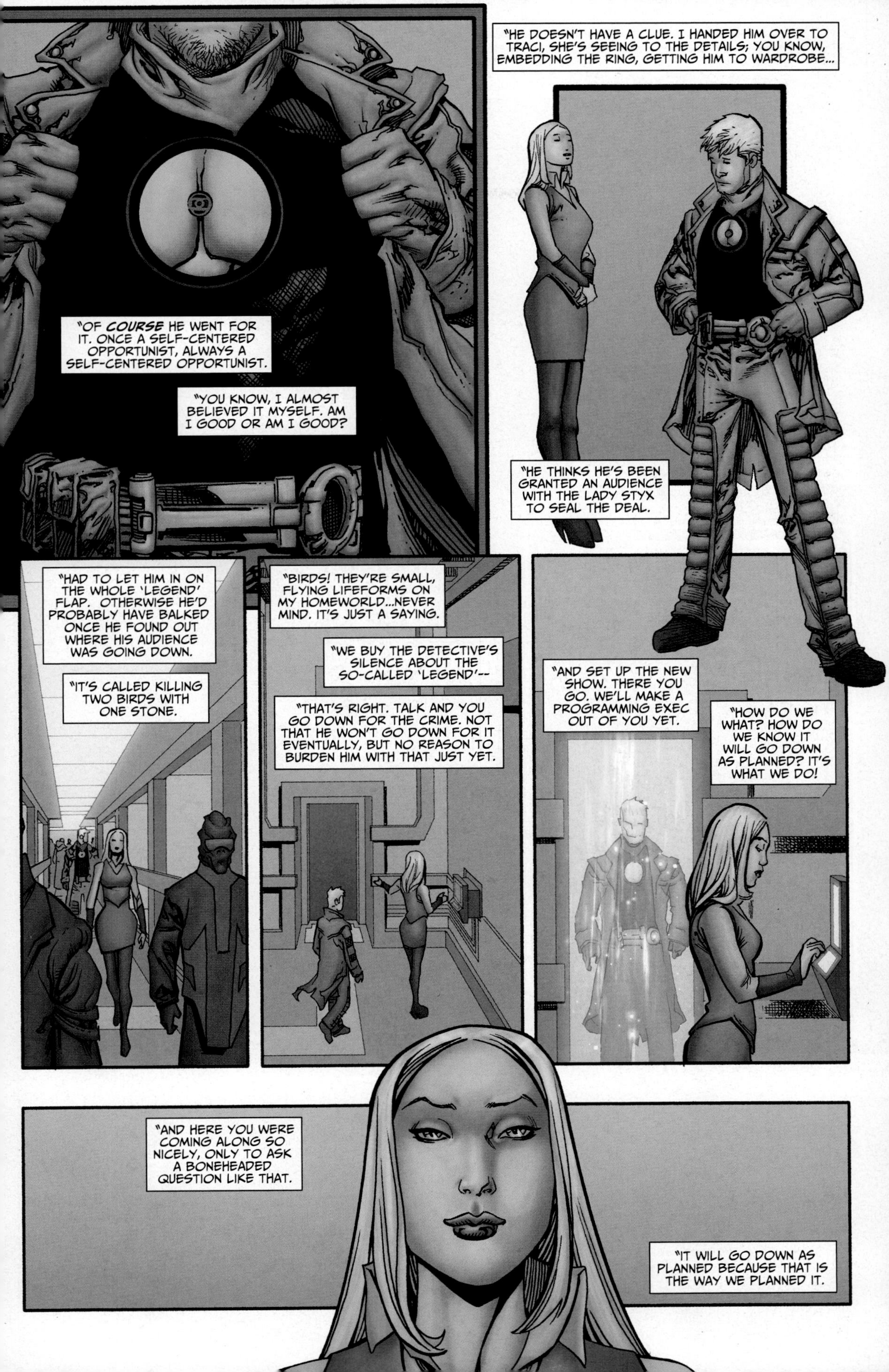
"OF COURSE HE WENT FOR IT. ONCE A SELF-CENTERED OPPORTUNIST, ALWAYS A SELF-CENTERED OPPORTUNIST.
"YOU KNOW, I ALMOST BELIEVED IT MYSELF. AM I GOOD OR AM I GOOD?
"HE DOESN'T HAVE A CLUE. I HANDED HIM OVER TO TRACI, SHE'S SEEING TO THE DETAILS; YOU KNOW, EMBEDDING THE RING, GETTING HIM TO WARDROBE...
"HE THINKS HE'S BEEN GRANTED AN AUDIENCE WITH THE LADY STYX TO SEAL THE DEAL.
"HAD TO LET HIM IN ON THE WHOLE 'LEGEND' FLAP. OTHERWISE HE'D PROBABLY HAVE BALKED ONCE HE FOUND OUT WHERE HIS AUDIENCE WAS GOING DOWN.
"IT'S CALLED KILLING TWO BIRDS WITH ONE STONE.
"BIRDS! THEY'RE SMALL, FLYING LIFEFORMS ON MY HOMEWORLD...NEVER MIND. IT'S JUST A SAYING.
"WE BUY THE DETECTIVE'S SILENCE ABOUT THE SO-CALLED 'LEGEND'--
"THAT'S RIGHT. TALK AND YOU GO DOWN FOR THE CRIME. NOT THAT HE WON'T GO DOWN FOR IT EVENTUALLY, BUT NO REASON TO BURDEN HIM WITH THAT JUST YET.
"AND SET UP THE NEW SHOW. THERE YOU GO. WE'LL MAKE A PROGRAMMING EXEC OUT OF YOU YET.
"HOW DO WE WHAT? HOW DO WE KNOW IT WILL GO DOWN AS PLANNED? IT'S WHAT WE DO!
"AND HERE YOU WERE COMING ALONG SO NICELY, ONLY TO ASK A BONEHEADED QUESTION LIKE THAT.
"IT WILL GO DOWN AS PLANNED BECAUSE THAT IS THE WAY WE PLANNED IT.

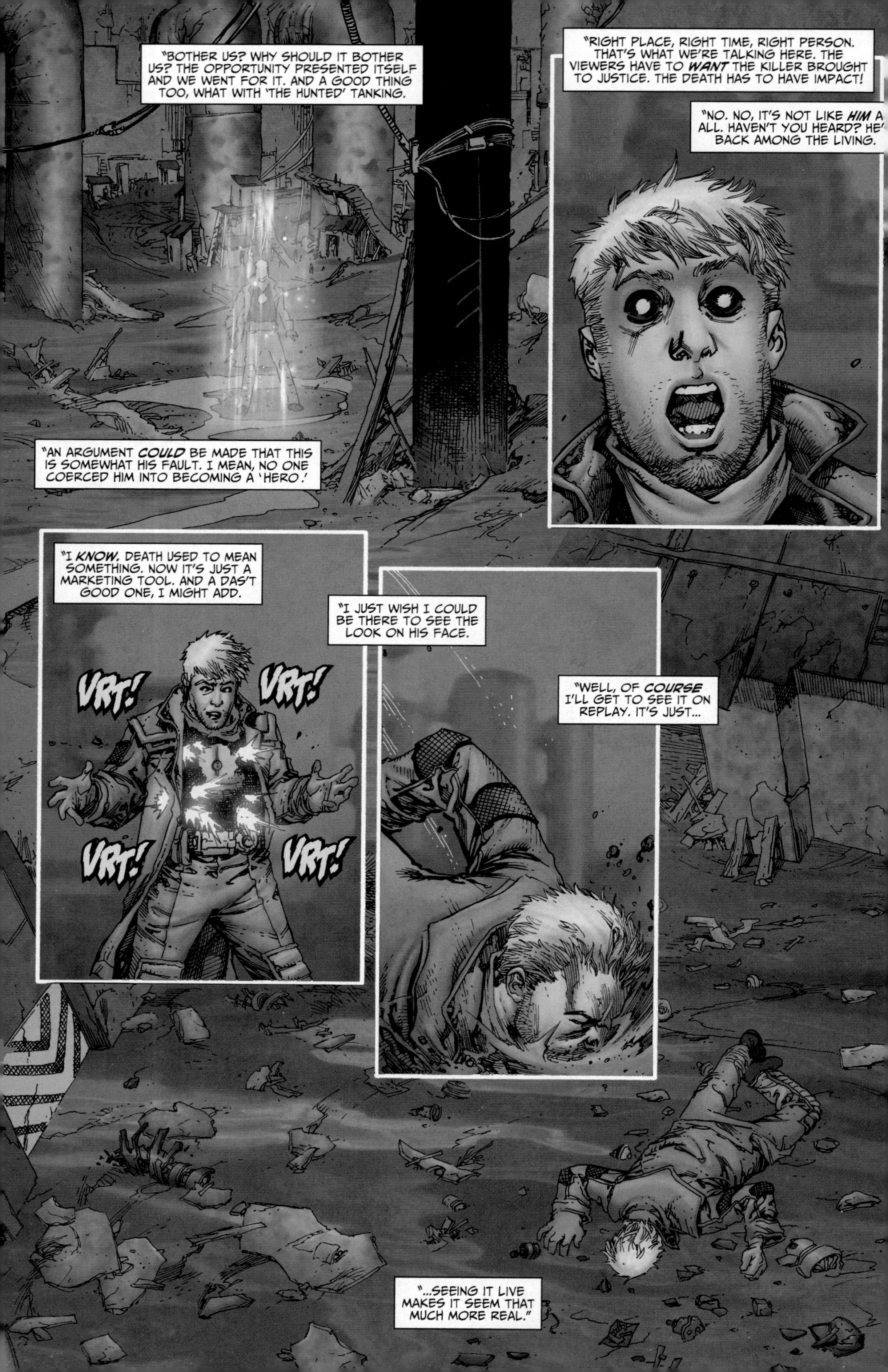
"BOTHER US? WHY SHOULD IT BOTHER US? THE OPPORTUNITY PRESENTED ITSELF AND WE WENT FOR IT. AND A GOOD THING TOO, WHAT WITH 'THE HUNTED' TANKING.
"AN ARGUMENT COULD BE MADE THAT THIS IS SOMEWHAT HIS FAULT. I MEAN, NO ONE COERCED HIM INTO BECOMING A 'HERO.'
"RIGHT PLACE, RIGHT TIME, RIGHT PERSON. THAT'S WHAT WE'RE TALKING HERE. THE VIEWERS HAVE TO WANT THE KILLER BROUGHT TO JUSTICE. THE DEATH HAS TO HAVE IMPACT!
"NO. NO, IT'S NOT LIKE HIM A ALL. HAVEN'T YOU HEARD? HE' BACK AMONG THE LIVING.
"I KNOW. DEATH USED TO MEAN SOMETHING. NOW IT'S JUST A MARKETING TOOL. AND A DAS'T GOOD ONE, I MIGHT ADD.
VRT!
VRT!
VRT!
VRT!
"I JUST WISH I COULD BE THERE TO SEE THE LOOK ON HIS FACE.
"WELL, OF COURSE I'LL GET TO SEE IT ON REPLAY. IT'S JUST...
"...SEEING IT LIVE MAKES IT SEEM THAT MUCH MORE REAL."

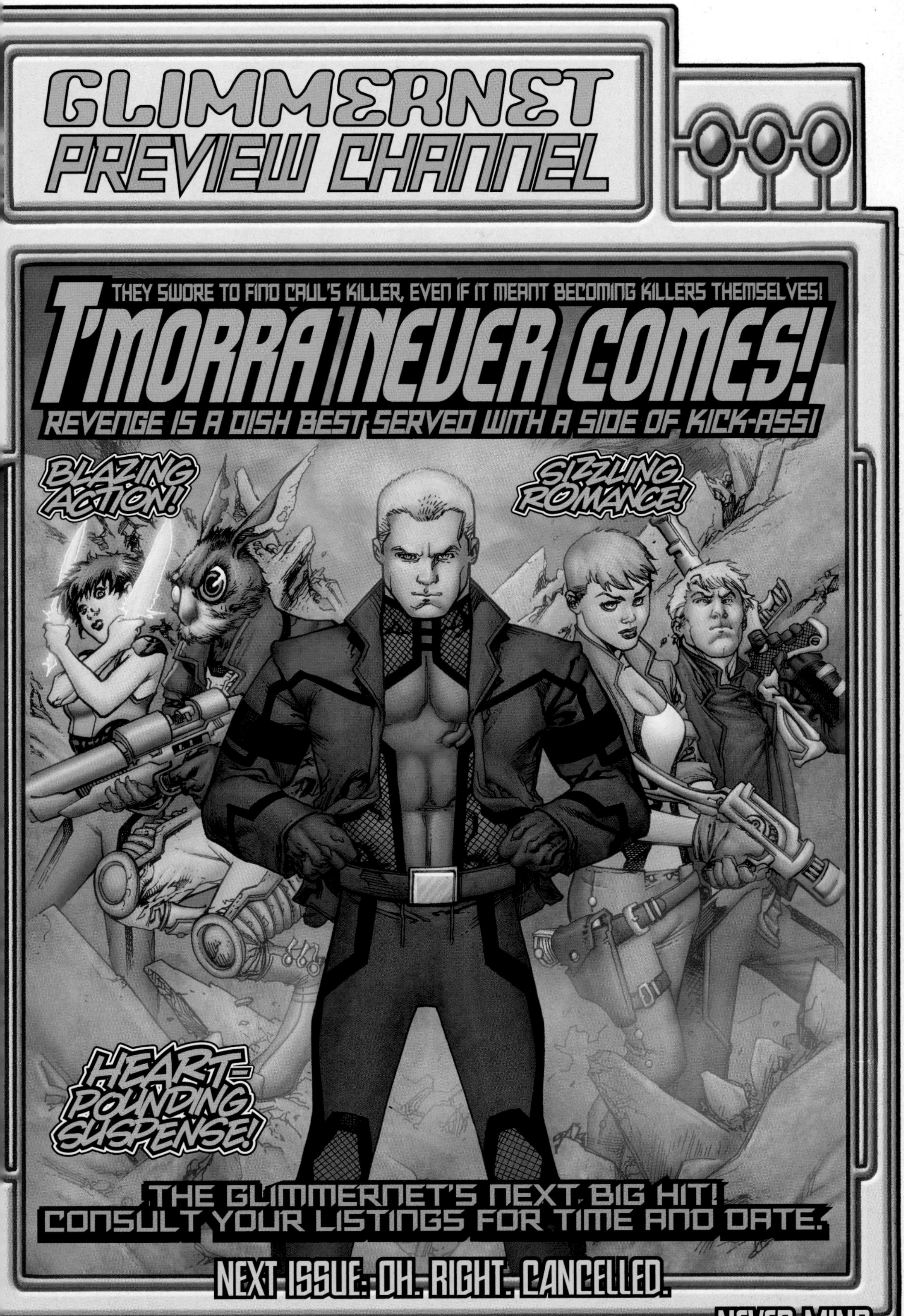
GLIMMERNET
PREVIEW CHANNEL
THEY SWORE TO FIND CAUL'S KILLER, EVEN IF IT MEANT BECOMING KILLERS THEMSELVES!
T'MORRA NEVER COMES!
REVENGE IS A DISH BEST SERVED WITH A SIDE OF KICK-ASS!
BLAZING ACTION!
SIZZLING ROMANCE!
HEART-POUNDING SUSPENSE!
THE GLIMMERNET'S NEXT BIG HIT!
CONSULT YOUR LISTINGS FOR TIME AND DATE.
NEXT ISSUE: OH. RIGHT. CANCELLED.
NEVER MIND.

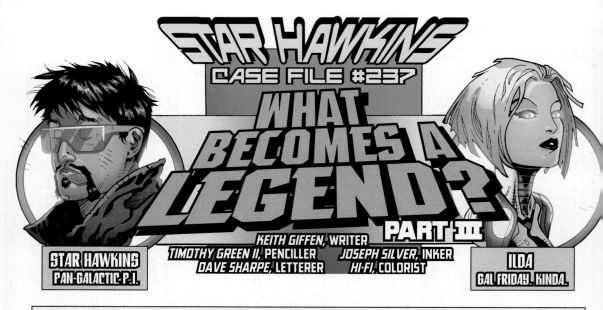

STAR HAWKINS

CASE FILE #237

WHAT BECOMES A LEGEND?

PART III

KEITH GIFFEN, WRITER

TIMOTHY GREEN II, PENCILLER   JOSEPH SILVER, INKER

DAVE SHARPE, LETTERER   HI-FI, COLORIST

STAR HAWKINS
PAN-GALACTIC P.I.

ILDA
GAL FRIDAY. KINDA.

EVERY CULTURE HAS ITS LEGEND(S) -- THE BOGEYMAN, SANTA CLAUS, BIGFOOT, AND SO ON. ON *TOLERANCE*, THE LEGEND OF CHOICE IS THE ONE ABOUT THE LONGEST-RUNNING "HUNTED" CONTESTANT. PAN-GALACTIC PRIVATE INVESTIGATOR *STAR HAWKINS* HAS JUST DISCOVERED THAT NOT ONLY DOES THIS LEGENDARY CONTESTANT EXIST, BUT THAT SHE'S THE ABSOLUTE RULER OF THE ENTIRE TENEBRIAN DOMINION, *THE LADY STYX.*

WHAT DO I DO? BOW? GENUFLECT?

SEEING HOW YOU'RE ACTING LIKE A PANICKY SCHOOLGIRL, YOU MIGHT TRY A CURTSY.

YOU'RE *NOT* HELPING!

AND THIS COMES AS A SURPRISE TO YOU?

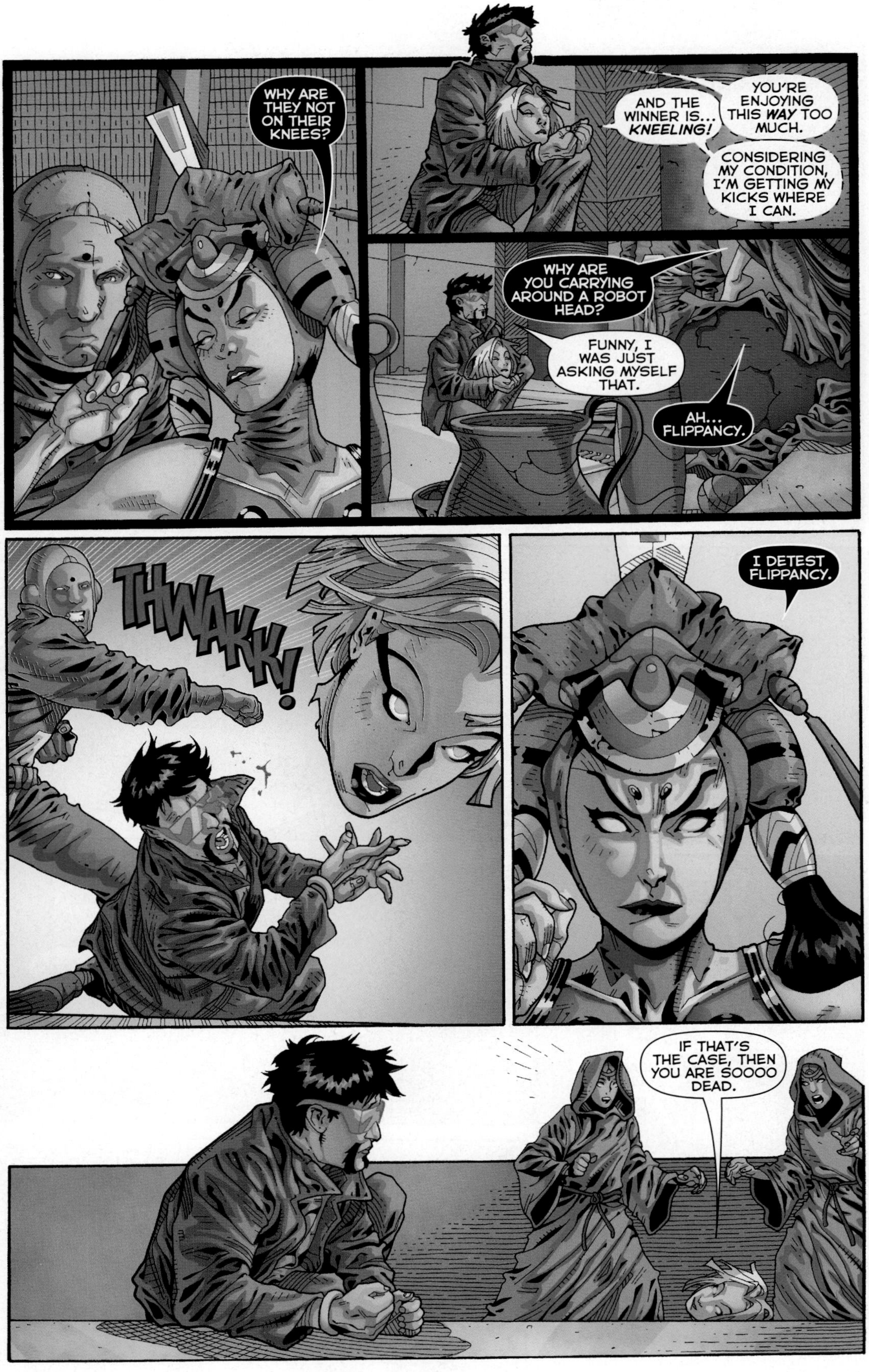
WHY ARE THEY NOT ON THEIR KNEES?
AND THE WINNER IS... KNEELING!
YOU'RE ENJOYING THIS WAY TOO MUCH.
CONSIDERING MY CONDITION, I'M GETTING MY KICKS WHERE I CAN.
WHY ARE YOU CARRYING AROUND A ROBOT HEAD?
FUNNY, I WAS JUST ASKING MYSELF THAT.
AH... FLIPPANCY.
THWAKK!
I DETEST FLIPPANCY.
IF THAT'S THE CASE, THEN YOU ARE SOOOO DEAD.

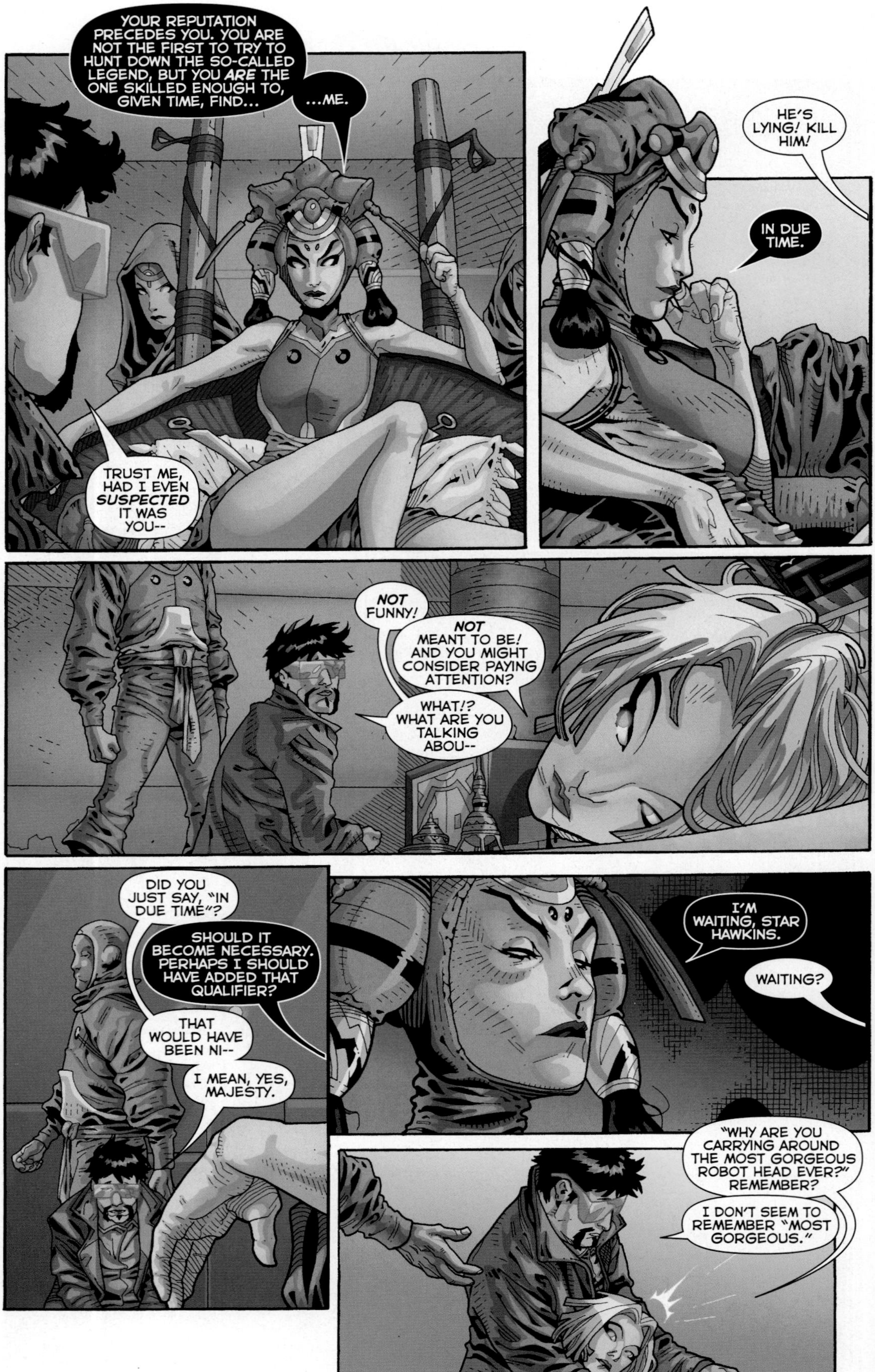
YOUR REPUTATION PRECEDES YOU. YOU ARE NOT THE FIRST TO TRY TO HUNT DOWN THE SO-CALLED LEGEND, BUT YOU *ARE* THE ONE SKILLED ENOUGH TO, GIVEN TIME, FIND...
...ME.
TRUST ME, HAD I EVEN *SUSPECTED* IT WAS YOU--
HE'S LYING! KILL HIM!
IN DUE TIME.
NOT FUNNY!
NOT MEANT TO BE! AND YOU MIGHT CONSIDER PAYING ATTENTION?
WHAT!? WHAT ARE YOU TALKING ABOU--
DID YOU JUST SAY, "IN DUE TIME"?
SHOULD IT BECOME NECESSARY. PERHAPS I SHOULD HAVE ADDED THAT QUALIFIER?
THAT WOULD HAVE BEEN NI--
I MEAN, YES, MAJESTY.
I'M WAITING, STAR HAWKINS.
WAITING?
"WHY ARE YOU CARRYING AROUND THE MOST GORGEOUS ROBOT HEAD EVER?" REMEMBER?
I DON'T SEEM TO REMEMBER "MOST GORGEOUS."

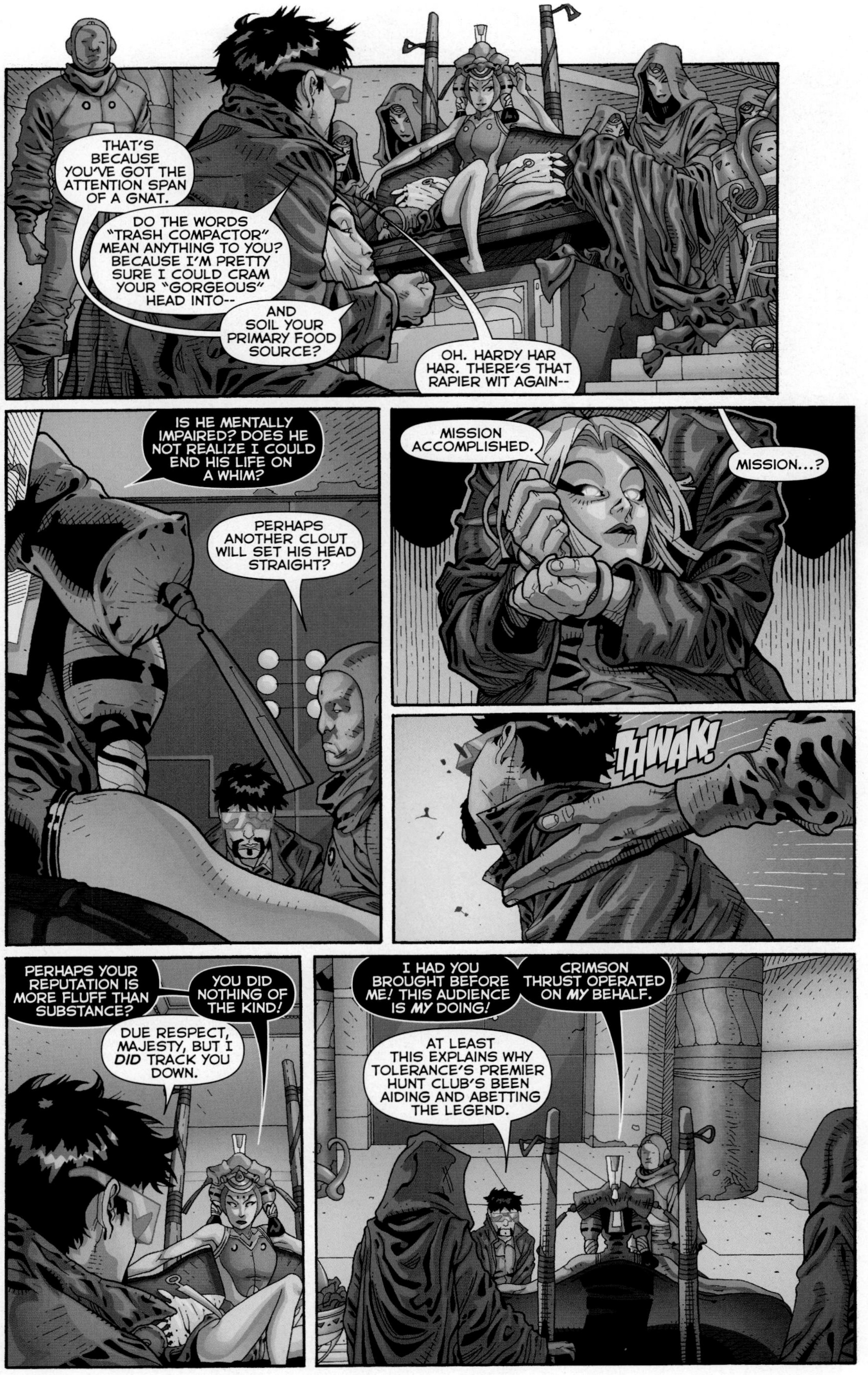
THAT'S BECAUSE YOU'VE GOT THE ATTENTION SPAN OF A GNAT.
DO THE WORDS "TRASH COMPACTOR" MEAN ANYTHING TO YOU? BECAUSE I'M PRETTY SURE I COULD CRAM YOUR "GORGEOUS" HEAD INTO--
AND SOIL YOUR PRIMARY FOOD SOURCE?
OH. HARDY HAR HAR. THERE'S THAT RAPIER WIT AGAIN--
IS HE MENTALLY IMPAIRED? DOES HE NOT REALIZE I COULD END HIS LIFE ON A WHIM?
PERHAPS ANOTHER CLOUT WILL SET HIS HEAD STRAIGHT?
MISSION ACCOMPLISHED.
MISSION...?
THWAK!
PERHAPS YOUR REPUTATION IS MORE FLUFF THAN SUBSTANCE?
YOU DID NOTHING OF THE KIND!
DUE RESPECT, MAJESTY, BUT I DID TRACK YOU DOWN.
I HAD YOU BROUGHT BEFORE ME! THIS AUDIENCE IS MY DOING!
CRIMSON THRUST OPERATED ON MY BEHALF.
AT LEAST THIS EXPLAINS WHY TOLERANCE'S PREMIER HUNT CLUB'S BEEN AIDING AND ABETTING THE LEGEND.

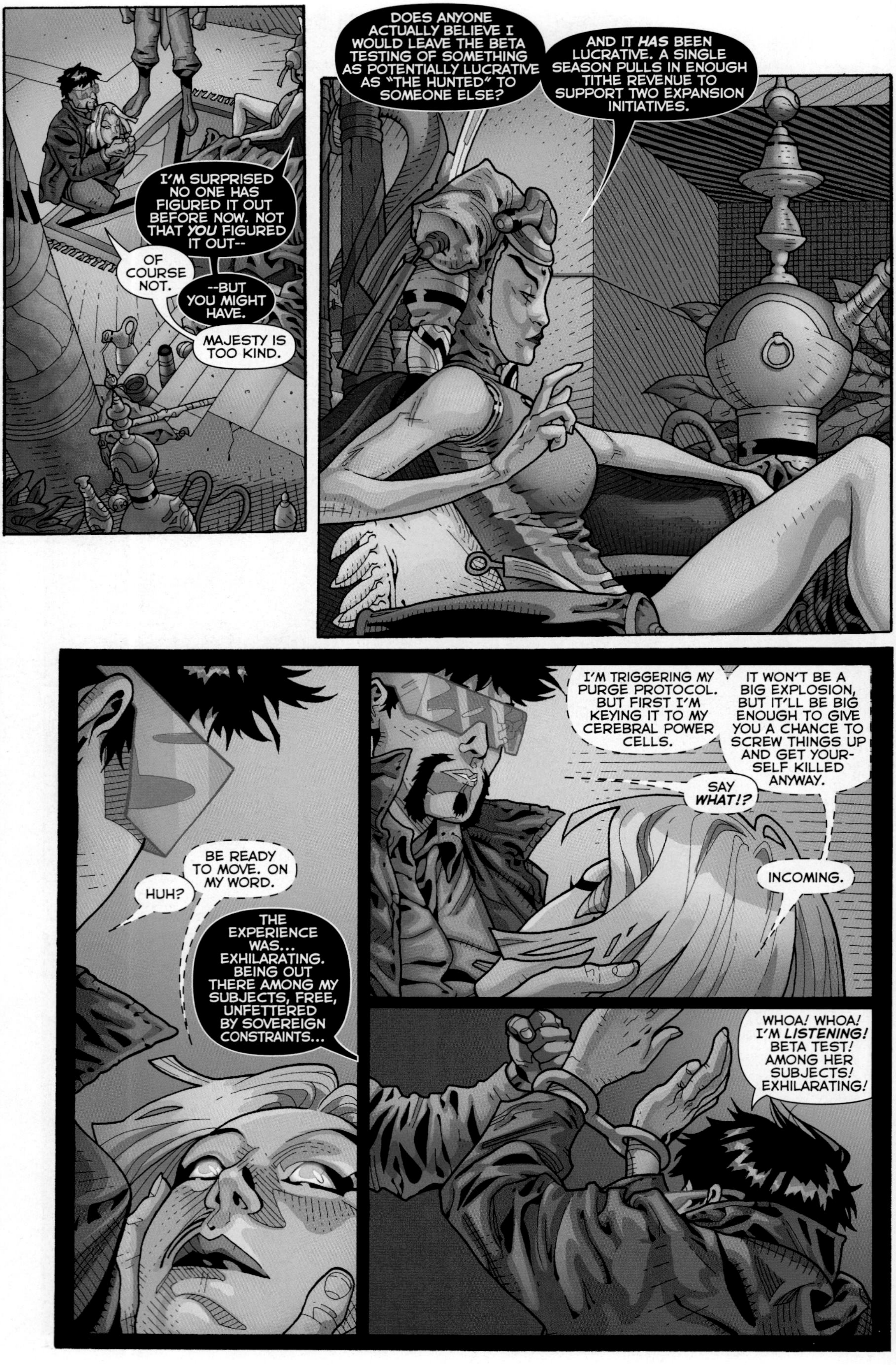
I'M SURPRISED NO ONE HAS FIGURED IT OUT BEFORE NOW. NOT THAT *YOU* FIGURED IT OUT--
OF COURSE NOT.
--BUT YOU MIGHT HAVE.
MAJESTY IS TOO KIND.
DOES ANYONE ACTUALLY BELIEVE I WOULD LEAVE THE BETA TESTING OF SOMETHING AS POTENTIALLY LUCRATIVE AS "THE HUNTED" TO SOMEONE ELSE?
AND IT *HAS* BEEN LUCRATIVE. A SINGLE SEASON PULLS IN ENOUGH TITHE REVENUE TO SUPPORT TWO EXPANSION INITIATIVES.
BE READY TO MOVE. ON MY WORD.
HUH?
THE EXPERIENCE WAS... EXHILARATING. BEING OUT THERE AMONG MY SUBJECTS, FREE, UNFETTERED BY SOVEREIGN CONSTRAINTS...
I'M TRIGGERING MY PURGE PROTOCOL. BUT FIRST I'M KEYING IT TO MY CEREBRAL POWER CELLS.
IT WON'T BE A BIG EXPLOSION, BUT IT'LL BE BIG ENOUGH TO GIVE YOU A CHANCE TO SCREW THINGS UP AND GET YOUR-SELF KILLED ANYWAY.
SAY *WHAT!?*
INCOMING.
WHOA! WHOA! I'M *LISTENING!* BETA TEST! AMONG HER SUBJECTS! EXHILARATING!

TO MAKE A LONG STORY SHORT-- AND HASTEN YOUR DEATH--I FOUND THE EXPERIENCE PLEASANT ENOUGH THAT I OPTED TO "DROP MYSELF INTO THE GAME" REGULARLY.

AT GREAT RISK TO MY WELL-BEING, I MIGHT ADD.

I'LL BET.

APPARENTLY, MY LITTLE SOJOURNS GAVE BIRTH TO THIS...LEGEND NONSENSE. I SUPPOSE WERE I MORE COMMON, I WOULD FIND IT FLATTERING. AS IT STANDS, I FIND IT BENEATH MY NOTICE.

UNLESS SOMEONE LIKE YOU COMES SNOOPING AROUND AND GETS TOO CLOSE TO THE TRUTH. THEN I FIND IT INTOLERABLE.

NOW!

!?!

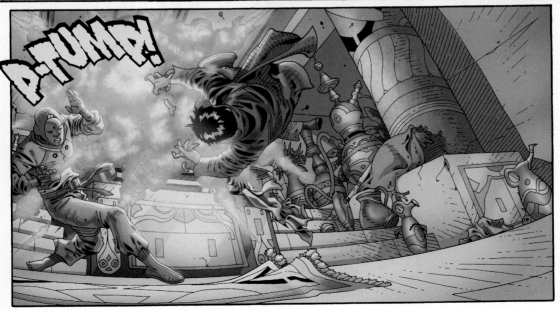

P-TUMP!

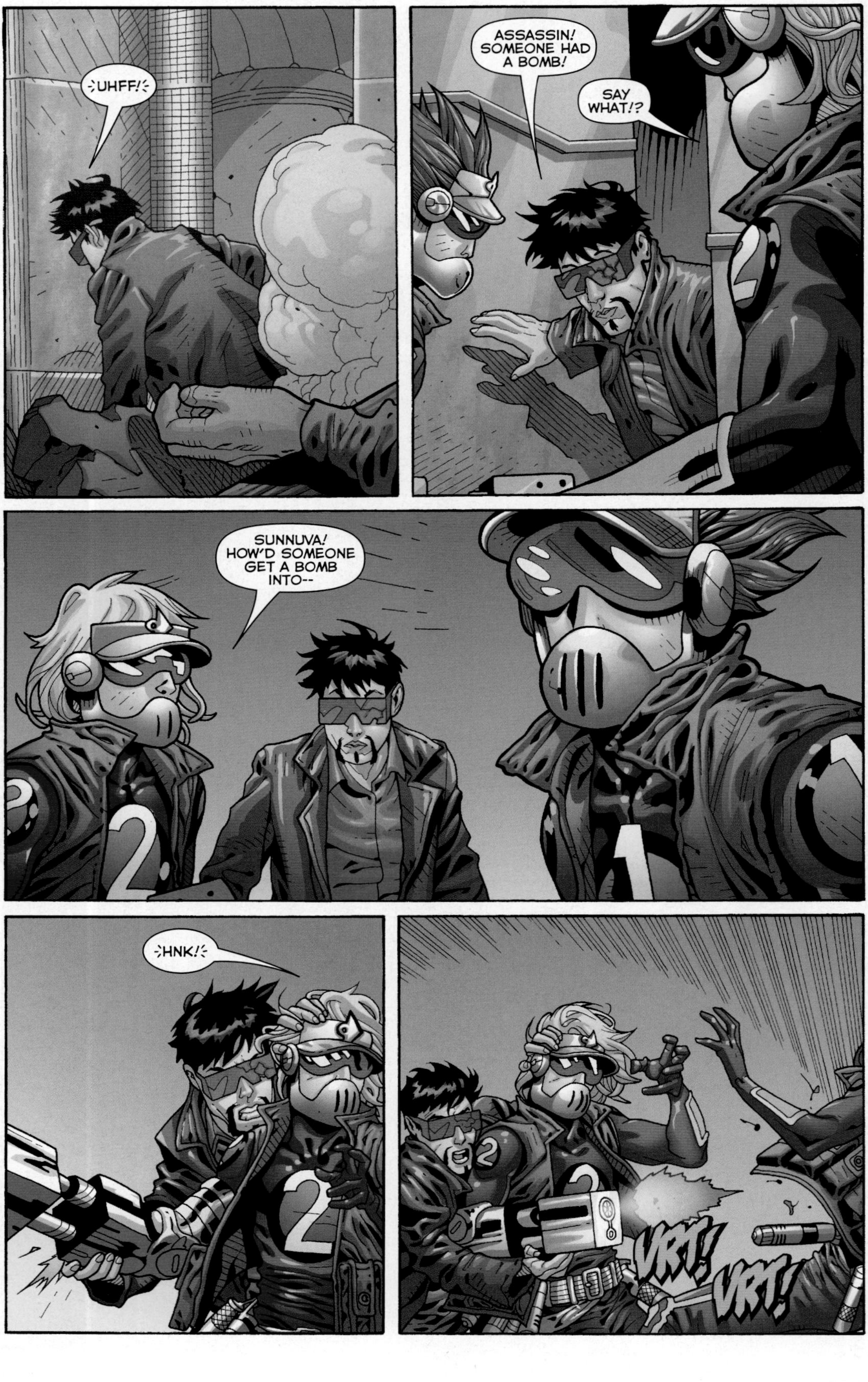
UHFF!
ASSASSIN! SOMEONE HAD A BOMB!
SAY WHAT!?
SUNNUVA! HOW'D SOMEONE GET A BOMB INTO--
HNK!
VRT!
VRT!

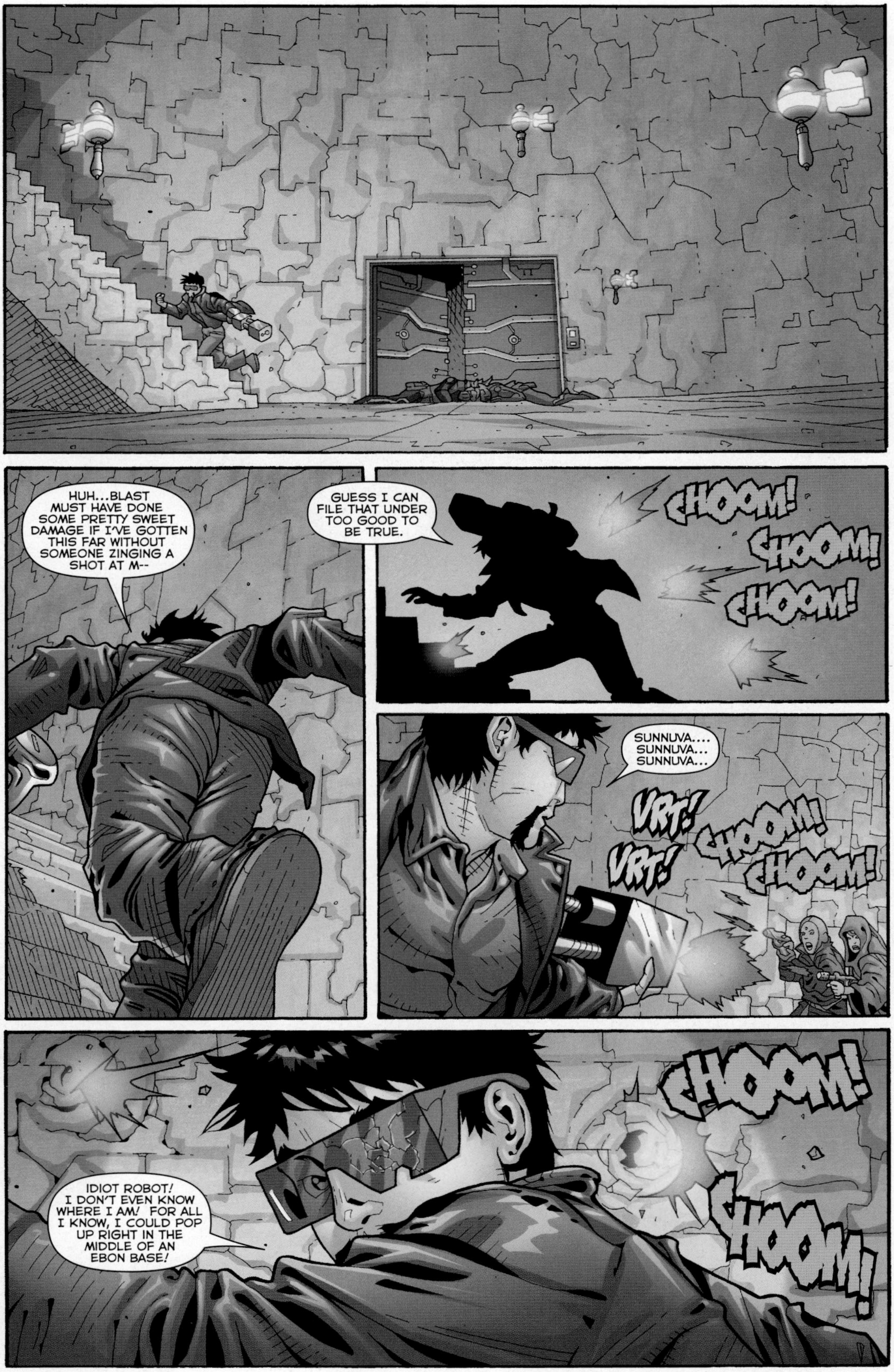
HUH...BLAST MUST HAVE DONE SOME PRETTY SWEET DAMAGE IF I'VE GOTTEN THIS FAR WITHOUT SOMEONE ZINGING A SHOT AT M--
GUESS I CAN FILE THAT UNDER TOO GOOD TO BE TRUE.
CHOOM!
CHOOM!
CHOOM!
SUNNUVA.... SUNNUVA... SUNNUVA...
VRT!
VRT!
CHOOM!
CHOOM!
IDIOT ROBOT! I DON'T EVEN KNOW WHERE I AM! FOR ALL I KNOW, I COULD POP UP RIGHT IN THE MIDDLE OF AN EBON BASE!
CHOOM!
CHOOM!

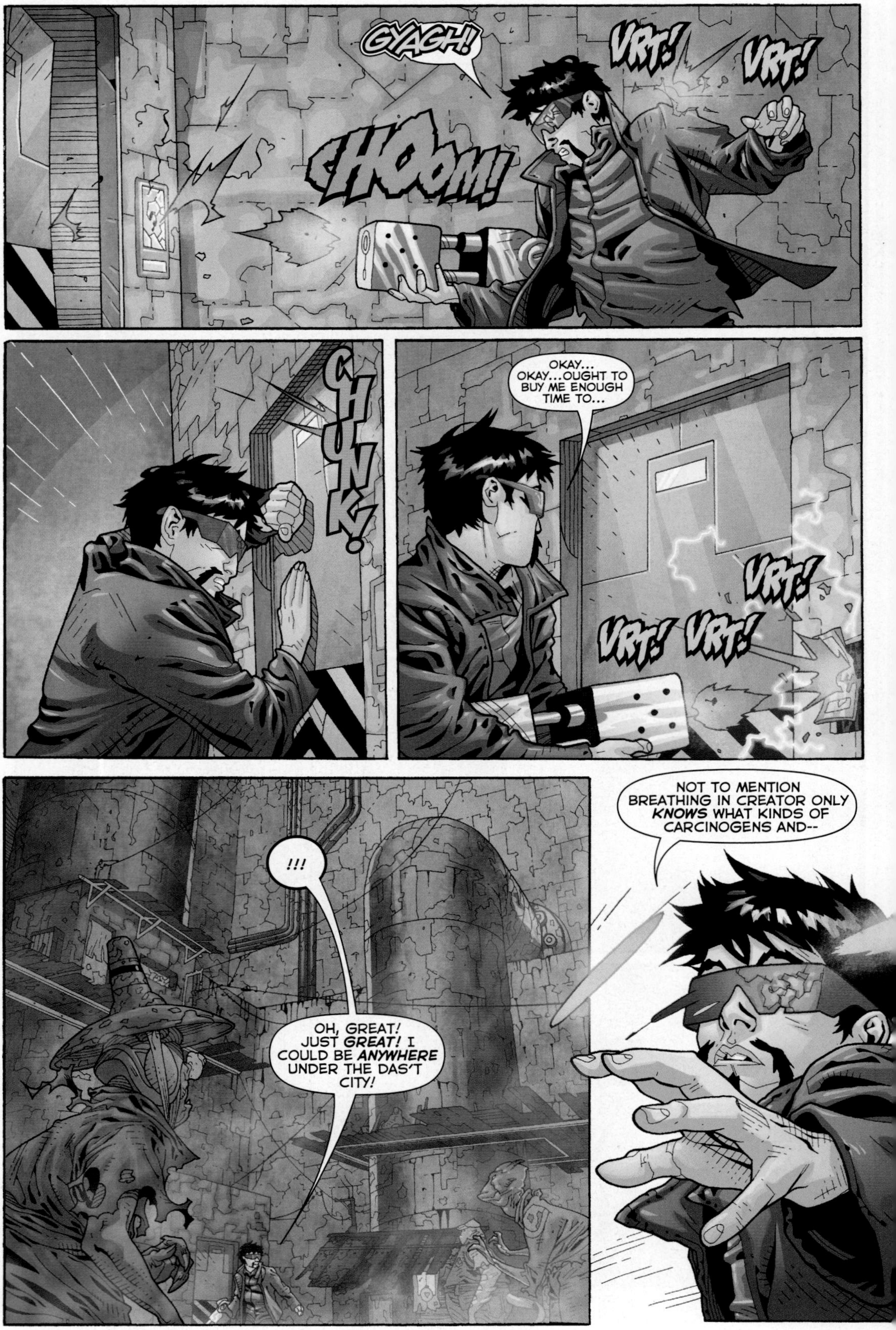
GYAGH!
VRT! VRT!
CHOOM!
CHUNK!
OKAY... OKAY...OUGHT TO BUY ME ENOUGH TIME TO...
VRT!
VRT! VRT!
!!!
OH, GREAT! JUST GREAT! I COULD BE ANYWHERE UNDER THE DAS'T CITY!
NOT TO MENTION BREATHING IN CREATOR ONLY KNOWS WHAT KINDS OF CARCINOGENS AND--

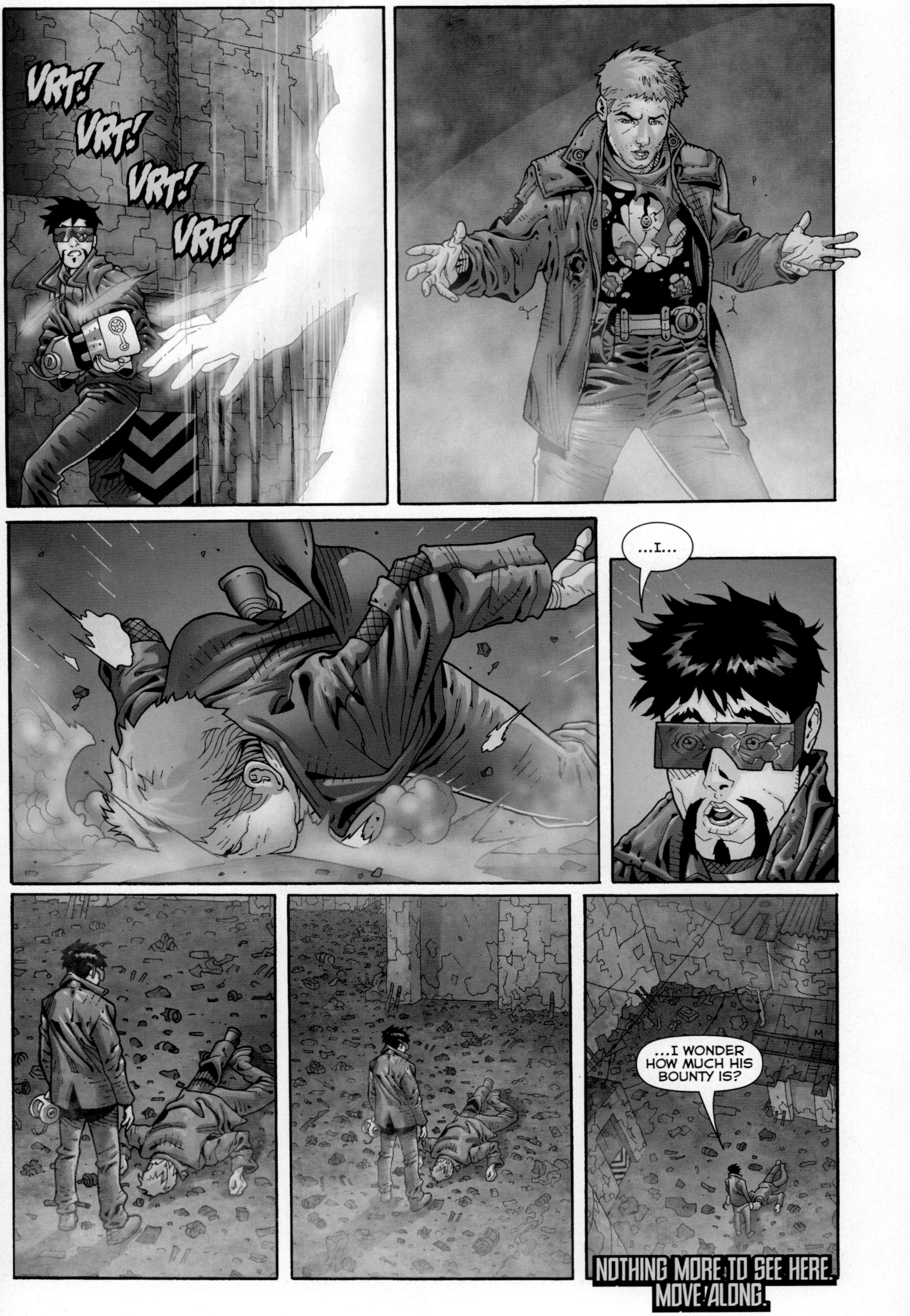
VRT! VRT! VRT! VRT!
...I...
...I WONDER HOW MUCH HIS BOUNTY IS?
NOTHING MORE TO SEE HERE. MOVE ALONG.

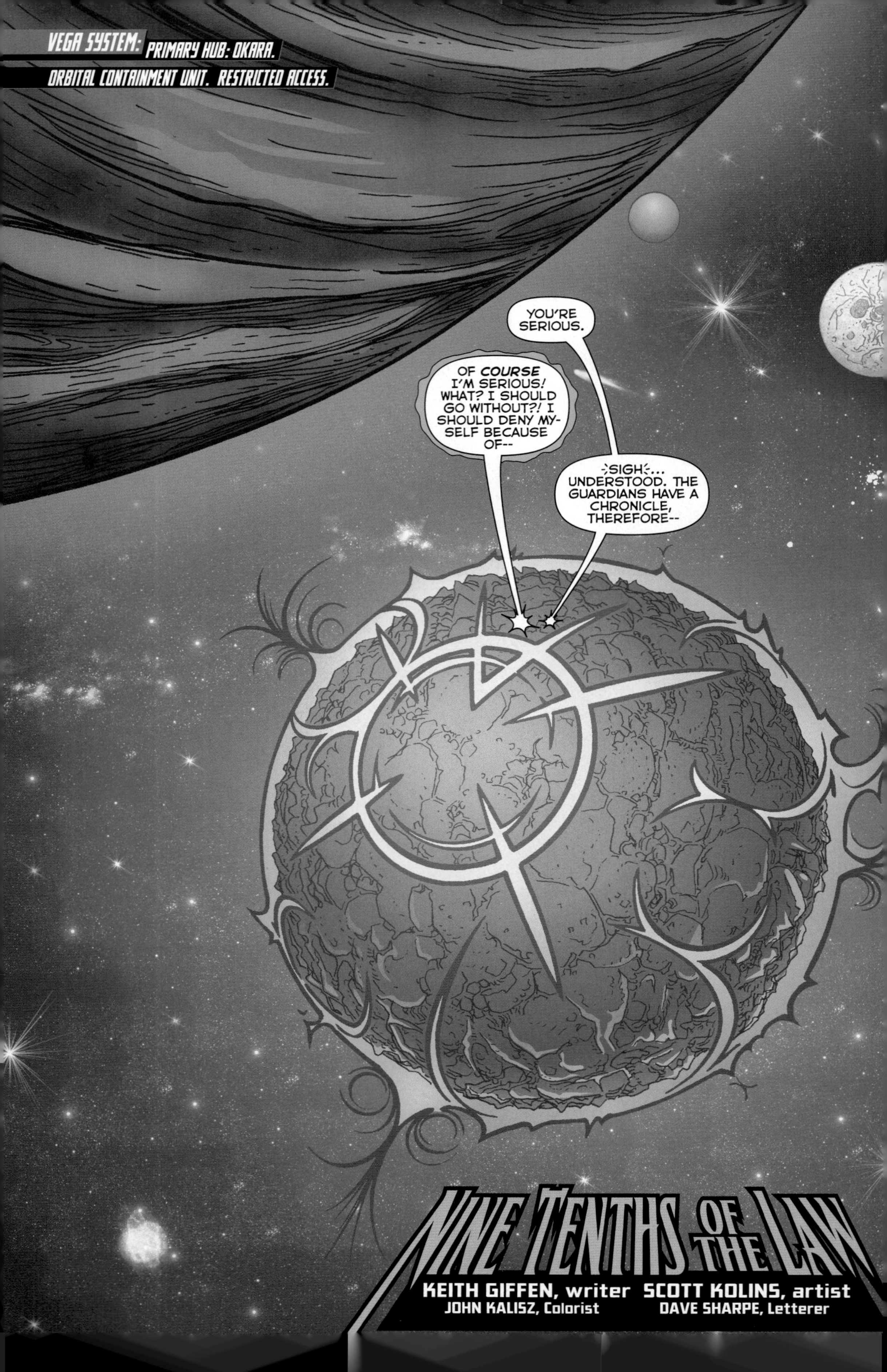
VEGA SYSTEM: PRIMARY HUB: OKARA.
ORBITAL CONTAINMENT UNIT. RESTRICTED ACCESS.
YOU'RE SERIOUS.
OF COURSE I'M SERIOUS! WHAT? I SHOULD GO WITHOUT?! I SHOULD DENY MY-SELF BECAUSE OF--
-SIGH-... UNDERSTOOD. THE GUARDIANS HAVE A CHRONICLE, THEREFORE--
NINE TENTHS OF THE LAW
KEITH GIFFEN, writer SCOTT KOLINS, artist
JOHN KALISZ, Colorist DAVE SHARPE, Letterer

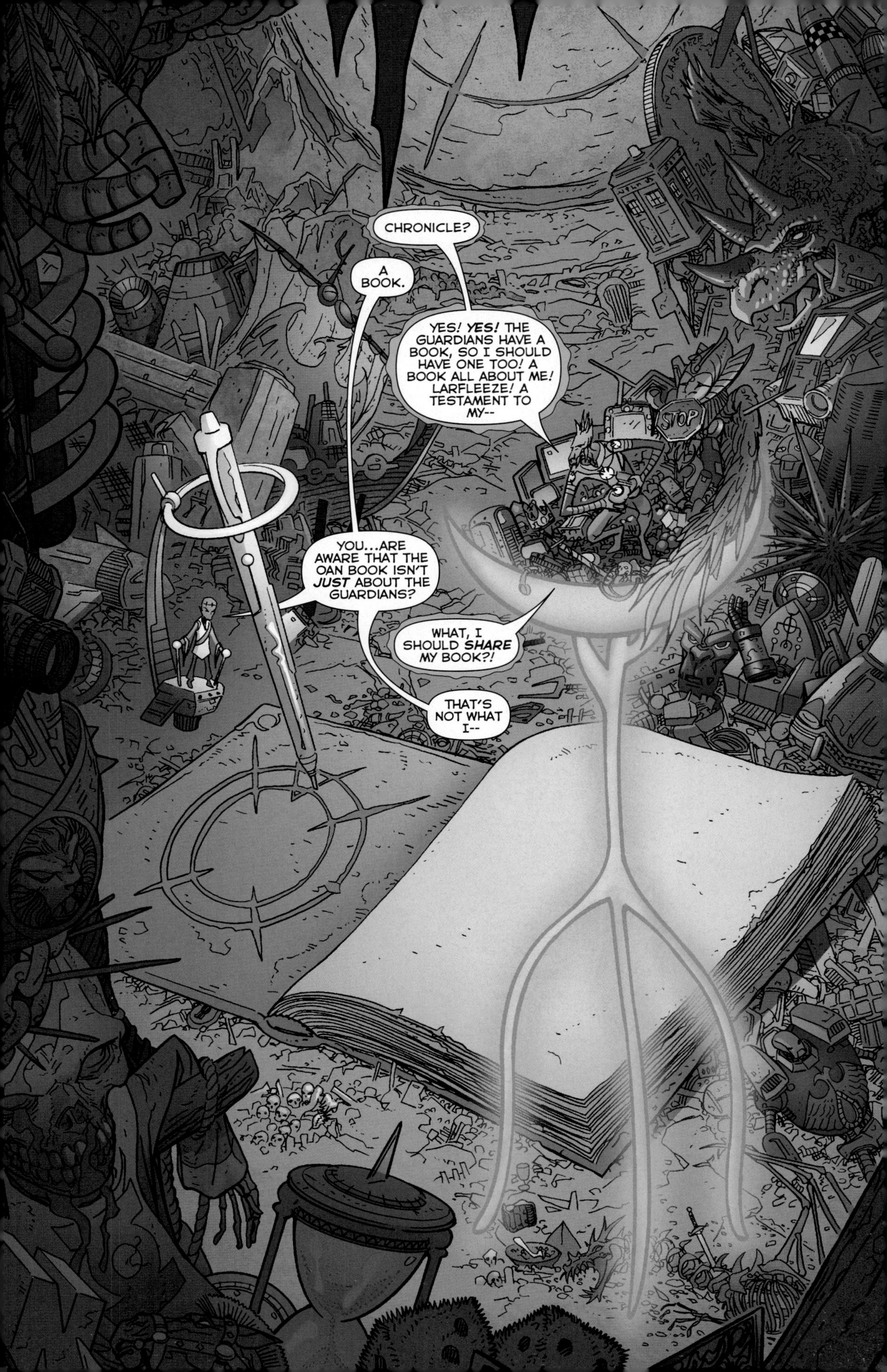
CHRONICLE?
A BOOK.
YES! YES! THE GUARDIANS HAVE A BOOK, SO I SHOULD HAVE ONE TOO! A BOOK ALL ABOUT ME! LARFLEEZE! A TESTAMENT TO MY--
YOU...ARE AWARE THAT THE OAN BOOK ISN'T JUST ABOUT THE GUARDIANS?
WHAT, I SHOULD SHARE MY BOOK?!
THAT'S NOT WHAT I--
STOP

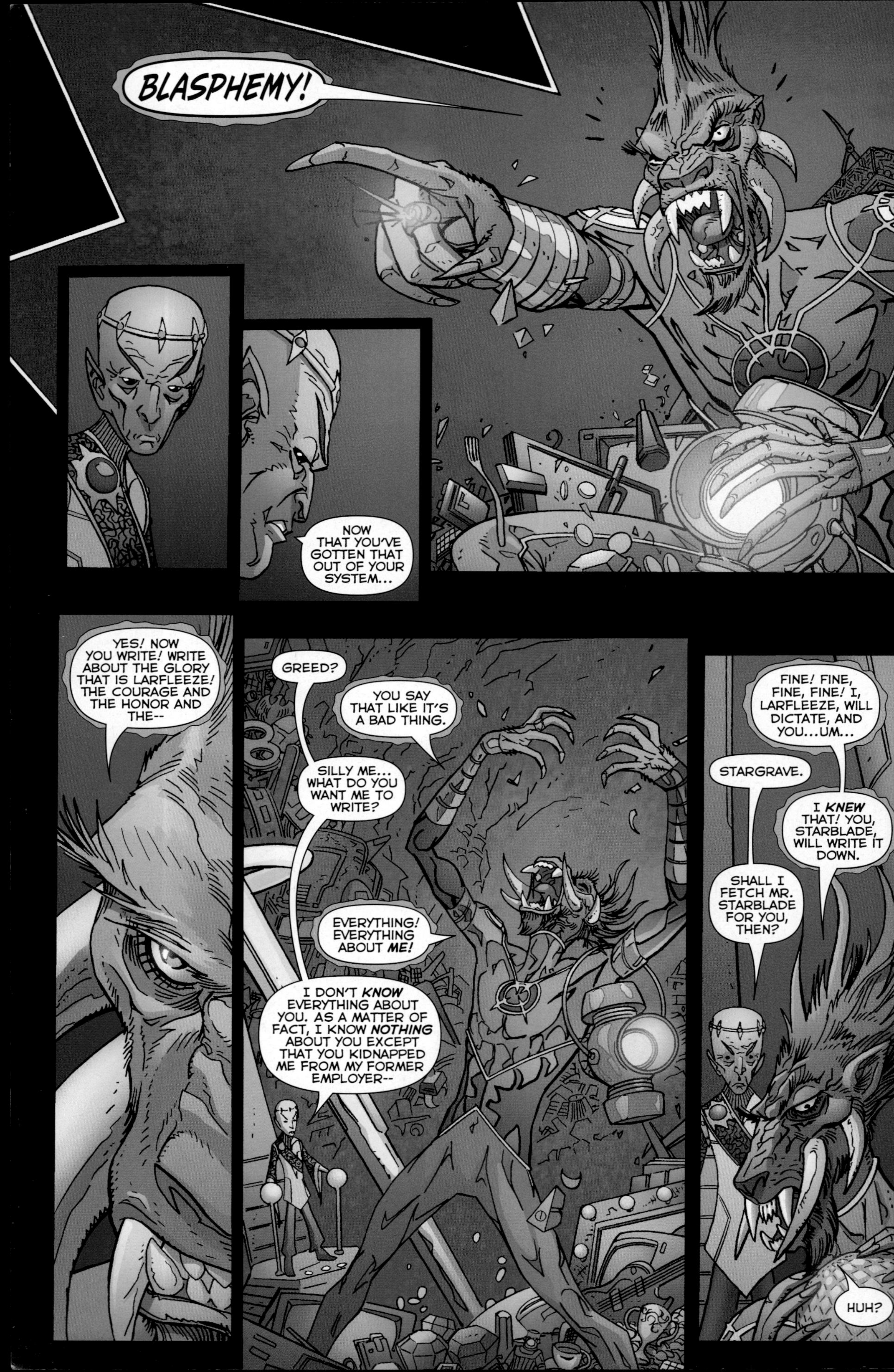
BLASPHEMY!
NOW THAT YOU'VE GOTTEN THAT OUT OF YOUR SYSTEM...
YES! NOW YOU WRITE! WRITE ABOUT THE GLORY THAT IS LARFLEEZE! THE COURAGE AND THE HONOR AND THE--
GREED?
YOU SAY THAT LIKE IT'S A BAD THING.
SILLY ME... WHAT DO YOU WANT ME TO WRITE?
EVERYTHING! EVERYTHING ABOUT ME!
I DON'T KNOW EVERYTHING ABOUT YOU. AS A MATTER OF FACT, I KNOW NOTHING ABOUT YOU EXCEPT THAT YOU KIDNAPPED ME FROM MY FORMER EMPLOYER--
FINE! FINE, FINE, FINE! I, LARFLEEZE, WILL DICTATE, AND YOU...UM...
STARGRAVE.
I KNEW THAT! YOU, STARBLADE, WILL WRITE IT DOWN.
SHALL I FETCH MR. STARBLADE FOR YOU, THEN?
HUH?

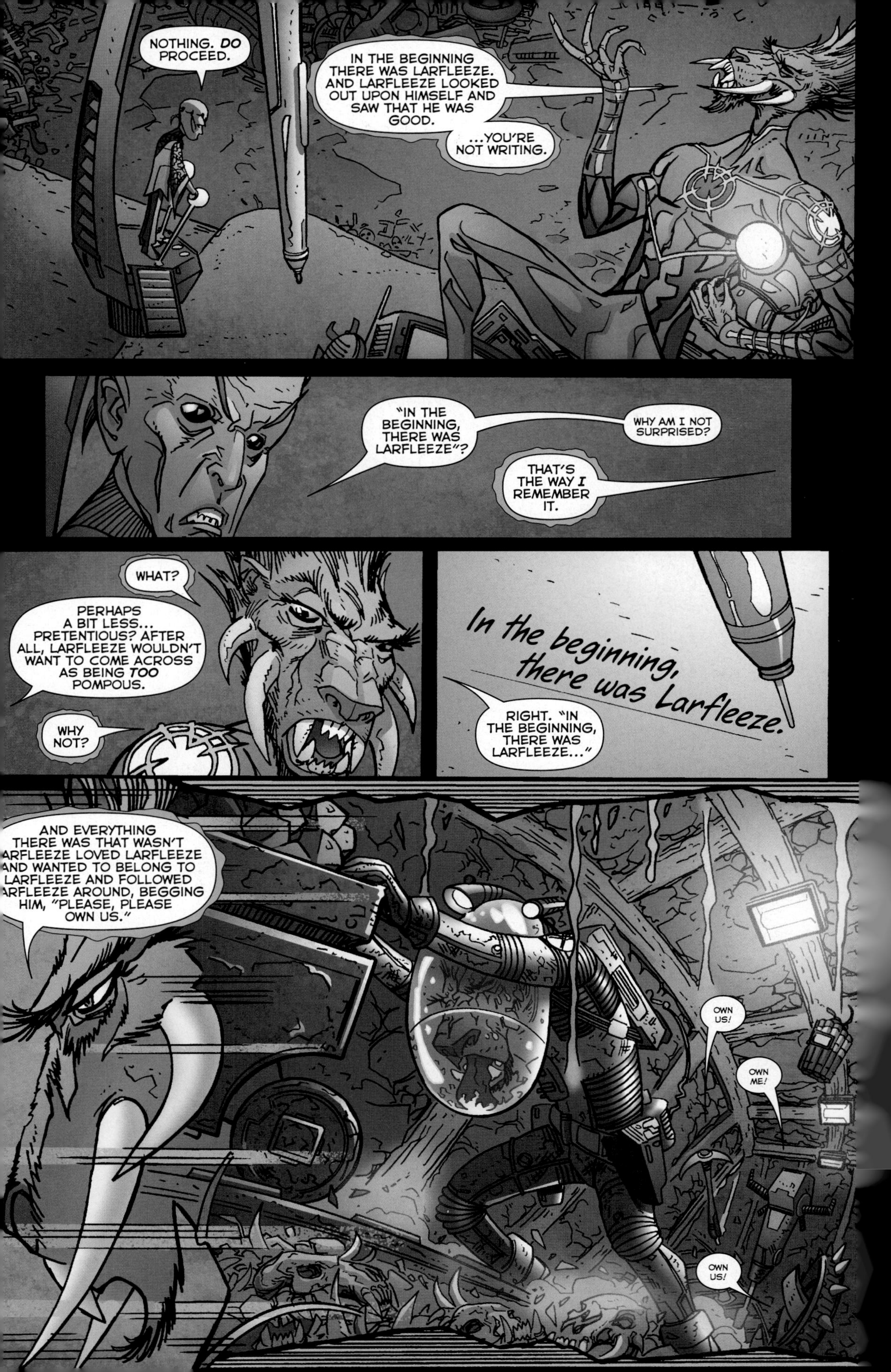
NOTHING. DO PROCEED.
IN THE BEGINNING THERE WAS LARFLEEZE. AND LARFLEEZE LOOKED OUT UPON HIMSELF AND SAW THAT HE WAS GOOD.
...YOU'RE NOT WRITING.
"IN THE BEGINNING, THERE WAS LARFLEEZE"?
WHY AM I NOT SURPRISED?
THAT'S THE WAY I REMEMBER IT.
WHAT?
PERHAPS A BIT LESS... PRETENTIOUS? AFTER ALL, LARFLEEZE WOULDN'T WANT TO COME ACROSS AS BEING TOO POMPOUS.
WHY NOT?
In the beginning, there was Larfleeze.
RIGHT. "IN THE BEGINNING, THERE WAS LARFLEEZE..."
AND EVERYTHING THERE WAS THAT WASN'T LARFLEEZE LOVED LARFLEEZE AND WANTED TO BELONG TO LARFLEEZE AND FOLLOWED LARFLEEZE AROUND, BEGGING HIM, "PLEASE, PLEASE OWN US."
OWN US!
OWN ME!
OWN US!

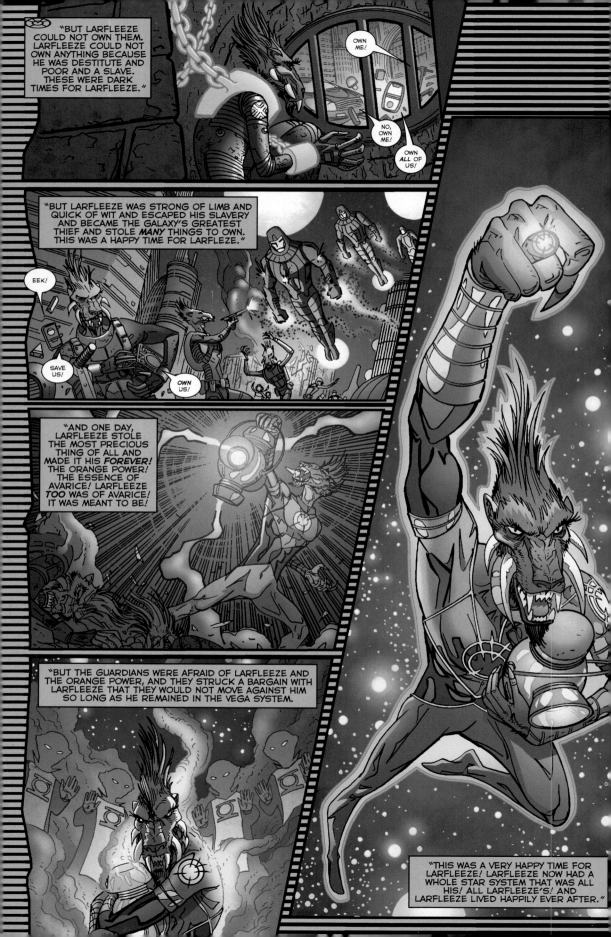

"BUT LARFLEEZE COULD NOT OWN THEM. LARFLEEZE COULD NOT OWN ANYTHING BECAUSE HE WAS DESTITUTE AND POOR AND A SLAVE. THESE WERE DARK TIMES FOR LARFLEEZE."

OWN ME!

NO, OWN ME!

OWN ALL OF US!

"BUT LARFLEEZE WAS STRONG OF LIMB AND QUICK OF WIT AND ESCAPED HIS SLAVERY AND BECAME THE GALAXY'S GREATEST THIEF AND STOLE MANY THINGS TO OWN. THIS WAS A HAPPY TIME FOR LARFLEZE."

EEK!

SAVE US!

OWN US!

"AND ONE DAY, LARFLEEZE STOLE THE MOST PRECIOUS THING OF ALL AND MADE IT HIS FOREVER! THE ORANGE POWER! THE ESSENCE OF AVARICE! LARFLEEZE TOO WAS OF AVARICE! IT WAS MEANT TO BE!

"BUT THE GUARDIANS WERE AFRAID OF LARFLEEZE AND THE ORANGE POWER, AND THEY STRUCK A BARGAIN WITH LARFLEEZE THAT THEY WOULD NOT MOVE AGAINST HIM SO LONG AS HE REMAINED IN THE VEGA SYSTEM."

"THIS WAS A VERY HAPPY TIME FOR LARFLEEZE! LARFLEEZE NOW HAD A WHOLE STAR SYSTEM THAT WAS ALL HIS! ALL LARFLEEZE'S! AND LARFLEEZE LIVED HAPPILY EVER AFTER."

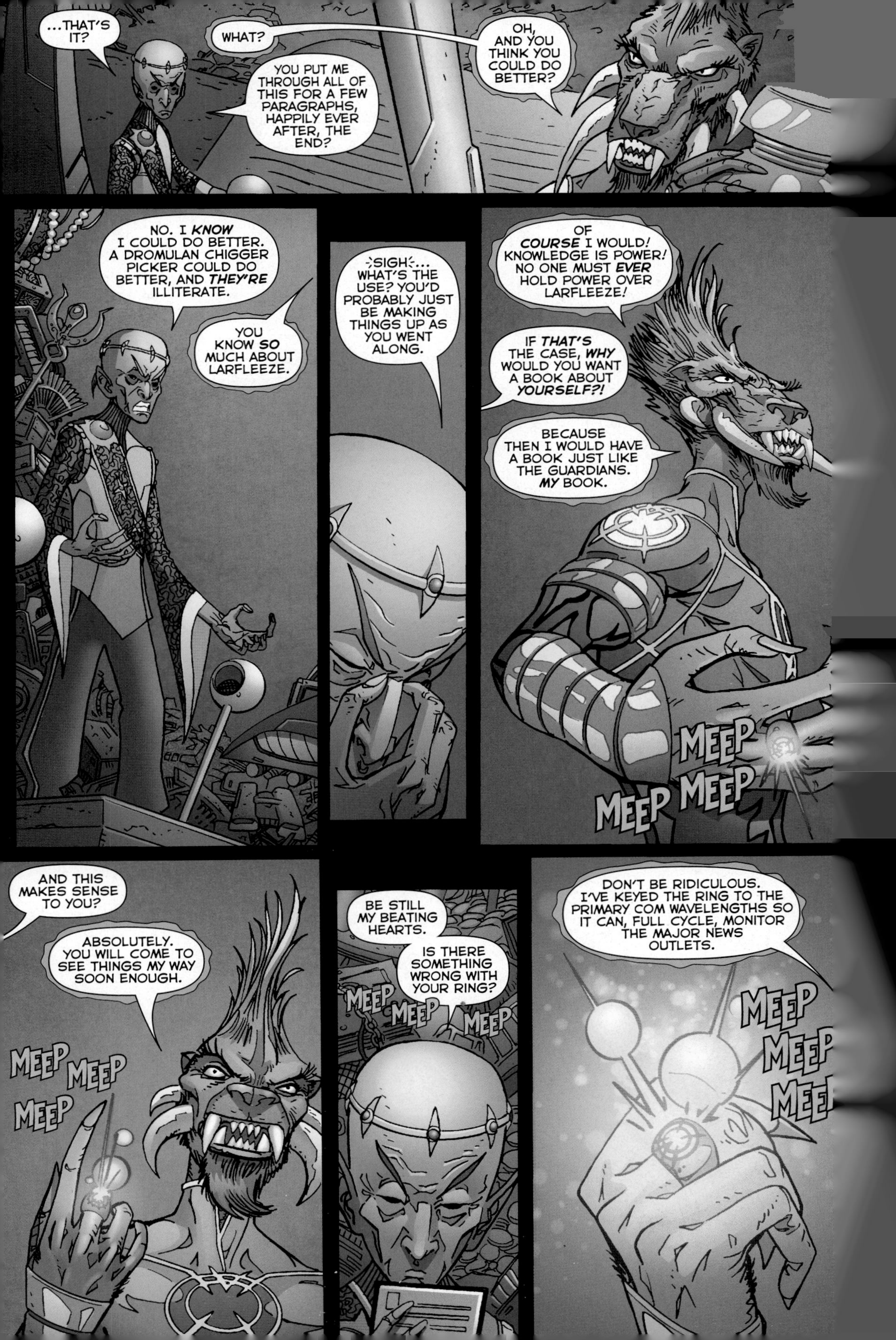
...THAT'S IT?
YOU PUT ME THROUGH ALL OF THIS FOR A FEW PARAGRAPHS, HAPPILY EVER AFTER, THE END?
WHAT?
OH, AND YOU THINK YOU COULD DO BETTER?
NO. I KNOW I COULD DO BETTER. A DROMULAN CHIGGER PICKER COULD DO BETTER, AND THEY'RE ILLITERATE.
YOU KNOW SO MUCH ABOUT LARFLEEZE.
SIGH... WHAT'S THE USE? YOU'D PROBABLY JUST BE MAKING THINGS UP AS YOU WENT ALONG.
OF COURSE I WOULD! KNOWLEDGE IS POWER! NO ONE MUST EVER HOLD POWER OVER LARFLEEZE!
IF THAT'S THE CASE, WHY WOULD YOU WANT A BOOK ABOUT YOURSELF?!
BECAUSE THEN I WOULD HAVE A BOOK JUST LIKE THE GUARDIANS. MY BOOK.
MEEP MEEP MEEP MEEP
AND THIS MAKES SENSE TO YOU?
ABSOLUTELY. YOU WILL COME TO SEE THINGS MY WAY SOON ENOUGH.
MEEP MEEP MEEP
BE STILL MY BEATING HEARTS.
IS THERE SOMETHING WRONG WITH YOUR RING?
MEEP MEEP MEEP
DON'T BE RIDICULOUS. I'VE KEYED THE RING TO THE PRIMARY COM WAVELENGTHS SO IT CAN, FULL CYCLE, MONITOR THE MAJOR NEWS OUTLETS.
MEEP MEEP MEEP

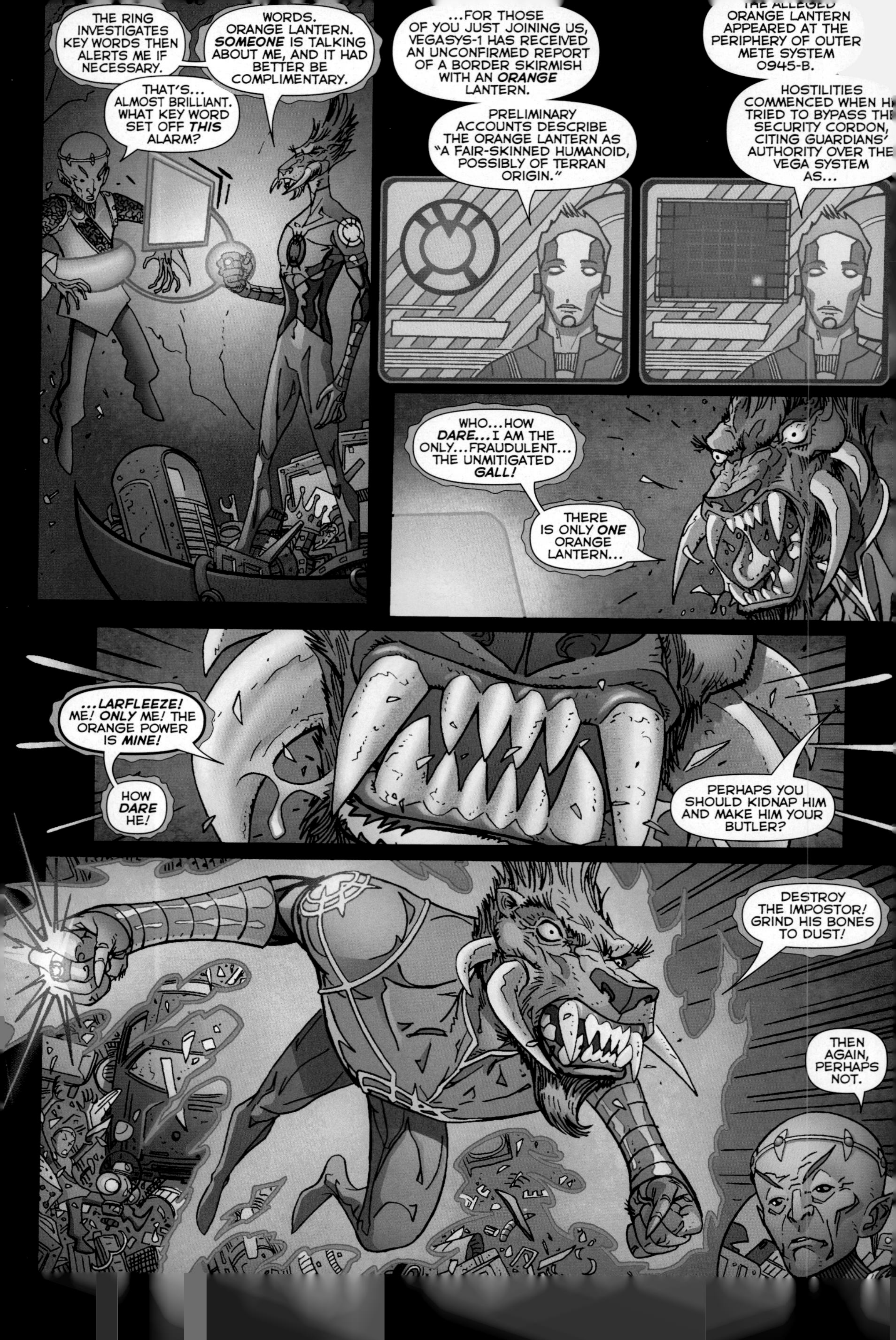

THE RING INVESTIGATES KEY WORDS THEN ALERTS ME IF NECESSARY.
THAT'S... ALMOST BRILLIANT. WHAT KEY WORD SET OFF *THIS* ALARM?
WORDS. ORANGE LANTERN. *SOMEONE* IS TALKING ABOUT ME, AND IT HAD BETTER BE COMPLIMENTARY.
...FOR THOSE OF YOU JUST JOINING US, VEGASYS-1 HAS RECEIVED AN UNCONFIRMED REPORT OF A BORDER SKIRMISH WITH AN *ORANGE* LANTERN.
PRELIMINARY ACCOUNTS DESCRIBE THE ORANGE LANTERN AS "A FAIR-SKINNED HUMANOID, POSSIBLY OF TERRAN ORIGIN."
ORANGE LANTERN APPEARED AT THE PERIPHERY OF OUTER METE SYSTEM 0945-B.
HOSTILITIES COMMENCED WHEN H TRIED TO BYPASS TH SECURITY CORDON, CITING GUARDIANS' AUTHORITY OVER THE VEGA SYSTEM AS...
WHO...HOW *DARE*...I AM THE ONLY...FRAUDULENT... THE UNMITIGATED *GALL!*
THERE IS ONLY *ONE* ORANGE LANTERN...
...LARFLEEZE! ME! *ONLY* ME! THE ORANGE POWER IS *MINE!*
HOW *DARE* HE!
PERHAPS YOU SHOULD KIDNAP HIM AND MAKE HIM YOUR BUTLER?
DESTROY THE IMPOSTOR! GRIND HIS BONES TO DUST!
THEN AGAIN, PERHAPS NOT.

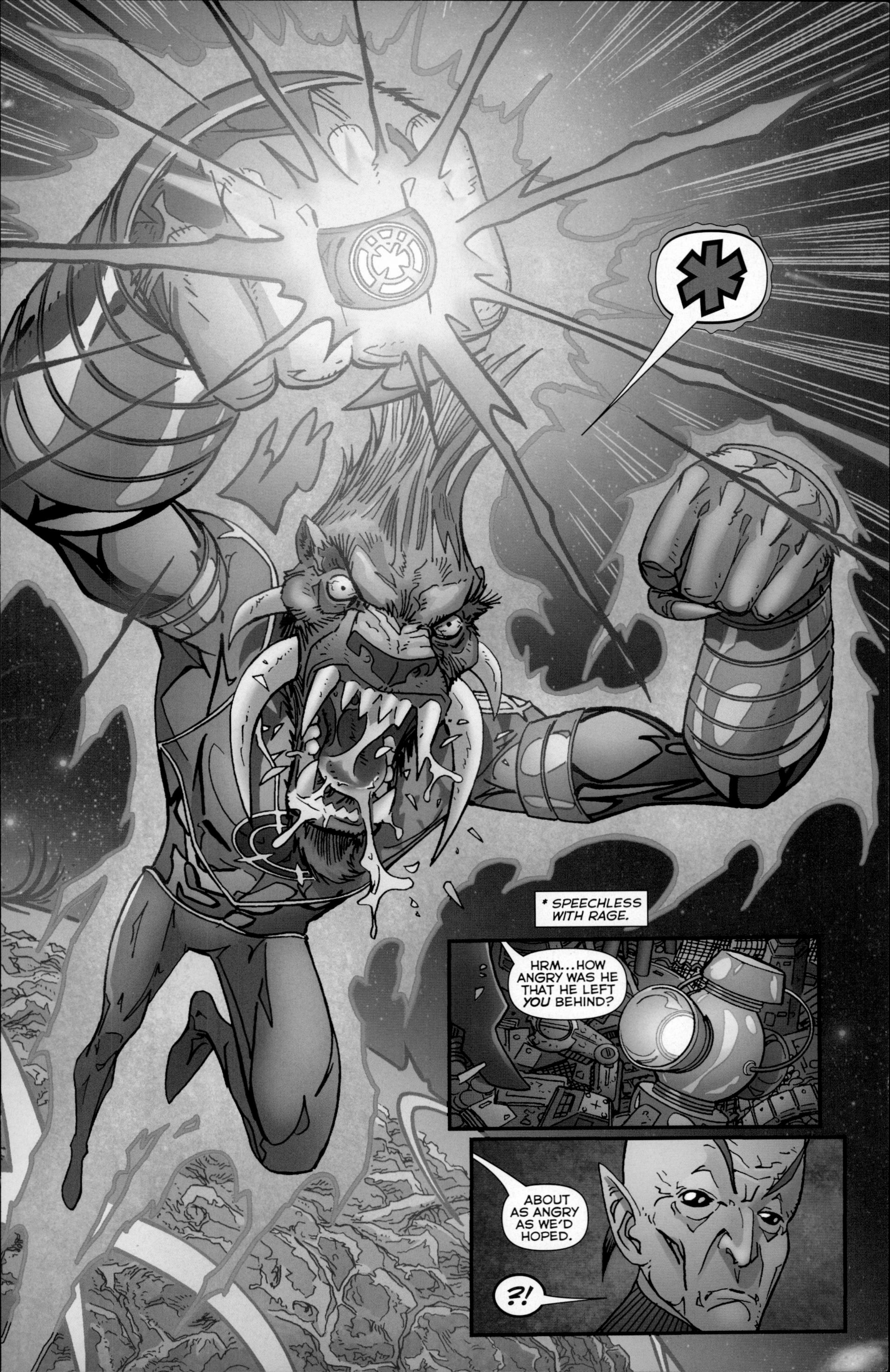
*
* SPEECHLESS WITH RAGE.
HRM...HOW ANGRY WAS HE THAT HE LEFT YOU BEHIND?
ABOUT AS ANGRY AS WE'D HOPED.
?!

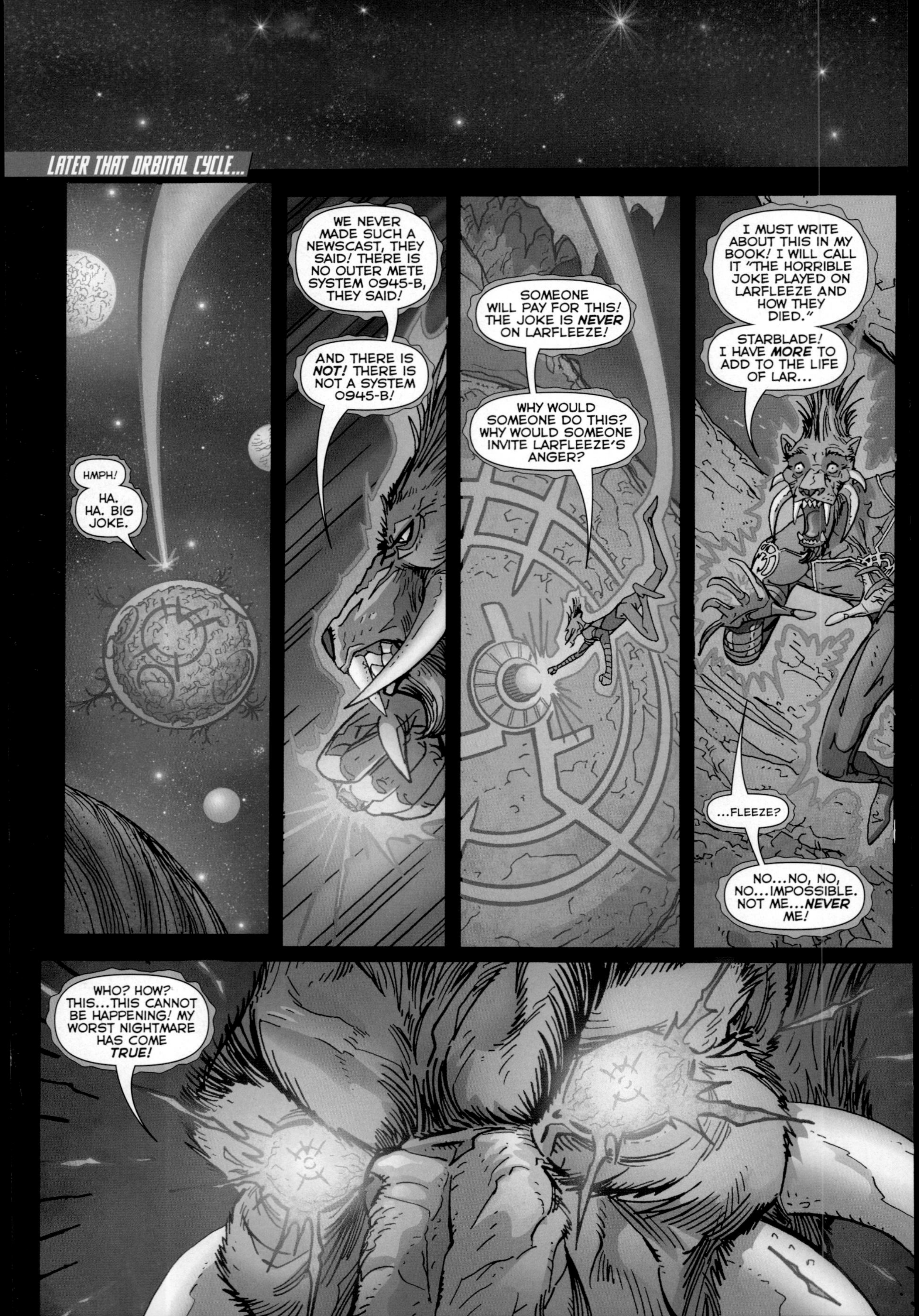
LATER THAT ORBITAL CYCLE...
HMPH!
HA. HA. BIG JOKE.
WE NEVER MADE SUCH A NEWSCAST, THEY SAID! THERE IS NO OUTER METE SYSTEM 0945-B, THEY SAID!
AND THERE IS NOT! THERE IS NOT A SYSTEM 0945-B!
SOMEONE WILL PAY FOR THIS! THE JOKE IS NEVER ON LARFLEEZE!
WHY WOULD SOMEONE DO THIS? WHY WOULD SOMEONE INVITE LARFLEEZE'S ANGER?
I MUST WRITE ABOUT THIS IN MY BOOK! I WILL CALL IT "THE HORRIBLE JOKE PLAYED ON LARFLEEZE AND HOW THEY DIED."
STARBLADE! I HAVE MORE TO ADD TO THE LIFE OF LAR...
...FLEEZE?
NO...NO, NO, NO...IMPOSSIBLE. NOT ME...NEVER ME!
WHO? HOW? THIS...THIS CANNOT BE HAPPENING! MY WORST NIGHTMARE HAS COME TRUE!

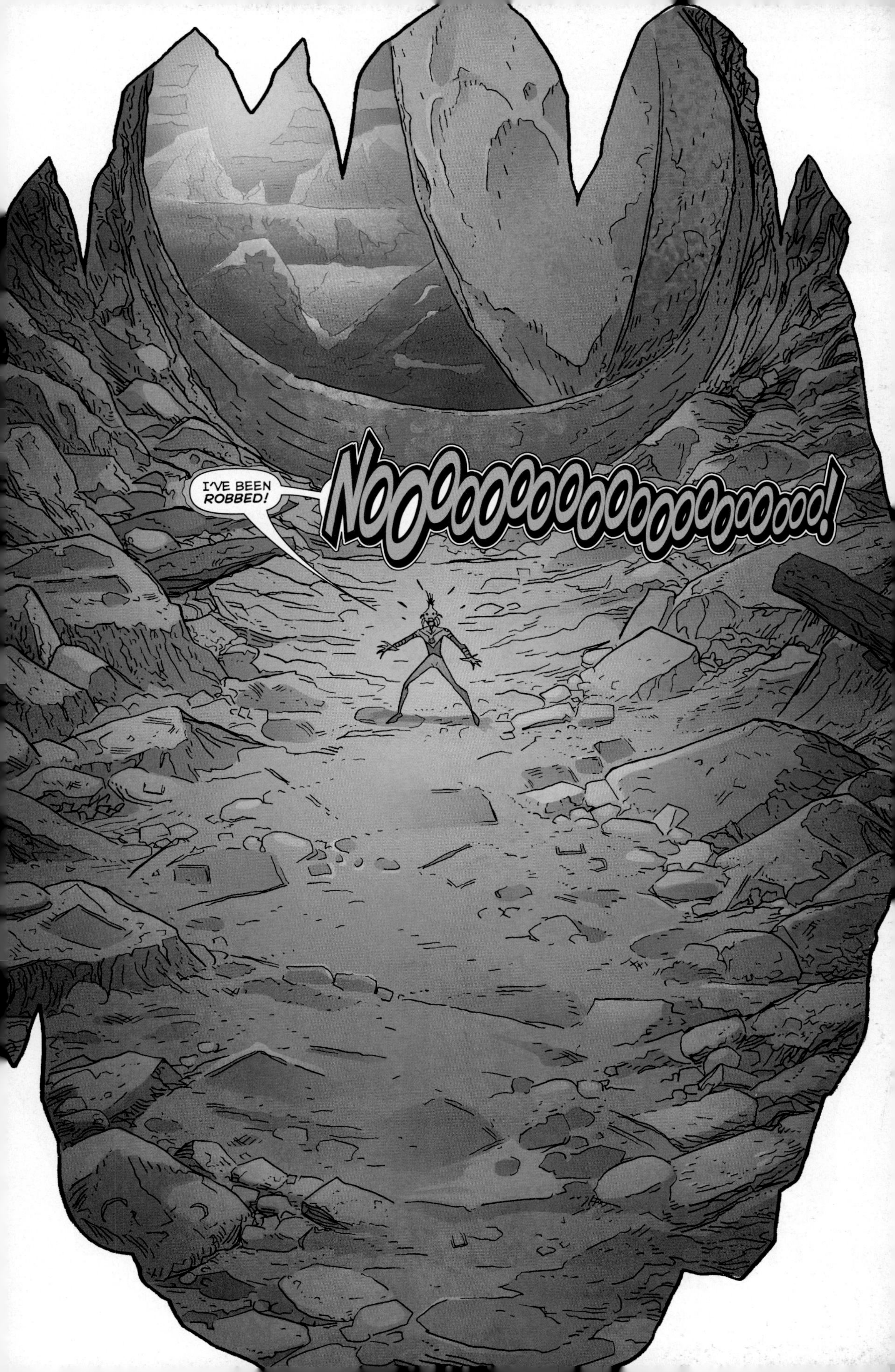
I'VE BEEN ROBBED!
NOOOOOOOOOOOOOOOOOOOOOOOO!

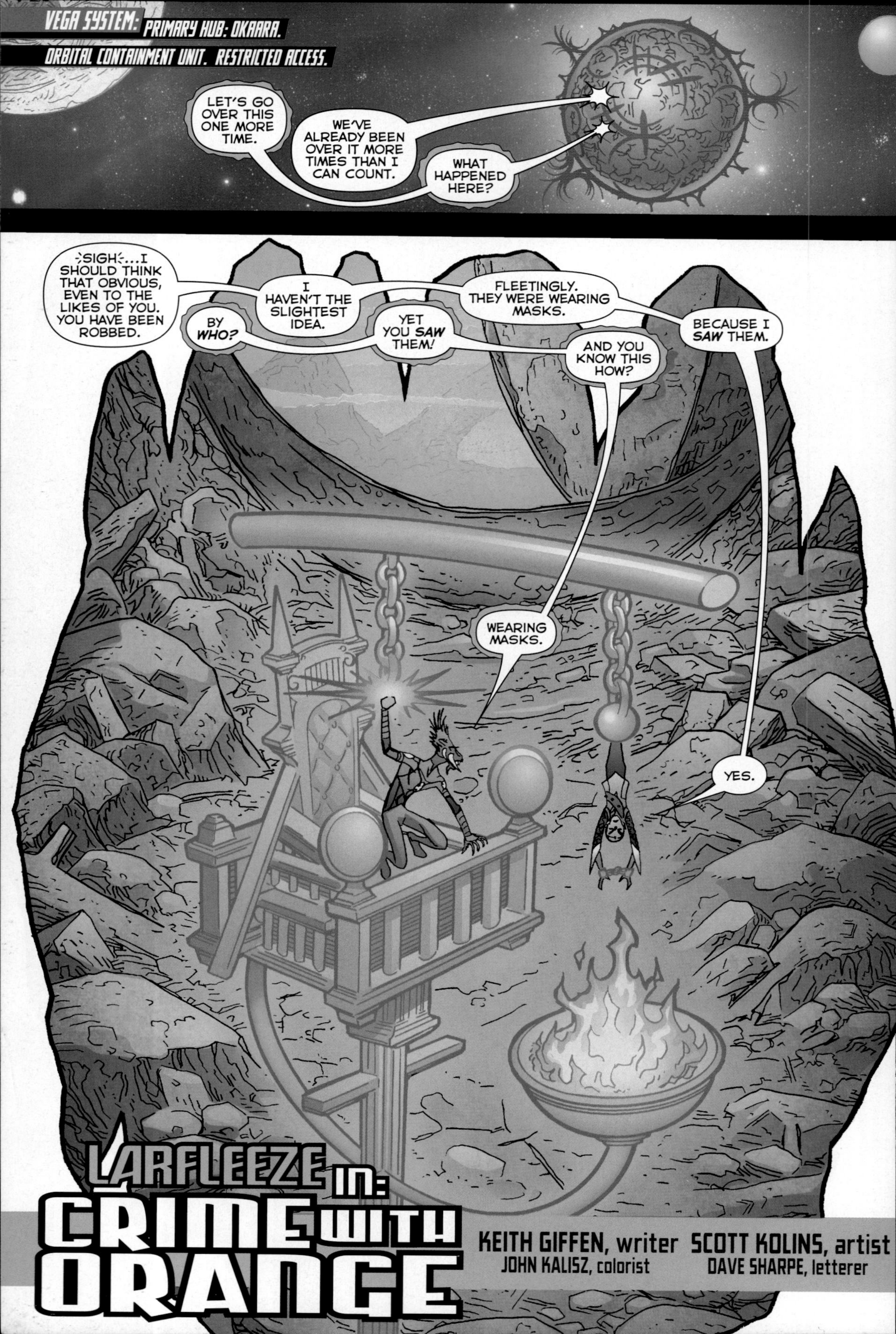
VEGA SYSTEM: PRIMARY HUB: OKAARA.
ORBITAL CONTAINMENT UNIT. RESTRICTED ACCESS.
LET'S GO OVER THIS ONE MORE TIME.
WE'VE ALREADY BEEN OVER IT MORE TIMES THAN I CAN COUNT.
WHAT HAPPENED HERE?
SIGH...I SHOULD THINK THAT OBVIOUS, EVEN TO THE LIKES OF YOU. YOU HAVE BEEN ROBBED.
BY WHO?
I HAVEN'T THE SLIGHTEST IDEA.
YET YOU SAW THEM!
FLEETINGLY. THEY WERE WEARING MASKS.
AND YOU KNOW THIS HOW?
BECAUSE I SAW THEM.
WEARING MASKS.
YES.
LARFLEEZE IN:
CRIME WITH ORANGE
KEITH GIFFEN, writer SCOTT KOLINS, artist
JOHN KALISZ, colorist DAVE SHARPE, letterer

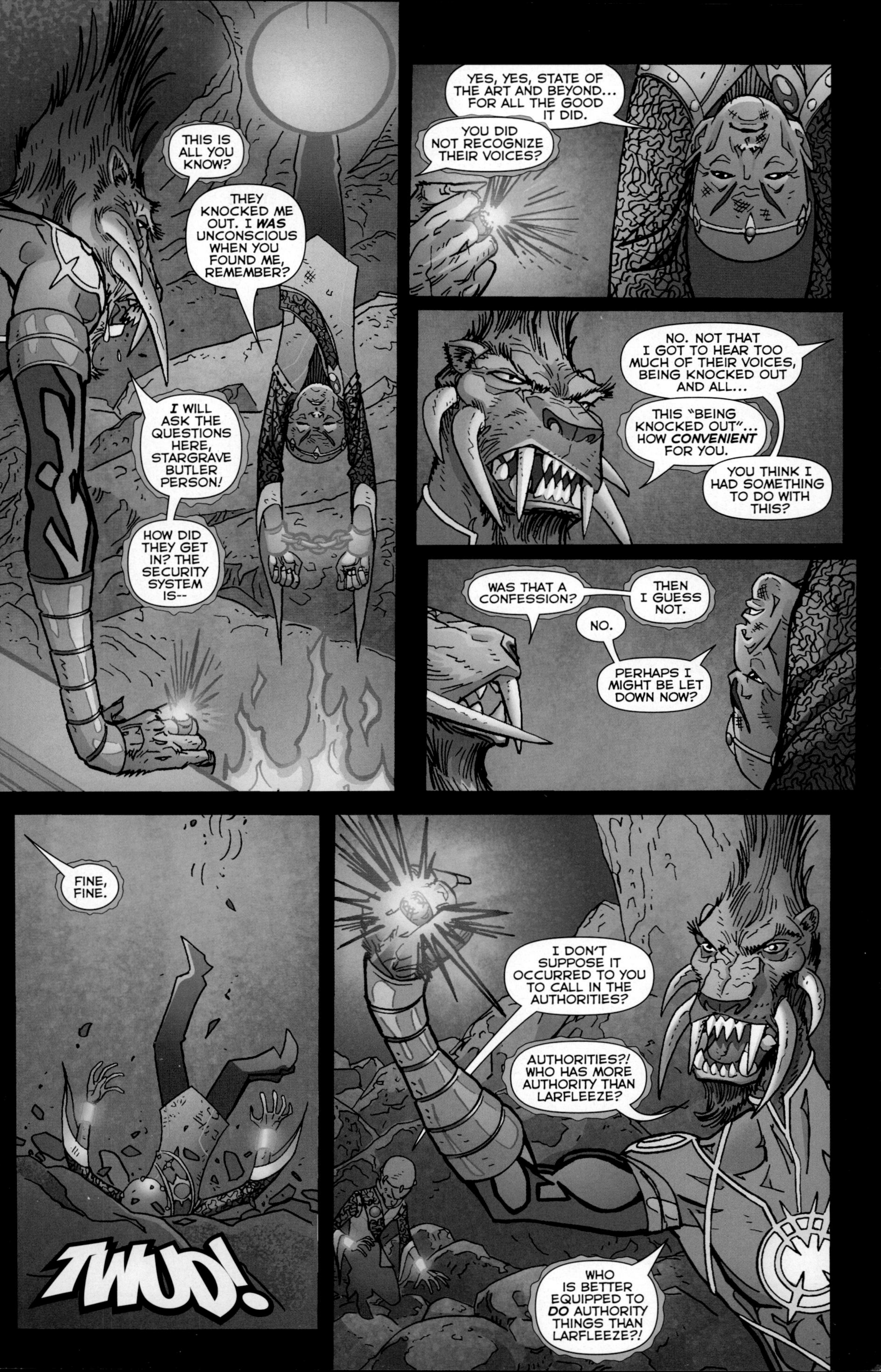
THIS IS ALL YOU KNOW?
THEY KNOCKED ME OUT. I *WAS* UNCONSCIOUS WHEN YOU FOUND ME, REMEMBER?
I WILL ASK THE QUESTIONS HERE, STARGRAVE BUTLER PERSON!
HOW DID THEY GET IN? THE SECURITY SYSTEM IS--
YES, YES, STATE OF THE ART AND BEYOND... FOR ALL THE GOOD IT DID.
YOU DID NOT RECOGNIZE THEIR VOICES?
NO. NOT THAT I GOT TO HEAR TOO MUCH OF THEIR VOICES, BEING KNOCKED OUT AND ALL...
THIS "BEING KNOCKED OUT"... HOW *CONVENIENT* FOR YOU.
YOU THINK I HAD SOMETHING TO DO WITH THIS?
WAS THAT A CONFESSION?
NO.
THEN I GUESS NOT.
PERHAPS I MIGHT BE LET DOWN NOW?
FINE, FINE.
TWUD!
I DON'T SUPPOSE IT OCCURRED TO YOU TO CALL IN THE AUTHORITIES?
AUTHORITIES?! WHO HAS MORE AUTHORITY THAN LARFLEEZE?
WHO IS BETTER EQUIPPED TO *DO* AUTHORITY THINGS THAN LARFLEEZE?!

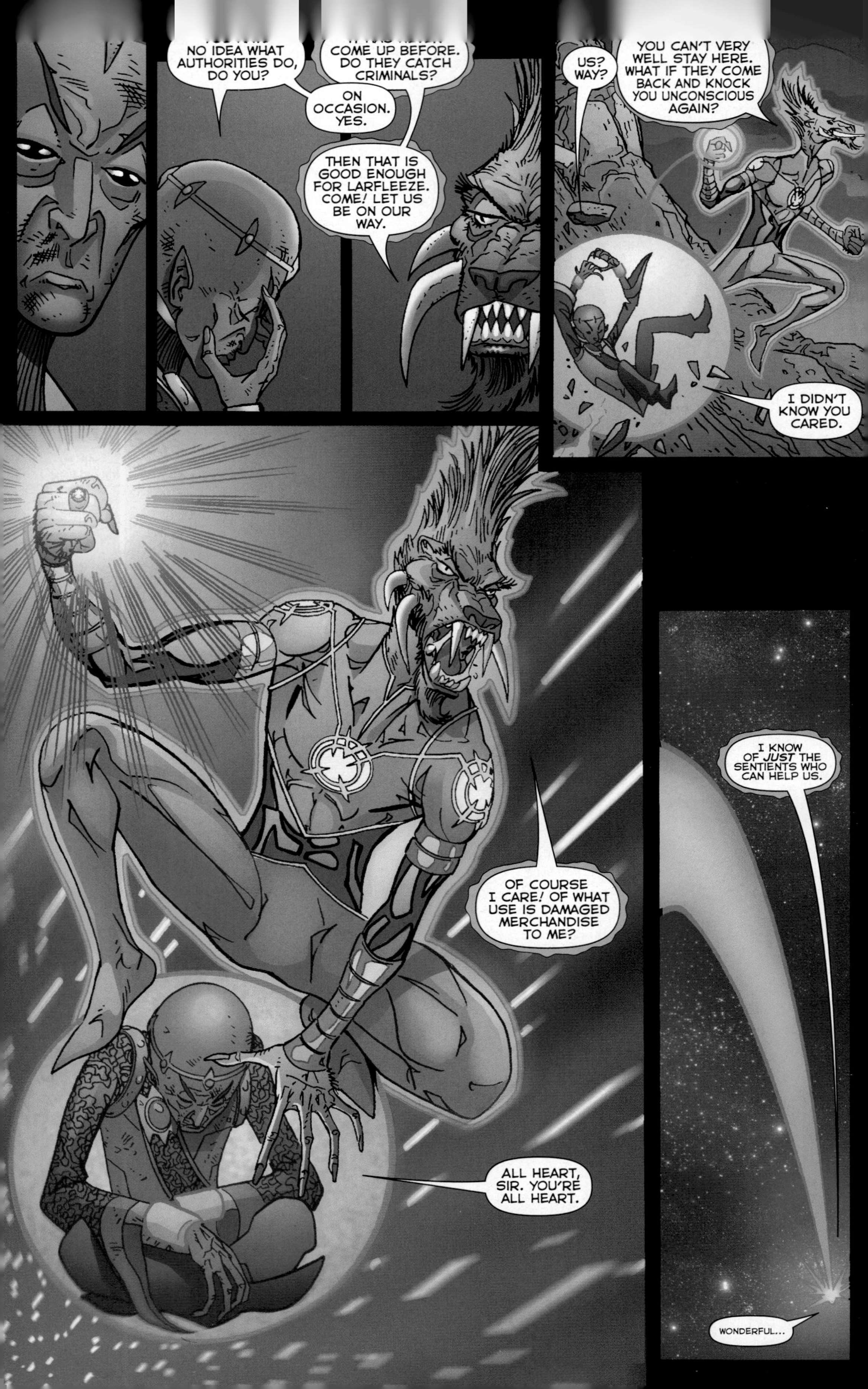
NO IDEA WHAT AUTHORITIES DO, DO YOU?
COME UP BEFORE. DO THEY CATCH CRIMINALS?
ON OCCASION. YES.
THEN THAT IS GOOD ENOUGH FOR LARFLEEZE. COME! LET US BE ON OUR WAY.
US? WAY?
YOU CAN'T VERY WELL STAY HERE. WHAT IF THEY COME BACK AND KNOCK YOU UNCONSCIOUS AGAIN?
I DIDN'T KNOW YOU CARED.
OF COURSE I CARE! OF WHAT USE IS DAMAGED MERCHANDISE TO ME?
ALL HEART, SIR. YOU'RE ALL HEART.
I KNOW OF *JUST* THE SENTIENTS WHO CAN HELP US.
WONDERFUL...

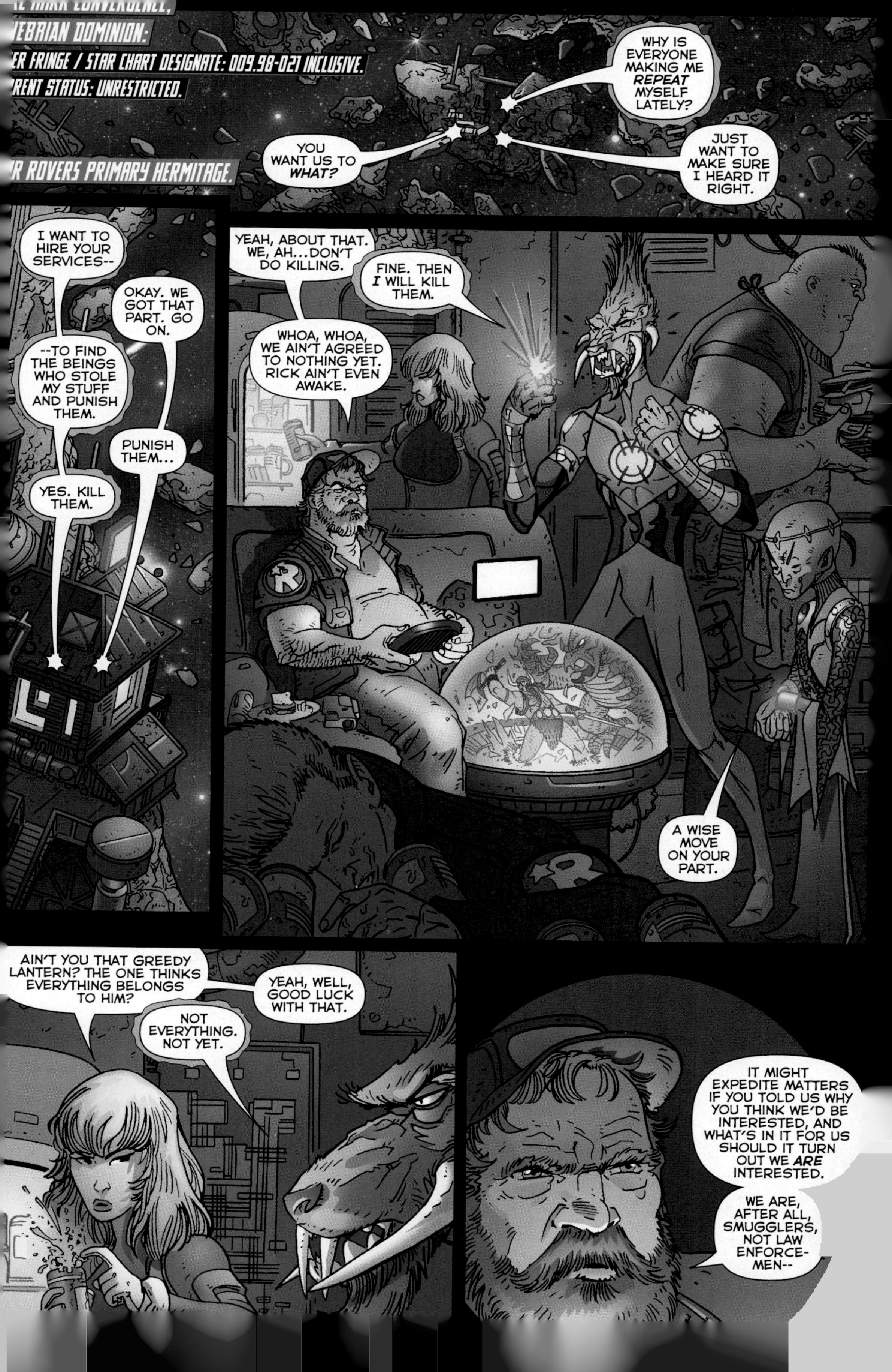
VEBRIAN DOMINION:
ER FRINGE / STAR CHART DESIGNATE: 009.98-021 INCLUSIVE.
RENT STATUS: UNRESTRICTED.
R ROVERS PRIMARY HERMITAGE.
YOU WANT US TO WHAT?
WHY IS EVERYONE MAKING ME REPEAT MYSELF LATELY?
JUST WANT TO MAKE SURE I HEARD IT RIGHT.
I WANT TO HIRE YOUR SERVICES--
OKAY. WE GOT THAT PART. GO ON.
--TO FIND THE BEINGS WHO STOLE MY STUFF AND PUNISH THEM.
PUNISH THEM...
YES. KILL THEM.
YEAH, ABOUT THAT. WE, AH...DON'T DO KILLING.
FINE. THEN I WILL KILL THEM.
WHOA, WHOA, WE AIN'T AGREED TO NOTHING YET. RICK AIN'T EVEN AWAKE.
A WISE MOVE ON YOUR PART.
AIN'T YOU THAT GREEDY LANTERN? THE ONE THINKS EVERYTHING BELONGS TO HIM?
NOT EVERYTHING. NOT YET.
YEAH, WELL, GOOD LUCK WITH THAT.
IT MIGHT EXPEDITE MATTERS IF YOU TOLD US WHY YOU THINK WE'D BE INTERESTED, AND WHAT'S IN IT FOR US SHOULD IT TURN OUT WE ARE INTERESTED.
WE ARE, AFTER ALL, SMUGGLERS, NOT LAW ENFORCE-MEN--

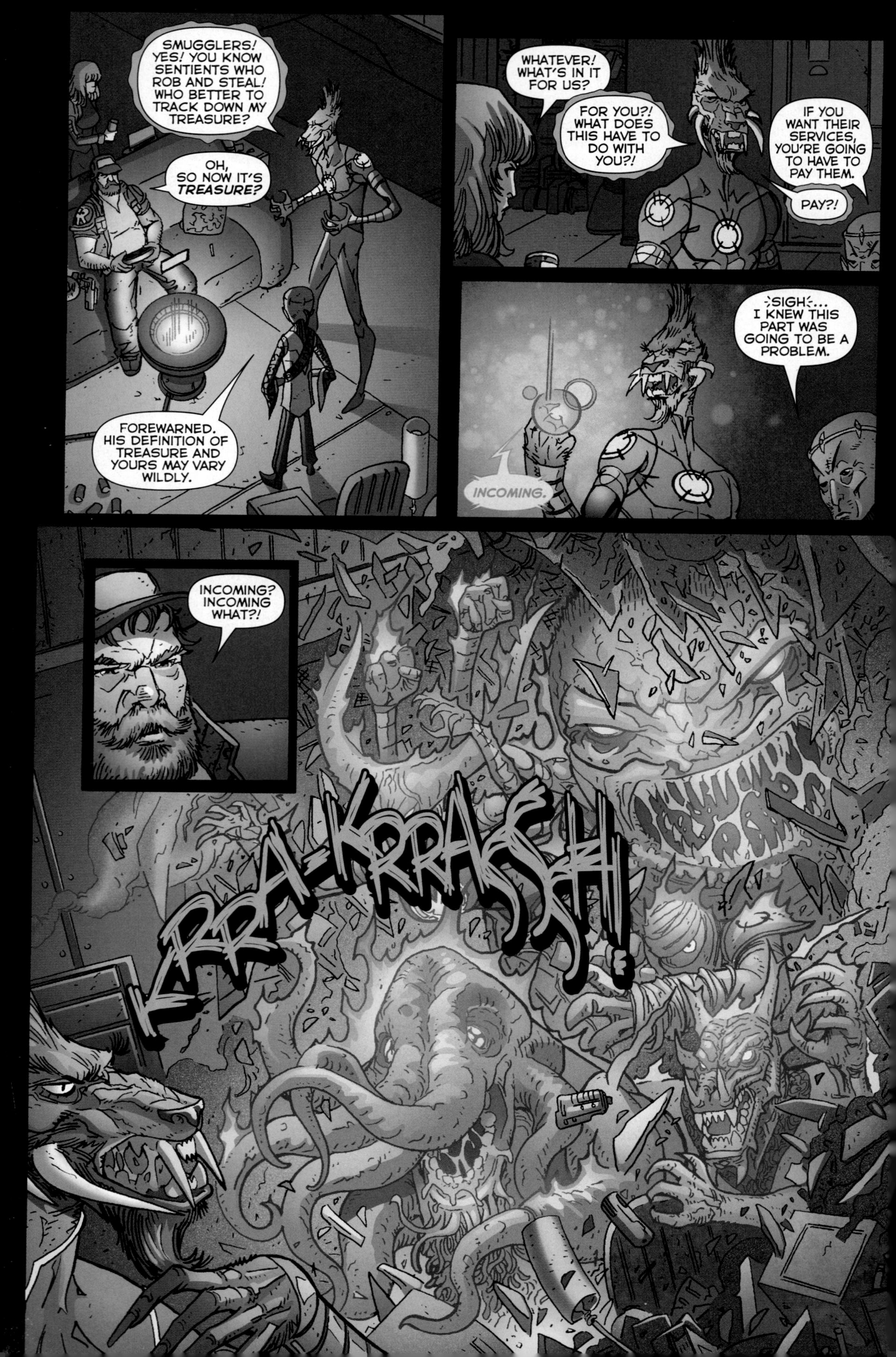
SMUGGLERS! YES! YOU KNOW SENTIENTS WHO ROB AND STEAL! WHO BETTER TO TRACK DOWN MY TREASURE?
OH, SO NOW IT'S *TREASURE?*
FOREWARNED. HIS DEFINITION OF TREASURE AND YOURS MAY VARY WILDLY.
WHATEVER! WHAT'S IN IT FOR US?
FOR YOU?! WHAT DOES THIS HAVE TO DO WITH YOU?!
IF YOU WANT THEIR SERVICES, YOU'RE GOING TO HAVE TO PAY THEM.
PAY?!
SIGH... I KNEW THIS PART WAS GOING TO BE A PROBLEM.
INCOMING.
INCOMING? INCOMING WHAT?!
KRRA-KRRASSH!

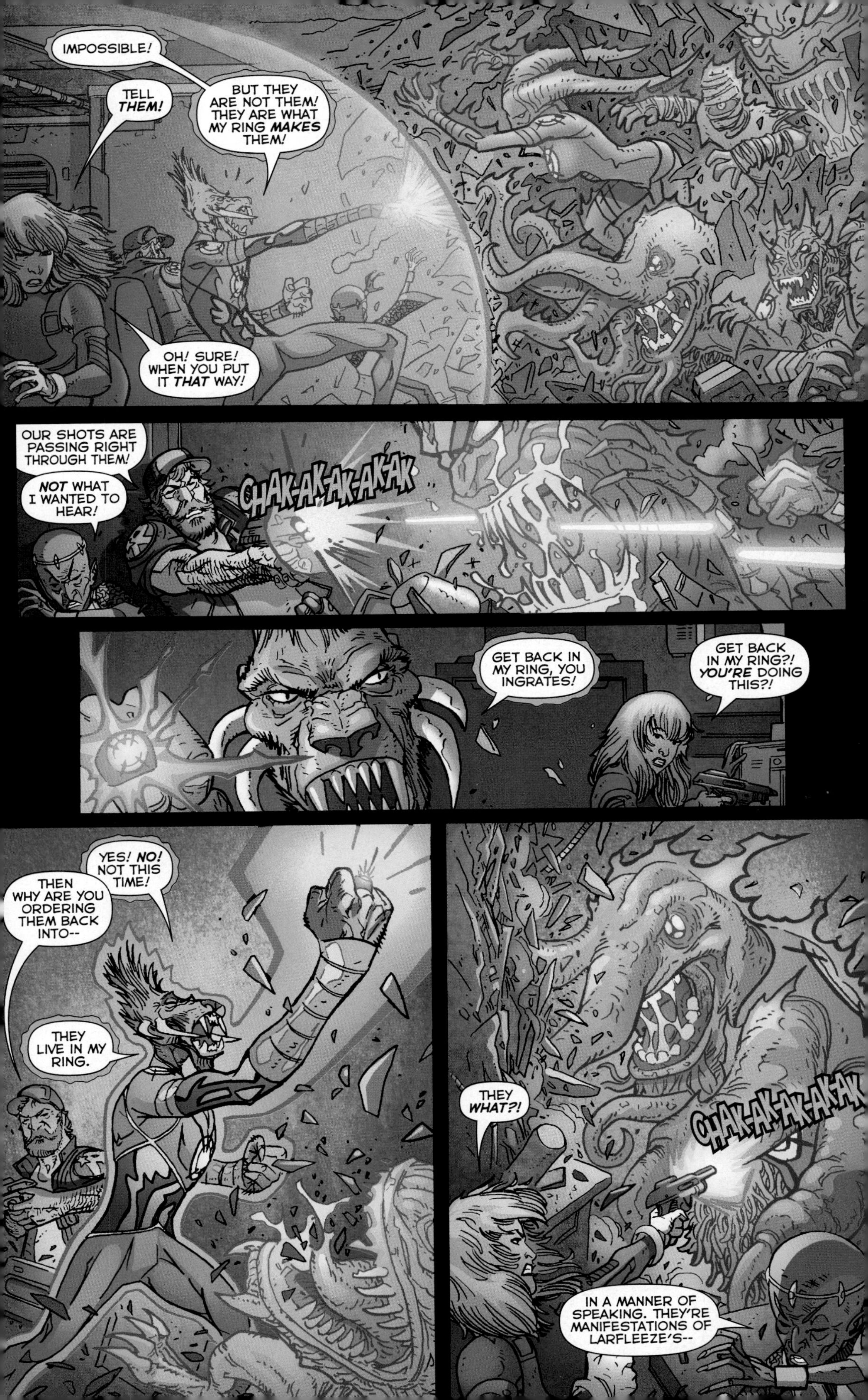

IMPOSSIBLE!
TELL *THEM!*
BUT THEY ARE NOT THEM! THEY ARE WHAT MY RING *MAKES* THEM!
OH! SURE! WHEN YOU PUT IT *THAT* WAY!
OUR SHOTS ARE PASSING RIGHT THROUGH THEM!
NOT WHAT I WANTED TO HEAR!
CHAK-AK-AK-AK-AK
GET BACK IN MY RING, YOU INGRATES!
GET BACK IN MY RING?! *YOU'RE* DOING THIS?!
YES! *NO!* NOT THIS TIME!
THEN WHY ARE YOU ORDERING THEM BACK INTO--
THEY LIVE IN MY RING.
THEY *WHAT?!*
CHAK-AK-AK-AK-AK
IN A MANNER OF SPEAKING. THEY'RE MANIFESTATIONS OF LARFLEEZE'S--

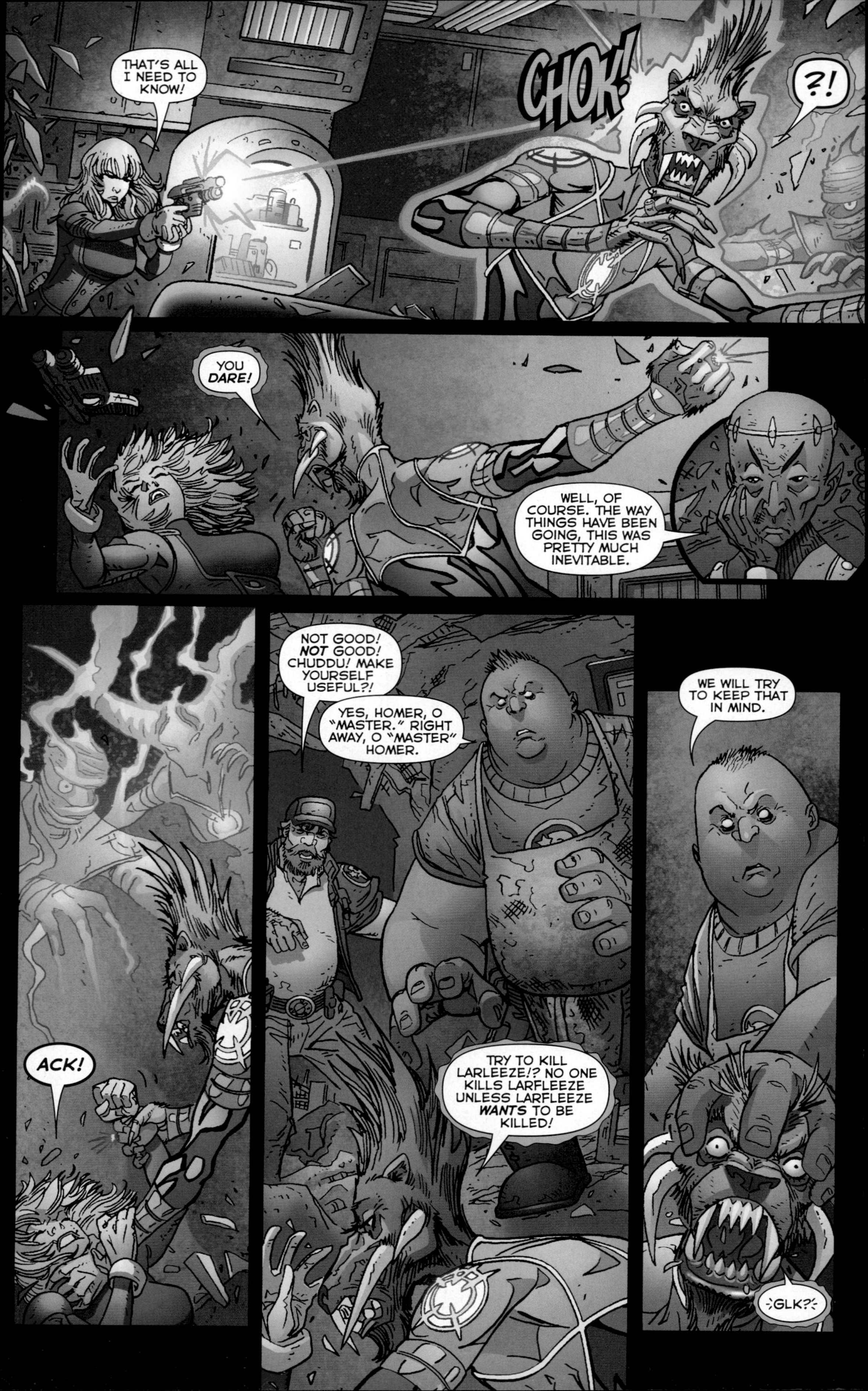

THAT'S ALL I NEED TO KNOW!
CHOK!
?!
YOU DARE!
WELL, OF COURSE. THE WAY THINGS HAVE BEEN GOING, THIS WAS PRETTY MUCH INEVITABLE.
ACK!
NOT GOOD! NOT GOOD! CHUDDU! MAKE YOURSELF USEFUL?!
YES, HOMER, O "MASTER." RIGHT AWAY, O "MASTER" HOMER.
TRY TO KILL LARLEEZE!? NO ONE KILLS LARFLEEZE UNLESS LARFLEEZE WANTS TO BE KILLED!
WE WILL TRY TO KEEP THAT IN MIND.
GLK?

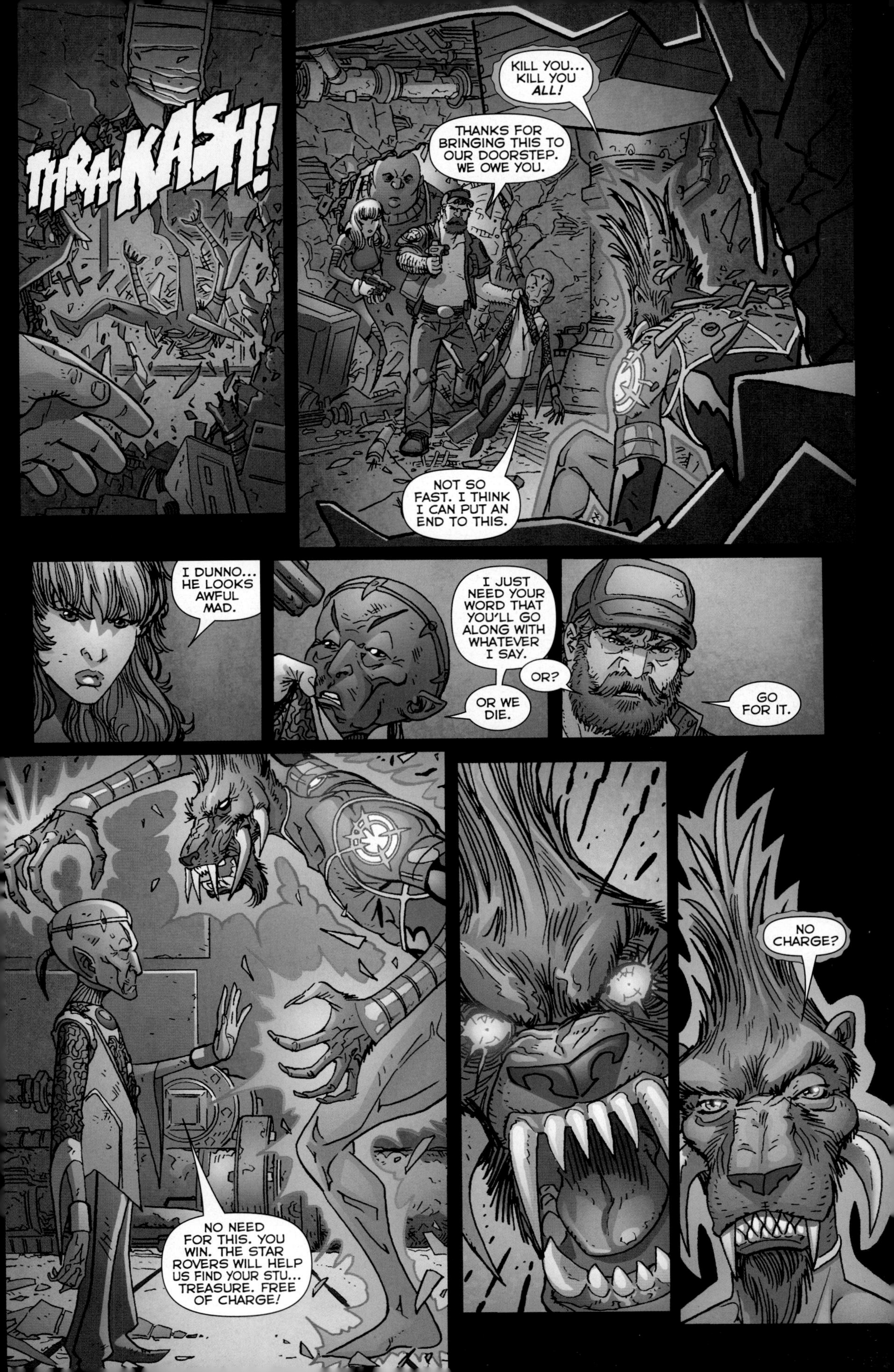
THRA-KASH!
KILL YOU... KILL YOU ALL!
THANKS FOR BRINGING THIS TO OUR DOORSTEP. WE OWE YOU.
NOT SO FAST. I THINK I CAN PUT AN END TO THIS.
I DUNNO... HE LOOKS AWFUL MAD.
I JUST NEED YOUR WORD THAT YOU'LL GO ALONG WITH WHATEVER I SAY.
OR?
OR WE DIE.
GO FOR IT.
NO NEED FOR THIS. YOU WIN. THE STAR ROVERS WILL HELP US FIND YOUR STU... TREASURE. FREE OF CHARGE!
NO CHARGE?

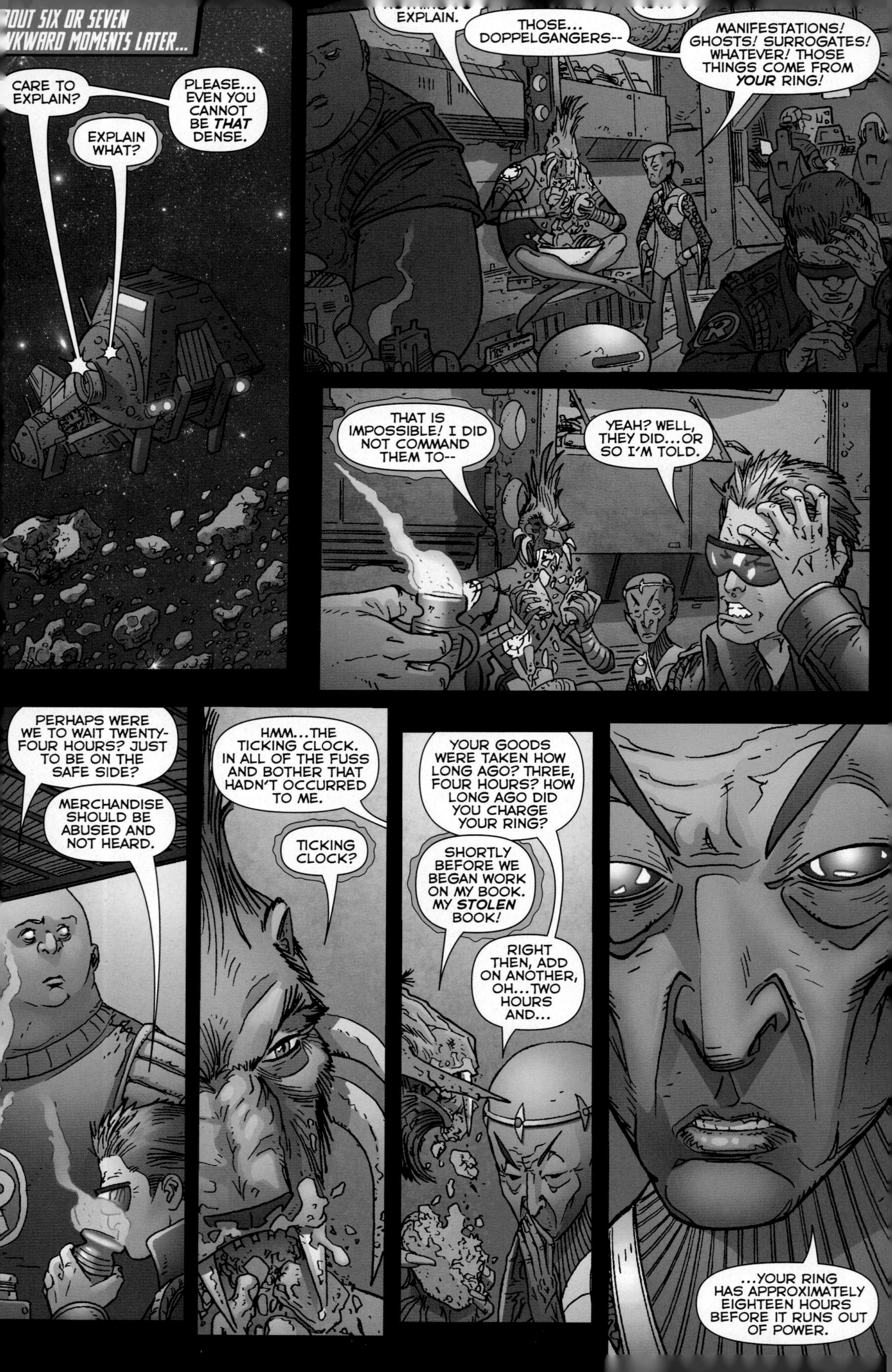
OUT SIX OR SEVEN
WKWARD MOMENTS LATER...
CARE TO EXPLAIN?
PLEASE... EVEN YOU CANNOT BE *THAT* DENSE.
EXPLAIN WHAT?
EXPLAIN.
THOSE... DOPPELGANGERS--
MANIFESTATIONS! GHOSTS! SURROGATES! WHATEVER! THOSE THINGS COME FROM *YOUR* RING!
THAT IS IMPOSSIBLE! I DID NOT COMMAND THEM TO--
YEAH? WELL, THEY DID...OR SO I'M TOLD.
PERHAPS WERE WE TO WAIT TWENTY-FOUR HOURS? JUST TO BE ON THE SAFE SIDE?
MERCHANDISE SHOULD BE ABUSED AND NOT HEARD.
HMM...THE TICKING CLOCK. IN ALL OF THE FUSS AND BOTHER THAT HADN'T OCCURRED TO ME.
TICKING CLOCK?
YOUR GOODS WERE TAKEN HOW LONG AGO? THREE, FOUR HOURS? HOW LONG AGO DID YOU CHARGE YOUR RING?
SHORTLY BEFORE WE BEGAN WORK ON MY BOOK. MY *STOLEN* BOOK!
RIGHT THEN, ADD ON ANOTHER, OH...TWO HOURS AND...
...YOUR RING HAS APPROXIMATELY EIGHTEEN HOURS BEFORE IT RUNS OUT OF POWER.

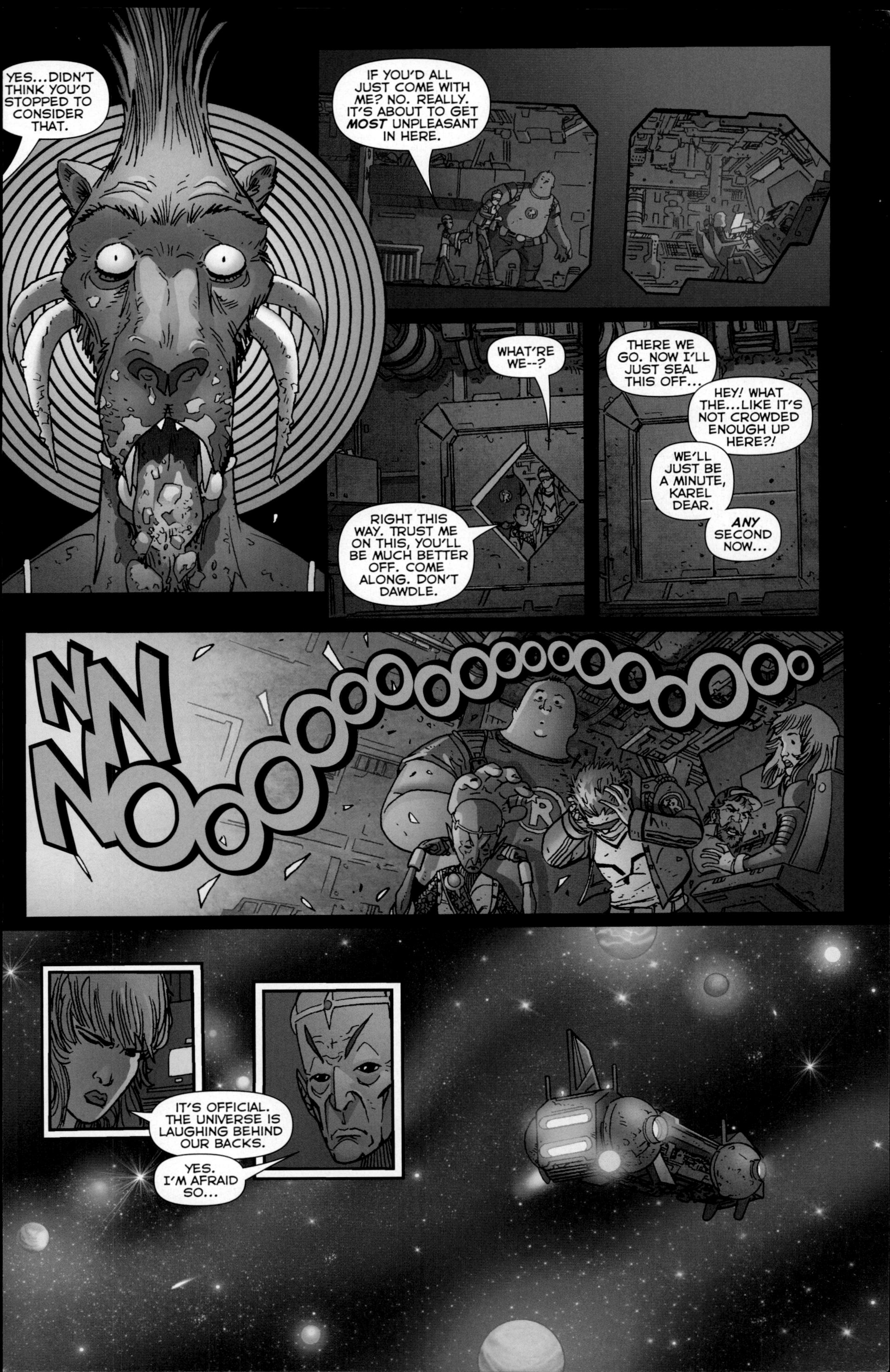

YES...DIDN'T THINK YOU'D STOPPED TO CONSIDER THAT.
IF YOU'D ALL JUST COME WITH ME? NO. REALLY. IT'S ABOUT TO GET MOST UNPLEASANT IN HERE.
WHAT'RE WE--?
RIGHT THIS WAY. TRUST ME ON THIS, YOU'LL BE MUCH BETTER OFF. COME ALONG. DON'T DAWDLE.
THERE WE GO. NOW I'LL JUST SEAL THIS OFF...
HEY! WHAT THE...LIKE IT'S NOT CROWDED ENOUGH UP HERE?!
WE'LL JUST BE A MINUTE, KAREL DEAR.
ANY SECOND NOW...
NNNOOOOOOOOOOOOOOOOOOOOOO
IT'S OFFICIAL. THE UNIVERSE IS LAUGHING BEHIND OUR BACKS.
YES. I'M AFRAID SO...

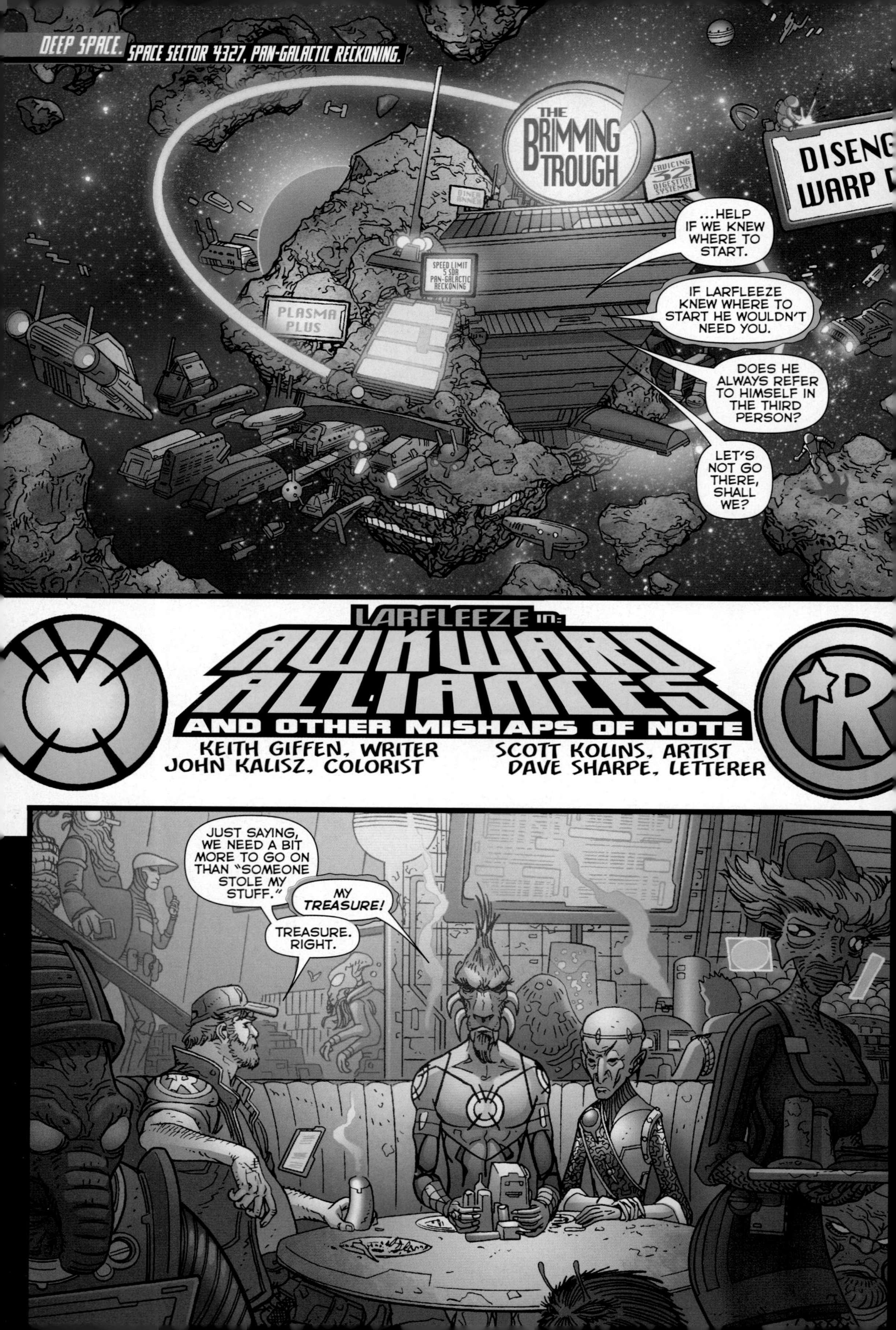
DEEP SPACE.
SPACE SECTOR 4327, PAN-GALACTIC RECKONING.
THE BRIMMING TROUGH
SPEED LIMIT 5 SDR PAN-GALACTIC RECKONING
PLASMA PLUS
DISENG
WARP
...HELP IF WE KNEW WHERE TO START.
IF LARFLEEZE KNEW WHERE TO START HE WOULDN'T NEED YOU.
DOES HE ALWAYS REFER TO HIMSELF IN THE THIRD PERSON?
LET'S NOT GO THERE, SHALL WE?
LARFLEEZE IN:
AWKWARD ALLIANCES
AND OTHER MISHAPS OF NOTE
KEITH GIFFEN, WRITER
JOHN KALISZ, COLORIST
SCOTT KOLINS, ARTIST
DAVE SHARPE, LETTERER
JUST SAYING, WE NEED A BIT MORE TO GO ON THAN "SOMEONE STOLE MY STUFF."
MY *TREASURE!*
TREASURE. RIGHT.

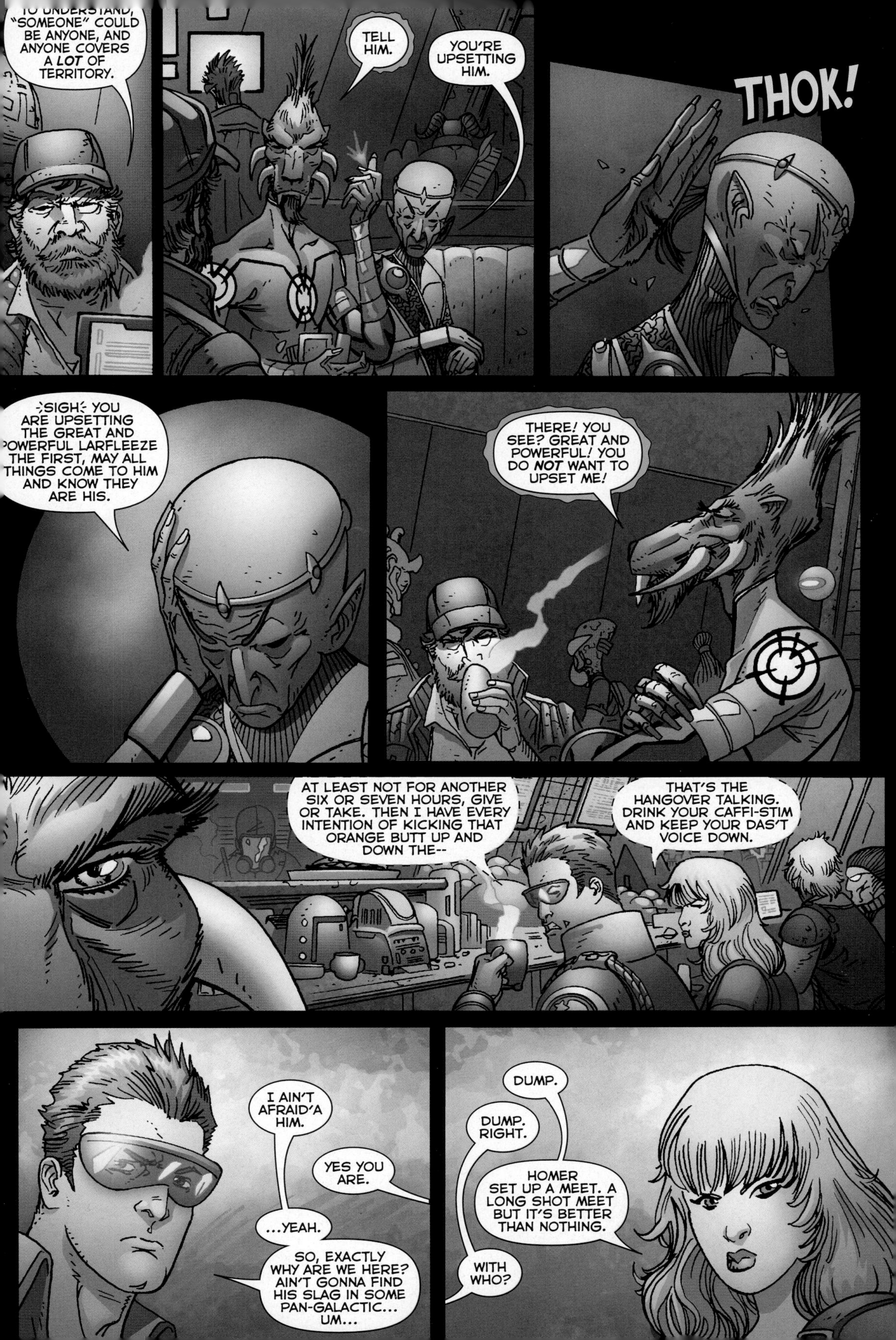
TO UNDERSTAND, "SOMEONE" COULD BE ANYONE, AND ANYONE COVERS A *LOT* OF TERRITORY.
TELL HIM.
YOU'RE UPSETTING HIM.
THOK!
-SIGH- YOU ARE UPSETTING THE GREAT AND POWERFUL LARFLEEZE THE FIRST, MAY ALL THINGS COME TO HIM AND KNOW THEY ARE HIS.
THERE! YOU SEE? GREAT AND POWERFUL! YOU DO *NOT* WANT TO UPSET ME!
AT LEAST NOT FOR ANOTHER SIX OR SEVEN HOURS, GIVE OR TAKE. THEN I HAVE EVERY INTENTION OF KICKING THAT ORANGE BUTT UP AND DOWN THE--
THAT'S THE HANGOVER TALKING. DRINK YOUR CAFFI-STIM AND KEEP YOUR DAS'T VOICE DOWN.
I AIN'T AFRAID'A HIM.
YES YOU ARE.
...YEAH.
SO, EXACTLY WHY ARE WE HERE? AIN'T GONNA FIND HIS SLAG IN SOME PAN-GALACTIC... UM...
DUMP.
DUMP. RIGHT.
HOMER SET UP A MEET. A LONG SHOT MEET BUT IT'S BETTER THAN NOTHING.
WITH WHO?

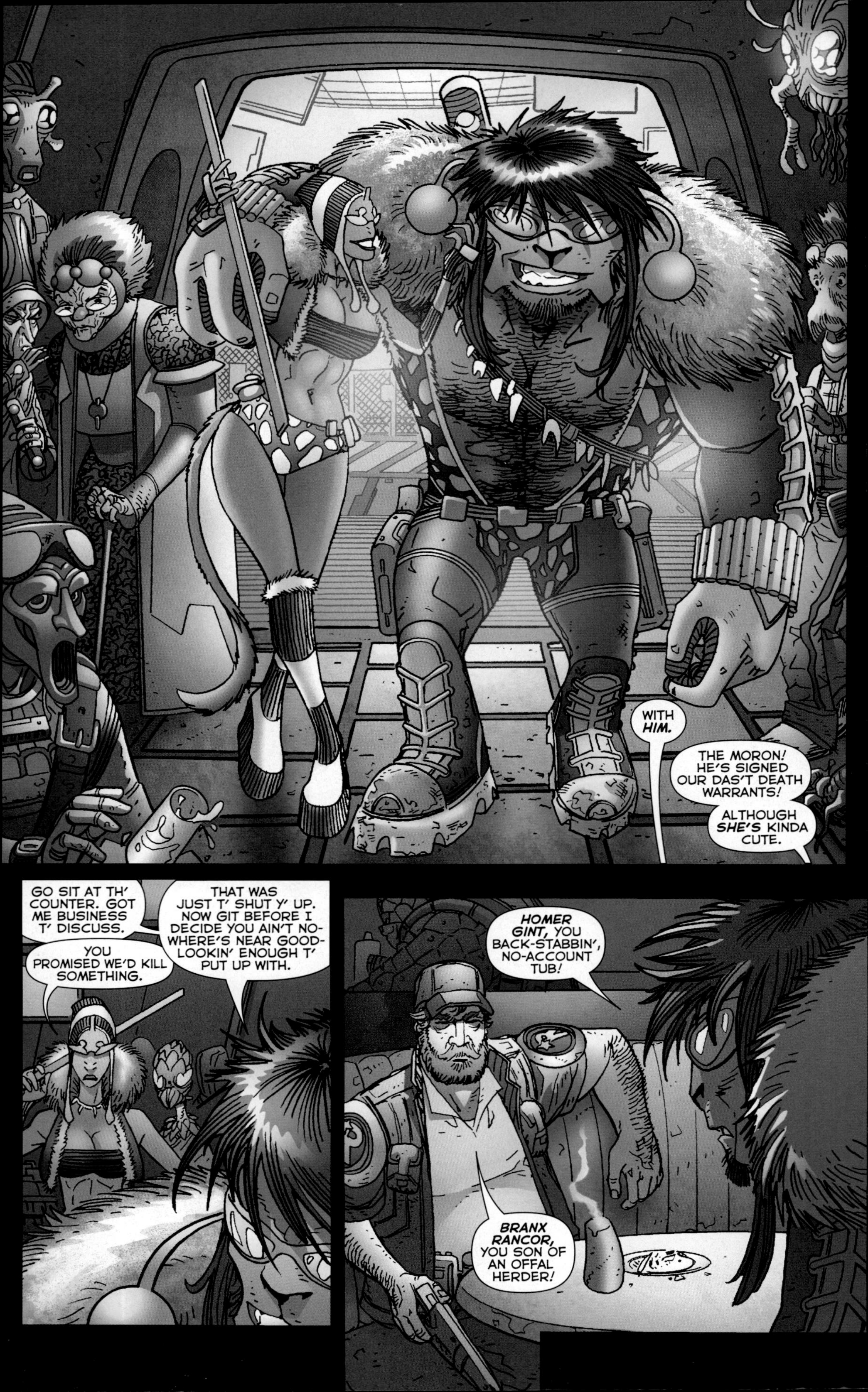
WITH HIM.
THE MORON! HE'S SIGNED OUR DAS'T DEATH WARRANTS!
ALTHOUGH SHE'S KINDA CUTE.
GO SIT AT TH' COUNTER. GOT ME BUSINESS T' DISCUSS.
YOU PROMISED WE'D KILL SOMETHING.
THAT WAS JUST T' SHUT Y' UP. NOW GIT BEFORE I DECIDE YOU AIN'T NO-WHERE'S NEAR GOOD-LOOKIN' ENOUGH T' PUT UP WITH.
HOMER GINT, YOU BACK-STABBIN', NO-ACCOUNT TUB!
BRANX RANCOR, YOU SON OF AN OFFAL HERDER!

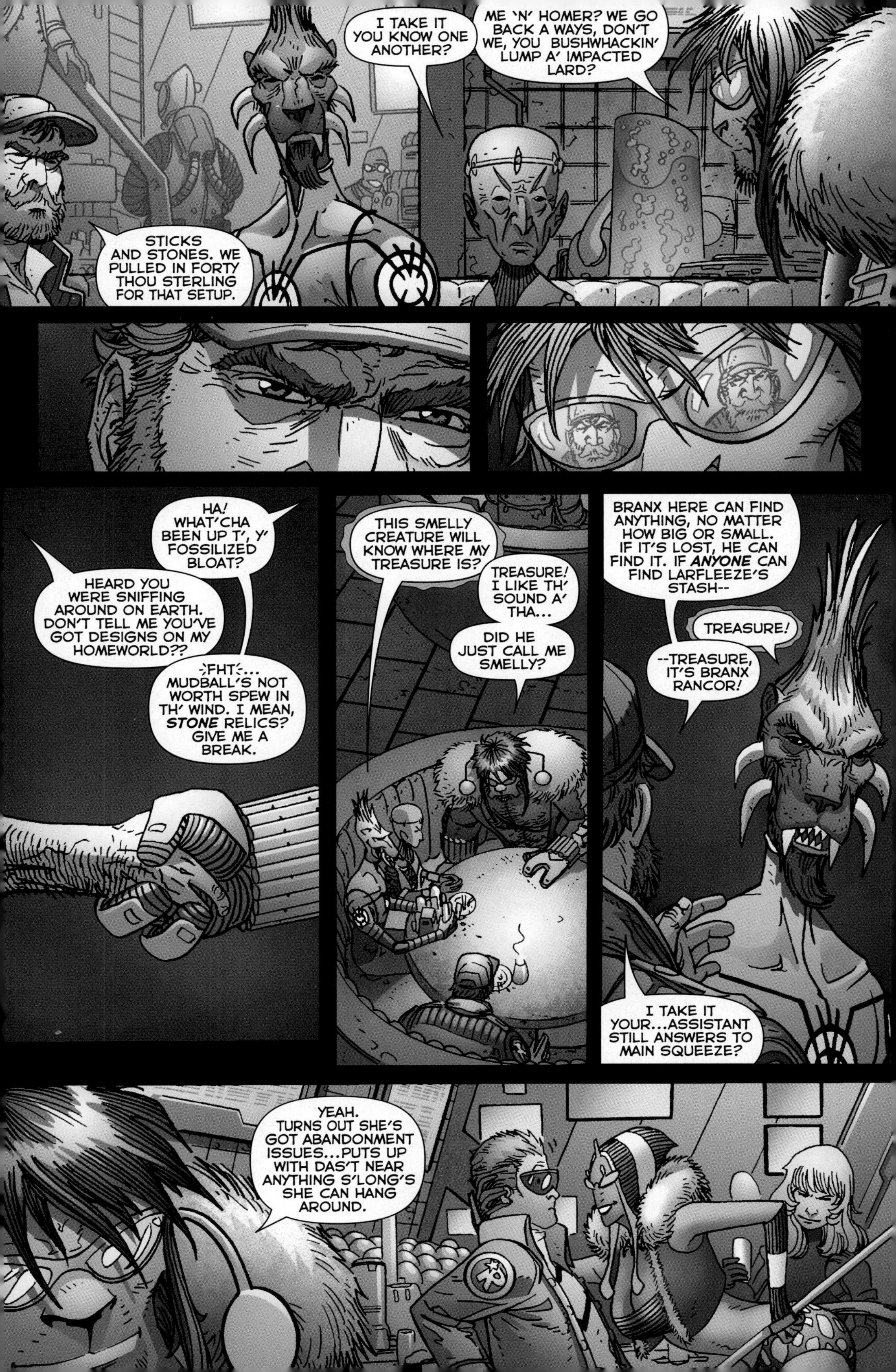
I TAKE IT YOU KNOW ONE ANOTHER?
ME 'N' HOMER? WE GO BACK A WAYS, DON'T WE, YOU BUSHWHACKIN' LUMP A' IMPACTED LARD?
STICKS AND STONES. WE PULLED IN FORTY THOU STERLING FOR THAT SETUP.
HA! WHAT'CHA BEEN UP T', Y' FOSSILIZED BLOAT?
HEARD YOU WERE SNIFFING AROUND ON EARTH. DON'T TELL ME YOU'VE GOT DESIGNS ON MY HOMEWORLD??
-FHT-... MUDBALL'S NOT WORTH SPEW IN TH' WIND. I MEAN, *STONE* RELICS? GIVE ME A BREAK.
THIS SMELLY CREATURE WILL KNOW WHERE MY TREASURE IS?
TREASURE! I LIKE TH' SOUND A' THA...
DID HE JUST CALL ME SMELLY?
BRANX HERE CAN FIND ANYTHING, NO MATTER HOW BIG OR SMALL. IF IT'S LOST, HE CAN FIND IT. IF *ANYONE* CAN FIND LARFLEEZE'S STASH--
TREASURE!
--TREASURE, IT'S BRANX RANCOR!
I TAKE IT YOUR...ASSISTANT STILL ANSWERS TO MAIN SQUEEZE?
YEAH. TURNS OUT SHE'S GOT ABANDONMENT ISSUES...PUTS UP WITH DAS'T NEAR ANYTHING S'LONG'S SHE CAN HANG AROUND.

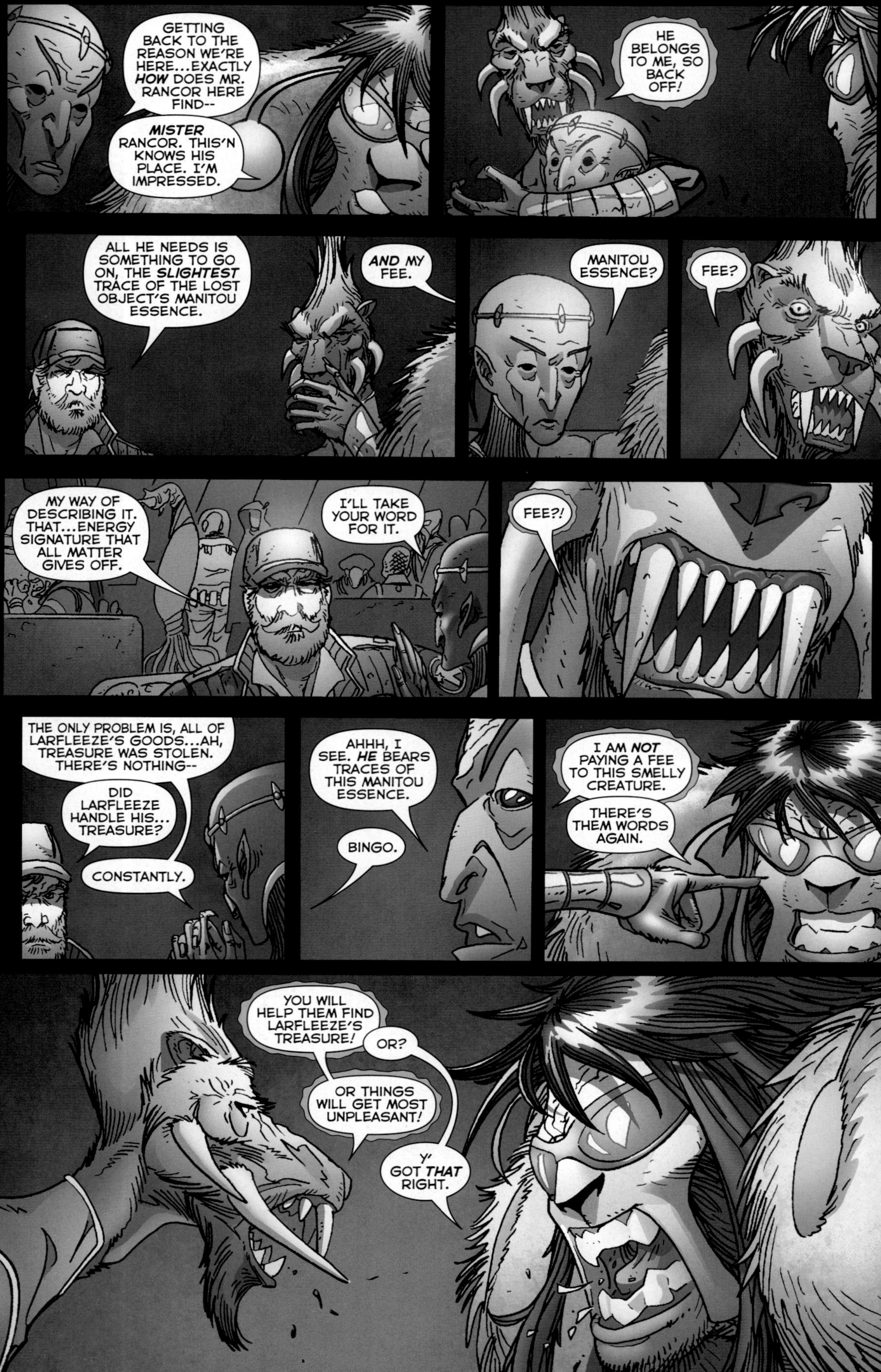
GETTING BACK TO THE REASON WE'RE HERE...EXACTLY *HOW* DOES MR. RANCOR HERE FIND--
MISTER RANCOR. THIS'N KNOWS HIS PLACE. I'M IMPRESSED.
HE BELONGS TO ME, SO BACK OFF!
ALL HE NEEDS IS SOMETHING TO GO ON, THE *SLIGHTEST* TRACE OF THE LOST OBJECT'S MANITOU ESSENCE.
AND MY FEE.
MANITOU ESSENCE?
FEE?
MY WAY OF DESCRIBING IT. THAT...ENERGY SIGNATURE THAT ALL MATTER GIVES OFF.
I'LL TAKE YOUR WORD FOR IT.
FEE?!
THE ONLY PROBLEM IS, ALL OF LARFLEEZE'S GOODS...AH, TREASURE WAS STOLEN. THERE'S NOTHING--
DID LARFLEEZE HANDLE HIS... TREASURE?
CONSTANTLY.
AHHH, I SEE. *HE* BEARS TRACES OF THIS MANITOU ESSENCE.
BINGO.
I AM *NOT* PAYING A FEE TO THIS SMELLY CREATURE.
THERE'S THEM WORDS AGAIN.
YOU WILL HELP THEM FIND LARFLEEZE'S TREASURE!
OR?
OR THINGS WILL GET MOST UNPLEASANT!
Y' GOT *THAT* RIGHT.

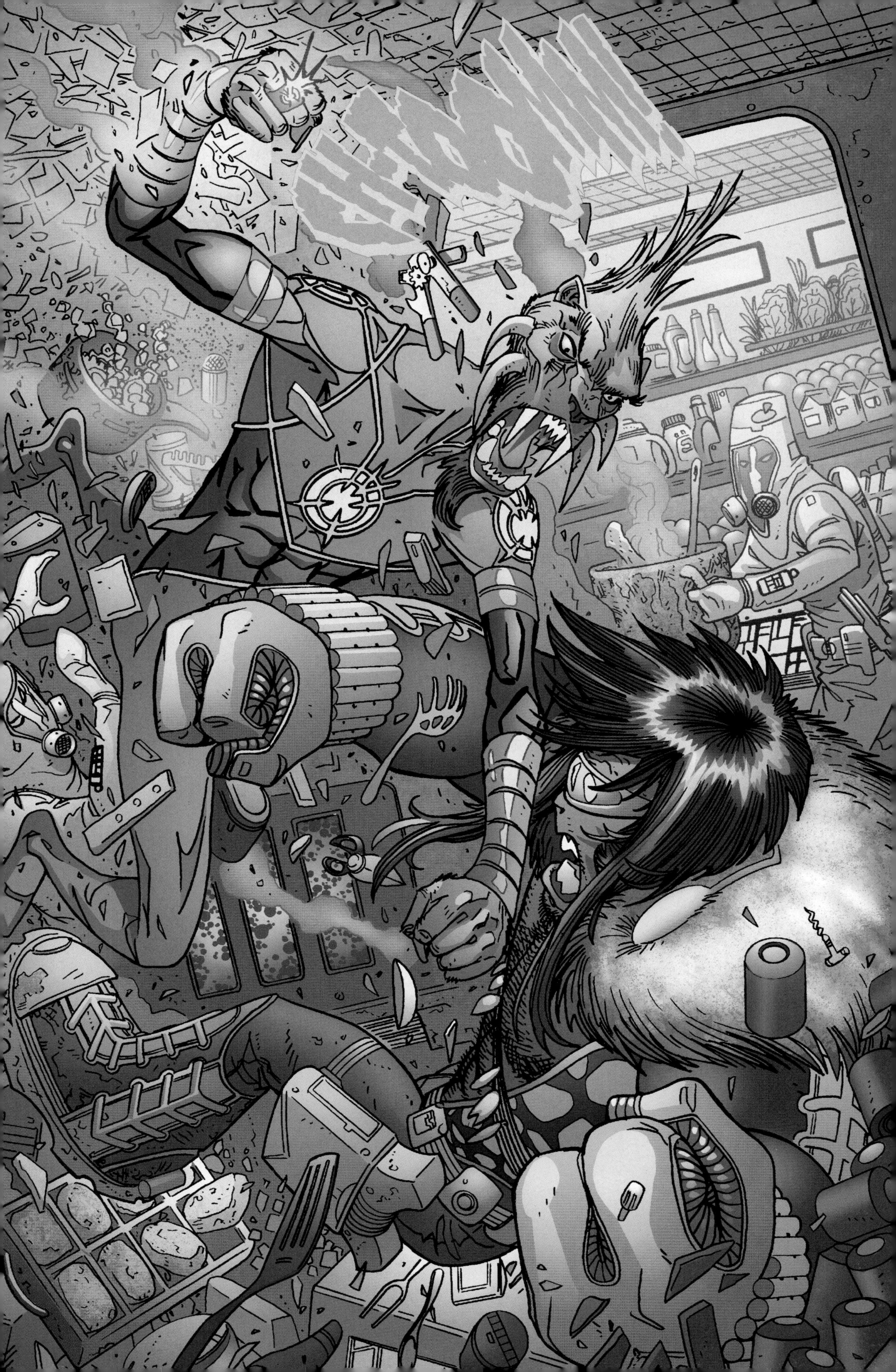

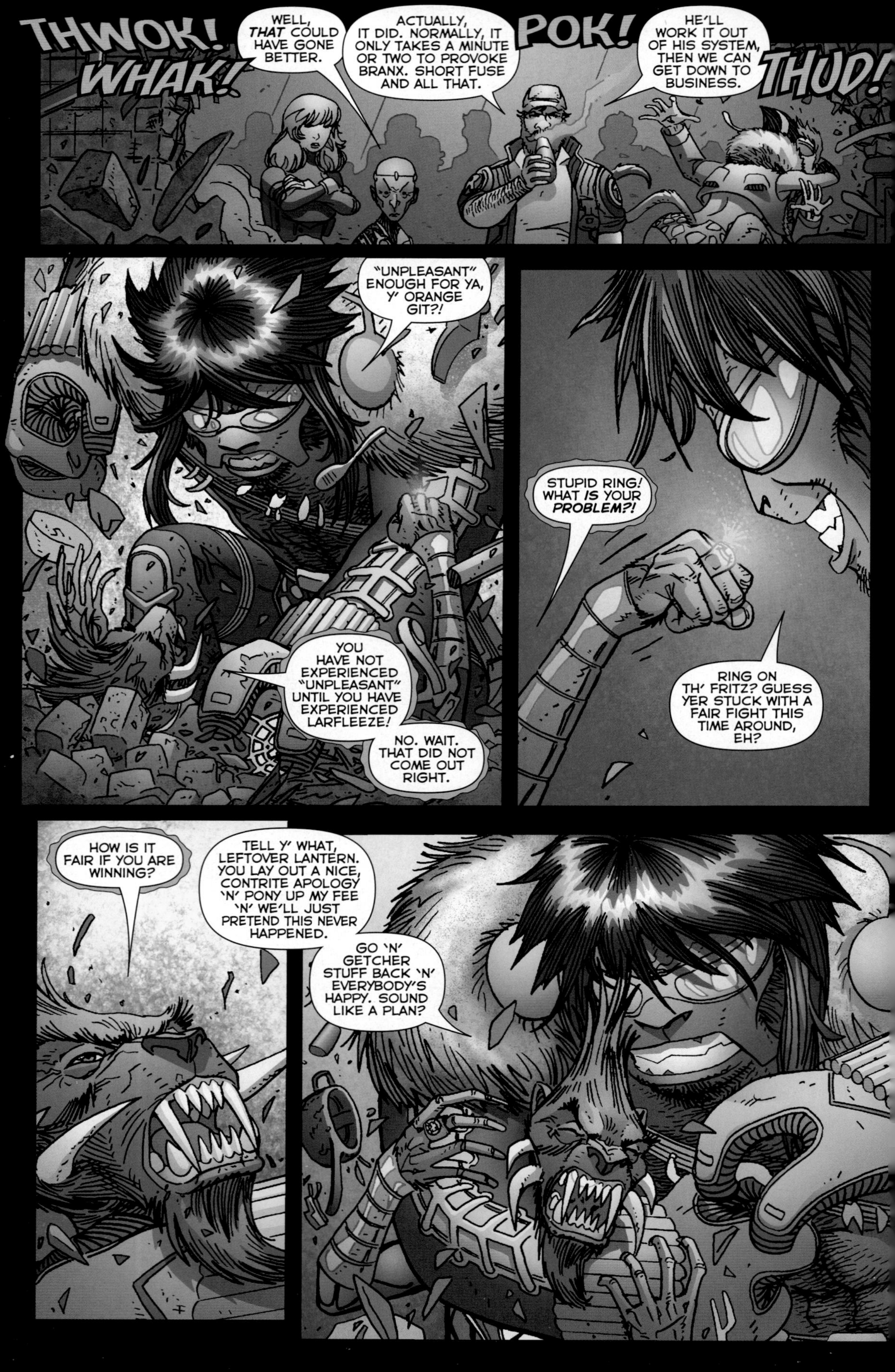
THWOK!
WHAK!
WELL, THAT COULD HAVE GONE BETTER.
ACTUALLY, IT DID. NORMALLY, IT ONLY TAKES A MINUTE OR TWO TO PROVOKE BRANX. SHORT FUSE AND ALL THAT.
POK!
HE'LL WORK IT OUT OF HIS SYSTEM, THEN WE CAN GET DOWN TO BUSINESS.
THUD!
"UNPLEASANT" ENOUGH FOR YA, Y' ORANGE GIT?!
YOU HAVE NOT EXPERIENCED "UNPLEASANT" UNTIL YOU HAVE EXPERIENCED LARFLEEZE!
NO. WAIT. THAT DID NOT COME OUT RIGHT.
STUPID RING! WHAT IS YOUR PROBLEM?!
RING ON TH' FRITZ? GUESS YER STUCK WITH A FAIR FIGHT THIS TIME AROUND, EH?
HOW IS IT FAIR IF YOU ARE WINNING?
TELL Y' WHAT, LEFTOVER LANTERN. YOU LAY OUT A NICE, CONTRITE APOLOGY 'N' PONY UP MY FEE 'N' WE'LL JUST PRETEND THIS NEVER HAPPENED.
GO 'N' GETCHER STUFF BACK 'N' EVERYBODY'S HAPPY. SOUND LIKE A PLAN?

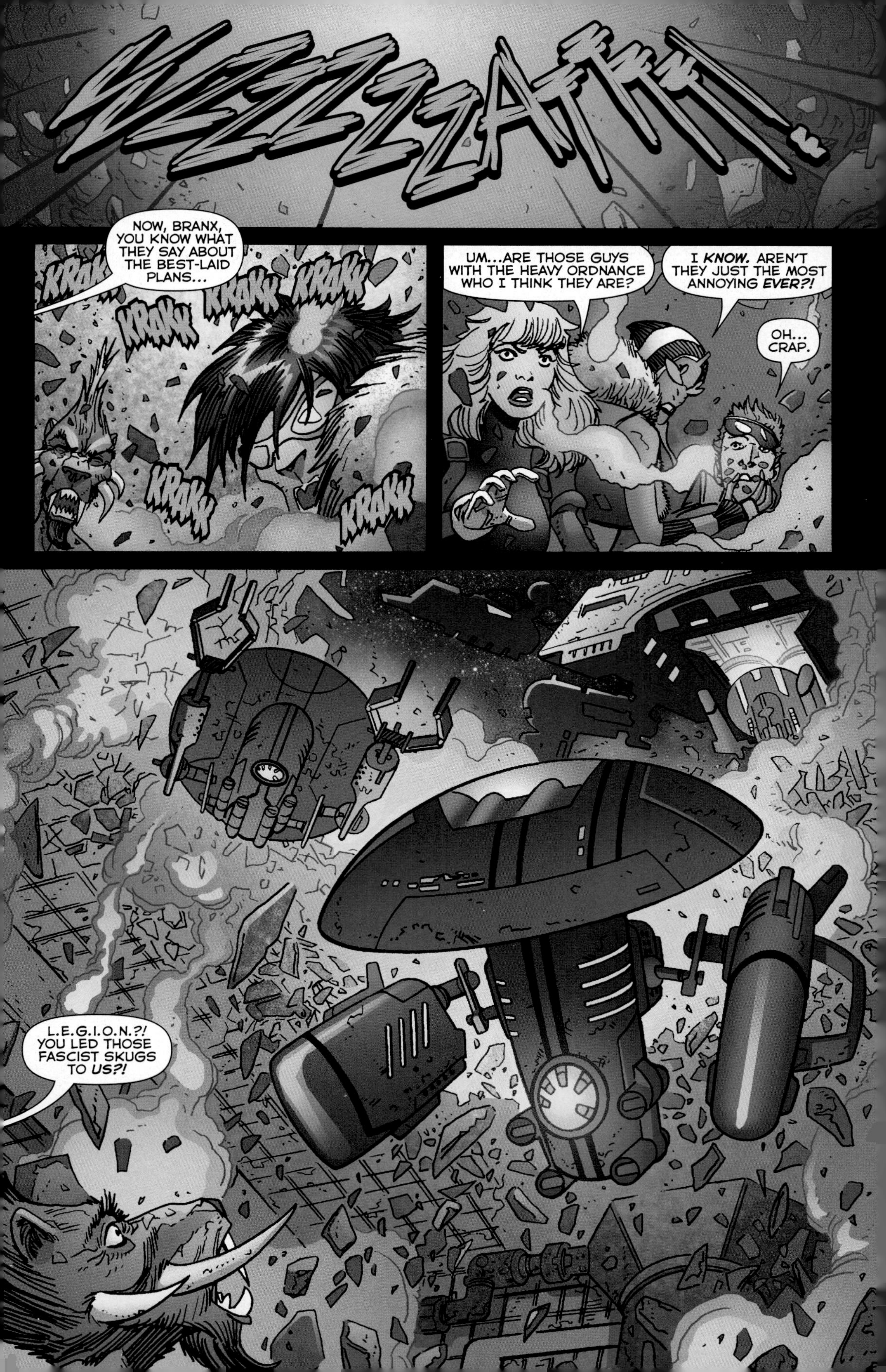
VZZZZZAAATTT!!
NOW, BRANX, YOU KNOW WHAT THEY SAY ABOUT THE BEST-LAID PLANS...
KRAKK KRAKK KRAKK KRAKK KRAKK KRAKK
UM...ARE THOSE GUYS WITH THE HEAVY ORDNANCE WHO I THINK THEY ARE?
I KNOW. AREN'T THEY JUST THE MOST ANNOYING EVER?!
OH... CRAP.
L.E.G.I.O.N.?! YOU LED THOSE FASCIST SKUGS TO US?!

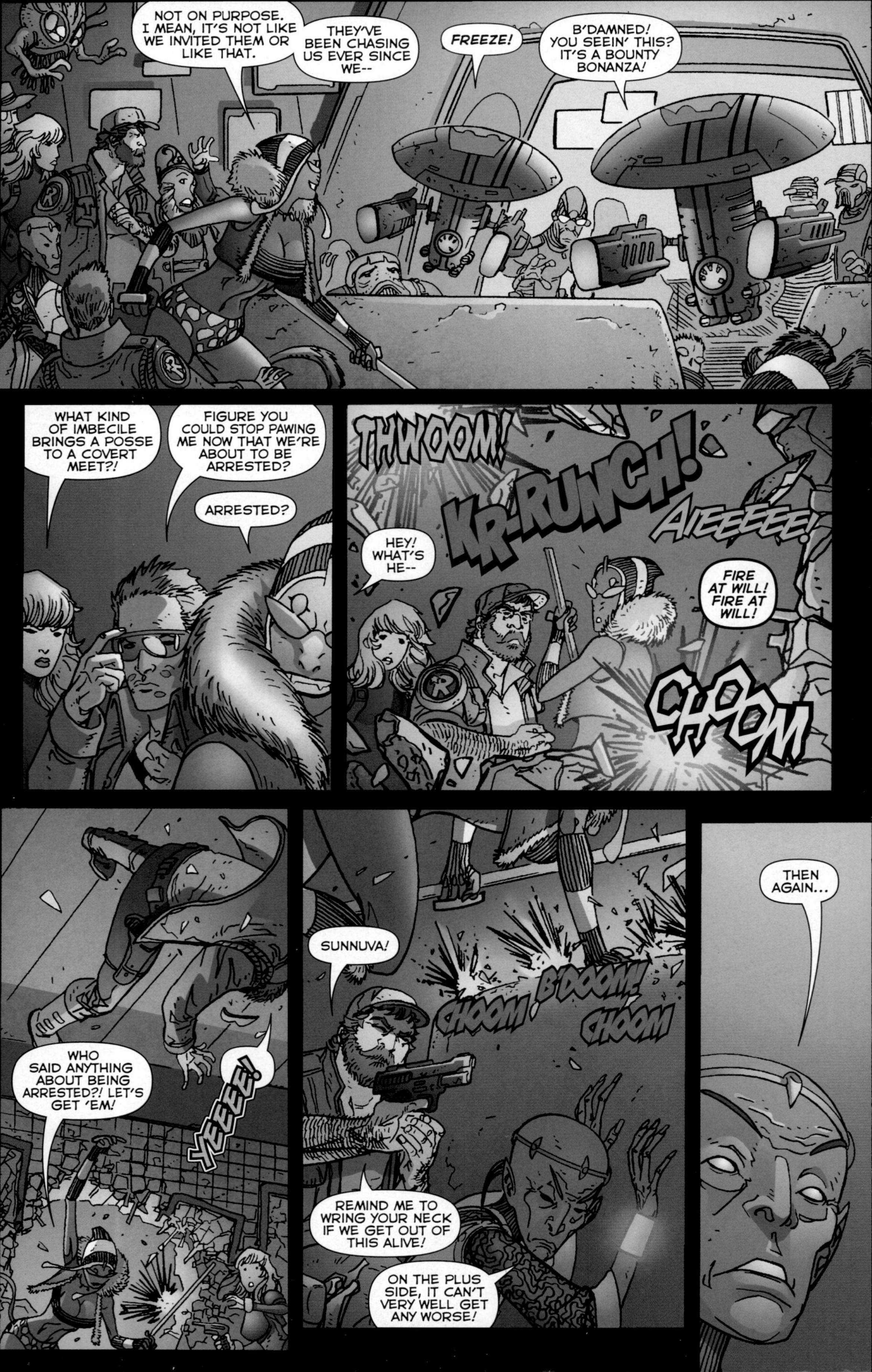
NOT ON PURPOSE. I MEAN, IT'S NOT LIKE WE INVITED THEM OR LIKE THAT.
THEY'VE BEEN CHASING US EVER SINCE WE--
FREEZE!
B'DAMNED! YOU SEEIN' THIS? IT'S A BOUNTY BONANZA!
WHAT KIND OF IMBECILE BRINGS A POSSE TO A COVERT MEET?!
FIGURE YOU COULD STOP PAWING ME NOW THAT WE'RE ABOUT TO BE ARRESTED?
ARRESTED?
THWOOM!
KR-RUNCH!
AIEEEEEE!
HEY! WHAT'S HE--
FIRE AT WILL! FIRE AT WILL!
CHOOM
WHO SAID ANYTHING ABOUT BEING ARRESTED?! LET'S GET 'EM!
YEEEEE!
SUNNUVA!
CHOOM
B'DOOM!
CHOOM
REMIND ME TO WRING YOUR NECK IF WE GET OUT OF THIS ALIVE!
ON THE PLUS SIDE, IT CAN'T VERY WELL GET ANY WORSE!
THEN AGAIN...

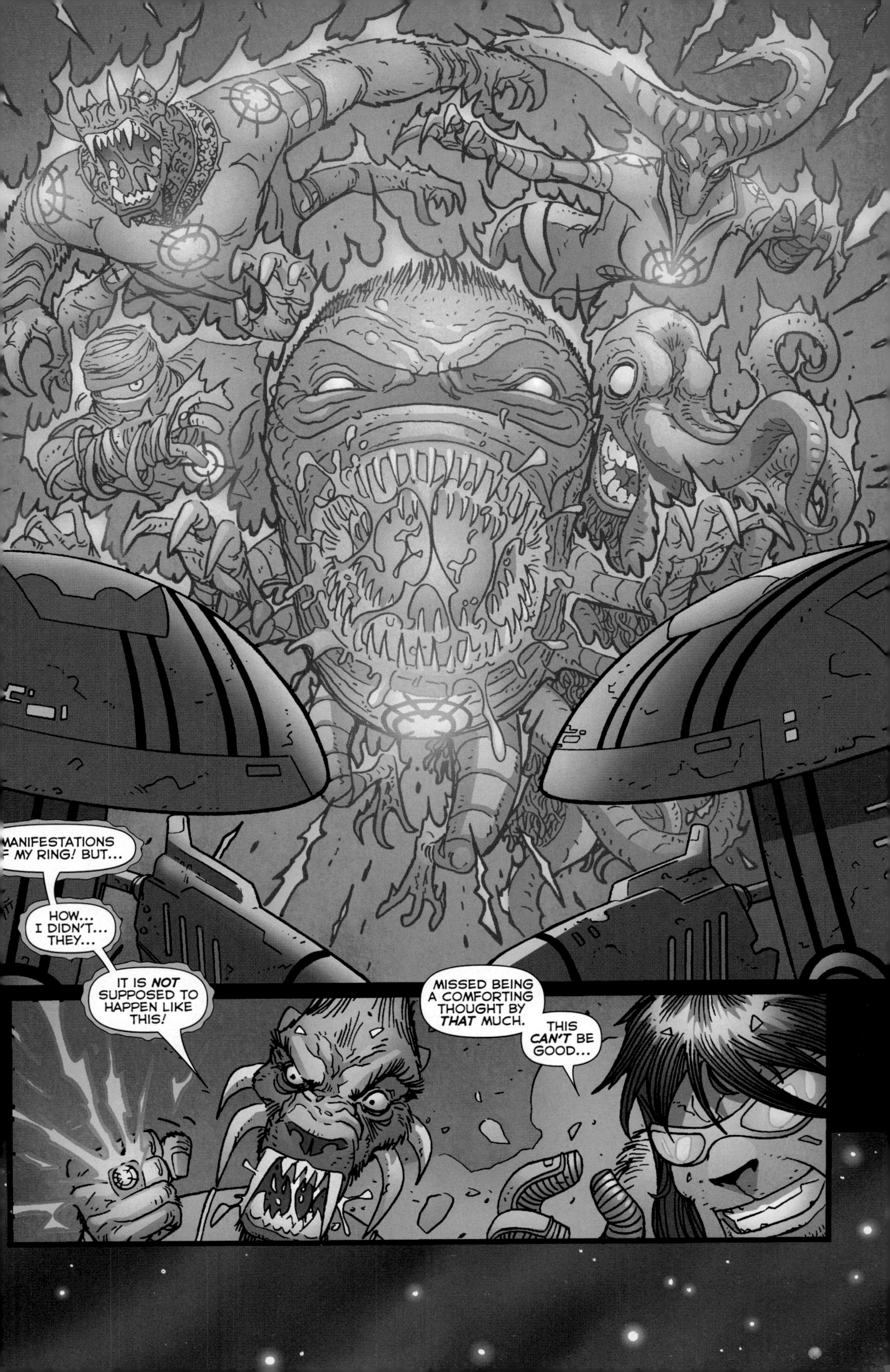
MANIFESTATIONS
F MY RING! BUT...
HOW...
I DIDN'T...
THEY...
IT IS NOT
SUPPOSED TO
HAPPEN LIKE
THIS!
MISSED BEING
A COMFORTING
THOUGHT BY
THAT MUCH.
THIS
CAN'T BE
GOOD...

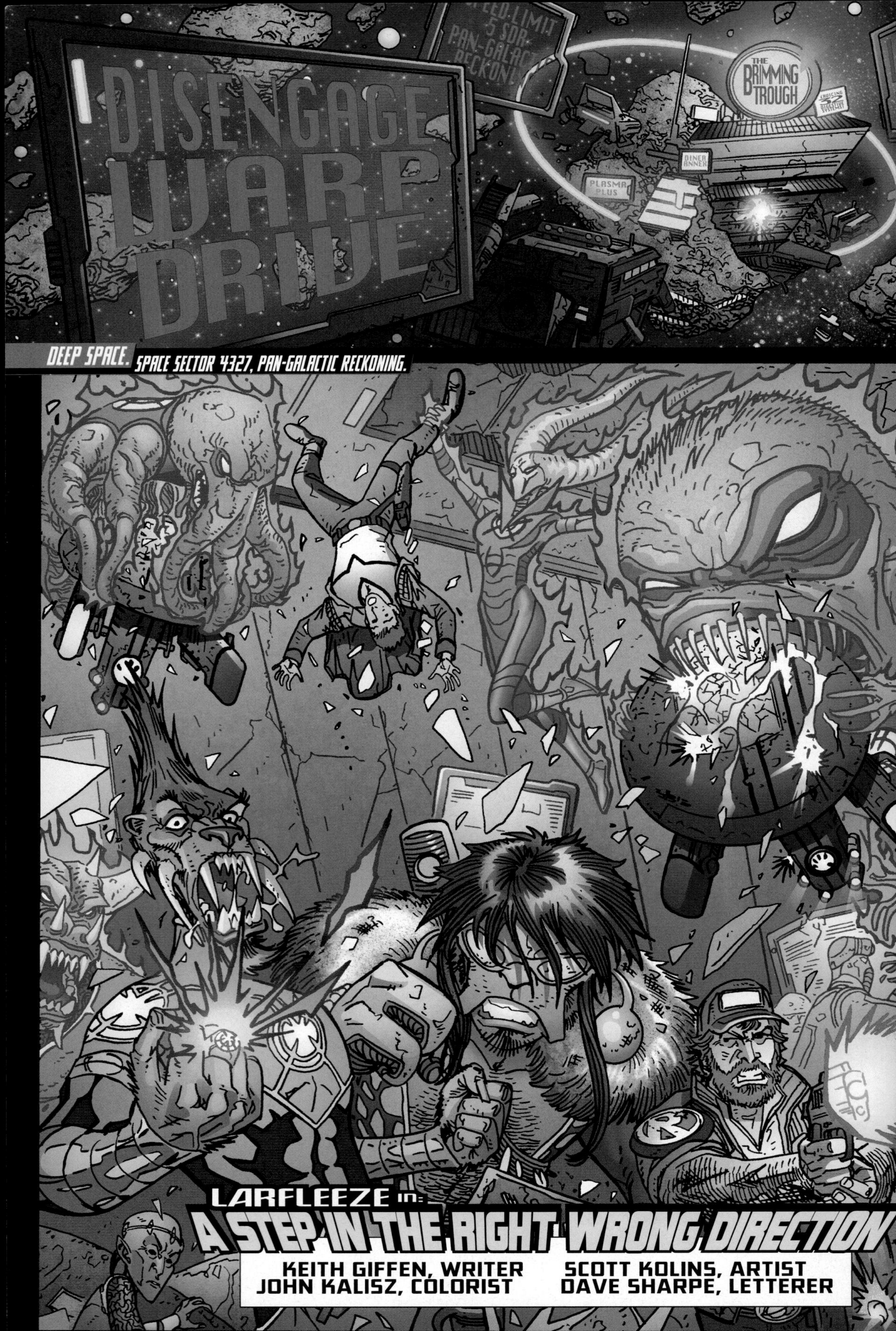

DISENGAGE WARP DRIVE
SPEED LIMIT 5 SDR PAN-GALACTIC RECKONING
THE BRIMMING TROUGH
DINER ANNEX
PLASMA PLUS
DEEP SPACE.
SPACE SECTOR 4327, PAN-GALACTIC RECKONING.
LARFLEEZE IN:
A STEP IN THE RIGHT WRONG DIRECTION
KEITH GIFFEN, WRITER
SCOTT KOLINS, ARTIST
JOHN KALISZ, COLORIST
DAVE SHARPE, LETTERER

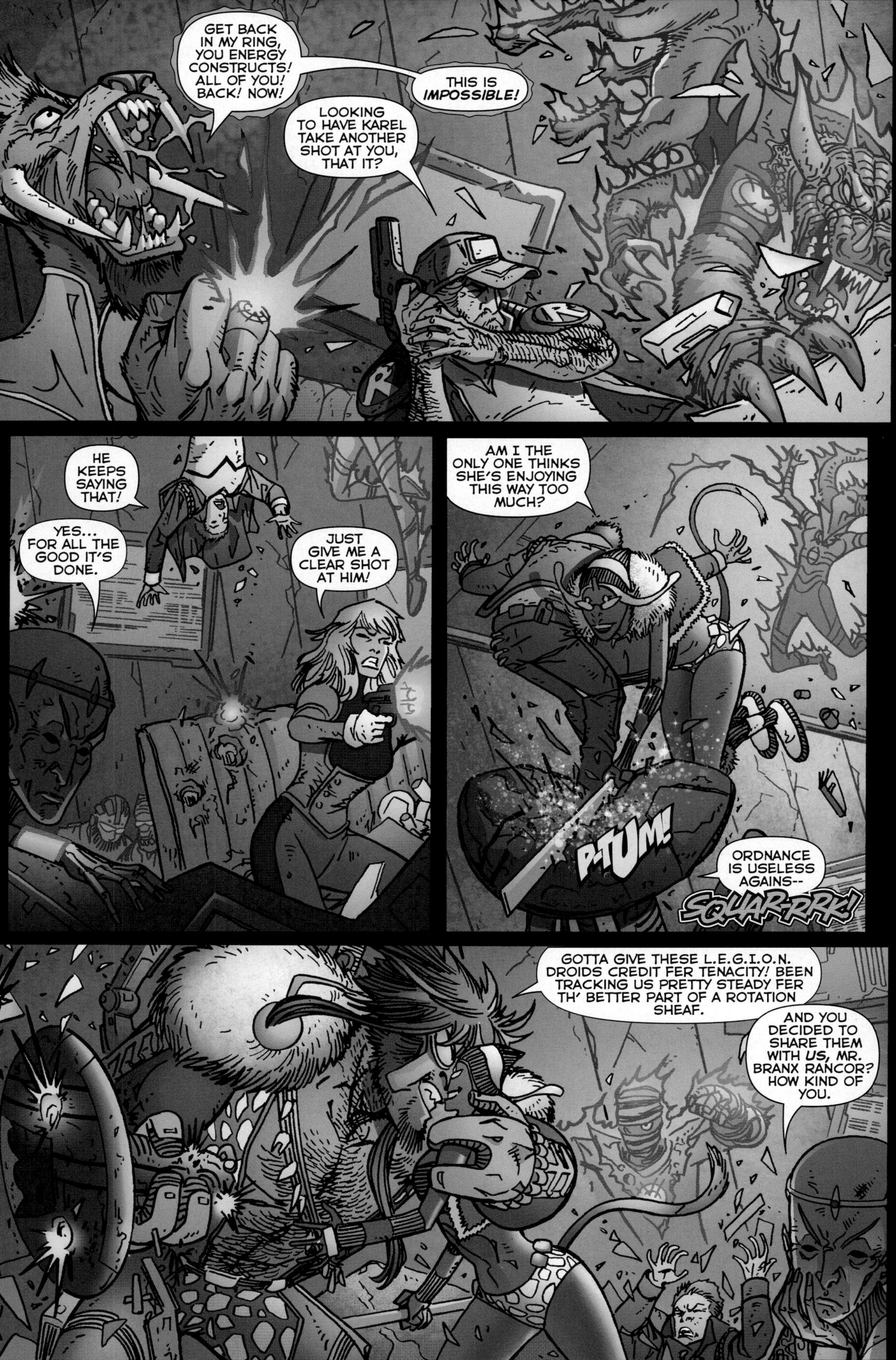
GET BACK IN MY RING, YOU ENERGY CONSTRUCTS! ALL OF YOU! BACK! NOW!
THIS IS IMPOSSIBLE!
LOOKING TO HAVE KAREL TAKE ANOTHER SHOT AT YOU, THAT IT?
HE KEEPS SAYING THAT!
YES... FOR ALL THE GOOD IT'S DONE.
JUST GIVE ME A CLEAR SHOT AT HIM!
AM I THE ONLY ONE THINKS SHE'S ENJOYING THIS WAY TOO MUCH?
P-TUM!
ORDNANCE IS USELESS AGAINS--
SQUAR-RRK!
GOTTA GIVE THESE L.E.G.I.O.N. DROIDS CREDIT FER TENACITY! BEEN TRACKING US PRETTY STEADY FER TH' BETTER PART OF A ROTATION SHEAF.
AND YOU DECIDED TO SHARE THEM WITH US, MR. BRANX RANCOR? HOW KIND OF YOU.

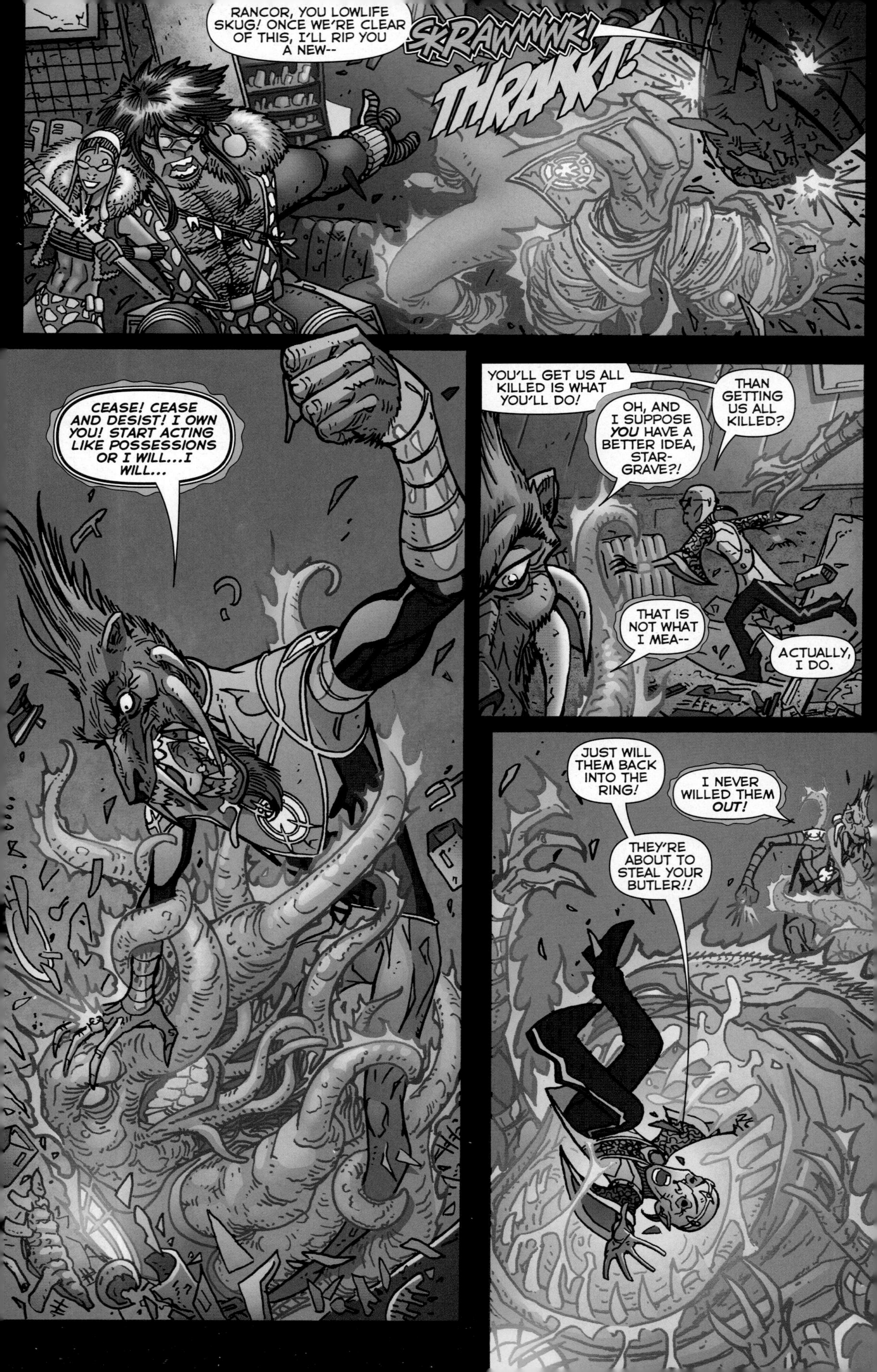
RANCOR, YOU LOWLIFE SKUG! ONCE WE'RE CLEAR OF THIS, I'LL RIP YOU A NEW--
SKRAWWWK!
THRAKT!
CEASE! CEASE AND DESIST! I OWN YOU! START ACTING LIKE POSSESSIONS OR I WILL...I WILL...
YOU'LL GET US ALL KILLED IS WHAT YOU'LL DO!
OH, AND I SUPPOSE YOU HAVE A BETTER IDEA, STAR-GRAVE?!
THAN GETTING US ALL KILLED?
THAT IS NOT WHAT I MEA--
ACTUALLY, I DO.
JUST WILL THEM BACK INTO THE RING!
I NEVER WILLED THEM OUT!
THEY'RE ABOUT TO STEAL YOUR BUTLER!!

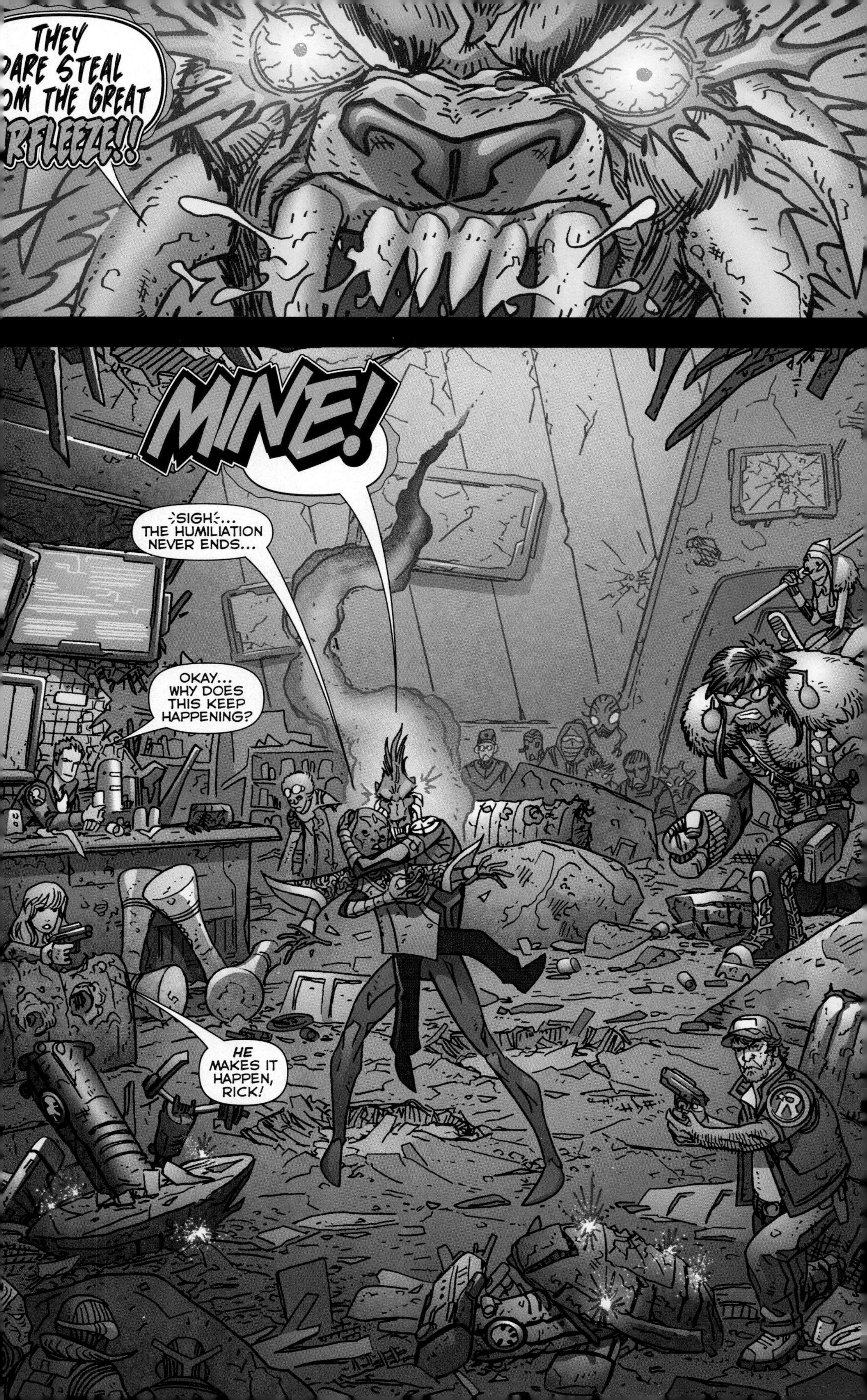
THEY DARE STEAL
OM THE GREAT
RFLEEZE!!
MINE!
SIGH... THE HUMILIATION NEVER ENDS...
OKAY... WHY DOES THIS KEEP HAPPENING?
HE MAKES IT HAPPEN, RICK!

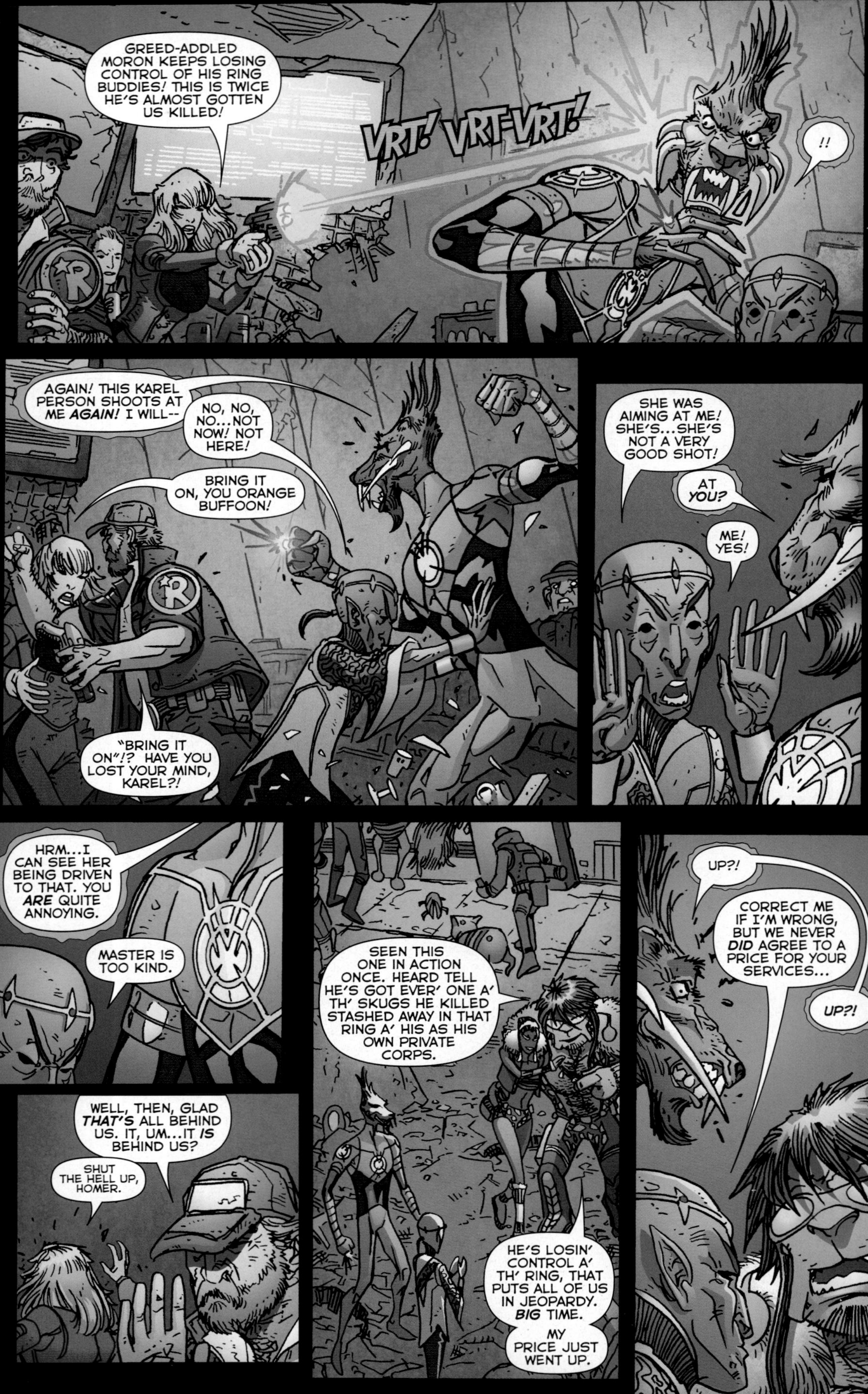
GREED-ADDLED MORON KEEPS LOSING CONTROL OF HIS RING BUDDIES! THIS IS TWICE HE'S ALMOST GOTTEN US KILLED!
VRT! VRT-VRT!
!!
AGAIN! THIS KAREL PERSON SHOOTS AT ME *AGAIN!* I WILL--
NO, NO, NO...NOT NOW! NOT HERE!
BRING IT ON, YOU ORANGE BUFFOON!
"BRING IT ON"!? HAVE YOU LOST YOUR MIND, KAREL?!
SHE WAS AIMING AT ME! SHE'S...SHE'S NOT A VERY GOOD SHOT!
AT *YOU?*
ME! YES!
HRM...I CAN SEE HER BEING DRIVEN TO THAT. YOU *ARE* QUITE ANNOYING.
MASTER IS TOO KIND.
WELL, THEN, GLAD *THAT'S* ALL BEHIND US. IT, UM...IT *IS* BEHIND US?
SHUT THE HELL UP, HOMER.
SEEN THIS ONE IN ACTION ONCE. HEARD TELL HE'S GOT EVER' ONE A' TH' SKUGS HE KILLED STASHED AWAY IN THAT RING A' HIS AS HIS OWN PRIVATE CORPS.
HE'S LOSIN' CONTROL A' TH' RING, THAT PUTS ALL OF US IN JEOPARDY. *BIG* TIME.
MY PRICE JUST WENT UP.
UP?!
CORRECT ME IF I'M WRONG, BUT WE NEVER *DID* AGREE TO A PRICE FOR YOUR SERVICES...
UP?!

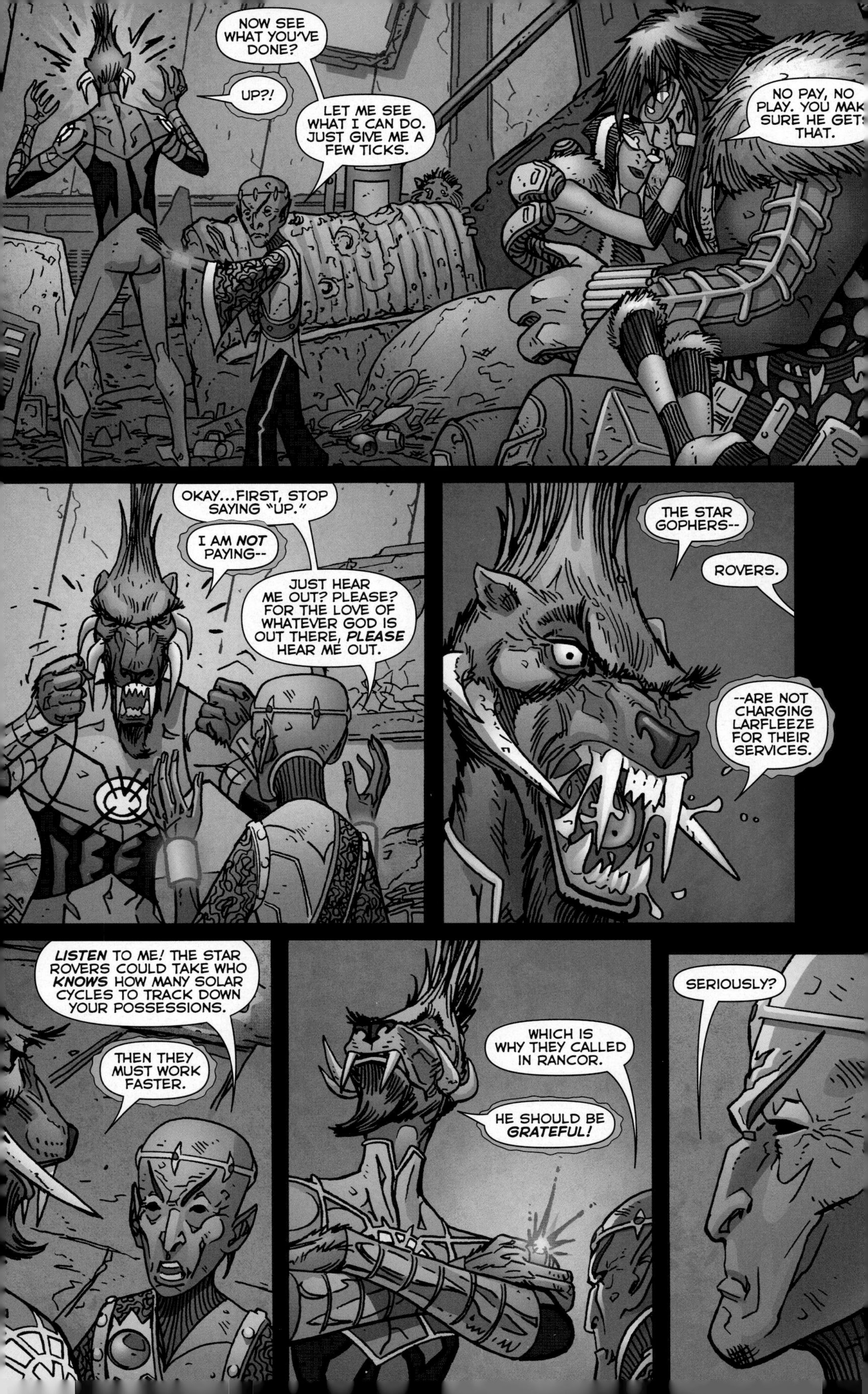
NOW SEE WHAT YOU'VE DONE?
UP?!
LET ME SEE WHAT I CAN DO. JUST GIVE ME A FEW TICKS.
NO PAY, NO PLAY. YOU MAK SURE HE GET THAT.
OKAY...FIRST, STOP SAYING "UP."
I AM *NOT* PAYING--
JUST HEAR ME OUT? PLEASE? FOR THE LOVE OF WHATEVER GOD IS OUT THERE, *PLEASE* HEAR ME OUT.
THE STAR GOPHERS--
ROVERS.
--ARE NOT CHARGING LARFLEEZE FOR THEIR SERVICES.
LISTEN TO ME! THE STAR ROVERS COULD TAKE WHO *KNOWS* HOW MANY SOLAR CYCLES TO TRACK DOWN YOUR POSSESSIONS.
THEN THEY MUST WORK FASTER.
WHICH IS WHY THEY CALLED IN RANCOR.
HE SHOULD BE *GRATEFUL!*
SERIOUSLY?

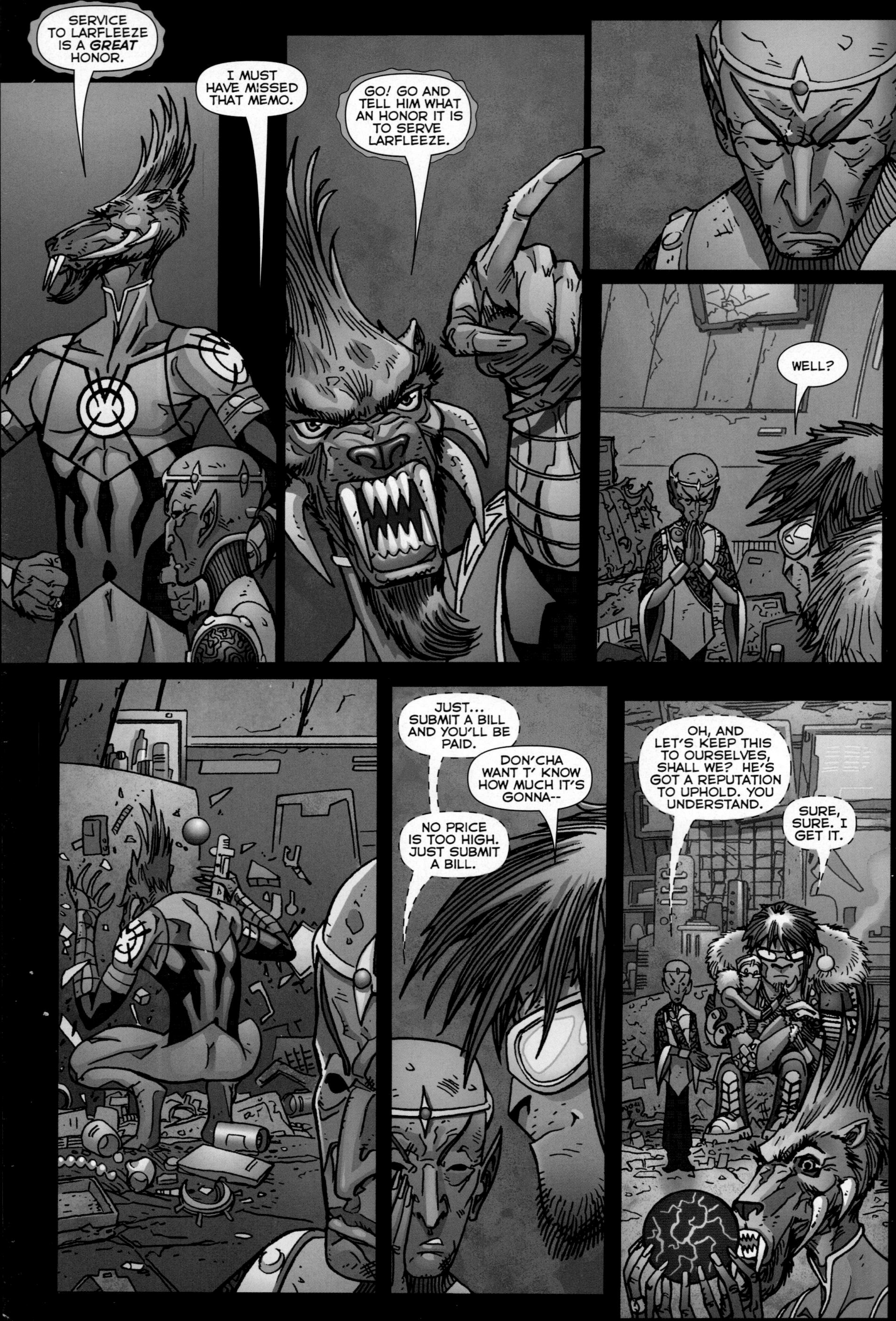

SERVICE TO LARFLEEZE IS A *GREAT* HONOR.
I MUST HAVE MISSED THAT MEMO.
GO! GO AND TELL HIM WHAT AN HONOR IT IS TO SERVE LARFLEEZE.
WELL?
JUST... SUBMIT A BILL AND YOU'LL BE PAID.
DON'CHA WANT T' KNOW HOW MUCH IT'S GONNA--
NO PRICE IS TOO HIGH. JUST SUBMIT A BILL.
OH, AND LET'S KEEP THIS TO OURSELVES, SHALL WE? HE'S GOT A REPUTATION TO UPHOLD. YOU UNDERSTAND.
SURE, SURE. I GET IT.

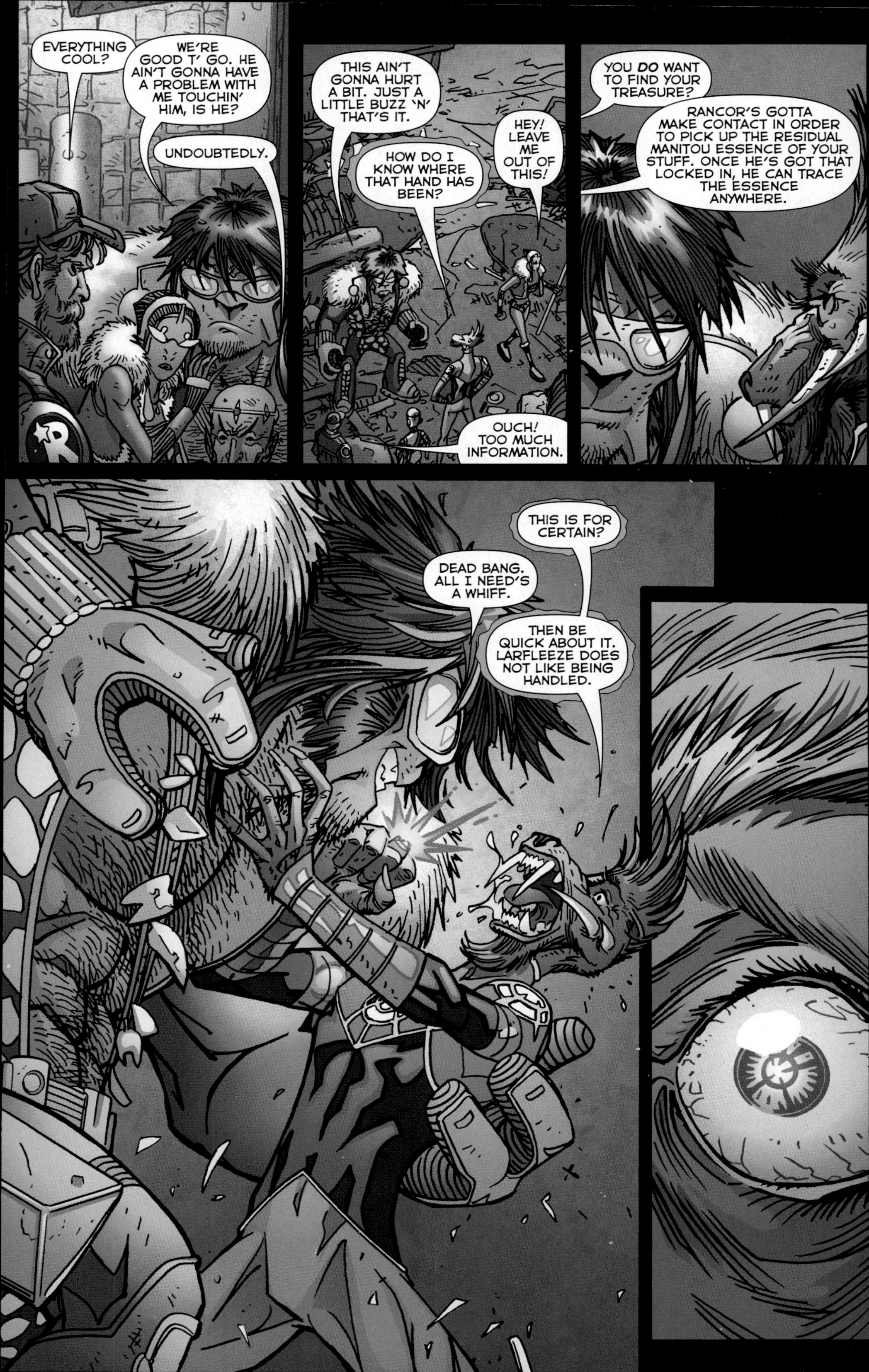
EVERYTHING COOL?
WE'RE GOOD T' GO. HE AIN'T GONNA HAVE A PROBLEM WITH ME TOUCHIN' HIM, IS HE?
UNDOUBTEDLY.
THIS AIN'T GONNA HURT A BIT. JUST A LITTLE BUZZ 'N' THAT'S IT.
HOW DO I KNOW WHERE THAT HAND HAS BEEN?
HEY! LEAVE ME OUT OF THIS!
OUCH! TOO MUCH INFORMATION.
YOU DO WANT TO FIND YOUR TREASURE?
RANCOR'S GOTTA MAKE CONTACT IN ORDER TO PICK UP THE RESIDUAL MANITOU ESSENCE OF YOUR STUFF. ONCE HE'S GOT THAT LOCKED IN, HE CAN TRACE THE ESSENCE ANYWHERE.
THIS IS FOR CERTAIN?
DEAD BANG. ALL I NEED'S A WHIFF.
THEN BE QUICK ABOUT IT. LARFLEEZE DOES NOT LIKE BEING HANDLED.

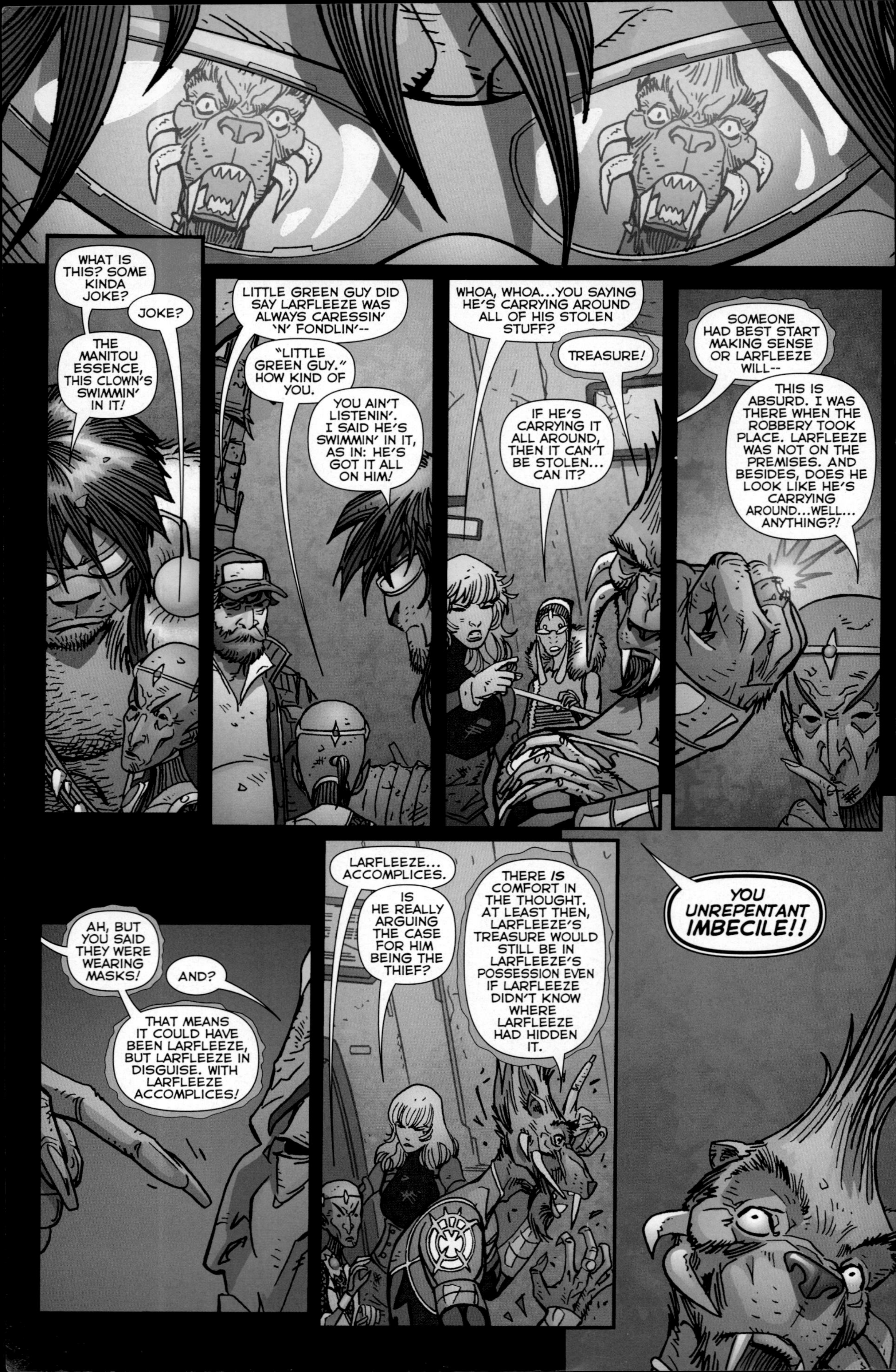

WHAT IS THIS? SOME KINDA JOKE?
JOKE?
THE MANITOU ESSENCE, THIS CLOWN'S SWIMMIN' IN IT!
LITTLE GREEN GUY DID SAY LARFLEEZE WAS ALWAYS CARESSIN' 'N' FONDLIN'--
"LITTLE GREEN GUY." HOW KIND OF YOU.
YOU AIN'T LISTENIN'. I SAID HE'S SWIMMIN' IN IT, AS IN: HE'S GOT IT ALL ON HIM!
WHOA, WHOA...YOU SAYING HE'S CARRYING AROUND ALL OF HIS STOLEN STUFF?
TREASURE!
IF HE'S CARRYING IT ALL AROUND, THEN IT CAN'T BE STOLEN... CAN IT?
SOMEONE HAD BEST START MAKING SENSE OR LARFLEEZE WILL--
THIS IS ABSURD. I WAS THERE WHEN THE ROBBERY TOOK PLACE. LARFLEEZE WAS NOT ON THE PREMISES. AND BESIDES, DOES HE LOOK LIKE HE'S CARRYING AROUND...WELL... ANYTHING?!
AH, BUT YOU SAID THEY WERE WEARING MASKS!
AND?
THAT MEANS IT COULD HAVE BEEN LARFLEEZE, BUT LARFLEEZE IN DISGUISE. WITH LARFLEEZE ACCOMPLICES!
LARFLEEZE... ACCOMPLICES.
IS HE REALLY ARGUING THE CASE FOR HIM BEING THE THIEF?
THERE IS COMFORT IN THE THOUGHT. AT LEAST THEN, LARFLEEZE'S TREASURE WOULD STILL BE IN LARFLEEZE'S POSSESSION EVEN IF LARFLEEZE DIDN'T KNOW WHERE LARFLEEZE HAD HIDDEN IT.
YOU UNREPENTANT IMBECILE!!

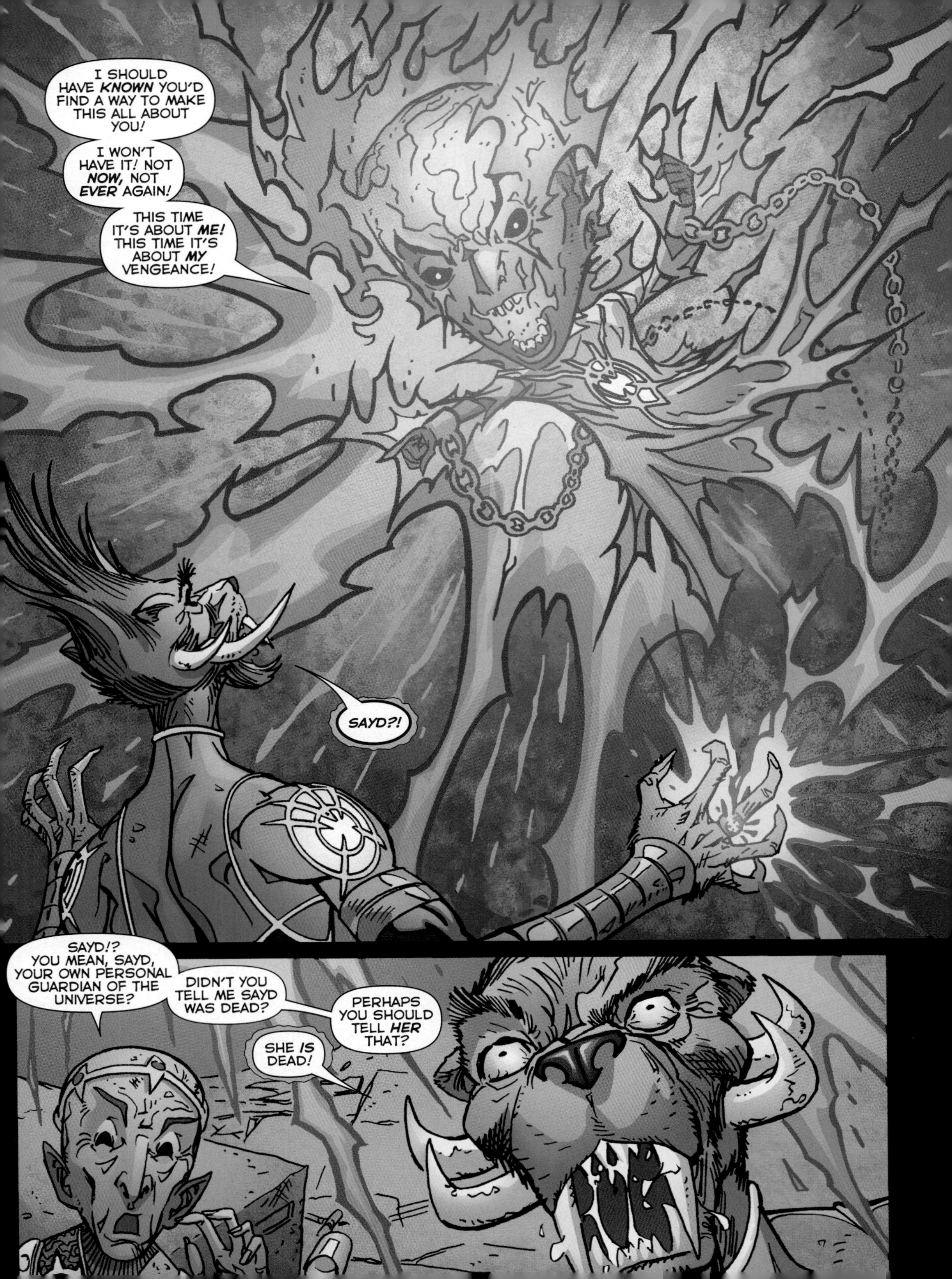
I SHOULD HAVE KNOWN YOU'D FIND A WAY TO MAKE THIS ALL ABOUT YOU!
I WON'T HAVE IT! NOT NOW, NOT EVER AGAIN!
THIS TIME IT'S ABOUT ME! THIS TIME IT'S ABOUT MY VENGEANCE!
SAYD?!
SAYD!? YOU MEAN, SAYD, YOUR OWN PERSONAL GUARDIAN OF THE UNIVERSE?
DIDN'T YOU TELL ME SAYD WAS DEAD?
PERHAPS YOU SHOULD TELL HER THAT?
SHE IS DEAD!

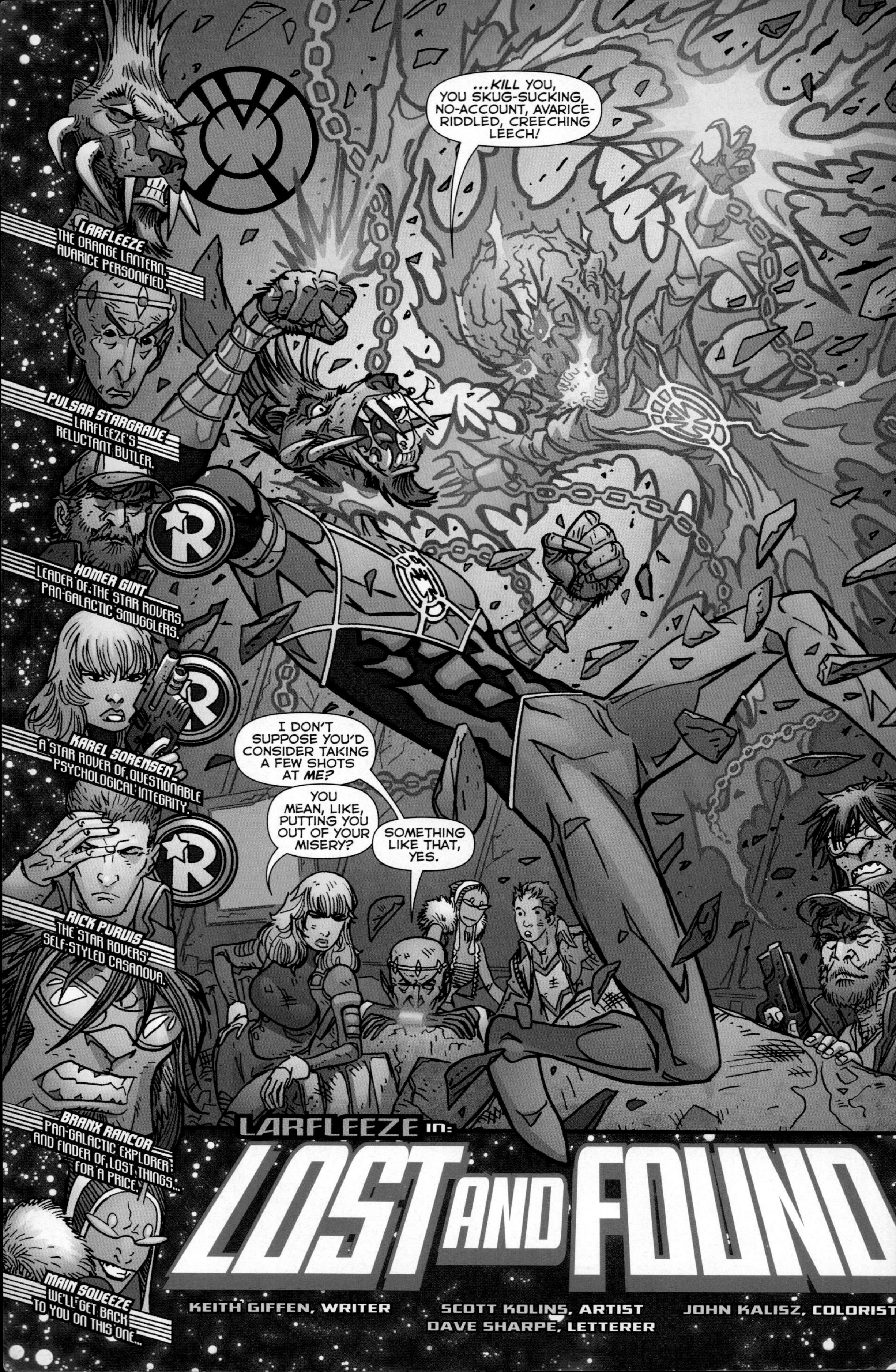
...KILL YOU, YOU SKUG-SUCKING, NO-ACCOUNT, AVARICE-RIDDLED, CREECHING LEECH!
LARFLEEZE
THE ORANGE LANTERN. AVARICE PERSONIFIED.
PULSAR STARGRAVE
LARFLEEZE'S RELUCTANT BUTLER.
HOMER GINT
LEADER OF THE STAR ROVERS, PAN-GALACTIC SMUGGLERS.
KAREL SORENSEN
A STAR ROVER OF QUESTIONABLE PSYCHOLOGICAL INTEGRITY.
RICK PURVIS
THE STAR ROVERS' SELF-STYLED CASANOVA.
BRANX RANCOR
PAN-GALACTIC EXPLORER AND FINDER OF LOST THINGS... FOR A PRICE.
MAIN SQUEEZE
WE'LL GET BACK TO YOU ON THIS ONE...
I DON'T SUPPOSE YOU'D CONSIDER TAKING A FEW SHOTS AT ME?
YOU MEAN, LIKE, PUTTING YOU OUT OF YOUR MISERY?
SOMETHING LIKE THAT, YES.
LARFLEEZE IN:
LOST AND FOUND
KEITH GIFFEN, WRITER
SCOTT KOLINS, ARTIST
DAVE SHARPE, LETTERER
JOHN KALISZ, COLORIST

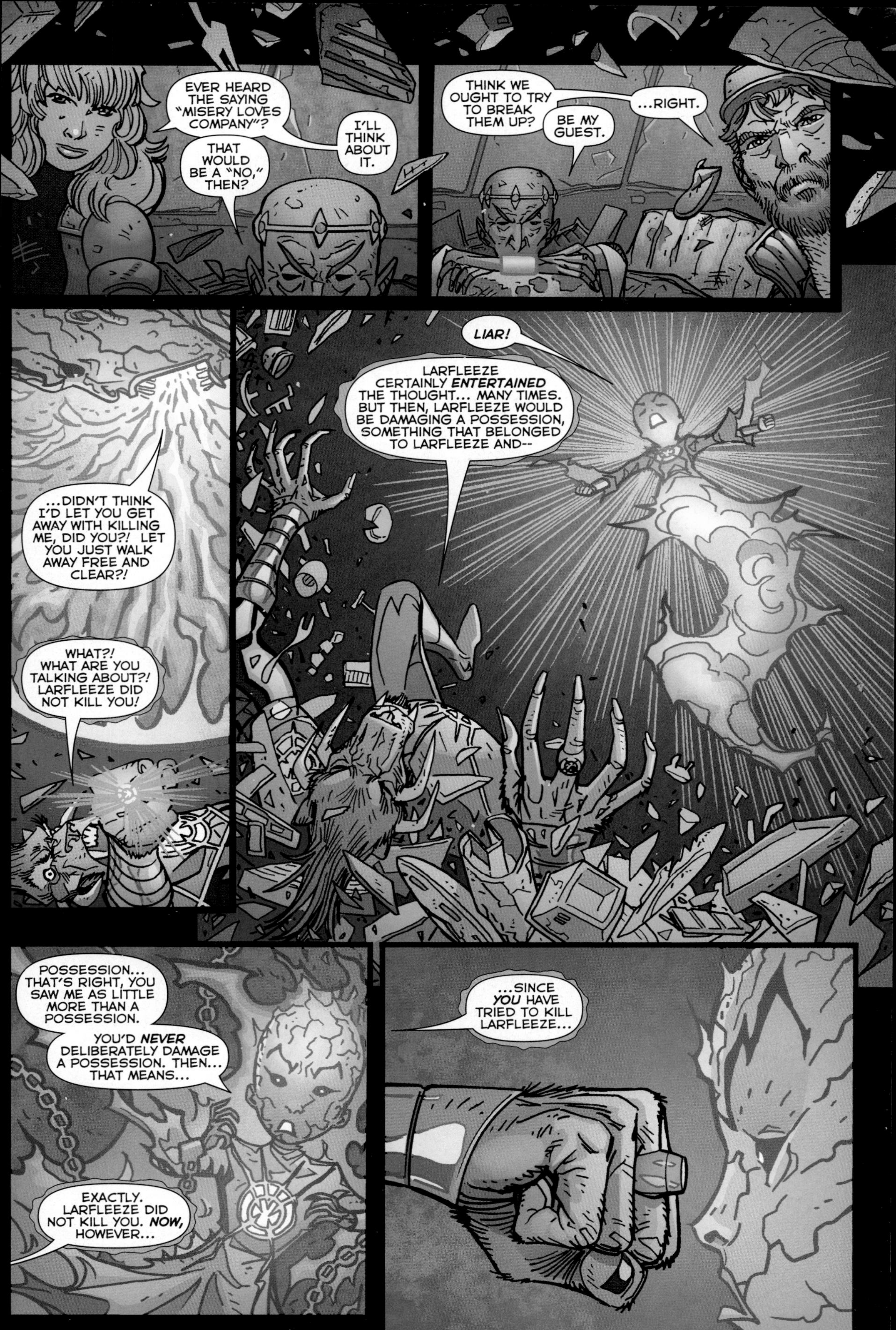
EVER HEARD THE SAYING "MISERY LOVES COMPANY"?
I'LL THINK ABOUT IT.
THAT WOULD BE A "NO," THEN?
THINK WE OUGHT TO TRY TO BREAK THEM UP?
...RIGHT.
BE MY GUEST.
LIAR!
LARFLEEZE CERTAINLY ENTERTAINED THE THOUGHT... MANY TIMES. BUT THEN, LARFLEEZE WOULD BE DAMAGING A POSSESSION, SOMETHING THAT BELONGED TO LARFLEEZE AND--
...DIDN'T THINK I'D LET YOU GET AWAY WITH KILLING ME, DID YOU?! LET YOU JUST WALK AWAY FREE AND CLEAR?!
WHAT?! WHAT ARE YOU TALKING ABOUT?! LARFLEEZE DID NOT KILL YOU!
POSSESSION... THAT'S RIGHT, YOU SAW ME AS LITTLE MORE THAN A POSSESSION.
YOU'D NEVER DELIBERATELY DAMAGE A POSSESSION. THEN... THAT MEANS...
EXACTLY. LARFLEEZE DID NOT KILL YOU. NOW, HOWEVER...
...SINCE YOU HAVE TRIED TO KILL LARFLEEZE...

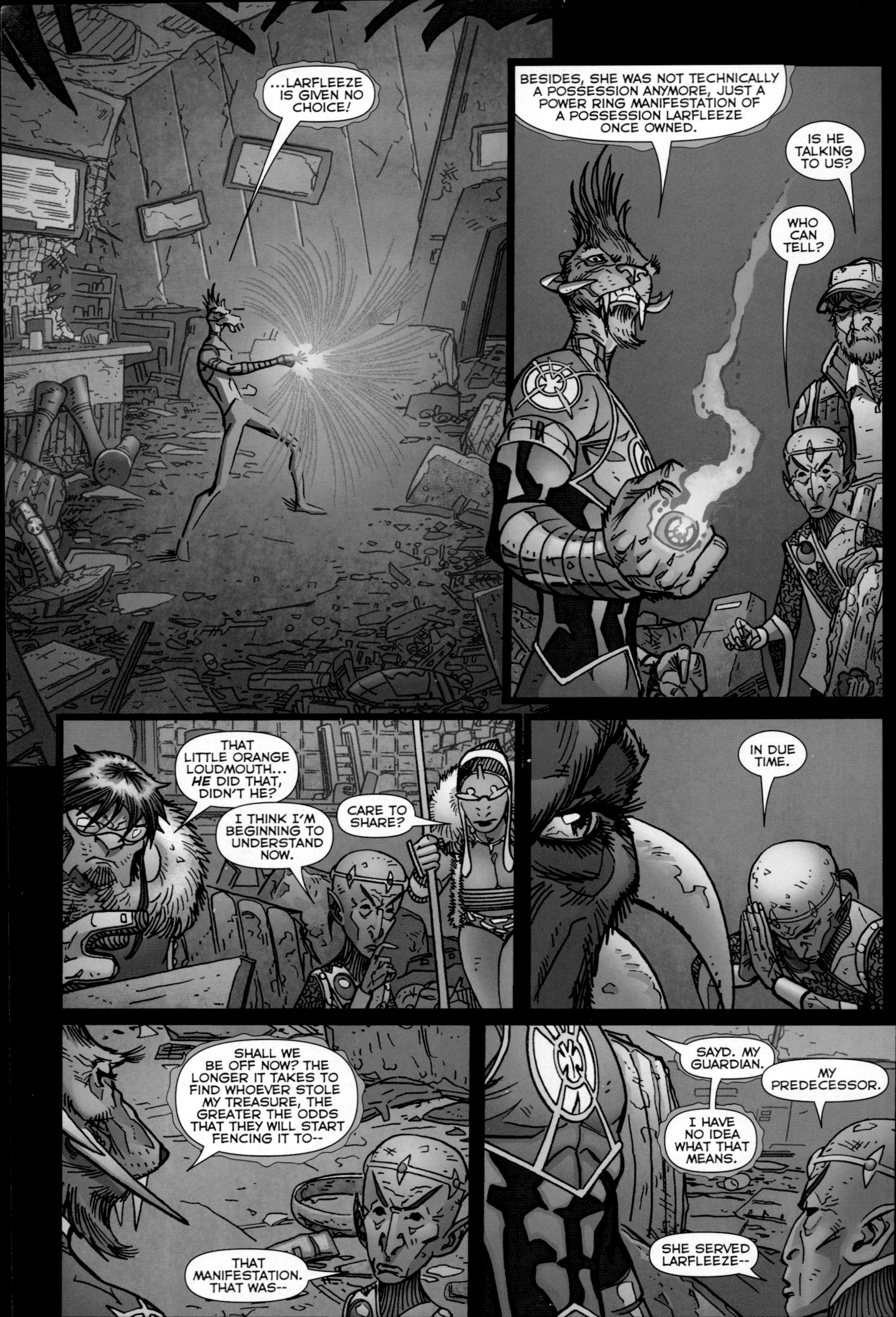
...LARFLEEZE IS GIVEN NO CHOICE!
BESIDES, SHE WAS NOT TECHNICALLY A POSSESSION ANYMORE, JUST A POWER RING MANIFESTATION OF A POSSESSION LARFLEEZE ONCE OWNED.
IS HE TALKING TO US?
WHO CAN TELL?
THAT LITTLE ORANGE LOUDMOUTH... **HE** DID THAT, DIDN'T HE?
I THINK I'M BEGINNING TO UNDERSTAND NOW.
CARE TO SHARE?
IN DUE TIME.
SHALL WE BE OFF NOW? THE LONGER IT TAKES TO FIND WHOEVER STOLE MY TREASURE, THE GREATER THE ODDS THAT THEY WILL START FENCING IT TO--
THAT MANIFESTATION. THAT WAS--
SAYD. MY GUARDIAN.
MY PREDECESSOR.
I HAVE NO IDEA WHAT THAT MEANS.
SHE SERVED LARFLEEZE--

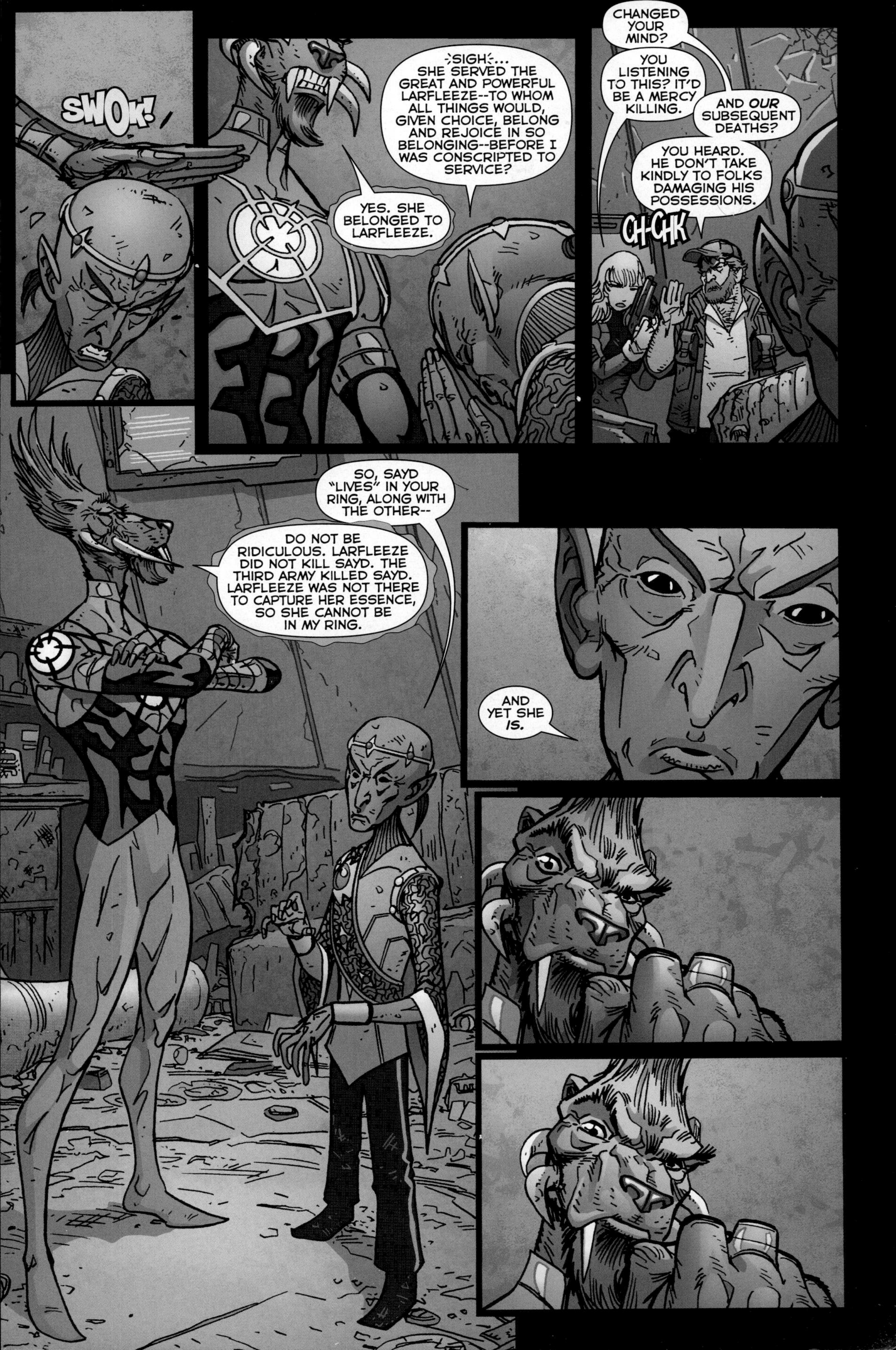
SWOK!
-SIGH-... SHE SERVED THE GREAT AND POWERFUL LARFLEEZE--TO WHOM ALL THINGS WOULD, GIVEN CHOICE, BELONG AND REJOICE IN SO BELONGING--BEFORE I WAS CONSCRIPTED TO SERVICE?
YES. SHE BELONGED TO LARFLEEZE.
CHANGED YOUR MIND?
YOU LISTENING TO THIS? IT'D BE A MERCY KILLING.
AND OUR SUBSEQUENT DEATHS?
YOU HEARD. HE DON'T TAKE KINDLY TO FOLKS DAMAGING HIS POSSESSIONS.
CH-CHK
SO, SAYD "LIVES" IN YOUR RING, ALONG WITH THE OTHER--
DO NOT BE RIDICULOUS. LARFLEEZE DID NOT KILL SAYD. THE THIRD ARMY KILLED SAYD. LARFLEEZE WAS NOT THERE TO CAPTURE HER ESSENCE, SO SHE CANNOT BE IN MY RING.
AND YET SHE IS.

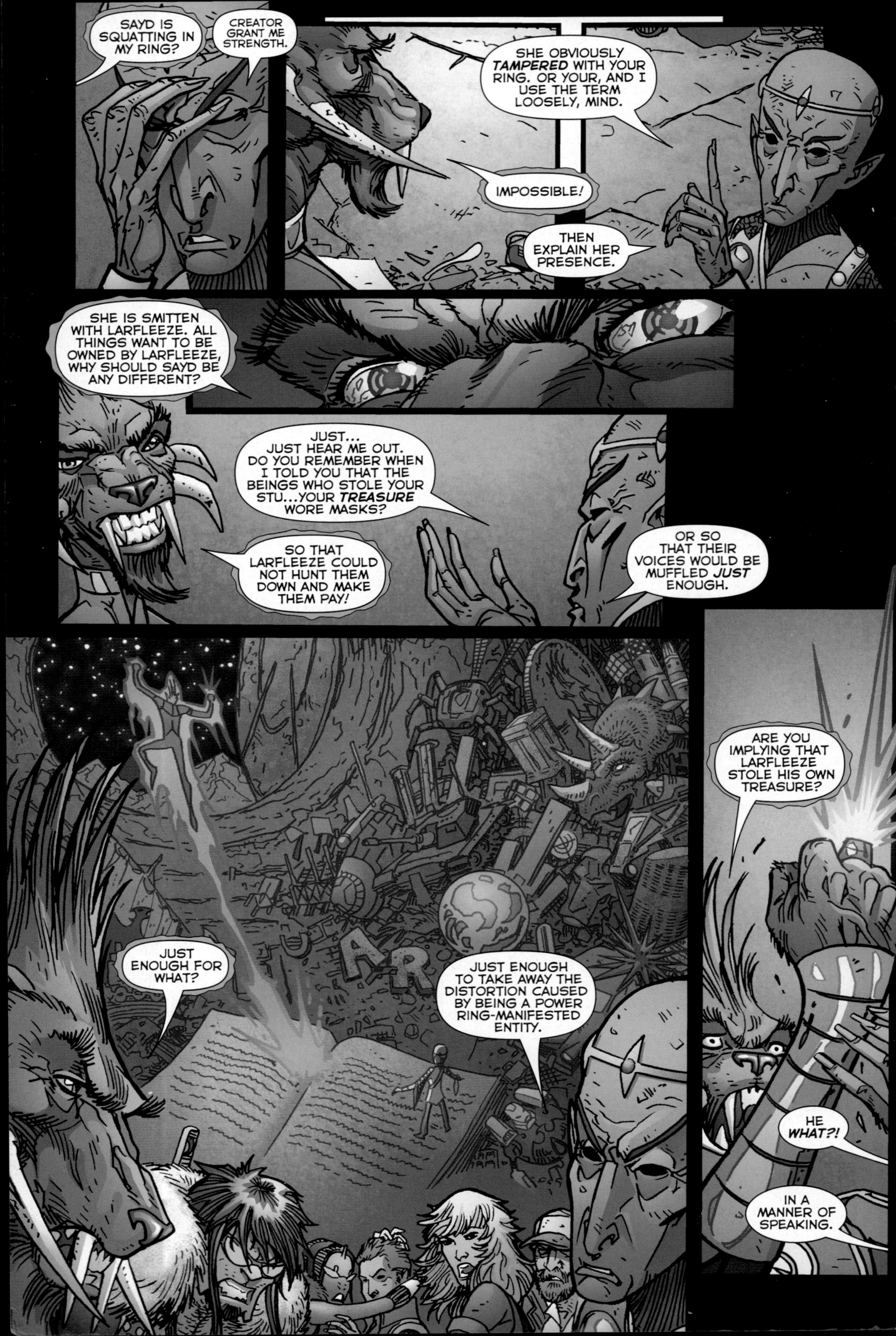
SAYD IS SQUATTING IN MY RING?
CREATOR GRANT ME STRENGTH.
SHE OBVIOUSLY TAMPERED WITH YOUR RING. OR YOUR, AND I USE THE TERM LOOSELY, MIND.
IMPOSSIBLE!
THEN EXPLAIN HER PRESENCE.
SHE IS SMITTEN WITH LARFLEEZE. ALL THINGS WANT TO BE OWNED BY LARFLEEZE, WHY SHOULD SAYD BE ANY DIFFERENT?
JUST... JUST HEAR ME OUT. DO YOU REMEMBER WHEN I TOLD YOU THAT THE BEINGS WHO STOLE YOUR STU...YOUR TREASURE WORE MASKS?
SO THAT LARFLEEZE COULD NOT HUNT THEM DOWN AND MAKE THEM PAY!
OR SO THAT THEIR VOICES WOULD BE MUFFLED JUST ENOUGH.
JUST ENOUGH FOR WHAT?
JUST ENOUGH TO TAKE AWAY THE DISTORTION CAUSED BY BEING A POWER RING-MANIFESTED ENTITY.
ARE YOU IMPLYING THAT LARFLEEZE STOLE HIS OWN TREASURE?
HE WHAT?!
IN A MANNER OF SPEAKING.

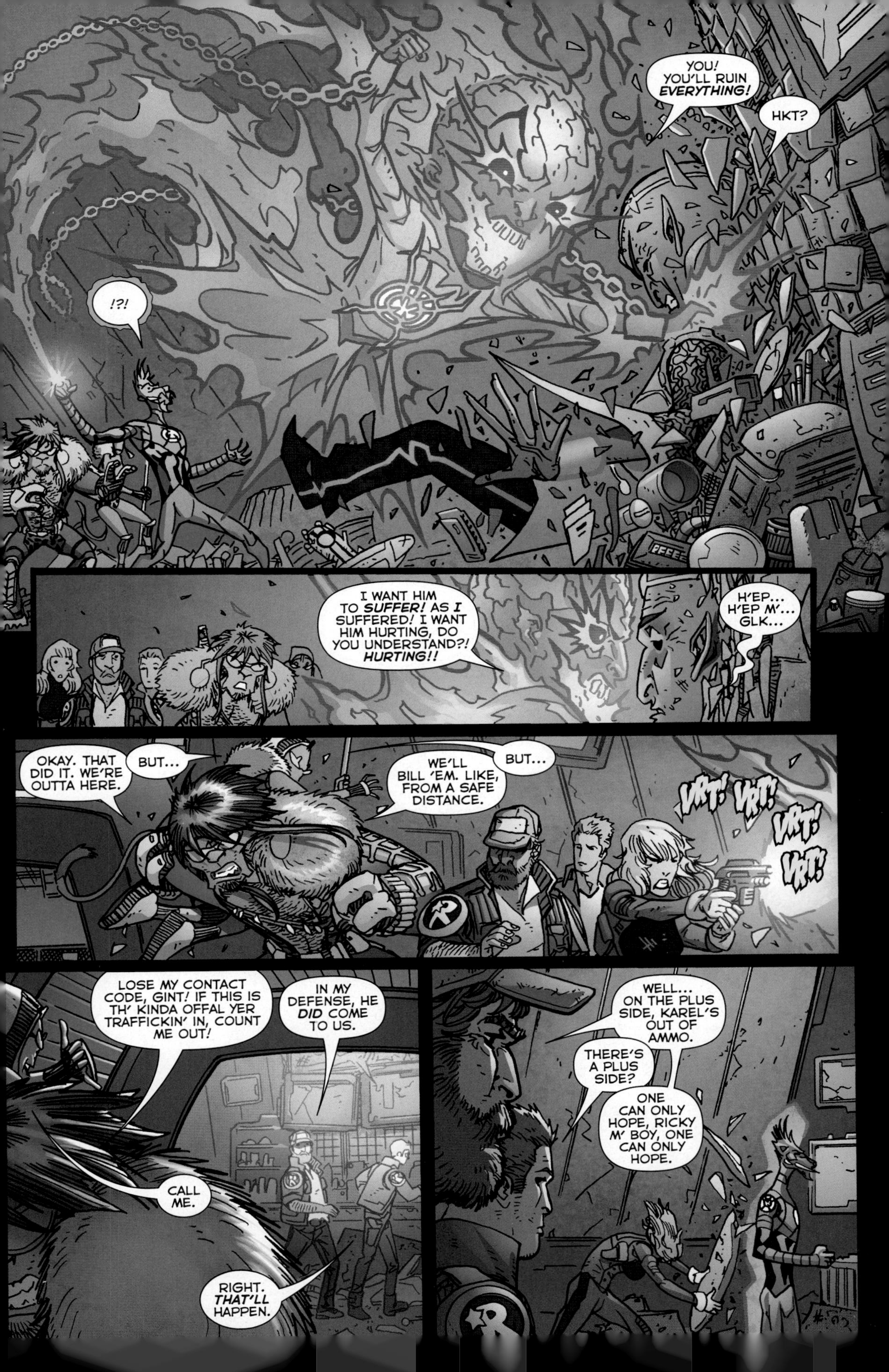
YOU! YOU'LL RUIN EVERYTHING!
HKT?
!?!
I WANT HIM TO SUFFER! AS I SUFFERED! I WANT HIM HURTING, DO YOU UNDERSTAND?! HURTING!!
H'EP... H'EP M'... GLK...
OKAY. THAT DID IT. WE'RE OUTTA HERE.
BUT...
WE'LL BILL 'EM. LIKE, FROM A SAFE DISTANCE.
BUT...
VRT! VRT! VRT! VRT!
LOSE MY CONTACT CODE, GINT! IF THIS IS TH' KINDA OFFAL YER TRAFFICKIN' IN, COUNT ME OUT!
IN MY DEFENSE, HE DID COME TO US.
CALL ME.
RIGHT. THAT'LL HAPPEN.
WELL... ON THE PLUS SIDE, KAREL'S OUT OF AMMO.
THERE'S A PLUS SIDE?
ONE CAN ONLY HOPE, RICKY M' BOY, ONE CAN ONLY HOPE.

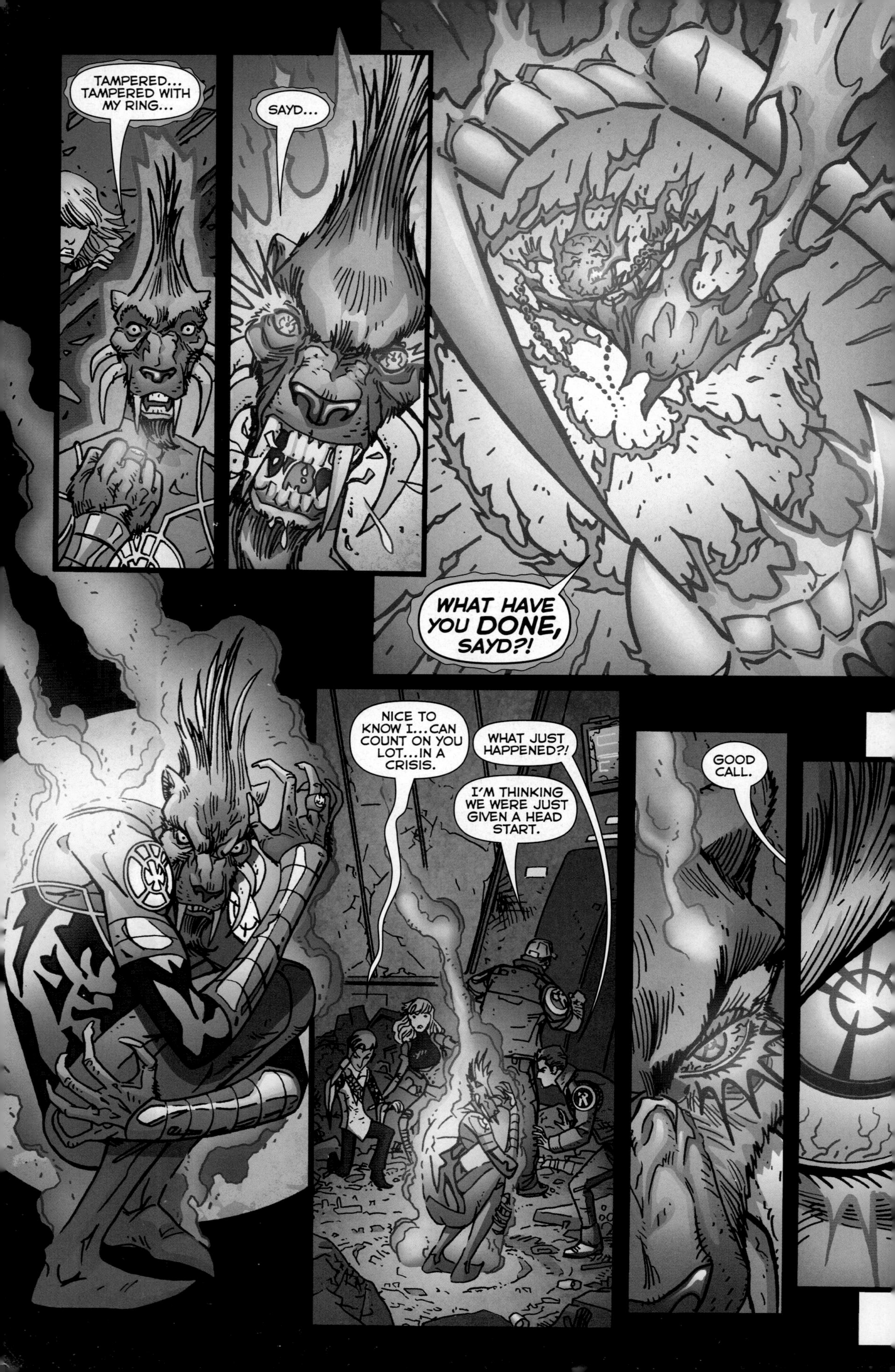
TAMPERED... TAMPERED WITH MY RING...
SAYD...
WHAT HAVE YOU DONE, SAYD?!
NICE TO KNOW I...CAN COUNT ON YOU LOT...IN A CRISIS.
WHAT JUST HAPPENED?!
I'M THINKING WE WERE JUST GIVEN A HEAD START.
GOOD CALL.

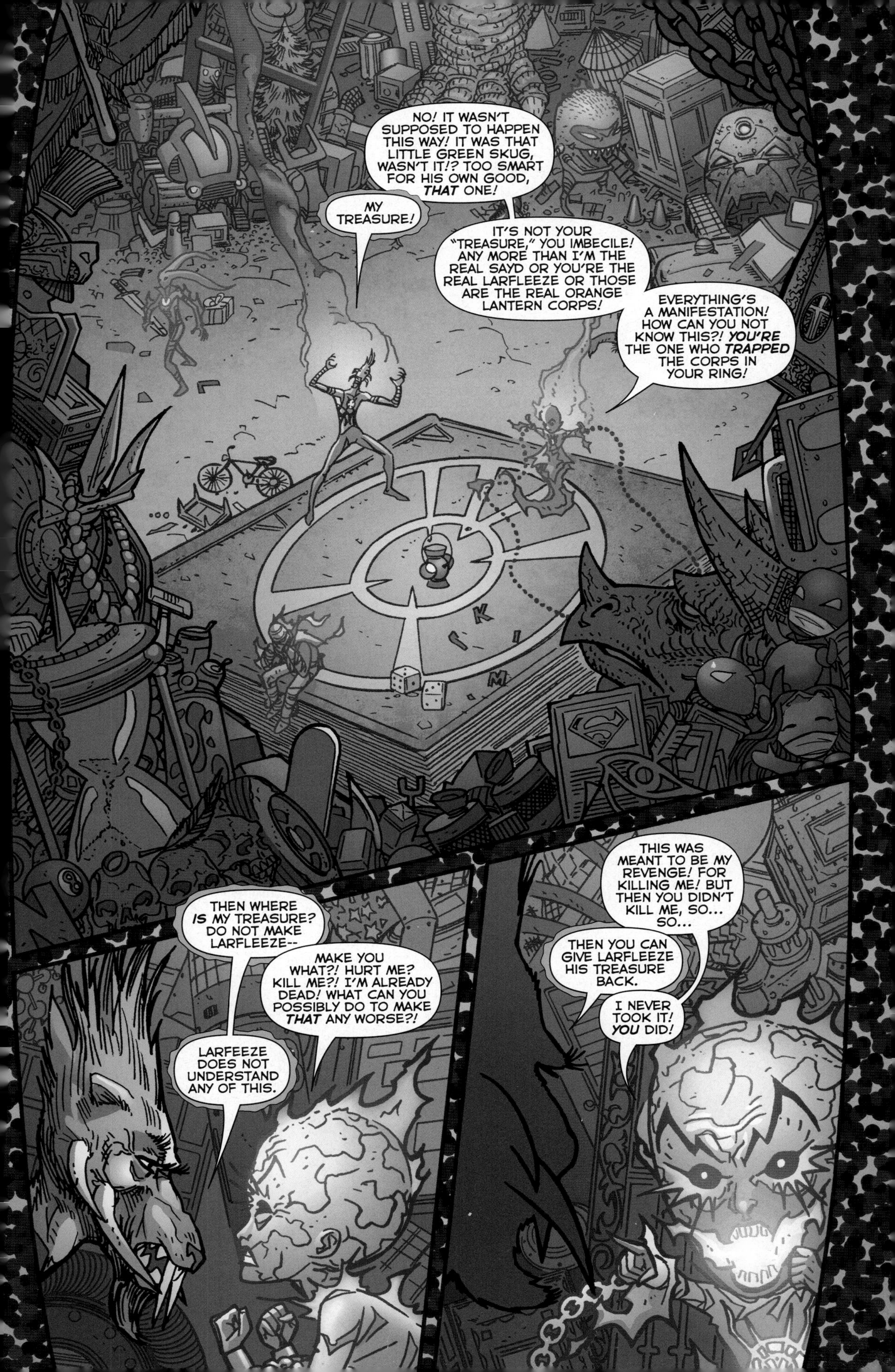
NO! IT WASN'T SUPPOSED TO HAPPEN THIS WAY! IT WAS THAT LITTLE GREEN SKUG, WASN'T IT!? TOO SMART FOR HIS OWN GOOD, THAT ONE!
MY TREASURE!
IT'S NOT YOUR "TREASURE," YOU IMBECILE! ANY MORE THAN I'M THE REAL SAYD OR YOU'RE THE REAL LARFLEEZE OR THOSE ARE THE REAL ORANGE LANTERN CORPS!
EVERYTHING'S A MANIFESTATION! HOW CAN YOU NOT KNOW THIS?! YOU'RE THE ONE WHO TRAPPED THE CORPS IN YOUR RING!
THEN WHERE IS MY TREASURE? DO NOT MAKE LARFLEEZE--
MAKE YOU WHAT?! HURT ME? KILL ME?! I'M ALREADY DEAD! WHAT CAN YOU POSSIBLY DO TO MAKE THAT ANY WORSE?!
LARFLEEZE DOES NOT UNDERSTAND ANY OF THIS.
THIS WAS MEANT TO BE MY REVENGE! FOR KILLING ME! BUT THEN YOU DIDN'T KILL ME, SO... SO...
THEN YOU CAN GIVE LARFLEEZE HIS TREASURE BACK.
I NEVER TOOK IT! YOU DID!

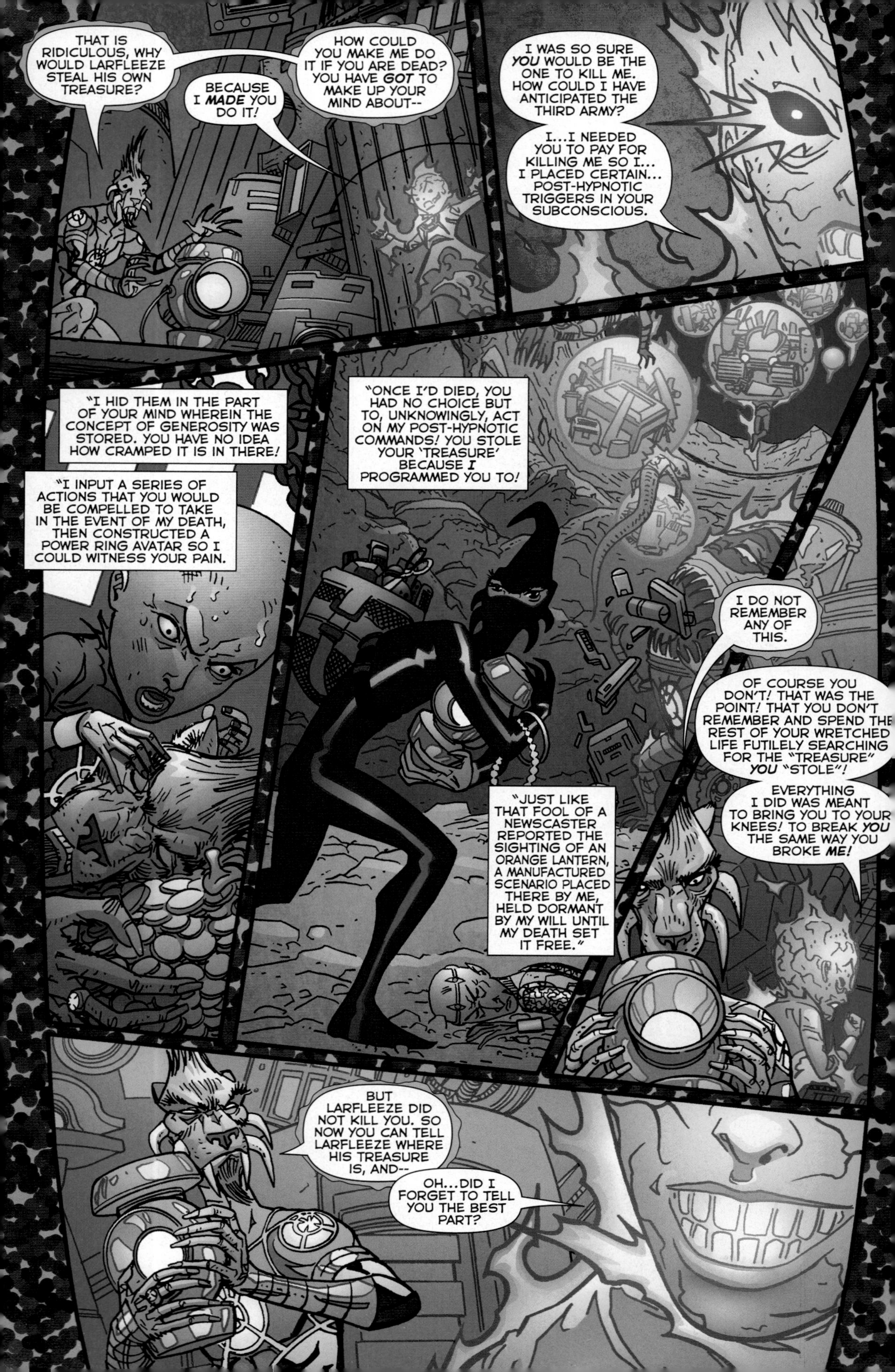
THAT IS RIDICULOUS, WHY WOULD LARFLEEZE STEAL HIS OWN TREASURE?
BECAUSE I *MADE* YOU DO IT!
HOW COULD YOU MAKE ME DO IT IF YOU ARE DEAD? YOU HAVE *GOT* TO MAKE UP YOUR MIND ABOUT--
I WAS SO SURE *YOU* WOULD BE THE ONE TO KILL ME. HOW COULD I HAVE ANTICIPATED THE THIRD ARMY?
I...I NEEDED YOU TO PAY FOR KILLING ME SO I... I PLACED CERTAIN... POST-HYPNOTIC TRIGGERS IN YOUR SUBCONSCIOUS.
"I HID THEM IN THE PART OF YOUR MIND WHEREIN THE CONCEPT OF GENEROSITY WAS STORED. YOU HAVE NO IDEA HOW CRAMPED IT IS IN THERE!
"I INPUT A SERIES OF ACTIONS THAT YOU WOULD BE COMPELLED TO TAKE IN THE EVENT OF MY DEATH, THEN CONSTRUCTED A POWER RING AVATAR SO I COULD WITNESS YOUR PAIN.
"ONCE I'D DIED, YOU HAD NO CHOICE BUT TO, UNKNOWINGLY, ACT ON MY POST-HYPNOTIC COMMANDS! YOU STOLE YOUR 'TREASURE' BECAUSE *I* PROGRAMMED YOU TO!
"JUST LIKE THAT FOOL OF A NEWSCASTER REPORTED THE SIGHTING OF AN ORANGE LANTERN, A MANUFACTURED SCENARIO PLACED THERE BY ME, HELD DORMANT BY MY WILL UNTIL MY DEATH SET IT FREE."
I DO NOT REMEMBER ANY OF THIS.
OF COURSE YOU DON'T! THAT WAS THE POINT! THAT YOU DON'T REMEMBER AND SPEND THE REST OF YOUR WRETCHED LIFE FUTILELY SEARCHING FOR THE "TREASURE" *YOU* "STOLE"!
EVERYTHING I DID WAS MEANT TO BRING YOU TO YOUR KNEES! TO BREAK *YOU* THE SAME WAY YOU BROKE *ME!*
BUT LARFLEEZE DID NOT KILL YOU. SO NOW YOU CAN TELL LARFLEEZE WHERE HIS TREASURE IS, AND--
OH...DID I FORGET TO TELL YOU THE BEST PART?

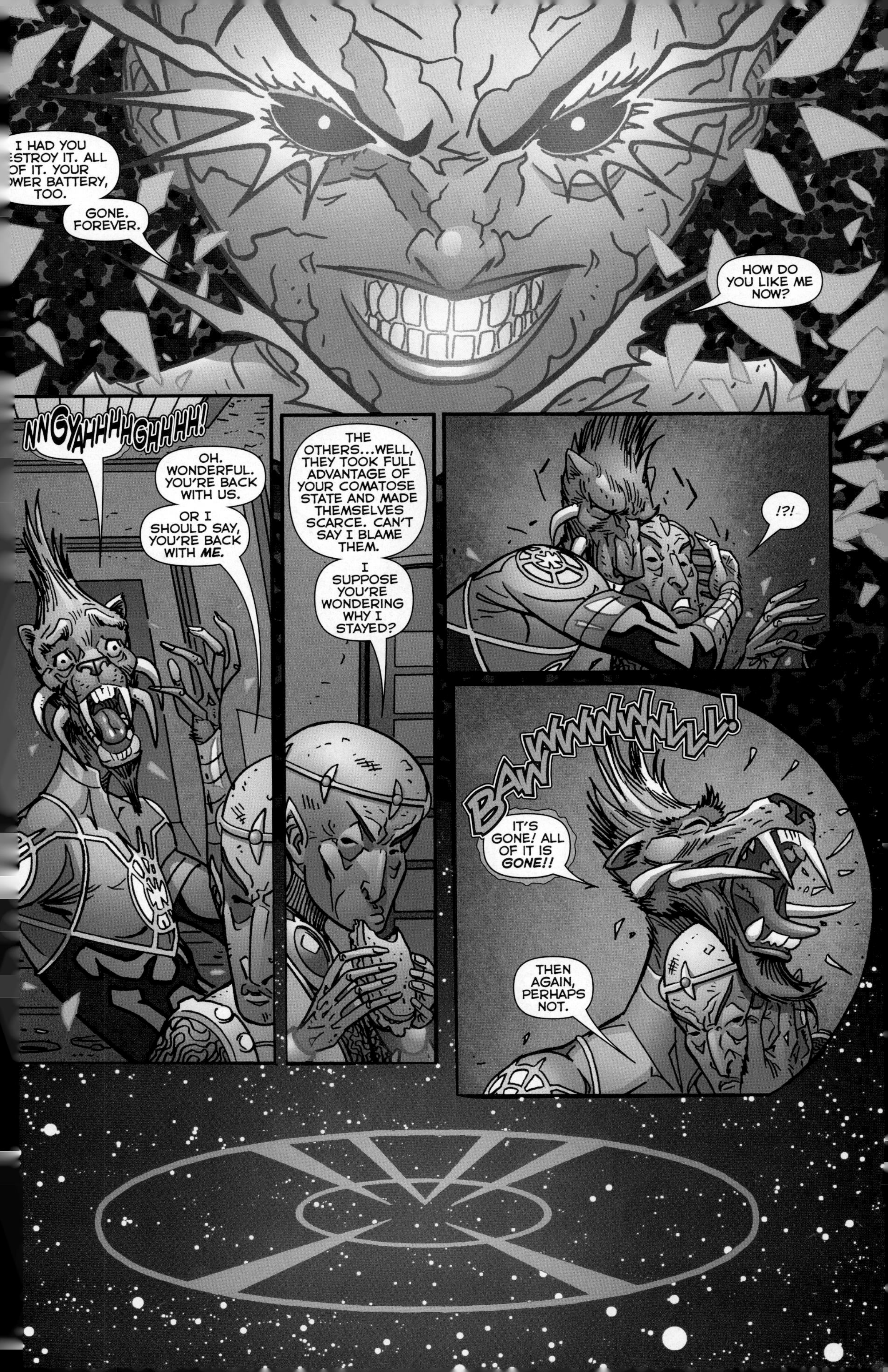
I HAD YOU ESTROY IT. ALL OF IT. YOUR OWER BATTERY, TOO.
GONE. FOREVER.
HOW DO YOU LIKE ME NOW?
NNGYAHHHHGHHHH!
OH. WONDERFUL. YOU'RE BACK WITH US.
OR I SHOULD SAY, YOU'RE BACK WITH ME.
THE OTHERS...WELL, THEY TOOK FULL ADVANTAGE OF YOUR COMATOSE STATE AND MADE THEMSELVES SCARCE. CAN'T SAY I BLAME THEM.
I SUPPOSE YOU'RE WONDERING WHY I STAYED?
!?!
BAWWWWWWLL!
IT'S GONE! ALL OF IT IS GONE!!
THEN AGAIN, PERHAPS NOT.

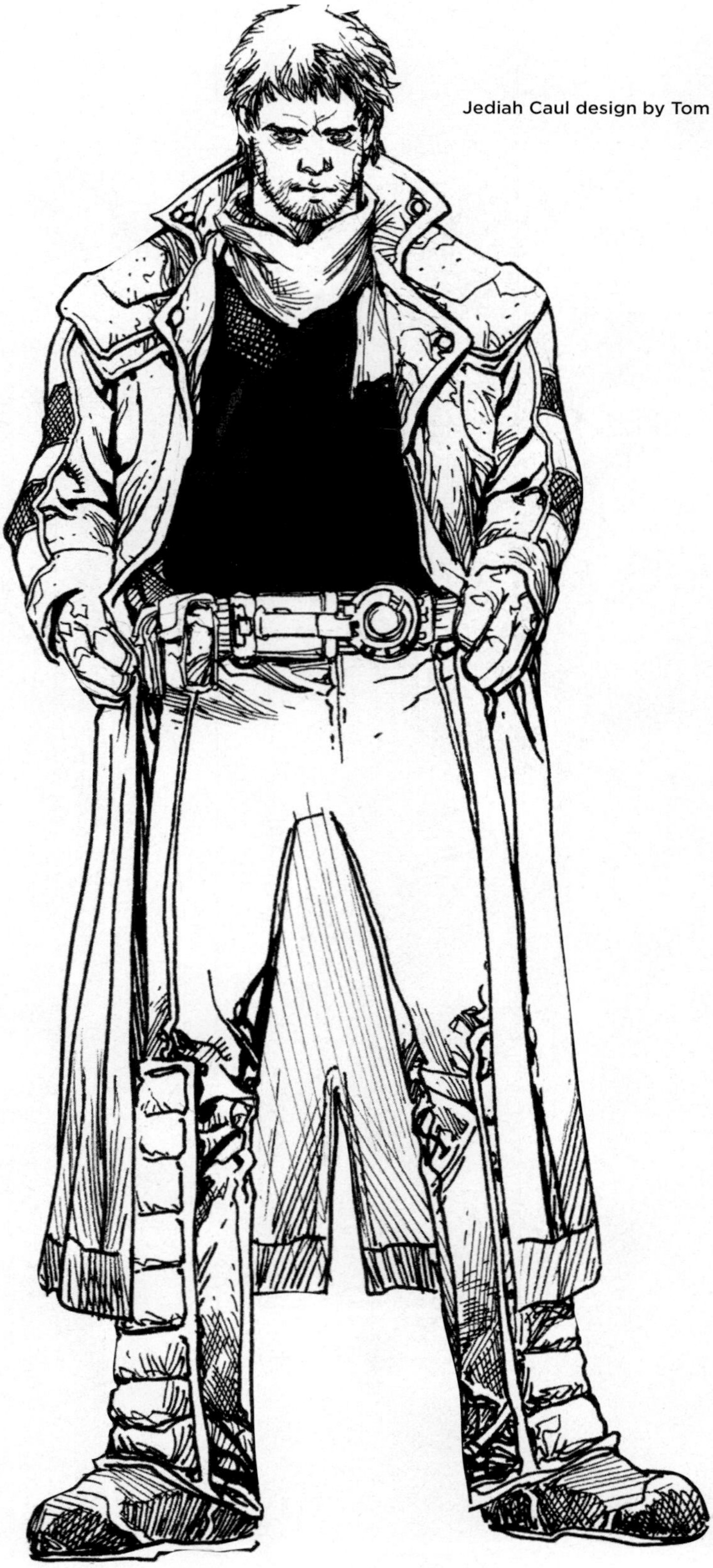

Jediah Caul design by Tom Raney

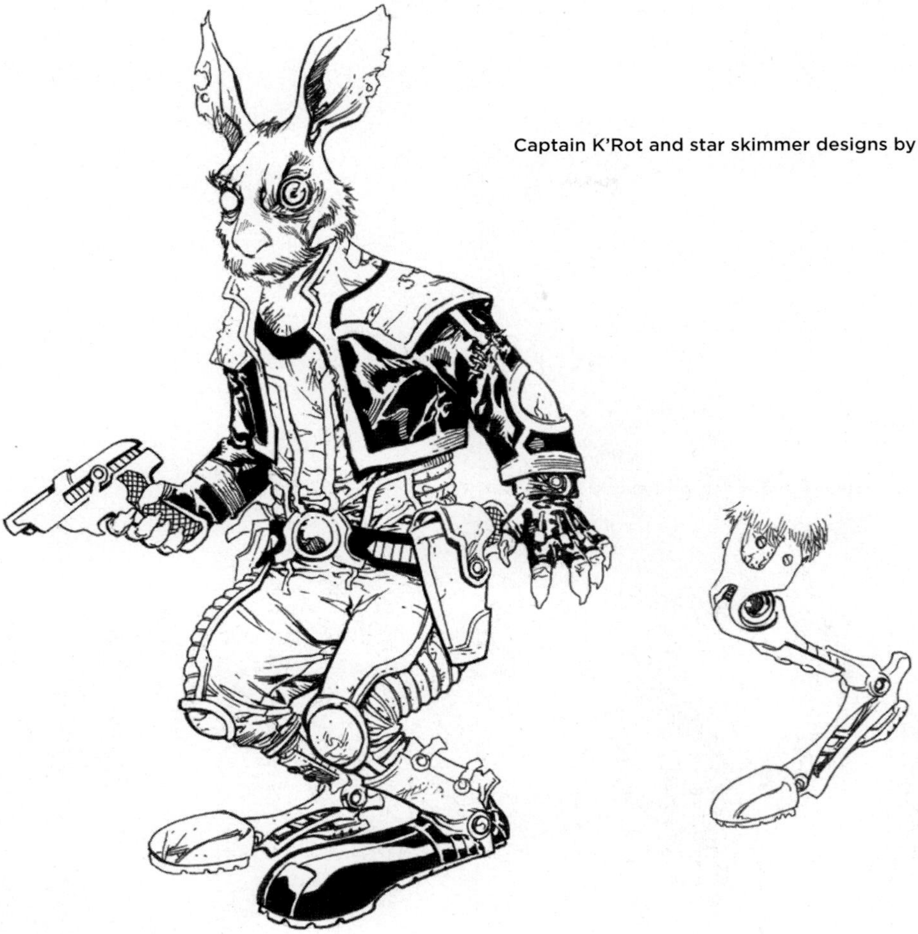

Captain K'Rot and star skimmer designs by Tom Raney

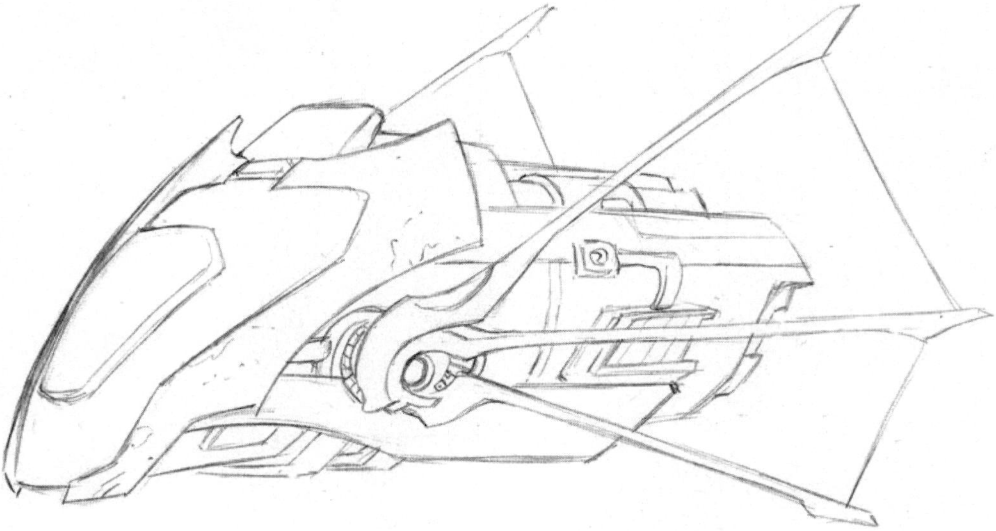

Stealth and space cabbie designs by Tom Raney

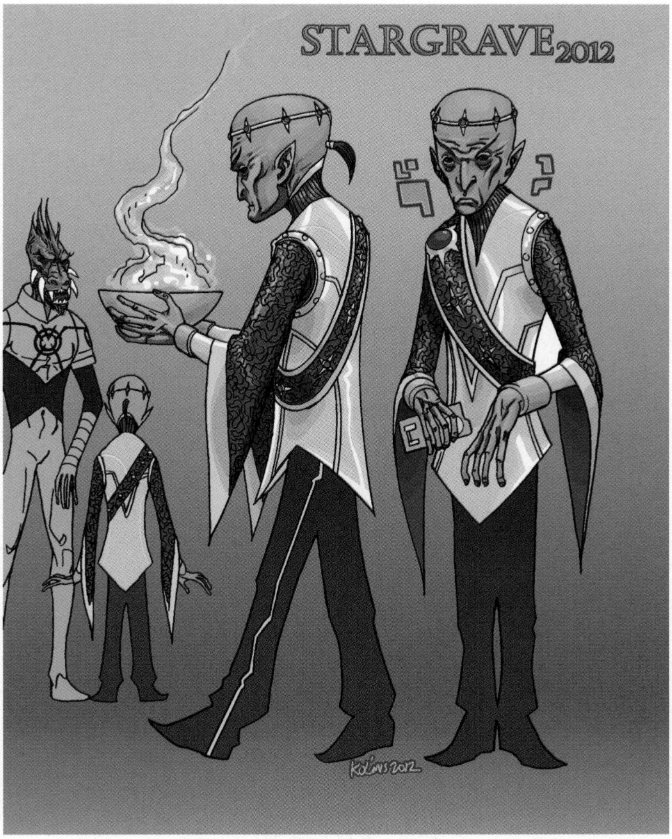
STARGRAVE2012
KOLINS 2012

Stargrave and Rancor designs by Scott Kolins

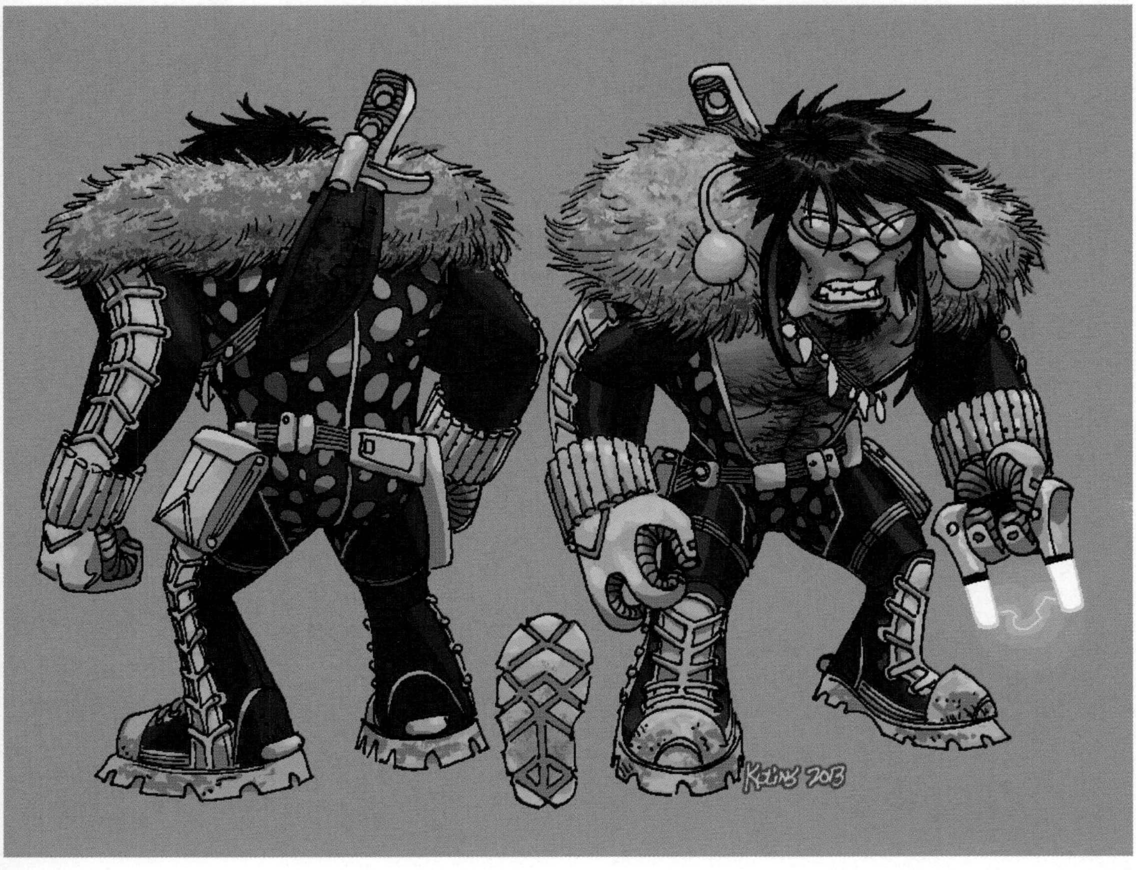
KOLINS 2013

Star Hawkins and Ember designs by Tom Raney

THRESHOLD
UNUSED COVER FOR ISSUE #1

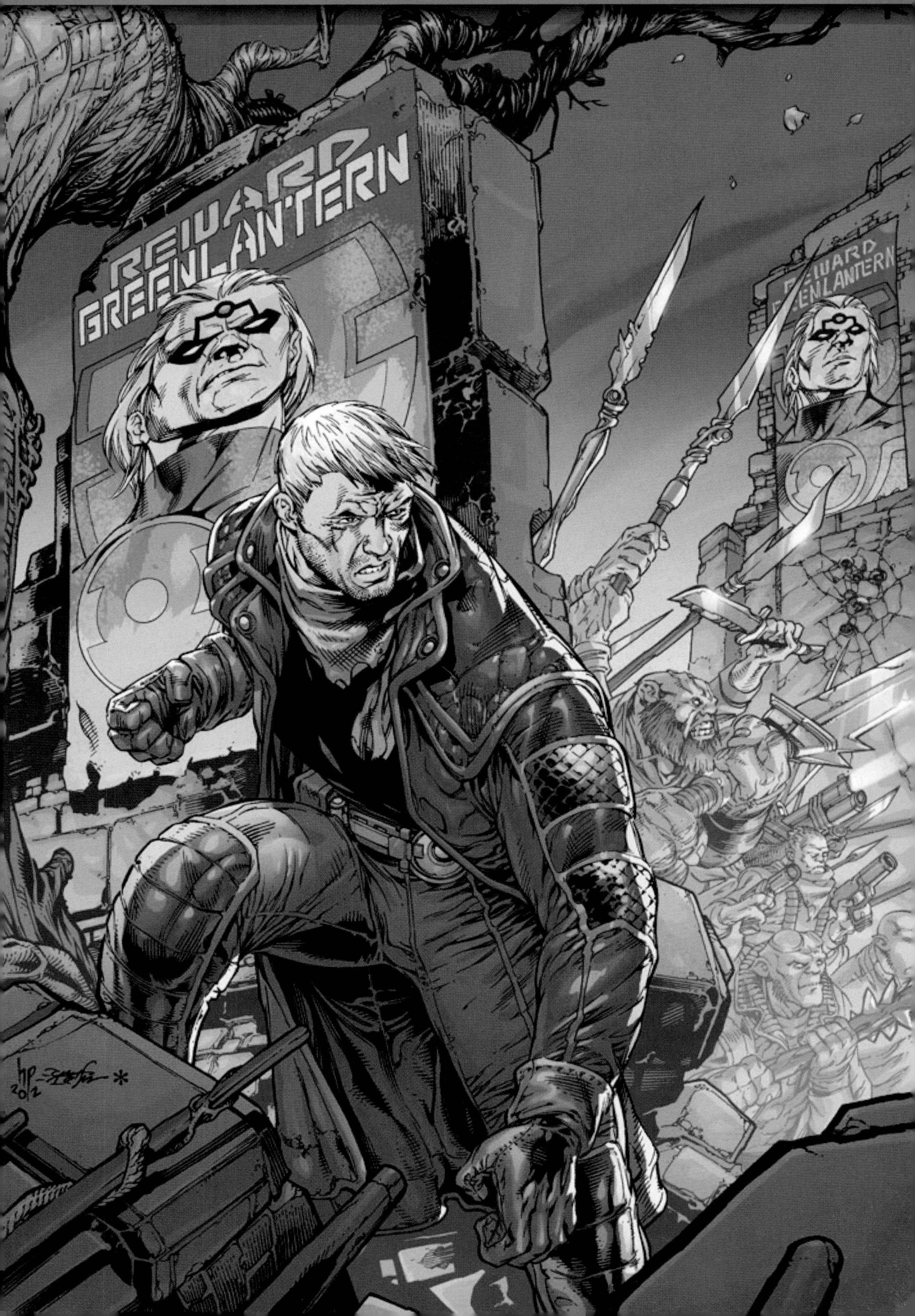
REWARD
GREEN LANTERN
REWARD
GREEN LANTERN

FROM THE WRITER OF *JUSTICE LEAGUE* & *THE FLASH*

GEOFF JOHNS
GREEN LANTERN: REBIRTH

GREEN LANTERN:
BRIGHTEST DAY

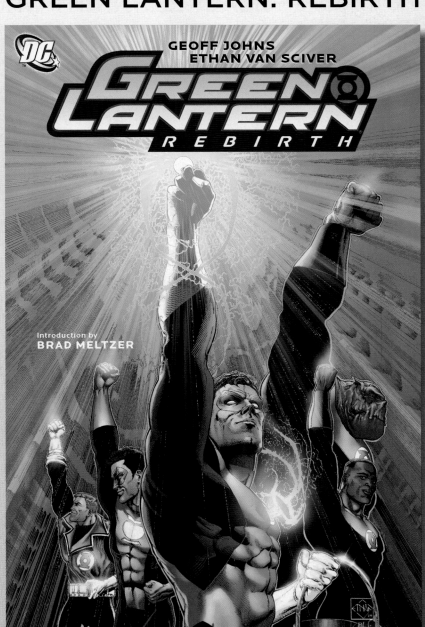

GEOFF JOHNS
ETHAN VAN SCIVER

Green Lantern: Rebirth

Introduction by
BRAD MELTZER

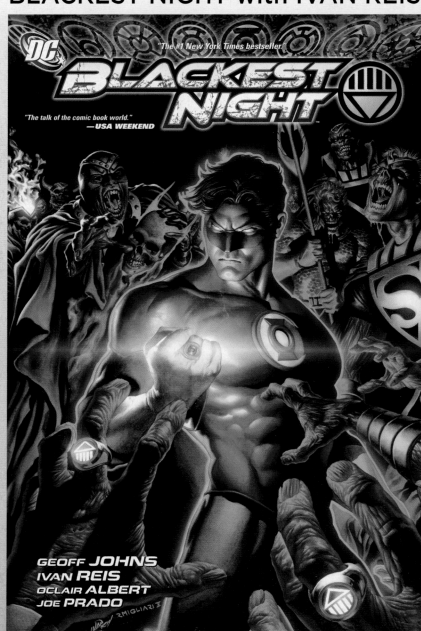

DC COMICS™

TALES OF THE 31ST CENTURY SUPER-TEAM

"One of the greatest comic book runs of all-time."
—COMIC BOOK RESOURCES

FROM LEGENDARY WRITER

PAUL LEVITZ

with KEITH GIFFEN

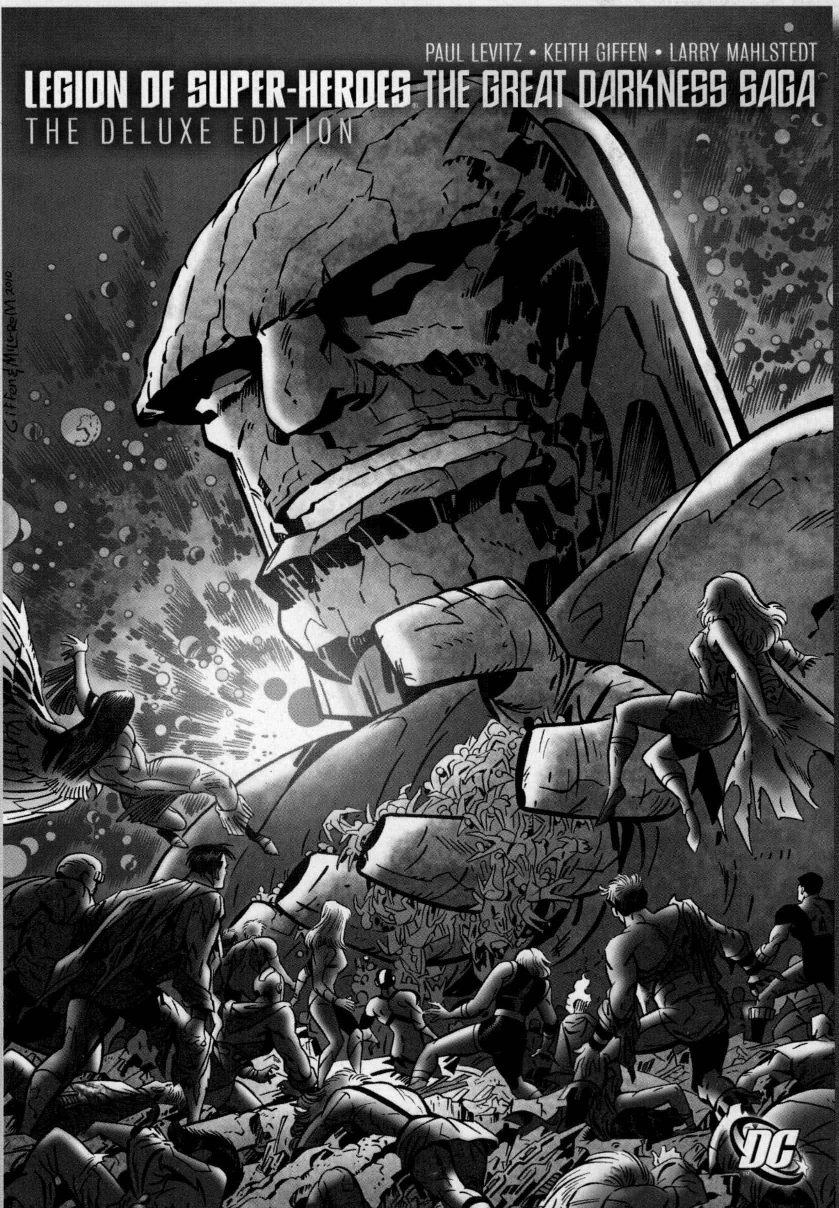
PAUL LEVITZ • KEITH GIFFEN • LARRY MAHLSTEDT
LEGION OF SUPER-HEROES THE GREAT DARKNESS SAGA
THE DELUXE EDITION

LEGION OF SUPER-HEROES: THE CURSE

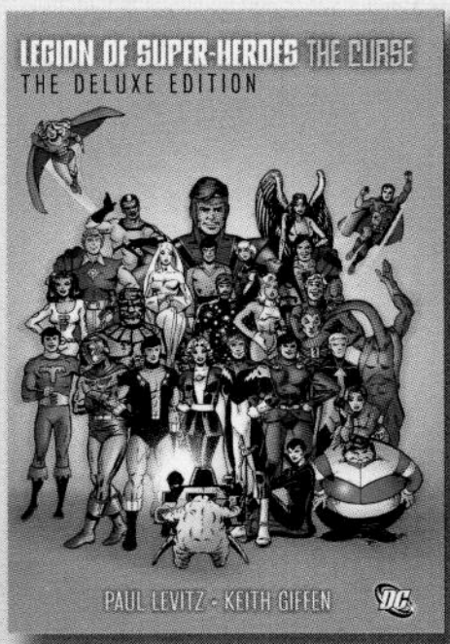
LEGION OF SUPER-HEROES THE CURSE
THE DELUXE EDITION
PAUL LEVITZ · KEITH GIFFEN

with KEITH GIFFEN

LEGION OF SUPER-HEROES: THE CHOICE

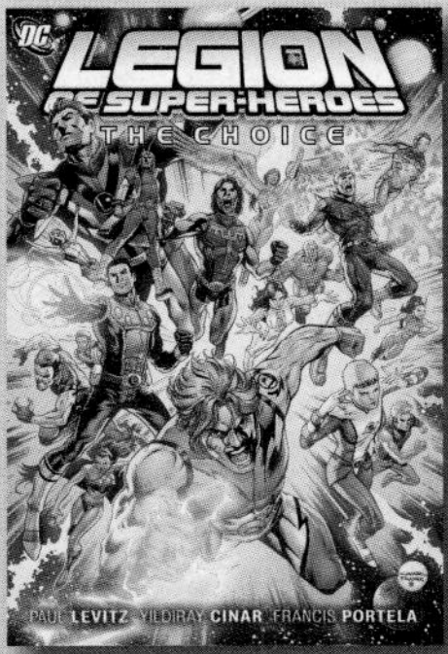
LEGION OF SUPER-HEROES
THE CHOICE
PAUL LEVITZ · YILDIRAY CINAR · FRANCIS PORTELA

with YILDIRAY CINAR

ALSO AVAILABLE

LEGION OF SUPER-HEROES: EYE FOR AN EYE
with KEITH GIFFEN

LEGION OF SUPER-HEROES: CONSEQUENCES
with YILDIRAY CINAR

LEGION OF SUPER-HEROES: WHEN EVIL CALLS
with PHIL JIMENEZ & YILDIRAY CINAR

"[A] comic legend." —ROLLING STONE

"[Grant Morrison is] comics' high shaman." —WASHINGTON POST

"[Grant Morrison] is probably my favorite writer. That guy has more ideas in his pinky than most people do in a lifetime." — Gerard Way from MY CHEMICAL ROMANCE

FROM THE WRITER OF *ALL-STAR SUPERMAN* AND *BATMAN & ROBIN*

GRANT MORRISON
with HOWARD PORTER

JLA VOL. 2

with HOWARD PORTER

JLA VOL. 3

with HOWARD PORTER

JLA VOL. 4

with HOWARD PORTER, FRANK QUITELY and ED McGUINNESS

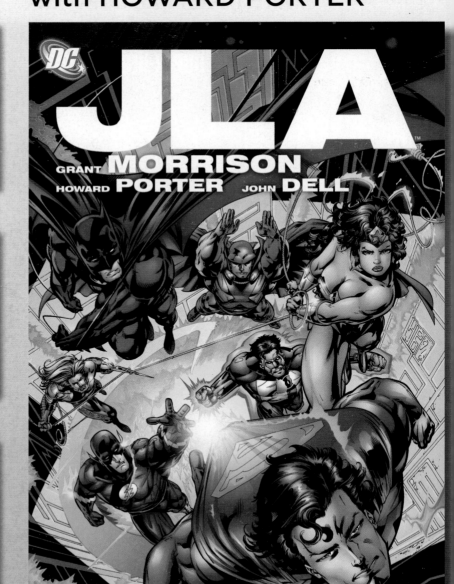